Understanding Statistics
in the Social Sciences

Understanding Statistics in the Social Sciences

William Ray Arney

The Evergreen State College
Olympia, Washington

W. H. FREEMAN AND COMPANY • NEW YORK

Library of Congress Cataloging-in-Publication Data

Arney, William Ray.
  Understanding statistics in the social sciences.

  Includes index.
  1. Social sciences—Statistical methods.   I. Title.
HA29.A74   1990   300'.1'5195   89-11943
ISBN 0-7167-2006-X

Printed in the United States of America

1 2 3 4 5 6 7 8 9   VB   8 9

Contents

Interlude A
Suicide: Individual Will or Social Regularity 86

5
Probability 92

6
Probability Distributions 123

7
Sampling and an Introduction to Decision Making 163

10
Introduction to Association and Statistical Independence 256

11
Measures of Association for Discrete Variables 287

Interlude C
Statistical Doubletalk? 317

12
Measures of Association for Continuous Variables   325

Interlude D
Political History of Correlation   383

13
Analysis of Variance: The Case of Multiple Means   386

Preface

The premise of this book is that statistics is like a language. You have to learn a language if you want to communicate with others who know it. This is as true for statistics as it is for Spanish or French. Following directly from this premise are several pedagogical positions reflected in this text.

First, if a student has a good, personal reason for learning statistics, she or he will learn the material more easily. I encourage students to find data sets that are of *compelling personal interest* to them. I encourage students to pursue their own questions, using their own data when possible. One student entered my class on quantitative analysis as an avowed, self-described "radical, pyro-feminist English major." She did the very best work in that class because she had arrived on day one with a data set on coeducation under her arm. She said, "I have to analyze this. Can you help me?" There is no motivation like self-motivation. Three data sets are appended to this text. The student who does not have a data set of his or her own should refer to these data sets to see if they can spark any interest.

Second, I think one learns a language best by hearing it and by speaking it. I try to "speak" to the reader throughout the pages of this book. I often "say" the same thing in several different ways so that the student can "hear" how the language, with its nuances, might be used in everyday (statistical) parlance. I encourage students to talk to themselves and to talk in class so that they can hear themselves, as well as others, speaking this slightly foreign language.

Third, much of the text and many of the end-of-chapter exercises are built around three data sets (which are found in Appendix A) and a very limited number of other examples. The text elaborates the analysis of these data sets and examples as it introduces more and more sophisticated statistical techniques. I believe that if a student studies a limited number of examples or studies a single data set carefully and systematically, he or she will appreciate better the links among central statistical concepts.

If there is a bias in this book, it favors understanding statistics over calculating them. I dwell occasionally on a topic (e.g., degrees of freedom) that might be dispensed with more quickly in a more formula-oriented text. And I sometimes relegate to a chapter supplement the formulas for calculating certain statistics. I am interested in having students arrive at an understanding of the logic behind the formulas. The emphasis here is on statistical reasoning and the "forms of statistical argument," not computation, even though formulas are given, explained, and discussed.

I have written this book with the reader—the person who now holds this book in hand—constantly in mind. I have tried to respect the fact that you are devoting time to this work. In return, I hope you will have me in mind as you read this book. If you find yourself "talking back" to this book, I hope you will think of yourself as talking back to me. Take (a little more) time to write to me and tell me what you have to say. Write to me at The Evergreen State College, Olympia, Washington 98505. I'm here—very likely in the rain—waiting.

I express my appreciation to the following people: Professor Thomas Li-Ping Tang generously provided me with original data from his dissertation. That data is reproduced in Appendix A and is used extensively throughout the text. I am grateful to the Literary Executor of the late Sir Ronald A. Fisher, F.R.S. to Dr. Frank Yates, F.R.S. and the Longman Group Ltd., for permission to reprint Table III from their book *Statistical Tables for Biological, Agricultural and Medical Research* (6th Edition 1974). I co-taught statistics and research methods courses with Joel Levine at Dartmouth College and, several times, with David Paulsen at The Evergreen State College. I learned much from both of them. Thanks also to Jerry Lassen and Jaime C. Kooser with whom I also co-taught classes at Evergreen. David Paulsen and Russ Lidman used this text in a previous draft in one of their classes. Thanks to them for helpful comments and thanks to their students for suffering through a mimeographed, unimproved version of this effort. I am grateful to the following reviewers for helpful comments: William R. Kelly, University of Texas; John Collette, University of Utah; Robert K. Leik, University of Minnesota; James R. Schwenke, Kansas State University; Lawrence G. Felice, Baylor University; Milton J. Brawer, Western Michigan University, and a special word of thanks for Susan Reiland for her very helpful detailed review of an early draft of the manuscript.

Finally, thanks to Debbie and John for their understanding. This book is dedicated to my parents, John Wilson Arney and Grace Kuhn Arney, for all of *their* understanding through the years.

William Ray Arney

To the Student

"What good are statistical formulae, which students can learn in a fortnight, if they do not learn as well the forms of statistical argument?"[1] This brief, rhetorical question posed by Philip Rieff sets the stage for this introduction to statistics. You could learn most of the statistical formulas for which you would ever have a use in two weeks of dedicated study. With a little more dedication, you could quickly become a person whom others would consult concerning the use of statistical technique. It is unlikely, however, that after two weeks you would understand fully what you were doing as you skillfully but rather thoughtlessly analyzed reams of data. It is unlikely that you would appreciate what Rieff called "the forms of statistical argument."

The forms of statistical argument have a surprisingly short history. Most of the statistical techniques you will learn in this introductory course were invented in the late nineteenth or early twentieth century. The theme of this book is taken from one of the first papers on "The Study of Statistics in Colleges and Technical Schools." The paper, written in 1890 by Francis A. Walker, says, in part:

> During the past twenty or even ten years there has been an astonishingly rapid development of historical and economic studies in our higher institutions of learning. . . . Unfortunately, while this rapid development of historical and economic work has been going on, a branch of study which has the highest virtue at once to train the hand of the historical or the economic scholar and to furnish him with professional tools of the first importance has been almost wholly neglected. I refer to statistics, whose very methods are hardly known to the great majority of our economists and historians. . . . There are, indeed, a few schools where a little elementary instruction has, of recent years, been given in the use of figures as a means of testing sociological conclusions; but in no one of them has

the full proper course of statistics been established. It cannot be long, however, before the growing interest in economics and history will compel the recognition of statistics as a distinct and an important part of the curriculum of every progressive institution. The main difficulty will be to find the men [sic] who have had the training at once severe and liberal, which will qualify them to inspire and direct these studies.[2]

Walker was calling for curricular reform so that statistics would become an important part of university studies in economics, history, sociology, and so on. The only problem was that few people could teach this new subject.

The few students of statistics there were in the 1890s were taught many of the things you will learn from this book. As Walker put it,

The pupil is taught to look up the data relating to a given subject, as these may be found scattered through long series of official reports; to bring the various statements together, to examine them as to their proper comparability, to test their accuracy by all means which may be available, and to put them together into tables. The student is further taught to work out the percentages involved and to set one class of facts into relation with others; ... and finally to make diagrams or charts.[3]

Students in the nineteenth century were, however, taught more in their courses on statistics than we would ever think of teaching in modern courses. Statistics courses in the major universities usually discussed the doctrine of free will. Is human behavior the result of individuals who act of their free will or the result of some social, economic, or psychological law? Walker was confident that students who dedicated themselves to the "long and laborious training" necessary to become proficient in numerical reasoning would "educe from thousands of pages closely packed with figures some hitherto unsuspected law of human life or conduct."[4] For others, whether people are free and willful or whether they act according to social and economic laws remained an open question. Regardless of an instructor's orientation, early training in statistics always contained a "liberal" aspect. Statistics courses had a political dimension, in the largest sense of the term "political."

Today we seldom consider the politics of statistics. Each of us tends to be in one of two opposed camps. Either we believe statistical reasoning has an important place in the administration of social and political life, or we are hypercritical of statistics and spout clichés such as, "There are lies, there are damn lies, and there are statistics." In my view, neither camp provides a comfortable place to stand. Both camps leave the meaning of the phrase "the forms of statistical argument" unexamined, the former by uncritically embracing statistical reasoning, the latter by dismissing statistics outright.

This book stakes out a third camp and invites you into it. The book covers all basic statistical formulas and provides an easy entry into the statistician's culture and language. At the same time as it offers this training, this book alerts you to the inescapable political dimension of statistical reasoning. It does so, first, by pointing out the pervasiveness of statistical arguments in modern life and, second, by attending, briefly and occasionally, to the history of statistics. Statistics arose at a peculiar time in history, and the discipline reflects and reinforces the world view prevalent at the end of the nineteenth century. This book tries to give you both some facility with statistical formulas and a healthy, appropriately critical attitude toward the forms of statistical argument.

· · ·

NOTES

1. Philip Rieff, *Fellow Teachers*, Delta, New York, 1973.

2. Francis A. Walker, "The Study of Statistics in Colleges and Technical Schools," *Technology Quarterly*, February 1890, quoted in Helen Mary Walker, *Studies in the History of Statistical Method*, William and Wilkens Co., Baltimore, Md., 1929, p. 150.

3. Ibid.

4. Ibid., p. 151.

Understanding Statistics
in the Social Sciences

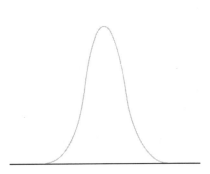

. . .

The Logic of
Statistical Analysis

Your father phones and says, "I got bad news today. Now I need some advice."

He explains that he has had a chronic, nagging chest pain for a little over a year. He finally decided to have it checked by physicians at the medical college nearby. His physician told him that he has "chronic stable angina." He says, "The doctor says there's a lot of technical stuff about my condition that she can tell me, but she says the bottom line is that I need to have bypass surgery. I told her I wanted to talk to you first. What do you think?"

How do you respond? How do you formulate advice when your father or another person is faced with a decision like this?

There are lots of ways to make a decision or to help another person make a decision. Many people simply rely on the doctor's judgment. "Doctor knows best" is the flag they fly, so if the doctor prescribes surgery, surgery it will likely be. People also rely on "local knowledge," anecdotes about what happened to friends and to friends of friends: "Remember George? Terrible. Was in the hospital for weeks after a bypass. Then just sort of drifted off. Lot of good surgery will do you!" Or, "Gosh, Maria was a wreck before her bypass. Couldn't walk, much less jog. Look at her now—running marathons! Remarkable. And her friend Pat— same thing. Surgery's marvelous. You've got no choice. Have it."

There is another way to help someone make such a decision. You could find out if anyone has assessed the effectiveness of bypass surgery in a scientific way. A trip to the library would show you that, indeed, someone has. In fact, many people have. One study, in particular, compared bypass surgery to medical therapy (taking pills under a physician's supervision) for your father's condition. It was a large study conducted by the Veterans Administration (VA) hospitals across the country. It was published in the prestigious *New England Journal of Medicine* by Dr Marvin Murphy and associates.[1]

The study was conducted to answer an important question in medicine and health policy: Is it better, in terms of the survival of patients, to subject a patient with chronic stable angina to bypass surgery or to treat the condition with pills and close supervision? Surgery is more costly than pills, both to individuals and to society. It would be valuable to know that surgery is a better form of treatment before the personal and political decisions are made to pay for it.

The study began with clinical interviews of 5,538 patients. Of that number, 596 were found to meet all the criteria for entry into the study. That is, they had chronic stable angina, and they had no signs of the diseases that were already known to be better treated with surgery. Once a patient was in the study, he was randomly assigned either to have surgery or to be treated with medications. The two groups, after random assignment, were identical in virtually every respect. The 286 people assigned to have surgery had bypasses done within 2 months of assignment to the surgery group. The 310 treated with pills were followed by their physicians for several years.

The principal outcome in which physicians were interested was survival. Did a higher proportion of those who underwent surgery survive, or did more of those treated medically survive? The answer, assessing survival 3 years after treatment, was that *there was not a statistically significant difference between the two groups.* That is, the study did not provide data that would allow anyone to claim that surgery is better than pills.

An editorial in the *New England Journal of Medicine* pointed out that bypass surgery is very expensive. It added, "If the principle espoused by many economists and political leaders is accepted—namely, that the total national resources for health care are now more or less fixed—the enormous funds already being devoted to this procedure divert support available for other, perhaps more necessary aspects of medical care."

Social and health policy is one thing. The question you face is, what advice do you give your father? Before you offer that advice, you should know a little more about the meaning of that crucial sentence, "There is not a statistically significant difference between the two groups."

· · ·

THINKING STATISTICALLY

The rest of this book is devoted to helping you develop the skills you need to understand the above sentence well. However, now you can begin to develop a rudimentary understanding of the logic underlying such an utterance.

In truth, there *was* a difference in the survival rates of the two groups 36 months after entry into the study. Of those treated medically, 87 percent were alive 3 years after entry, and 88 percent of those who had surgery were alive. Numbers like these—"87 percent of those treated medically" and "88 percent of those who had surgery"—are *statistics*. They are *descriptive statistics*. They describe the data from the study. They describe the experience of 596 *cases* for which data on the *variable* "survival" were available. The statistics say that among the people *in the study*, surgery was ever so lightly better than drug therapy.

Science always begins with a *sample* and seeks to generalize to a *population* from which the sample came. In this case you have a sample of surgically treated patients with a survival rate of 88 percent who come from a population of all (previous and potential) surgically treated patients and a sample of medically treated patients with a survival rate of 87 percent who come from a population of all medically treated patients. The logic of making an *inference* from a sample to a population goes like this: After a look at the descriptive statistics, you discover that the study favours surgery. But the samples may have come from populations in which the survival rates are the same; that is, there may be no difference in the experience of surgically and medically treated groups. *Simply by chance* two samples having different survival rates could have been selected from their respective populations, which have identical survival rates. The likelihood of there being a difference in such samples decreases as the magnitude of the difference between the samples increases. However, even very large differences between the samples are possible if the samples came from populations between which there is, in fact, no difference. The question in this instance is, is it reasonable to claim that these samples, with their 1 percentage point difference in survival rate, came from populations that had different survival rates? The answer is that you may make the claim, but the likelihood of such a claim's being wrong is very high. It is not reasonable to make such a claim. And, in fact, *inferential statistics* will provide a precise meaning for the term "reasonable."

What do you tell your father? You can say that if he meets all the criteria that people had to meet to become a subject in this study, and if he is interested in making his decision solely on the basis of survival, the best available statistical evidence says he should flip a coin to make the decision to have surgery or to take the pills. There is no evidence to assert that one treatment is better than the other.

Your father probably will not like this kind of advice. He will probably say that, in fact, there are a lot of things to think about: the quality of life (not just its length), the cost of the operation, the stress that an operation would put on your mother, the difficulty he has always had in following doctors' orders to take pills on a prescribed regimen, etc. At this point, you would have to go back to the library—and back through the process of thinking statistically about all these other variables—to search for any statistical evidence that will help him make a decision within this expanded decision-making space. In fact, you would find that there are other, much more recent studies of this problem. You would at least want to pay attention to data of a more recent vintage.

· · ·

REVIEW: HOW THE STUDIES WORK

It is important that you follow the logic of this example. You will gain the technical skills necessary to fill in the details as you progress through this book. The logic is summarized in Figure 1.1.

First, any scientific study begins with a question to be answered or a decision to be made. The question in this case is, Is surgery better, in terms of survival, than medical therapy for treating chronic stable angina?

Step	Example
1. Decide question to answer or decision to make	Is surgery better, in terms of survival, or is medical treatment better for chronic stable angina?
2. Imagine population to which question applies	Population 1: medically treated cases; population 2: surgically treated cases
3. Select samples	Random assignment of all cases to surgical or medical treatment
4. Describe experience of samples	Survival (surgical): 88% Survival (medical): 87%
5. Make inference into population	Decision: not to assert that samples come from populations with different survival rates

FIGURE 1.1 Thinking of science statistically.

Second, you imagine the population or populations for which this is an appropriate question, that is, for which the variable of interest can be measured. In this example, there are two populations: people with chronic stable angina who have bypass surgery and people with chronic stable angina who follow drug therapy.

Third, since you cannot study whole populations, you select representative samples from the populations of interest. In this case the samples were chosen by taking every person entering the cardiac care units of the VA hospital system after the start of the study, determining if he met the criteria for entrance into the study, and then randomly assigning him to have surgery or to be treated and followed medically.

Fourth, you describe the experience of the samples. The descriptive statistics show that the sample assigned to surgery fared a little better than the sample assigned to medical treatment.

Fifth, you make an inference: what can be reasonably said about the populations from which these samples came, on the basis of your knowledge about the samples? You could claim that the "surgery" population had a higher survival rate than the "medical" population. The likelihood of such a claim's being wrong is very high. I would decide not to make such a claim.

Finally, answer the question posed by the study or make a decision. In this case, the data do not support the conclusion that surgery is better than medical treatment of chronic stable angina.

A Word of Caution

The account of this particular study is long, and the logic probably seems unnecessarily complex and convoluted. But this study is very simplified and somewhat extracted from its context. As you learn statistics, you will understand the complexities and learn to go through all the steps quickly, so that answering a question or making a decision will not be such a long process. However, you will never be able to fully extract a statistical study from its human context.

This study of the treatment of chronic stable angina drew an unprecedented number of letters to the editor of the *New England Journal of Medicine*. Some criticized the study's design. Others asserted that the surgeons who performed the surgeries were not using the best available surgical procedures (and, therefore, their work should not be compared to medical treatment). Still others asserted that survival ought not to be the only variable against which the efficacy of treatment is measured. On the other side, some said that for all its faults, this study was the best available and ought to become the basis for all future studies. Others said that this study only proved what was well known before and asked why it had taken so long to get such data out for public discussion. Others were ready to use the results to set public health care policy. The debate was a highly charged, emotional one.

What do you do? First, you need to learn statistics, so that you can read studies like this one to help you answer a question that you face. You should be able to read such studies yourself and not have to rely on "experts" to interpret the results for you. Second, you must think about the context of the statistical studies. You need to understand statistics and the people who use them. Only then can you become a wise as well as a competent and informed consumer of statistical information.

The ASARCO Smelter Debate: Another Example

Near Tacoma, Washington, there is a copper smelter that began operation near the turn of the century. In 1922 to 1923, ASARCO, the owner of the smelter, built an arsenic refinery which quickly became one of the principal sources of arsenic in the United States. Even after installation of pollution control devices in 1951 and improvements in pollution control technology since, the smelter dusted the Tacoma area with an estimated 130 tons of arsenic every year, Arsenic can cause cancer. In fact, statistical studies of workers in arsenic refineries show that workers have a much higher than average chance of dying of lung cancer. Based on those studies of workers inside refineries and on estimates of arsenic emissions, the Environmental Protection Agency (EPA) estimated that the residents of Tacoma who lived around the refinery could expect to experience between 1 and 17 deaths from arsenic-induced lung cancer each year. In 1983 and 1984, the EPA held a series of meetings with residents of Tacoma to see whether they felt the federally allowed arsenic emssion standard should be lowered.

The meetings were heated. Workers from the plant knew that lowering the emission standard would cost them their jobs since the plant owners would not install equipment to bring the plant into compliance with proposed lower standards. Other residents felt the risk of cancers outweighed the threatened loss of jobs. They were especially afraid for the children who went to school in the shadow of the smelter and who had elevated levels of arsenic in their hair and in their urine. The debates were emotional. One worker, on a nationally televised news program, was asked point-blank, "If it could be proved with certainty that the smelter is causing one extra lung-cancer death each year, would you favor closing the smelter?" He thought for quite a while before answering in a quiet voice, "No. It's not worth 500 jobs."

Into the middle of the controversy came a team of state epidemiologists (statisticians who study the incidence and distribution of mortality and sickness). They said it might be possible to determine if the smelter was causing excess deaths from lung cancer. The problem was to separate arsenic-induced lung cancer from lung cancer caused by smoking. They reasoned: If a large cohort of non-smokers could be followed for an extended period of time, it should be possible to detect the predicted excess incidence of lung cancer [the excess over what is expected based on rates for the whole United States population]."[2] Actually following a group of nonsmokers would take years, but the epidemiologists took advantage of a little experiment nature had conducted for them. They noted that women who died of lung cancer before 1970 constituted a group in which smoking was not prevalent. "Smoking only became popular among women during the 1940s," they wrote. "Since lung cancer takes many years to develop, mortality among women is only now reflecting the health effects of cigarette use during the 1940s and 1950s." So they compared women's death rate from lung cancer in Tacoma from 1935 to 1969 to the national women's death rate from lung cancer for the same period. If the arsenic refinery were causing excess deaths, the Tacoma women's death rate from lung cancer would be higher than the national death rate.

Do you see the logic here? The researchers had a sample from a population made mostly of nonsmokers from the Tacoma area (which means the population was exposed to high levels of arsenic). Based on the EPA's ideas and information, that population was expected to have a higher death rate from lung cancer than the population in the whole country, a population consisting largely of nonsmokers who were not exposed to high levels of arsenic. The overall population—the "unexposed" population—had a known death rate from lung cancer. The statistical question was, Did the Tacoma sample come from a population (the "exposed" population) whose death rate from lung cancer was higher than the death rate of the unexposed population.[2]

As it turned out, death rates for the area immediately around the smelter, for Tacoma, and for the country in which Tacoma is located were lower than the national rates. From these sample data and inferential statistics, one could not conclude that the death rate of the exposed population was higher than that of the unexposed population. Floyd Frost, a state epidemiologist, wrote to William Ruckelshaus, then Director of the EPA, "The study provides no evidence of excess lung cancer in the Tacoma area, even at the relatively high arsenic emission levels for the period covered (1935—1969)."[3]

The Outcome

Does that settle the issue? Does the EPA just accept the facts and stop its effort to lower the emission standards? The data in this case tell a clear story. The data point out that the government should be concerned about arsenic-induced lung cancer among workers in refineries, but the EPA should not be concerned about excess deaths in the Tacoma area. Shouldn't policy follow directly from the data?

Well, of course, the data did not close the books on the smelter debate. Why? Because the smelter debate was a political debate in which a report like Floyd Frost's is just another point available for use in the argument. Frost's work may carry more weight than the argument of the worker who would trade 500 jobs for one death annually or of the parents concerned about arsenic in their children's

urine, but not because Frost's work is any more truthful than the worker's judgment or the parents' concern. Statistical work may gain more respect simply because, in our culture, we tend to value statistical arguments more than emotional
ones. Frost's work enters the debate on the same terms as the worker's view or
the parent's statement: All are initially fragments in a conversation, statements in
a debate.

· · ·

STATISTICS AS LANGUAGE

Statistics is just like a language. If you want to understand people who use statistics to convey messages, you have to know statistics, too. If you want to be
able to talk back to people who know statistics, you have to develop rudimentary
statistical skills at the very least. Knowing statistics, like knowing French, German,
or Swahili, does not make you a better person. It just makes you a more capable
person in circumstances that call for knowledge of a special language. You will
move more easily among people who speak in terms of rates, regressions, means
and moments, samples, populations, and margins of error if you, too, can use those
terms knowledgeably.

   You have to make a decision: Is it important to you to be able to speak this
language? Would you like to participate in this curious culture? You need not say
yes. Lots of people travel easily through Germany or Kenya with the aid of an
interpreter. Others make their way through foreign lands by smiling, shouting,
pointing, grunting, and miming. There will always be someone willing to tell you
what statistical procedure to use to answer questions using a data set, and there
will always be someone to interpret the statistics for you as they come pouring
out of a computer. You could live life well without a working knowledge of statistics. So before spending the time it takes to learn this new language, you should
decide whether you have a reason to learn it. If you have a reason, your path to
understanding statistics will be smooth. If you are, at this point, using this book
to satisfy major requirement or to get a statistics course on your record, make
your life easier: Find a reason for learning this peculiar language of statistics.

Learning Statistics as a New Language

You should try to learn statistics just as you would learn a new language. Learn
the vocabulary and the rules by which "words" can be strung together to make
sense. When you learn that the *sample variance* is "the sum of the squared deviations about the mean divided by the number of observations minus 1," just
accept that as you accept the definitions of foreign words. (Doesn't that definition
sound foreign to you?) Do not worry, at first, about the *meaning* of the word
"variance." Just learn the definition. Later, as your vocabulary grows, you will

begin to understand and appreciate the rule-governed relationship between variance and other statistical concepts. The meaning of "variance" will become clear
to you as you learn about and appreciate the web of relationships in which the
concept of variance is embedded. A term like "electric switch" gains meaning in
the complex web of relationships among "electric switch" and "light fixture,"
"house," "room," "darkness," "wiring," "voltage," and so on. "Variance" gains
meaning in the web of relationships among "variance" and "mean," "correlation,"
"coefficient of determination," "normal distribution," "standard error," "sampling
distribution," and so on. Go slowly. Build your vocabulary carefully. Develop a
clear understanding of the rules governing relationships among concepts. The
meanings will be clear in time.

As you begin to learn statistics, talk to yourself. Talk your way through problems. Explain every step to yourself. (And do not deceive yourself! If you cannot
explain something to yourself, you do not understand it. Refresh your memory
before going on.) As you become more comfortable with the language of statistics,
you will not need to talk yourself through each and every definition and rule.
You will gradually begin to speak as a native. You will become fluent, graceful,
and correct.

Finally, use your resources well. You cannot learn a language easily by sitting
down with a textbook and a battery of language tests. You learn a language by
immersing yourself in the culture of that language. You listen to the fast talk of
expert speakers. You find tutors willing to tolerate your stumbling attempts to
utter the simplest phrases. You have a pocket dictionary handy at all times. So
you should do the same with statistics. Become conscious of the everyday uses of
statistics. Listen to how other people use statistics. Read newspapers and watch
television. Statistics are everywhere. Try to understand people who sound fluent
in statistics and statistical reasoning. Also use your instructors well. Ask questions,
expect helpful corrections to your statistical "vocabulary" and "grammar." Expect
to make many mistakes, but learn from them. And above all, refer often to this
book and other statistics texts. Professional statisticians do not keep all the statistical formulas in their heads. There is no reason to. Everyone refers to a text or
reference book as needed. While you are learning statistics, refer often to books.
Your dependence on them will decrease as your expertise grows.

Do not expect to become an expert overnight. Your first exposure to statistics
can only introduce you to terms and concepts and to a few elementary applications. Your skills will sharpen as you use statistics to do projects that are important
to you.

You should also keep everything in perspective. It does not reflect badly on
you to make mistakes as you learn statistics. You will learn the language more
easily if you can laugh at your mistakes in the same spirit as a native speaker
laughs at your desperate attempts to find a bathroom or order a meal in a foreign
country. You can make the study of statistics a very serious business; you will
enjoy it more if you choose to make it fun.

· · ·

A STATISTICAL CULTURE

Although learning statistics is easier if you have a compelling personal reason to do so, there is another reason to learn this material: self-defense. By learning statistics you do more than gain the ability to talk to and understand statisticians. You gain the tools for participating more fully in our decidedly statistical culture.

It is difficult to think of a modern problem that is not amenable to a statistical analysis of some sort. Florence Nightingale, nicknamed "the passionate statistician," wrote in 1891 to Francis Galton about the kinds of investigations she would undertake if she were appointed to a "statistical Professorship or Readership at the University of Oxford."[4] Her list of proposed inquiries is very modern. She would study the effects of nutrition on poor children. She would evaluate Forster's Act, the late nineteenth-century version of Head Start, to see "what proportion of children forget their whole education after leaving school" and to see "what are the methods and what are the results . . . in preventing primary education from being a waste." She was curious about the effect of "legal punishment—i.e., the deterrent or encouraging effects upon crime of being in jail." And she would investigate the effects of the workhouses: "What is the proportion of names which from generation to generation appear the same in Workhouse records? What is the proportion of children de-pauperised or pauperised by the workhouse?" To conclude her letter, Nightingale solicited from Galton some ideas on *"how to use these statistics in order to legislate for and to administer our national life* with more precision and experience." Her concerns were strikingly modern, and they remain an indication of how important statistical method has become to our "national life." We use quantitative methods to investigate all aspects of modern society.

Opinion Polls

In this century we supplement quantitative investigations of social problems with the ubiquitous public opinion poll. The Gallup and Harris organizations are permanent fixtures on the modern political scene. Major television networks and newspapers have their own polling organizations that can have the opinions of a representative sample of the U.S. population on any issue within 3 days.

You can tell you live in a statistical culture because one automatic, virtually "natural" response to almost any problem is, "Do a (statistical) study." Consider the Warner Amex Cable Communications' QUBE, an interactive television system that allows Warner to "do a study" almost instantaneously. A set of buttons installed on the television sets of subscribers to the QUBE interactive television system in Columbus, Ohio, allows them to respond to such questions as "What effect do you think Reaganomics will have on the economy? Do you think it will (1) greatly help, (2) somewhat help, (3) make no difference, (4) somewhat hurt, (5) greatly hurt?" Each viewer presses a numbered button. Then a computer scans the subscribers' responses and prints summaries on the TV screen. You know we are a statistical culture when statistics is so closely linked with a cultural icon like the TV set.

Experts have different views of this system. Some feel that the 'QUBE system is a "potentially powerful ally of democracy" that will "enhance the quality of communication and reinforce civic exchanges." Others feel that registering an opinion from inside one's home does not contribute to democratic forms of government since "a compilation of opinions does not make a civic culture; such a culture demands a deliberative process in which people engage one another as citizens." One great fear about interactive TV systems that scan viewers' sets every 6 seconds is that the system might invade the privacy of the subscribers' homes. The system could check how many people watched a particular show or how many watched a political advertisement, and it could register viewers' instant responses to advertisements and shows in addition to their responses to opinion poll questions.

When the people at Warner got wind of this criticism of their system, they did the natural thing. They did a study. They used their QUBE system to ask people if the system was an invasion of privacy. "The Television Explosion," a Public Broadcasting System program, reported that in response to the poll 70 percent of QUBE subscribers said they were not worried about the system's invading their privacy. This, according to one commentator, "settled the matter as far as QUBE was concerned."[5]

Statistics is so much a part of our culture that the response to criticism of the statistical way of thinking is very likely to be a statistical response. Be aware. Learn statistics so you can understand more about this life we share.

$$\bullet \quad \bullet \quad \bullet$$

NOTES

1. Marvin L. Murphy, Herbert N. Hultgren, Katherine Detre, James Thomson, Timothy Takaro, and participants of the Veterans Administration Cooperative Study, "Treatment of Chronic Stable Angina: A Preliminary Report of Survival Data of the Randomized Veterans Administration Cooperative Study," *New England Journal of Medicine* 297(12):621–627, Sept. 22, 1977.

2. Floyd Frost, Sam Milham, Lucy Harter, and Cheryl Bayle, "Tacoma-Area Lung Cancer Study," mimeograph, Olympia: Department of Social and Health Services, State of Washington, 1984.

3. Ibid.

4. Letter from Florence Nightingale to Francis Galton, dated Feb. 7 1891, entitled, "Scheme for Social Physics Teaching," in Karl Pearson, *Life, Letters and Labours of Francis Galton*, Vol. 2, Cambridge, England: Cambridge University Press, 416–418.

5. Jean Bethke Elshtain, " 'Interactive' TV: Democracy and the QUBE Tube," *The Nation* 235:108–110, Aug. 7–14, 1982.

2

▼

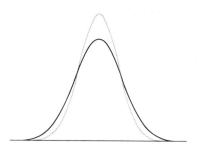

. . .

Variables and Hypotheses

This chapter introduces the bases of scientific thought: variables and hypotheses. Scientific thinking is familiar to you. Your task now is to cast your own, somewhat individualized, understanding of science into commonly accepted scientific language.

. . .

CASES AND VARIABLES

Science begins with the individual *case*. The first task in reading or planning a scientific study is to decide what you want to study—what you want to analyze. What is your *unit of analysis*? Psychologists generally study people—the personality traits and behavioral tendencies of people. An individual person is the unit of analysis, and each person is a case. Physiological psychologists are usually more interested in people's (or animals') brains. The individual brain is a case that is analyzed chemically or electrically. Sociologists typically analyze groups and are concerned with a group's cohesiveness, the stratification of a society (which is a very large group), or the level of equality in a face-to-face interaction of two people (which is a very small group). The sociologists' unit of analysis is the group, and he or she is concerned principally with characteristics of groups that cannot be apprehended just by studying the individuals of that group. Economists study economies, economic policies, and the economic behavior of people. Always make sure you know what unit of analysis is the focus of a study and what a case is.

Science is concerned with cases because certain of their aspects can be measured. These aspects or characteristics of cases are called *variables.* In the vocabulary of statistics "variable" is a critical word. A variable is a collection of categories. The number of categories in the collection may be finite or infinite. Regardless of the number of categories in the collection, in order for the collection to be a variable, it must satisfy two criteria. The categories must be (1) mutually exclusive and (2) totally inclusive. At this stage in the development of your language skills, just memorize this definition: *A variable is a collection of categories that is mutually exclusive and totally inclusive.*

(Throughout this book, I will first define a term and then explain each part of the definition. As you build your vocabulary, the meaning of the term will become clear as you comprehend the relationship of one concept to the many other concepts in the language.)

The first element of the definition of "variable" says a variable is a collection of categories. The categories that constitute a variable are descriptors of a single characteristic of the cases. One characteristic of people is height. One collection of categories that describes height is the collection of the two categories "tall" and "short." The two categories "tall" and "short" taken together are the variable "height." One characteristic of a nation is the crude birthrate, or the number of children born each year per 1000 people in the population at midyear. One collection of categories that describes the birthrate is $\{0, 0.1, 0.2, 0.3, \ldots, 1.0, 1.1, \ldots\}$. A characteristic of groups is their decision-making style. One collection of categories that describes a decision-making style is "democratic," "bureaucratic," and "dictatorial." The variable "decision-making style" is the collection of these three categories.

The second part of the definition of "variable" says that a collection of categories describing a characteristic is a variable if the categories are (1) mutually exclusive and (2) totally inclusive. This simply means that there is one—and only one—category to which each case can be assigned.

Consider the characteristic of people called "age." Is the collection of categories $\{0-5, 5-10, 10-15, \ldots, 75-80\}$ a variable? Look at Figure 2.1. The first three cases can be assigned unambiguously to one and only one category each. The

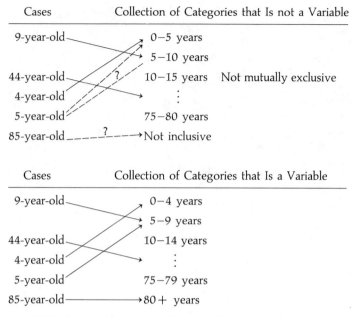

FIGURE 2.1 Assignment of cases to categories by "age".

9-year-old goes in the category of 5–10 years. The 44-year-old goes in the category of 40–45 years. The 4-year-old is, without question, in the category of 0–5 years. But what about the 5-year-old? She could go into either category—0–5 years or 5–10 years. Her assignment is ambiguous because the categories are not *mutually exclusive*.

What about the 85-year-old? She cannot find a category to which she belongs because the collection of categories stops at age 80. The categories are not *totally inclusive* of every possible case.

The bottom half of Figure 2.1 shows a collection of categories that is a variable since they are totally inclusive and mutually exclusive. For every imaginable case there is a category to which it can be unambiguously assigned.

· · ·

KINDS OF VARIABLES: LEVELS OF MEASUREMENT

There are four kinds of variables—nominal, ordinal, interval, and ratio—as shown in Table 2.1. These names refer to the way in which a characteristic of a case is measured. The distinctions among kinds of variables are important because some statistics are appropriate for one kind of variable but not for others.

A *nominal variable* is one whose categories simply have names. The variable "attitude toward abortion"—measured by a yes, no, or don't-know response to

TABLE 2.1 Levels of Measurement for Variables

Type of Variable	Categories Have:			
	Names	Order	Intervals	Ratios
Nominal	Yes	No	No	No
Ordinal	Yes	Yes	No	No
Interval	Yes	Yes	Yes	No
Ratio	Yes	Yes	Yes	Yes

the question, Do you think abortion should be okay if a woman's health is endangered by her pregnancy?—is a nominal variable. The categories just have names, "yes," "no," and "don't know."

By contrast, an *ordinal variable* is a collection of categories that have names *and* at an inherent order among them. There is no inherent way to order "yes," "no," and "don't know." There is, however, an inherent order to the categories "low," "moderate," and "high." A variable such as "self-reported enthusiasm for punk rock" for which one used the categories "low," "moderate," and "high" would be an ordinal variable.

An *interval variable* is a variable in which the distance between the categories has meaning. The categories of an interval variable have names, they have an inherent order among them, and the intervals between them are meaningful. Fahrenheit temperature is an example of an interval variable. The distance between −2 degrees Fahrenheit (−2°F) and −1°F is the same as that between 101°F and 102°F. The intervals are meaningful. Compare the variable "temperature" to the variable "enthusiasm" mentioned above. It does not make sense to talk about the distance between "low" and "moderate" or the distance between "moderate" and "high." Distance has no meaning for ordinal variables. Meaningful distance is the defining characteristic of an interval variable.

Ratio variables are distinguished from interval variables by the meaningfulness of the ratios of categories. If the ratios are meaningful then the category "zero" is meaningful as well. If "zero" means that no amount of the quantity is present, then the variable is a ratio variable. Now 0°F does not mean there is no temperature, that is, no molecular movement. Fahrenheit temperature is not a ratio variable, and consequently a glass of wine served at 50°F cannot be said to be 1.25 times as warm as a glass of water served at 40°F. The ratio between the two temperatures on the Fahrenheit scale—50/40 = 1.25 in this case—is meaningless. The Kelvin scale for temperature, however, is a ratio measure of temperature. Now 0 Kelvin (K) means no temperature, no molecular movement, and a body at 5000 K* can be said to be twice as warm as a body at 2500 K. Income is also a ratio variable. A

---

* Note that no degree symbol is used with kelvin.

person making \$20,000 is making 1.33 times the income of a person making \$15,000. A person with zero income has no dollars.

Some people speak only of the distinction between discrete and continuous variables. *Continuous variables* have measurement scales with an infinite number of categories, where each category can be named by a point on the real number line. A case can be assigned to any point in an interval by using any fractional number desired, if the variable being measured is continuous. A *discrete variable* consists of categories to which integer numbers can be assigned. (Integers are whole numbers, containing no fractions.) There is no possibility of assigning a case to a spot between categories of a discrete variable.

Caution: The way in which a variable is measured—the way in which its categories are constructed—determines the kind of variable it is. The variable "age" seems inherently to be a continuous, ratio-level variable since a person can be any number of years plus any fraction of a year old and because "0 years of age" is meaningful. However, age measured by the collection {0−4 years, 5−9 years, 10−14 years, . . .} is a discrete variable. You can, for example, assign the integer 1 to the category 0−4 years, the integer 2 to the category 5−9 years, 3 to the category 10−14 years, and no assignment is possible between categories 1 and 2 or between categories 2 and 3. "Age" measured by determining a person's exact age in years and fractions of years is a continuous variable, while "age" measured by assignment to a specified age range is a discrete variable.

· · ·

DATA SETS

It is useful now to take a closer look at the three data sets in Appendix A. Examining the data sets will help solidify the concepts of case and variable. If this discussion of all three data sets is too much for you at this point, skip some of it and come back when you need to know something about the variables in these studies.

Any data set is characterized by the number of cases and number of variables per case, and the data set can be presented in a *case-by-variable matrix*. Appendix A shows the case-by-variable matrix for each data set.

Social Indicators: Countries Data Set

Consider the first data set. (Figure 2.2 contains reproductions of portions of each data set.) This data set contains 5 social indicators for 142 countries. What is a "case" in this data set? Obviously, a country is a case. There are 142 cases. How many variables are there? It is tempting to say 5, but this would not be technically correct. Actually, there are 6 variables per case—the 5 social indicators plus the variable "country." "Country" is obviously a nominal variable since the categories

Countries Data Set

Country	Doctors per 100,000	Urbanization, %	Per Capita Income, $	Male Life Expectancy, years	Literacy Rate, %
Afghanistan	51	—	168	39.9	12
Albania	—	38.0	490	64.9	75
Algeria	19	52.0	1600	52.9	36
Angola	6	—	500	37.0	12
Argentina	192	72.0	2331	65.2	93

Internal-Motivation Experiment 1

Task Label	Protestant Work Ethic	Leisure Ethic	Type A Personality	Anagrams Solved	Time Spent on Word Game
1	66	59	51	13	80
1	98	39	45	37	—**
1	82	43	48	17	40
1	101	49	47	20	—**

** Data not available for this subject.

Hospital Cost

Doctor	DRG	Compli- cations	Dis- charges	ALOS	Non-special- ization, %	Total Cost, $	Surgery, % of Total Cost	Diagnosis, % of Total Cost	Materials and Technology, % of Total Cost
01	370	1	1	5.0	50	2527	2	3	20
01	371	0	4	4.0	50	1962	3	17	
02	370	1	2	4.0	47	1673	4	3	21
02	371	0	7	4.4	47	2513	7	9	14

FIGURE 2.2 Data sets: Case-by-variable matrices.

are simply names. All other variables in this data set are ratio variables. For each of the 5 social indicator variables, zero means there is nothing there—no urbanization, no literacy, no life expectancy, and so on—and a ratio of one level to another for any of the 5 variables is meaningful.

A Social Psychology Experiment: A Two-Part Data Set

The second data set in Figure 2.2 is from two experiments about internal motivation and is a little more complicated. First, this single data set actually consists of two separable data sets, one from experiment 1 and the other from experiment 2, which is discussed at the end of the chapter. What is a case? In both experiments a case is an experimental subject. Researchers Tang and Baumeister used volunteer undergraduate students at Case Western Reserve University for the first experiment and volunteer undergraduates from the National Taiwan University, Taiwan, Republic of China, for the second experiment. There were 60 subjects (cases) in experiment 1 and 40 subjects in experiment 2.

In experiment 1, there are six variables (see the second part of Figure 2.2): "task label," "Protestant work ethic," "leisure ethic," "Type A personality," "anagrams solved" during the experimental period, and "time spent on word game" during a 15-minute observation period.

"Task label" is a nominal variable. It consists of two categories, "leisure" and "work." "Task label" refers to the way in which the researcher introduced the experiment to a subject; in particular, it refers to how the researchers described the task of solving anagrams. Some subjects were told they were taking part in a study of "work," that the task of solving anagrams was like the work of a clerk or a secretary or an historian, and the researcher, upon leaving the room, encouraged the subject to "work hard." The subjects given these instructions were in the "work" category of the variable "task label." The other subjects were told that they were taking part in a study of leisure-time activities, that solving anagrams is like doing crossword puzzles or playing Scrabble, and they were told to "have fun." These subjects were in the "leisure" category of "task label."

The next three variables in the data set are the subject's scores on three psychological tests. Each test consisted of a series of statements, each of which was scored on a scale of 1 ("does not apply to me") to 7 ("applies strongly to me"). The work-ethic scale had 19 items on it; the subject could score between 19 (19×1) and 133 (19×7). The higher the score, the stronger the subject's endorsement of the Protestant work ethic. The leisure-ethic scale consisted of 10 items, so a subject could score between 10 and 70. Once again, higher scores indicated a greater endorsement of a leisure ethic. The Type A personality scale contained 9 items. Higher scores on this scale indicated a person was hard-driving, competitive, and, according to other research, more prone to have a heart attack later in life. These three variables are clearly ordinal variables. They are not interval variables since the distance between each point on the scale is not really meaningful.

"Anagrams solved" indicates the number of anagrams a person completed during a 15-minute period. It is a ratio variable.

"Time spent on word game" during the observation period is a indicator of a person's willingness to continue doing a task even when not required to do so. After the 15-minute period during which the subject solved anagrams, the researcher entered the room and asked if the subject would mind pretesting material that the researcher planned to use in another series of experiments. The subjects were given a choice of three different task; one was a word construction task very similar to the problem of solving anagrams. The researcher then left the room to observe the subject through a one-way mirror and recorded the number of seconds during a 15-minute observation period that the subject spent on the word construction task. "Time spent on word games" is an indicator of a person's internal motivation. This variable is also a ratio variable.

The reasons why the researchers were interested in these variables are explained later. The variables for the second experiment are explained in an exercise at the end of this chapter.

Hospital Costs Data Set

The third data set is more complicated still. It contains information about average hospital costs for obstetric procedures. A case in this data set is more complicated than a case in the other data sets, so a little background is necessary.

In 1984, the U.S. government began a simplified scheme of paying hospitals to take care of patients on Medicare and Medicaid, the government's medical insurance programs for the elderly and the poor. Instead of paying hospitals whatever they charged, the government decided to pay a fixed rate based on the diagnosis made for each case. So regardless of how much a hospital charges for an appendectomy and how much it might spend on a patient undergoing an appendectomy, the government pays a fixed appendectomy fee. (The scheme is a little more complicated than this since it accounts for regional and local differences in hospital costs, but this gives you the basic idea of the policy.) The diagnosis for which the government pays is expressed by a number, the number of a *diagnostically related group* (DRG for short). DRGs 370 to 384 are in the obstetric group. For example, DRG 370, is "cesarean section with complications." DRG 373 is "vaginal delivery without complicating diagnosis." If the hospital can provide care to an individual patient for less than what the government pays for that person's discharge DRG, the hospital pockets the difference. If the cost is more than what the government pays, the hospital must make up the difference out of its own funds.

Clearly, this DRG-based reimbursement scheme provides an incentive to hospitals to reduce costs. One means of reducing costs is to let all physicians know how much his or her patients cost and whether his or her average charges for a particular DRG are above or below the average cost incurred by patients of all physicians practicing in the hospital. Across the country, hospitals conduct workshops to show physicians whether they are high-cost or low-cost physicians, in the hope that high-cost doctors will learn from their low-cost colleagues how to move their patients out of the hosptial faster and how to provide good medical care at a lower cost. Appendix A shows the kind of data hospitals are using in these efforts.

With that as background, you can understand what a case is in this data set and what aspects of each case are measured by the variables in this case-by-variable matrix. A case in this data set consists of a physician-DRG pair. So the first case (first line) is information for physician 01's behavior with respect to DRG 370. You can see that each case is not just a doctor because the second line of the data set also contains information about physician 01, but it shows his or her costs for DRG 371. You can also see that a case is not a DRG because DRG 370 appears in lines 1 and 10 (among others) of the data set. So in this data set a case is a physician-DRG pair. A case is defined by a physician's number, in the first column of the case-by-variable matrix, and the DRG number, in the second column of the matrix.

Besides physician number and DRG number, there are eight other variables in this data set. The third variable indicates whether a DRG has a complicating diagnosis. This variable has the value 1 if there is a complicating diagnosis and 0 if not. But since the DRG name tells you whether there is a complicating diagnosis, why create another variable that is redundant with one aspect of the variable "DRG"? Look at the data set. There is nothing about the DRG *numbers* that readily indicates whether a complication was present or not. It so happens that DRGs 370, 372, and 383 are diagnoses with complications. All other DRGs are diagnoses without complications. But there is nothing about the numbers that makes the distinction. This "complications" variable makes an explicit part of the data set the aspect of each case that can be characterized by the two categories "complications present" or "complications not present."

The variable "discharges" is the number of discharges a physician had in a specific DRG. Physician 01 discharged one person who had a cesarean section with complications (DRG 370). The same doctor also discharged 28 patients with a diagnosis of "vaginal delivery without complicating diagnosis."

ALOS stands for average length of stay. It is the average number of days spent in the hospital by the physician's patients in the specified DRG.

"Nonspecialization" is the percentage of DRGs (in which a physician discharged at least one patient) that are not in the obstetric group. If a physician discharged a lot of patients in nonobstetric DRGs, the percentage of DRGs for which the physician discharged patients not in the obstetric group would be high and you would surmise that the physician tends not to specialize in obstetrics. If the percentage is small, the physician tends to treat only obstetric patients. For example, the physician who discharged patients in DRGs 17, 26, 84, 121, 370, 371, 424, and 456 would have discharged patients in two obstetric DRGs and in six nonobstetric DRGs. The doctor would have a nonspecialization score of $6/(2 + 6) = 6/8 = 75$ percent.

The next variable in the data set is the average total cost of a patient's care by the specified physician in the specified DRG. So, on average, a "normal," medically inconsequential delivery (DRG 373) by physician 01 cost $1074 in hospital charges. This cost included room and board, any specialty care and clinical support (including the use of an emergency-room physician), surgical costs, charges for diagnostic work, and charges for material and technology. The final three variables in the data set show the percentages of total cost devoted to surgery, diagnosis, and materials and technology (including drugs).

. . .

STATISTICS AS DATA REDUCTION

Among other things, statistics are tools for data reduction. *Data* are, according to one dictionary, "things known or assumed."[1] Statistics are useful when you have large amounts of data—lots of things known or assumed—that you want to make more manageable so that you can analyze them.

For example, suppose that for 1500 people you know each person's name, age, sex, occupation, and number of years of school completed; whether the person would approve of abortion if a pregnancy endangered a woman's life; and whether the person had been out of work and looking for a job for at least 1 week in the last year. Then you would know seven things about each person. You would know everything in Table 2.2, the case-by-variable matrix for this data set. You would know $7 \times 1500 = 10,500$ things. That is a large number of things to know.

Statistics are tools that will reduce the amount of data that you have to work with. Suppose you calculated the *average* age and *average* number of years of school completed and the *percentage* of the 1500 people who are female, the *percentage* who are blue-collar workers, the *percentage* of people who would approve of abortion if a woman's life were endangered by the pregnancy, and the *percentage* of people unemployed for at least 1 week in the last year. Those six numbers, those six *statistics*, would give you some idea of the characteristics of this particular group of 1500 people. In fact, as groups of 1500 people go, you would know quite a lot about *this* group of 1500 by knowing just those six numbers. A reduction from 10,500 pieces of data to 6 statistics is a sizable data reduction. Data reduction is one of the major tasks of statistics.

TABLE 1.1 Case-by-Variable Matrix for 1500 People and 7 Variables

				Variables			
Case no.	Name	Age	Sex	Occupation	Schooling	Approve Abortion	Unemployed
1	K. Page	32	F	Court reporter	14	Yes	No
2	J. James	63	M	Farmer	12	No	No
3	R. McCaw	45	M	Student	15	No	No
1499	G. Smotley	14	M	—	7	No	—
1500	J. Seams	52	F	Psychiatrist	22	—	No

To reduce the data from 10,500 pieces to 6 numbers, you paid a price: You lost a lot of information. You know the average age and number of years of school completed, but you do not know from those six statistics the age of the oldest or youngest person in the group. Nor do you know the average number of years of school completed by those who have completed at least 12 years of school. You could calculate other statistics such as the highest and lowest age. You could also calculate statistics on subsets of the sample such as those who have completed at least 12 years of school. These other statistics would give you a sense of the diversity among these 1500 people. Even with these other statistics, you still could not determine which person was the oldest or the youngest. Data become more manageable through data reduction, but information is lost in the process.

There is a general rule in statistics: *To gain the summary information that statistics provide, you lose other information.* It may be more useful to know the average unemployment rate for the 50 states than to know the unemployment rates and the names of each of the 50 states. It is certainly much easier to remember a single number—the average unemployment rate—than it is to remember 50 numbers paired with 50 names. But you pay a price for choosing a statistic over the original data. At some time, you may want to know how many Southern states have unemployment rates above 10 percent. The single statistic, the average unemployment rate for the 50 states, does not contain the information you need to find the answer you want.

Losing information is not necessarily bad. In everyday language, every time you speak or write a word, you give up information about "things known or assumed." If you say to a friend, "Look at that person," you have given up a lot of information that you know or assume by choosing the word "person." Is the person a man or woman, old or young, disheveled or neatly dressed? Did you perhaps assume that she or he was from another country? Why did you choose to omit that information from your statement? We always use information selectively. It would be impossible to do otherwise. Words, when used well, convey necessary information to a knowledgeable listener, even though the selection of a particular word means giving up or losing information you have at your command. The same is true in statistics. Statistics, when used well, convey necessary information to a knowledgeable listener, even though some information contained in a data set is lost to the conversation.

· · ·

HYPOTHESES

A hypothesis is a statement that you think is true but which you can test. The following sounds like a simple declarative statement: The percentage of people in the United States who believe abortion should be okay if a woman's life is in danger from the pregnancy is greater than 50 percent. It is a declarative statement, and I believe it to be true. The statement becomes a hypothesis when I am willing to test it to see if it is true. I could test this hypothesis by using data from sample surveys and inferential statistics to make an inference from a sample to the population from which the sample came; so the statement is a hypothesis.

Often hypotheses are statements about relationships between variables. For example, the researchers in the internal motivation experiments were interested in the relationship between what a task was called ("work" or "leisure," the variable "task label") and the internal motivation the subject might have to continue doing the task when not required to do so. You probably have your own ideas (hypotheses) about what happens. How do you feel when you tell your friends, "Sorry, but I've got to go *work* on my statistics now"? Lousy, right? In the words of the researchers, "[when] extrinsic rewards cause the task to be perceived as work, . . . this perception . . . diminishes the motivation to do it."[2] This sounds reasonable enough, but they went a little further:

> We predicted that among subjects who endorse the work ethic, labeling the task as work would increase their tendency to choose to perform that activity later on. Among subjects who do not endorse the value of work, however, "turning play into work" by means of labeling the task may, we predicted, reduce their subsequent inclination to perform that task.[3]

So this is the hypothesis: Among those people told they were to do some "work," low-work-ethic subjects will not have the internal motivation to continue a task, but high-work-ethic subjects will.

The variable of principal interest here is "internal motivation." It is called the *dependent variable* in the hypothesis because its level is thought to be dependent on the level of another variable, "work ethic." "Work ethic" is called the *independent variable* because in this hypothesis it is not dependent on any other variable.

Sometimes it helps to diagram a hypothesis. A simple, two-variable hypothesis is diagramed thus:

Independent variable → Dependent variable

Sometimes the arrow connecting the two variables means "causes," but it need not mean that. Establishing a cause-and-effect relationship between two variables is very difficult. (Causality is discussed in Chapter 10.) Science may ultimately wish to discover what causes something to happen, but science is concerned first with discovering relationships between variables. Diagraming a hypothesis merely serves to distinguish the dependent variable from the independent variable, and it need not indicate a causal relationship.

How would you diagram the hypothesis from the first internal motivation experiment? First, determine which is the dependent and which the independent variable. The dependent variable, the variable of principal interest, is "internal motivation," or in this case willingness to continue doing a task when not required to do so. The independent variable is "work ethic." The diagram would look like this:

$$\text{Work ethic} \xrightarrow{+} \text{Internal motivation}$$

The plus sign indicates that higher levels of "work ethic" tend to go with higher levels of "internal motivation." There is a positive relationship between the two variables.

Remember, a hypothesis states a *possible* relationship between variables. The hypothesis does not have to be true. It only has to be testable. It has nothing to do with individual cases. Some individuals in experiment 1 will probably be high-work-ethic people showing little internal motivation. Others will be low-work-ethic people with high internal motivation. No matter. As long as high-work-ethic people *tend* to be more internally motivated than low-work-ethic people, the hypothesis will be supported. And even if the data do not support the hypothesis, there is no cause for concern. A hypothesis only needs to be falsifiable, not true.

Note: An exercise at the end of the chapter introduces you to internal-motivation experiment 2, its variables, and the hypothesis *it* was designed to test. Be sure to read that exercise carefully.

• • •

KEY CONCEPTS IN THIS CHAPTER

Henceforth, at the end of each chapter, a reference list of key concepts is given. The list gives the page where a concept or formula is introduced.

Case   12
Case-by-variable matrix   16
Data reduction   21
Dependent variable   23
Hypothesis   22
Independent variable   23
Statistical tools (statistics)   21
Unit of analysis   12
Variable   13
     Continuous variable   16
     Discrete variable   16
     Interval variable   14
     Nominal variable   15
     Ordinal variable   15
     Ratio variable   15

. . .

NOTES

1. The word "data" is a plural noun and technically takes a plural verb. So we say, "Data *are* simply . . . ." The singular of "data" is "datum." "Datum" refers to a single piece of data. The work "data" is sometimes constructed as a singular noun, especially if it refers to a data set. For example, one might say, "The opinion poll data *shows* [instead of *show*] that attitudes toward abortion are becoming more liberal."

2. Thomas Li-Ping Tang and Roy F. Baumeister, "Effects of Personal Values, Perceived Surveillance, and Task Labels on Task Preference: The Ideology of Turning Work into Play," *Journal of Applied Psychology* 68:99–105, 1984. Copyright 1984 by the American Psychological Association. Reprinted by permission.

3. Ibid., p. 99.

. . .

EXERCISES

Chapter 2

1. Think about the concept "religious belief" or "religious affiliation," the concept measured by asking on a questionnaire, What is your religion?

   a. Construct a variable called "religion" that has two categories.
   b. Construct a variable "religion" that has five categories.
   c. Construct a variable "religion" that has a dozen categories.
   d. What kind of variable is "religion"? Is it a different kind of variable depending on the number of categories it has?

   2. Suppose you have surveyed a college class, using the measurement device in Exercise 1, and constructed a variable with four categories. You find there are 90 Protestants, 60 Catholics, 20 Jews, and 5 who identify themselves as "other." You could use this measuring device for other classes and determine how many people in each class identified themselves with each religion. Construct a new variable called "religion's popularity" based on the number of respondents in each religion. This new variable would rank the four religions according to the number of professed adherents you discovered in the survey. Use the following steps as aids:

   a. When you ask the question, What is your religion?, the individual respondent is the unit of analysis and the variable is "religion." Each individual was a case. What is the unit of analysis for the variable "religion's popularity"? That is, what is a case for the variable "religion's popularity"?

   b. "Catholic," "Protestant," "Jewish," and "other" were the categories
   of the variable "religion." What categories did you use to construct
   the variable "religion's popularity"?
   c. How would you assign each case in this exercise to the categories
   you formed?

3. Internal-Motivation Experiment 2

Based on the results of the first experiment, Tang and Baumeister proposed
a second study. Some subjects in experiment 1 spent a lot of time on the word
game. This might have been due to internal motivation, the intrinsic reward that
comes from doing the task. However, it might have been due to a desire to please
the experimenter who, the subjects may have suspected, may have had an interest
in their behavior. To see if the time spent on the word game was dependent on
internal motivation or on "self-presentational concerns" (the desire to please the
investigator), the researchers first put each of the 40 subjects in experiment 2
through a process just like that in experiment 1. Then, in each case, the subject
was taken to another room. On the table in that room were a jigsaw puzzle and a
series of anagrams.

Subjects were randomized into two experimental conditions. One-half were
told that the experimenter wanted them to fill out a questionnaire. The experimenter made an excuse to leave the subject alone in the room for 15 minutes. The
subject thought he was simply being left alone and that the researcher had no
interest in how he spent the time. In fact, the subject was observed, and the amount
of time spent doing anagrams was recorded. In the public condition, the experimenter told the subject she or he was to "pretest" the jigsaw puzzle and anagram
game for use in future projects. The subject was asked to determine which was
more difficult. In the public condition, the subject thought the researcher had an
interest in how he spent the time.

In both conditions, the researcher timed the seconds spent on the anagrams
during the 15-minute period. "Time spent on word game" is the dependent variable
in this study. The researchers also administered scales on "Protestant work ethic,"
"leisure ethic," and "Type A personality."

   a. In Appendix A, the experimental variable is called "observation
   type" and consists of the categories "public" and "private." Can you
   think of a better name for this variable?
   b. Construct a hypothesis relating the experimentally manipulated
   variable "observation type" to the dependent variable "time spent
   on word game."
   c. What kind of variable is "observation type"?
   d. Among people who score high on the Protestant work-ethic scale,
   what do you think is the relationship between "observation type"
   and "time spent on word game"? Among people who score low on the
   Protestant work-ethic scale, what relationship do you think exists

between "observation type" and "time spent on word game"?
Formulate your hypotheses.

e. Do you think there would be a relationship between "Type A
personality" and "time spent on word game" in either experiment?

f. Take as your unit of analysis, for the moment, an experiment—a
whole experiment. You have two cases: experiment 1 and experiment 2.
Construct a nominal variable that has two categories such that
experiment 1 is assignable to one category and experiment 2 is
assignable to the other category. (Do not simply construct a variable
consisting of categories named "1" and "2.") What is the name
of this variable?

4. What kind of variables are these?

a. Number of pages in a book
b. Number of stripes on the U.S. flag
c. Unemployment rate in Winden County
d. Number of unemployed people in Winden County
e. Car colors
f. Book titles
g. Types of scholars
h. Football players' numbers
i. Cards in a playing deck

5. John Gardner wrote a fairy tale called "The Griffin and the Wise Old Phil-
osopher." It is based on the idea that wherever a griffin goes, it causes human beings
around it to become completely befuddled and confused. That happens whenever
the griffin in the story travels out of his castle and among the human beings in
the town. No human seems capable of doing anything! But then the griffin gets
a little befuddled and confused himself, because some human beings seem to have
gotten some things done between his visits. If he visits the same person twice,
both times the griffin sees a person who is befuddled and confused and unable to
do anything. But that human being appears to have accomplished some tasks between visits from the griffin.

Let us turn the premise of the story into a statement: Whenever a griffin is
present, human beings are befuddled and confused and incapable of accomplishing
anything; and whenever griffins are not present, human beings can function effec-
tively and accomplish things.

a. Is the statement falsifiable by a griffin?
b. Is the statement falsifiable by a human being?
c. Is this statement falsifiable at all? That is, is this statement a hypothesis?

6. Calvin Trillin says that he has a foolproof method to keep the planes he
flies on from crashing. He just refuses to reset his watch to the time zone of his

destination until he lands there. His technique for keeping the planes in the air has not failed yet.

   a. Derive a hypothesis from this practice. What is the dependent variable? What is the independent variable? How are these two variables related?

   b. What would be required for the hypothesis to be falsified?

   c. List three difficulties would you face if you wanted to test this hypothesis.

7. For each pair of variables, do three things:

   a. State what a case is.

   b. Construct a hypothesis relating each pair of variables. Remember that a hypothesis does not have to be true; it just has to be testable. Briefly discuss the reasoning that led to your hypothesis.

   c. Describe, as precisely as you can, how you might measure the dependent variable in each instance.

Pair	Independent Variable	Dependent Variable
1	River temperature	Trout population in river
2	Average hours of daylight in a forest	Percentage of forest's population that is deciduous
3	Age of person	Person's score on standardized scholastic achievement test
4	Number of keys on person's key ring	Person's power is an organization
5	Number of cars passing over roadway	Maintenance cost of roadway
6	Average snowfall in city	Productivity of city's workforce
7	Number of catalogs mailed by college admissions office	College enrollment
8	Number of admissions to an area hospital	Area's death rate
9	Pints of blood donated by a factory's workforce	Level of workforce's esprit de corps
10	Quality of parts shipped from a company	Company's profit
11	Budget of city's fire department	Annual loss due to fire in city
12	Prison population of state	Average length of prison sentences in criminal cases in state
13	Number of exercises a student works in the statistics text	Student's grade in statistics course

3

▼

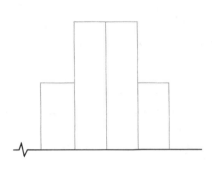

• • •

Frequency Distributions

You know that a variable is a mutually exclusive and totally inclusive collection of categories. Each category in the collection is one of various descriptors of some specific characteristic of the cases. To begin to describe a data set, it is helpful to know how the cases are distributed across the categories of a variable. If you have a sample of 1500 people, how many are white-collar workers and how many blue-collar workers? How many are 0 to 4 years old, how many 5 to 9 years old, how many 10 to 14 years old, and so on? These are questions about the *frequency* with which cases fall into the various categories of a variable. These questions concern how cases *distribute* themselves across the categories of a variable. In general, these questions involve the *frequency distribution* of cases on a particular variable.

· · ·

A BEGINNING EXAMPLE

Table 3.1 contains the leisure-ethic scores of the 40 cases in internal-motivation experiment 2. Table 3.2 shows how many cases fall in each category of the variable. The first column shows the category. It contains all possible categories from a score of 10 to 70. The second column is the tally of the cases in each category. The third column is the frequency of cases in each category. The frequency of cases is equal to the number of tally marks in the category.

So what good is that? Well, you can see immediately that the lowest score in the data set is not equal to the lowest possible score and that the highest score in the sample is not equal to the highest possible score. The lowest score is 30, and the highest is 58. You can also see, in a way that you cannot with the original data, that the scores are spread out across the categories between 30 and 58, perhaps with a slight tendency to clump around the upper 40s. From this elaborate frequency distribution, you can get some idea of the *pattern* of the distribution of the cases on the variable.

If you are interested in the *pattern* of distribution of cases on a variable, it is sometimes helpful to restructure a frequency distribution. Instead of listing all the categories, it is useful to form *classes* of categories and make a frequency distribution of cases across those classes.

In this example, it might be helpful to form classes consisting of five categories each. Look at Table 3.3. There are 12 classes; each one is numbered: $i = 1, 2, 3, \ldots, 12$. The second column of Table 3.3 shows the *boundaries* of each class. Next is the tally of cases in the class. Then there is a column of frequencies. The frequency in classs 1 is designated f_1. Since there are no cases in class 1, which contains scores 10, 11, 12, 13, and 14, we know that $f_1 = 0$. There are four cases in class 5, which has class boundaries at 30 and 34, so $f_5 = 4, f_6 = 8, f_7 = 8, f_8 = 11,$

TABLE 3.1 Leisure-Ethic Scores
for the 40 Cases in Internal-
Motivation Experiment 2

31	48	44	46	43
47	48	48	51	46
50	48	34	54	47
51	38	39	39	55
42	50	45	40	50
37	38	30	35	47
37	55	32	38	52
41	44	47	41	58

TABLE 3.2 Frequency Distribution of Leisure-Ethic Scores from Table 3.1

Category	Tally	Frequency	Category	Tally	Frequency
10		0	41	||	2
11		0	42	||	2
12		0	43	|	1
13		0	44	||	2
14		0	45	|	1
15		0	46	||	2
16		0	47	||||	4
17		0	48	||||	4
18		0	49		0
19		0	50	|||	3
20		0	51	||	2
21		0	52	|	1
22		0	53		0
23		0	54		0
24		0	55	||	2
25		0	56		0
26		0	57		0
27		0	58	|	1
28		0	59		0
29		0	60		0
30	|	1	61		0
31	|	1	62		0
32	|	1	63		0
33		0	64		0
34	|	1	65		0
35	|	1	66		0
36		0	67		0
37	||	2	68		0
38	|||	3	69		0
39	||	2	70		0
40	|	1			

TABLE 3.3 Frequency Distribution of Leisure-Ethic Scores from Table 3.1 with Classes of Five Categories Each

Class i	Class Boundaries	Tally	Frequency f_i	Relative Frequency
1	10−14		0	0
2	15−19		0	0
3	20−24		0	0
4	25−29		0	0
5	30−34	||||	4	4/40
6	35−39	⊬⊬ |||	8	8/40
7	40−44	⊬⊬ |||	8	8/40
8	45−49	⊬⊬ ⊬⊬ |	11	11/40
9	50−54	⊬⊬ |	6	6/40
10	55−59	|||	3	3/40
11	60−64		0	0
12	65 +		0	0

and so on. In general, the frequency of cases in class i is designated f_i, where i can be any value from 1 to 12 in this example.

Table 3.3 also shows the *relative frequency* with which cases fall into these constructed classes of the variable "leisure ethic." The relative frequency of class i is defined as f_i/n, where n is the total number of cases in the sample. In this example, $n = 40$. Class 5 occurs 4/40ths or 10.0 percent of the time in the sample. Class 6 occurs 8/40ths or 20.0 percent of the time.

All this information can be depicted in a *frequency histogram*, or simply a *histogram*. A histogram is a picture composed of rectangles each of a length proportional to the relative frequency of a class. The rectangle is constructed over a class interval which is placed along a line at the bottom of the picture.

Figure 3.1 shows a histogram based on the information in Table 3.3. Along the bottom, or horizontal axis, of the histogram the class intervals are displayed. Along the left side, or vertical axis, is a line showing frequency. The rectangles rise above the class intervals to the height of the frequency of cases in the class. The length of each rectangle is proportional to the relative frequency of cases in each category. This gives you a very good idea about the overall distribution of cases across the classes. (*Note:* The jagged part of the bottom scale indicates that some of the scale has been left out of the picture.)

A histogram is useful. Not only does it show you the pattern of distribution of cases across the categories of a variable, but also it can be used to find, for example, the relative frequency of broad classes of scores, say, scores in the class of 45 or more. The relative frequency of a broad class of scores (such as scores of 45 or more) is equal to the proportion of the area of the histogram covered by

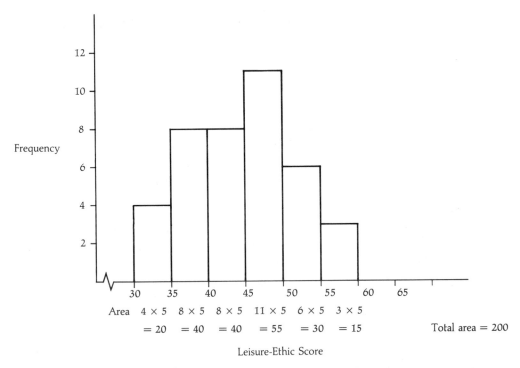

FIGURE 3.1 Frequency histogram of leisure-ethic scores.

the rectangles over the part of the scale of interest. The bottom lines of Figure 3.1 show the areas of each rectangle in the histogram. From these you find that the total area covered by the histogram is 200 units. The area covered by rectangles from a score of 45 and up is $55 + 30 + 15 = 100$ units. The relative frequency of cases with leisure-ethic scores of 45 or more is 100/200, or 50 percent. This example may seem trivial since you could obtain the relative frequency simply by adding the relative frequencies of classes 8 through 12 from Table 3.3. But the notion that *the area under a part of a histogram corresponds to the relative frequency* will be useful later as things get more complicated.

What good is the relative frequency? It may seem like just so much busywork to divide the frequency by the total number of cases in the sample. But think about the experiment from which these data came. The researchers are, of course, interested in describing the data on the 40 cases in the sample, and the histogram does this. However, they are scientists interested in generalizing to the population from which this sample came. How would you respond if you were asked, How many people in the population from which this sample came have a leisure-ethic score of 45 or more? You might be tempted to say, "How should I know?" In a way, this would be a proper response. You don't know anything about the population from which this sample came—not even its size. But you could use information from the sample to estimate that about 50 percent of the people in the population (regardless of the population's size) scored 45 or more on the leisure-ethic scale.

I will have much more to say about estimates of this sort later. For now, note that the relative frequency of occurrences in a sample reveals something about the population from which the sample came.

Dice

Consider a demonstration I performed recently.[1] I said to a group of students, "Let's construct a frequency distribution of many throws of two dice. To speed the data collection, we'll have Beth throw this red pair and Bill throw this white pair. You two throw the dice, add the spots showing, and report the total to me. I'll construct a quick-and-dirty frequency distribution and eventually a histogram from the data."

What is the variable? Obviously, the variable is "sum of spots showing on two dice." What collection of categories constitutes this variable? The variable can assume values 2, 3, 4, . . . , 12. A throw of two dice cannot total less than 2 or more than 12, and the result must always be a whole number. This collection of categories {2, 3, . . . , 12} is a variable since each throw can be assigned to one and only one category.

Let's pause for a moment because you know something about throwing dice. Over the long run, there should be more 7s than any other number because there are more combinations of two dice that add to 7 than there are combinations that add to any other number. In fact, there are 6 ways to obtain a 7 (first die = 1, second die = 6, or 1−6; first die = 2, second die = 5, or 2−5; 3−4; 4−3; 5−2; 6−1) out of the 36 possible combinations of the two dice. There is only one way to obtain a 2 (1−1), and there is one way to obtain a 12 (6−6). So, over the long run, we should obtain 6 times as many 7s as 2s or 12s. There are 2 ways out of 36 possible combinations to get a 3 (1−2 and 2−1), so over the long run there should be 3 times as many 7s as 3s and twice as many 3s as 2s or 12s. By the same reasoning, there should be 3 times as many 7s as there are 11s. All 36 combinations of two dice are shown in Figure 3.2.

By following this logic for all categories, the *theoretical* distribution of throws of two dice looks like Figure 3.3. This is the relative-frequency histogram for the

			Die 2			
Die 1	1	2	3	4	5	6
1	2	3	4	5	6	7
2	3	4	5	6	7	8
3	4	5	6	7	8	9
4	5	6	7	8	9	10
5	6	7	8	9	10	11
6	7	8	9	10	11	12

FIGURE 3.2 Thirty-six combinations of two dice.

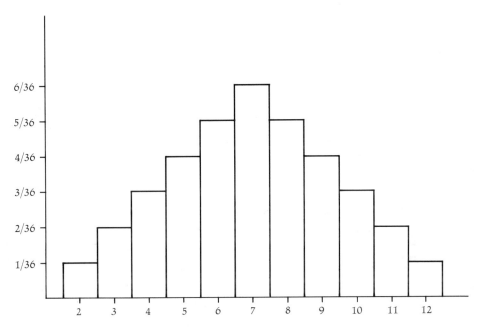

FIGURE 3.3 Theoretical distribution of the variable "sum of two dice." Relative-frequency histogram for "sum of two dice."

population of throws of two dice. The distribution is symmetric. That is, both sides of the distribution are shaped the same. And the distribution is shaped like steps of a staircase since the variable is a discrete variable. Figure 3.3 is the distribution one would expect to see after many, many throws of two dice.

"Now," I said, "begin to collect some sample data." I recorded Bill's throws with Xs and Beth's throws with Os. I placed one mark opposite the category in which a particular roll fell. I tried to make each mark about the same size so the marks would seem to form a "bar" (made of individual marks) proportional in length to the number of throws in a category. In this way I "tallied" the cases in each category and, at the same time, formed the basis for drawing a histogram. (I recorded the distribution sideways just in case some number showed up often and made me run off the top of the chalkboard.)

After every 10 throws by each person, I also counted the number of throws in each category and recorded the count to the right of each bar. The array of counts is called the *frequency distribution*.

After 10 throws each, the distribution looked like that in Figure 3.4. This does not look at all like what one might expect. "Why?" I asked the students. "Not enough throws," came the unanimous reply. Remember that the theoretical distribution is the distribution of the sample data that one would expect over the very long run. Twenty cases are not a very long run. "Roll more," I told Beth and Bill, taking the advice of the class.

i	Throws	f_i
2	X	1
3	X	1
4	O	1
5	OOOO	4
6	X X	2
7	X X	2
8	X	1
9	O	1
10	XOXO	4
11	OOX	3
12		0

FIGURE 3.4 Distribution after 20 throws, 10 from Bill's dice (X) and 10 from Beth's (0).

After 60 rolls, 30 by each person, the distribution of 60 cases looked like that in Figure 3.5. What do you think of that distribution?

The distribution does not look like the theoretical distribution. There are many more 5s and 10s than one would expect. Why? "Roll more," most of the class said. "Rigged dice," came the muted protest of one fellow in the back. Another student

i	Throws	f_i
2	X	1
3	X	1
4	OOXOX	5
5	OOOOX X XOXOOXX	13
6	X X X X	4
7	X X X X X X X X	8
8	X XOXO	5
9	OOOOOXO	7
10	XOXOOOOXOOO	11
11	OOXOO	5
12		0
		$n = 60$

FIGURE 3.5 Distribution after 60 throws, 30 from Bill's dice (X) and 30 from Beth's dice (0). Also shown is frequency distribution f_i, $2 < i < 12$.

i	Throws	f_i
2	X X	2
3	X X X	3
4	O O X O X X O O	8
5	O O O O X X X O X O O X X X O X	16
6	X X X X X O O X	8
7	X X X X X X X X X X	10
8	X X O X O O X	7
9	O O O O O X O X X O X O O X X O	16
10	X O X O O O O X O O O O O O O O X X O	19
11	O O X O O O O O X O	10
12	X	1
		$n = 60$

FIGURE 3.6 Distribution of 100 throws, 50 from Bill's dice (X) and 50 from Beth's (0).

came to the defense of the rest of the class and argued that the distribution in Figure 3.5 is a possible result from 60 throws of fair dice. It just so happens that in this particular sample of 60 throws, there are a lot of 5s and 10s. "Besides," he argued, "you can see that with 60 throws, the shape of the distribution is 'more like' the theoretical distribution than the distribution with only 20 throws. More 7s have been obtained, and 2s, 3s, 11s, and 12s have not come." His conclusion: "Roll more." And roll more they did.

Figure 3.6 shows the distribution after 100 throws. Just as I was about to ask, "What next?" the fellow who had proposed the rigged dice spoke: "I'd like to see Beth's dice. She has not rolled even one 7. Her dice roll 9s and 10s and 11s with a very high frequency; 4s, 5s, and 6s with lower frequency; and they never roll a 7." He looked at Beth's dice and found they were, indeed, peculiar. One die had two sides with 3 spots, two sides with 4 spots, and two sides with 5 spots. The other die had two 6s, two 1s, and two 5s. You cannot roll a 7 with these dice. The now-honorable doubter worked out the theoretical distribution for these fixed dice. That is, he figured out the 36 possible combinations of the dice and found that the distribution for fixed dice looks like Figure 3.7. The upper part of that figure shows the 36 combinations of these dice, and the lower part shows the relative-frequency distribution expected of these dice.

Because I had kept information on whose dice were thrown for each throw by recording Beth's throws with an O and Bill's with an X, I could split the distribution in Figure 3.6 into two distributions, one for Beth's dice and the other for

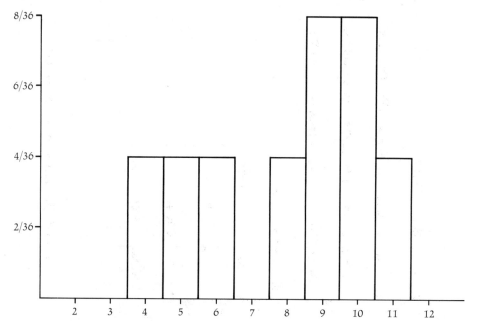

Die 1	Die 2					
	1	1	5	5	6	6
3	4	4	8	8	9	9
3	4	4	8	8	9	9
4	5	5	9	9	10	10
4	5	5	9	9	10	10
5	6	6	10	10	11	11
5	6	6	10	10	11	11

FIGURE 3.7 Thirty-six possible combinations of the fixed dice (upper panel), and the theoretical distribution of the fixed dice (lower panel).

Bill's dice. These two distributions are shown in Figure 3.8. They are each called a *conditional distribution* because I have "conditioned" the original distribution on another factor. In this case, I conditioned on the names of the people throwing the dice. The distributions are called *conditional distributions* because we have made two conditional selections of cases. One selection is made *if* the name of the thrower is "Bill," and the other is made *if* the thrower is "Beth." The conditional form in the English language is *if,* so the notion of a conditional distribution should not be foreign to you.

Several lessons are embedded in this example. One is trivial. You now know how to construct a frequency distribution and a histogram. You just take each case, determine the category to which the case belongs, and keep track of how many cases end up in each category. A listing of the number of cases by category is a

i	Bill's Throws	f_i		i	Beth's Throws	f_i
2	XX	2		2		
3	XXX	3		3		
4	XXX	3		4	OOOOO	5
5	XXXXXXX	8		5	OOOOOOOO	8
6	XXXXX	6		6	OO	2
7	XXXXXXXXXX	10		7		0
8	XXXX	4		8	OOO	3
9	XXXXXX	6		9	OOOOOOOOOO	10
10	XXXXX	5		10	OOOOOOOOOOOOOO	14
11	XX	2		11	OOOOOOOO	8
12	X	1		12		

FIGURE 3.8 Two conditional distributions of dice throws, one for Bill's and one for Beth's throws.

frequency distribution. A histogram is a pictorial representation of the frequency distribution. The length of each bar in a histogram represents the number of cases in the category relative to the numbers of cases in other categories.

The second lesson is not so trivial. It goes something like this: "A scientist is always skeptical. Trust your instincts." This double injunction is not necessarily a contradiction. Think about the common practice of rolling dice. You know, in advance, what the distribution of lots of throws of two dice is going to look like. When the distribution in the example failed to look like it "should," most people found a way to explain the discrepancy: "Roll more." When one fellow got suspicious, a little reasoning by classmates talked him out of his position, at least temporarily. Only after a lot more evidence was collected, and only after the skeptic was able to put his position pointedly, clearly, and forcefully, did others agree that the dice might be rigged. Trusting your own intuition and investigating hunches will often save you time and, sometimes, considerable embarrassment. Acting on your intuition when the majority of a community of scientists are against you may be difficult, but it is necessary.

The third lesson is more subtle. If I had not kept track of the results of the throws for the separate sets of dice by using Xs and Os, the information needed to inquire statistically into the difference between the sets of dice would have been lost. The class would have been left with an odd distribution consisting of all Xs which I could have easily transformed into a familiar, traditional histogram. Without the information conveyed by the Xs and Os, discovering that one set of dice was behaving oddly could have taken much, much longer. The moral is this: Retain as much information as you possibly can as you conduct statistical inquiries.

• • •

EXPLORATORY DATA ANALYSIS

Statistician John W. Tukey has developed a scheme for, as he puts it, "scratching down numbers" that essentially creates a histogram, that preserves more information than a traditional histogram does, that does not require a great degree of carefulness (even though it requires thoughtfulness), and that can be done with pencil and paper. He calls his scheme a "stem-and-leaf display."[2] The exercise with the dice created a kind of stem-and-leaf display.

Tukey[2] recommends that you always begin your scratching by putting a line down the paper. Then you let your "stems" go across the page as I did. Each stem is labeled, as for the dice, with some category that represents the numerical value of the cases to be put onto that stem. You enter each case on the appropriate stem by adding a "leaf." The leaf is not just an X, because the leaf should contain some information about the case. In the dice example, each leaf contained information about the name of the thrower. Tukey's scheme is useful because it keeps you in close touch with the data. If you use a computer to analyze your data, there is a tendency to pay attention only to the output, not to the input, the raw data. If you just scratch down numbers, you get a better "feel" for the raw data.[3]

• • •

PER CAPITA INCOME: AN EXAMPLE

Now let's play with what you know. Turn to Appendix A. How would you construct a frequency distribution for per capita income, one of the variables in the first data set?

First, you notice that per capita income is a continuous, ratio variable. It has no discrete categories like 2, 3, 4, . . . , 12 for the dice. So the first task is to construct classes into which the cases can be sorted. There are no firm rules for determining the number of classes you should use. The only "rule" is that the result of your operation should be informative.[4] Your frequency distribution or histogram should tell you at a glance something that is difficult to determine from simply scanning the raw data. Beyond that rule, trial and error (and experience, as you gain it) are your guides.

First, scan all 142 values of per capita income. Do it quickly. Just get a sense of what small and large values the variable can assume.

In this data set, lots of values have only three digits. That is, there are a lot of cases with per capita income less than $1000. There are several cases above $10,000, and there are a bunch of cases between $1000 and $10,000. At least we know from the quick scan that the frequency distribution must start at 0 and go up to $16,000.

$0–$4999	120
$5000–$9999	15
$10,000–$14,999	5
$15,000+	2

FIGURE 3.9 Frequency distribution for per capita income.

How large should the classes be? This is the tricky part. Having larger classes means fewer classes, which means simplicity of presentation. But simplicity of presentation means bulldozing all the subtlety out of the data, if there is any in the first place. Smaller classes will reveal finer features of the data; but constructing a histogram with smaller classes means more classes, which means a "busier" frequency distribution or histogram. A busier frequency distribution can muddle the subtlety. By trial and error you need to strike a compromise between conveying information and making the presentation easy to understand. It is sometimes not an easy compromise to make.

I quickly constructed a frequency distribution with four classes. It is shown in Figure 3.9. The first three classes are $5000 wide. They extend from $0 to $4999, from $5000 to $9999, and from $10,000 to $14,999. The fourth class is for all cases of $15,000 or more. What does the figure say? It says that very few countries have an annual per capita income of $5000 or more. It says little else. It tells us nothing about the fine structure of the great bulk of the countries that lie below the $5000 mark. This distribution is not very helpful, in my opinion. You need a stem-and-leaf diagram that zooms in on the mass of countries below $5000.

What happens if you reduce the category size to $1000? Figure 3.10 shows the resulting frequency distribution. This analysis is more useful. It shows that most countries still fall in the lowest class. That is, most countries have per capita incomes below $1000. Also the number of countries in each $1000 category declines sharply up to the $5000 level. Between $5000 and $10,000, countries are sprinkled rather evenly. Then there are a few countries here and there up to the two countries that lie at $15,000 or more. Clearly, there are two *outliers*, or cases that are very different from all the other cases. Figure 3.10, more clearly than Figure 3.9, makes it obvious that these two high-income countries are very different, since Figure 3.9 shows the gap between them and the countries next in line. Overall, this diagram is fairly useful. It has quite a few classes, but not too many, at least to my eyes.

Tukey, in his exploratory data analysis, encourages us to put names of outliers on graphs to get a sense of what might be accounting for the odd values. Are the two high-income countries flukes caused by high oil prices, for example? Well, the highest-income country is the United Arab Emirates, an oil producer. However, next down the list is Switzerland. Next come two oil states, but they are followed by three industrial states—Luxembourg, Belgium, and Canada. Looking at the data

Per Capita Income, $	10	20	30	40	50	60	70	f_i
0–999	**************************************							76
1000–1999	*********%							21
2000–2999	*****%							11
3000–3999	****							8
4000–4999	**							4
5000–5999	%							1
6000–6999	**%							5
7000–7999	*%							3
8000–8999	*							2
9000–9999	**							4
10,000–10,999	*%	Belgium, Canada, Luxembourg						3
11,000–11,999	*	Kuwait, Saudi Arabia						2
12,000–12,999								0
13,000–13,999								0
14,000–14,999								0
15,000–15,999	%	Switzerland						1
16,000 +	%	United Arab Emirates						1

FIGURE 3.10 A stem-and-leaf frequency distribution for per capita income. An asterisk represents two cases; a percent sign represents one case.

this closely suggests that there is more than one determinant of high per capita income.

How about a frequency distribution with smaller categories still? Figure 3.11 shows the stem-and-leaf design that results with classes $500 wide. It says pretty much the same thing as Figure 3.10. Most countries are very low in per capita income; there is a rapid decline in the number of countries per category up to $5000; there is an even sprinkling of countries up to about $10,000; and there are a few outliers.

Figure 3.11 is much more difficult to grasp, though, than Figure 3.10. It seems to me unmanageably long. Since it is so long and conveys little more information than Figure 3.10, I would choose Figure 3.10 to present the distribution of the variable "per capita income." Your choice may be different depending on the circumstances in which you are presenting your analysis. The lesson is this: You pay a price for choosing either simplicity or complexity of presentation. The prices differ, and you have to choose which you prefer to pay.

I added another feature to Figure 3.11. I made the "leaves" on the stems out of letters instead of meaningless marks like asterisks or percent signs. Each letter

Hundreds	10	20	30	40	50
0	ACACOSACCAOCCCSCSONAOCACCCCOCOCACAOOCOCCCACCAOOCCAAC				
5	CCCSCOOONNAAAAOACNCSCACCC				
10	AAOCOAANSCAAS				
15	EOSSSAAN				
20	SEEOEAO				
25	EEES				
30	OEEAEE				
35	EE				
40	CE				
45	AE				
50					
55	E				
60	EOC (C = Libya)				
65	EO				
70					
75	OEE				
80	A				
85	N (United States)				
90	EE				
95	EE				
100	NE				
105	E				
110	A				
115	A				
120		N = North and Central America			
125		S = South America			
130		A = Asia			
135		E = Europe			
140		C = Africa			
145		O = Other			
150	E				
155					
160	A				

FIGURE 3.11 A third distribution of per capita income, with smaller categories.

designates the region of the world in which the country is located. I may have classified countries incorrectly, but for now I'm just scratching down these numbers based on my imperfect knowledge of world geography. Classification errors notwithstanding, there are lots of African countries in the low-income part of the display and lots of European countries in the upper-income regions. It might have been better to classify Central American countries separately with South American instead of North American countries, but that's the value of hindsight. This stem-and-leaf display strongly suggests that there are gross regional differences in income as well as the country-to-country differences shown in Appendix A.

· · ·

NECESSARY INFORMATION

In this chapter you have been introduced to the simple techniques that make data more informative. A frequency distribution, a histogram, and a stem-and-leaf diagram are helpful because they give descriptive, summary pictures of large amounts of data. Just as in choosing class-interval sizes in this last example, however, the choice of how to present data—how to make data more informative—is not always clear. You will have to decide which statistical presentations contain the information you want to convey. You need to decide which information is necessary and which is not.

As in language, no information is inherently necessary. You make choices about the information you wish to convey, based on the context in which you find yourself.

When you are speaking, your context determines, to a degree, your choice of words. You would probably not say, "Look at that person," in front of Madison Square Garden on the night of a big game, because there would be so many people in your field of vision. That is, you would not say, "Look at that person" unless you did something else that would change the context to make your statement meaningful. Pointing would change the context. Prefacing your statement with a remark about a particular kind of person, so that a companion's attention would be focused on a limited category of people, would change the context. If you did nothing to change the context, you would have to add other information to enable your statement to communicate anything special: "Look at that person wearing the funny blue hat with the red patch on it."

The data you choose to analyze and the statistical analyses you perform depend, similarly, on the context in which you find yourself. If you are working for a lobbying organization supporting a bill granting a woman the right to have an abortion if her life is endangered by the pregnancy, the hypothetical data set on the 1500 people discussed in Chapter 2 may be very useful, since it contains respondents' answers to just that question. If you were a politician wondering simply how people feel about abortion, those data would not be very useful because people's feelings about abortion differ depending on the reasons given for having one. There is, for example, about a 40-percentage-point difference in approval of abortion when a woman's life is endangered, on the one hand, and when the woman is married and simply does not want any more children, on the other. The data set mentioned above would be even less useful in a context where the important question was, How liberal are people's political views today? The context in which

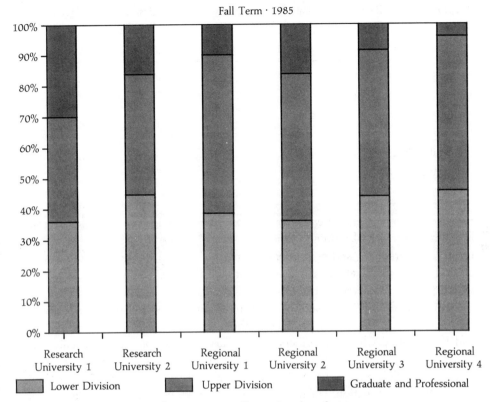

Fall Term · 1985

FIGURE 3.12 Enrollment by class division.

you find yourself determines the kinds of questions that are important; and questions, in turn, determine what information is necessary.

Here is a small example from a state higher education policy-making board. The staff of the board presented Figure 3.12 in the context of a discussion about the emphasis that various institutions of the state should give to upper- and lower-level work. The scale on the left is a percentage scale, and the components of the bars above each school show the percentages of each student body enrolled in lower-division courses, upper-division courses, and graduate and professional training. The policy-making board used this chart to argue that the six state institutions were "surprisingly similar" in the proportions of their efforts devoted to lower-division work (with all the institutions having about 40 percent of their enrollment in the lower division). The context for this discussion was a proposal that the two research universities, in the future, emphasize upper-level, graduate, and professional courses and that the regional universities emphasize lower-division enrollment.

A faculty member from Research University 1 got the original data, shown in Table 3.4. On the basis of the original data, he argued that because of sheer size,

TABLE 3.4 Enrollment in Six State Institutions by Class Division

Institution	Total Enrollment	Lower Division	Upper Division	Graduate and Professional
Research University 1	35,878	13,275	11,840	10,763
Research University 2	17,107	7,185	7,014	2,908
Regional University 1	5,206	1,978	2,656	572
Regional University 2	8,413	3,112	3,871	1,430
Regional University 3	4,500	1,890	2,115	495
Regional University 4	2,365	1,106	1,254	95

the research universities already "carry most of the burden" of upper-level, graduate, and professional training. "The data show," he said, "that 74 percent of all upper-level, graduate, and professional training is done at the research universities already; so to worry about 'emphasis' seems silly to me. The emphasis is already where you say you want it to be."

Is this a case of "you can prove anything with statistics"? No. It is a case of this faculty member's trying to change the context (through his deft argument) and thus change what is considered "necessary information" in the debate. The change hinges on the interpretation of the word "emphasis." The staff was interested in relative emphasis *within* institutions. In *that* context, Figure 3.12 contains the necessary information. The faculty member was trying to argue that "emphasis" should be judged *across* institutions and specifically *between* the research universities and the regional universities. If he were successful in having his interpretation of "emphasis" accepted as part of the terms of the debate, his information (which comes from the same data) would be considered the necessary information. To know what the best answer is, you have to understand the terms of the question.

. . .

KEY CONCEPTS IN THIS CHAPTER

Class   30
    Class boundaries   30
Conditional distribution   38
Estimation   33
Frequency   29
Frequency distribution   29, 35
Histogram (frequency histogram)   32
Outliers   41
Relative frequency   32
Stem-and-leaf display   40
Theoretical distribution   34

$$\cdots$$

NOTES

1. Joel Levine first showed me this demonstration. He also told me of the shop just off Times Square in New York City that sells the required set of dice.

2. John W. Tukey, *Exploratory Data Analysis*, Addison-Wesley, Reading, Mass., 1977.

3. As was probably inevitable, there are now computer programs to do exploratory data analysis. This is odd but true.

4. And there are always criticisms of unequivocal statements like this. H. A. Sturges ("The Choice of a Class Interval," *Journal of the American Statistical Association*, March 1926) recommends that you find the number of categories by the formula $k = 1 + 3.3 \log n$, where n is the number of cases in the sample and k is the number of categories used in the histogram.

$$\cdots$$

EXERCISES

Chapter 3

1. Consider the Type A personality scores of those people in internal-motivation experiment 2.

    a. Write down the scores of those in the "private" condition and scan them.

    b. Write down the smallest and the largest scores and the total number of scores.

    c. Select class boundaries by which to group scores.

    d. Tally the scores in each class, and construct a frequency distribution f_i.

    e. Make a frequency histogram of the scores.

    f. Repeat steps (**a**) through (**e**) for those in the "public" condition.

    g. Was there any reason to expect, before you did steps (**a**) through (**f**), that the frequency distributions would differ? Are they different? If so, how and why?

2. Construct a frequency distribution for "urbanization" from the first data set in Appendix A.

    a. Pick appropriate class boundaries, and construct the frequency distribution f_i.

    b. Construct a histogram for "urbanization."

    c. Describe the distribution's shape.

3. This problem is concerned with the variable "time spent on word game" in experiment 1.

    a. Construct a histogram for the variable.

    b. Now condition the distribution on the categories of variable "task label."

    c. Take one of the conditional distributions from part (**b**) and condition it on the variable "Protestant work ethic." (Divide "Protestant work ethic" into two categories. Assign subjects to a "high" work-ethic group and a "low" work-ethic group in a way that seems appropriate to you.)

    d. Use the statistics developed in parts (**b**) and (**c**) to make a statement about the hypothesis on which the experiment is based.

4. Develop a hypothesis about the relationship between the Protestant work-ethic score and the leisure-ethic score. Use data from either internal-motivation experiment to test the hypothesis.

    a. Construct histograms of the dependent variable for two levels of the independent variable.

    b. Based on the analysis, decide if the hypothesis is supported.

The following exercises are not related to the data sets at the end of the book.

5. Fifty people crossing a campus square were asked how many pets they owned. Here are their answers:

1	0	1	2	0	0	0	2	1	0
3	2	1	0	0	0	0	1	2	0
5	1	0	1	0	0	1	2	3	4
3	2	1	0	0	2	1	1	0	0
4	2	1	0	1	7	1	0	0	1

    a. Construct a frequency distribution for the variable "number of pets owned."

    b. Draw a histogram of the frequency distribution.

    c. If it would make sense to form classes, do so and construct another frequency distribution and histogram.

6. Thirty people coming to a medical clinic had their temperatures taken. Here are the results, in degrees Fahrenheit:

98.2	98.2	98.7	98.3	101.5	98.9
98.8	98.7	102.6	104.7	99.2	99.1
98.6	98.8	99.9	100.1	98.3	99.1
103.5	104.0	100.1	97.9	98.1	98.2
98.6	98.9	98.7	98.8	98.6	98.7
100.1	101.4	102.1	102.5	98.2	98.6

a. Construct a frequency histogram using classes 1°F in width.
b. Construct a frequency histogram using classes 0.5°F wide.
c. Would you gain helpful information by decreasing the class width? In what contexts would the first histogram be helpful? In what contexts would the second one be helpful?
d. Describe the distribution of temperatures.
e. Name three variables that might be used as independent variables to form hypotheses to account for the differences in temperature. That is, treat "temperature" as a dependent variable and form three hypotheses.

7. Here are the percentage changes experienced by 25 stocks from one day to the next:

−2.7	3.0	1.7	1.8	2.7
0.1	0.6	−3.7	−2.1	−1.8
−0.9	−1.2	−0.7	−3.5	1.6
1.1	10.6	−4.2	−3.7	−5.2
0.6	−5.1	−0.9	−1.2	1.1

a. Construct a frequency histogram using classes 2 percent in width.
b. What is the relative frequency of stocks going up? Calculate this from the raw data.
c. What is the relative frequency of stocks going down? Calculate this from the histogram.
d. Based on this small sample, did the market as a whole go up or down? Why?

8. The following data show the age of the head of household for 30 families and whether there are children:

Age of Head	Children	Age of Head	Children	Age of Head	Children
27	Yes	29	Yes	27	Yes
22	No	35	Yes	17	No
29	No	54	Yes	37	Yes
32	Yes	42	No	40	No
35	Yes	19	No	41	Yes
22	No	62	Yes	18	No
18	No	54	Yes	21	Yes
21	Yes	49	Yes	44	No
29	No	32	No	49	Yes
30	No	19	No	61	No

a. Develop a hypothesis about the relationship between these two variables. Do this without reference to the data.
b. Construct a frequency histogram of age of heads of household.
c. Construct two conditional frequency distributions or histograms for age of head of household, one for families with children and the other for families without children.
d. Construct a stem-and-leaf diagram of age of head of household and put a Y (yes) or N (no) for the leaves.
e. Construct a frequency distribution for the variable "children present."
f. Construct a stem-and-leaf diagram of "children present," and use numbers that represent a case's "age" for leaves. (You could use a 1 for a head of household under 20, a 2 for a person in his or her twenties, and 3 for someone in her or his thirties, and so on.)
g. Which diagram—(b), (c), (d), (e), or (f)—best helps you determine whether the data support the hypothesis? Is the hypothesis supported?

9. The following data are taken from neighborhood gardens that are planted with the same variety of corn and that use the same brand of fertilizer. For all 35 gardens, data were collected on the average length (in inches) of the ears of corn produced and on the amount of fertilizer applied per 100 square feet (ft^2) of garden.

Fertilizer	Ear Length	Fertilizer	Ear Length	Fertilizer	Ear Length
5.8	6.4	8.1	7.6	8.9	5.9
9.7	7.8	10.1	7.1	4.6	6.7
8.8	5.4	3.2	6.8	7.8	6.4
5.2	7.9	5.4	6.7	1.0	6.2
0.0	6.5	4.5	6.1	10.0	7.0
3.2	6.2	6.7	5.9	1.7	7.0
5.6	7.1	8.9	6.9	0.0	6.9
9.1	6.8	15.1	7.1	7.9	7.1
10.2	6.9	4.0	7.2	1.1	6.4
3.2	7.1	0.0	7.1	8.4	6.7
0.0	7.0	1.7	7.6	8.1	6.5
2.0	8.1	3.2	8.1		

a. Develop a hypothesis about the relationship between the two variables.

b. Make frequency distributions and histograms for both variables.
c. Divide the independent variable into two classes (high and low fertilizer use, or large and small ears of corn, depending on which is the independent variable in your hypothesis).
d. Do conditional distributions of the dependent variable for both categories of the independent variable.
e. Make a stem-and-leaf diagram of the dependent variable with leaves that designate the level of the independent variable.
f. Use your diagrams to decide if the hypothesis is supported by the data.

10. Here are data for 45 students on study time and grades. Study time is divided into high (H), medium (M), and low (L).

Study Time	Grade	Study Time	Grade	Study Time	Grade
H	A	M	A	L	A
H	C	M	B	L	C
H	B	M	C	L	B
H	C	M	C	L	C
H	A	M	B	L	A
H	A	M	A	L	C
H	B	M	C	L	C
H	C	M	A	L	C
H	A	M	C	L	D
H	D	M	C	L	B
H	A	M	A	L	A
H	B	M	B	L	C
H	C	M	B	L	C
H	A	M	D	L	B
H	A	M	D	L	C

a. Develop a hypothesis about the relationship between these two variables.
b. Test the hypothesis by using appropriate techniques.

11. Here are data on age and intelligence quotient (IQ) for 50 people. Age is divided into two categories, young (Y) and old (O).

Age	IQ	Age	IQ
Y	89	O	107
Y	100	O	86
Y	90	O	100
Y	97	O	101
Y	102	O	98
Y	104	O	97
Y	120	O	87
Y	115	O	104
Y	91	O	105
Y	82	O	100
Y	100	O	108
Y	102	O	102
Y	107	O	97
Y	94	O	92
Y	91	O	84
Y	98	O	101
Y	102	O	107
Y	100	O	89
Y	110	O	92
Y	101	O	94
Y	91	O	108
Y	86	O	110
Y	88	O	112
Y	107	O	115
Y	117	O	90

a. Develop a hypothesis about the relationship between the two variables.
b. Test the hypothesis.

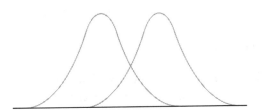

• • •

Describing Distributions: Measures of Central Tendency and Dispersion

Frequency distributions are the statistical pictures worth a thousand words. But sometimes just a few well-chosen words are sufficient to convey the necessary information about a distribution. In Table 3.4, which contains data on the distribution of students (the cases) across the six state institutions (the categories of the variable "place of enrollment"), you know quite a lot about enrollment if you know only that "The institution most heavily enrolled is Research University 1." In Figure 3.8, the conditional distributions of Bill's and Beth's throws of the dice, you know a lot if you know that Bill's distribution seems to have its center at a lower point on the scale than Beth's. You know still more if you know that Bill's distribution also seems a bit more spread out than Beth's.

Distributions can be described in terms just like these. Where does a distribution center itself? How spread out is the distribution? This chapter discusses the statistics that allow you to describe frequency distributions. This chapter is about the *descriptive statistics* that measure the central tendency and dispersion of frequency distributions.

In the early part of the nineteenth century, Adolphe Quetelet invented the term *"l'homme moyen,"* or "the average man," to describe a characteristic of a social aggregate. "Average man" was the first term that allowed people to talk about Man without mentioning men. The "average man" was an abstraction derived by taking the average of each important characteristic of all members of a group. Emile Durkheim (of whom more is said in Interlude A, following this chapter) wrote in *Suicide* of Quetelet's method:

> When Quetelet drew to the attention of philosophers the remarkable regularity with which certain social phenomena repeat themselves during identical periods of time, he thought he could account for it by the theory of the average man. . . . According to him, there is a definite type in each society more or less exactly reproduced by the majority, from which only the minority tends to deviate under the influence of disturbing causes.[1]

The concept of the average man was the foundation of descriptive statistics for one variable. The *average* is the first univariate statistic you will study in detail.

• • •

THE AVERAGE OR MEAN

You probably know, at least intuitively, what an average of a set of numbers is. The *arithmetic average*[2] is the sum of all the numbers divided by the number of numbers. If 6 students had examination scores 72, 68, 85, 92, 70, and 81, the arithmetic average would be the sum of all 6 scores, or $72 + 68 + 85 + 92 + 70 + 81 = 468$, divided by the number of scores, 6, so the arithmetic average score is $468/6 = 78$. The arithmetic average is called the *mean* in statistics. We would say, "The mean score on the test was 78."

No one scored 78, but remember that descriptive statistics do not refer to individual cases. Statistics like the mean are characteristics of entire groups of cases. A statistic is a descriptor of a group, not of an individual in the group.

The mean is a central point around which all the other cases are arrayed. The mean test score is a characteristic of a group of students who took a test. It is a measure of central tendency for the variable "test score."

The *mean* is defined as

$$\bar{X} = \frac{\sum\limits_{i=1}^{n} X_i}{n} \qquad (4.1)$$

This definition reads, "The mean of X is equal to the sum of the values of n cases on variable X divided by n, the number of cases." All the symbols in Formula (4.1) are explained below. For now, just accept that the formula and its rendering in English are equivalent.

Formula (4.1) is the arithmetic mean of a variable for a sample. If you have data on an entire population—say you had data on every person in the United States from a census of the population or on every company in the Fortune 500 from an annual survey of the 500 largest corporations—then the mean of a variable is expressed as

$$\mu = \frac{\sum_{i=1}^{N} X_i}{N} \tag{4.2}$$

The Greek letter μ (pronounced "mew") is a *population parameter*. It is calculated in the same way as the sample statistic $\bar{X}$: Sum the values of all the cases in the population on variable X, and divide by the number of cases. *Note* that N (capital) designates the number of cases in a population while n (lowercase) designates the number of cases in a sample.

This is your first formal introduction to the difference between a population parameter and a sample statistic. Usually you will not calculate population parameters because you will not have information on every case in a population. You will usually calculate a sample statistic and use it to *estimate* a corresponding population parameter. Now $\bar{X}$ is a good *estimator* of the population mean μ. (The criteria for a good estimator are discussed later, in Chapter 9.) For now, let's take apart Formulas (4.1) and (4.2) to be sure to understand every element completely. (Some of you will not need the detailed, step-by-step description that follows. When you understand the formula and its relationship to the concept, skip to the next section under "Examples.")

In Formula (4.1), $\bar{X}$, read "X bar," denotes the sample mean of any variable X. Similarly, $\bar{Y}$ is the mean of variable Y. A bar over a letter indicates that the symbol refers to the *mean* of the variable designated by the letter. As you know, μ is the population mean. Sometimes people add a subscript to μ designating the variable to which the population mean refers. So μ_X is the population mean of variable X, and μ_Y is the population mean of variable Y.

Now X_i is the value of case i (where i is an integer) on variable X. In the series of test scores, X_1 is the value of the first case on the variable "score." In the example above, $X_1 = 72$. In Formula (4.1), the integer i can assume any value from 1 to n, the number of cases. In the example above, $n = 6$ and i can be 1, 2, 3, 4, 5, or 6.

The $\sum$ sign is a *summation operator*. It is a very important symbol in the language of statistics, and your good efforts to understand its use and meaning will be well repaid.

Using the $\sum$ symbol is a shorthand way of saying, "Take the sum of . . . ." And $\sum_{i=1}^{n} X_i$ means, "Take the sum of all the X_is as you let i range over all possible values it can assume: 1, 2, . . . , n." So $\sum_{i=1}^{6} X_i$ means $X_1 + X_2 + X_3 + X_4 + X_5 + X_6$.

A summation operator works like this: First, let i equal 1 and add X_1 to what you start with, 0. Then let $i = 2$ and add X_2 to the quantity you already have, X_1. Next add X_3 to the sum you have so far, $X_1 + X_2$, and so on until you let $i = n$, where n is 6 in this case, and add X_6 to $X_1 + X_2 + X_3 + X_4 + X_5$. The summation operator is especially valuable if you have large amounts of data. It simplifies expressions involving sums of many cases.

Now you see why $(\sum_{i=1}^{n} X_i)/n$ is the average, or mean, of a set of n numbers in a sample. It is the sum of the numbers divided by the number of numbers.

Examples

Go back to the dice throwing. What is the mean of Bill's throws? The data are shown in Figure 3.8. The number of cases is the number of throws, so $n = 50$. You can add the 50 cases in a straightforward way. The sum of all the cases is $2 + 2 + 3 + 3 + 3 + 4 + \cdots + 11 + 11 + 12 = 341$. The arithmetic average of his throws is $341/50 = 6.82$.

What is the mean of Beth's throws? By the same sort of calculation the mean of Beth's throws is $414/50 = 8.28$.

Are Bill's dice different from Beth's? Of course, you know now that they are. But if you had only this statistical information, would you suspect that the two pairs of dice were different? To put the question in a statistical manner, we have a sample of size 50 drawn from the population of all the throws of Bill's dice. And we have a sample of size 50 drawn from the population of all the throws of Beth's dice. The scientific question is whether the population of throws of Bill's dice is the same as or different from the population of throws of Beth's dice. The populations would be different if, for example, they had different population means. We cannot answer the question with certainty since we cannot know the nature of the (infinite) populations of throws of two dice for either Bill's dice or Beth's dice. That is, we cannot determine empirically the population means of the throws of two dice.

However, we do have two sample means. If you had to estimate the population mean for Bill's dice based on the information contained in the sample, you should estimate that mean to be 6.82. Likewise, an estimate of the mean of Beth's population of all throws of her dice would be 8.28. It seems as though the samples may have come from different populations since the centers of the two sample frequency distributions are so different. For now, I will assert that the means of the two populations are different. In a later chapter, you will learn how to determine the likelihood that my assertion is incorrect.

Now turn to another data set. What is the mean hospital charge to patients treated by physician 01 in the third data set of Appendix A? To find this mean, you need to add the number of patients treated by physician 01 and find the total charges for those patients. The total number of patients is easy to find. It is the sum of the discharges in each of the nine diagnostically related groups (DRGs) in which physician 01 discharged patients. Physician 01 treated 46 ($= 1 + 4 + 1 + 28 + 2 + 1 + 1 + 2 + 6$) patients. What are the total hospital charges for them? You might be tempted to add the "total cost" figures for the nine DRGs used by physician 01. But remember that the variable "total cost" in the data set is, in fact, the total *average* cost charged to patients in that DRG. Physician 01's one patient in DRG 370 was charged exactly $2527. However, the four patients in DRG 371 were charged an *average* of $1962. Some were charged more, and others were charged less. But all together those patients were charged 4 times the average cost, or 4 × $1962 = $7848. The one patient in DRG 372 paid $740. The 28 patients in DRG 373 were charged 28 × $1074 = $30,072. The sum of all the charges to patients of physician 01 is the sum of all such multiplications. The total charges to physician 01's patients are

$$
\begin{array}{r}
1 \times 2527 \\
+ \ 4 \times 1962 \\
+ \ 1 \times \ \ 740 \\
+28 \times 1074 \\
+ \ 2 \times 1434 \\
+ \ 1 \times 3197 \\
+ \ 1 \times 1053 \\
+ \ 2 \times \ \ 158 \\
+ \ 6 \times \ \ 521 \\
\hline
\$51{,}747
\end{array}
$$

To find the average cost to patients of physician 01, divide this total charge by the number of patients physician 01 treated. The mean charge is $51,747/ 46 = $1125.

The mean indicates the central tendency of a variable, but "central" has a special, peculiar meaning. Suppose each case were a 1-ounce (oz) weight and the cases were placed along a board based on their distances from each other. The mean would be at the point, if you placed a fulcrum under the board, where the board would balance. In fact, this is exactly how Quetelet thought of the mean, or the "average." The mean is sensitive to how distant cases are from each other. To see the effect of the mean's sensitivity on distance, consider the per capita incomes of the second 10 cases in Appendix A. The mean of these 10 cases in $1732.40. Now eliminate the case with the largest per capita income, Belgium. The mean of the remaining nine cases is $724.90. One case with a large value makes a difference of more than $1000 in the mean in this small sample. Belgium is way out on one end of the balance board and requires several low-income countries to balance its effects. The mean is a measure of central tendency that is very sensitive to outliers. A few cases with very high or very low values can make a large difference in the mean.

· · ·

THREE OTHER MEASURES OF CENTRAL TENDENCY

The Median

Some measures of central tendency are insensitive to outliers. You have probably thought of at least one already. Why not just line up all the cases from the lowest to the highest and take the value of the middle case? That certainly would be a measure of central tendency. In fact, the "middlemost value," as Sir Francis Galton, one of the earliest statistical pioneers, called it, is a well-respected measure of central tendency called the *median*. If the cases are ordered from the lowest value to the highest value, the median is the point on the number line that divides the sample exactly in half. If there are an odd number of cases in the sample, then the value of the $(n + 1)/2$ case, counting up from the lowest-valued case, is the median. If there are an even number of cases, the median lies between the $n/2$ and the $(n + 2)/2$ case. You could say that the median is the value of the $(n + 1)/2$ case—even though there is no $(n + 1)/2$ case—if there are an even number of cases since $(n + 1)/2$ has a ".5" on the end if there are an even number of cases. If there are 10 cases, there is no $(10 + 1)/2 = 5.5$ case. By convention, the median of an even number of cases is the arithmetic average of the two middle cases in the series. If there are 10 cases, the median is the arithmetic average of the fifth and sixth cases, counting up from the lowest-valued case.

Caution: Cases in a case-by-variable matrix are *usually not ordered* from lowest value to highest value. Usually you must reorder the cases in a data set before finding the median. Do not use the numerical order in a case-by-variable matrix to find the $(n + 1)/2$ case. Find the $(n + 1)/2$ case only after ordering the cases from low to high values.

What is the median of the 105 cases for which there are data on urbanization? If there are 105 cases, the middle case is the $(105 + 1)/2$, or the 53d, case. The cases have to be ordered from lowest to highest. If you do that, the 53d case is Ecuador, which has a 42.8 percent urbanization. And 42.8 percent is the median urbanization rate. It is the middlemost value for urbanization. It is exactly in the center of all 105 cases.

The data from internal-motivation experiment 2 are arrayed in decreasing order of Protestant work-ethic score for each experimental condition. What is the median work-ethic score for the "public" condition? That is, what is the *conditional median* if the experimental condition is "public"? There are 20 cases, so the median is the value of the $(20 + 1)/2 = 10.5$ case. The median is the average of the 10th and 11th cases, counting from the lowest-value case. The 10th case from the bottom of the list—and in this instance you can use the order in the list, because the list is ordered according to numerical value—has a work-ethic score of 83, and the 11th case has a score of 84. The median is the average of 83 and 84, or $(83 + 84)/2 = 83.5$.

What is the median per capita income in the first data set? There are 142 cases, so the median is the value of the 71.5 case. In fact, it is the average of the values of the two middle cases, the 71st and 72d cases. These two cases—which you would find by sorting the cases from lowest to highest value and then counting from the bottom of the list—are Mongolia, which has a per capita income of $750, and Nicaragua, which has a per capita income of $825. The average of these two values is $787.50, the median per capita income of the 142 countries. The median divides the sample exactly in half.

The median urbanization of 42.8 percent is very close to the mean urbanization of 43.2 percent, but the median per capita income of $787.50 is not at all close to the mean per capita income of $2335.40. Why? Per capita income has several cases with very large values; it has several high-value outliers that tilt the balance toward them and consequently pull the mean toward them. The distribution of the per capita income is said to be *skewed*. In particular, it is said to be *skewed positively*, in the direction of the elongated tail of the distribution. (Look at the stem-and-leaf diagram in Chapter 3.) The distribution of urbanization is relatively symmetric. (You will see this when you construct it in an exercise at the end of the chapter.) Neither tail in the distribution of urbanization is noticeably longer than the other. There are no urbanization outliers to pull the mean decidedly higher or lower than the median.

A skewed distribution will have very different mean and median values. The distribution is skewed in the direction of the mean. If the mean is higher than the median, the distribution is skewed positively; if the mean is lower than the median, the distribution is skewed negatively. If the median and the mean are about the same, the distribution is probably *symmetric* about its center.

The Trimean

John Tukey invented a measure of central tendency that is based on the median but has some sensitivity to the skew and is not as sensitive to outliers as the mean is. The measure is called the *trimean* and is defined as a weighted average of the median and the upper and lower quartiles. To understand this definition, you need to know what the quartiles are.

The *upper quartile* is the point on the number line above which one-quarter (hence the name "quartile") of the cases lie. The *lower quartile* is the point on the number line below which 25 percent of the cases lie. (The median is sometimes called the *middle quartile* because it, together with the upper and lower quartiles, divides a batch of data into four parts.) You can find the lower quartile, designated Q_1, and the upper quartile, designated Q_3, by the following formulas:

$$Q_1 = 0.25n + 0.5 \qquad\qquad (4.3a)$$

$$Q_3 = 0.75n + 0.5 \qquad\qquad (4.3b)$$

If the result for either one has a ".5" on the end, then the quartile is the average of the two numbers whose ranks fall above and below the result. If the result following the decimal point is anything but 5, round the result to the nearest integer. Then the quartile is the value of the case whose rank from the lowest-valued case is given by the result.

For example, we can find the quartiles for per capita income. The lower, or first, quartile, is at rank

$$Q_1 = 0.25n + 0.5 = 0.25(142) + 0.5 = 36$$

The first quartile is the value of the 36th case. The value of the 36th case—once the data have been ordered from the lowest value to the highest value—is $330, so the first quartile is at $330. The third, or upper, quartile is at rank

$$Q_3 = 0.75n + 0.5 = 0.75(142) + 0.5 = 107$$

It is equal to the value of the 107th case, or $2711.

We said the trimean is equal to a "weighted average" of the median and the two quartiles. The trimean gives more weight to the median, the central value, than it does to the quartiles. Specifically,

$$\text{Trimean} = \frac{Q_1 + 2M + Q_3}{4} \tag{4.4}$$

where M is the median. The trimean of per capita income is thus

$$\frac{330 + 2(787.5) + 2711}{4} = \$1154$$

The fact that the trimean is larger than the median tells you that the distribution of per capita income is skewed positively. You can see, however, that the trimean is not as far from the median as the mean is. The trimean is less sensitive than the mean to the outliers in a distribution.

The Mode

There is one more measure of central tendency, the mode. The *mode* is the category that contains the largest number of cases. The mode is always easy to find if you have a histogram or a stem-and-leaf display because the mode is the bump. The mode for per capita income in Figure 3.10 is $0 to $999. The mode is the category that has the most cases in it. The modal category for Bill's 50 throws of dice is 7. The modal category for Beth's throws is 10.

Choosing a Measure of Central Tendency

The most frequently used measures of central tendency are the mean, the median, and the mode. It is appropriate to calculate the mean, median, and mode if a variable is continuous and you have constructed a frequency distribution with discrete categories. If a variable is *ordinal*, the mean has no meaning since distance between categories of an ordinal variable is not meaningful, and the concept of distance is important because of the "balance board" idea underlying the mean. However, you can calculate the median for an ordinal variable since the median requires only that the cases be capable of being ordered from lowest to highest. If a variable is *nominal*, i.e., if it has no inherent numerical order among its categories, you cannot even calculate the median because there is no way to order the cases. You can determine only that variable's mode. The mode does not depend on either distance or order. In response to the question, "Should books on homosexuality be removed from the public library?," suppose that 88 percent responded no, 10 percent said yes, and 2 percent gave no answer or didn't know. Then the mode for this variable is "no." The variable has no median since the cases cannot be ordered from lowest to highest on the variable "response," and the variable has no mean since distance between categories "yes" and "no" is meaningless. This is your first example of the principle that certain statistics are appropriate only for certain kinds of variables. Now review Table 2.1 to make sure you understand the different levels of measurement for variables.

· · ·

SUMMARY

Your vocabulary building has begun. You know that a scientist thinks in terms of variables and relationships between variables. Science begins with the statement of a falsifiable relationship between variables; that statement is called a *hypothesis*. The first task following the formation of a hypothesis, which is an act of imagination, is the description of variables, which is a practical matter for descriptive statistics. Variables have characteristics of their own. One way to begin describing a variable is to say something about its central tendency. You can say which category of the variable occurs most frequently by calculating the mode. You can find the middle of an ordered set of cases by calculating the median. And you can say something about the balance point of a set of cases—the measure of central tendency that takes into consideration the distances between cases—by calculating the mean. Measures of central tendency are one characteristic of variables.

The center of a distribution is not the only characteristic, however. Some variables are more spread out than others. In the next section we discuss measures of dispersion.

· · ·

MEASURES OF DISPERSION

Science is interested in change. Two underlying goals of science are prediction and control—making things change in a predictable manner so that events can be controlled. Change may be the principal problem for Western philosophy and modern science, but change sometimes takes a long time to measure. Very early in the history of modern science, attention was focused on the more rudimentary notion of *difference*. Instead of watching something change over a long time, science often turns its analytic attention to differences at one point in time.

Quetelet, once again, was a pioneer of this kind of thinking. He was interested in how people develop intellectually and morally. He felt he could quantitatively assess moral development by observing a person's behavior over time. But to assess just one person's moral development in this way would take, literally, a life-time. He proposed, instead, the idea of observing many people at one point in time and examining the differences among them to see if there were a pattern to the differences based on the subjects' ages. By doing this, he was not able to study the "moral development of a person," but he could study the variable "moral development" across a large number of people. Instead of examining data collected on a single case over time in order to study change, Quetelet suggested collecting data on many cases at a single point in time to study differences. Data collected on a single case over time are called *time-series data*, and data collected on many cases at one time are called *cross-sectional data*.

Quetelet's legacy remains with us today because most scientific research is done with cross-sectional data—data that provide a stop-action photograph of a phenomenon. Information on processes is often developed by inferring a time dimension into cross-sectional data. So, for example, information on "moral development," which is clearly a process, is discovered by inferring time into cross-sectional data collected from people of different ages. A researcher might study the "moral development" of people who are 10 years old and people who are 15 years old right now. If there is a difference between these two groups of people, the researcher might very well conclude that the difference is due to "develop-ment," the change that occurs in most individuals—the "average" individual—between the ages of 10 and 15. To make this inference, one has to assume that people who are 10 years old now will, in 5 years, be like the people who are 15 years old now. Obviously, this kind of inference must be made with caution. You should be aware that researchers often make this assumption without explicitly saying so. They do this because research using cross-sectional data is much easier to carry out.

The previous section provided tools for describing the central tendency of a group of cross-sectional data. Means, medians, modes, and trimeans allow you to compare different groups of data by comparing the points where various groups "center." Women, on average, score higher than men on tests of knowledge and ability in the humanities. Men, on average, are taller than women. Cars on the freeway, on average, travel faster than cars on residential streets. A measure of central tendency is one characteristic of a group of data, and it can be used for gross comparisons like these. Measures of central tendency can be used to measure differences *between* groups of data.

In this section we provide tools for measuring the dispersion of data. We discuss measures of difference *within* a single group of data. Cars on the freeway might travel faster than cars on residential streets on average, but anyone who has been on a metropolitan freeway at rush hour knows that not all cars on freeways travel faster than cars on residential streets. There are differences among the speeds of cars on freeways. There is some dispersion among cases (the cars). The variable "speed" contains some variation.

There are many different methods for measuring dispersion within a group of data. In this chapter we discuss the range, semi-interquartile range, variance, standard deviation, and coefficient of variation, all of which measure dispersion, or variation, within a group of data.

The Range

The simplest way to measure difference in a group is to determine the range of values that a variable actually assumes in a set of cases. The range of values assumed is just determined by noting the values of the highest-value and lowest-value cases. The highest- and lowest-value cases are called the *extremes.* Sometimes, for interval or ratio variables, the range is expressed as a function of the difference between the extremes. You take the difference between the maximum and minimum values in the data set and add a 1 to the last significant digit of the result. If the result of the subtraction is 106, add 1 to get a range of 107. If the result of the substraction is 0.45, add 0.01 to get a range of 0.46. The effect of this addition of 1 in the last significant digit is to include both extremes in the single value for the range.

Table 4.1 lists the per capita incomes of the first 10 cases and the second 10 cases from the first data set in Appendix A. (These data are used throughout this chapter, so look closely at the table now.) What are the ranges of the two sets of data in Table 4.1? In the first set Australia has the highest per capita income, at $7720. Bangladesh is the lowest-value case with a per capita income of $85. The data range from $85 to $7720. The difference of $7635 + $1 ($7720 − $85 + $1) = $7636 is the range of this set. The range of the second 10 cases is from $70 to $10,800 for a range of $10,731. (Note that the range can be expressed in two ways: by noting the lowest and highest values and by taking the difference and adding 1 in the last significant digit.)

The second set has a wider range of values. Using the range as a measure of dispersion, you would say the second set of 10 countries shows more dispersion or more variability than the first set. The range is the simplest measure of dispersion and the easiest to calculate. It tells you something about dispersion within

TABLE 4.1 Per Capita Incomes of the First 10 and Second 10 Countries from Appendix A

First 10 Cases		Second 10 Cases	
Country	Per Capita Income, $	Country	Per Capita Income, $
Bangladesh	85*	Cameroon	628
Afghanistan	168	Barbados	1,450
Albania	490	Belgium	10,800
Angola	500	Bhutan	70
Algeria	1,600	Benin	162
Argentina	2,331	Bolivia	477
Bahamas	3,310	Bulgaria	2,100
Bahrain	4,967	Burma	113
Austria	6,739	Brazil	1,523
Australia	7,720	Botswana	544

* Data are reordered from lowest- to highest-value cases.

data sets—the two sets of countries in this case. The range has the disadvantage that it tells you nothing about how the data are distributed between the lowest- and highest-value cases.

The Semi-interquartile Range

The range is a measure of dispersion that is extremely sensitive to outliers. Only the extreme values in a data set are used to calculate the range. In the second data set used above, Belgium is far above the second case, Bulgaria, which has a per capita income of $2100. If Belgium were dropped from the data set, the range of the remaining nine cases would be $2031 instead of $10,731.

A more complicated measure of dispersion that is not very sensitive to outliers is the semi-interquartile range. The *semi-interquartile range* is defined as the average distance of the upper and lower quartiles from the median. The median and upper and lower quartiles were defined in the previous section.

Once you have the quartiles for a set of data, calculating the semi-interquartile range is easy. Remember that the semi-interquartile range is the average distance of the upper and lower quartiles from the median. Let us make one change in notation here and say the median is sometimes called the *second quartile* and is designated Q_2. So the collection of quartiles Q_1, Q_2, and Q_3, where $Q_2 = M$, divides a set of data into four parts. The distance of the upper quartile from the median is $Q_3 - Q_2$. The distance of the lower quartile from the median is $Q_2 - Q_1$. The average of these two distances from the median—the semi-interquartile range—is

$$\frac{(Q_3 - Q_2) + (Q_2 - Q_1)}{2} = \frac{Q_3 - Q_1}{2} \tag{4.5}$$

Formula (4.5) is the semi ("half") interquartile range ("distance between the upper and lower quartiles").

For the 10 cases on the left side of Table 4.1, the second quartile, or the median, is the value of the $(10 + 1)/2 = 5.5$ case, or the average of the 5th and the 6th cases after the cases have been ordered from lowest to highest in per capita income. The median for those 10 cases is $(1600 + 2331)/2 = \$1965.50$.

The first quartile is the value of the $0.25(10) + 0.5$ case; it is the value of the 3d case, counting up from the lowest-value case. The first quartile for these data is \$490. The third quartile is the value of the $0.75(10) + 0.5$ case, or the value of the 8th case. For these data, the upper quartile is \$4967.

The semi-interquartile range for the data on the left side of Table 4.1 is calculated from the quartiles determined above: $(Q_3 - Q_1)/2 = (4967 - 490)/2 = \$2239$.

The semi-interquartile range for the data on the right side of Table 4.1 is \$681. Thus the quartiles are closer to the median in the second group of data than in the first group of data.

By using the semi-interquartile range as a measure of dispersion, the second data set appears *less* dispersed, less variable, more tightly packed (all these terms mean the same thing) than the first data set.

To say that the semi-interquartile range shows the first set of countries is more dispersed than the second set does *not* contradict the conclusion derived from using the range as a measure of dispersion. It just shows that different statistics have different properties. The semi-interquartile range is insensitive to outliers; the range is sensitive to outliers. Because the second data set contains an outlier, the range indicates that the set is very spread out while the semi-interquartile range indicates the set is less variable. If you want to understand statistics, you need to learn not only the formulas, but also the *meanings* of the statistical formulas.

If you have not done so already, construct frequency distributions or histograms or stem-and-leaf displays for the two data sets in Table 4.1. Mine are shown in Figure 4.1. Clearly the data for the first 10 countries are more spread out than the data for the second 10 countries. Nine of the second 10 cases are rather tightly grouped near the low end of the scale. The semi-interquartile range reflects the *general tendency* to group or to spread out better than the range does. The larger the semi-interquartile range, the more spread out the data are in general.

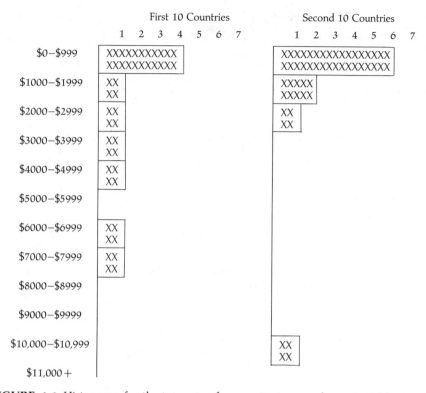

FIGURE 4.1 Histograms for the two sets of per capita income shown in Table 5.1, the first and second 10 countries from Appendix A.

Box-and-Whisker Plots

John Tukey, once again, has devised a masterful way of displaying differences between batches of data by using five statistics you know how to calculate. His *box-and-whisker plots* are based on the median, the lower and upper quartiles, and the extremes of a batch of data.

You construct a box-and-whisker plot thus: First, along the edge of the paper, make a line that has on it a number scale big enough to cover the range of values in the data set. To do a box-and-whisker plot for per capita income, put down a scale that ranged from $0 to $16,000. Then put a short, horizontal line at the first quartile's level on the scale and a similar line at the third quartile's level on the scale. Make the "box" by connecting the right sides and the left sides of the two horizontal lines with vertical lines. Next put a horizontal line inside the box at the median's level on the scale. That line marks the central tendency of the batch of data. Finally, extend a straight line (a "whisker") from the middle of the top of the "box" to the upper extreme's level on the scale and another line from the middle of the bottom of the box to the lower extreme's level on the scale.

Figure 4.2 shows two box-and-whisker plots of per capita income, one for the first 10 countries in Table 4.1 and the other for the second 10. I've scratched in

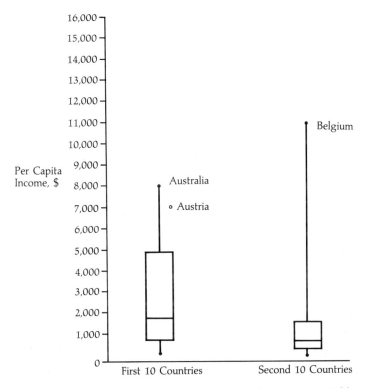

FIGURE 4.2 Box-and-whisker plots for two sets of countries in Table 4.1.

the names of some of extreme-value countries. This display quickly shows that the second set of countries is centered lower on the scale; tends to be fairly tightly grouped in a narrow, low range of values; but has an anomalous outlier, Belgium, at its upper extreme. Box-and-whisker plots are very useful devices for quickly apprehending the central tendency and the general character of the dispersion in a data set.

The Variance

The semi-interquartile range is a measure of dispersion for ordinal variables. It requires only that it be possible to order cases from lowest to highest. The semi-interquartile range does not take into consideration distances between cases. For example, Belgium counted as just one more case in the calculation of the semi-interquartile range of the second set of 10 values of per capita income. Belgium could have had a value of $10,000,000 or $2200, and the semi-interquartile range would still have been equal to $681.

A measure of dispersion that takes into consideration not only the order of cases but also the distances between them is the *variance*. The variance is a measure of dispersion for interval and ratio variables. Distances between cases must be meaningful in order to calculate the variance, so you cannot calculate the variance of an ordinal or nominal variable.

The *variance* of a variable is defined as the average of the squared deviations around the mean of the variable. The symbol for the variance of a variable for a population is σ^2. (Since σ is the lowercase Greek sigma, σ^2 is "sigma squared.") Sometimes a subscript is added to denote the variable to which σ^2 refers. Thus σ_x^2 is the population variance of variable X, and σ_y^2 is the population variance of Y. Expressed mathematically, the variance is

$$\sigma^2 = \frac{\sum_{i=1}^{N} (X_i - \mu)^2}{N} \tag{4.6}$$

Now, let's connect each part of the verbal definition of the variance—"average of the squared deviations around the mean"—to the mathematical expression in Formula (4.6). First, consider "deviations around the mean": $X_i - \mu$ is a single deviation from the population mean. It is the difference between the value of case i on variable X, denoted X_i, and the population mean of X, denoted μ. The difference tells you how far a single case deviates from the center of a distribution, where the center is indicated by the mean.

Second, consider "*squared* deviations around the mean." Obviously, $(X_i - \mu)^2$ is a squared deviation around the mean. You take a single deviation from the mean and square it.

Finally, consider "*average* of the squared deviations around the mean." Formula (4.6) is, in fact, an arithmetic average. It says to sum all N squared deviations from the mean and to divide by the number of cases N. That is an average of the squared deviations around the mean, and the average of the squared deviations around the mean is the variance σ^2.

Since the variance is a measure of dispersion, it is supposed to measure the spread of a distribution. The variance does just this. Each term that is figured into the average is positive (since each deviation is squared), so it does not matter whether a "deviation" is positive or negative to begin with. That is, it does not matter if a case lies above or below the mean. Averaging the squared deviations around the mean allows for the fact that some data sets have more cases than others. You would not want a measure of dispersion to get larger simply by adding cases, because then it would be a measure of the size of the data set in addition to being a measure of dispersion. These are some of the rationales for the definition of the variance as the average of the squared deviations from the mean, but the blunt fact is that the variance is the average of the squared deviations from the mean because that is how statisticians define the variance. Statisticians find this definition useful because it fits so well with other statistical concepts. Ever since R. A. Fisher said in 1918 that it was "desirable [to use the average squared deviation from the mean as a] measure of variability" and added, "We shall term this quantity the Variance,"[3] everyone who learns statistics learns that the average squared deviation around the mean is the variance. You should learn that, too.

Formula (4.6) is for the population variance. Recall that you rarely have information on all the cases in a population. So what is the variance of a variable in a sample? It is very tempting to substitute into Formula (4.6) $\bar{X}$, the sample mean, for μ, the population mean, and n, the number of cases in the sample, for N, the number of cases in the population. If you did that, however logical it might seem, you would not get a correct answer. The sample variance of a variable, denoted s^2 (or with a subscript, s_x^2 or s_y^2, for example), is

$$s^2 = \frac{\sum\limits_{i=1}^{n} (X_i - \bar{X})^2}{n - 1} \tag{4.7}$$

Formula (4.7) is similar to Formula (4.6) (with sample statistics substituted for population parameters), but the denominators are slightly different.

The denominator in Formula (4.7) is $n - 1$, not simply n, as you might have expected. Why? One answer is, that's just the way things are in this funny world of statistics. A better answer starts with the concept of a "good estimator," a term encountered earlier. Recall that $\bar{X}$, the sample mean, is a good estimator of μ, the population mean. If you put n in the denominator of Formula (4.7), the result would not be a good estimator of σ^2. In fact, a denominator of n in Formula (4.7) would cause you to consistently underestimate σ^2. So statisticians correct for that systematic underestimation—that *bias*— by using $n - 1$ for the denominator. Formula (4.7), just as it is given above, is a good estimator of σ^2. And s^2 is a good estimator of σ^2. So N is the denominator for the population variance σ^2, and $n - 1$ is the denominator for the sample variance s^2.

Now let's calculate the variance of per capita income for the sample of 10 countries on the left side of Table 4.1. All the relevant calculations are shown in Table 4.2. The first column contains the name of each case. The second column contains the value of each case on the variable "per capita income." Sum the values in that column and divide by the number of cases, 10, to calculate the sample mean. The mean of this sample of 10 cases is $2791, and it is at the bottom of the second column.

The third column contains the deviation of each case from the mean, or $X_i - \bar{X}$. Notice that some of the deviations are positive and others are negative. The sum of the 10 deviations is zero, because the mean is the balance point for all the cases. For every unit of positive deviation from the mean there is one unit of negative deviation from the mean.

The last column contains the square of each deviation from the mean, or $(X_i - \bar{X})^2$. The sum of the squared deviations around the mean—sometimes just called the *sum of squares*—is 71,262,010. The variance is found by dividing the sum of squares by the number of deviations, 10, minus 1, so the variance is 7,918,001. That is the *sample variance* of those 10 numbers.

TABLE 4.2 Calculation of Variance for Data on Left Side of Table 4.1

Case	Value $\bar{X}_i$	Deviation $X_i - \bar{X}$ $(X_i - 2791)$	Squared Deviation $(X_i - \bar{X})^2$
Bangladesh	85	−2,706	7,322,436
Afghanistan	168	−2,623	6,880,129
Albania	490	−2,301	5,294,601
Angola	500	−2,291	5,248,681
Algeria	1,600	−1,191	1,418,481
Argentina	2,331	−460	211,600
Bahamas	3,310	519	269,361
Bahrain	4,967	2,176	4,734,976
Austria	6,739	3,948	15,586,704
Australia	7,720	4,929	24,295,041
	Sum = 27,910	Sum = 0	Sum = 71,262,010
	Mean = 2,791		Variance = 7,918,001

What does it mean that the variance is 7,918,001? Nothing yet, because we have no other terms to which we can connect "variance." We just say that the variance of these 10 numbers is 7,918,001.

A "Calculation Formula" for the Variance

There is a slightly shorter way to calculate the variance. Using Formula (4.7) requires you to make two "passes" through the data, one to calculate the mean and the other to calculate the squared deviations around the mean. Formula (4.8) shows a shortcut method for calculating the variance. It requires only one pass through the data.

$$s^2 = \frac{\sum\limits_{i=1}^{n}(X_i - \bar{X})^2}{n-1} = \frac{\sum\limits_{i=1}^{n}X_i^2 - \frac{\left(\sum\limits_{i=1}^{n}X_i\right)^2}{n}}{n-1} = \frac{n\sum\limits_{i=1}^{n}X_i - \left(\sum\limits_{i=1}^{n}X_i\right)^2}{n-1} \quad (4.8)$$

The calculation of the variance for the countries on the right side of Table 4.1 that uses this "computational formula" or "calculation formula" for the variance is shown in Table 4.3. The variance of those 10 cases is 10,501,202.

Note: The computational formula for the sample variance is algebraically equivalent to the other formula for the sample variance. Formulas (4.7) and (4.8) are equivalent. You can use either one since they both give the same results.

TABLE 4.3 Calculation of Variance for Data on
Right Side of Table 4.1 Using the Shortcut Method

Case	Value	(Value)^2
Bhutan	70	4,900
Burma	113	12,769
Benin	162	26,244
Bolivia	477	227,529
Botswana	544	295,936
Cameroon	628	394,384
Barbados	1,450	2,102,500
Brazil	1,523	2,319,529
Bulgaria	2,100	4,410,000
Belgium	10,800	116,640,000
	Sum = 17,867	126,433,791

$$(\text{Sum})^2 = 319,229,689$$

$$\sum_{i=1}^{10} X_i^2 - \frac{\left(\sum_{i=1}^{10} X_i\right)^2}{10} = 126,433,791 - \frac{319,229,689}{10}$$

$$= 94,510,822$$

$$s^2 = 94,510,822/(10-1)$$

$$= 10,501,202$$

Notice that the variance of the second 10 numbers is larger than the variance of the first 10 numbers. Using the variance as a measure of dispersion, you would conclude that the second 10 numbers were more dispersed than the first 10 numbers.

So now we know that the second 10 numbers are more dispersed (according to the ranges) and less dispersed (according to the semi-interquartile ranges) and more dispersed (according to the variances) than the first 10 numbers, right? This is a classic example of lying with statistics, right? It just shows you can prove anything with statistics, right? Wrong. The variance, like the range, is a measure of dispersion that is sensitive to outliers. Variance, unlike the semi-interquartile range, takes distance into consideration. In`fact, the variance *squares* the distances, so the effect of outliers is somewhat magnified in the calculation of the variance. Consider what happens to the variance of the second set of 10 numbers if you once again eliminate Belgium. The variance of the remaining 9 numbers is 530,578, almost one-twentieth of the variance of the original 10 countries. The inclusion of a single outlier, Belgium, inflated the variance by a factor of 20. The variance is a measure of dispersion that is very sensitive to outliers, particularly if the size of the sample is small.

You cannot "prove anything" with statistics. You cannot "lie with statistics," unless, of course, you are talking to someone who does not understand statistics. If you understand that the range and the variance are measures of dispersion which are sensitive to outliers and that the semi-interquartile range is a measure of dispersion which is not sensitive, then a statement like the following alerts you to the fact that the second data set contains outliers: The range and the variance show that the second data set is more dispersed than the first, but the semi-interquartile range shows that the first data set is more dispersed than the second. Understanding statistics protects you from being deceived by people who might try to prove anything with statistics.

Standard Deviation

The *standard deviation* of a variable is the positive square root of the variance. The sample standard deviation, not surprisingly, is denoted by the square root of s^2, or just plain s. It sometimes carries a subscript like s_x, to denote the standard deviation of X. The formula is straightforward:

$$s = \sqrt{s^2} = \sqrt{\frac{\sum_{i=1}^{n}(X_i - \bar{X})^2}{n-1}} \tag{4.9}$$

The standard deviation of the first data set from Table 4.1 is $\sqrt{7{,}918{,}001}$, or 2814, and the standard deviation of the second set of per capita income in Table 4.1 is 3240. The general interpretation of the standard deviation is the same as that of the variance: The larger the standard deviation, the more dispersed the data set.

Historically, the standard deviation appeared before the variance. Karl Pearson used the term "standard deviation" in 1894,[4] more than 20 years before Fisher coined the term "variance." Standard deviation comes after variance here because it requires pushing one more button on your calculator. After you have calculated the variance, just press the square root button to get the standard deviation. The standard deviation is used extensively in inferential statistics, and we have much to say about it later.

One important difference between the standard deviation and the variance is the units in which each statistic is expressed. Variance is expressed in units squared. The variance of per capita income, for example, is expressed in terms of "dollars squared," which is not an easy term to understand intuitively. The standard deviation, or the square root of the variance, is expressed in terms of raw units, dollars in the case of per capita income. That makes the standard deviation a somewhat more appealing measure of dispersion.

$\bullet\ \bullet\ \bullet$

COEFFICIENT OF VARIATION

The coefficient of variation C is a measure of relative dispersion. The *coefficient of variation* for a variable is defined as the sample standard deviation of the variable divided by the variable's sample mean:

$$C = \frac{s_x}{\bar{X}} \tag{4.10}$$

The coefficient of variation has several advantages over the standard deviation and the variance.

First, the coefficient of variation controls for the magnitude of the values of the cases. Consider the 10 countries on the right side of Table 4.1, the set of countries containing statistically troublesome Belgium. With Belgium included, the standard deviation is 3240 around a mean of $1786. With Belgium excluded, the standard deviation of the remaining countries is 728 around a mean of $785. Naturally the variation is greater with Belgium included. But the mean of the data with Belgium included is also higher, so in a sense there is more room for cases to deviate around the (higher) mean if Belgium is included. You would expect the variance and standard deviation to be larger with Belgium included than with Belgium excluded, all other things being equal. The coefficient of variation standardizes for the average value of cases in a data set and gives you a sense of *relative variation*, variation relative to the magnitude of the mean. The coefficient of variation for the data set with Belgium included is $3240/1786 = 1.81$, and C with Belgium excluded is $728/785 = 0.93$. The coefficients of variation indicate that the data with Belgium included are still more dispersed than with Belgium excluded, but the difference, after the differences in the means of the two data sets are taken into consideration, is only a factor of 2, not a factor of 5, as the raw standard deviations indicated. The coefficient of variation should be used to compare variability of data sets that have very different means.

The second advantage of the coefficient of variation over the standard deviation is that it is a unitless number. The coefficient of variation can be used to compare the variability of two data sets that are measured in different units. (The standard deviation is a measure of dispersion expressed in the units of the variable, dollars in the case of per capita income. The mean is a measure of central tendency expressed in the units of the variable. Dividing the standard deviation by the mean yields a unitless number.)

To see why the unitlessness of the coefficient of variation is useful, consider the following example: Two high school classes take achievement tests. One class takes the Scholastic Aptitude Test (SAT) and has a mean score of 520 with a standard deviation of 80. The other takes the American College Test (ACT) and has a mean score of 14 with a standard deviation of 2.24. On the face of it, the first class's scores seem to be much more variable than the second class's scores since a standard deviation of 80 is much larger than a standard deviation of 2.24. But you know that the two tests are scored on different scales. SAT scores range from 200 to 800, and ACT scores range from 1 to 36. The tests are scored in different units, so to compare variations in test scores, you must standardize for the original units of measurement. You should compare the variability of the first class's scores to that of the second by using the coefficient of variation. For the first class, $C = 80/520 = .16$. For the second class, $C = 2.24/14 = .16$. The two classes had equal dispersions of scores around their respective means.

A word of caution about the coefficient of variation is in order. Use it only when the variable(s) under consideration has (have) a natural floor at zero. If the mean were less than zero, C would be negative, and a statistic that indicated there was negative variation would be difficult to interpret.

· · ·

SUMMARY: COMPARING DISTRIBUTIONS

In this chapter we discussed characteristics of distributions. Distributions of cases, just like the cases themselves, are distinguished by their characteristics. Characteristics that distinguish one case in the first data set (a country) from another include a country's urbanization rate or per capita income. Characteristics that distinguish one distribution from another include central tendency, dispersion, and skewness, three familiar terms. Two distributions can differ from one another on one, two, or three of these characteristics. The distributions in Figure 4.3 are both

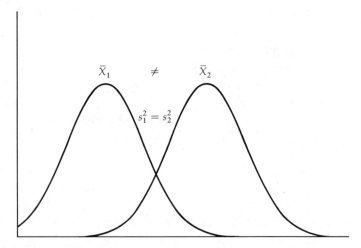

FIGURE 4.3 Two distributions with unequal means but equal variances and skewness.

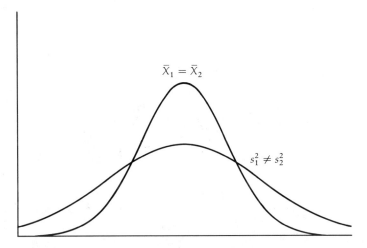

FIGURE 4.4 Two symmetric distributions with equal means but unequal variances.

symmetric (that is, they are not skewed) and they have equal variances, but they differ because they have different means. The two distributions in Figure 4.4 are both symmetric and they have equal means, but they have different variances. Figure 4.5 shows two distributions with equal means and variances, but one is skewed and the other is not. These are the kinds of comparisons you can make, using the statistics you have already learned.

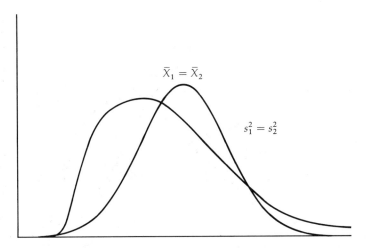

FIGURE 4.5 Two distributions with equal means and variances. One distribution is symmetric; the other is skewed.

• • •

READING COMPUTER OUTPUT

Most data analysis today is done by computer. Many standard programs will do all the statistical techniques in this book (and more). They are available for computers big and small. Although it is not our purpose to teach you to use any particular statistical analysis program, we will show you how to read the output from one such program. The program is called SPSS-X Batch System. SPSS-X is a trademark of SPSS Inc. of Chicago, Illinois, for its proprietary computer software.

Figures 4.6 through 4.9 contain analyses of the variable "male life expectancy." All these figures were produced directly by SPSS-X.

28 NOV 88	SPSS-X RELEASE 2.0A FOR DATA GENERAL AOS/VS				
MLE	MALE LIFE EXPECTANCY				
MEAN	55.038	MEDIAN	56.900	STD DEV	12.152
VARIANCE	147.680	RANGE	48.000	MINIMUM	25.000
MAXIMUM	73.000	SUM	7540.199		
VALID CASES	137	MISSING CASES	5		

FIGURE 4.6 Summary statistics for male life expectancy.

All the terms in Figure 4.6, which is a set of summary statistics, are familiar to you. It shows the MINIMUM and MAXIMUM values of male life expectancy (25.0 and 73.0 years) and the difference between them, which is the RANGE. (SPSS-X does not add 1 to the difference between extremes, so both extremes are not included in the calculation of this RANGE.) SUM is simply the sum of all the values of the cases for which there are data on this variable. At the bottom of the figure, you see that this analysis is for "VALID CASES 137 MISSING CASES 5." Five cases in the data set do not have values of male life expectancy, so SUM is the sum of values of the remaining 137 cases. MEAN is, of course, the mean male

28 NOV 88	SPSS-X RELEASE 2.0A FOR DATA GENERAL AOS/VS				
MLE1	RECODED MALE LIFE EXPECTANCY				

VALUE LABEL	VALUE	FREQUENCY	PERCENT	VALID PERCENT	CUM. PERCENT
25 YR OF LESS	1.00	1	0.7	0.7	0.7
25.1−30 YR	2.00	1	0.7	0.7	1.5
30.1−35 YR	3.00	3	2.1	2.2	3.6
35.1−40 YR	4.00	15	10.6	10.9	14.6
40.1−45 YR	5.00	19	13.4	13.9	28.5
45.1−50 YR	6.00	12	8.5	8.8	37.2
50.1−55 YR	7.00	15	10.6	10.9	48.1
55.1−60 YR	8.00	10	7.0	7.3	55.5
60.1−65 YR	9.00	18	12.7	13.1	68.6
65.1−70 YR	10.00	34	23.9	24.8	93.4
70.1 YR OR MORE	11.00	9	6.3	6.6	100.0
		5	3.5	MISSING	
	TOTAL	142	100.0	100.0	

FIGURE 4.7 Frequency distribution for male life expectancy.

life expectancy. It is SUM divided by 137. The mean male life expectancy is 55.0 years. The MEDIAN is 56.9 years. The VARIANCE is 147.7, and the standard deviation (STD DEV) is the square root of the variance, or 12.1.

Figure 4.7 shows a frequency distribution of male life expectancy. To get the computer to produce this figure, we had to instruct the computer to "recode" the

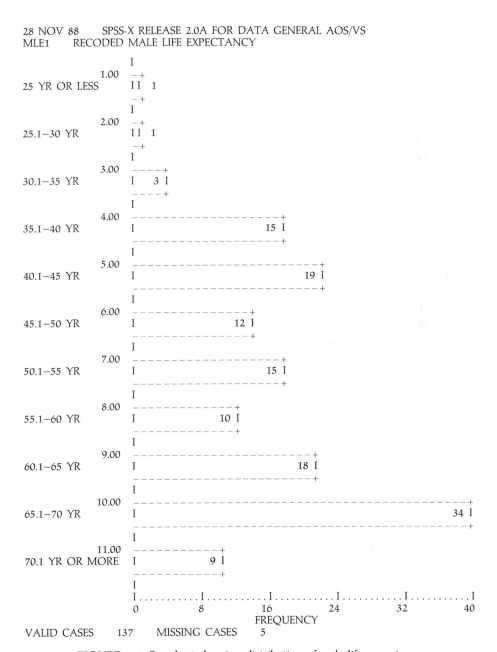

FIGURE 4.8 Bar chart showing distribution of male life expectancy.

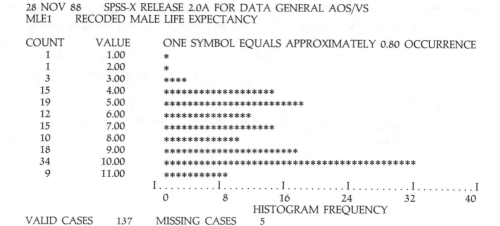

28 NOV 88   SPSS-X RELEASE 2.0A FOR DATA GENERAL AOS/VS
MLE1   RECODED MALE LIFE EXPECTANCY

```
COUNT     VALUE      ONE SYMBOL EQUALS APPROXIMATELY 0.80 OCCURRENCE
  1        1.00      *
  1        2.00      *
  3        3.00      ****
 15        4.00      ******************
 19        5.00      ***********************
 12        6.00      **************
 15        7.00      ******************
 10        8.00      *************
 18        9.00      *********************
 34       10.00      *******************************************
  9       11.00      ***********
                     I.........I.........I.........I.........I.........I
                     0         8        16        24        32        40
                                       HISTOGRAM FREQUENCY
VALID CASES     137    MISSING CASES     5
```

FIGURE 4.9 Histogram showing distribution of male life expectancy.

variable "male life expectancy" (which is a continuous variable) into 11 discrete classes. The class boundaries are shown at the left of the figure. The number that the computer assigns to each class is shown under VALUE. Next comes the frequency with which the cases fall into each class. Note that the final line in the figure lists the five missing cases as MISSING. The column headed PERCENT is the percentage of the original 142 cases falling into each class and into the MISSING category. And VALID PERCENT is the percentage of all valid (that is, non-missing) cases in each class. Finally, CUM PERCENT is the cumulative percentage of cases contained in categories up to and including the category under consideration.

Figures 4.8 and 4.9 are two pictorial representations of the data in Figure 4.7. Figure 4.8 is a bar chart, and Figure 4.9 is a histogram. Each gives roughly the same information but presents it differently. The bar chart lists class boundaries at a space between its bars. The histogram does not list the class boundaries, but it puts its "bars" right next to each other. A bar chart is generally better for presenting nominal variables, and a histogram is better for presenting ordinal variables.

· · ·

KEY CONCEPTS IN THIS CHAPTER

. . .

NOTES

1. Emile Durkheim, *Suicide: A Study in Sociology*, translated by George Simpson, The Free Press, a Division of Macmillan, Inc., New York, 1951, 1979, p. 300.

2. We use the adjective "arithmetic" because there are other kinds of averages. There is, for example, the *geometric average*, a statistic not discussed in this book.

3. R. A. Fisher, "The Correlation between Relations on the Supposition of Mendelian Inheritance," *Transactions of the Royal Society of Edinburgh* 52:399, 1918.

4. Karl Pearson, "Contributions to the Mathematical Theory of Evolution—I: On the Dissection of Asymmetrical Frequency Curves," *Philosophical Transactions* A185: 88, 1894.

· · ·

EXERCISES

Chapter 4

Note to Computer Users: These exercises were written for students who do not use computers to do these exercises. So when an exercise says to "select 10 countries . . . , " for example, this is done in the interest of making the calculations simpler. If you are doing these exercises with a computer, adapt them. Instead of selecting, say, the first 10 countries, select a random sample of 10 countries. If there is no reason to make any selection, do the analysis on the whole data set. Your instructor will guide you on this matter.

1. This question concerns the data on social indicators in Appendix A.

   a. Select 10 countries, however you wish, from the list in Appendix A.
   b. Calculate the mean per capita income for that sample. Does your answer seem reasonable? That is, look at the values. Does your mean value seems close to the center of the 10 values?
   c. Now select another 10 countries.
   d. Calculate the mean per capita income for this data set.
   e. Are the sample means different from the overall per capita income mean of $2335.40? Why?

2. This question concerns Type A personality scores in internal-motivation experiment 2. It is related to Exercise 1 in Chapter 3.

   a. Find the conditional mean of Type A personality for the "private" subjects in internal-motivation experiment 2.
   b. Compare the mean found in part (a) to the conditional mean of Type A personality for the "public" subjects.
   c. Is there any reason to expect the two means to differ?
   d. Which is the easier comparison to make? (i) Comparing histograms as you did in Chapter 3; (ii) comparing means. Which comparison is better? What is the difference between "easier" and "better," if there is a difference?

3. Look back to your answers to Exercise 2 in Chapter 3, a question concerning urbanization from the first data set in Appendix A.

   a. Where is the mode?
   b. What is the mean of the variable?
   c. Construct a box-and-whisker plot of urbanization.

4. This question concerns Protestant work-ethic scores in internal-motivation experiment 1.

    a. Calculate the conditional mean Protestant work-ethic score for the first 10 cases assigned to each of the experimental conditions in internal-motivation experiment 1. (If you are using a computer, calculate the conditional mean for all the scores in this group.)

    b. If the means are different, why?

    c. What might it mean for the experiment if the overall conditional means are the same for the two experimental groups? What might it mean if the conditional means are different?

5. Calculate the mean Protestant work ethic for the first 10 subjects in internal-motivation experiment 2.

    a. Compare the mean for these 10 subjects to the conditional means calculated in Exercise 4.

    b. Develop a plausible explanation for the difference in scores between experiments.

6. This question concerns "time spent on word game" in experiment 1. It is related to Exercise 3 in Chapter 3.

    a. Calculate the conditional means for the two distributions constructed previously.

    b. Use the statistics developed in part (a) to make a statement about the hypothesis on which the experiment is based.

7. Exercise 4 in Chapter 3 is concerned with the relationship between the Protestant work-ethic score and leisure-ethic score.

    a. Determine conditional measures of central tendency for the two conditional distributions.

    b. Based on this analysis, is the hypothesis supported?

    c. Compare this analysis (in terms of its being easier and/or better) to the analysis you did in Chapter 3.

8. This question concerns the average length of stay (ALOS) in the hospital cost data set.

    a. What is the mean ALOS for DRG 373, "vaginal delivery without complicating diagnosis," for *physicians*? That is, use "physician" as your unit of analysis.

    b. What is the overall ALOS for *patients* diagnosed as DRG 373?

    c. Why is there a difference between the answers in parts (a) and (b)?

9. What are the conditional mean "average total costs" for (i) procedures with complications and (ii) procedures without complications? If you are not using a computer, use information only for physicians 01, 02, and 03 in this analysis.

10. What is the mean charge to patients of physician 02? Formulate two reasonable hypotheses to account for the difference between this physician's mean charge and the mean charge of physician 01 calculated in the text. How could your hypothesis be tested?

11. What is the average total cost to patients for physician 05? Is there anything in the data set that would suggest why his or her average cost is different from that of physician 01, which was calculated in the text?

12. Develop a hypothesis that might account for differences in the percentage of total cost that is devoted to "material and technology." Test the hypothesis.

13. The specialization score for each physician does not vary across the DRGs in which she or he discharged patients. For example, the specialization score is 50 percent for physician 01 regardless of whether you look at DRG 370, 371, 372, or any other DRG. Why is there no variation in the specialization score across DRGs for every physician?

14. This question continues to examine the specialization score.

    a. What is the range of specialization scores across all 22 physicians?
    b. What are the three quartiles Q_1, Q_2, and Q_3 of "specialization score"?
    c. What is the semi-interquartile range of specialization scores?
    d. What is the variance of "specialization"?
    e. How would you describe the distribution—the place where the distribution centers, its shape, and its dispersion—of specialization scores?
    f. Do a box-and-whisker plot of specialzation scores.

15. Calculate the semi-interquartile range for the first 15 countries that have "urbanization" scores. What does this statistic tell you about "urbanization?

16. In internal motivation experiment 1, is the distribution of "time spent on the word game" for those in the "work" condition very different from the distribution of "time spent" for those in the "leisure" condition?

    a. Do the distributions "center" at the same place or at different places?
    b. Are the distributions shaped differently? (Use whatever kind of presentation is appropriate to answer this question.)
    c. Are the ranges different?
    d. Are the "spreads" or dispersions different? (Use whatever measures of dispersion are appropriate to answer this question.)

17. It could be argued that the group assigned to the "work" condition and the group assigned to the "leisure" condition in experiment 1 are different if they solved different numbers of anagrams or if there was a big difference in the number of anagrams solved by members within each of the two groups. If the groups are different, that would mean that randomization of experimental subjects did not yield two comparable groups. Would you say that the two groups are roughly the same or different on the basis of anagrams solved?

18. Is there more variation among the first 10 Protestant work-ethic scores or among the first 10 Type A personality scores in experiment 1? The following steps will help you answer this question.

    a. Find the mean, variance, and standard deviation of the first 10 Protestant work-ethic scores.
    b. Find the mean, variance, and standard deviation of the first 10 type A personality scores.
    c. Calculate the coefficient of variation for the two variables.
    d. Compare the coefficients of variation and answer the question.

19. How would you describe the differences between the first 10 entries for the variable "doctors per 100,000 population" (Afghanistan through Belgium) and the second 10 entries for the same variable (Benin through Central African Republic)?

20. Consider the first 15 cases in the first data set that have a value for the variable "literacy rate" (Afghanistan through Brazil).

    a. What is the mean literacy rate for this set of countries?
    b. What is the range of values?
    c. What is the variance of literacy rate?
    d. What is the standard deviation of literacy rate?
    e. Now divide the group into two subgroups. The first subgroup consists of those countries with per capita incomes of $1000 or more. The second subgroup consists of countries with per capita incomes of less than $1000.
    f. Calculate the conditional means, ranges, variances, and standard deviations of the two subgroups.
    g. Do box-and-whisker plots for the two subgroups of data.
    h. Explain the differences between statistics for the overall group of 15 countries and the statistics of the two subgroups.
    i. Explain the differences between the statistics for the two subgroups. Pay particular attention to a difference in variances (or standard deviations), if there is any.

    The following exercises are concerned with the data in Exercises 5 through 11 in Chapter 3.

21. This question refers to the data in Exercise 5, Chapter 3, on the number of pets owned.

    a. What is the modal number of pets owned? That is, what is the mode of the distribution you constructed?
    b. What is the mean number of pets owned?
    c. Based on the statistics in (**a**) and (**b**), is the distribution skewed? Which way? Does your assessment based on the statistics agree with the picture of the distribution you produced earlier?
    d. Do a box-and-whisker plot of the variable "number of pets owned."

22. This question refers to the data on temperatures in Exercise 6, Chapter 3.

   a. What is the mean temperature recorded?
   b. What are the variance and the standard deviation of this sample of temperatures?
   c. Would you characterize this distribution as unimodal or bimodal? That is, is there one bump or two in the distribution?

23. This question refers to the data in Exercise 7, Chapter 3, on stock price changes.

   a. What are the mean, median, mode, variance, and standard deviation of stock price changes?
   b. Estimate the percentage change in the whole market based on the data in this sample.
   c. If you knew that all 11 stocks that went up were computer and airline stocks and all 14 stocks that went down were oil-related stocks, would that knowledge increase or decrease your confidence in the estimate of the overall market that you made in part **(b)**?

24. This question concerns the data on age of head of household and children being present in the family, Exercise 8, Chapter 3.

   a. What is the conditional mode of the variable "children present" for heads of household under the age of 30? What is the conditional mode for head of household 30 years and over?
   b. What is the conditional mean age of heads of household with children present? What is the conditional mean age of heads of household without children present?
   c. Which data—those calculated in **(a)** or **(b)**—better help you decide if the hypothesis you formed earlier is supported by the data? Is the hypothesis supported?

25. This question refers to the data in Exercise 9, Chapter 3, on neighborhood gardens.

   a. Construct a box-and-whisker plot of corn ear length for those who used more than the mean amount of fertilizer.
   b. Construct a box-and-whisker plot of corn ear length for those who used less than the mean amount of fertilizer.
   c. Compare the two box-and-whisker plots. Does using more fertilizer increase corn ear length?

26. This question refers to the data in Exercise 10, Chapter 3, on grades and study time.

   a. Find the conditional modes and medians of grade level for each level of study time.

    b. Is it possible to find conditional mean grades for each level of study time? If so, do it.

    c. Does a higher level of study time tend to be associated with a higher grade level?

    d. On the basis of these data, would you urge an individual who wanted to increase a grade to study more? Why? (That is, what assumptions did you make in order to generalize from these data to any individual?)

27. This question refers to the data in Exercise 11, Chapter 3, on age and IQ.

    a. What are the overall mean, median, variance, and standard deviation of the IQ scores?

    b. What are the conditional means and standard deviations of IQ for the two age groups?

    c. Is increasing age associated with higher IQ? If you are puzzled by the result, and have not done so, look up the definition of "IQ" in the dictionary.

A

▾

Suicide: Individual Will or Social Regularity?

. . .

There are three "Interludes" in the text. Treat them as such—no exercises, no big deal, perhaps of some interest.

In the section "To the Student," I mentioned that in the earliest statistics courses, you would have learned statistical formulas and at the same time would have studied liberal topics like the doctrine of free will. Statistics was a troublesome discipline to those who had staked their individual philosophies and their lives together in the forms of the polities they constituted on the notion that people are inherently free. Quetelet had developed the necessary logicial tools to talk about social regularities that are observable without reference to (supposedly free) individuals. He wrote in 1832:

Thus we pass from one year to another with the sad perspective of seeing the same crimes reproduced in the same order and calling down the same punishments in the same proportions. Sad condition of humanity! . . . We might enumerate in advance how many individuals will stain their hands in the blood of their fellows, how many will be forgers, how many will be poisoners, almost can we enumerate in advance the births and deaths that should occur. There is a budget we pay with frightful regularity; it is that of prisons, chains, and the scaffold.[1]

The behavior of populations was more predictable, Quetelet thought, than the behavior of individuals.

Karl Pearson, a very famous statistician of the late nineteenth and early twentieth centuries, wrote of Florence Nightingale, "Her statistics were more than a study, they were indeed a religion. . . . To understand God's thoughts, she held we must study statistics, for they are the measure of His purpose. The study of statistics was for her a religious duty."[2] Her faith lay in the social regularities that revealed the nature of providence. Her faith was not grounded on the concept of a free and willful individual.

Emile Durkheim was a sociologist who began his work late in the nineteenth century. His fledgling discipline took root in the ground prepared by the "forms of statistical argument." In one of his works, *Suicide*,[3] Durkheim took an act— killing oneself—that seems on the face of it a most individual act of will and showed that the act is, in fact, a social regularity. He would say that suicide obeys social laws. *Suicide* repays close study even today because it is a rigorous demonstration of scientific method that develops support for an intriguing hypothesis: "Social integration in groups, more than individual traits, accounts for differences in propensity to suicide."

Durkheim developed his hypothesis somewhat in opposition to Quetelet's theory of the "average man." Durkheim thought the theory of the average man could not account for suicide because only a tiny minority of people in a population ever killed themselves. As he put it, "In countries where [suicide] is most common, 300 or 400 cases per million inhabitants at the most are found. It is radically excluded by the average man's instinct of self-preservation; the average man does not kill himself."[4]

Durkheim developed a hypothesis that he thought accounted for the fact that some people become the exception to the propensity for people in groups to be, in Quetelet's terms, of a "definite type . . . more or less exactly reproduced by the majority." Durkheim studied the effects of one variable, social integration, on another variable, suicide. The dependent variable in Durkheim's hypothesis is propensity to commit suicide. Durkheim's question was, do individual-level variables or society-level variables provide the best explanation of differences in propensity to commit suicide? Is suicide a topic of study principally for psychologists or for sociologists?

Durkheim is engaging in classical scientific behavior. He is examining two competing hypotheses to see if one explains a phenomenon better than the other. The two hypotheses can be diagramed:

Social variables → Suicide

Individual variables → Suicide

He asks which hypothesis is more effective at explaining differences in suicide rates.

Durkheim begins his book *Suicide* with an inquiry into the explanatory power of psychological variables. Most people who had studied suicide before Durkheim thought suicide was related to insanity or alcoholism or some other, perhaps psychopathic condition. Durkheim reasoned that if pathological, psychological conditions account for suicide, then groups with larger percentages of insane or alcoholics should have higher suicide rates. He examined data from European countries like those in Table 1. (This is only one of many tables Durkheim examined.)

Durkheim did not have any statistical techniques with which to describe his data. The statistics he "should" have used had not been invented. But anyone can see from Table 1 that there is no relationship between a country's rank on the independent variable, insanity rate, and a country's rank on the dependent variable, suicide rate. Some countries, like Scotland, have a high insanity rate and a low suicide rate. Saxony has a low insanity rate and a high suicide rate. Some countries are high on both variables (Denmark); some are low on both (Bavaria). There is no general tendency for countries with high insanity rates to have high suicide rates and countries with low insanity rates to have low suicide rates, as the psychological hypothesis relating insanity and suicide would suggest.

TABLE 1 Relations of Suicide and Insanity in Different European Countries

Country	Insane per 100,000 Inhabitants	Suicides per 100,000 Inhabitants	Rank Order of Countries	
			Insanity	Alcoholism
Norway	180 (1855)	107 (1851–1855)	1	4
Scotland	164 (1855)	34 (1856–1860)	2	8
Denmark	125 (1847)	258 (1846–1850)	3	1
Hannover	103 (1856)	13 (1856–1860)	4	9
France	99 (1856)	100 (1851–1855)	5	5
Belgium	92 (1858)	50 (1855–1860)	6	7
Wurtemberg	92 (1853)	108 (1846–1856)	7	3
Saxony	67 (1861)	245 (1856–1860)	8	2
Bavaria	57 (1858)	73 (1846–1856)	9	6

TABLE 2 Religious Composition of States and Suicide

States	Average Suicides per Million Inhabitants
Protestant	190
Mixed (Protestant and Catholic)	96
Catholic	58
Greek Catholic	40

After testing a lot of hypotheses and using traits of individuals as the independent variable, Durkheim concluded that a statement that says suicide is best explained by such variables is not supported by the data. He abandoned this hypothesis and took up the task of testing its competitor, the statement that suicide is a social phenomenon best explained by social variables.

Durkheim's insights about the social nature of suicide sprang from his observation that suicide rates vary with the religious composition of countries, states, provinces, and other geographical areas. The first table he presents showing the relationship between religious composition and suicide is reproduced in Table 2. Protestant states have much higher suicide rates than predominantly Catholic states. This relationship held for provinces within states, too.

Could the difference in suicide rates be due to differences in the way the two religions think about and treat suicide, Durkheim wondered? No, he says, "They both prohibit suicide with equal emphasis; not only do they penalize it morally with great severity, but both teach that a new life begins beyond the tomb where men are punished for their evil actions, and Protestantism as well as Catholicism numbers suicide among them."[5] The explanation of the difference in rates must be found elsewhere.

Durkheim finds the explanation of differences in suicide rates in the "only essential difference" between the religions, namely, in the fact that Protestants are permitted much greater freedom of personal inquiry than Catholics. Durkheim developed a concept to account for the differences he saw and then used this concept—a social variable—as an independent variable in other hypotheses about suicide. Durkheim believed that the greater the sense of *community* a religion provides, the lower the suicide rate would be. But he was willing to generalize this statement so that the hypothesis did not apply only to religions. He believed, generally, that

$$\text{Social integration} \rightarrow \text{Suicide}$$

where the relationship is negative: The higher the integration of a community, religious or not, the lower the suicide rate.

The dependent variable is the suicide rate, and the independent variable is social integration. The unit of analysis is a social group. "Integration" is a characteristic of groups, and Durkheim is analyzing groups to understand the relationship between two aspects of groups, their integration, and their suicide rate.

Out of this general idea, Durkheim first formulated the specific, testable hypothesis that people living in families tend to have a lower suicide rate than people not living in families. People living in families are more socially integrated, he reasoned, and thus should have lower suicide rates. That was Durkheim's hypothesis.

Durkheim collected lots of data on the effects of family life on suicide. Some of those data are shown in Table 3. Those data show that men and women from all age groups, except those 16 to 25 years old, have much higher suicide rates if they are not married than if they are married. He also found that unmarried women with children have lower suicide rates than unmarried women without children. Children, presumably, provide the former group with social integration that the latter group does not have.

After much effort to show that suicide is best understood as the result of social, not psychological, factors, Durkheim finally committed himself to a bold statement:

> It is not mere metaphor to say of each human society that it has a greater or lesser aptitude for suicide. . . . Each social group really has a collective inclination for the act, quite its own, and the source of all individual inclination, rather than their result.[6]

Of course, science never stops testing hypotheses. In fact, Durkheim's hypotheses are still the inspiration of a good deal of social science today. The techniques we use are more sophisticated. The logic is the same.

TABLE 3 Suicides per 100,000 Inhabitants of each Sex, of like Marital Status and Age

	Age, Yr						
	16–25	26–35	36–45	46–55	56–65	66–75	76+
Men							
Married	10.51	10.58	18.77	24.08	26.29	20.76	9.48
Unmarried	5.69	25.73	66.95	90.72	150.08	229.27	333.35
Women							
Married	2.63	2.76	4.15	5.55	5.70	7.09	7.64
Unmarried	2.99	6.14	13.23	17.05	25.98	51.93	34.69

. . .

NOTES

1. Adolphe Quetelet, *Nouveaux Memoires de l'Academie des Science et Belles Lettres de Bruxelles* 7:87, 1832.

2. Karl Pearson, *The Life, Letters and Labours of Francis Galton*, vol. 2, Cambridge University Press, Cambridge, England, 1914–1930, p. 414.

3. Emile Durkheim, *Suicide; A Study in Sociology*, translated by George Simpson, The Free Press, a Division of MacMillan, Inc., New York, 1951.

4. Ibid., p. 302.

5. Ibid., p. 157.

6. Ibid., pp. 299, 309–310.

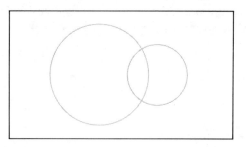

. . .

Probability

Now you can use statistics to describe distributions of cases on single variables. Once data are described, it would be useful to know whether the data in hand justify making any claims beyond themselves. Do you have a basis for asserting anything about cases that might exist in the world but which are not included in the data set you have used descriptive statistics to characterize? A question about generalizability from your data is an inferential question. The inferential question—mentioned several times previously—asks whether you can make any inferences about unobserved cases in the whole population of cases based on the sample of observed cases. *Inferential statistics* is a branch of statistics that parallels descriptive statistics and that is used to answer this question.

You have seen the terms "sample" and "population." Most of the time you work with only a (small) portion of all possible cases. If you do not have in hand absolutely all cases of a certain type, then you are working with a sample of cases. A *sample* is a selection of cases from all possible cases. All possible cases taken together are called the *population* of cases.

Samples are "drawn," you say, from a population. Descriptive statistics describe variables that are characteristics of cases in the sample. If a sample is representative of the population from which it was drawn, inferential statistics allow you to make inferences from a sample to the population from which the sample was drawn.

For example, 41 percent of the 1404 people interviewed during the General Social Survey (GSS) of 1980 said that abortion should be okay for any reason. This statistic—"41 percent of those interviewed said that . . ."—tells you nothing directly about the population of the United States from which this sample was drawn. It would be nice if the data from the GSS could be used to say something about the U.S., population as a whole, which numbered some 225 million at the time of the survey, especially since the data in the survey are very expensive to collect. In the whole population, what is the level of approval of abortion? Can anything be said about the approval rate in the population based on the data in the sample? That is an inferential question for which inferential statistics will be useful.

We said that inferential statistics can be used to make inferences from a sample to a population *if the sample is representative of the population from which it was drawn.* The question of representativeness is a tough one. Since you generally know little about a whole population, how do you know if a sample is representative of it? You almost always decide about the representativeness of a sample based on how the sample was drawn. If you interviewed 1404 people whom you or your friends know about their attitudes toward abortion, that group of 1404 people would not be terribly representative of the U.S. population, because we all tend to know people who are pretty much like ourselves. Your group would probably not include people who are very unlike you. The GSS chooses its sample differently. It divides the country into census tracts. Then it *randomly* selects tracts so that poor and rich, predominantly white and predominantly nonwhite, and urban and rural neighborhoods are included in the selection. Then within census tracts, the GSS *randomly* chooses a residential block and selects houses on the block from which to choose its respondents. This complicated procedure, which relies on the *randomness* of selection at several points, produces a sample that is representative of all the people in the United States 18 years or older who are not in institutions. The GSS sample of the U.S. population is randomly selected. *Therefore*, the sample is representative of the U.S. population, and information from the GSS is indicative of opinions of people in the whole population.

Ensuring representativeness of samples is a central problem in scientific research, and it is discussed briefly in the next chapter. For now, you need to know about the potential problem posed by nonrepresentativeness so that you can ask whether a sample is representative. If a sample is representative, you can make inferences from it to the population from which it was drawn. If a sample is not representative, there is no statistical procedure that will help you make inferences beyond the sample.

All inferences from samples to populations are made in a probabilistic way. That is, you can never make a claim about a population with certainty, no matter how large or how representative the sample. You will always have some degree of uncertainty. Probability is the science of uncertainty. You make inferences and then tell people the likelihood of your inferences being wrong. To make statements about likelihood, you have to know something about probability.

. . .

PROBABILITY DEFINED

You live with probabilities. You probably (see!) understand probability reasonably well, even though you might not have a formal, mathematical scheme by which you could express that understanding. Already in working through this text, you have used elementary concepts in probability.

Even though probability is a concept you encounter every day, developing a generally acceptable definition of the term is difficult. Philosophers of science and mathematics have difficulty agreeing on the meaning of probability, so we should not feel any inadequacy because of difficulties we might encounter. So let's begin with a familiar example.

Yesterday, the weather forecaster said, "The probability of rain today is 20 percent." Today she said, "The probability of rain is 85 percent." What exactly does the forecaster mean when she says, "The probability of rain is 85 percent"? First, she is saying that she is not certain that it will rain. Probabilistic statements are, first, statements of uncertainty. A statement of probability is an expression of uncertainty about the occurrence of one event out of a range of possible events. In the case of weather forecasting, it will either "rain" or "not rain." The forecaster is absolutely certain that there will be weather today, but there is some uncertainty about the *kind* of weather—the specific event out of a range of possibilities—that will occur. A probabilistic statement tells you the likelihood of occurrence of a particular event relative to the likelihood of occurrence of all possible events.

A friend of the forecaster says that on any day of the year it will either rain or not rain, so the chance of rain must always be 50-50, 50 percent, or .50. "Right?" he says smugly. The forecaster does not think that way, but it is worth exploring why. When the forecaster says the chance of rain is 85 percent today after saying that the chance was .2 yesterday, she is saying that today is different from yesterday. That is, the *conditions* today are different from the conditions yesterday. Today there is a large low-pressure area situated 200 miles (mi) west of the broadcast station, the barometer is falling, and the sky is cloudy. Yesterday, the barometer was stable, there were few clouds, and the low-pressure system had not formed yet. The conditions on the two days are different. Today's set of conditions is conducive to rain; yesterday's set was not. A forecaster uses historical data to assess the probability of rain under a specific set of conditions. She can make these statements because historical records indicate that on days when there was a low-pressure system about 200 mi west of the station, the barometer was dropping, and the sky was cloudy, it was more likely to rain than not. In fact, 85 percent of the days when those conditions were present, it rained. Fifteen percent of the time when conditions were like that, it did not rain. Similarly, on 20 percent of the days when there was no low-pressure system, no clouds, and a steady barometer, it rained. Under those same conditions, 80 percent of the time it did not rain. Similar conditions do not always guarantee the same outcome. The outcome is always uncertain to some degree, so one makes probabilistic statements about such events.

This example points toward an adequate definition of probability:

> The *probability* of an event is the relative frequency with which an event occurs over the long run under similar conditions.

Let's take apart that definition.

Essential Prior Definitions

We need to formalize some commonsense ideas to understand the definition fully. To appreciate the concept of "event," as in "the probability of an event . . . ," you must understand the concepts of "experiment," "outcome," and "sample space."

An *experiment* is a process that leads to an observation. Common sense says that an experiment is something you do in a laboratory: set up equipment, mix chemicals, weigh, measure, write in a notebook, and so on. The concept as it is used here includes laboratory experiments (since laboratory experiments are each a "process that leads to an observation"), but this concept of experiment is more general. An experiment can be a process like "see if it rains during a 24-hour period and record the result." Or an experiment can be "roll two dice, add the faces that show, and record the result." Or "roll four dice, two red, two white; add the faces that are up on the white dice; subtract from that the sum of the faces of the red dice that are touching the surface on which the dice rest; record the result." An experiment is any general but specifiable process that leads to an observation.

An *outcome* is the result of a particular experiment. All the experiments described above are general processes that lead to some general kind of observation. "See if it rains" does not tell you whether it rained on a particular day; it tells you what to do on any day in general to conduct the experiment. An outcome is the observation made at the conclusion of one iteration of the experiment. An outcome for the first experiment described above might be "It rained." An outcome of the second might be "11." An outcome is a particular result that occurs as a result of following the instructions of a general experimental procedure.

A *sample space* is the set of all possible outcomes of an experiment. The sample space of an experiment is, by convention, a set of outcomes that is collectively denoted S. The sample space of the first experiment S_1, is

$$S_1 = \{\text{"It rained," "It did not rain"}\}$$

There are two possible outcomes for each observation, two outcomes that might be the result of the general process that leads to an observation. The sample space of the second experiment S_2 is familiar to you. It is

$$S_2 = \{2, 3, 4, 5, 6, 7, 8, 9, 10, 11, 12\}$$

Each outcome in a sample space is called a *sample point*. The number of sample points in a given sample space is denoted $n(S)$. For the first experiment $n(S_1) = 2$. For the second experiment $n(S_2) = 11$, and $n(S_3) = 35$ for the third.

Definition of Probability

Finally, we return to the original definition of probability. The definitions of "experiment," "outcome," and "sample space" permit a clear definition of "event," a key word.

An *event* is any subset of sample points from a sample space. An event might be a simple outcome, one point in a sample space. For example, {"It rained"} is a subset of the sample space $S_1 = \{\text{"It rained," It did not rain"}\}$. It is very possible for someone to be interested in the probability of the simple event $A_1 - \{\text{"It rained"}\}$. But an event can be more than a simple outcome of an experiment. We might be interested, in the case of the second experiment, in the probability of event $A_2 = \{11 \text{ or } 12\}$. Now $A_2 = \{11 \text{ or } 12\}$ is a subset of the sample space, so according to the definition it is an event, but it is not just a simple outcome.

In the definition, the phrase "the probability of an event . . . " says a probability (a number or a percentage) is associated with one event out of a sample space. Each event A has a probability associated with it. The probability of event A is designated $P(A)$.

The definition stipulates that the probability of an event must be a relative frequency over the long run *under similar conditions*. If you throw a die, usually you assume that the corners of the die remain the same, the table remains level, the ground remains stable, the shake you give the die is similar across many such shakes, the spots on the faces of the die remain the same, and so on. If the conditions change, all bets are off, or at least they should be. A statement about the probability of an event assumes that conditions stay the same over the long run during which relative frequency is calculated.

The definition also says that the probability of any single event is a *relative frequency*. The concept of relative frequency is familiar. A relative frequency is the frequency of an event relative to the frequency of all possible events. If you roll a fair die 100 times and a 1 turns up 22 times, the relative frequency of a 1 is 22, the number of times a 1 turned up, divided by 100, the total number of events.

So the relative frequency of a 1 is 22/100 = .22. Don't get confused: .22 is *not* the probability of getting a 1 on one throw of a fair die. Why? Because there is one other, important part of the definition.

Probability is a relative frequency *over the long run*. You would have to throw a die many, many times to determine the probability of the event "1" by this method; 100 throws is not an especially long run. How long is long enough?

I spent a morning throwing my set of rigged dice to determine the relative frequency of 10 over the long run. I threw the dice 500 times. The first time I threw the dice, I got a 9. The relative frequency of getting 10 over this very short run of one throw was 0 (the number of 10s) divided by 1 (the number of throws), or 0. The second throw was also a 9. The relative frequency of 10 was 0 over two throws. The third throw was a 4, so the relative frequency of 10 was still 0. The fourth throw was a 10. The relative frequency was then 1 (the number of 10s thrown) divided by 4 (the number of throws), or .25. The fifth roll was an 8; the relative frequency went down to 1/5 = .20. The sixth throw was a 4, and the relative frequency of 10 became .166. I got two more 10s over the next four throws, so after 10 throws the relative frequency of 10 was 3/10 = .30.

Ten throws are not a "long run." Figure 5.1 shows the relative frequency of 10 over 500 throws, with the relative frequency recalculated after every 10 throws.

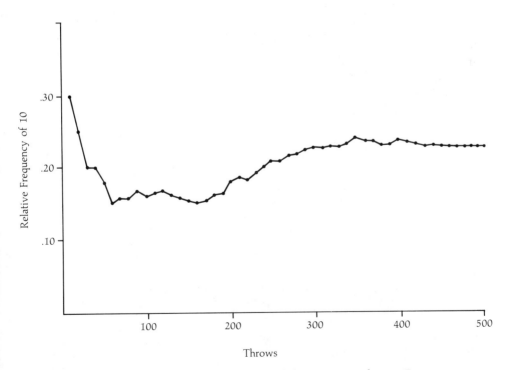

FIGURE 5.1 Relative frequency of 10 from fixed dice over 500 throws. Frequency is recalculated every 10 throws.

The leftmost point on the chart is at .30, the relative frequency of 10 after 10 throws. I got two 10s during the next 10 rolls. That gave me a total of five 10s out of 20 throws. The relative frequency of 10 after 20 throws was 5/20 = .25, as the graph shows. After 30 throws, I had six 10s for a relative frequency of .20.

From Figure 5.1, over the long run the probability of getting a 10 on a single throw of the fixed dice is about .22. The line seems to converge on .22. This experiment illustrates how probabilities can be determined *empirically*. You conduct an experiment many, many times and determine the relative frequency with which an event occurs.

Figure 5.1 reveals one major problem with empirical probabilities. If you happened to stop repeating the experiment after 100 trials—which seems like a fairly long run—you would conclude that the probability of getting a 10 is about .15 or .16. The graph of relative frequency does not stabilize around .22 until 300 or 400 trials have been conducted. And 400 trials of even the simplest experiment like throwing two dice takes a long time.

Theoretical Probability

Fortunately, there is another approach to determining probability, a *theoretical* approach. You can determine the probability of an event based on a theory about the way a small part of the world works. In fact, the doubting student did just that for the dice when I conducted my demonstration. His arguments are in Chapter 3. Figure 5.2 is a slight variation of Figure 3.7. It shows the sample space for the experiment "Throw two fixed dice, add the faces showing, and record the score."

		Die 1				
	1	1	5	5	6	6
3	(3, 1) 4	(3, 1) 4	(3, 5) 8	(3, 5) 8	(3, 6) 9	(3, 6) 9
3	(3, 1) 4	(3, 1) 4	(3, 5) 8	(3, 5) 8	(3, 6) 9	(3, 6) 9
4	(4, 1) 5	(4, 1) 5	(4, 5) 9	(4, 5) 9	(4, 6) 10	(4, 6) 10
4	(4, 1) 5	(4, 1) 5	(4, 5) 9	(4, 5) 9	(4, 6) 10	(4, 6) 10
5	(5, 1) 6	(5, 1) 6	(5, 5) 10	(5, 5) 10	(5, 6) 11	(5, 6) 11
5	(5, 1) 6	(5, 1) 6	(5, 5) 10	(5, 5) 10	(5, 6) 11	(5, 6) 11

Die 2 (row labels at left)

FIGURE 5.2 Thirty-six combinations of two fixed dice and sums of two faces in each instance.

Figure 5.2 shows the 36 possible combinations of the two rigged dice and the sums of the two faces for each combination. If the fixed dice are otherwise fair and are fairly thrown, then, in theory, each face has an equal chance of turning up. If that is true, then, in theory, each of the 36 possible two-dice combinations has an equal chance of occurring. That is, in theory, each outcome shown in Figure 5.2 has a probability of 1/36 associated with it.

What, then, is the probability of event $A = \{10\}$ on one throw of the fixed dice? What is $P(A) = P(10)$? Note that event $A = \{10\}$ is not a simple outcome since there are eight outcomes—the eight sample points in boxes—that produce a 10. So, in theory, the probability of getting a 10 is $8 \times 1/36 = 8/36$. The theoretical probability of getting a 10 on any given throw is $8/36 = .2222$.

We can hardly fail to notice that the empirical probability on which the line in Figure 5.1 converges is remarkably close to the theoretical probability calculated on the basis of commonsense ideas about the way dice roll. This is not a coincidence. There is a mathematical law that connects the notion of empirical probability and theoretical probability. The *law of large numbers* says that as you increase the number of times that an experiment is repeated, the relative frequency with which an event occurs approaches the theorical probability of the event for a single trial. The law of large numbers provides assurance that you need not repeat an experiment many, many times to determine the probability of an event. You usually rely on a theory to determine the probability of an event's occurring during a single trial of the experiment.

Diagrammatic Approaches to Probability

There are two convenient schemes for diagraming possible outcomes of an experiment: grids and trees. Both approaches help you visualize the points in a sample space.

Let's start with a classical "balls in an urn" probability problem. There are two balls in an urn, one red and the other blue. The experiment is, "Shake the urn, draw one ball, record its color, return the ball to the urn, shake the urn, draw another ball, and record its color." The observation consists of two colors of balls in an order, first drawn followed by second drawn. A *probability tree* diagram of this experiment is shown in the top part of Figure 5.3. The first draw has two possible outcomes, red or blue. The second draw also has two possible outcomes, red or blue. Each branch of the tree represents one possible result of an aspect of the experiment. Each endpoint on the tree represents one point in the sample space of the experiment. The first outcome—one point in the sample space—is the point (1st = red, 2nd = red), or (red, red). The second point is (red, blue). The third point is (blue, red), and the fourth point is (blue, blue).

This experiment can also be represented on a grid. The bottom part of Figure 5.3 shows the *probability grid* for this experiment. Each point formed by the intersection of grid lines is a point in the sample space. Recall that in the dice experiment we used a grid to represent the 36 points in the sample space. Each

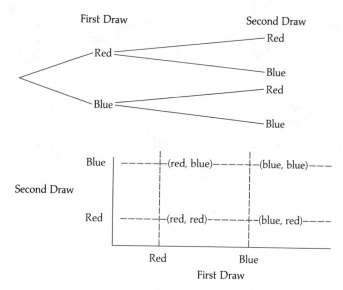

FIGURE 5.3 Probability tree and probability grid representation of the two-balls-in-the-urn experiment.

combination of selections of the two balls or faces of the two dice corresponds to one point in the sample space.

Probability trees have one advantage over grids. They are not so confusing when there are more than two aspects to an experiment. For example, if the experiment were, "Give birth to three children (no multiple births) and record the

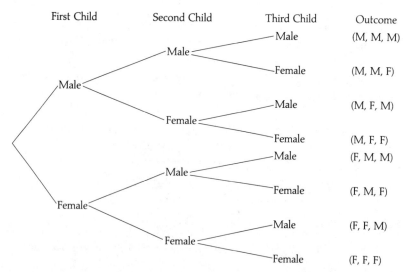

FIGURE 5.4 Probability tree of outcomes of "have three children" experiment.

sex of each," you would need a three-dimensional grid to represent the points in the experiment's sample space. However, Figure 5.4 shows the eight possible outcomes easily on a probability tree.

Probability When Outcomes Are Equiprobable

Trees and grids allow you to assess immediately the probability of an event if all the outcomes have the same probability of occurring. If outcomes have the same probability of occurring, you say, "The outcomes are *equiprobable.*" If all the points in a sample space are equally likely to occur, then the probability of an event A is the ratio of the number of points in event A to the number of points in the sample space, or

$$P(A) = \frac{n(A)}{n(S)}$$

Once again, this is a rule you have already used since it is an intuitive rule. In the dice experiment, each of the 36 outcomes was equally likely to occur. In that experiment, the number of points in the space was 36, so $n(S) = 36$. If event A is $A = \{10\}$, then $n(A) = 8$. Eight outcomes comprise event $A = \{10\}$. The probability of getting a 10 on one throw of the rigged dice is

$$P(10) = \frac{n(A)}{n(S)} = \frac{8}{36} = .222$$

What is the probability of getting a family of three singly born children that has at least two males if the outcomes in Figure 5.4 are equally likely? In that experiment, $n(S) = 8$. Four outcomes (the first, second, third, and fifth from the top) have at least two males in them. So if $A = \{$"at least two males"$\}$, $n(A) = 4$, and

$$P(A) = \frac{n(A)}{n(S)} = \frac{4}{8} = 0.5$$

Finally, what is the probability of getting a family with exactly two female children? If $A = \{$"exactly two females"$\}$, $n(A) = 3$, so $P(A) = 3/8 = .375$.

• • •

PROPERTIES OF PROBABILITIES

You must learn several properties of probability to understand the logic and concepts of inferential statistics. The first property is that *the probability associated with an event varies between 0 and 1,* or to express it mathematically,

$$0 \le P(A) \le 1$$

In words, the probability of A, or $P(A)$, is always greater than or equal to 0 and less than or equal to 1. If the probability of event A is 0, the event never occurs; if the probability A is 1, the event always occurs. In the experiment "Have three children . . . ," the probability of event $A = \{\text{three children}\}$ is 1. It always happens that you have three children if you do this experiment. If the event of interest is $A = \{\text{rain}\}$ in the experiment "See if it rains . . . ," then $0 \leq P(\text{rain}) \leq 1$, that is, the probability of rain is between 0 and 1 on any given day.

The second property is that the *probabilities of all possible outcomes of an experiment sum to 1*. To express it mathematically,

$$\sum_{A = \text{all outcomes}} P(A) = 1$$

This means, first, that some outcome must always occur. If you perform an experiment, an outcome will definitely occur.

This simple idea means, second, that if you know the probability of an event's occurring $P(A)$, then the probability of the event's not occurring, sometimes written $P(\bar{A})$, is $1 - P(A)$ since an event must either occur or not occur. And $\bar{A}$, the notation used to describe the event "not A," is called the *complement* of event A. The probability of $\bar{A}$ (the complement of A) $P(\bar{A})$ is always equal to $1 - P(A)$. The probability of getting a 10 from the fixed dice is .222. The complement of event $A = \{10\}$ is event $\bar{A} = \{4, 5, 6, 8, 9, 11\}$. The probability of not getting a 10 (that is, the probability of getting a 4, 5, 6, 8, 9, or 11) is

$$P(\overline{10}) = 1 - P(10) = 1 - .222 = .778$$

Simple Addition Rule

The third property of probability is a little more complicated: *If two events are mutually exclusive, then the probability of occurrence of one event or the other is the sum of the individual probabilities of the two events*. If A and B are mutually exclusive, then

$$P(A \text{ or } B) = P(A) + P(B) \tag{5.1}$$

This rule holds only for mutually exclusive events.

Mutually exclusive events are two events defined so that if one event occurs, the other cannot. If you throw a 7 with two fair dice, that precludes you from also throwing a 10 on the same throw. Events $A_1 = \{7\}$ and $A_2 = \{10\}$ are mutually exclusive events. By comparison, the two events $A_1 = \{7 \text{ or less}\}$ and $A_2 = \{7 \text{ or more}\}$ for one throw of two fair dice are not mutually exclusive. The occurrence of event A_1 does not preclude the occurrence of event A_2. If, for example, you throw a 7, both event A_1 and event A_2 have occurred.

The simple addition rule can be extended. If $A_1, A_2, \ldots, A_k$ are all mutually exclusive, then the probability of occurrence of one of them during a single trial of an experiment is

$$P(A_1 \text{ or } A_2 \text{ or } \ldots \text{ or } A_k) = P(A_1) + P(A_2) + \cdots + P(A_k)$$

This rule is called the *simple addition rule* of probability.

You have used this addition rule already even though you have done so implicitly. Look at Figure 5.2 again. The probability of any single outcome shown in the figure is 1/36. To find the probability of getting a 10 on any throw, you want to know the probability of getting the outcome in row 3 and column 5 (4, 6 = 10) or the outcome in row 3 and column 6 (4, 6 = 10) *or* the outcome in row 4 and column 5 *or* the outcome in row 4 and column 6 *or* any of the outcomes in the lower box. This probability is expressed as

$P[(4, 6) \text{ or } (4, 6) \text{ or } (4, 6) \text{ or } (4, 6) \text{ or } (5, 5) \text{ or } (5, 5) \text{ or } (5, 5) \text{ or } (5, 5)]$
$\quad = P(4, 6) + P(4, 6) + P(4, 6) + P(4, 6) + P(5, 5) + P(5, 5) + P(5, 5) + P(5, 5)$
$\quad = 1/36 + 1/36 + 1/36 + 1/36 + 1/36 + 1/36 + 1/36 + 1/36$
$\quad = 8/36$

Here's a slightly more complicated example. An urn contains four balls, a white plain (WP) ball, a white striped (WS) ball, a black plain (BP) ball, and a black striped (BS) ball. The experiment is to draw twice from the urn, replacing the ball drawn first after recording its type. The observation is the combination of two types of balls drawn. Figure 5.5a shows the sample space for this experiment. Is event $A_1 = \{$two black balls$\}$ mutually exclusive of event $A_2 = \{$at least one white ball$\}$? Figure 5.5b shows these two events. The outcomes that comprise event A_1 are in the lower right corner of the grid. The outcomes in event A_2 are all the other outcomes in the grid. The two subsets of outcomes do not overlap. If an outcome in one subset of outcomes occurs, an outcome in the other set cannot. Events A_1 and A_2 are mutually exclusive. Since this is so, the simple addition rule applies in calculating the probability of getting two black balls *or* at least one white ball:

$$P(A_1 \text{ or } A_2) = P(A_1) + P(A_2) = \frac{1}{4} + \frac{3}{4} = 1$$

In fact, $A_1 = \bar{A}_2$, or A_1 is the complement of A_2.

Is event $A_3 = \{$both balls are striped$\}$ mutually exclusive of event $A_4 = \{$both balls are same color$\}$? No. Look at Figure 5.5c. Two outcomes—(WS, WS) and

	White plain	White striped	Black plain	Black striped
White plain	(WP, WP)	(WP, WS)	(WP, BP)	(WP, BS)
White striped	(WS, WP)	(WS, WS)	(WS, BP)	(WS, BS)
Black plain	(BP, WP)	(BP, WS)	(BP, BP)	(BP, BS)
Black striped	(BS, WP)	(BS, WS)	(BS, BP)	(BS, BS)

(a)

	White plain	White striped	Black plain	Black striped	
White plain	(WP, WP)	(WP, WS)	(WP, BP)	(WP, BS)	A_2
White striped	(WS, WP)	(WS, WS)	(WS, BP)	(WS, BS)	
Black plain	(BP, WP)	(BP, WS)	(BP, BP)	(BP, BS)	A_1
Black striped	(BS, WP)	(BS, WS)	(BS, BP)	(BS, BS)	

(b)

	White plain	White striped	Black plain	Black striped
White plain	(WP, WP)	(WP, WS)	(WP, BP)	(WP, BS)
White striped	(WS, WP)	(WS, WS)	(WS, BP)	(WS, BS)
Black plain	(BP, WP)	(BP, WS)	(BP, BP)	(BP, BS)
Black striped	(BS, WP)	(BS, WS)	(BS, BP)	(BS, BS)

A_4, A_3

(c)

Key: WP = White plain
WS = White striped
BP = Black plain
BS = Black striped

FIGURE 5.5 Sample space of an experiment involving four balls. (*a*) Sample space. (*b*) Sample space with events A_1 = {two black balls} and A_2 = {at least one white ball} shown. (*c*) Sample space with events A_3 = {both balls striped} and A_4 = {both balls the same color}.

(BS, BS)—are common to both events. The simple addition rule cannot be applied to calculate the probability of getting both balls striped or both balls of the same color. The case is more complicated and is taken up below.

Venn diagrams help you see what it means for events to be mutually exclusive. The rectangle in Figure 5.6 contains all the points in the sample space of the four-ball experiment. The circles marked A_1 and A_2 contain the sample points in each event. There is no overlap between the circles. The events are mutually exclusive. In Figure 5.6*b*, there is an overlap or intersection, between events A_3 and A_4. Events A_3 and A_4 are not mutually exclusive.

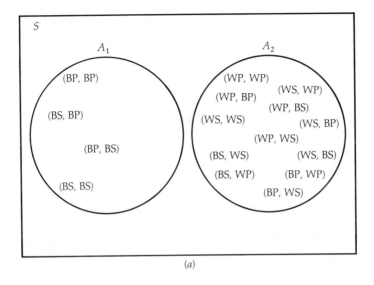

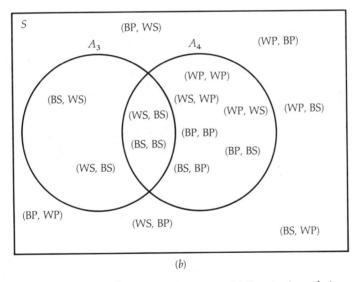

FIGURE 5.6 Venn diagrams of events in Figure 5.5. (*a*) Events A_1 and A_2 are mutually exclusive events. (*b*) Events A_3 and A_4 are not mutually exclusive events.

Simple Multiplication Rule

The simple addition rule gives the probability that one event *or* the other will occur. What is the probability that one event *and* the other will occur? If two events *A* and *B* are independent of each other, then

$$P(A \text{ and } B) = P(A) \cdot P(B) \qquad (5.2)$$

The probability of occurrence of two independent events is the product of the probabilities of each event. The rule is extended to multiple events as long as all the events are independent of one another:

$$P(A_1 \text{ and } A_2 \text{ and } \ldots \text{ and } A_k) = P(A_1) \cdot P(A_2) \cdots P(A_k)$$

Some states run lotteries called *triple-choice games*. The winning number is selected by mixing three sets of balls, each numbered from 1 to 9 (or in some cases 0 to 9), in three separate machines. One ball is drawn from each machine. The three drawings are made independently of one another. The winning number is the combination of three numbers chosen. What is the probability of getting a 9 from the first machine, a 6 from the second, and a 3 from the third? Expressed mathematically, if $A_1 = \{\text{first machine} = 9\}$, $A_2 = \{\text{second machine} = 6\}$, and $A_3 = \{\text{third machine} = 30\}$, what is $P(A_1 \text{ and } A_2 \text{ and } A_3)$? There are nine balls in each machine, and each has an equal chance of being selected, so the probability of getting any given ball from one of the machines is 1/9. That is, $P(A_1) = 1/9$, $P(A_2) = 1/9$, and $P(A_3) = 1/9$. Since the events are independent,

$$P(A_1 \text{ and } A_2 \text{ and } A_3) = P(A_1) \cdot P(A_2) \cdot P(A_3)$$
$$= 1/9 \cdot 1/9 \cdot 1/9 = 1/279 = .0014 = .14\%$$

or slightly greater than 0.1 percent.

In the previous paragraphs, we relied on your commonsense notion of "independence" of two events. As with everything in this language of statistics, commonsense terms have a formal meaning. Formally, *two events are independent of each other if the occurrence of one event does not affect the probability of occurrence of the other event.* Drawing a 9 from the first machine in the triple-choice game does not affect the probability of drawing a 6 (or any other ball, for that matter) from the second machine. Having a child of one sex for the first birth does not normally affect the probability of having a female (or a male) child for the second birth. (However, books are available to help parents "choose the sex" of their baby. If a couple's having a male child made them decide to try to have female child on their second try, and if the advice of these manuals worked, then the outcomes of two births would not be independent of each other. The events would be *dependent*.)

Technically, two events A and B are said to be independent if

$$P(B|A) = P(B) \qquad \text{or} \qquad P(A|B) = P(A)$$

where $P(B|A)$ is the symbol for the *conditional probability* of event B given event A. It is the probability of occurrence of event B given that event A has already occurred. The definition of independence says that two events A and B are independent if the conditional probability of occurrence of event B given that A has already occurred is exactly equal to the probability of occurrence of event B (without reference to event A). Or, the definition continues, A and B are independent if the probability of A given B is equal to the probability of A.

Let's return once more to the sample space of the two fixed dice. Let $D_1 =$ {both dice show the same number} and $D_2 =$ {10}. You know $P(D_2) = 8/36$. What is $P(D_1)$? There are only four points in the space where the faces of the dice are the same: the four combinations of two 5s. So $P(D_1) = 4/36$. What, now, is the conditional probability, $P(D_1 | D_2)$, the probability of the two visible faces of the dice being the same given that you have rolled a 10? If a 10 has been rolled, then one of the eight combinations boxed in Figure 5.2 must have occurred. Four of those eight outcomes also belong to the event "both dice show the same number." Over the long run, the relative frequency of both dice showing the same number given that a 10 has been rolled is $4/8 = 1/2$. So $P(D_1 | D_2) = 1/2$. Since $P(D_1 | D_2) \neq P(D_1)$, events D_1 and D_2 are not independent. Events D_1 and D_2 are dependent.

General Multiplication Rule

The notions of independence and conditional probability lead to a general multiplication rule. In general (i.e., whether events are independent or not),

$$\begin{aligned} P(A \text{ and } B) &= P(A) \cdot P(B|A) \\ &= P(B) \cdot P(A|B) \end{aligned} \tag{5.3}$$

The probability of occurrence of both A and B is equal to the probability of one event times the conditional probability of the other, given that the first has occurred.

In the example of the fixed dice, what is the probability of getting a 10 and having both dice show the same number? That is, what is $P(D_1 \text{ and } D_2)$? The general multiplication rule gives

$$\begin{aligned} P(D_1 \text{ and } D_2) &= P(D_2) \cdot P(D_1|D_2) \\ &= 8/36 \cdot 1/2 = 8/72 = 1/9 \end{aligned}$$

If you knew $P(D_2|D_1)$, you could check the equivalence of the general multiplication rule. What is the probability of getting a 10 given that both faces of the dice are the same? If both faces show the same number, both faces must be 5s on these fixed dice. So, it is always the case that if both faces show the same number, a 10 will occur. That is,

$$P(D_2|D_1) = 1$$

Consequently,

$$P(D_1 \text{ and } D_2) = P(D_1) \cdot P(D_2|D_1) = 1/9 \cdot 1 = 1/9$$

Let's calculate the probability of winning a lottery that requires you to match all six numbers drawn from a single mixing machine that contains 40 numbered balls. You need to know the probability

$$P(E_1 \text{ and } E_2 \text{ and } E_3 \text{ and } E_4 \text{ and } E_5 \text{ and } E_6)$$

where E_1 = 1st ball drawn matches one of six numbers selected
   E_2 = 2d ball drawn matches one of remaining five numbers
   E_3 = 3d ball drawn matches one of remaining four numbers
   E_4 = 4th ball drawn matches one of remaining three numbers
   E_5 = 5th ball drawn matches one of remaining two numbers
   E_6 = 6th ball drawn matches one remaining number

First, what is $P(E_1)$? (The probability tree for this experiment is shown in Figure 5.7.) There are 40 points in the sample space. Event E_1 contains six points, six numbers that you have chosen as your lottery numbers. So $P(E_1) = 6/40$. What is $P(E_1 \text{ and } E_2)$? Following the general multiplication rule, we get

$$P(E_1 \text{ and } E_2) = P(E_1) \cdot P(E_2 \mid E_1)$$

Hit = match of a number
Miss = no match of a number

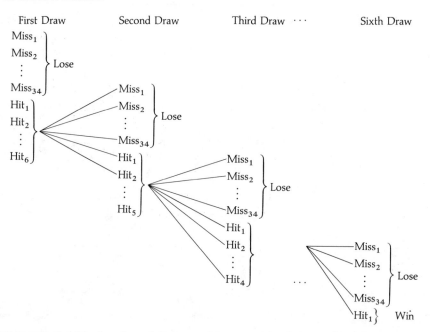

FIGURE 5.7 Probability tree for a lottery requiring a match of six numbers drawn from 40 numbered balls.

If event E_1 has occurred—that is, the first ball drawn has matched one of the numbers chosen—then there are 39 balls remaining in the mixing machine and 5 numbers left to match. The probability that the second ball matches one of the five remaining numbers given that the first ball matched one of the six is $P(E_2|E_1) = 5/39$.

$$P(E_1 \text{ and } E_2) = P(E_1) \cdot P(E_2|E_1) = (6/40)(5/39) = 30/1560$$

What is $P(E_1 \text{ and } E_2 \text{ and } E_3)$? Once again using the general multiplication rule, we get

$$P(E_1 \text{ and } E_2 \text{ and } E_3) = P(E_1 \text{ and } E_2) \cdot P(E_3|E_1 \text{ and } E_2)$$

If event "E_1 and E_2" has occurred, there are 38 remaining balls in the mixing machine and four remaining numbers to match. The probability that the third ball will match one of the four remaining numbers, given that the first two have matched, is $P(E_3|E_1, \text{ and } E_2) = 4/38$. Then

$$P(E_1 \text{ and } E_2 \text{ and } E_3) = P(E_1 \text{ and } E_2) \cdot P(E_3|E_1 \text{ and } E_2)$$
$$= (30/1560)(4/38) = 120/59{,}280$$

Following this logic gives

$$P(E_1 \text{ and } E_2 \text{ and } E_3 \text{ and } E_4) = (120/59{,}280)(3/37) = 360/2{,}193{,}360$$

$$P(E_1 \text{ and } E_2 \text{ and } E_3 \text{ and } E_4 \text{ and } E_5) = (360/2{,}193{,}360)(2/36)$$
$$= 720/78{,}960{,}960$$

and

$$P(E_1 \text{ and } E_2 \text{ and } E_3 \text{ and } E_4 \text{ and } E_5 \text{ and } E_6) = (720/78{,}960{,}960)(1/35)$$
$$= 720/2{,}763{,}624{,}600$$

It's your money.

General Addition Rule

If events are not mutually exclusive, then the simple addition rule for probability does not apply. If A and B are not mutually exclusive events, then

$$P(A \text{ or } B) = P(A) + P(B) - P(A \text{ and } B) \tag{5.4}$$

This rule is most easily understood if you look at a Venn diagram. Figure 5.8*a* shows two mutually exclusive events. The probability of occurrence of one or the other is simply the sum of the separate probabilities according to the simple

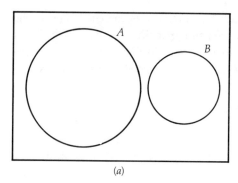
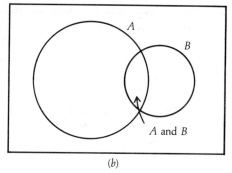

(a)   (b)

FIGURE 5.8 Venn diagrams demonstrating the general addition rule. (*a*) Two events
are mutually exclusive. (*b*) Two events are not mutually exclusive.

addition rule. If A and B are not mutually exclusive, as in Figure 5.8*b*, there is an
area of overlap. If you added $P(A)$ and $P(B)$, you would be "counting" the points
contained in the overlapping area *twice*. The general addition rule subtracts the
area of overlap once.

Back to the four-balls experiment. What is the probability of getting two
striped balls or two balls of the same color? In the terms used earlier, $A_3 = \{$both
balls striped$\}$, $A_4 = \{$both balls the same color$\}$. What then is $P(A_3$ or $A_4)$?
The sample space contains 16 points, so $n(S) = 16$. And $n(A_3) = 4$, so $P(A_3) =$
$4/16 = 1/4$. Also $P(A_4) = 8/16 = 1/2$. But the events are not mutually exclusive, so you cannot apply the simple addition rule and claim that $P(A_3$ or $A_4) =$
$3/4$. We need to find

$$P(A_3 \text{ or } A_4) = P(A_3) + P(A_4) - P(A_3 \text{ and } A_4)$$

To find the last term on the right side, note that two events are common to events
A_3 and A_4, so $n(A_3$ and $A_4) = 2$. Consequently, $P(A_3$ and $A_4) = 2/16 = 1/8$,
and

$$P(A_3 \text{ or } A_4) = 1/4 + 1/2 - 1/8 = 5/8$$

In words, the probability of getting both balls striped or both balls of the same
color on one run of the experiment is $5/8$.

$\bullet \quad \bullet \quad \bullet$

USING THE PROPERTIES OF PROBABILITY

The several properties of probability discussed in the previous section can be used
in combination to solve relatively complicated problems in probability. Here are
several examples.

First, consider an example in which only the simple addition rule and the simple multiplication rule are used. What are the probabilities of various combinations of gender in three births if the probabilities of having a male and a female child are exactly reflected in real-world data? The *sex ratio* is defined as the number of males per 100 females of a given age. The *sex ratio at birth*—the number of male babies born per 100 female babies born—is not 100 in real life. In fact, there are about 105 males born for every 100 females. The sex ratio at birth is about 105. What is the probability of a single birth producing a male child? The relative frequency of males relative to the total number of births over the long run is $P(\text{male}) = 105/(105 + 100) = .51$. So what is the probability of a family of three singly born children consisting of exactly two female children? Figure 5.9 shows the probability tree for this experiment with the probability of each branch placed on the branch.

The event $A = \{\text{exactly two females}\}$ consists of outcomes O_4, O_6, and O_7. So what is $P(A)$ when

$$P(A) = P(O_4 \text{ or } O_6 \text{ or } O_7)$$

The three outcomes are mutually exclusive. If one occurs, neither of the other two can occur. That means the simple addition rule [Formula (5.1)] applies and

$$P(A) = P(O_4 \text{ or } O_6 \text{ or } O_7) = P(O_4) + P(O_6) + P(O_7)$$

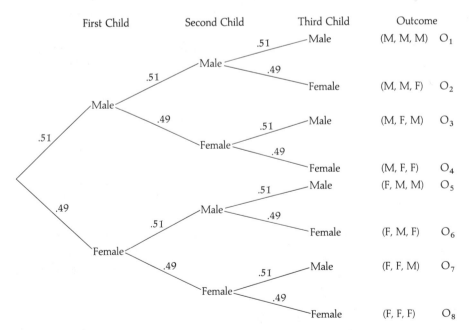

FIGURE 5.9 Probability tree for the experiment "have three children" with probabilities of each branch inserted on the branches.

What is $P(O_4)$? Outcome O_4 is reached through a combination of prior outcomes. Specifically,

$$O_4 = (\text{1st birth} = \text{male and 2d birth} = \text{female and 3d birth} = \text{female})$$

These three births are independent of one another since the probability of the second birth being a female is not affected by the prior birth of a male. Always $P(\text{female}) = .49$ and $P(\text{male}) = .51$. So the simple multiplication rule [Formula (5.2)] says

$$
\begin{aligned}
P(O_4) &= P(\text{1st birth} = \text{male and 2d birth} = \text{female and 3d birth} = \text{female}) \\
&= P(\text{1st} = \text{male}) \cdot P(\text{2d} = \text{female}) \cdot P(\text{3d} = \text{female}) \\
&= (.51)(.49)(.49) = .1225
\end{aligned}
$$

And $P(O_6)$ and $P(O_7)$ can be calculated in the same way and are equal to the same number. So

$$
\begin{aligned}
P(A) &= P(O_4 \text{ or } O_6 \text{ or } O_7) = P(O_4) + P(O_6) + P(O_7) \\
&= .1225 + .1225 + .1225 = .3675
\end{aligned}
$$

which is slightly less than the probability of having exactly two females in three single births if the probability of having a male is the same as the probability of having a female. [Recall that if $P(\text{male}) - P(\text{female})$, then $P(A) = .375$.]

The next example uses the more general rules. Suppose that the probability of a student in a class being, in fact, a poor student who does not comprehend the material at the end of the course is .1, and the probability of a student's being a good student is .9. Then suppose that the probability of the instructor's making a correct judgment about each student is .85. That is, the probability of the instructor's passing a good student is .85, and that of failing a poor student is also .85. Out of a class of 200 students, how many students will pass?

You need to express this problem in terms of probabilities. The first part is simple:

$$P(\text{good student}) = .9 \qquad P(\text{poor student}) = .1$$

The second part of what you are given is a conditional probability. The instructor's making a "correct judgment" means two things: (1) A student passes *if* he or she is a good student worthy of passing, and (2) A student fails *if* she or he is a poor student and should not pass. To express it mathematically,

$$P(\text{fail} \mid \text{poor student}) = .85 \qquad P(\text{pass} \mid \text{good student}) = .85$$

The question asks, What is $P(\text{pass})$?

The students who pass consist of two groups: good students who pass and poor students who pass. These are mutually exclusive groups, so the simple addition rule [Formula (5.1)] applies, and

$$P(\text{pass}) = P(\text{good student and pass}) + P(\text{poor student and pass})$$

However, the judgment the instructor makes about a student is not independent of the quality of the student. Thus the terms on the right side of the equation, $P(\text{good student and pass})$ and $P(\text{poor student and pass})$, need to be determined from the general multiplication rule [Formula (5.3)]. The first term is

$$P(\text{good student and pass}) = P(\text{good student}) \cdot P(\text{pass}|\text{good student})$$
$$= (.9)(.85) = .765$$

The second term is

$$P(\text{poor student and pass}) = P(\text{poor student}) \cdot P(\text{pass}|\text{poor student})$$

The second factor on the right, the conditional probability of passing given that one is a poor student, is not given directly in the problem. However, the instructor who passes someone who is a poor student has made an "incorrect" decision. An "incorrect" decision is the complement of a "correct" decision, which means

$$P(\text{pass}|\text{poor student}) = 1 - P(\text{fail}|\text{poor student})$$
$$= 1 - .85 = .15$$

And so

$$P(\text{poor student and pass}) = P(\text{poor student}) \cdot P(\text{pass}|\text{poor student})$$
$$= (.1)(.15) = .015$$

Finally, the probability of passing the class is

$$P(\text{pass}) = .765 + .015 = .78$$

So 78 percent of the students will pass. Applying that probability to a class of 200 students means that $.78(200) = 156$ students will pass.

As a final example, determine the probability of a poor student's passing this class (which means someone would be certified when he or she is incompetent). In words that are close to the meaning of mathematical symbols, what is the probability of a student being, in fact, a poor student once the decision to pass the student has been made? Expressed symbolically, what is the following?

$$P(\text{poor student}|\text{pass})$$

TABLE 5.1 Distribution of 200 Students into Four Possible Outcomes

Actual Quality	Pass	Fail	Total
Good student	$156 - 3 = 153$	$44 - 17 = 27$	180
Poor student	3*	$20 - 3 = 17$	20
Total	156*	$200 - 156 = 44$	200

* Calculated in an example.

Rearranging terms in Formula (5.3) to find the conditional probability gives

$$P(\text{poor student} \mid \text{pass}) = \frac{P(\text{poor student and pass})}{P(\text{pass})}$$

$$= \frac{P(\text{poor student}) \cdot P(\text{pass} \mid \text{poor student})}{P(\text{pass})}$$

$$= \frac{(.1)(.15)}{.78} = 1.9 \text{ percent}$$

The students having to pass the scrutiny of an instructor whose judgments are correct only 85 percent of the time reduces the percentage of poor students released from the school as certified from 10 percent (the original proportion of students who are poor achievers) to 1.9 percent.

There is a cost for this screening. Table 5.1 shows how the 200 students in this class are distributed into the four possible outcomes. You know from the information given in the problem that 90 percent, or 180 students, are good students and 20 students are poor achievers. In the first part of this example, you found that 156 students will pass the course. That means 22 percent, or 44, of them will fail. Only 1.9 percent of the 156 students who pass will be poor students. That means there are 3 poor students who passed. Of those who passed $156 - 3 = 153$ are good students, and $20 - 3 = 17$ of the poor students failed. Finally, $44 - 17 = 180 - 153 = 27$ good students failed. Of the good students 15 percent did not pass.

· · ·

KEY CONCEPTS IN THIS CHAPTER

· · ·

EXERCISES

Chapter 5

1. Here is a series of balls-in-an-urn experiments. For each experiment list the sample space and determine the probability requested.

    a. Four balls are in the urn. Three are red, and one is blue. One ball is drawn. What is the probability that the ball is red? What is the probability that the ball is blue? What is the probability of the ball being yellow?

    b. Five balls are in the urn. Two are red, two are blue, and one is yellow. One ball is drawn. What is the probability that the ball is red? What is the probability that the ball is blue? What is the probability of the ball being yellow?

    c. One ball is in the urn. It is red. One ball is drawn. What is the probability that the ball will be red? What is the probability that the ball will have corners?

d. Four balls are in the urn. Two are red, two are black. Two balls are drawn. What is the probability that both will be black? What is the probability that one will be red and one will be black?

2. An experiment consists of tossing a coin 4 times.

  a. If an outcome consists of "number of heads," what is the sample space?
  b. If an outcome consists of a collection of heads and tails in the order obtained, what is the sample space?

3. Two dice—one red, one white—each have the following six faces: 1, 1, 3, 3, 5, 5.

  a. Suppose an experiment consists of rolling the two dice and recording the sum of the two faces showing.
    (i) What is the sample space?
    (ii) What is the probability of getting a 6?
    (iii) What is the probability of getting a 10?
    (iv) What outcomes comprise the event "even number"? What is the probability of getting an even number on one throw?
    (v) What outcomes are in the event "a number greater than 4"? What is the probability of that event?
  b. An experiment consists of recording the number that shows on a die by the die's color.
    (i) What is the sample space?
    (ii) What is the probability of the red die's showing a 1 and the white die's showing a 3?
    (iii) What is the probability of the event "red die less than 3 and white die 3 or higher"?
    (iv) What is the probability of the event "even number"?
    (v) What is the probability that both dice show a 5?

4. An experiment consists of flipping a coin and rolling one of the fixed dice in exercise 3.

  a. What is the sample space of this experiment?
  b. Find the following:
    (i) $P(\text{coin} = \text{head})$
    (ii) $P(\text{coin} = \text{head and die} = 3)$
    (iii) $P(\text{coin} = \text{head and die} = \text{even number})$
    (iv) $P(\text{coin} = \text{head or die} = \text{odd number})$
    (v) $P(\text{coin} = \text{head and die} = 3 \text{ or } 5)$
    (vi) $P(\text{die} = 3 | \text{coin} = \text{head})$
    (vii) $P(\text{coin} = \text{head} | \text{die} = 3)$
  c. Is event $\{\text{coin} = \text{head}\}$ independent of event $\{\text{die} = 3\}$?
  d. Is event $\{\text{coin} = \text{head}\}$ mutually exclusive of event $\{\text{die} = 3\}$?

5. Toss two coins 100 times. Record the number of heads obtained on each throw.

   a. What is the sample space of this experiment?
   b. Make a graph showing the relative frequency of the outcome "one head." Plot the relative frequency every five throws.
   c. On the graph in **(b)**, plot the relative frequency of "two heads." Plot the relative frequency every five throws.
   d. Make a probability grid or tree for this experiment.
   e. What is the theoretical probability of getting "one head"?
   f. Is the answer in **(e)** the same as the level on which the graph constructed in **(b)** converges? Why?

6. Here are some outcomes in a sample space and the probabilities of each one occurring. The outcomes are mutually exclusive.

Outcome	1	2	3	4	5	6	7
Probability	.50	.10	.10	.05	.05	.05	.05

   a. What is the probability of getting outcome 7 on one run of this experiment?
   b. Over the long run, how many more times should outcome 7 occur than outcome 6?
   c. What is the probability of occurrence of outcome 6 or outcome 7 on one run of this experiment?
   d. Over the long run, how many more times should outcome 7 occur than the event consisting of {outcome 4 or outcome 5 or outcome 6}?
   e. Are there any other outcomes besides these seven in the sample space? Explain.

7. Suppose that $P(H) = .7$ and $P(K) = .1$ and $P(L) = .1$ and H, K, and L are mutually exclusive events in sample space S.

   a. Draw a Venn diagram of space S.
   b. Find $P(H \text{ or } K)$.
   c. Find $P(\bar{H})$.
   d. Find $P(\bar{K})$.
   e. Find $P(H \text{ or } K \text{ or } L)$.
   f. Find $P(H \text{ and } K)$.
   g. Find $P(K \text{ and } L)$.

8. One female is selected at random from a population. The probability that she is a mother is .3. The probability that she works is .4. Are the events "mother" and "works" mutually exclusive? Determine the probability that this person is a working mother if you can. If you cannot do that, explain why not.

9. Here are three experiments. Are the events listed (separated by a semi-colon) mutually exclusive?

   a. Four balls are in an urn. One is black; three are white. Two separate draws are made and the color of each ball is recorded. The ball is replaced after the first draw.

      (i) Black on the first draw; white on the second draw
      (ii) Black on both draws; white on both draws
      (iii) Black on both draws; white on the first draw
      (iv) One black ball, one white; white on the first draw
      (v) Both balls white; at least one white ball

   b. Two dice with the following faces are thrown, the numbers on each are noted, and the sum of the two faces is recorded.

      Die 1:   1, 3, 5, 7, 9, 11

      Die 2:   2, 4, 6, 8, 10, 12

      (i) Sum is an odd number; die 2 = 2.
      (ii) Die 1 = 1; die 2 is less than 5.
      (iii) Die 1 is less than 6, and die 2 is less than 5; sum is greater than 10.
      (iv) Sum is 11 or less; dice show adjacent integers (for example, 1 and 2).
      (v) Sum is greater than 19; both dice show single-digit numbers.

   c. A couple has three births, each of which may be a single birth or a twin birth.

      (i) At least one twin birth; a family of three or more children
      (ii) At least one twin birth; a family with at least three male children
      (iii) No twin births; a family with at least three male children
      (iv) A family of four children; no twin births

10. If $P(H) = .3$ and $P(K) = .7$ and H and K are independent events, find:

   a. $P(H \text{ and } K)$
   b. $P(K \text{ and } H)$
   c. $P(H|K)$
   d. $P(K|H)$

11. Suppose $P(H) = .3$ and $P(K) = .4$ and $P(H|K) = .1$.

   a. Are H and K independent events?
   b. What is $P(H \text{ and } K)$?
   c. What is $P(H \text{ or } K)$?

    d. Draw a Venn diagram showing events H and K in sample space S. Write the probabilities $P(H)$, $P(K)$, $P(H$ and $K)$, $P(H$ or $K)$, and $P(\bar{H}) + P(\bar{K})$ in the appropriate places in the sample space.

    e. Are H and K mutually exclusive events?

12. Suppose $P(R) = .5$, $P(S) = .2$, $P(T) = .2$, $P(R$ and $S) = .1$, $P(R$ and $T) = .1$, and $P(S$ and $T) = 0$.

    a. Find $P(R$ or $S)$.
    b. Find $P(S$ or $T)$.
    c. Find $P(R$ or S or $T)$.
    d. What is $P(R|T)$?
    e. Find $P(T|R)$.
    f. What is $P(S|T)$?
    g. If you have not already done so, construct a Venn diagram of these events in sample space F.
    h. Are R and S mutually exclusive? How about S and T?
    i. Are R and S independent? How about S and T?

13. Suppose $P(A) = .6$, $P(B) = .4$, $P(C) = .3$, $P(A$ and $B) = .3$, $P(A$ and $C) = .2$, and $P(B$ and $C) = .1$.

    a. Construct a Venn diagram of these events in a sample space.
    b. Find the following:
      (i) $P(A$ or $B)$
      (ii) $P(A$ or B or $C)$
      (iii) $P(A$ and B and $C)$
      (iv) $P(A|B$ or $C)$
      (v) $P(A|B$ and $C)$
      (vi) $P(A$ or $B|C)$
    c. Are any of the three pairs of events mutually exclusive?
    d. Are any of the three pairs of events independent?

14. Of the people attending a rock concert 85 percent are teenagers. Of the people attending 65 percent are females while 70 percent of the teenagers are females. One person is selected at random to meet with the stars of the show. What is the probability that the person is

    a. a male
    b. a female teenager
    c. a male who is not a teenager?

15. There are three red balls and three blue balls in an urn. Three balls are selected.

    a. If you replace the selected ball after recording its color, what is the probability of getting three red balls?

b. If you do not replace the selected balls after recording the color, what is the probability of getting three red balls?

16. Records at a college show that the probability of a student's passing a quarter is .97.

a. If passing one quarter is independent of passing another quarter, what is the probability of passing two quarters? Three quarters? Four?

b. If the probability of passing one quarter, given that you have failed one previously, is .75, what is the probability of passing one quarter? What is the probability of passing one quarter and failing the next? What is the probability of passing one quarter and failing the next two? What is the probability of failing three quarters in a row?

17. A man said, "Every day that I go to work, it's a '50-50' chance that I won't have that job at the end of the day". What is the probability that he will last one full workweek (5 days) if continued employment on each day is independent of continued employment on every other day?

18. Ace Marbles sells marbles in bags of five. Ace bags its marbles from a large supply that is 50 percent clear marbles and 50 percent solid colors.

a. Find the probability that a bag will contain all clear or all solid marbles.

b. What is the probability that a bag will contain exactly two clear marbles?

c. Find the probability that a bag will contain at least three solid marbles.

19. Ace Marbles loads its bags of five marbles each from a batch that contains 25 percent clear marbles and 75 percent solid-color ones.

a. Find the probability that a bag will contain all clear marbles.

b. What is the probability that a bag will contain exactly two clear marbles?

c. Find the probability that a bag will contain at least three solid-color marbles.

20. Suppose the "have children" experiment required that a couple have four singly born children. Suppose, furthermore, that the probability of having a female is the same as the probability of having a male. What is the probability of the following outcomes?

a. Exactly one female child
b. No female children
c. At least one male child
d. At least three children of the same sex

21. Suppose the probability of getting an A in calculus is .20 and the probability of getting an A in physics is .19. Of those who get an A in calculus, 80 percent also get an A in physics.

    a. What is the probability of getting an A in both subjects?
    b. What is the probability of getting an A in physics for someone who gets an A in calculus?
    c. What is the probability of not getting an A in either subject?

22. Suppose a voter is selected at random from a town whose population is distributed in the following way:

		Will Vote, %		
		Democrat	Republican	Total
	Democrat	40	15	55
Registered	Republican	5	40	45
	Total	45	55	100

What is the probability that the voter selected will be the following?

    a. A Democrat
    b. A voting Republican
    c. A Democrat voting Democratic
    d. A *crossover voter* (a person who votes the opposite party from his or her registration)
    e. Voting Democratic if he or she is a Democrat
    f. Voting Republican if she or he is a Democrat

23. Suppose two voters were selected randomly (and the selections were independent) from the town described in Exercise 22. Find the following probabilities:

    a. Both are Republicans.
    b. Both are Democrats.
    c. Both vote Democratic.
    d. Both are crossover voters.
    e. Both vote their party allegiances.

24. Suppose a store sells widgets in packets of 3. The probability of a widget being defective is .10. The store says it will give you two packets of widgets free if any of the widgets in the packet you purchase are defective.

    a. What is the probability of getting a packet with exactly one defective widget?
    b. What is the probability that at least one widget will be defective in any given packet?
    c. If 100 customers buy one packet of widgets each, how many free packets of widgets should the store expect to distribute?

25. In an example in the text, 1.9 percent of poor students passed a course when an instructor made a correct judgment about the students only 85 percent of the time. By how much would the instructor have to increase his or her "correct judgment" rate to reduce the percentage of poor students passing the course to 1 percent?

26. Somebody messed with the spelling checker on the word processor you use for your papers. It now identifies only 98 percent of the incorrectly spelled words. If you misspell words 25 percent of the time, how many words in a 2000-word essay would be misspelled if you did not use the checker? How many would be misspelled if you did use the defective checker?

27. The probability of a day being cloudy is .6. The probability of rain on any given day is .48, but the probability of rain if it is cloudy is .8. What is the probability of a cloudy, rainy day? What is the probability of a cloudy day with no rain? What is the probability of a day having no clouds and no rain? Does it ever rain without clouds?

28. You pick cards from a pack of 52.

   a. What is the probability of getting an ace on one draw?
   b. What is the probability of drawing two face cards if you do not replace the first card drawn?
   c. What is the probability of drawing a spade or a diamond?
   d. What is the probability of a card being a face card if the card is black?

29. What is the probability of getting one 6–6 (double-6) in three throws of two fair dice? If you throw at least one 6–6 in the three throws, what is the probability of getting a 6–6 on the next throw?

CHAPTER

6

▼

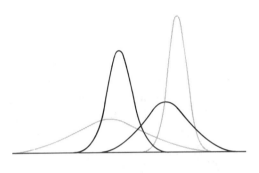

. . .

Probability Distributions

In Chapter 5 you learned about probability, specifically the probability of an event. This chapter extends that basic idea and provides an overview of *probability distributions*. Recall that frequency distributions are tables showing the pattern of frequencies of cases across the categories of a variable, and a frequency histogram is a picture of a frequency distribution. Similarly, a probability distribution is a table that shows the pattern of probabilities across the events in a sample space, and a probability histogram is a picture of a probability distribution. This chapter introduces you to the general notion of a probability distribution, for both discrete and continuous variables, and to two specific probability distributions, the binomial distribution and the normal distribution.

· · ·

RANDOM VARIABLES AND
PROBABILITY DISTRIBUTIONS

A probability distribution shows you the pattern of probabilities across all events in a sample space. More technically and more correctly, a probability distribution shows you the probabilities associated with each value of a random variable. Before we can define "probability distribution," you need to know what a random variable is.

A *random variable* is a numerically valued function defined on a sample space. Random variables are denoted by lowercase letters such as x or y. We will treat the definition of "random variable" like all others so far and take it apart.

A random variable x is, first, a numerically valued "function." But what is a function? Remember from high school algebra a function assigns every value in its domain to one and only one value in its range. A function provides a "map" from a domain of objects into a range of objects, and the map is structured so that an object in the domain is mapped onto one and only one object in the range. Two objects in the domain can be mapped onto the same object in the range, but a single object in the domain cannot be mapped onto two objects in the range.

The rest of the definition tells you about a random variable's domain and range. By saying that a random variable is a *numerically valued* function, the definition says that the range into which objects are mapped is a set of numbers. (It is not more specific than that.) The range is not a set of names, places, or other objects; it is just numbers. To define a random variable on a sample space means that the domain of a random variable is the sample space of some experiment. That's it. A random variable is a function that provides a map from a sample space into a set of numbers.

Some specific examples will help you understand this general definition. Figure 6.1*a* shows, in general, what a random variable is. It is a map from a sample space of an experiment into a set of numbers. Figure 6.1*b* shows a random variable x associated with the roll of two fair dice. The outcomes in the sample space are the sums of the faces showing after the roll of two dice, the familiar 2, 3, 4, . . . , 12. It is very easy to map the outcomes in this sample space into a set of numbers since the outcomes are numbers already. Figure 6.1*b* shows the most commonsensical map from the sample space into a set of numbers: Outcome "2" is mapped onto the number 2, outcome "3" onto the number 3, and so on up through outcome "12", which is mapped onto the number 12.

The outcomes of the four-ball experiment have no numbers immediately associated with them. However, it is possible to construct random variables based on this experiment. Figure 6.1*c* shows one such random variable y. Variable y is a map from the sample space to a set of numbers; y is the random variable "number of black balls drawn." Notice that every element in the range is a number, so y is numerically valued, y is defined for every point in the sample space, and

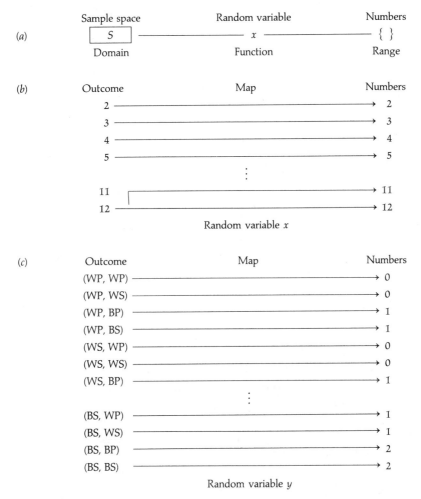

FIGURE 6.1 A random variable is a numerically valued function defined on a sample space. (*a*) General form of a random variable. (*b*) Random variable *x* mapping from sample space of the experiment "sum of two fair dice" into a set of numbers. (*c*) Random variable *y* maps from the sample space of the solid-color, striped balls experiment into a set of numbers. And *y* is the variable "number of black balls drawn."

y assigns each element in the domain (each outcome of the experiment) to one and only one element in the range (a number). Because *y* meets all these criteria, *y* is a random variable.

Finally, consider "age." A person can be assigned to any age, expressed numerically. You determine a person's age and map that onto a number consisting of a whole number and a fraction.

The random variable "age" is different from the random variables "number of black balls drawn" and "sum of two fair dice," and this difference suggests an important distinction in random variables. Random variables can be either discrete or continuous. A random variable is a *discrete random variable* if the set of numbers into which it maps points in a sample space contains a countable number of numbers. Random variables x and y, discussed above, are discrete random variables. The "number of female children in a family of three singly born children" is also a discrete random variable. If the range of a random variable is the real number line, then it is a *continuous random variable*. "Age" expressed as a whole number plus any given fraction and variables like the "speed of a car" are continuous random variables, since any fraction of a mile per hour can be assigned to the speed of any given car.

• • •

PROBABILITY DISTRIBUTIONS FOR DISCRETE RANDOM VARIABLES

A *probability distribution for a discrete random variable x* is a function $P(x)$ that shows the probability of each value of the random variable.

Once again, the term "function" appears in this definition. The definition says that a probability distribution $P(x)$ maps from its domain of all values of the random variable x into its range of probabilities. Probability distributions may be presented in tables or in pictures like probability histograms.

Figure 6.2 shows the probability distribution of the random variable "number of black balls drawn" in the four-ball experiment. It shows several ways to present a probability distribution. Figure 6.1c shows that the random variable can assume the value 0, 1, or 2. The range of y is the set of numbers $\{0, 1, 2\}$. These values are the *domain* of the function $P(y)$, which maps each of these values into a probability, the probability of occurrence of each value.

You calculate these probabilities in the usual way. Of the 16 outcomes in the sample space of this experiment (shown in Chapter 5), 4 have the value of $y = 0$, so $P(0) = 4/16 = 1/4$. There are eight outcomes in the sample space that the random variable y maps onto the value $y = 1$, so $P(1) = 8/16 = 1/2$. There are four outcomes that the function y maps onto the value $y = 2$, so $P(2) = 4/16 = 1/4$.

Figure 6.2a shows a table of these values of the probability distribution $P(y)$. Figure 6.2b shows a graphical representation of the same probability distribution. You can immediately see from this representation the relative probabilities associated with the values of the random variable. For example, you can see that the probability of getting a 1 is twice as great as that of getting a 0 or a 2. This representation—called a *line graph*—gives you a better idea of the pattern of probabilities than Figure 6.2a does. Finally, and most typically, Figure 6.2c shows a probability histogram. The probability histogram has the advantage, like the frequency histogram, that the relative area covered by the rectangles is the probability with which a compound event like "one or more black balls" occurs.

Figures 3.3 and 3.7 are also probability histograms for discrete random variables. Look at them again. The first is a probability distribution for the random

y	$P(y)$
0	$4/16 = 1/4$
1	$8/16 = 1/2$
2	$4/16 = 1/4$

(*a*)

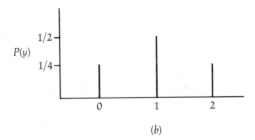

(*b*)

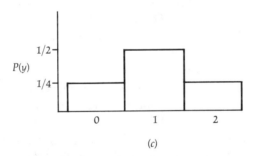

(*c*)

FIGURE 6.2 Probability distribution for random variable "number of black balls drawn." (*a*) Tabular presentation of probability distribution. (*b*) Line graph of probability distribution. (*c*) Probability histogram of probability distribution.

variable "sum of two fair dice." The second is a probability distribution for the random variable "sum of two fixed dice." Each figure pictorially presents the probabilities associated with each value of the random variable under consideration.

If a distribution is to be a *probability* distribution, it must, of course, obey all the laws and properties of probabilities. Specifically, all probabilities in the distribution must follow the first and second properties of probability, namely,

1. For every value of x, $0 \leq P(x) \leq 1$.

2. $\displaystyle\sum_{\text{all } x} P(x) = 1$

These are the same properties discussed in Chapter 5, but they have been translated to the language of random variables rather than the language of events.

Mean and Variance of Discrete Random Variables

Once probabilities are displayed in a histogram, your first reaction should be, "I have the tools to describe distributions. I can describe that distribution in terms of where it centers and how dispersed it is." Probability distributions have mean values and variances. That is, random variables, like other variables, are characterized by their mean values and variances.

Probability distributions are not distributions of cases. In fact, they do not refer to anything you observe. Probability distributions are *theoretical* distributions. They are based on theories about the way some part of the world (having children, throwing dice, drawing balls from an urn) works. They give the *theoretical* relative frequency with which a range of events occurs over the (infinitely) long run. Since probability distributions are theoretical, you need a different method from "sum the cases and divide by the number of cases" to find the mean of the distribution. Both means and variances of probability distributions for random variables are expressed in terms of "expected values."

The mean of a theoretical probability distribution for a discrete random variable x is the *expected value of x*. The expected value of x is denoted $E(x)$. The expected value of x is "expected" in the sense that over the long run $E(x)$ is the most characteristic value of the variable.

The concept of expected value is easier to grasp if you can make an intuitive leap from the mean of a sample, which you understand well, to the mean of an infinitely large (hence, theoretical) population. Let's try to make that leap with an example of fixed dice.

Figure 6.3*a* is a frequency histogram for a sample of 500 throws of fixed dice. This histogram shows the frequencies with which each of the values of the variable "sum of two dice" appears in one sample of 500 cases. What is the mean of this sample of 500 throws? It is

$$\bar{X} = \frac{\sum_{x=2}^{12} x \cdot f_x}{n}$$

$$= \frac{4 \cdot 51 + 5 \cdot 60 + 6 \cdot 53 + 8 \cdot 50 + 9 \cdot 109 + 10 \cdot 112 + 11 \cdot 65}{500}$$

$$= \frac{4038}{500} = 8.076$$

Now imagine a sample that is much, much larger, say a sample of 9,000,000 throws. Over this very long, but not yet infinite, run, the distribution of throws would begin to look very much like the (theoretical) distribution of throws shown in Figure 6.3*b*. It would not happen exactly, but close to 1 million throws would be 4s, about 1 million would be 5s, . . . , about 2 million would be 10s, and so on,

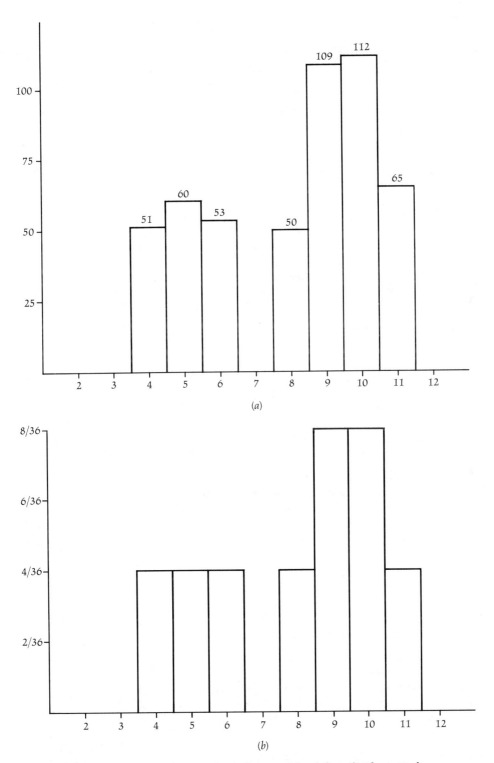

FIGURE 6.3 (*a*) Actual distribution of 500 throws of fixed dice. (*b*) Theoretical probability distribution of the random variable "sum of two fixed dice." (*c*) Distribution of a sample of 9,000,000 throws based on the theoretical probability distribution.

x	$P(x)$	f_x
2	0	0
3	0	0
4	1/9	1,000,000
5	1/9	1,000,000
6	1/9	1,000,000
7	0	0
8	1/9	1,000,000
9	2/9	2,000,000
10	2/9	2,000,000
11	1/9	1,000,000
12	0	0

(c)

FIGURE 6.3 (Continued)

as shown in Figure 6.3c. The mean of this very large sample of 9 million is

$$\bar{X} = \frac{\begin{array}{c} 4 \cdot 1{,}000{,}000 + 5 \cdot 1{,}000{,}000 + 6 \cdot 1{,}000{,}000 + 8 \cdot 1000{,}000 \\ + 9 \cdot 2{,}000{,}000 + 10 \cdot 2{,}000{,}000, + 11 \cdot 1{,}000{,}000 \end{array}}{9{,}000{,}000}$$

$$= 4(1/9) + 5(1/9) + 6(1/9) + 8(1/9) + 9(2/9) + 10(2/9) + 11(1/9)$$

$$= 8.00$$

The mean of this large sample is 8.00.

But notice something about the form of the last equation. It says that if the (large) sample exactly follows the probability distribution (the distribution of cases that would result over the infinitely long run), then the mean of the distribution is

$$4 \cdot P(4) + 5 \cdot P(5) + 6 \cdot P(6) + 8 \cdot P(8) + 9 \cdot P(9) + 10 \cdot P(10) + 11 \cdot P(11)$$

or in general

$$\sum_{x=2}^{12} x \cdot P(x)$$

This is the equation for the mean value μ of the random variable x whose probability distribution is given by $P(x)$. In fact, the expected value of x is defined as

$$E(x) = \sum_x x \cdot P(x) \tag{6.1}$$

and the expected value of x is equal to the mean of x, or μ_x. Formula (6.1) says that to find the mean of x, or μ, take each value of x, multiply it by the probability with which the value occurs, and sum these products over all values of x.

What is the mean number of black balls you could expect to draw in the four-ball experiment? Using the information from Figure 6.2a,

$$E(y) = \sum_y y \cdot P(y) = 0 \cdot 1/4 + 1 \cdot 1/2 + 2 \cdot 1/4 = 1$$

You can see that the distribution in Figure 6.2c is symmetric and centers on $y = 1$. Over many, many repetitions of the experiment "draw two balls and record the number that are black," you could expect to draw, on average, one black ball.

What is the mean value of the random variable "sum of two fair dice," the mean of the distribution in Figure 3.3? The probability distribution is

x	2	3	4	5	6	7	8	9	10	11	12
$P(x)$	1/36	2/36	3/36	4/36	5/36	6/36	5/36	4/36	3/36	2/36	1/36

and the expected value is

$$
\begin{aligned}
E(x) &= \sum_x x \cdot P(x) \\
&= 2 \cdot 1/36 + 3 \cdot 2/36 + 4 \cdot 3/36 + 5 \cdot 4/36 + 6 \cdot 5/36 + 7 \cdot 6/36 \\
&\quad + 8 \cdot 5/36 + 9 \cdot 4/36 + 10 \cdot 3/36 + 11 \cdot 2/36 + 12 \cdot 1/36 \\
&= 7.00
\end{aligned}
$$

which is obviously where that distribution centers and is, in a commonsense way, the "expected value" of the throw of two fair dice.

You can calculate the *variance* of a theoretical distribution also. The variance σ^2 is the expected value of the squared deviation of the random variable x from its mean μ, or

$$\sigma^2 = E[(x - \mu)^2]$$

Using reasoning similar to that for the mean, we get

$$\sigma^2 = E[(x - \mu)^2] = \sum_x (x - \mu)^2 \cdot P(x) \tag{6.2}$$

You can use Formula (6.2) to calculate the variance of random variables in all the probability distributions discussed so far. In the four-ball experiment, the variance of y, the number of black balls drawn, is

$$
\begin{aligned}
\sigma^2 &= \sum_y (y - \mu)^2 \cdot P(y) \\
&= (0 - 1)^2 \cdot 1/4 + (1 - 1)^2 \cdot 1/2 + (2 - 1)^2 \cdot 1/4 \\
&= (1)(1/4) + (0)(1/2) + (1)(1/4) = 1/2
\end{aligned}
$$

Variances can be used to compare the dispersion of two random variables. Which distribution is more dispersed, the distribution of the variable "sum of two fair dice" or the distribution of the variable "sum of two fixed dice"? For the fair dice,

$$\sigma^2 = (2 - 7)^2(1/36) + (3 - 7)^2(2/36) + (4 - 7)^2(3/36)$$
$$+ (5 - 7)^2(4/36) + (6 - 7)^2(5/36) + (7 - 7)^2(6/36)$$
$$+ (8 - 7)^2(5/36) + (9 - 7)^2(4/36) + (10 - 7)^2(3/36)$$
$$+ (11 - 7)^2(2/36) + (12 - 7)^2(1/36)$$
$$= 5.83$$

For the fixed dice,

$$\sigma^2 = (4 - 8)^2(1/9) + (5 - 8)^2(1/9) + (6 - 8)^2(1/9)$$
$$+ (8 - 8)^2(1/9) + (9 - 8)^2(2/9) + (10 - 8)^2(2/9)$$
$$+ (11 - 8)^2(1/9)$$
$$= 5.33$$

The random variable "sum of two fair dice" is more dispersed than the random variable "sum of two fixed dice" because the variance of the former is larger than the variance of the latter.

· · ·

BINOMIAL DISTRIBUTION

A law student attends a seminar once a week for 4 weeks. There are eight students in the class. Every week, two students are selected randomly to present one case each. (The two students are selected each week without regard to the fact that they may have been selected before.) What is the probability that a student will be called on to present no cases during the 4 weeks? What is the probability that she will be called upon to present one case? What is the probability she will have to present two cases, three cases, and four cases? Expressed mathematically, what is the probability distribution of the random variable "number of cases presented by an individual during the 4-week course"? And if this experiment were applied to all students over the long run, how many cases should the average student expect to present during a 4-week seminar? Mathematically, what is the expected value of the random variable "number of cases presented"?

   This problem obviously involves a probability distribution of a discrete random variable. The variable, call it y, is "number of cases presented during 4 weeks." The probability of having to present a case in any one week is 2 (the number of students selected to present) divided by 8 (the number of students attending) = .25. Knowing just this, you can use a probability tree to figure out all the outcomes of this experiment and the probability associated with each outcome. And from that you can construct a probability distribution of the random variable y. The tree and the resulting distribution are shown in Figure 6.4.

Outcome

Week 1	Week 2	Week 3	Week 4	Random Variable	Number of Yeses	Probability
No	No	No	No	NNNN	0	$(.75)(.75)(.75)(.75) = .3164$
			Yes	NNNY	1	$(.75)(.75)(.75)(.25) = .1055$
		Yes	No	NNYN	1	$(.75)(.75)(.25)(.75) = .1055$
			Yes	NNYY	2	$(.75)(.75)(.25)(.25) = .0352$
	Yes	No	No	NYNN	1	$(.75)(.25)(.75)(.75) = .1055$
			Yes	NYNY	2	$(.75)(.25)(.75)(.25) = .0352$
		Yes	No	NYYN	2	$(.75)(.25)(.25)(.75) = .0352$
			Yes	NYYY	3	$(.75)(.25)(.25)(.25) = .0117$
Yes	No	No	No	YNNN	1	$(.25)(.75)(.75)(.75) = .1055$
			Yes	YNNY	2	$(.25)(.75)(.75)(.25) = .0352$
		Yes	No	YNYN	2	$(.25)(.75)(.25)(.75) = .0352$
			Yes	YNYY	3	$(.25)(.75)(.25)(.25) = .0117$
	Yes	No	No	YYNN	2	$(.25)(.25)(.75)(.75) = .0352$
			Yes	YYNY	3	$(.25)(.25)(.75)(.25) = .0117$
		Yes	No	YYYN	3	$(.25)(.25)(.25)(.75) = .0117$
			Yes	YYYY	4	$(.25)(.25)(.25)(.25) = .0039$

Random Variable	Number of Yeses	Probability	Probability distribution
NNNN	0	$(.75)(.75)(.75)(.75) = .3164$	Zero yeses .3164
NNNY	1	$(.75)(.75)(.75)(.25) = .1055$	One yes
NNYN	1	$(.75)(.75)(.25)(.75) = .1055$	.1055
NNYY	2	$(.75)(.75)(.25)(.25) = .0352$	.1055 .4220
NYNN	1	$(.75)(.25)(.75)(.75) = .1055$	.1055
NYNY	2	$(.75)(.25)(.75)(.25) = .0352$	.1055
NYYN	2	$(.75)(.25)(.25)(.75) = .0352$	Two yeses
NYYY	3	$(.75)(.25)(.25)(.25) = .0117$	.0352
YNNN	1	$(.25)(.75)(.75)(.75) = .1055$	.0352
YNNY	2	$(.25)(.75)(.75)(.25) = .0352$	.0352 .2112
YNYN	2	$(.25)(.75)(.25)(.75) = .0352$	.0352
YNYY	3	$(.25)(.75)(.25)(.25) = .0117$	.0352
YYNN	2	$(.25)(.25)(.75)(.75) = .0352$	.0352
YYNY	3	$(.25)(.25)(.75)(.25) = .0117$	Three yeses
YYYN	3	$(.25)(.25)(.25)(.75) = .0117$	.0117
YYYY	4	$(.25)(.25)(.25)(.25) = .0039$	.0117 .0468
			.0117
			.0117
			Four yeses .0039

FIGURE 6.4 Finding the probability distribution for the random variable "number of cases presented in 4 weeks".

How many points are there in the sample space? There are four aspects to this experiment, and each aspect has two possible results, so there are

$$n(S) = (2)(2)(2)(2) = 16$$

points in the sample space. Every one of these 16 outcomes is shown on the figure.

What is the probability of each outcome? For the first one, since all four aspects of the experiment (being selected or not each week) are independent.

$$P(\text{no and no and no and no}) = P(\text{no}) \cdot P(\text{no}) \cdot P(\text{no}) \cdot P(\text{no})$$
$$= (.75)(.75)(.75)(.75) = .3164$$

For the second,

$$P(\text{no and no and no and yes}) = P(\text{no}) \cdot P(\text{no}) \cdot P(\text{no}) \cdot P(\text{yes})$$
$$= (.75)(.75)(.75)(.25) = .1055$$

For the fourth outcome,

$$P(\text{no and yes and yes and yes}) = P(\text{no}) \cdot P(\text{yes}) \cdot P(\text{yes}) \cdot P(\text{yes})$$
$$= (.75)(.25)(.25)(.25) = .0352$$

Notice that, in general, if there are s yeses in an outcome (and consequently $4 - s$ noes, then the probability of an outcome in which there are s yeses is

$$P(4 - s \text{ noes and } s \text{ yeses}) = (.75^{4-s})(.25^s)$$

From this, you can find the probability of getting an outcome that has any specified number of yeses in it. If s is the number of yeses in the outcome, then

$$P(s = 0) = (.75^{4-0})(.25^0) = .3164$$
$$P(s = 1) = (.75^{4-1})(.25^1) = .1055$$
$$P(s = 2) = (.75^{4-2})(.25^2) = .0352$$
$$P(s = 3) = (.75^{4-3})(.25^3) = .0117$$
$$P(s = 4) = (.75^{4-4})(.25^4) = .0039$$

There is only one outcome where $s = 0$ and $s = 4$, so the overall probability of getting an outcome with zero yeses is .3164, and the overall probability of getting an outcome with four yeses is .0039. But for the other events, $s = 1$, 2, or 3, there is more than one outcome. To figure the overall probability, you need to know how many outcomes produce the events "one yes," "two yeses," or "three yeses" and then multiply that number by the probability of getting each of those outcomes.

You could use Figure 6.4 to determine the number of outcomes that map onto each category of the random variable y and then use the simple addition rule to determine the overall probability of having a specific number of yeses in the outcome. That is done in the last section of the figure. So, for example, there are four outcomes with one yes in them. The probability of having to present one case is .1055 + .1055 + .1055 + .1055 = .4220. But this procedure could get tedious for large sample spaces.

You could use another tool to find the number of outcomes that have a specific number of yeses in them. How can you calculate the number of outcomes in the sample space that have one yes in them? You can use a mathematical technique for calculating the number of *combinations* of M objects that can be selected, without regard to order, from a collection of N objects. In this case, you begin with a collection of $N = 4$ "objects," or weeks in which one might be asked to present a case. The question is, How many ways are there to select a combination of those N objects so that there is one yes in them, one week in which one has to present? In general, the number of combinations of M objects from a collection of N objects is given by

$$\binom{N}{M} = \frac{N!}{M!(N-M)!} \tag{6.3}$$

where the exclamation point means "factorial." Recall that $N! = N(N-1)(N-2)\cdots 1$, and by definition $0! = 1$. In this problem, you want to know the number of combinations of selections from a collection of $N = 4$ objects that results in $M = 1$ yes. How many collections of "exactly one presentation" can be selected from the collection of four "possible presentations"? In other words, what is $\binom{4}{1}$? Well,

$$\binom{4}{1} = \frac{4!}{1!(4-1)!} = \frac{4 \cdot \cancel{3} \cdot \cancel{2} \cdot \cancel{1}}{1(\cancel{3} \cdot \cancel{2} \cdot \cancel{1})} = 4$$

the number of outcomes in the figure with one yes. Knowing the number of outcomes with one yes and knowing $P(s = 1)$, the probability of each outcome that involves one presentation, you can calculate the overall probability of having to give exactly one presentation:

$$P(x = 1) = \binom{4}{1}P(s = 1) = (4)(.1055) = .422$$

What is the probability of having to give exactly two presentations? It is equal to the number of combinations in which you have to give exactly two presentations (out of the 4 weeks) times the probability of each of those outcomes. Mathematically,

$$P(x = 2) = \binom{4}{2} P(s = 2) = \frac{4!}{2!(4-2)!}(.0352)$$

$$= \frac{4 \cdot 3 \cdot 2 \cdot 1}{(2 \cdot 1)(2 \cdot 1)}(.0352) = (6)(.0352) = .2112$$

And, finally, what is the probability of having to give three presentations?

$$P(x = 3) = \binom{4}{3} P(s = 3) = \frac{4!}{3!(4-3)!}(.0117)$$

$$= \frac{4 \cdot 3 \cdot 2 \cdot 1}{(3 \cdot 2 \cdot 1)(1)}(.0117) = (4)(.0117) = .0468$$

But now you have all the information you need to construct the probability distribution:

No. case presentations y	0	1	2	3	4
P(y)	.3164	.4220	.2112	.0468	.0039

You can check that this is a probability distribution by making sure that it obeys the first two properties of probability. It obeys the first since all values of $P(y)$ are greater than or equal to 0 and less than or equal to 1. It obeys the second since all the probabilities sum to 1.0 (allowing for roundoff error).

Finally, how many cases should a law student expect to present on average? That is, what is the mean of this distribution?

$$E(y) = \sum_y y \cdot P(y)$$

$$= (0)(.3164) + (1)(.4220) + (2)(.2112) + (3)(.0468) + (4)(.0039)$$

$$= 1.0$$

This problem is an example of a *binomial experiment* that results in a *binomial probability distribution*. You say that the random variable y is a *binomial random variable*. In general, a binomial experiment has the following characteristics:

1. The experiment involves n identical trials.
In our example, a trial was a "week in seminar." There were 4 weeks, so $n = 4$.

2. Each trial results in one of two results, conventionally called a *success* or a *failure*.

In our example, each trial (each week) resulted in a student's having to present a case or not having to present a case. It makes no difference which one is called the success and which the failure. If presenting a case is the success, then not presenting is the failure.

3. The probability of getting a success on each trial is always the same, and it is equal to p. The probability of a failure is always $q = 1 - p$.

In our example, if presenting a case was a "success," then $p = .25$. The probability of not presenting a case, a failure, was always $q = 1 - p = .75$.

4. The trials are independent.

In our example, the chance of having to present one week was not affected by having presented or not having presented previously. Students were chosen randomly to present a case each week.

5. The binomial variable of interest is the number of successes obtained in n trials.

In our example, the variable of interest was called y and was the number of cases a student would have to present during the $n = 4$ weeks.

If an experiment meets all five criteria, it is a *binomial experiment*. The probability distribution associated with the experiment—the probability distribution of the random variable x—is a *binomial distribution*. The binomial distribution $P(x)$ gives the probability of x for any value x might assume and

$$P(x) = \binom{n}{x} p^x q^{n-x} \tag{6.4}$$

Formula (6.4) is precisely the formula applied for each value of y in the example above.

Another example will help solidify this concept in your mind. You have already studied a binomial experiment without giving it that name. The "have three children" experiment is a binomial experiment because

1. The experiment involves $n = 3$ identical trials. Each trial consists of having a child.

2. Each trial results in one of two possible outcomes, a female child or a male child. (Depending on your biases, you denote one a success, the other a failure. I'll reveal my bias by saying that having a female child is a success.)

3. The probability of getting a female child (a success) on each trial is always $p = .49$. The probability of getting a male child is always $q = 1 - p = .51$.

4. The trials are independent.

5. The variable of interest is y, the number of females in a family of three singly born children.

This is a binomial experiment, so the probability distribution $P(y)$ will follow a binomial distribution, and

$$P(y) = \binom{n}{y}p^y q^{n-y} = \binom{3}{y}(.49^y)(.51^{3-y})$$

The probability distribution is

Number of females y	0	1	2	3
$P(y)$	.1327	.3823	.3674	.1176

Note that $P(2)$, the probability of having exactly two females, is the same as in Chapter 5 (allowing for roundoff error).

Mean and Variance of a Binomial Random Variable

If you know that a random variable x is distributed according to the binomial distribution, it is easy to find the mean and variance of x.

Consider the following progression. If there is one trial, then $n = 1$, and

$$E(x) = \sum_x x \cdot P(x) = 0(q) + 1(p) = p$$

If there are two trials, $n = 2$, and

$$E(x) = \sum_x x \cdot P(x) = 0(q^2) + 1(2pq) + 2(p^2)$$
$$= 2pq + 2p^2 = 2[p(1-p) + p^2]$$
$$= 2p$$

If there are three trials, $n = 3$, and

$$E(x) = \sum_x x \cdot P(x) = (0)(q^3) + (1)(3pq^2) + (2)(3p^2q) + (3)(p^3)$$
$$= 3p(q^2 + 2pq + p^2) = 3p(q + p)^2$$
$$= 3p(1 - p + p)^2 = 3p$$

And so on. In general,

$$E(x) = \mu = np$$

For the law school students, $E(x) = np = (4)(.25) = 1.0$, the same mean as calculated earlier. In the "have three children" experiment, the expected number of females is $E(y) = np = 3(.49) = 1.47$.

The variance of a binomial distribution is easy to find, too:

$$E(x - \mu)^2 = \sigma^2 = npq$$

The variance of the random variable "number of female children" in the "have three children" experiment is

$$\sigma^2 = npq = (3)(.49)(.51) = .75$$

The variance of the number of cases presented by the law school students is $npq = (4)(.25)(.75) = .75$.

Using a Binomial Table

Suppose you come to class utterly unprepared for the surprise quiz that greets you. You blankly stare at a 10-question, true/false quiz that bears no relationship to your reading of the night before. You decide to answer the questions randomly. What is the probability of your getting a passing score of at least seven answers correct?

This is a binomial experiment where the probability of getting a correct answer (a success) on each trial is $p = .5$. There are $n = 10$ questions or trials (and, for once, the word "trial" seems appropriate). If y is the random variable "number correct," you need to find the probability

$$P(y = 7 \text{ or } y = 8 \text{ or } y = 9 \text{ or } y = 10)$$

which, according to the simple addition rule, is

$$P(y = 7) + P(y = 8) + P(y = 9) + P(y = 10)$$

Table B.1 in Appendix B lists binomial coefficients for a variety of n's and x's, and Table B.2 lists probabilities for a variety of n's, x's, and p's. For this experiment, you want the section of Table B.2 where $n = 10$. That section is reproduced as Figure 6.5. Go to the column where $p = .5$ and then go down to the row where $x = 7$. That probability, the first circled in Figure 6.5, is $P(y = 7) = .117$. (Notice that our experiment is expressed in terms of the random variable y while the table is expressed in terms of the random variable x. No matter.) The next place down the column shows $P(y = 8) = .044$; then $P(y = 9) = .010$; and finally $P(y = 10) = .001$. The chance of passing the quiz is $P(y \geq 7) = .117 + .044 + .010 + .001 = .172$, or just over a 17 percent chance of passing. On average, you could expect to answer $np = (10)(.5) = 5$ questions correctly.

Learning to use these tables will save you a lot of calculation time.

n	x	.01	.05	.10	.20	.30	.40	p .50	.60	.70	.80	.90	.95	.99	x
10	0	904	599	349	107	028	006	001	0+	0+	0+	0+	0+	0+	0
	1	091	315	387	268	121	040	010	002	0+	0+	0+	0+	0+	1
	2	004	075	194	302	233	121	044	011	001	0+	0+	0+	0+	2
	3	0+	010	057	201	267	215	117	042	009	001	0+	0+	0+	3
	4	0+	001	011	088	200	251	205	111	037	006	0+	0+	0+	4
	5	0+	0+	001	026	103	201	246	201	103	026	001	0+	0+	5
	6	0+	0+	0+	006	037	111	205	251	200	088	011	001	0+	6
	7	0+	0+	0+	001	009	042	(117)	215	267	201	057	010	0+	7
	8	0+	0+	0+	0+	001	011	(044)	121	233	302	194	075	004	8
	9	0+	0+	0+	0+	0+	002	(010)	040	121	268	387	315	091	9
(10)	10	0+	0+	0+	0+	0+	0+	(001)	006	028	107	349	599	904	10

FIGURE 6.5 Portion of the binomial distribution table. Portion shown is for an experiment with 10 trials, $p = .5$.

· · ·

PROBABILITY DISTRIBUTIONS FOR CONTINUOUS RANDOM VARIABLES

Figure 6.6 shows a frequency histogram for 500 values of χ^2 (χ^2 is chi squared, or the Greek letter χ, pronounced "kai," raised to the second power). Do not worry at this point what a χ^2 is. All you need to know is that it is a continuous random variable. It can assume any nonnegative value on the real number line. Figure 6.6 was constructed by grouping the 500 values of χ^2 into classes 0.5 unit wide.

You could use this figure to estimate the *empirical* probability (the relative frequency in this sample) of getting a χ^2 of any given size. For example, you could estimate the empirical probability of getting a χ^2 between 0 and 1. The relative frequency of χ^2 in that range is $119 + 100/500 = .438$. Or you could calculate the empirical probability of getting a χ^2 of any size or larger. For example, the empirical probability of getting a χ^2 of 12 or more is zero. There is no area under boxes beyond 12. What, though, is the probability of getting a χ^2 of 10 or greater? There are four cases that lie at 10.0 or above, so the empirical probability of getting 10 or greater is $4/500 = .008$.

But notice something about that phrase "you could estimate the probability of getting a χ^2 *of any given size*." In fact, using Figure 6.6, you cannot estimate the probability of getting a χ^2 of, say, exactly 3.21768. It does not make sense to talk of a probability of getting a particular, exact value for a continuous random variable.

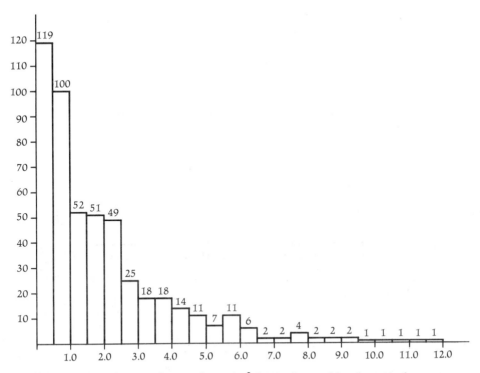

FIGURE 6.6 Distribution of 500 values of χ^2 from 3-by-2 tables showing the joint distribution of 150 cases, each drawn from a population in which the two variables were not associated.

Remember that probability corresponds to area under a distribution. There is no area under a single point on a distribution. Area is captured only by a range of values. You estimate the probability of getting a value in a specified *range* of a continuous variable. In the examples above, we estimated the empirical probability of getting a χ^2 *between 0 and 1*, that is, $P(0 < \chi^2 < 1)$, and the probability of getting a χ^2 greater than 10 that is, $P(\chi^2 > 10)$. Both say that we are to find the probability of getting a χ^2 that lies within a specific range of values (one range is closed, the other open). With continuous random variables, you must always assess the probability of the random variables assuming a value within a specific range.

You assess the probability that a continuous random variable will assume a value in a range by using the variable's *probability density function*. A probability density function for random variable x is designated $f(x)$. A probability density function is defined so that the total area under the curve $f(x)$ is equal to 1.0 and so that the area lying above a specified interval, bounded by points a and b, is equal to the probability of the random variable's assuming a value in that interval. That is, the area under $f(x)$ above the interval $a < x < b$ is $P(a < x < b)$.

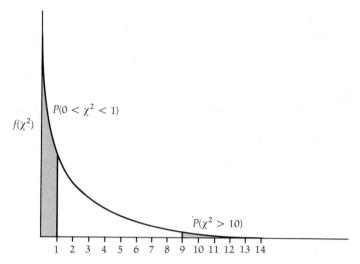

FIGURE 6.7 Theoretical distribution of χ^2 with areas corresponding to probabilities discussed in text.

Figure 6.7 shows the theoretical probability density function $f(x)$ for the theoretical population of χ^2 values from which the sample of 500 in Figure 6.6 came. This is an important distribution in statistics that you will encounter again. For now, think of it merely as an example of a probability density function for a continuous random variable, and look at the two shaded areas. These areas correspond to the areas used in the estimation of empirical probabilities earlier. The first is $P(0 < \chi^2 < 1)$; the second is $P(\chi^2 > 10)$. These areas can be calculated precisely, and the actual areas under the curve in the figure over the two intervals $0 < \chi^2 < 1$ and $\chi^2 > 10$ are close to the empirical probabilities estimated earlier.

In general, with continuous random variables:

1. Use a probability density function $f(x)$ as the probability distribution,

2. Estimate probabilities of the random variable's assuming a value in a specified interval bounded by a and b; that is, estimate the probability that x will be in the interval $a < x < b$.

3. Find the probability by calculating the proportion of the area under the curve $f(x)$ that lies above the interval $a < x < b$. The probability is $P(a < x < b)$. You will generally use a precalculated table to look up these values.

You will encounter a number of probability density functions as you read through this book, but these principles apply to them all.

. . .

NORMAL DISTRIBUTION

Now you are ready to study the most familiar, famous, and, to some, frightening probability distribution of all, the *normal distribution*. There is no need to be frightened. It is just another probability distribution that operates according the principles outlined above.

The normal distribution, shown in Figure 6.8, has not been around forever. In fact, Abraham De Moivre discovered this distribution and published his thoughts on it in a pamphlet for his friends on November 12, 1733.[1] (Trivia buffs, take note.) The distribution became known as the great *Law of Error* since it described very well errors in the measurement of many things. In the early part of the nineteenth century, Pierre Simon, the Marquis de Laplace, and Karl Friedrich Gauss applied the Law of Error to the study of recorded variations in astronomical observations. When one observes the orbits of planets, there is some error in measurement each time one looks through the telescope. Laplace and Gauss used the probabilistic law of error—which said that errors in measurement are distributed symmetrically around the true value of a phenomenon with errors decreasing as one moved away from that true value—to determine the most likely orbits of the planets. The work of Gauss is so important in the history of mathematics that the normal distribution is sometimes called the *Gaussian distribution*. If you encounter that term, do not worry that you will have to learn a new set of mathematics. "Gaussian distribution" is just another name for the "normal distribution."

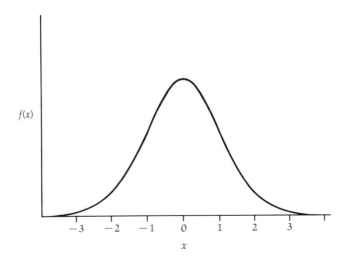

FIGURE 6.8 The normal distribution.

Later in the nineteenth century, Sir Francis Galton applied probabilistic thinking, and specifically the normal distribution, to the study of variations in human traits. Perhaps better than anyone before him, Galton understood the importance of using probability to study variation. In his book *Natural Inheritance*, he wrote of the normal distribution,

> I know scarcely anything so apt to impress the imagination as the wonderful form of cosmic order expressed by the "law of frequency of Error." The law would have been personified by the Greeks and deified, if they had known of it. It reigns with serenity and in complete self-effacement among the wildest confusion. . . . It is the supreme law of Unreason. Whenever a large sample of chaotic elements are taken in hand and marshalled in the order of their magnitude, an unsuspected and most beautiful form of regularity proves to have been latent all along.[2]

Galton was saying that you could make sense out of apparent nonsense; you could understand the incomprehensible; you could perceive regularity in the irregular— if only you looked from the right perspective. The perspective provided by the normal distribution and the rest of probability theory applies to the world in which you and I live every day.

The normal distribution is special for two reasons. First, it describes lots of different variables very well. IQ scores, errors in measurements of the orbits of planets, measures of product quality in many manufacturing processes, and many more kinds of data are distributed according to the normal distribution. (You say that these variables are *normally distributed*.) Second, and more important with regard to inferential statistics, the normal distribution is the basis of many inferential tests.

The normal distribution is a probability density function for a continuous variable x. The height of the normal distribution $f(x)$ at any point x is given by

$$f(x) = \frac{1}{\sqrt{2\pi \cdot \sigma}} e^{-(1/2)[(x-\mu)/\sigma]^2}$$

What an equation! Of all the things in life not worth remembering, that is near the top of my list. However, it is useful to look at the equation because it tells you something important. The right side of the equation contains the random variable x (which is the domain of the probability density function), two constants π and e (equal to approximately 3.1416 and 2.7183, respectively), and two parameters μ and σ. The size and shape of a normal distribution are determined completely by the values of μ and σ. Of course, μ is the mean of the distribution, and σ is its standard deviation. Figure 6.9 shows several normal distributions that have different μ's and σ's. Each centers on its mean, and each is dispersed according to the relative size of σ.

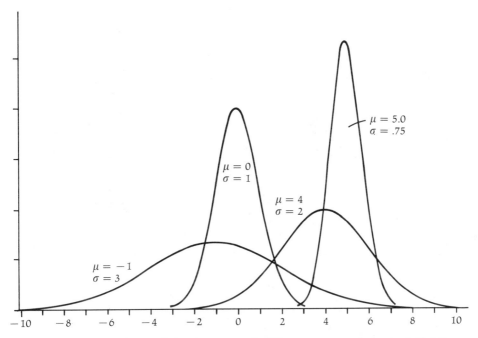

FIGURE 6.9 Several normal distributions with different means and standard deviations.

Obviously, *the* normal distribution is not just *a* normal distribution. It is a whole family of distributions, one for every possible combination of μ and σ.

It would be hopeless to try to construct tables of the areas under all possible normal distributions so that people could find the probability of any event from a variable normally distributed with any given mean μ and any given standard deviation σ. But, in fact, you need only the probabilities from *one* normal distribution to be able to find probabilities from any other normal distribution. The only distribution you need is the *standard normal distribution*, the normal distribution that has a mean μ equal to 0 and a standard deviation σ equal to 1. Appendix B contains a table, Table B.3, that shows the fraction of the area under the standard normal distribution that lies to the right of a given point a. That area is equal to the probability that the random variable x will assume a value greater than a. That is, the area is equal to $P(x > a)$.

The values in Table B.3 give you the probability of getting a value greater than a on any single draw from a population in which variable x is distributed according to the standard normal distribution. So what is the probability of drawing, on any given draw, a case that has a value of greater than 0 on the continuous random variable that has a mean of 0 and a standard deviation of 1 and is normally distributed? That's easy. Look at the row where $z = 0$, and read the probability

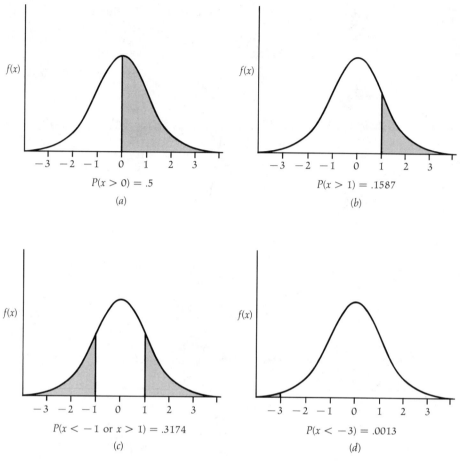

FIGURE 6.10 Examples of probabilities for the standard normal distribution.

of .50. This is shown graphically in Figure 6.10a. But you should know this without looking it up. The standard normal distribution is symmetric about its mean of 0. So one-half the area lies above 0, and one-half the area lies below 0. The probability of getting a case with a value of greater than 0 would necessarily be .50.

What is the probability of getting, on any given draw, a case with a value greater than 1 on this variable that is distributed according to a standard normal distribution? If $z = 1$, the table says .1587 of the total area under the normal distribution lies to the right of that point. The probability of getting a case with a value greater than 1 is about .16. You say, $P(x > 1) = .16$. See Figure 6.10b.

If the outcome of an event were distributed according to a standard normal distribution, what would be the probability of getting an outcome of less than -1 or more than 1? That is, in the standard normal distribution, what is $P(x < -1$ or $x > 1)$? Look at Figure 6.10c. Since the events "$x < -1$" and "$x > 1$" are mutually exclusive, the simple addition rule applies, so

$$P(x < -1 \text{ or } x > 1) = P(x < -1) + P(x > 1)$$

You already know that $P(x > 1) = .1587$. What, then, is $P(x < -1)$? Look at Table B.3 in Appendix B. At $z = -1$, you see the value .8413, but that is the probability of getting a value of x *larger than* -1. That is, $P(x > -1) = .8413$. You want the proportion of the area that is *not* to the right of -1; you want the probability of the complement of "$x > -1$." To find the probability of a complement, recall that you subtract the probability of the event from 1, so

$$P(x < -1) = 1 - P(x > -1) = 1 - .8413 = .1587$$

The answer to the question, then, is

$$P(x < -1 \text{ or } x > 1) = .1587 + .1587 = .3174$$

This is shown in Figure 6.10c.

There is a quicker way to assess the value of $P(x < -1)$. You could note, once again, that the normal distribution is symmetric. If .1587 of the total area under the distribution lies above $+1$, then an equal amount must lie in the other tail to the left of -1. So .1587 of the total area will lie in either tail. The total area in both tails is $2(.1587) = .3174$, the same value as determined above.

What is the probability $P(-1 < x < 1)$? That is, what is the probability of an outcome's falling in the interval bounded by -1 and 1? That interval is the complement of the interval "$x < -1$ and $x > 1$," so $P(-1 < x < 1)$ is the area *not* shaded in Figure 6.10c, or

$$P(-1 < x < 1) = 1 - P(x < -1 \text{ and } x > 1) = 1 - .3174 = .6826$$

About 68 percent of the time, a random standard normal variable will fall between -1 and 1.

Try one more exercise on the standard normal distribution. What is the probability of getting an outcome of less than -3 if the process is distributed according to the standard normal distribution? That is, what is $P(x < -3)$? Look at Figure 6.10d. First, recognize that $P(x < -3)$ is the probability of the complement of $x > -3$, so

$$P(x < -3) = 1 - P(x > -3)$$

The probability of getting a case with a value of *more* than -3 is .9987, so the probability of getting a case with a value of less than -3 is $1 - .9987 = .0013$. There is a very small chance, little more than 1 in 1000, of getting an outcome of -3 or less if the event is distributed according to the standard normal distribution.

Applications

To move beyond the simple, tiring problem of looking up answers in a table, you need to understand how to use the standard normal distribution, with its mean of 0 and standard deviation of 1, to calculate probabilities in *nonstandard* normal distributions, those where $\mu \neq 0$ or $\sigma \neq 1$.

The nice thing about the normal distribution is that the area under the curve and over an interval bounded a given number of standard deviations from the mean is the same regardless of the mean or the standard deviation of the normal distribution in question. On *any* normal distribution, 32 percent of the area under curve lies above 1 standard deviation above the mean and below 1 standard deviation below the mean (the example in Figure 6.10*b*). On any normal distribution, 68 percent of the area under the distribution lies between 1 standard deviation below the mean and 1 standard deviation above the mean. That is, $P(-1\sigma < x < 1\sigma) = .68$ regardless of the parameters of the normal distribution. Similarly, between -2 and $+2$ standard deviations of the mean of any normal distribution lies about 95 percent of the area under the distribution.

Here is a common application of the normal distribution: IQ scores are normally distributed with a mean of 100 and a standard deviation of 10. Of all IQ scores, then, 68 percent fall between 1 standard deviation below the mean ($100 - 10 = 90$) and 1 standard deviation above the mean ($100 + 10 = 110$). The probability of selecting a person from the population who has an IQ between 90 and 110 is .68. The probability of selecting a person with an IQ between 80 and 120 (i.e., within 2 standard deviations of the mean) is $P(80 < IQ < 120) = .9544$.

To use a standard normal distribution, you must convert raw data like IQ scores to standard units, in which an increment or decrement of 1 unit equals a move up or down of 1 standard deviation. You also need to convert the raw data so that their mean is zero. That is, you need to *standardize* the normally distributed variable so that a standard normal distribution is a good descriptor of it. Standardization consists of two operations: converting the data so the mean is 0 and converting them so that the standard deviation is 1.

The conversion of the data so the mean is 0 is accomplished by subtracting the mean of the data from each raw score. The second operation—the conversion of the data so the standard deviation is 1—is accomplished by dividing each raw score by the standard deviation. In general, you do a "z transformation" on all raw data points where

$$z = \frac{x - \mu}{\sigma}$$

For example, to convert IQ scores to standard units, you subtract the mean IQ of 100 from each raw score and divide the result by the standard deviation of 10:

$$z_{IQ} = \frac{IQ - \mu}{\sigma_{IQ}} = \frac{IQ - 100}{10}$$

An IQ of 120 converted or standardized in this way becomes $(120 - 100)/10 = 2.0$. This standardization indicates that an IQ of 120 lies 2.0 standard deviations above the mean IQ score. If you do not know the population parameters μ and σ but you believe the variable is normally distributed, then you can still do a z transformation, using the sample statistics $\bar{X}$ and s_x. In that case

$$z = \frac{X - \bar{X}}{s_x}$$

To see how standardization works, consider the following example. Suppose you know that the number of squirts per refill of 7 ounces (oz) of liquid handsoap is distributed as in Figure 6.11. Figure 6.11 is well described by a normal distribution, but it has a mean of 84 and a standard deviation of 10.5. Since proper marketing of the product depends on knowing such things, suppose you wanted to find the probability of a person's getting more than 100 uses from a single refill, which, the marketing manager tells you, would make the soap refill last, on average, 2.5 days longer than if the person got the mean of 84 squirts from the refill. You can see from Figure 6.11 that you need to know the fraction of the area of the distribution that lies to the right of the arrow. You could look up that fraction easily if the distribution had a mean of 0 and a standard deviation of 1, but it doesn't. You have to standardize the distribution by calculating how many standard units above

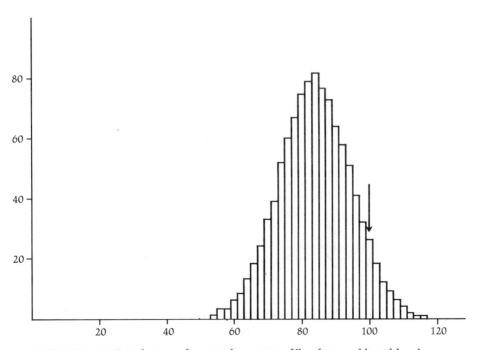

FIGURE 6.11 Distribution of squirts from 640 refills of 7 oz of liquid handsoap.

the mean of 84 the value of 100 lies. You know that 100 lies $100 - 84 = 16$ raw units (squirts) above the mean. The standard deviation is 10.5, so 16 squirts is $16/10.5 = 1.52$ standard deviations above the mean. Because this is now a standard unit, you can use the standard normal distribution to find out how much of the area of the distribution lies beyond $z = 1.52$. If x is the random variable "number of squirts," then $P(x > 1.52) = .064$. Just over 6 percent of the time a person will get 100 or more uses from a 7-oz refill of liquid handsoap. On the basis of such data analyses, great business decisions are made.

One more example: Brokers in a large stock brokerage firm have a mean wage from commissions on sales of $60,000. The variable "wages" of brokers is normally distributed with a standard deviation of $8000. At the end of the year, a broker is fired if he or she has not made at least $40,000 from commissions on sales. What percentage of brokers are let go at the end of the year? To answer that question, look at Figure 6.12. You need to know how many standard deviations below the mean $40,000 is. The standard score corresponding to $40,000 is

$$z = \frac{40,000 - 60,000}{8000} = \frac{-20,000}{8000} = -2.5$$

and $P(z < -2.5) = .006$. Fewer than 1 percent of the brokers are let go because they could not earn $40,000 or more.

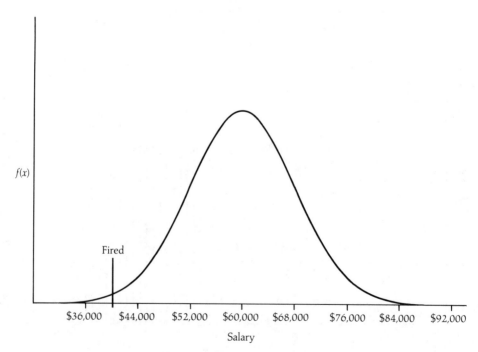

FIGURE 6.12 Broker's salary example.

• • •

NORMAL APPROXIMATION OF THE BINOMIAL DISTRIBUTION

Figure 6.13 shows four binomial distributions. They all have in common that p, the probability of a success, is equal to .3. They differ because n, the number of trials, increases from 4 to 25. Several things happen as n increases. First, the distribution shifts to the right. You expect that since the mean of a binomial is equal to np. If p remains the same while n increases, the mean of the distribution increases. Second, the distribution becomes more symmetric. Third, and most important for purposes of this discussion, the distribution looks less and less like a set of stair steps and more and more like a smooth curve. In particular, it looks more and more like a normal distribution.

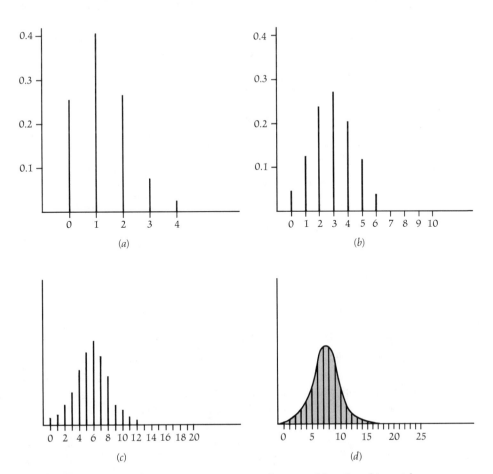

FIGURE 6.13 From discrete to continuous random variables. Four binomial distributions for $p = .3$ with increasing n. (a) $n = 4$. (b) $n = 10$. (c) $n = 20$. (d) $n = 25$.

In general, the probability distribution for a binomial random variable comes to look more and more like a normal distribution as the number of trials increases. In fact, under certain conditions, the normal distribution is a good approximation for the binomial distribution. To see what that means, and how you can apply the fact that the normal distribution is a good approximation of the binomial, let's look at the following example.

Ace Marbles sells marbles in bags of 25. The company fills its bags from an enormous batch of marbles that consists of 30 percent clear marbles and 70 percent cat's-eyes. The company knows that bags with more clear marbles sell better than bags with few clear marbles, and the company knows that bags with three or fewer clear marbles tend not to sell at all. What is the probability that a bag with have 3 or fewer clear marbles in it?

"Number of clear marbles" is the result of a binomial experiment and is a binomial random variable. Each bag is one experiment, and each experiment consists of 25 "trials." A trial is the selection of one marble for the bag. The probability of a success (the selection of a clear marble) on each trial is $p = .3$. If y is the random variable "number of clear marbles" in a bag, you are asked to find $P(y \leq 3)$. Figure 6.14 is a binomial probability distribution for this problem, and the shaded area shows the probability in question. (Figure 6.14 is a magnified histogram version of the line graph in Figure 6.13d since that distribution applies here.) You could calculate this by

$$P(y = i) = \binom{25}{i}(.3)^i(.7)^{25-i} \qquad i = 0, 1, 2, 3$$

but this is a tedious calculation. You can look this up in an expanded version of the binomial table at the back of the book, and you will find that

$$P(y \leq 3) = P(y = 0) + P(y = 1) + P(y = 2) + P(y = 3)$$
$$= .000 + .002 + .007 + .024 = .033$$

or a little more than 3 percent of the bags will have 3 or fewer clear marbles in them.

But in this book you do not have a table suitable to this purpose. Figure 6.14 looks very much like a normal distribution. You can use the normal distribution to approximate this distribution and answer the question.

There is one tricky aspect to such an approximation. Look closely at the rectangle over the 3 in Figure 6.14. The base of that rectangle covers the interval from 2.5 to 3.5. Now y is a discrete random variable, so it cannot assume values like 2.75; but when you find the single probability $P(y = 3)$, you are actually finding the area covered by a histogram that extends over an interval from 2.5 to 3.5. When you find the probability $P(y \leq 3)$, you are finding an area covered by several

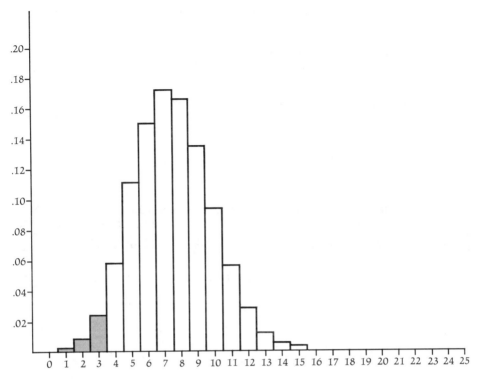

FIGURE 6.14 Normal approximation of binomial distribution.

histograms that extends up to 3.5. If you use a normal distribution, which is a distribution for a continuous random variable that can assume values like 2.75, it makes sense to find $P(y < 3.5)$ when you are interested in $P(y \leq 3)$. To find $P(y \leq 3)$ for a discrete random variable, you find $P(y < 3.5)$ for its corresponding continuous random variable approximation.

Figure 6.14 is not a standard normal distribution since it does not have a mean of 0 and a standard deviation of 1. Its mean is at $np = (25)(.3) = 7.5$. Its variance is $npq = (25)(.3)(.7) = 5.25$, so its standard deviation is $\sqrt{5.25} = 2.29$. Now to find $P(y < 3.5)$, you need to know how many standard deviations below the mean of 7.5 the value $y = 3.5$ falls. The standard score corresponding to $y = 3.5$ is

$$z = \frac{3.5 - 7.5}{2.29} = -1.75$$

So $P(z < -1.75) = P(y < 3.5)$. Using the table for the standard normal distribution, you find that $P(y < 3.5) = .0401$. So approximately 4 percent of the time bags with an average of 7.5 clear marbles in them will have 3 or fewer clear marbles in them. The answer obtained this way is not exactly equal to the answer obtained by using a binomial distribution, but that is why this technique is called a *normal approximation* of the binomial distribution.

We said the normal distribution can be used to approximate a binomial distribution under certain conditions. In general, you can use this approximation when both np, the number of trials times the probability of a success, and nq, the number of trials times the probability of a failure, are greater than or equal to 5.

· · ·

NOTES

1. Abraham De Moivre, *Approximatio ad Summam Terminorum Binomii*, Nov. 12, 1733. Reprinted in R. C. Archinbald, "A Rare Pamphlet of Moivre and Some of His Discoveries," *Isis* 8: 671–676, October 1926, plus a facsimile of the *Approximatio*.

2. Francis Galton, *Natural Inheritance*, Macmillan, London, 1888, p. 86.

· · ·

KEY CONCEPTS IN THIS CHAPTER

· · ·

EXERCISES

Chapter 6

1. Here are some experiments. You are to create random variables that map the outcomes of the experiments into sets of numbers. In each case, describe the map.

    a. There are four balls in an urn. Three are red; one is blue.

      (i) Describe the random variable x = "number of red balls in 4 draws" if each ball is replaced after being drawn and its color is recorded.

     (ii) Describe the random variable y = "number of red balls in 4 draws" if the balls are not replaced after being drawn.

    (iii) Eight draws are made, and the ball is replaced after its color is recorded. Describe the variable z = "number of times a ball drawn is a different color from the ball drawn just before it."

    b. Refer to the coin-tossing experiment in Exercise 2, Chapter 5. A coin is tossed 4 times.

      (i) Describe the random variable m = "number of heads."

     (ii) Create a random variable that maps the collection of heads and tails in the order obtained into a set of numbers. (*Hint*: You can use any set of numbers in any numerical base.)

    c. Refer to the dice-throwing experiment, Exercise 3, Chapter 5. Two dice (one red, one white) are tossed, and each has the following faces: 1, 1, 3, 3, 5, 5.

      (i) Describe the random variable x = "sum of two dice."

     (ii) Create a random variable y that maps from the event "an even number" into a set of numbers.

    (iii) Create a random variable z that preserves both the color and the number of both dice.

2. Which of the following are discrete random variables and which are continuous random variables?

    a. The time it takes to prepare a tax return
    b. The number of pages in a book
    c. The time you wait in a college registration line
    d. The distance from your house to your friends' houses
    e. The number of chipped coffee cups you own
    f. The number of poorly exposed pictures in a roll of film

3. Which of the following are probability distributions? Explain.

a.
x	0	1	2	3
$P(x)$	1/8	$-1/8$	1/2	1/2

b.
y	17	26	35	40	41
$P(y)$	.05	.50	.05	.30	.10

c.
z	0	1	2	3	4	5
$P(z)$	.22	.22	.22	.22	.22	.22

4. Here is a probability distribution for the random variable x.

x	0	1	2	3	4	5
$P(x)$	1/8	1/4	1/4	1/8	1/8	1/8

a. Make a probability histogram of the distribution.
b. Find $\mu = E(x)$.
c. Find $E(x^2)$.
d. Find σ_x^2 and σ_x.

5. Here is an empirical distribution of 500 throws of a set of three fair dice:

Number	Throws	Number	Throws
3	1	11	44
4	8	12	60
5	13	13	59
6	26	14	38
7	39	15	27
8	57	16	15
9	62	17	7
10	41	18	3

a. Construct a histogram of the variable "sum of three fair dice."
b. Describe the variable by using appropriate statistics.

   c. Using the histogram, calculate the empirical probability of getting each of the following outcomes on a single throw of three fair dice:

      (i) Probability of getting a 4

      (ii) Probability of getting a 4 or a 5

      (iii) Probability of getting a 4 or a 13

      (iv) Probability of getting an 8 or lower

      (v) Probability of getting a 9 or higher

      (vi) Probability of getting a 14 or higher

      (vii) Probability of getting an even number

      (viii) Probability of getting three 6s

   d. Construct the theoretical probability distribution for the random variable "sum of three fair dice."

   e. Put the probability histogram for this random variable on the same graph (but use a probability scale) as the frequency histogram.

   f. Find the theoretical probability of:

      (i) Getting a 4

      (ii) Getting a 4 or a 5

      (iii) Getting a 4 or a 13

      (iv) Getting an 8 or lower

      (v) Getting a 9 or higher

      (vi) Getting a 14 or higher

      (vii) Getting an even number

      (viii) Getting three 6s

6. Here is a theoretical distribution of one throw of three fixed dice, which is not the same as the fixed dice discussed earlier.

$$\frac{1/18}{\underline{\hspace{1cm}}} + \frac{1/9}{\underline{\hspace{1cm}}} + \frac{3/18}{\underline{\hspace{1cm}}} + \frac{2/9}{\underline{\hspace{1cm}}} + \frac{5/18}{\underline{\hspace{1cm}}} + \frac{3/9}{\underline{\hspace{1cm}}} +$$

```
 3
 4 X X X X
 5 X X X X
 6 X X X X X X X X
 7 X X X X X X X X
 8 X X X X X X X X X X X X
 9 X X X X X X X X X X X X
10 X X X X X X X X
11 X X X X X X X X
12 X X X X
13 X X X X
14
15
16
17
18
```

a. Verify that this is a probability distribution.
b. Describe the theoretical distribution by finding its mean, variance, and standard deviation.
c. Calculate the following:
   (i) Probability of getting a 4
   (ii) Probability of getting a 4 or a 5
   (iii) Probability of getting a 4 or a 13
   (iv) Probability of getting an 8 or lower
   (v) Probability of getting a 9 or higher
   (vi) Probability of getting a 14 or higher
   (vii) Probability of getting an even number
   (viii) Probability of getting three 6s

7. This problem uses the experiment in Exercise 9(**a**), Chapter 5. Four balls are in an urn; three are white and one is black. Two separate draws are made, the first ball is replaced after being drawn, and the colors are recorded.

a. Construct the probability distribution of "number of black balls drawn."
b. Calculate the mean number of black balls drawn and the variance and standard deviation of that random variable.
c. Construct the probability distribution for the random variable "number of white balls drawn."
d. Calculate the mean and variance of this distribution.
e. Why are the probability distributions in parts (**a**) and (**c**) different?

8. This problem uses the experiment in Exercise 9(**c**), Chapter 5. A couple has three births. Each one may be a single birth or twins. Suppose the probability of a twin birth is .03.

a. Construct the probability distribution of the number of twin births.
b. What is the mean number of twin births?
c. What is the mean resulting family size? (You should be able to determine the mean family size without constructing the probability distribution of the variable "family size.")

9. Refer to Exercise 17, Chapter 5. If the man says that it's 50-50 that he will be employed at the end of each day, but he originally plans to work 3 weeks (15 working days), then do the following:

a. Construct a probability distribution of the variable "number of days worked."
b. How long should this man realistically "expect" to work?

10. This question refers to Exercise 18, Chapter 5. Ace Marbles sells marbles in bags of 5 which it fills from a batch of marbles that consists of 50 percent clear marbles and 50 percent solid-color marbles.

    a. Construct the probability distribution of the number of clear marbles in a bag.

    b. Find the mean number of clear marbles in a bag.

    c. Determine the probability that a bag will have 2 or fewer clear marbles. Make this determination by using the probability distribution.

11. This question refers to Exercise 19, Chapter 5. Ace Marbles fills the same bags but from a batch of marbles that is 25 percent clear and 75 percent solid.

    a. Construct the probability distribution of the number of clear marbles in a bag.

    b. Find the mean number of clear marbles in a bag.

    c. Determine the probability that a bag will have 2 or fewer clear marbles. Make this determination by using the probability distribution.

12. Refer to the defective widget problem, Exercise 24, Chapter 5. Widgets come in packets of three. The probability that a widget is defective is .10.

    a. Construct the probability distribution of the number of defective widgets in a bag.

    b. Find the mean number of defective widgets in a bag, and find the standard deviation of the variable "number of defective widgets."

13. Here are the approximate probabilities of getting a χ^2 greater than the specified value x. (*Caution:* The χ^2 distribution is, like the normal distribution, a family of distributions. This one is different from the one used in the text.)

x	$P(\chi^2 > x)$	x	$P(\chi^2 > x)$
0	1	11	.13
1	.994	12	.10
2	.96	13	.07
3	.89	14	.05
4	.79	15	.035
5	.67	16	.025
6	.53	17	.018
7	.41	18	.012
8	.32		
9	.25		
10	.18		

    a. Find $P(\chi^2 > 12)$.

    b. Find $P(\chi^2 < 14)$.

    c. Find $P(1 < \chi^2 < 10)$.

    d. Find $P(\chi^2 < 2 \text{ or } \chi^2 > 12)$.

14. Find the area that lies in the region(s) indicated on a standard normal distribution:

    a. $P(x > 1.5)$
    b. $P(x < 2.6)$
    c. $P(x < -1.5)$ or $P(x > 1.5)$
    d. $P(-4 < x < 4)$
    e. $P(-2.5 < x < 2.5)$
    f. $P(x < 3.1$ or $x > 2.5)$
    g. $P(x < 0$ or $x > 0)$
    h. $P(x < 0$ or $x < -1.5)$

15. Find the probabilities indicated for the normal distribution with mean μ_x and standard deviation σ_x.

    a. $P(x > 150)$ when $\mu_x = 130$ and $\sigma_x = 15$
    b. $P(x < 1.65)$ when $\mu_x = 2.15$ and $\sigma_x = 0.18$
    c. $P(-2.8 < x < 2.8)$ when $\mu_x = 1.4$ and $\sigma_x = 1.4$
    d. $P(-2.8 < x < 2.8)$ when $\mu_x = 0$ and $\sigma_x = 1.4$
    e. $P(1.1 < x < 2.2)$ when $\mu_x = 0$ and $\sigma_x = 1.4$

16. This problem requires you to use the standard normal distribution in a different way from that required by the previous two exercises.

    a. Find x such that $P(z > x) = .5$.
    b. Find x such that $P(-x < z < x) = .5$.
    c. Find y such that $P(z < -y$ or $z > y) = .5$.
    d. Find y such that $P(z < -y$ or $z > y) = .05$.
    e. Find y such that $P(z > y) = .05$.

17. Find k if x is a normal random variable.

    a. $P(x > k) = .5$ if $\mu_x = 800$ and $\sigma_x = 2000$
    b. $P(-k < x < k) = .2$ if $\mu_x = 0$ and $\sigma_x^2 = 4$
    c. $P(x < -k$ or $x > k) = .01$ if $\mu_x = 110$ and $\sigma_x^2 = 150$

18. In a certain state, men's salaries are normally distributed with a mean of $18,500 and a standard deviation of $3500. On average, a woman earns $14,750.

    a. The women's average salary is what percentage of the men's average salary?
    b. The average woman makes more money than what percentage of all the men in the state?

19. A computer sales company finds that if a computer does not fail to function in the first 24 hours of operation, it will run without a failure for an average of 15 months. "Time to first failure" is normally distributed with a standard deviation of 3 months. The company "burns in" each computer it sells by leaving it running continuously for 24 hours before sending it to the customer. The company wants to write a warranty so that it has to fix only 10 percent of the machines under that warranty.

    a. How long should the warranty period be?

    b. Out of 1000 computers sold, how many will run for 2 years before their first failure?

    20. One-Hour Foto Service knows that its mean time to develop a roll of film is 48 minutes and that the "time to develop" is a normally distributed random variable with a standard deviation of 5 minutes. If the business wants to make an average of $9.00 per roll of film developed but it does developing free on every roll that takes more than 1 hour to develop, how much should the business charge to develop each roll?

    21. Students answer each question on a 50-minute multiple-choice examination in 45 seconds, on average. Their "time to answer" is normally distributed with a variance of 100 seconds. How many questions should be on a test that the instructor wants only one-half the class to finish in one-half hour?

    22. "Age at marriage" is normally distributed with a mean, for the U.S. population, of 27.3 years. The standard deviation of the variable is 3.1 years.

    a. What is the probability that a person will be married by age 21?

    b. What is the probability that a person will marry between the ages of 25 and 29?

    c. What is the probability that a person will marry after his or her 35th birthday?

    23. Use the binomial distribution table in Appendix B (Table B.2) to construct four binomial probability distributions in the form of histograms or line graphs. Use the same "probability of success" p for all four (but don't use $p = .3$ as in the example in the text). Vary n, the number of trials, from 3 to 20. Describe the differences among the distributions.

    24. Use the binomial distribution table in Appendix B (Table B.2) to construct four binomial probability distributions in the form of histograms or line graphs. Let $n = 20$ in all four. Vary p, the probability of success, from .1 to .9. Describe the differences among the distributions.

    25. For this problem, use the distribution with $n = 12$ constructed in Exercise 23.

    a. Find the exact probability that $x \geq 7$, using the table in the back of the book.

    b. Find the approximate probability of $P(x > 6.5)$, using the normal approximation to the binomial. Note: You will have to have chosen p in the range 0.42–0.58 for this approximation to work.

    26. Suppose the "have children" experiment was carried to its biological extreme and the procedure was to "have as many children as biologically possible."

Population experts have used a combination of the fertility experiences of Indian villagers (who begin having children as early as possible but who do not continue throughout their reproductive lives) and of Hutterites (who begin childbearing late but continue until it is biologically impossible to have more children) to estimate that the biological maximum fertility is about 32 children per woman.

  a. If the probability of having a female child is .51 and the probability of having a male child is .49, what is the exact expected value of the random variable "number of male children"?
  b. What is the exact standard deviation of that random variable?
  c. What is the approximate probability of having 20 or more male children?
  d. What is the approximate probability of having fewer than 5 male children?

  27. In the past, Fudge and Company has hired 20 percent of the people who apply for jobs. The company expects to have 100 openings during the next year.

  a. If the company has 400 applicants, what is the approximate probability that the company will fill all its openings?
  b. If the company has 600 applicants, what is the approximate probability that the company will fill all its openings?
  c. How many applications should Fudge accept to make the chance of not filling all the positions less than 5 percent?

  28. In an office, about 5 percent of the coffee cups get broken each year. There are 50 employees in the office.

  a. Melissa is an employee. What is the probability that her cup will be broken in 1 yr?
  b. What is the probability that Melissa's cup will be broken in 2 years?
  c. What is the approximate probability that, in 1 year, more than 5 percent of the employees' cups will be broken?
  d. What is the approximate probability that the employees will have a really good year and no cups will be broken?

  29. Suppose 5000 high school students apply for admission to a college. There are 1000 openings. The director of admissions knows that the college's *yield rate* (the percentage of admitted students who actually arrive on campus in the fall) is 65 percent. Approximately how many students should be admitted to make it 99 percent likely that the class of 1000 will be filled?
  30. A machine that makes "fillipsies" is readjusted after it produces a batch of 100 in which there are more than 4 defective fillipsies. If the probability that any given fillipsy is defective is 0.05 (and that probability remains constant), approximately how many batches of 100 will be produced before the machine is adjusted?

CHAPTER

7

▼

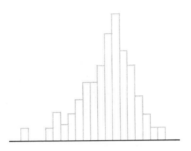

. . .

Sampling and an Introduction to Decision Making

"Take a random sample." It is a simple sentence that expresses a crucial concept in statistical reasoning. Random sampling is the basis for making inferences from samples into populations. If a sample is not drawn randomly from its parent population, no amount of statistical sophistication will allow you to use probabilistic techniques to make argumentative jumps from samples to populations. Random selection allows you to use probability theory to make claims about a population based solely on your knowledge of a sample.

The excursion into probability has been a long one, so a little review is in order.

Descriptive statistics allow you to describe variables in samples. Science wants to be able to generalize from samples to populations. You can never be certain about generalizations. There is always some uncertainty involved in making a generalization from a known sample to an unknown population. Probability is the science of uncertainty. So generalizations are made as probabilistic statements. That is why you need the rigorous grounding in probability that the previous chapters provided. But to make any generalizations at all, a sample must be randomly selected from its parent population. We now turn to the simple, essential concept of random selection.

· · ·

RANDOM SAMPLES

A *random sample* is one selection of cases from a population where the selection follows a procedure called random sampling. That seems like a circular definition, but it points out an important conceptual issue about random samples. To assess whether a sample is random, first you focus not on the sample itself, but on the *procedure* by which the sample was selected.

Random sampling is a procedure that gives every element of a population consisting of N elements an equal chance of being selected on each of n draws. In probabilistic terms, if D_i is the outcome "element i is drawn," then

$$P(D_i) = P(D_j) \qquad \text{for all } i, j = 1, 2, \ldots, N$$

You say, "A sample of size n has been randomly selected from a population of size N" if random sampling has been followed.

Let us use a nearly trivial example to illustrate. Suppose you were interested in the grade-point averages (GPAs) of students kept after school during a given week. Staff restrictions permit you to determine only three grade points. During the week of interest, six students are kept after school: Susan, Karen, Bill, Calvin, Russ, and Derek. You need to select a random sample of size 3 ($n = 3$) from this population of size 6 ($N = 6$). In order for the sample to be randomly selected, according to the definition, you need a procedure that makes three selections such that every name has an equal chance of being selected each time. One reasonable procedure would be this: (1) Assign a number from 1 to 6 to each name. (2) Roll a fair die 3 times and enter into the sample the student whose name corresponds to the number that turns up. This procedure is random since each name has a 1/6 chance of being selected on each draw. Figure 7.1a shows all the possible samples of size $n = 3$ that can be selected in this way.

Perhaps you are surprised by the composition of some of the samples. The first sample in Figure 7.1a, for instance, consists of Susan and Susan and Susan! This is not very representative of the population of six students since five of the six

Susan Susan Susan	Karen Karen Calvin	Calvin Calvin Susan
Susan Susan Karen	Karen Karen Russ	Calvin Calvin Karen
Susan Susan Bill	Karen Karen Derek	Calvin Calvin Bill
Susan Susan Calvin	Karen Bill Calvin	Calvin Calvin Russ
Susan Susan Russ	Karen Bill Russ	Calvin Calvin Derek
Susan Susan Derek	Karen Bill Derek	Calvin Russ Derek
Susan Karen Bill	Karen Calvin Russ	Russ Russ Russ
Susan Karen Calvin	Karen Calvin Derek	Russ Russ Susan
Susan Karen Russ	Karen Russ Derek	Russ Russ Karen
Susan Karen Derek	Bill Bill Bill	Russ Russ Bill
Susan Bill Calvin	Bill Bill Susan	Russ Russ Calvin
Susan Bill Russ	Bill Bill Karen	Russ Russ Derek
Susan Bill Derek	Bill Bill Calvin	Derek Derek Derek
Susan Calvin Russ	Bill Bill Russ	Derek Derek Susan
Susan Calvin Derek	Bill Bill Derek	Derek Derek Karen
Susan Russ Derek	Bill Calvin Russ	Derek Derek Bill
Karen Karen Karen	Bill Calvin Derek	Derek Derek Calvin
Karen Karen Susan	Bill Russ Derek	Derek Derek Russ
Karen Karen Bill	Calvin Calvin Calvin	

(*a*)

Susan Karen Bill	Susan Calvin Russ	Karen Calvin Derek
Susan Karen Calvin	Susan Calvin Derek	Karen Russ Derek
Susan Karen Russ	Susan Russ Derek	Bill Calvin Russ
Susan Karen Derek	Karen Bill Calvin	Bill Calvin Derek
Susan Bill Calvin	Karen Bill Russ	Bill Russ Derek
Susan Bill Russ	Karen Bill Derek	Calvin Russ Derek
Susan Bill Derek	Karen Calvin Russ	

(*b*)

FIGURE 7.1 (*a*) Random samples of size 3 from a population of size 6 population elements: Susan, Karen, Bill, Calvin, Russ, and Derek. (*b*) Simple random samples of size 3 from a population of size 6 population elements: Susan, Karen, Bill, Calvin, Russ, and Derek.

are left out, you say. But remember two things. First, this sample would be a random sample as long as it was selected by random sampling. It is possible for an unrepresentative sample to be selected by a random sampling procedure. Second, the fact that a sample is random only gives you *a basis for arguing* that your sample is representative of the population. After the fact, an opponent may argue that the sample resulting from a random sampling procedure is not representative. The argument that you have in reply is that random sampling is the only way, before the fact, to be able to *hope* for representativeness after the fact. Random sampling does not guarantee representativeness. It merely eliminates, before the fact, some of the biases that guarantee nonrepresentativeness.

The procedure described above—in which every element in the population has an equal chance of being selected on each draw—is called *very simple random sampling* (VSRS for short). It is also known as *sampling with replacement*. On the first draw, a population element is selected at random. It is replaced in the selection pool. This element is at risk of being drawn again as you make subsequent selections. In a very simple random sample, every element i in a population of size N has a probability of $P(D_i) = 1/N$ of being selected on all n draws.

Sometimes random samples are drawn *without replacement*. Once an element is selected for inclusion in the sample, it is withdrawn from the selection pool so that it may not be drawn again. Such a procedure is called *simple random sampling* (SRS). SRS ensures that a sample will not contain repetitive information. Once Susan, or anyone else, is selected from the population and information about her is entered in the sample, SRS makes sure that all subsequent draws will enter different information (data about other cases) in the sample.

In a simple random sample, every combination of n elements out of the N population elements has the same probability of being selected. You know how to find the number of combinations of n elements out of a collection of N elements. If we use the notation

$$C_n^N = \binom{N}{n}$$

then the number of combinations of n elements taken from a collection of N objects is C_n^N. In the example above, simple random sampling would make it equally likely that any one of the

$$C_3^6 = \frac{6 \cdot 5 \cdot 4 \cdot 3 \cdot 2 \cdot 1}{(3 \cdot 2 \cdot 1)(3 \cdot 2 \cdot 1)} = \frac{120}{6} = 20$$

combinations of three students from the population of six would be selected. Figure 7.1*b* shows the 20 samples of three students that could be selected by an SRS procedure. In general, simple random sampling is a procedure that makes the probability of each of the C_n^N samples being selected equal to $1/C_n^N$.

The example above is "nearly trivial" since the number of possible samples is so small. Consider the problem of selecting a sample of 10 students from a school of 1500. Using SRS, you would need a procedure that ensured that each of the

C^{1500}_{10} samples (which is an extraordinarily large number of samples) is equally likely to be selected.

There is a difference between very simple random sampling (VSRS) and simple random sampling (SRS). The decision to replace an element (VSRS) or not to replace it (SRS) obviously affects the probability of any given sample being selected. In the example above, the probability of the sample consisting of Susan, Russ, and Derek being selected using SRS is 1/20. The probability of the same sample's being selected using VSRS is 1/56, almost one-third its probability of selection under an SRS scheme. The probability of the sample consisting of Susan, Susan, and Susan being selected using SRS is zero. The difference has obvious practical importance if the population from which you are drawing is small. As the population gets larger, the difference is of less and less importance in practice. The inferential statistics you will study are based on the idea of a VSRS. However, SRS methods are sometimes employed when large samples are being studied since the effect of using SRS is not great when populations are large.

Using a Random Number Table

Random sampling is a simple idea. It is not always easy to do. There are some famous examples of seemingly random procedures that were, in fact, not random.

One state's lottery was found to be rigged. Like many states, this one used a machine that mixed Ping-Pong balls with an air blower. A videotape of the drawing showed that some balls tended to bounce around near the bottom of the machine and so did not have the same chance as the others of being selected from a tube at the top of the mixer. The balls were impounded, and some were found to have been weighted. Actually, the investigation was initiated when a computer discovered that another process which should have been random was not: the betting for the week was going too heavily toward some numbers (the nonweighted balls as it turned out) and away from others. The conclusion: Crime, dastardly crime, had struck at the lottery. And it took very, very little to change the weight of a single Ping-Pong ball and thereby the fortunes of the state's bettors.

The first draft lottery conducted by the Selective Service System may not have been random either. Some 366 identical capsules containing all possible birth dates were mixed in a bowl and drawn. Those men with the first birth date selected were the first to be drafted. Statistician John Ware found that dates in the last 6 months of the year tended to be selected early and dates in the first 6 months of the year tended to be selected late in the draw. If, in fact, each date in the bowl had an equal probability of being selected on each draw, Ware estimated that the chances were less than 5 in 1000 that the dates would have come out of the bowl in the pattern they did. Ware speculated, "In the course of shuffling the capsules, the months tended to stay together. The first 6 months may have been placed in the bowl first and they tended to stay together and be drawn last." But—and this is very important—Ware based his speculations about the nonrandomness of the procedure *on the basis of the outcome* of the draw. The sample that resulted from the drawing was not impossible to obtain from an SRS procedure. In fact, Ware's argument was that if you did such a drawing 1000 times, you would expect about 5 drawings to show the degree of imbalance in selection shown by this particular drawing. Ware was not arguing that the sample selected was an impossible one if an SRS procedure had been used; he was arguing only that the sample was an *unlikely* one. Ware thought it so unlikely that he "guessed" (his word) that the procedure was not, in fact, simple random sampling. The moral of this tale is that random sampling may result in unlikely samples. You may use unlikeliness to raise suspicions about the randomness of the procedure that created the result, but the degree of unlikeliness of a result does not *prove* a selection procedure was nonrandom. Randomness is determined by the procedure, not by the outcome.

A good procedure for conducting random sampling involves the use of a table of random numbers. Such a table is Table B.4 (in Appendix B), and the first part of that table is reproduced in Figure 7.2.

I.	1 — 4	5—8	9—12	13—16	17—20	21—24	25—28	29—32
1	74 44	80 91	21 41	40 25	98 81	57 12	30 13	24 93
2	72 59	62 28	26 74	90 62	91 20	70 31	19 10	23 06
3	33 76	63 60	48 79	23 76	28 61	87 65	79 30	38 27
4	78 02	65 54	17 61	60 15	00 81	18 07	66 38	88 33
5	32 46	64 91	77 63	26 35	94 81	54 90	10 70	10 66
6	19 68	47 39	30 75	39 71	13 14	55 59	25 38	79 00
7	06 34	06 19	72 70	53 47	57 70	04 07	54 81	04 98
8	62 23	31 49	29 34	39 38	99 54	66 13	94 08	17 03
9	97 69	04 44	89 07	31 84	66 59	86 21	61 78	60 26
10	71 00	49 40	32 08	38 57	58 59	69 72	31 52	94 75
11	32 40	60 49	51 52	47 01	29 40	59 31	14 60	26 91
12	63 42	42 91	61 34	02 22	44 76	88 32	06 36	71 39
13	09 20	12 10	05 86	08 66	45 84	84 80	69 45	65 08
14	62 50	89 39	48 02	24 64	45 60	20 27	83 65	33 82
15	73 95	05 00	52 98	08 57	74 19	05 58	27 46	23 26
16	62 43	84 11	42 38	74 13	04 57	80 26	28 04	20 52
17	07 00	14 93	55 80	14 27	69 56	24 43	30 82	55 08
18	83 26	52 43	70 61	67 23	07 36	49 78	40 25	09 66
19	14 67	02 60	21 02	64 47	54 86	62 88	81 12	28 29
20	33 60	94 02	89 25	44 73	03 85	01 95	17 85	70 51
21	02 73	10 59	69 74	76 11	57 27	04 63	94 15	74 96
22	75 46	82 03	13 43	64 34	96 68	23 86	38 49	83 98
23	79 06	02 26	58 82	81 17	91 27	44 27	71 89	17 90
24	85 16	88 13	08 97	13 08	73 28	25 34	79 27	16 34
25	37 30	30 55	08 17	55 15	93 34	10 60	00 95	60 26

FIGURE 7.2 Part of the Random Number Table from Appendix B.

To use a random number table to do a very simple random sample, you do the following:

1. Assign to every element of a population a unique number between 1 and N.
2. Enter the random number table at a random starting point.
3. Move through the random number table in a preselected, random direction to choose n elements numbered from 1 to N.
4. The sample consists of those n elements whose numbers are selected.

For example, suppose a university has a policy of checking Ph.D. dissertations for errors of spelling and grammar. It does these checks by randomly selecting 10 pages from each dissertation and checking only those pages. How would the staff select 10 pages from a Ph.D. dissertation of 800 pages to check for errors of spelling and grammar? To illustrate how this might be done, I will use Figure 7.2 as a random number "generator."

First, every page in the dissertation would be assigned a number from 1 to 800. Second, I enter the random number table at a random starting point. To do this, I need another random selection device. I open my phone book and put a pencil on the page. I take the phone numbers I have pointed to as a random number device. I will take the last two digits of the first number I find as the row entry into the table if that number is 25 or less. I will take the fourth and fifth digits of the second number I select as the column entry as long as those digits are 32 or less. (Can you guess why I would not use the *first two digits* of a phone number?) My entry point, selected this way, is row 19 and column 27.

Third, I will move through the table in a randomly selected direction. I will move through the table in the direction my watch's second hand is pointing . . . now. It points ←. So I look at the three digits in row 19 and column 27, row 19 and column 26, and row 19 and column 25. Those digits form the number 118. Page 118 is part of the sample. The next three digits, moving in the same direction, form the number 882. There is no page 882 in the population of pages, so I go on. The next three digits (in columns 21, 20, and 19) are 6, 6, and 8, respectively, so into the sample goes page 668. When I get to the beginning of row 19, I move up to row 18 (since I am going "backward"). The resulting sample of 10 pages consists of pages 118, 668, 457, 446, 201, 206, 207, 641, 669, and 52 (52 consists of the digits 0–5–2). There are no pages repeated in the sample, even though the procedure allowed for that possibility.

Why bother with such a cumbersome process? Why not just select 10 pages "at random"? The problem lies with human beings. The selections humans make "at random" are not random selections. In the example above, if I were doing the selecting, I would probably have selected a few pages from the beginning of the dissertation, a few from the middle, and a lot from the end ("knowing," at least subconsciously, that errors will be more frequent near the end of the work, but knowing also that I need a few pages that are not from the end in order to make the selection a "random" one).

Reason not with randomness. Just use a random device, like a random number table, to make truly random selections.

Sampling in Practice

In practice, sampling is usually done by mixing random sampling with some form of nonrandom or purposeful sampling. I will mention three forms.

Systematic samples use a random starting point for the sample and then follow some "system" for selecting elements from the population for inclusion in the sample. The Veterans Administration study of chronic stable angina, discussed on the opening pages of this book, used a systematic sampling procedure. The system was "take *every* patient complaining of . . . ; evaluate the patient for inclusion in the study; everyone who meets the following criteria . . . is in the sample." A common sampling procedure involves randomly selecting a starting point on a list (a list like "all names in the phone book" or "all people registered at a college") and including every *k*th (for example, 4th, 7th, 12th, 107th) person on the list in the sample.

A *cluster sample* involves clustering elements of a population, randomly selecting a cluster from which to pick, and then randomly selecting an element from the clusters. The General Social Survey (GSS), mentioned earlier, uses a multilevel cluster sampling procedure to select its sample, which must be representative of the United States population. First, the GSS clusters all elements of the population (the non-institutionalized population of the United States over 18 years of age) into census tracts. Within those clusters, the GSS forms clusters by blocks within the tracts and then by households within the blocks. The GSS randomly chooses census tracts, blocks from within the chosen tracts, and households from within the chosen blocks. Finally, a member of the chosen household is picked at random. That person is included in the sample. Cluster samples are cheaper than simple random samples, but they usually have greater error in them.

Finally, many studies are conducted by using *stratified random sampling*. Stratified random sampling is especially useful if you want to make comparisons between or among subgroups of a population. A stratified random sample begins by dividing a population into subpopulations. These subpopulations are the *strata* from which elements of the population are selected randomly. For example, if you wanted to compare women's salaries to men's salaries, you would want a sampling procedure that guarantees a mixture of sexes in the resulting sample. VSRS and SRS make no guarantees. To perform stratified random sampling, you would stratify the population into one stratum of women and one stratum of men. Then random sampling from each stratum makes the sample a random sample that includes both groups.

When one subgroup is very small relative to another subgroup in a population, it is sometimes desirable to sample disproportionately more people from the smaller stratum. For example, if you wanted to compare blacks' salaries to whites' salaries, you would stratify the population into blacks and whites and then purposefully oversample from the black stratum. You might purposefully make 25 percent of the final sample black when, in fact, blacks constitute about 12 percent of the United States population. In the final analysis, you can make adjustments for such purposeful overrepresentation. In fact, many computer programs of statistical analysis provide a means to adjust all analyses for over- and underrepresentation created by stratified random sampling.

Sampling in practice is a sophisticated business. The task of sampling is to provide a basis for arguing that a sample is representative of the population from which it is drawn. Regardless of the complexity of the sampling scheme, at the heart of the project must be a procedure that involves some form of random selection.

$$\bullet \quad \bullet \quad \bullet$$

SAMPLING DISTRIBUTIONS

Why is random selection of a sample so important? Until now, we have said, "because it is the basis for claiming that the sample is representative of its parent population." But random sampling, in fact, allows you only to use probabilistic reasoning and probabilistically based statistical theory to generalize. To "generalize" means that you can make a statement about a population based on a sample and know that the degree to which your statement about the population deviates from the truth about the population is due solely to sampling error. Deviations from the truth are due to the chance involved in selecting one sample from among the many possible samples.

For example, if you know that a sample mean is equal to $\overline{X}$, you can make a statement about the population mean μ. In fact, you can say that, to the best of your knowledge, the population mean μ is "equal to $\overline{X}$." If the sample was randomly drawn, then any difference between your statement that μ is "equal to $\overline{X}$" and the true value of μ is due strictly to sampling error, to chance introduced by selecting one sample from the many possible.

There is a way to quantify sampling error and to describe it. Sampling error is described by a sampling distribution of a sample statistic. A *sampling distribution of a sample statistic* is the distribution of the sample statistic for all possible samples (of a specific size) that can be drawn from the parent population. Let's pursue an old example to break down this definition.

Remember the six students kept after school? They formed a population of size 6. Suppose their grade-point averages are: Susan, 2.1; Karen, 2.6; Bill, 2.3; Calvin, 1.2; Russ, 3.0; Derek, 2.4. The definition of "sampling distribution of a sample statistic" says you need to take all possible samples of a specific size from the population. Figure 7.1*a* lists all possible samples of size $n = 3$. Let's use them. Then the definition says you must calculate a sample statistic for all the samples.

2.1	2.4	2.6	2.6	2.4	3.0	2.4
2.1	2.1	2.6	2.3	1.2	3.0	2.4
2.1	2.3	2.6	2.3	1.2	3.0	
2.1	2.3	2.6	2.3	1.2	3.0	
2.1	2.1	2.3	2.3	1.2	3.0	
2.1	2.1	2.6	2.3	1.2	2.4	
2.3	2.4	2.4	2.3	1.2	2.4	
2.1	2.6	2.6	2.3	2.4	2.4	
2.6	2.6	2.4	2.3	3.0	2.4	

(a)

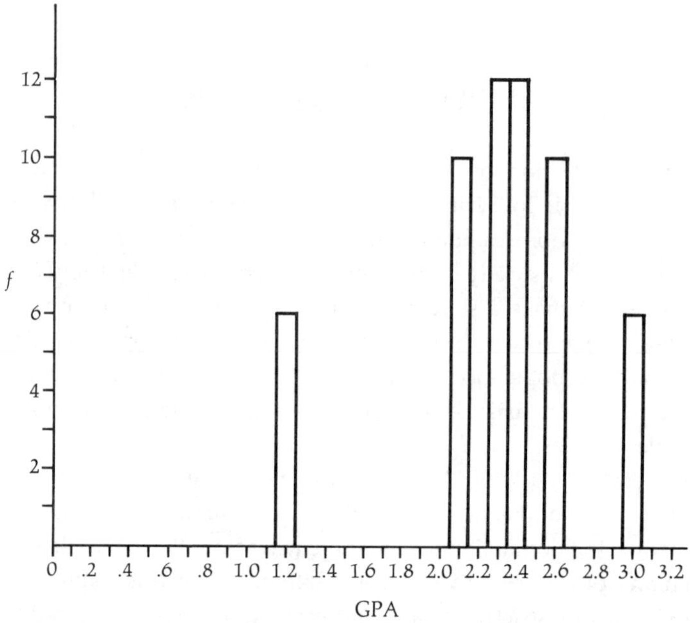

GPA

(b)

FIGURE 7.3 (a) Median grade point averages for all 56 samples of size 3 from a population of six. (b) Histogram of median grade points for 56 samples.

Figure 7.3a gives the *median* grade-point average (GPA) for all 56 samples. Once you have calculated the designated sample statistic—the median in this case—for all possible samples of a specific size, the definition says to form a distribution of these values. Figure 7.3b is a histogram of the 56 medians in Figure 7.3a. Thus distribution is, by definition, the *sampling distribution of the median* for samples of size 3.

A sampling distribution shows how a sample statistic is distributed across all possible samples that can be taken from a population. A sampling distribution shows the values a sample statistic can assume and the relative frequency with which the sample statistic assumes each value. That is, a sampling distribution is a probability distribution for a random variable, and the random variable for which a sampling distribution is a probability distribution is a sample statistic. That may sound confusing, but if you apply your knowledge of the terms in that sentence, it makes good sense.

To work backward through the confusion, the sentence says that a sample statistic is a random variable. How can a statistic, which describes a characteristic of a variable, be a random variable? Simple. Does a sample statistic meet the criteria for being a random variable? Taking a sample from a population is an *experiment*. The *procedure* is to randomly select a sample of a specific size n from a population of size N. The *sample space* of this experiment is all C_n^N possible samples. Each *point* in the sample space is an *observation* of a single iteration of the experiment: a single sample of size n. Now, recall that a *random variable* is a function that maps points in the sample space into a set of numbers. This function assigns one number to every point in the sample space of the experiment. A sample statistic does precisely this. For each sample, the median assigns a single numerical median value to each sample. Likewise, the mean assigns a single numerical mean value to the sample, and the range assigns a single number to a sample. Any sample statistic can be thought of as a function that maps any sample onto a single number. Consequently, a sample statistic is a random variable.

The sentence then says a sampling distribution is a probability distribution for the sample statistic. The sampling distribution is a probability distribution because it shows you the relative frequency with which each value of the sample statistic occurs in the sample space. For example, in the "students after school" case, Figure 7.3 shows that it is possible to get a sample of size 3 in which the median GPA is 3.0. The likelihood of this happening is 6/56 or about 0.11. A median GPA of 3.0 is much less likely than getting a median GPA between 1.75 and 2.25. The latter occurs with a probability of 35/56, or about 62 percent of the time.

The sampling distribution shows you the nature of the error in a sample statistic—its deviation from the true value of a statistic in the population (also called, remember, a *population parameter*)—that is strictly due to the chance of drawing one sample from the many possible. The true population median for the population of six students is 2.35. The sampling distribution of the median (Figure 7.3*a*) has a mean value of 2.30, very close to the true value. You say, "The expected value of the median is 2.30." (Remember, the median is a random variable; the sampling distribution of the median is a probability distribution, so the mean of the sampling distribution of the median is the "expected value of the median.") The range of the sampling distribution of the median (Figure 7.3*b*) is $(3.0 - 1.2) + 0.1 = 1.9$. The standard deviation of the sampling distribution of the median is .46, and the distribution is skewed slightly to the left. Overall, you expect, strictly by the luck of the draw, that the sample median will be a little lower than the true median in the population.

    A sampling distribution of a sample statistic can be constructed for any sample statistic. Figure 7.4a shows the *mean* GPAs for the 56 three-person samples that can be drawn from the population of six students. The expected value of the mean—the mean of the sampling distribution of the mean—is 2.267, which is exactly equal to the true mean GPA of the six students.

2.100	2.367	2.500	2.667	2.567	2.700	2.000
2.267	1.867	2.133	2.300	1.200	2.867	2.600
2.167	2.467	2.733	2.233	1.500	2.767	
1.800	2.267	2.533	2.400	1.667	2.400	
2.400	2.100	2.033	1.933	1.567	2.800	
2.200	1.900	2.633	2.533	1.800	2.400	
2.333	2.500	2.433	2.333	1.600	2.300	
1.967	2.600	2.267	2.167	2.200	2.467	
2.567	2.433	2.067	1.967	3.000	2.367	

(a)

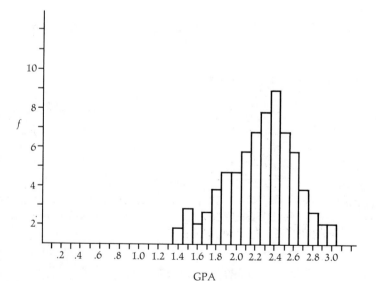

FIGURE 7.4 (a) Mean grade point averages for all 56 samples of size 3 from a population of 6. (b) Histogram of mean grade points for 56 samples.

• • •

CENTRAL-LIMIT THEOREM

The examples in the previous section had very small sample spaces. There were only 56 points in the space formed by VSRS of samples of size 3 from a population of 6. Suppose the population in question had the 142 countries listed in the first data set in Appendix A. Suppose, then, that you used SRS to take samples of size 10. There would be C^{142}_{10} samples in the sample space. That's a very large number, and that population is not very large. Even if a population were known (which is rarely the case), it would be impractical to construct the sampling distribution of a sample statistic by taking all possible samples from the population, calculating the sample statistic for each sample, and then forming the distribution of the sample statistics. Fortunately, in the case of the sample mean statistical theory can tell you a lot about the sampling distribution of the mean, without your having to do a lot of calculations. The *central-limit theorem* deals with the sampling distribution of the mean.

As a starting point for understanding the central-limit theorem, a computer took 500 random samples of size 10 from the list of 142 countries and calculated the mean of each sample. The distribution that resulted is shown in Figure 7.5. Compare this to the distributions of incomes in Figures 3.9, 3.10, and 3.11. This

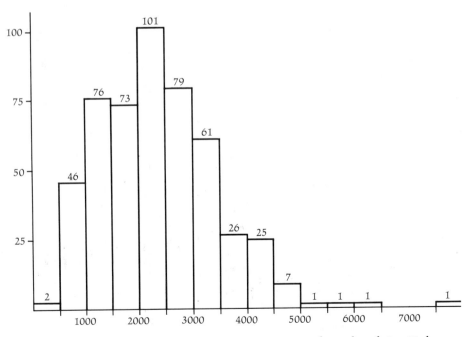

FIGURE 7.5 Distribution of 500 mean per capita incomes of samples of size 10 drawn randomly from list of 142 countries.

distribution is unimodal and slightly skewed, and (as the computer says) it has a mean of 2335.84 and a standard deviation of 1036.34. Remember that this is a distribution of 500 sample means, but the distribution of means has a mean of its own. Even though the distribution of sample means is slightly skewed, it is much less skewed than the original distribution. It is also less dispersed than the original distribution of per capita income, which had a standard deviation of 3293.2, more than 3 times the standard deviation of this distribution of sample means.

This example will help you grasp the subtlety and beauty of one of the most interesting and least obvious facts in statistics. The *central-limit theorem* says that if you take all possible random samples of size n from a population that has a mean of μ and a standard deviation of σ for some variable, then the sampling distribution of the mean has three properties:

1. The mean of the sampling distribution, denoted $\mu_{\bar{x}}$, is equal to μ, the mean of the variable in the population,

2. The standard deviation of the sampling distribution, denoted $\sigma_{\bar{x}}$, is equal to $\sigma/\sqrt{n}$, the standard deviation of the variable in the population divided by the square root of the sample size.

3. The sampling distribution is normally distributed if the variable is normally distributed in the population. In addition, the sampling distribution will be approximately normally distributed if n is fairly large (say, greater than 30). Furthermore, the approximation of the normal distribution increases as the sample size increases.

The third property of the central-limit theorem—that the sampling distribution of the mean approximates the normal distribution regardless of the shape of the distribution of the original variable—lets you use knowledge of the normal distribution to say something about the sampling distribution of the mean. To see how powerful this theorem is, let us begin with a very nonnormal variable and see what happens as we construct a distribution of means of random samples of various sizes.

Look at Figure 7.6. Figure 7.6a shows the theoretical probability distribution of the throw of one fair die. It has a mean of 3.5 and a standard deviation of 1.71.

I took 500 random samples of size $n = 2$ from this population and calculated the mean of each sample. The distribution of 500 means of samples of size $n = 2$ is shown in Figure 7.6b. (This is technically not a sampling distribution since we have not taken *all* possible random samples of size 2 from the population. But this distribution is an empirical approximation of the sampling distribution of the mean.) You can see that this distribution is more like a normal distribution than the original uniform (flat) distribution. It is symmetric and slopes off on either side of the mean. It has a mean of 3.43, close to the population mean of $\mu = 3.5$, as the central-limit theorem predicted. According to the central-limit theorem, the standard deviation of the sampling distribution of the mean when $n = 2$ is $\sigma/\sqrt{n} = 1.71/\sqrt{2} = 1.21$. The standard deviation of this approximation of the sampling distribution is 1.205—very close.

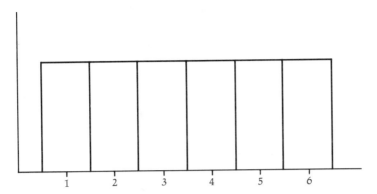

FIGURE 7.6 (*a*) Theoretical distribution of the throw of one fair die.

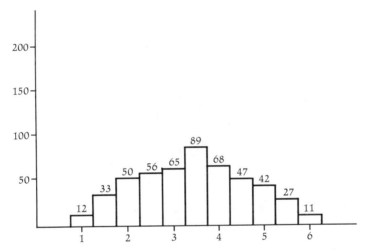

FIGURE 7.6 (*b*) Distribution of means of 500 samples of size 2 of throws of one die.

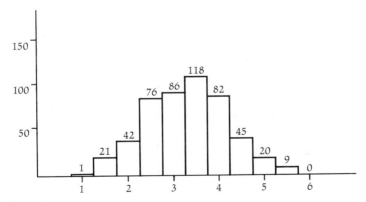

FIGURE 7.6 (*c*) Distribution of means of 500 samples of size 4 of throws of one die.

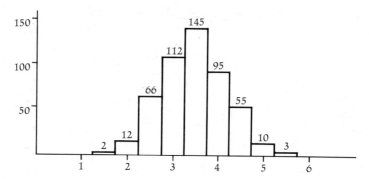

FIGURE 7.6 (*d*) Distribution of 500 means of 500 samples of size 6 of throws of one die.

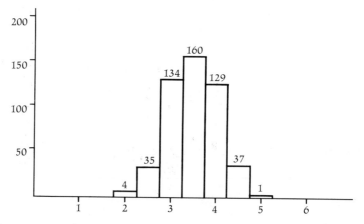

FIGURE 7.6 (*e*) Distribution of 500 means of samples of size 10 of throws of one die.

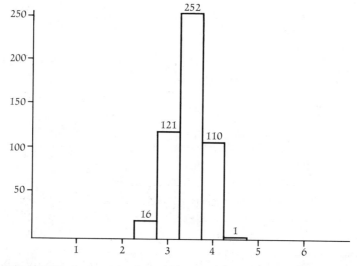

FIGURE 7.6 (*f*) Distribution of 500 means of samples of size 20 of throws of one die.

Figure 7.6c through f shows what happens as you increase the sample size to 4, then 6, then 10, and finally 20. The sampling distribution of the mean always has a mean of $\mu_{\bar{X}} = 3.5$. Each empirical distribution of 500 sample means is centered near 3.5 (with $n = 4$, mean $= 3.44$; $n = 6$, mean $= 3.46$; $n = 10$, mean $= 3.48$; $n = 20$, mean $= 3.50$).

The central-limit theorem says the distribution will narrow since the denominator of the formula for the standard deviation of the sampling distribution increases as the sample size increases. (As n increases, $\sqrt{n}$ also increases, so $\sigma/\sqrt{n}$ decreases). The following table shows the standard deviation of the sampling distribution of the mean for each sample size and the calculated standard deviations of the distributions in Figure 7.6b through f.

Figure	Sample Size n	$\dfrac{\sigma}{\sqrt{n}}$	Standard Deviation of Empirical Distribution
7.6b	2	1.21	1.20
7.6c	4	0.86	0.90
7.6d	6	0.70	0.68
7.6e	10	0.54	0.53
7.6f	20	0.38	0.36

The empirical approximation is very close to the actual values of the standard deviations of each sampling distribution.

After you make one minor addition to your vocabulary, we will discuss the usefulness of all this material. Saying "standard deviation of the sampling distribution of the mean" is very cumbersome. Statisticians call the standard deviation of any sampling distribution simply the *standard error*. The term helps you remember that the sampling distribution describes errors in the estimation of population parameters that are due to sampling. If the distribution is a sampling distribution of the mean, then the standard deviation of the sampling distribution of the mean is the *standard error of the mean*.

"Standard error" is the term you see on computer output. Figure 7.7 shows statistical descriptions of three variables in the social indicators data set. The first variable, male life expectancy, has a MEAN of 55.038. (You saw this before, in Figure 4.6.) Just next to that is S. E. MEAN, the standard error of the mean or the standard deviation of the sampling distribution of the mean. It is 1.038. The computer assumes that the 137 countries for which data exist are a sample drawn from a larger population. It does not know σ, the standard deviation of male life expectancy in the population, so the computer estimates the standard error of the mean by dividing the sample standard deviation (12.152) by the square root

VARIABLE MLE   MALE LIFE EXPECTANCY

MEAN	55.038	S.E. MEAN	1.038	STD DEV		12.152
VARIANCE	147.680	KURTOSIS	−1.149	S.E. KURT		1.986
SKEWNESS	−.302	S.E. SKEW	.207	RANGE		48.000
MINIMUM	25.000	MAXIMUM	73.000	SUM		7540.199

VALID OBSERVATIONS   137   MISSING OBSERVATIONS   5

- -

VARIABLE INC   INCOME PER CAPITA

MEAN	2335.401	S.E. MEAN	276.356	STD DEV	3293.158
VARIANCE	10844887.363	KURTOSIS	3.869	S.E. KURT	1.987
SKEWNESS	2.052	S.E. SKEW	.203	RANGE	15930.000
MINIMUM	70.000	MAXIMUM	16000.000	SUM	331627.000

VALID OBSERVATIONS   142   MISSING OBSERVATIONS   0

- -

VARIABLE URBAN   URBANIZATION PERCENTAGE

MEAN	42.234	S.E. MEAN	2.350	STD DEV	24.085
VARIANCE	580.082	KURTOSIS	−.963	S.E. KURT	1.982
SKEWNESS	.199	S.E. SKEW	.236	RANGE	91.500
MINIMUM	3.500	MAXIMUM	95.000	SUM	4539.599

VALID OBSERVATIONS   105   MISSING OBSERVATIONS   37

FIGURE 7.7 Computer output showing "standard errors" of various sample statistics.

of the number of cases in the sample (VALID OBSERVATIONS = 137). Hence, the standard error of the mean is $12.152/\sqrt{137} = 1.038$.

Notice that the printout also contains values for S. E. KURT and S. E. SKEW. These are the standard error of the kurtosis and the standard error of the skewness, respectively. We mentioned skewness earlier, but we did not quantify it. It can be quantified, so skewness is a sample statistic that is also a random variable, and so it has a sampling distribution which has a standard error. Kurtosis is a sample statistic, too. It measures the "pointedness" or "flat-headedness" of a distribution. It also has a sampling distribution, and the computer includes its standard error in the printout.

Applications: Introduction to Decision Making

Now, consider the use of the standard error of the mean. The throws of a fair die are distributed as in Figure 7.6a. What is the probability of throwing a single die 100 times and having the faces sum to more than 400?

First, translate "throwing a single die 100 times and having the faces sum to more than 400" to statistical language. "Throwing a single die 100 times" means "drawing a sample of size 100," doesn't it? And "having the faces sum to more than 400" means that the sample of size 100 would have a mean of more than 4.0

(400/100). Since the sample size is large, the central-limit theorem says the sampling distribution of the mean will be approximately normally distributed. The sampling distribution will have a mean of 3.5, the population mean. The standard deviation of the sampling distribution (its standard error) will be $\sigma/\sqrt{n} = 1.71/\sqrt{100} = .171$.

"Sample mean" is a continuous random variable whose probability distribution is approximately that shown in Figure 7.8. You need to find the probability that the continuous random variable "sample mean" will exceed 4.0. Phrased this way, this is a familiar problem.

To solve it, you need to convert the mean of 4.0 to a standard score by subtracting from it the mean of the sampling distribution. So, in standard units, you want to know the probability of getting a score $(4.0 - 3.5)/.171 = 2.92$ standard units above the mean of the standard normal distribution. Look at the standard normal table (Table B.3) in Appendix B. The probability of getting a score that high is only .0018, or $P(z > 2.92) = .0018$. Much less than 1 percent of the time you would roll a single die 100 times and have the faces sum to more than 400.

Now try a more complicated and potentially more practical example. Suppose a woman named Beth comes to your party from her statistics class carrying her own set of dice. You observe her and determine that over the course of 50 throws,

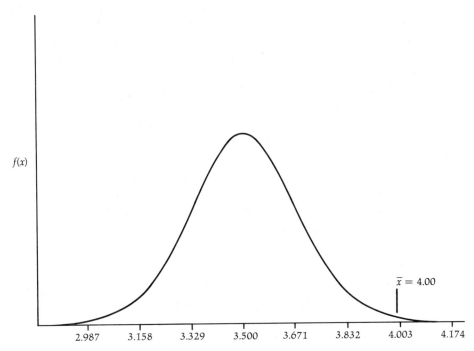

FIGURE 7.8 Normal distribution with mean 3.5 and standard error of .171 which is the sampling distribution of the mean of a throw of a fair die.

the average of the sum of the two dice is 8.28. Do you let Beth continue to play with her dice? Now 8.28 is higher than the expected value of the average of 7.0, but is it too high to give up your faith that Beth is using fair dice? You have all the tools to decide now.

First, you need to express what you know about fair dice in a statistically precise way. You know that the population of throws of fair dice is shaped like the distribution in Figure 6.7a. You know that the mean of that population distribution is $\mu = 7.0$. You can also calculate the standard deviation of that population distribution: $\sigma = 2.40$. The statistical question is this: Is it reasonable to say Beth's sample of 50 throws actually came from that population that has $\mu = 7.0$ and $\sigma = 2.40$?

Using the information you have and the central-limit theorem, you can say that the sampling distribution of the mean for sample size 50 has a mean of 7.0 and is approximately normal since the sample size is larger than 30, and the standard error is $2.40/\sqrt{50} = .34$. Then you can determine how many standard-error units Beth's sample mean of 8.28 is from the mean of the sampling distribution. It is $(8.28 - 7.0)/(2.40/\sqrt{50}) = 1.28/.34 = 3.76$ standard units above the mean. What is the probability of getting a value at least that large when drawing from a standard normal distribution? Look at Table B.3. $P(z \geq 3.76) = .0001$ or so. The probability is .0001 that Beth would obtain a sample mean of 8.28 (in a sample of size 50) if, in fact, she were playing with fair dice. *She may still be playing with fair dice.* (And this is a crucial step in statistical reasoning.) Beth may have had a very odd set of 50 rolls of her (fair) dice. How odd? Well, odd to the tune of 1 in 10,000. Remember that you are making a probabilistic statement about Beth's dice. You cannot be certain that Beth is playing with fixed dice because, on average, about 1 sample out of every 10,000 samples of size 50 will have a mean higher than 8.28.

At this point you have to make a decision: Ask Beth to play with the house dice, or let her continue to use her own. You would weigh many factors in this decision: the degree of your friendship with Beth, other folks' testimony about her good character, the potential embarassment to everyone involved in asking Beth to change dice, and so on. You would include all these factors in a reasoning process incorporating the fact that the odds are about 1 in 10,000 that she has a fair pair of dice. Then you have to decide what to do. (Okay. I admit I would ask Beth to play with the house dice. But you should realize that this admission tells you something only about *me, not* about the true nature of Beth's dice.)

· · ·

KEY CONCEPTS IN THIS CHAPTER

· · ·

EXERCISES

Chapter 7

1. Consider the set of numbers $\{0, 4, 6, 10, 12\}$ to be a population.

   a. List all possible samples of size $n = 2$ that could result from applying a very simple random sampling (VSRS) scheme to this population.

   b. On the list made in part (**a**), circle all those samples that could result from applying a simple random sampling (SRS) scheme to this population.

   c. Construct the sampling distribution of the mean for samples of size $n = 2$.

   d. Construct the sampling distribution of the median for samples of size $n = 2$.

   e. If there is a difference between the distributions constructed in parts (**c**) and (**d**), explain why. If there is no difference, explain why.

   f. Construct the sampling distribution of the range of samples of size $n = 2$.

   g. What are the expected values of the sample mean, sample median, and range? Compare these expected values to the actual mean, median, and range of the population of numbers. Discuss your findings.

2. Consider the set of numbers $\{1, 4, 7, 10, 13\}$ to be a population.

   a. List all possible samples of size $n = 3$ that could result from applying a VSRS scheme to this population.

   b. On the list made in part (**a**), circle all those samples that could result from applying an SRS scheme to this population.

    c. Construct the sampling distribution of the mean for samples of size $n = 3$.

    d. Construct the sampling distribution of the median for samples of size $n = 3$.

    e. If there is a difference between the distributions constructed in (c) and (d), explain why. If there is no difference, explain why.

    f. Construct the sampling distribution of the range of samples of size $n = 3$.

    g. What is the expected value of the sample mean? Of the sample median? Of the range? Compare these expected values to the actual mean, median, and range of the population of numbers; discuss your findings.

    3. Use the random number table to select 25 random samples of four two-digit numbers. Pick a random starting point and move through the table in a randomly selected direction. The first eight numbers you encounter will give you four two-digit numbers. (For example, the series 80271445 yields the numbers 80, 27, 14, and 45.) The next eight numbers will give you a second sample of four two-digit numbers, and so on.

    a. Calculate the means of each of the 25 samples.

    b. Construct a histogram of the means of the 25 samples.

    c. What is the mean value of these 25 means?

    d. If the digits in the random number table are, in fact, random, what should be the mean of all two-digit numbers in the table?

    e. Describe the expected relationship between the value of the mean found in part (c) and the mean you guessed in part (d). Describe the *actual* relationship. If there is a difference, why?

    4. Here is a population of numbers:

7	1	6	6	12	4	3	14	0	2
4	2	2	7	6	2	18	10	1	3
2	1	0	2	2	2	7	8	5	11
8	7	4	6	2	1	7	4	8	11
0	12	14	1	4	1	2	7	6	5
5	2	1	0	1	8	6	4	1	0

    a. Use the random number table to select 25 samples of size $n = 4$ from this population. Describe your strategy of sampling.

    b. Calculate the mean and the median of each sample.

    c. Construct histograms of the means and medians.

    d. Describe the distribution constructed in part (c), using appropriate statistics.

e. Describe the expected and actual relationships between the descriptions in part (**d**) and the true mean and median of the population of numbers.

5. Here is a probability distribution of a random variable X in a population:

X	0	1	2	3
$P(X)$	1/3	1/3	1/6	1/6

a. List all the samples of size $n = 3$ that can be taken from this population.
b. Determine the probability of each sample's being chosen. Put it next to the mean of each sample.
d. Construct a probability distribution of the random variable "mean of a sample of size $n = 3$."
e. What is $E(\bar{X})$? How does that number compare to $E(X)$?
f. What is $E[(\bar{X} - \mu)^2]$?

6. Here is a probability distribution for random variable X in a population:

X	1	2	4	5	7	8
$P(X)$	1/6	1/6	1/12	1/12	1/4	1/4

a. List all the samples of size $n = 2$ that can be taken from this population.
b. Calculate the mean of each sample and put it next to the sample.
c. Determine the probability of each sample's being chosen. Put it next to the mean of each sample.
d. Construct a probability distribution of the random variable "mean of a sample of size $n = 2$."
e. What is $E(\bar{X})$? How does that number compare to $E(X)$?
f. What is $E[(\bar{X} - \mu)^2]$?

7. Describe the sampling distribution of the mean (its shape, its central tendency, and a measure of its dispersion) if samples of size 7 are drawn from a normally distributed population with a mean of 1.0 and a standard deviation of 2.0.

8. Describe the sampling distribution of the mean (its shape, its central tendency, and a measure of its dispersion) if samples of size 3 are drawn from a population in which all values of the variable are equally likely and in which the mean is 5.7 and the standard deviation is .4.

9. Describe the sampling distribution of the mean (its shape, its central tendency, and a measure of its dispersion) if samples of size 500 are drawn from a population in which the variance is 17.4 and the mean is 180, but for which there is no other information about the distribution.

10. Describe the sampling distribution of the mean (its shape, its central tendency, and a measure of its dispersion) if samples of size 34 are drawn from a population that has a mean of 16, a mode of 18, a median of 17, and a standard deviation of 4.4.

11. What information besides that given in each part below do you need to describe the sampling distribution of the mean?

   a. Sample size of 40, population mean of 1.66
   b. Sample size of 4, population standard deviation of 40.7
   c. Sample size of 18, population variance of 17.9
   d. Sample size of 600, population mean of 11.4, coefficient of variation for the population of 17.1

12. Suppose a random sample of size n is drawn from a normally distributed population with mean $\mu = 0$ and a variance of $\sigma^2 = 100$. For each of the given sample sizes, give the mean and standard deviation of the sampling distribution of the mean.

   a. $n = 2$
   b. $n = 6$
   c. $n = 40$
   d. $n = 100$
   e. $n = 200$
   f. $n = 1000$
   g. $n = 1115$

13. Describe the sampling distribution of the mean for the following situations:

   a. $n = 10$, $\mu = 40$, $\sigma = 10$, parent population normally distributed
   b. $n = 100$, $\mu = 1.5$, $\sigma = 2.0$, parent population uniformly distributed
   c. $n = 40$, $\mu = 35$, $\sigma^2 = 35$, parent population normally distributed
   d. $n = 1000$, $\mu = 14$, $\sigma^2 = 78$, parent population's distribution shape unknown
   e. $n = 2$, $\mu = 162.4$, $\sigma = 32$, parent population's distribution shape unknown

14. If a random sample of size $n = 100$ is taken from a population with mean $\mu = 0$ and $\sigma = 10$, find the probabilities requested. Note that each is the probability of the sample mean falling in a specified range of values.

   a. $P(\bar{X} > 0)$
   b. $P(-2.0 < \bar{X} < 2.0)$
   c. $P(\bar{X} < 4.0)$
   d. $P(\bar{X} > 16)$

15. Back to the dice. Suppose someone claimed to be throwing three fixed dice where the probability distribution of the sum of the dice is thus

```
              1/18      2/18      3/18      4/18      5/18
         ---+----+----+----+----+
  3
  4   XXXX
  5   XXXX
  6   XXXXXXXX
  7   XXXXXXXX
  8   XXXXXXXXXXXX
  9   XXXXXXXXXXXX
 10   XXXXXXXX
 11   XXXXXXXX
 12   XXXX
 13   XXXX
 14
 15
 16
 17
 18
```

a. She throws the dice 32 times and gets the following results:

8	4	11	7	8	9	13	12
9	8	11	9	4	8	13	11
13	13	12	10	11	11	12	5
12	11	5	10	7	9	10	10

Is it reasonable to conclude that this sample was drawn from the population whose distribution is shown above?

b. She throws a different set of dice, which she claims is identical to her first set. She throws these 32 times with the following results:

8	6	10	9	8	9	9	10
9	11	8	7	3	11	8	7
9	3	9	6	10	8	9	9
10	7	9	4	9	7	6	4

Is it reasonable to claim that this sample was drawn from the population whose distribution is shown above?

16. Suppose family income in a community is normally distributed. The mean is $\mu = \$21{,}374$, and the standard deviation is $\sigma = \$2116$. A graduate student says he selected four people at random from the community for interviews. Their incomes are $20,500, $16,485, $14,750, and $8500. Is it likely that these people were, in fact, selected randomly from the community?

17. A candy-making machine is designed to produce 4-oz bars of chocolate. In fact, it produces bars that have a mean weight of 4 oz, where weight is normally distributed with a standard deviation of 0.10 oz. The machine is checked regularly by weighing samples of 100 bars. If the sample weighs less than 395 oz, the machine is assumed to be "off" and in need of adjustment. What is the probability that the machine will be considered "off" and adjusted if, in fact, it is actually performing according to its usual standards?

18. Suppose the candy makers in Exercise 17 wanted to set a new limit for the weight of a sample of 100 bars at which they would decide the machine needed adjusting. They want to set the limit so that the probability of the telltale sample's coming from a well-functioning machine (that produces bars with $\mu = 4$ oz and a standard deviation of 0.10 oz) is less than .01. What is the maximum weight to which they ought to set their limit?

19. Suppose a strain of corn produces ears with a mean length of 7 in and the length of an ear of corn is a normal random variable with a standard deviation of 1 in.

  a. What is the probability that a single ear of corn will be 8 in or more in length?
  b. What is the probability that a single ear of corn will be 9 in or more in length?
  c. If you randomly selected one ear from a garden, what is the probability that the ear will be 8 in or more?
  d. If you randomly selected 10 ears from a garden, what is the probability that the mean length of the ears will exceed 8 in?
  e. Suppose the distributor of the corn seed puts an advertisement in the paper and says, "We want to know your gardening secrets! Pick a random sample of 25 ears of our corn. If the mean length of your ears of corn exceeds 8 in, call our toll-free number and we'll come see what makes your garden grow." If 1000 people did this test, approximately how many gardens would the distributor have to visit?
  f. Devise a good scheme for selecting 25 ears of corn randomly from a garden. What is the probability that the average person will make a random selection from the garden?

20. A national achievement examination is known to produce a normal distribution of scores with a mean score of 50 and a standard deviation of 12.

  a. A student who scores better than 95 percent of the people taking the test is awarded a certificate of merit. What is the minimum score that will enable a student to get a certificate?

b. A class of 30 is awarded a certificate of merit if its mean score on the test exceeds the mean score of 95 percent of all other classes of 30 students taking the test. How high does the class mean score have to be in order for the class to get a certificate?

c. Which is harder to get, an individual certificate or a class certificate?

21. Certain brands of cassette tape are advertised as 90-minute tapes. In fact, the average playing time on the tapes is 91.2 minutes, and playing time is a normally distributed random variable with a standard deviation of .5 minute.

Suppose cassette tapes are sold in *packages of 3*:

a. If the manufacturer says, "If any tape has less than 90 minutes of playing time, return it and we'll send you two 90-minute tapes," What is the probability that any individual tape in the package will get returned?

b. Suppose the manufacturer says, "If the average playing time of these tapes is less than 90 minutes, send back the whole package and we'll send you two in the mail." What is the probability that a whole package will get returned?

Suppose cassette tapes are sold in *packages of 2*:

c. The manufacturer says, "If any of these tapes has less than 90 minutes of playing time, return it and we'll send you two 90-minute tapes." What is the probability that any individual tape in the package will get returned?

d. The manufacturer says, "If the average playing time of these tapes is less than 90 minutes, send back the whole package and we'll send you *two* in the mail." What is the probability that a whole package will get returned?

INTERLUDE

B

▼

Probability and culture

· · ·

You and I may live with probability, but not everyone in the history of the human race has, and not everyone alive today lives with probability in quite the same way as Western peoples do. Probability may seem like just another fact of life, but it has not always been so.

Most societies that have left artifacts and records played games of chance. Florence Nightingale David, writing in 1962,[1] notes that the talus (a polished heel bone of an animal like a deer, ox, or horse) was perhaps the first device used in games of chance. When it is thrown, the *talus* always lands in one of four positions. Egyptian tombs contained many fine tali. Some tomb walls have drawings of gamblers using a talus and various devices for keeping score. Even though ancient societies indulged in such games, none seems to have had any system for thinking probabilistically.

Historians now believe that probability, as a field of disciplined study, got its start during a 3-day coach ride during which the Chevalier de Mère—a worldly man known to have done a considerable amount of gambling—posed certain questions about the outcomes of repeated throws of dice to the mathematician Blaise Pascal. Some of the questions were easy. Mère, for example, asked Pascal how many throws of two dice it would take to give at least a 50-50 chance of getting one 6–6. Pascal solved that problem easily and gave the Chevalier the answer of 25. Other questions apparently led to a prolonged correspondence between Pascal and other mathematicians of the day, particularly Pierre de Fermat, and so was born the formal study of probability. That was in 1654, rather late in the history of games of chance.

French mathematicians including Bernoulli and Montmort made important contributions to the theory of probability in the eighteenth century. As we mentioned earlier, De Moivre discovered the normal distribution in 1733 while working on high-level mathematical ideas of interest to him and his circle of friends.

It was inevitable that the new ways of thinking would be applied to human beings as the objects of chance, but even late in the nineteenth century Francis Galton lamented the fact that he had so few data about human beings. To remedy the problem, he established an "anthropomorphic laboratory" at the 1884 International Health Exhibition. "By 1885 over 9000 people had paid the small fee and been measured for keeness of sight, color sense, 'judgment of eye,' hearing, highest audible note, breathing power, strength of pull and squeeze, swiftness of blow, span of arms, height standing and sitting, and weight. The offer of public prizes for the best-kept 'family records' brought in another body of important anthropomorphic data."[2] Galton and his students analyzed these data for years.

Using statistics to summarize data leads to a paradox of the modern age: Large *groups* of cases (individuals, flowers, rocks, nations, fruit flies, fraternities, whatever) become the principal focus of the investigator's attention; but contrary to some popular wisdom, the individual is *not* lost in the statistical shuffle. In fact, the individual case gains its individual definition through the attention paid to groups of cases, odd as that may sound. To be sure, the individual gains a definition very different from the one she or he had under a prescientific logic, but statistical reasoning is not inherently "depersonalizing." This paradox deserves some thought.

Under modern scientific logic and the Law of Error, what is an individual? An individual is a collection of errors. "Error" here is not a negative or critical term; it is simply descriptive. The Law of Error rules over the measurement of all an individual's "organs," the term the famous statistician Karl Pearson used when he talked about what we call "variables."[3] An individual occupies his or her individual place on the distribution of errors for every organ, every variable, like those measured Galton. A person is an individual because no other person occupies exactly his or her positions on the (potentially infinite) number of distributions of errors that the scientist has or can imagine. An individual is an absolutely unique collection of errors. You may not have a unique height or a unique liver size or a unique hair color or a unique IQ. But you are the only individual who has the unique combination of hair color, height, liver size, IQ, and so on, that you have. That combination of "errors" on distributions of variables is what you are. That combination of errors is, for the modern scientist following the traditions of the nineteenth century, the definition of your individuality. It is not surprising that the "cult of the individual" arises in a statistical culture.

Our particular approach to probabilistic thinking is both historically conditioned and culture-bound. Anthropologists tell us that not all cultures think in the same way. We wonder about the probability of rain, the probability of there being a pop quiz, the probability of a nuclear reactor meltdown, the probability of getting cancer (and the probability of surviving it). Members of our culture worry pretty much about the same things. We have a culturally specific *risk portfolio*—a selection of variables and processes that we have collectively chosen to think about in probabilistic terms. Mary Douglas and Aaron Wildavsky tell of the Lele, a people in Zaire who "suffered all the usual devastating tropical ills: fever, gastroenteritis, tuberculosis, leprosy, ulcers, barrenness, and pneumonia. In this world of disease, they focused mainly on being struck by lightning, the afflicition of barrenness, and one disease, bronchitis."[4] The Lele chose to think probabilistically about those things that they felt they could do something about. Of course, they had a very different list of concerns from the list we might have, but their culture encourages them to think about intervention in natural processes in a way that is radically different from our way of thinking. As you reflect on your study of probability, it will seem like the natural way to think about everything. It is a useful way to think; it is an essential way to think if you want to speak the language of statistics. It is not natural.

· · ·

NOTES

1. Florence Nightingale David, *Games, Gods and Gambling: The Origins and History of Probability and Statistical Ideas from Earliest Times to the Newtonian Era*, Hafner Publishing, London, 1962.

2. Donald A. MacKenzie, *Statistics in Britain, 1865–1930: The Social Construction of Scientific Knowledge*, Edinburgh University Press, Edinburgh, Scotland, 1981, p. 64.

3. Karl Pearson, "Mathematical Contributions to the Theory of Evolution III: Regression, Heredity and Panmixia," *Philosophical Transactions of the Royal Society*, A187:259, 1896.

4. Mary Douglas and Aaron Wildavsky, *Risk and Culture*, University of California Press, Berkeley, 1982.

8

▼

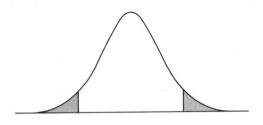

. . .

Hypothesis Testing and Decision Making

The last chapter ended with one having to make a decision about bothersome Beth who brought her own dice to the party. Recall, from the beginning of this book, that statistics is supposed to help you make decisions, decisions of the sort presented by Beth's dice and decisions of the sort presented by the father's heart problems. You now have all the tools you need to use statistics to help you make decisions. This chapter formalizes your already considerable knowledge of decision making and applies that knowledge to various circumstances encountered in statistical work.

· · ·

HYPOTHESIS TESTING

Statistics helps you make decisions under conditions of uncertainty. One way decisions are made under uncertainty is through *hypothesis testing*. In Beth's case, I came to my decision by having in mind a hypothesis about the way dice work and a suspicion (also a hypothesis) about Beth's dice. "If her dice are fair," I thought to myself, "the mean of her throws over the long run ought to be 7.0." That was one hypothesis. "Her dice area tending to roll sums higher than that. They may be rigged." That was another hypothesis. Statistics helped me make a decision about these competing hypotheses—her dice are fair/her dice are rigged—under conditions of uncertainty. I could not know for certain which hypothesis was actually true.

Remember, a hypothesis need not be true. It only has to be testable. Beth's 50 throws of her dice, and my knowledge of probability and statistics, allowed me to test the hypothesis "If her dice are fair, the mean of their sums should equal 7.0." The statistical, probabilistic analysis asked, If the hypothesis that Beth is playing with fair dice is true, how likely is it that one set of 50 throws would result in a mean sum of 8.28? The analysis concluded that if Beth were playing with fair dice, she would obtain a mean sum of 8.28 over 50 throws only about 1 out of 10,000 occasions that she rolled the dice 50 times. I rejected the hypothesis that Beth is playing with fair dice. So logically I had to accept the competing hypothesis: Over the long run, the mean of her dice is not equal to 7.0; Beth's dice are not fair dice.

This reasoning can be formalized in the following way:

First, we have a sample described by descriptive statistics. In the example, the relevant statistics are $\bar{X} = 8.28$ and $n = 50$.

Second, we want to generalize from this sample to the population from which this sample came. We want to make an *inference* from the sample into the population. That requires inferential statistics. One way to make an inference is to see if the sample data support, or fail to support, a hypothesis about a population parameter. In this example, the parameter of interest was the population mean μ. My knowledge of the behavior of fair dice led me to begin this inquiry with the hypothesis that $\mu = 7.0$. That is, if Beth were playing with fair dice, then the mean of the population from which this sample came is equal to 7.0. This hypothesis— the hypothesis that is true if my suspicions about Beth's dice are not correct—is called the *null hypothesis*. The null hypothesis is designated H_0. We write

$$H_0: \mu = 7.0$$

My suspicions about Beth's dice are embodied in a hypothesis called the *alternative hypothesis*. (The alternative hypothesis is also, sometimes, called the *research hypothesis*.) The alternative hypothesis is the logical complement of the null hypothesis. In a case where the null hypothesis is that the population mean, μ, equals

7.0, the alternative hypothesis must be that the population mean is *not* equal to 7.0. The alternative hypothesis is designated H_A, and you write,

$$H_A: \mu \neq 7.0$$

Finally, you conduct a test of the null hypothesis and make a decision. That test will always be a probabilistic test. You conduct it by first assuming the hypothesis is true and then calculating the likelihood of the sample described having been drawn from the population that has the parameter given in the null hypothesis. The test of the null hypothesis will always give you the probability of your being wrong if you decide to reject the null hypothesis. In Beth's case, I decided to reject the null hypothesis. I accepted the alternative and decided that Beth was probably playing with fixed dice. This decision may be incorrect. Beth may be playing with fair dice. The statistical test told me the probability of my being incorrect in my deciding Beth is playing with fixed dice is about 1 in 10,000. That is a risk *I* am willing to run as I ask Beth to play with house dice.

An essential element of this reasoning may seem a little convoluted at first, so you should attend to this closely. A statistical test of a hypothesis may provide you with a basis for rejecting a null hypothesis.. This is what happened in Beth's case. I rejected the null hypothesis and accepted its alternative. A statistical test of a hypothesis may not provide a basis for rejecting the null hypothesis. In that case, you merely *fail to reject* the null hypothesis. Your may have just thought, "Right. If I 'fail to reject' the null hypothesis, then I must be accepting it." Wrong. The tests of a hypothesis discussed here will not provide information that will permit you to accept a null hypothesis. You will only be able to draw the comparatively weak conclusion that you decide "not to reject" the null hypothesis.

To illustrate this central logical concept, consider Bill who comes later to the party with *his* own set of dice. His 50 rolls yield a mean sum of 6.82. Is he playing with fair or fixed dice? The test is the same as that applied to Beth. The null hypothesis and its alternative are

$$H_0: \mu = 7.0 \quad \text{and} \quad H_A: \mu \neq 7.0$$

You test the null hypothesis by assuming that it is true. If the null hypothesis is true, then, according to the central-limit theorem, the sampling distribution of the sample mean will be approximately normal and will have a mean $\mu_X = \mu = 7.0$ and a standard error of $2.40/\sqrt{50} = 0.34$. The sample mean of Bill's throws lies $6.82 - 7.0/0.34 = -0.53$ standard-error units away from the mean of this distribution. From the table of standard normal deviates (Table B.3), $P(z < -.53) = .298$. The probability of getting a sample mean more than .53 standard error units below the hypothesized mean of 7.0 is about 30 percent.

Should I reject the null hypothesis? Bill might be playing with fixed dice. If I reject the null hypothesis and conclude that he is playing with fixed dice, the probability that I am wrong in doing so is about 30 percent. Three times out of ten that I make a decision to reject the null hypothesis based on this kind of evidence, I will be wrong. I am not willing to run that level of risk of being wrong in these circumstances. Therefore, I decide not to reject the null hypothesis. Does that mean that the null hypothesis $\mu = 7.0$ is true and Bill is playing with fair dice? No. I have merely decided not to reject the null hypothesis (yet). I have insufficient evidence for rejecting the null hypothesis. I hold onto my suspicions.

In general, hypothesis testing is done as follows:

1. Formulate a null hypothesis and the alternative hypothesis about a population parameter.

2. Describe the sample, using appropriate descriptive statistics.

3. Determine the nature of the sampling distribution of the sample statistic if the sample came from a population characterized by the parameter in the null hypothesis.

4. Set a "level to reject." That is, decide what level of risk of being wrong in deciding to reject the null hypothesis is tolerable. The level to reject is denoted α.

5. Use the sampling distribution and appropriate sample statistics to calculate the probability that the observed sample statistic would have occurred if, in fact, the null hypothesis were true.

6. Compare the probability that the sample would have yielded the observed sample statistic if the null hypothesis were true to the "level to reject." If the probability is less than the level to reject, reject the null hypothesis and accept the alternative. If the probability is greater than the level to reject, do not reject the null hypothesis (but do not accept it either).

This general scheme is used in all hypothesis testing. The population parameters in question will change, the sampling distributions of the sample statistics will vary, but you will see this strategy used over and over throughout this chapter as some of these ideas get fleshed out.

· · ·

LARGE-SAMPLE HYPOTHESIS TESTING ABOUT A POPULATION MEAN

The examples concerning Beth's and Bill's dice involve *large-sample hypothesis testing about a population mean*. The examples both involved samples of 50, a "large" sample in the terms established by the central-limit theorem. And they were tests of hypotheses about the value of the mean of the random variable "sum of two dice" in the population from which the respective samples came. Each sample came either from a population with a mean sum of 7.0 or from a population in which the mean sum was not 7.0. The test helped me in each case, to make a decision to reject the null hypothesis or not.

One more example ought to solidify in your mind the idea and practice of large-sample hypothesis tests about population means.

The researcher in the internal-motivation experiments, Professor Tang, looks up from his computer terminal and says, "I'm no clinical psychologist, and my experiment was not really about this notion, but as I think back over my subjects, these students really seem driven. They seem almost compulsive. Frankly, I'm a little worried about them. If I had to guess, I would bet they're Type A personality scores are really high." Should he be worried about his students?

With many tests like the one for Type A personality, there are national "norms" against which specific samples can be compared to see if the samples are "really high" or not. Suppose the makers of the Type A personality test used in the internal-motivation experiments said that the national population on which the test was "normalized" scored a mean of 40.0 and had a variance of 70 (and, therefore, a standard deviation of 8.367). Is there reason to believe that the samples used in these experiments were drawn from populations that have mean scores greater than this national average?

To answer this question, just follow the steps of hypothesis testing:

First, for experiment 1, formulate the hypotheses—the null hypothesis and its alternative. In practice, the alternative hypothesis is usually formulated first. In this case, the researcher believes that the samples come from populations with a mean greater than the national norm. The research hypothesis is that $\mu > 40.0$. Thus, the alternative hypothesis is written

$$H_A: \mu > 40$$

The null hypothesis is that his student-subjects are, on average, just like everyone else or even lower than the national norm on type A personality. The null hypothesis is, then, that this sample came from a population with a mean of 40 or less:

$$H_0: \mu \leq 40$$

Second, once you have formulated the null and alternative hypotheses, describe the sample. Figure 8.1 shows a computer printout of descriptive statistics for both samples. The analysis of the first experiment includes only those 54 cases for whom complete data (including time spent on the word game) are available. For the first sample, the relevant statistic is $n = 54$, and the sample mean Type A score is 41.056, or 41.06.

Third, determine the nature of the sampling distribution of the sample statistic if, in fact, the null hypothesis is true and the sample came from a population that had a mean of 40.0. (The null hypothesis is that the mean is equal to *or less than* 40. Assuming that the mean is *equal to* 40 provides the most severe test of the hypothesis.) Since the sample in the first experiment is large, the central-limit theorem says that the sampling distribution of the sample mean is approximately normal, has a mean of $\mu_{\bar{x}} = \mu = 40.0$, and has a standard error of $\sigma/\sqrt{n} = 8.367/\sqrt{54} = 1.14$.

First Experiment

15:56:35   The Evergreen State College   DG MV/10000   AOS/VS 6.04

NUMBER OF VALID OBSERVATIONS (LISTWISE) = 54.00

VARIABLE	MEAN	STD DEV	MINIMUM	MAXIMUM	VALID N
TYPEA	41.056	8.762	19.000	57.000	54

Second Experiment

16:04:40   The Evergreen State College   DG MV/10000   AOS/VS 6.04

NUMBER OF VALID OBSERVATIONS (LISTWISE) = 40.00

VARIABLE	MEAN	STD DEV	MINIMUM	MAXIMUM	VALID N
TYPEA	43.250	8.236	18.000	59.000	40

FIGURE 8.1 Computer printout of descriptive statistics of Type A behavior for internal-motivation experiments 1 and 2.

Fourth, choose a level α to reject the null hypothesis . There will be much to say about choosing a level to reject shortly, but for now let me be somewhat arbitrary and say that we will reject the null hypothesis if the chance of being wrong when we do so is less than 1 in 20. My level to reject is $\alpha = .05$. I am unwilling to tolerate greater risk.

Fifth, calculate the probability of getting a sample mean of the size I observed if, in fact, the null hypothesis is true. Figure 8.2 is the sampling distribution of the mean if the null hypothesis is true. It shows a normal distribution with a mean of 40 and a standard error of 1.14. It also shows where the sample mean of 41.06 falls. This particular sample mean lies $41.06 - 40.0 = 1.06$ raw units from the hypothesized mean, or $1.06/1.14 = 0.93$ standard-error units above the mean. The probability of getting a sample mean at least that many standard-error units above the mean of 40 is $P(z > 0.93) = .32$.

Finally, compare the probability that a sample mean of the size observed would result from a single sample drawn from the population in which $\mu = 40$ to the level to reject. The probability of getting a sample mean of at least 41.06 if the null hypothesis is true is .32. If I decide to reject the null hypothesis, the chance of my being wrong in doing so is .32, about 1 in 3. I was willing to tolerate a risk of being wrong of only 1 in 20. I would run too great a risk in this case, so I decide not to reject the null hypothesis.

Conclusion: This sample does not provide evidence to support the claim that the population from which the sample came has a mean Type A score of more than 40.

What about the sample of Chinese students? Their mean, from Figure 8.1, is 43.250. The hypotheses are the same:

$$H_0: \mu > 40$$
$$H_A: \mu \leq 40$$

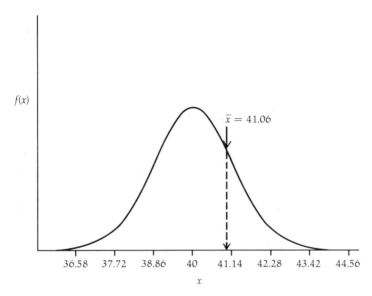

FIGURE 8.2 Sampling distribution of the mean for Type A scores in internal-motivation experiment 1.

Under the assumption that the null hypothesis is true, the sampling distribution of the sample mean is slightly different. It is still approximately normal, and it has a mean of $\mu_{\bar{x}} = \mu = 40.0$. But the standard error is larger. Since the standard error is $\sigma/\sqrt{n}$, the smaller the sample (the smaller n is), the larger the standard error. In this case, $n = 40$, so $\sigma/\sqrt{n} = 8.367/\sqrt{40} = 1.32$. The sample mean in this case is

$$z = \frac{43.25 - 40}{1.32} = 2.46$$

standard-error units above the mean. The probability of getting a mean at least that large if the null hypothesis is true is $P(z > 2.46) = .0069$. You would get a sample mean of at least 43.25 by drawing a sample of 40 from a population with a mean score of 40.0 less than 1 percent of the time. If I decide to reject the null hypothesis, the probability of my being wrong in doing so is less than 1 in 100. That is less than the risk of being wrong that I am willing to tolerate, the level of risk expressed in the level to reject. I decide to reject the null hypothesis and accept the alternative. *Conclusion:* This sample comes from a population with a mean type A personality score greater than 40.0.

Region of Rejection and Test Statistics

Setting a level to reject α makes you decide how much risk of being wrong you are willing to accept if you decide to reject the null hypothesis. A level to reject of $\alpha = .05$ means you are willing to be wrong 1 out of every 20 times you make a decision. A level to reject of $\alpha = .01$ means you are willing to be wrong only 1 out of 100 times. There is an easy way to graphically portray this level to reject on the appropriate sampling distribution. This method also permits easy the comparison between the level to reject and the probability of getting a sample statistic of the size your sample yielded if, in fact, the null hypothesis is true.

Consider a level to reject of $\alpha = .05$ and a sampling distribution that is normal. Establishing a level to reject means that you will reject the null hypothesis if the sample statistic is "too far" from the mean of the distribution. How far is "too far"? To put it precisely, you will reject the null hypothesis if the sample statistic falls beyond a point in the tail of the distribution beyond which lies 5 percent of the area under the curve. Look at Figure 8.3a. The shaded area is 5 percent of the area under the sampling distribution. Events on the number line directly under the shaded area occur 5 percent of the time. (That is, sample statistics that lie on the portion of the number line below the shaded region occur 5 percent of the time.) If a particular sample yields a statistic that falls on that part of the number line, the sample in question had less than a 1-in-20 chance of being selected from the population characterized by the parameter in the null hypothesis. If such a situation obtains, you have decided, before hand, to reject the null hypothesis. The section of the number line under the shaded area is called the *region of rejection*. Any time a sample statistic is in that region, you have decided to reject the null hypothesis.

Where is the lower boundary of the region of rejection in Figure 8.3a? It is the point on the number line beyond which 5 percent of the area under the distribution lies. Look at the table of normal deviates. That point on the number line is about 1.645 standard deviations above the mean. If you were working in the other tail, the boundary of 5 percent of the area under the distribution is 1.645 standard deviations below the mean.

To determine whether a sample statistic lies in the region of rejection, you use the sample statistic and the parameters of the sampling distribution to calculate a *test-statistic*. The test statistic gives the number of standard-error units that a sample statistic lies from the mean of its sampling distribution. If the test statistic falls in the region of rejection, you will reject the null hypothesis. If it falls outside the region of rejection, you will not reject the null hypothesis. If the level to reject were .05, the test statistic would have to be greater than 1.645 to fall in the region of rejection. If you were working in the left tail of the distribution, the test statistic would have to be less than -1.645.

Test statistics vary from hypothesis test to hypothesis test. For a large-sample test about a population mean, the test statistic is just like that calculated in all the examples above:

$$z = \frac{\bar{X} - \mu}{\sigma/\sqrt{n}}$$

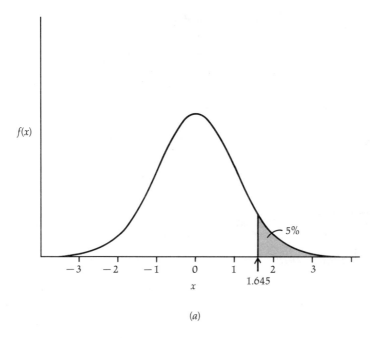

(a)

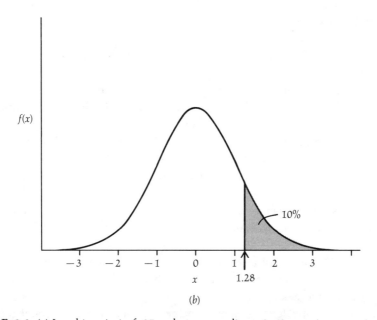

(b)

FIGURE 8.3 (a) Level to reject of .05 and corresponding rejection region on a standard normal distribution. (b) Level to reject of .10 and corresponding rejection region on a standard normal distribution.

Examining Type A personality scores of the samples in the internal-motivation experiments, we see that the region of rejection was just like that shown in Figure 8.3a. The test statistic had to exceed 1.645 in order to fall in the region of rejection. In the first experiment, $z = 0.93$, so I failed to reject the null hypothesis. In the second experiment, $z = 2.46$, greater than 1.645, so I decided to reject the null hypothesis.

What if you were willing to tolerate a risk of being wrong of 1 out of 10? How far from the mean of the sampling distribution would a sample statistic have to be? That is, how large would the test statistic have to be? Look at Figure 8.3b. The lower boundary of the shaded region is at $z = 1.28$. The region of rejection extends from 1.28 standard errors through infinity. If a test statistic is larger than 1.28, you can reject the null hypothesis and know that the chance of having incorrectly done so is 1 in 10.

Statistical Significance

It is necessary to add one more part of the statistical vocabulary if you want to be able to read the scientific literature. A term you will see in almost every scientific report is "*p* value." The *p value* is the approximate probability with which you would obtain a sample statistic of at least the size observed in your sample if, in fact, the null hypothesis is true. The *p* value is also called the *observed significance of the test*. In scientific papers, you will often see a statement like, "The test of the mean was statistically significant at the $p < .01$ level." Because this is such a common way of presenting statistical results, you need to understand this kind of phrase well.

The *p* value is equal to the proportion of the area under the sampling distribution that lies beyond the level of the sample statistic. In the case of Beth's dice, her sample mean was 3.76 standard-error units above the mean of the sampling distribution. The proportion of the area under the normal distribution beyond 3.76 standard deviations above the mean is $P(z > 3.76) = .0001$. That is the probability of drawing a sample of 50 from a population with a mean of 7.0 (that is, if the null hypothesis is true) and observing a sample mean of at least 8.28. You would write, "Beth's sample mean is statistically significant at the $p = .0001$ level." This phrase means that her sample mean is *significantly different* from the hypothesized population mean of 7.0.

Reporting the results of a statistical test using *p* values usually *implies* a rejection of the null hypothesis. However, by not being explicit, the researcher allows the reader to decide whether to reject the null hypothesis. If the reader would set the level to reject at a level greater than the *p* value, she or he would reject the null hypothesis along with the researcher. If the reader's level to reject were less than the *p* value, he or she would fail to reject the null hypothesis.

In the first internal-motivation experiment, $p = P(z > .93) = .32$. The observed significance of the test is $p = .32$. A result like this would usually be reported by saying, "The sample mean is not statistically significant $(p = .32)$," which means that the sample mean is not sufficiently different from the hypothesized population mean to justify a rejection of the null hypothesis. Saying that a test is "not significant" means that the researcher has decided not to reject the null hypothesis, that her or his level to reject is smaller than the observed significance of the test.

In general, first you choose a level to reject, the risk of incorrectly rejecting the null hypothesis that you are willing to tolerate. Then if the *p* value of the test is smaller than the level to reject, you reject the null hypothesis. If the *p* value is greater than the level to reject, you fail to reject the null hypothesis.

One-Tailed and Two-Tailed Tests

So far we have been conducting *one-tailed tests* about a population mean. That is, we determined the probability of a sample mean's having been taken from only one tail of the sampling distribution of the mean. In the example involving Beth's dice, we accepted the alternative hypothesis that $\mu > 7.0$. That is, we accepted the hypothesis that the actual mean of the population from which Beth's sample came lies in the upper tail of this distribution. The region of rejection is only in the upper tail.

Sometimes you want to determine only if a population mean is significantly different from some specified value without caring whether the population mean is greater than or less than the specified value. If you are concerned only about differences, you conduct a *two-tailed test* of statistical significance, and you construct a region of rejection that has two parts, one in the upper tail and one in the lower tail of the sampling distribution.

Consider this example. A graduate program in public administration admits a class of 40 students. On a Miller Analogy Test (MAT), the test required for admission, the class has an average score of 58.3. The director of the program asks her research assistant to determine whether it is possible to assure the school's administration that this entering class is no different from all people entering such programs throughout the country. The research assistant must determine whether there is a basis for claiming that this class came from a population different from the national population of all students entering public administration programs.

The makers of tests like the MAT often publish population means and standard deviations for various populations. Suppose the mean for all people entering graduate programs in public administration is 60.5 and the standard deviation is 10.7. That the sample mean for this one program is lower than the population mean is not the issue in the director's mind. She wants to know only whether she can claim that her class's mean score is not significantly different from the national mean. Since the mean score of the director's class is not exactly equal to the population mean of $\mu = 60.5$, maybe this sample was drawn from a population with a different mean. The alternative hypothesis, then, is

$$H_A: \mu \neq 60.5$$

This says that the mean score for the population from which this class came is not the same as the national mean score for all entering students. The null hypothesis is that the population from which this sample was drawn has a mean equal to 60.5, the overall population mean. That is,

$$H_0: \mu = 60.5$$

The sampling distribution of the mean is approximately normal, has a mean of $\mu_{\bar{x}} = \mu = 60.5$, and has a standard error of $\sigma/\sqrt{n} = 10.7/\sqrt{40} = 1.69$. The distribution is shown in Figure 8.4.

Suppose the director is willing to tolerate a 5 percent chance of incorrectly rejecting the null hypothesis. Where is the region of rejection? The director will reject the null hypothesis if the probability, overall, of doing so is 0.05. But if she cares only about a difference, a low-probability sample mean from either the left-hand tail or the right-hand tail would make her decision to reject an incorrect one. She has to construct a rejection region that is split into two parts to account for her indifference about whether the group's actual mean is high or low. One-half of the rejection region will be in the lower tail and one-half will be in the upper tail. The two parts of the rejection region will each capture 2.5 percent of the area under the distribution, so that the total area captured by the region is 5 percent. This area is shown on Figure 8.4.

The point on the standard normal distribution beyond which 2.5 percent of the area lies is $z = 1.96$. The bounds of the region of rejection on Figure 8.4 are 1.96 standard errors above the mean and 1.96 standard errors below the mean.

The test statistic, in this case, is

$$z = \frac{58.3 - 60.5}{1.69} = -1.3$$

The sample mean lies 1.3 standard-error units below the mean, as shown in Figure 8.4. It does not fall in the rejection region, so the researcher would not reject the null hypothesis. There is no basis for claiming that this sample comes from a population whose mean is different from the national mean of 60.5.

What is the observed significance of this test? What is the p value? Phrased another, equivalent way, what is the probability of getting a sample mean that is $60.5 - 58.3 = 2.2$ raw units from the population mean, either positively or negatively? That is, what is the probability that the sample mean came from the left tail of the distribution and was at least 2.2 raw units below the mean or that the mean came from the right tail and was at least 2.2 raw units above the mean?

Figure 8.5 shows the proportion of the area under the distribution that corresponds to this probability. Expressed mathematically, the question is, What is $P(\text{score} < \mu - 2.2 \text{ or score} > \mu + 2.2)$? From the simple addition rule of probability, this probability is equal to

$$P(\text{score} < \mu - 2.2) + P(\text{score} > \mu + 2.2)$$

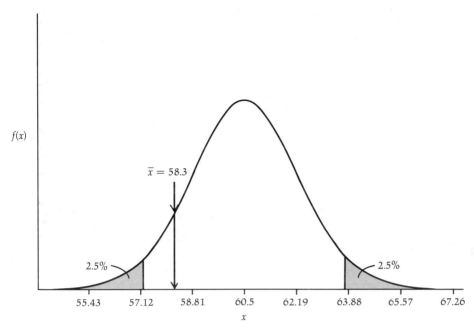

FIGURE 8.4 Two-tailed test of a hypothesis about the mean MAT.

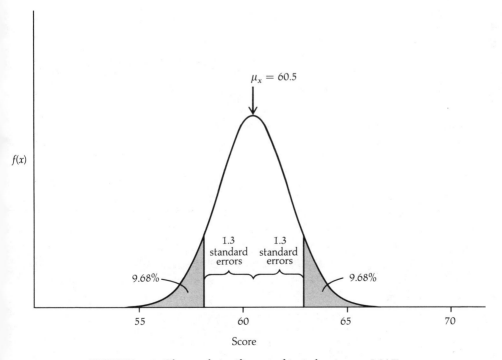

FIGURE 8.5 Observed significance of test about mean MAT score.

To determine the probabilities, we need to convert the raw scores to standard scores so that we can use the standard normal distribution. In standard scores,

$$z = \frac{\mu - 2.2 - \mu}{\sigma/\sqrt{n}} = \frac{-2.2}{10.7/\sqrt{40}} = -1.3$$

and

$$z = \frac{\mu + 2.2 - \mu}{\sigma/\sqrt{n}} = \frac{2.2}{10.7/\sqrt{40}} = 1.3$$

So we need to determine

$$P(z < -1.3) + P(z > 1.3)$$

We can look up $P(z > 1.3)$ directly in Appendix Table B.3:

$$P(z > 1.3) = .0968$$

Since the distribution is symmetric, $P(z < -1.3) = P(z > 1.3)$, and

$$P(z < -1.3) + P(z > 1.3) = .0968 + .0968 = .1936$$

The observed significance of the test is $p = .1936$, about 1 in 5. The risk involved in rejecting this null hypothesis is too high. I would not reject the null hypothesis, and urge the research assistant to do the same. I cannot conclude that the sample (this class) came from a population whose mean MAT score is different from that of all public administration students taking the test.

Note well how to calculate the observed significance of a test in a two-tailed test. Calculate the test statistic. Then determine the area under the distribution that lies beyond the positive value of the test statistic in the right-hand tail of the distribution. Add to that the area under the distribution that lies below the negative value of the test statistic in the left-hand tail.

What determines whether you do a one-tailed or a two-tailed test? Your research hypothesis. Nothing else. If your research hypothesis leads you to believe that the mean of the population from which your sample was drawn is greater than (or less than) some specified real number, then you must do a one-tailed test. Suppose you have no basis for thinking that the mean of the population from which your sample was drawn is either less than or greater than a specified number, but you want to know simply if there is a basis for claiming the mean of a variable in the population from which your sample was drawn is different from some specified number. Then you conduct a two-tailed test. Think carefully as you construct hypotheses; they will tell you what kind of test to conduct.

Setting a Level to Reject: Type I and Type II Errors

Two kinds of errors can be made in the decision about the null hypothesis. So far, we have talked only of one: the decision to reject the null hypothesis when it is, in fact, true. In statistical parlance, this kind of error is called a *Type I error*. Since R. A. Fisher emphasized the importance of Type I errors in his famous treatise on the topic, *The Design of Experiments*,[1] many people have focused exclusively on the issue of risk involved in rejecting a null hypothesis that is true.

Logically, however, there is another kind of error you can make, and in some situations it makes sense to focus on that kind of potential error. You can understand the other kind of error if you look at this table:

		Situation	
		H_0 is true	H_0 is false
Decision	Do not reject H_0	Correct decision	Type II error
	Reject H_0	Type I error	Correct decision

This table shows the relationship between decisions regarding the null hypothesis and the situation that exists. If you fail to reject a null hypothesis *and* it is true (the upper left corner of the table), or if you reject a null hypothesis and it is false (the lower right corner of the table), there is no problem. Both decisions are correct. The lower left cell shows a Type I error: You reject a null hypothesis that is true. The other kind of error you can make is called a *Type II error*. You can make the error of not rejecting a null hypothesis that is, in fact, false and should have been rejected. For example, a sample may have come from a population whose mean is different from the hypothesized population mean, and you may decide not to reject the null hypothesis. Bill may have been playing with fixed dice. If that were true, then you decided, rationally but incorrectly, that there was no basis for asking him to change dice. You would recognize this as an incorrect decision if you knew, in truth, that Bill had borrowed his teacher's funny dice before coming to the party.

You cannot simultaneously reduce the risk of committing both a Type I and a Type II error (unless you reduce the variance of the data by improving your sampling scheme). In fact, everything else being equal, as the risk of committing one type of error is reduced, the risk of committing the other type of error increases. (You can show this is true mathematically, but there is no need to go into that here.) Therefore, you have to decide which kind of error is more acceptable in the circumstances.

Suppose the circumstances of your research make it costly to conclude there is reason to believe that a sample came from a population in which the mean is different from the hypothesized population mean when, in fact, it came from a population characterized by the parameter in the null hypothesis. Then you should try to minimize the likelihood of making a Type I error. You should make the level to reject small. Suppose that it is more costly to conclude there is no basis for asserting a difference between the mean of the population from which your sample came and the hypothesized population mean when, in truth, there is a difference. Then you should try to reduce the risk of making a Type II error. To do that, raise the level to reject.

Consider two different research situations. First, you are an agency chief asked to devote a significant part of an education program budget to a narrowly focused effort for a small group of students. You decide that if you can be relatively well assured that the program will have an impact on students, you will do it; if not, you do not feel the expense can be justified since the client group is so small. You fund a pilot program to determine if the client group's mean test scores after the program exceed a nationally known standard achievement test score for students of this sort. But you want to write into the contract for the pilot program an instruction to the researchers that they must provide good assurance that the scores of these students are truly greater than the national mean score. In statistical language, you want to instruct the researchers to conduct a one-tailed test, and you want to tell the researchers, "Keep the chance of making a Type I error low." That is, you want to keep small the chance of incorrectly rejecting the null hypothesis that the students who participated in this program came from a population whose mean score is no different from a national mean score.

This instruction is fairly easy to translate. "Keep the chance of making a Type I error low" means to lower the level to reject the null hypothesis. You might even write into the contract a clause that would tell the researchers that they must not reject the null hypothesis unless the chances are less than 1 in 100 that they would be incorrectly rejecting it. That is, you could cause them to set their level to reject at, say, .01.

In making this decision, you would have to recognize, of course, that such a strategy would increase the likelihood of the researchers making a Type II error (a decision not to reject the null hypothesis if it were false). That is, the researchers would be increasing the risk of deciding that there was no basis for claiming the program had an effect when, in fact, it did improve students' scores. But because of your situation, you are willing to risk having no program in order to be relatively sure that a program, if funded, would work. That is the trade-off your judgment of the situation suggested to you.

The second situation puts you in the position of making funding decisions for research on cancer, a group of diseases on which the government "declared war" over a decade ago. Preliminary results from researchers might come to you in the form of mean number of years of survival of people who were treated with a drug. You could ask whether the sample of treated patients came from a population whose mean years of survival was greater than the known mean years of survival of patients who did not receive the drug. Your task would be to take these preliminary results and decide if further funding of research on drug X were merited.

What kind of error—type I or Type II—are you going to be more willing to make under these circumstances?

I would be more willing to make a Type II error in this case. That is, I would be willing to throw money at a drug that may not improve survival than I would be willing to withhold funding from a drug that, in truth, improves survival. Therefore, I might set my criterion for rejecting the null hypothesis rather high. I might be willing to run a $1/10$, or 1-in-10 ($\alpha = .10$), chance or even a $3/10$ chance ($\alpha = .30$) of being wrong in my decision to reject the null hypothesis in these circumstances. I make this decision because I dearly want to avoid the mistake of not funding research that would lead to the discovery of a drug that has a salutary effect on cancer.

The point of these two examples is that you must decide what kind of error you are more willing to make. You should make your decision knowing that there is always a trade-off. If you set your level to reject high, you are thereby deciding not to run a large risk of making a Type II error (the error of accepting a null hypothesis that is false). If you set your level to reject low, you are saying that a Type I error is more unacceptable and you would prefer not to reject a null hypothesis that is true.

One point is worth stressing again. You should make your decision regarding the level to reject the null *before you do the analysis.* You make the decision based on the circumstances in which you find yourself and on the costs associated with (1) the risk of rejecting a null hypothesis that is true and (2) the risk of accepting a null hypothesis that is false.

Summary: Rephrasing the Steps in Hypothesis Testing

So far, I have discussed only one type of hypothesis testing: large-sample tests about a population mean. But in the course of that discussion, many ideas have been introduced. Before discussing other types of tests, it may be useful to recapitulate the steps involved in hypothesis testing. In conducting a test about a population parameter, you must do the following:

1. Formulate a null hypothesis and the alternative hypothesis about a population parameter.
    (a) In practice, the alternative hypothesis is usually formulated first. The alternative hypothesis is the research hypothesis.
    (b) The null hypothesis and the alternative hypothesis are logically complementary.
    (c) Decide at this point whether a one-tailed or two-tailed test of the hypothesis appropriate.
2. Describe the sample, using appropriate descriptive statistics.
3. Determine the nature of the sampling distribution of the sample statistic if the sample came from a population characterized by the parameter in the null hypothesis.

4. Set a level to reject, α. That is, decide what level of risk of being wrong in deciding to reject the null hypothesis that you are willing to tolerate.

(a) Set the level to reject based on your relative willingness to commit a Type I or a Type II error.

(b) Based on the decision to conduct a one-tailed or two-tailed test, construct the region(s) of rejection on the sampling distribution.

5. Use the sampling distribution and appropriate sample statistics to calculate the probability that the observed sample statistic would have occurred if, in fact, the null hypothesis were true. That is, calculate the observed significance of the test or the p value.

6. Compare the probability that your sample would have yielded the observed sample statistic if the null hypothesis were true to the level to reject.

(a) If the sample statistic falls in the rejection region of the sampling distribution, reject the null hypothesis and accept the alternative. If the sample statistic falls outside the rejection region, do not reject the null hypothesis.

or (b) Compare the observed significance of the test (p value) to the level to reject. If the p value is smaller than the level to reject, reject the null hypothesis and accept the alternative. If the p value is larger than the level to reject, do not reject the null hypothesis.

· · ·

SMALL-SAMPLE HYPOTHESIS TESTS ABOUT A POPULATION MEAN

W. S. Gosset, a student of Karl Pearson's who took a job as research scientist at the Guinness Brewery in Dublin late in the nineteenth century, studied, among other things, how long Guinness stout would last before going bad. Guinness wanted to ship their beer to England, but they wanted to make sure it would last the trip. Gosset noted something odd when he looked closely at the distributions of mean survival times for small samples. The distributions were consistently "flatter" than a normal distribution, and their tails were consistently higher than those of a normal distribution. The distributions were more dispersed than the central-limit theorem said they should be. The larger his samples, the lower the tails would get and the more "mounded" the central area of the distribution became. Empirically, he discovered what the central-limit theorem shows to be true in theory: The larger the sample, the closer to normal the sampling distribution is. But what was Gosset to do for statistical tests of significance given that he was limited by circumstances (and, no doubt, by his employer) to drawing only a small number of testable draughts from the vats of that blackest of brews? He used his empirical results to develop, with the help of a mathematician, a family of distributions that accurately describe the sampling distribution of the mean for small samples. That family of distributions is called the *t distributions*. Gosset published his papers on small-sample statistics under the pseudonym "Student," so the *t* distributions came to be known as the *Student t distributions*.

The shape of the sampling distribution of the mean is different for small samples from that for large samples, but the approach to hypothesis testing remains the same. The central-limit theorem says that the sampling distribution of the mean is approximately normal for large samples *regardless* of the shape of the parent population's distribution. For small samples, there is no such promise. The shape of the sampling distribution of the mean for small samples depends very much on the shape of the parent population. If the underlying population is normally distributed, then the sampling distribution of the mean will be approximately normal. If you know that the underlying parent population is normally distributed, or if you can reasonably make that assumption, you can use the *t* distribution, which is "approximately normal," to conduct tests about a population mean.

For small samples, the sampling distribution of the mean is distributed according to a *t* distribution with a mean of μ and a standard error of $s_x/\sqrt{n}$, where s_x is the estimate of the population standard deviation. That is,

$$ s_x = \sqrt{\frac{\sum\limits_{i=1}^{n} (x_i - \bar{x})^2}{n-1}} $$

The shape of any one *t* distribution is dependent on the size of the sample involved: The smaller the sample, the higher the tails; the larger the sample, the closer to the normal the distribution becomes.

You must choose the appropriate *t* distribution to use. The choice of which *t* distribution from the family of distributions is determined by sample size. More accurately, the choice is determined by the number of "degrees of freedom" that remain in the data after the calculations required by the test have been performed. At this point, I will not discuss the meaning of "degrees of freedom." It is denoted "df," and for a test of one mean, df $= n - 1$. A sample of size $n = 5$ has 4 ($5 - 1 = 4$) degrees of freedom.

All the examples up to this point have been based on relatively large samples. A large sample is usually taken to mean one that has more than 30 cases in it. Why 30? Because if n is larger than 30, the *t* distribution is very much like the normal distribution. With $n > 30$, it becomes reasonable to use the normal distribution, even though some authors recommend using the *t* distribution until $n > 100$. Just which cutoff point you choose is not important; it *is* important that you choose a cutoff point knowing what you are doing.

Here is a problem involving small samples. I take a pair of dice out of my desk drawer (once again). I know that one pair in the drawer is fixed and the other is fair. I throw the dice I've picked 5 times. I get the following results:

Throw	1	2	3	4	5
Sum	11	6	10	8	11

So

$$\text{Mean} = 9.2 \qquad s_x = 2.17$$

This is a very suspicious sample, but can I conclude it was not taken from the population of throws of a pair of fair dice? Can I reject the null hypothesis that

$$H_0: \mu = 7.0$$

and accept the alternative hypothesis that

$$H_A: \mu \neq 7.0$$

First, I will answer the question *as if this were a large sample*, and I will use the standard normal distribution for an approximation of the sampling distribution of the mean. If the sample were taken from the population of throws of two fair dice and if I conducted the test as if the sampling distribution of the mean were normal (i.e, as if n were greater than 30), I would conclude that $\bar{X}$ is

$$z = \frac{\bar{X} - \mu}{s_x/\sqrt{n}} = \frac{9.2 - 7.0}{2.17/\sqrt{5}} = 2.27$$

standard units away from the mean of a standard normal distribution. Using a two-tailed test and setting the level to reject at 0.05, I would find

$$P = P(z < -2.27 \text{ or } z > 2.27) = .023$$

The observed significance of the test is smaller than the level to reject. I would reject the null hypothesis and conclude that the dice were rigged again. Figure 8.6 shows the normal distribution, the rejection region, and the place where the sample mean falls.

Intuitively, you should be able to see that if the size of a sample is small, the likelihood of getting an especially small or an especially large mean is greater than if the sample is large. A sample mean of 9.2 is suspiciously large, even for a sample of size 5, but you must test the null hypothesis against a distribution that accurately reflects the increased probability of getting a more extreme value of the sample mean from any given sample. You must use the t distribution.

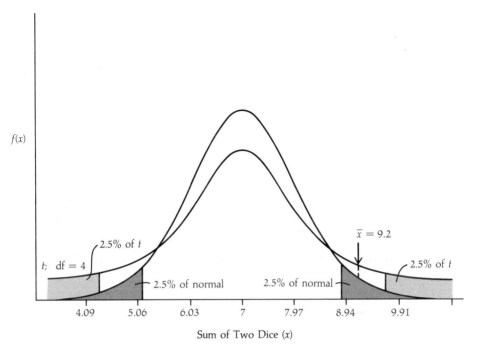

$f(x)$

2.5% of t

t; df = 4

2.5% of normal   2.5% of normal

$\bar{x} = 9.2$

2.5% of t

4.09   5.06   6.03   7   7.97   8.94   9.91

Sum of Two Dice (x)

FIGURE 8.6 Comparison of rejection regions in a normal distribution and a t distribution.

The table of t distributions, Table B.5 in the Appendix, is set up a little differently from the other tables. You decide, first, the proper row to use based on the degrees of freedom (df $= n - 1$). The table shows the area in either one tail or two tails of the distribution that lies beyond the value shown. The numbers in the table are the bounds of the region of rejection.

To use this table, you carry out the same calculations as you would for a large sample, but you use the appropriate t distribution to conduct the final test. To test the null hypothesis for the sample of 5 throws, you calculate the number of standard units from the population mean that the sample mean lies. The test statistic is

$$t = \frac{\bar{X} - \mu}{s_x/\sqrt{n}} = \frac{9.2 - 7.0}{2.17/\sqrt{5}} = 2.27$$

(Notice that you express these as "t" units, not "z" units as when you are working with the standard normal distribution.)

There are 5 cases in the sample, so df $= 5 - 1 = 4$. Look across the row marked df $= 4$, the fourth row from the top of Table B.5. Now 2.27 is between the first and second columns. Since you are interested only in whether the sample mean is *different* from the population mean, you must conduct a two-tailed test. This test statistic is in the region of rejection if the level to reject is .10, but it falls outside the rejection region for a level to reject of .05. I do *not* reject the null hypothesis in this case. I do not conclude that this sample came from a population whose mean is different from 7.0.

Suspicious sample or not, you cannot confidently come to any other conclusion. This example shows the importance of using small-sample statistical techniques when appropriate.

Superimposed on Figure 8.6 is the *t* distribution with its region of rejection. You can see that the sample mean, which fell inside the rejection region on the normal distribution, falls outside the rejection region on the *t* distribution.

Unknown Population Standard Deviation σ

Often, you do not know the population standard deviation of a variable σ. Remember that σ is used to calculate the standard error of the mean $\sigma/\sqrt{n}$. If you do not know σ, then you may use s, the sample standard deviation, as an estimate of σ. If the sample is large (say, more than 30 cases), the test statistic for a test about a population mean is

$$z = \frac{\bar{X} - \mu}{s/\sqrt{n}}$$

and you use the standard normal distribution as the sampling distribution on which to conduct the test. If the sample is small *and* the parent population is normally distributed, you use the now-familiar test statistic

$$t = \frac{\bar{X} - \mu}{s/\sqrt{n}}$$

and the *t* distribution with $n - 1$ degrees of freedom as the sampling distribution. In the previous section, we used s_x as an estimate of σ to calculate z, without saying anything about the substitution. Now let's make the case explicit. For example, suppose the publishers of the work-ethic scale used in the internal-motivation experiments told you that the mean of all people who had taken the English version of the test was 80.5. Could you conclude that the sample for experiment 2 was drawn from a population with a mean of 80.5? Since you do not know the standard deviation of "work ethic" in the population, you need to use the standard deviation of the sample as an estimate of the population parameter σ. You begin by formulating the hypothesis

$$H_A: \mu \neq 80.5$$

since the sample mean of 84.25 is not equal to the hypothesized population mean of 80.5. The null hypothesis is

$$H_0: \mu = 80.5$$

The sample standard deviation s is 9.34, so the estimate of the standard error is $9.34/\sqrt{40} = 1.48$. The test statistic is $z = 84.25 - 80.5/1.48 = 2.53$. The observed significance of this test, from a standard normal distribution, is $p = .012$ if a two-tailed test is employed. If my level to reject were greater than 0.012, I would conclude there is a significant difference between the sample mean and the population mean of the people who took the English version of the test. I reject the null hypothesis and conclude that this sample probably came from a population with a mean different from 80.5, the mean score of all English-speaking people who took the test.

· · ·

HYPOTHESIS TESTING ABOUT A POPULATION PROPORTION

In the 1980 General Social Survey (GSS), first respondents were asked if they thought abortion should be okay for several reasons, such as "if the pregnancy was the result of rape" or "if the woman is married and just doesn't want any more children." Then they were asked a general question: Do you think abortion should be okay for any reason? And 578 people said yes while 828 people said no. If a thoughtless legislator said to you, "I'll vote to legalize abortion if more than 40 percent of the people in the United States think it is okay," what would you advise her or him to do? Vote for or against?

In the sample, 41 percent of the respondents thought abortion was okay. But what about the population from which this sample came? Do more than 40 percent of the noninstitutionalized people over 18 years of age in the population of the United States think abortion is okay?

You can use this sample to test a hypothesis about a population proportion. If p is the proportion of people in the population who believe abortion should be okay, then the alternative, or research, hypothesis is

$$H_A: p > .40$$

The null hypothesis is

$$H_0: p \leq .40$$

Obviously, these hypotheses compel you to make a one-tailed test, but what is the nature of the sampling distribution of the sample proportion?

A population proportion is really a probability, a relative frequency over the long run. The population proportion p is the relative frequency with which people say yes to the question. Each sample is characterized by a sample proportion $\hat{p}$ (read "p hat"), the number of people in the sample who answered yes divided by the total number of people in the sample. The question is, What is the sampling distribution of $\hat{p}$?

To answer this, you need to think of a given sample as a binomial experiment consisting of n trials, where n is the number of cases in the sample, and with a probability of success equal to the true population proportion p. The binomial distribution then gives the exact probability distribution of the random variable "frequency of yes responses in the sample." If the sample size n is large, recall from Chapter 6, a binomial distribution is well approximated by a normal distribution. The normal approximation of the binomial distribution of frequency of successes has a mean of np and a variance of npq (and hence a standard deviation of $\sqrt{npq}$). You can convert this distribution of frequencies to a probability distribution of proportions by dividing each of the characteristics of the distribution by the number of cases in the sample n. Consequently, the distribution of a sample proportion $\hat{p}$ in a binomial experiment where p is the true probability of a success

1. Is approximately normal (if np and nq are both larger than 5 and if n is greater than 20)
2. Has a mean of p
3. Has a standard deviation of

$$\frac{\sqrt{npq}}{n} = \sqrt{\frac{npq}{n^2}} = \sqrt{\frac{pq}{n}}$$

which is approximately equal to $\sqrt{\hat{p}\hat{q}/n}$.

With the description of the sample and knowledge of the sampling distribution of the sample proportion, you are ready to do the calculations that will allow you to make a decision about the proportion of the population that said abortion should be okay. The sample proportion is

$$\hat{p} = 578/1406 = .411$$

The hypotheses are

$$H_0: p \le .4 \qquad H_A: p > .4$$

The test to be conducted is a one-tailed test. And let's set the level to reject at .01 to reduce the risk of a politically potent Type I error. The sampling distribution of the sample proportion $\hat{p}$ is approximately normal (since $n = 1406$, which is greater than 20, and $np = 578$ and $nq = 828$, both of which are greater than 5).

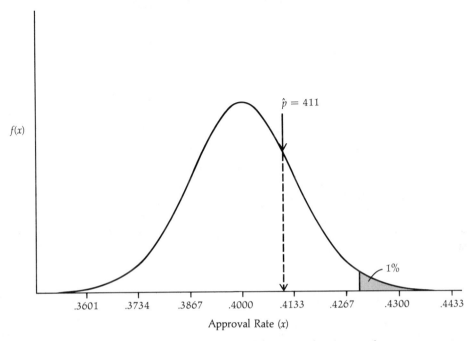

FIGURE 8.7 Normal approximation of binomial for a test about a population proportion.

The sampling distribution has a mean of $p = .4$ and a standard error of $\sqrt{\hat{p}\hat{q}/n} = \sqrt{(.411)(.589)/1406} = .013$. Figure 8.7 shows the sampling distribution and the rejection region. For a level to reject of .01, the lower bound of rejection region is at $z = 2.32$. The test statistic that tells you how many standard-error units the observed sample proportion $\hat{p}$ is from the mean of its sampling distribution is

$$z = \frac{\hat{p} - p}{\sqrt{\hat{p}\hat{q}/n}} = \frac{.411 - .400}{.013} = .85$$

This test statistic is not greater than the lower bound of the rejection region. *Conclusion:* Decide not to reject the null hypothesis. There is insufficient evidence to conclude that $p > .4$. In the population from which this sample came, you cannot say that more than .40 of the people think abortion should be okay. Memo to your legislator: Vote no.

What is the observed significance of the test? The probability of getting a sample proportion only .85 standard-error unit above the mean of the sampling distribution is fairly large, about $p = .20$. The chance of a decision to accept the alternative hypothesis (that the proportion of the population approving abortion is greater than .40) being incorrect would have been about 1 in 5. This is a high risk, especially for a politican who had already gone out on a limb by not insisting on "majority approval."

· · ·

HYPOTHESIS TESTS ABOUT TWO POPULATION MEANS

Instead of testing a hypothesis about a population mean, you often want to know if it is reasonable to claim that two independently drawn samples came from populations that have different means.

For example, Figure 8.8 shows the mean and standard deviations of per capita income for two subsets of the countries in Appendix A. The first subset is countries with urbanization equal to or below the median urbanization of 48.2 percent. The second subset is countries with urbanization greater than the median urbanization level. The mean incomes in these two samples are very different, $737.62 versus $4161.67. But what about the populations from which these samples came? Is there a basis for claiming that these samples came from populations with different mean per-capita incomes?

If you have two independent samples of sizes n_1 and n_2 with sample means $\bar{X}_1$ and $\bar{X}_2$ and variances s_1^2 and s_2^2, respectively, you can determine if it is reasonable to claim the means of the two populations from which the samples were drawn are different. That is, you begin with the alternative hypothesis that the population means are different

$$H_A: \mu_1 \neq \mu_2$$

or equivalently

$$H_A: \mu_1 - \mu_2 = 0$$

and you can test the null hypothesis that

$$H_0: \mu_1 = \mu_2$$

```
10:48:39        The Evergreen State College        DG MV/10000            AOS/VS 6.04
----                  DESCRIPTION OF SUBPOPULATIONS                       ----
CRITERION VARIABLE   INC      INCOME PER CAPITA
   BROKEN DOWN BY   URBANI
-----------------------------------------------------------------------------
```

VARIABLE	VALUE	LABEL	MEAN	STD DEV	CASES
FOR ENTIRE POPULATION			2433.3429	3121.7641	105
URBAN1	1.00	LOW URBANIZATION	737.6226	1103.5140	53
URBAN1	2.00	HIGH URBANIZATION	4161.6731	3549.2884	52

TOTAL CASES = 142 MISSING CASES = 37 OR 26.1 PCT.

FIGURE 8.8 Computer printout comparing samples of per capita income for countries with low and high urbanization.

ɔr equivalently

$$H_0: \mu_1 - \mu_2 = 0$$

The logic of this test is the same as before. You begin with a "what if." *What if* the null hypothesis is true? What, then, is the shape of the sampling distribution of the sample statistic known as the "difference between two independent sample means," $\bar{X}_1 - \bar{X}_2$?

By now you should know how such a sampling distribution is constructed. You begin with two populations that have equal means, so $\mu_1 - \mu_2 = 0$. Then you draw one sample of size n_1 from the first population, draw a sample of size n_2 from the second population, calculate the mean of each sample, subtract $\bar{X}_2$ from $\bar{X}_1$, and record the difference. You repeat that process until you have selected every possible combination of samples of size n_1 and n_2. The distribution of all the differences between means is the *sampling distribution of the difference between independent sample means.*

The sampling distribution of the difference between means has a mean of $\mu_{X_1 - X_2} = \mu_1 - \mu_2 = 0$. If you know the population variances of the populations σ_1^2 and σ_2^2, then the standard error of the sampling distribution $\sigma_{\bar{X}_1 - \bar{X}_2}$ is

$$\sigma_{\bar{X}_1 - \bar{X}_2} = \sqrt{\frac{\sigma_1^2}{n_1} + \frac{\sigma_2^2}{n_2}}$$

and the sampling distribution is normal. If you do not know σ_1^2 and σ_2^2 and the sample sizes are large, the standard error is approximately equal to

$$\sigma_{\bar{X}_1 - \bar{X}_2} \cong \sqrt{\frac{s_1^2}{n_1} + \frac{s_2^2}{n_2}}$$

To test the null hypothesis, you simply need to calculate how many standard units away from zero ($\mu_{\bar{X}_1 - \bar{X}_2} = \mu_1 - \mu_2 = 0$ if H_0 is true) the difference $\bar{X}_1 - \bar{X}_2$ is and use the standard normal distribution to determine the probability of getting a difference as large as $\bar{X}_1 - \bar{X}_2$ if, in fact, the samples were drawn from populations with equal means.

In the case of per capita income, the actual difference between the sample means is $\bar{X}_2 - \bar{X}_1 = 4161.67 - 737.62 = 3424.05$. If H_0 is true, then this statistic came from a sampling distribution with

$$\mu_{\bar{X}_1 - \bar{X}_2} = 0$$

and

$$\sigma_{\bar{X}_1 - \bar{X}_2} \cong \sqrt{\frac{s_1^2}{n_1} + \frac{s_2^2}{n_2}} = \sqrt{\frac{(1103.5)^2}{53} + \frac{(3549.3)^2}{52}} = 515.0$$

The test statistic is

$$\frac{(\bar{X}_1 - \bar{X}_2) - (\mu_1 - \mu_2)}{\sigma_{\bar{X}_1 - \bar{X}_2}} = \frac{3424.05 - 0}{515.0} = 6.64$$

Once again, the probability of getting a difference between sample means that large, if the population means are equal, is quite small. *Conclusion*: Reject H_0 and decide that the samples came from populations with unequal means.

This test was a two-tailed test inquiring only about difference. You can also conduct a one-tailed test of this sort. If you believe one population mean is greater than the other, you can test the null hypothesis that

$$H_0: \mu_1 - \mu_2 \leq 0 \qquad \text{or} \qquad H_0: \mu_1 - \mu_2 \geq 0$$

in the usual way.

Small Samples

If n_1 and n_2 are small, the sampling distribution of the differences between two independent sample means is not normally distributed. But under certain assumptions, the t distribution can be used. The important assumptions are the following:

1. The populations from which the two samples came are normally distributed.
2. The variances of the two populations are equal, or

$$\sigma_1^2 = \sigma_2^2$$

(Actually, the test described in this section is still useful if the populations are only approximately normal. Also if $n_1 = n_2$, the population variances can be very different from one another, and the test will still apply.)

If the requirements of normality and equal variances are met, or can be reasonably assumed to be operating, then the sampling distribution of $\bar{X}_1 - \bar{X}_2$ has the following characteristics:

1. It is shaped like a t distribution with $n_1 + n_2 - 2$ degrees of freedom.
2. It has a mean of $\mu_1 - \mu_2$.
3. It has a standard error well estimated by

$$\sqrt{\frac{(n_1 - 1)s_1^2 + (n_2 - 1)s_1^2}{n_1 + n_2 - 2} \left(\frac{1}{n_1} + \frac{1}{n_2} \right)}$$

Characteristic 3 is the estimate of the standard error by using a "pooled estimate of the variance" of the underlying populations. The estimated variances s_1^2 and s_2^2 are "pooled" to give one estimate of the underlying populations' variances, which is then used in the estimation of the standard error.

Consider a teacher who asserts that men score better than women in his class and offers as evidence the scores of the following 10 students, 6 men and 4 women:

Sex	M	F	F	M	F	F	M	M	M	M
Score	88	52	97	82	65	74	91	48	79	78

If men and women are independently drawn samples (they are not, for example, related to each other), then the independent sample means are 77.67 for males and 72.00 for females, and the sample variances are $s_m^2 = 237$ and $s_f^2 = 359$. Is it likely that the populations from which these samples were drawn (the populations of men and women in this grade level) have equal means on the variable "test score"? That is, can we reject the null hypothesis that

$$H_0: \mu_m = \mu_f \quad \text{or} \quad H_0: \mu_m - \mu_f = 0$$

and accept the alternative that men and women come from populations with the same means?

The absolute difference between means is $\bar{X}_m - \bar{X}_f = 77.67 - 72.00 = 5.67$. To calculate the number of standard units from zero this raw difference lies in the sampling distribution, we need to estimate the standard error of the sampling distribution when $n_m = 6$, $s_m^2 = 237$, $n_f = 4$, $s_f^2 = 359$. It is equal to

$$\sqrt{\frac{(6-1)237 + (4-1)359}{6+4-2}\left(\frac{1}{6} + \frac{1}{4}\right)} = 10.85$$

So the raw difference of 5.67 is only $t = 5.67/10.85 = 0.52$ standard units away from the sampling distribution mean of $\mu_m - \mu_f = 0$ (if, in fact, the population means are equal).

Look in the table of t distributions across the row at df $= n_m + n_f - 2 = 6 + 4 - 2 = 8$. The value $t = 0.52$ is to the *left* of the first column. That indicates that the probability of getting a t value at least that large is greater than .20 in conducting the required one-tailed test. So the difference betweeen means is not significantly different from zero since $p > .20$. You should not reject the null hypothesis, and you should not conclude that the mean value of "test score" in the population of men is different from that for women.

As a final example, let us ask whether physicians who tend to specialize in obstetrics keep their patients in the hospital longer for normal deliveries than do physicians who are not specialists. That is, I want to compare the average length of stay (ALOS) in DRG 373 (vaginal delivery without complications) for physicians with high specialization scores to the ALOS for the same DRG for physicians with low specialization scores. My hypothesis is that the mean ALOS for specialists is higher than that ALOS for nonspecialists. The research hypothesis is

$$H_A: \mu_S - \mu_N > 0$$

where S stands for specialists and N for nonspecialists. The null hypothesis is that

$$H_0: \mu_S - \mu_N \leq 0$$

The data for this test are shown in Table 8.1. I arbitrarily decided that the 11 physicians with the lower specialization scores were specialists and the others nonspecialists.

TABLE 8.1 Data to Compare Mean ALOS for Normal Deliveries by Specialists and Nonspecialists

Physician	Specialization Score, %	Specialist (S) or Nonspecialist (N)	ALOS for DRG 373, days
01	50	S	1.9
02	47	S	2.0
03	61	S	1.8
04	63	S	2.2
05	95	N	1.0
06	94	N	2.0
07	55	S	1.9
08	92	N	2.1
09	93	N	2.0
10	75	S	1.4
11	62	S	1.9
12	67	S	1.9
13	90	N	2.2
14	90	N	1.6
15	86	N	1.5
16	97	N	1.7
17	63	S	1.9
18	84	S	2.0
19	85	N	2.3
20	89	N	1.5
21	63	S	2.6
22	88	N	2.1

12:25:16 The Evergreen State College DG MV/10000 AOS/VS 6.04
------------------------------------- T-TEST ----------------------------

GROUP 1 — SPEC1   EQ   1.00
GROUP 2 — SPEC1   EQ   2.00

VARIABLE	NUMBER OF CASES	MEAN	STANDARD DEVIATION	STANDARD ERROR

ALOS   AVERAGE LENGTH OF STAY

GROUP 1	11	1.9545	.288	.087
GROUP 2	11	1.8182	.392	.118

* POOLED VARIANCE ESTIMATE * SEPARATE VARIANCE ESTIMATE

F VALUE	2-TAIL PROB.	* * *	T VALUE	DEGREES OF FREEDOM	2-TAIL PROB.	* *	T VALUE	DEGREES OF FREEDOM	2-TAIL PROB.
1.86	.343	*	.93	20	.363	*	.93	18.35	.364

FIGURE 8.9 Computer output comparing mean ALOS for normal births for specialists and nonspecialists.

Figure 8.9 shows a computer printout of a "*t* test" of the hypothesis listed above. Group 1 is the specialist group, and group 2 is the nonspecialist group. The specialists have a mean ALOS of 1.95 days, slightly longer than that of nonspecialists, whose mean ALOS is 1.81 days. At the bottom of the output you see a section called POOLED VARIANCE ESTIMATE. It says the value of the test statistic is $t = .93$. With $df = 20$ and our conducting a *two-tailed test*, the observed significance of the test is $p = .363$. That is fine, but the hypothesis dictated a one-tailed test. (The computer automatically calculates the significance of the test only for a two-tailed test.) The transition to a one-tailed test should not be a difficult one. The computer output means that 36.3 percent of the area under the *t* distribution lies in the upper tail above .93 standard-error unit above the mean *and* in the lower tail below .93 standard-error unit below the mean. One-half of that area, or about 18 percent, lies in each tail. If you were to conduct a one-tailed test, as required here, the observed significance of the test would be $p = \frac{1}{2}(.363) = .18$. The probability of being wrong if you decide to reject the null hypothesis is high—$p = .18$. I decide not to reject. I cannot claim, on the basis of these data, that specialists keep their "normal birth" patients in hospital longer than the nonspecialists.

Paired Samples

The tests of two means described so far all involve *independent samples*. A common and powerful experimental design has the researcher carefully match cases into pairs; subject one case from each pair to one experimental condition, subject the other member of the pair to another condition; and compare the results. Matching cases into pairs helps control the effects of extraneous factors that might influence the outcome of an experiment. However, matching pairs invalidates the tests described to this point since the "two samples" that result from such a selection are not independently drawn. The design dictates that the two samples be utterly dependent on one another. There is a way to overcome this difficulty. You conduct a *t test for a paired-difference experiment*.

Consider the following situation. A researcher is interested in the relative merits of two approaches to teaching music. Ten sets of identical twins are recruited for an experiment. One twin from each pair is randomly assigned to be taught by method 1. The other twin gets training via method 2. Musical ability is assessed after the training and is scored between 0 and 100. Pairing across experimental conditions controls for the effects of genetic complement and social upbringing, two factors known to affect musical ability. Because the pairing controls the effects of these two important factors, any differences in ability noted at the end of the training must have been due to the differences in methods, the researcher could argue.

The results of this experiment are shown in Figure 8.10*a*. If you treated the results of the experiment *as if* the samples under method 1 and method 2 were independent of one another, you would have to conclude that the null hypothesis cannot be rejected ($t = .54$, df $= 18$, $p > .20$ for a two-tailed test).

But this is odd. If you look at the results, in 9 out of the 10 pairs, method 2 produced better results than method 1. In a case like this, it is more appropriate to find the difference within each pair and then conduct a *t* test on the average difference score.

Figure 8.10*b* shows the appropriate sample statistics. The two samples are now considered as a single sample. It is a sample of difference scores, one for each of the 10 pairs. The mean difference score is $\bar{X}_{\text{diff}} = 4.9$. The standard deviation of the difference score is $s_{\text{diff}} = 4.7$. You can conduct a "single-sample *t* test" of the null hypothesis

$$H_0: \mu_{\text{diff}} = 0$$

and the alternative

$$H_A: \mu_{\text{diff}} = 0$$

You find that if the null hypothesis is true, then the mean difference of 4.9 lies

$$t = \frac{4.9 - 0}{4.7/\sqrt{10}} = 3.3$$

Twin Pair	Method 1	Method 2
1	68	74
2	51	55
3	42	56
4	81	84
5	72	68
6	31	39
7	61	68
8	71	74
9	82	84
10	19	25
	$\bar{X}_1 = 57.8$	$\bar{X}_2 = 62.7$
	$s_1 = 21.4$	$s_2 = 19.2$

(a)

Twin Pair	Method 1	Method 2	Difference
1	68	74	6
2	51	55	4
3	42	56	14
4	81	84	3
5	72	68	-4
6	31	39	8
7	61	68	7
8	71	74	3
9	82	84	2
10	19	25	6
		$\bar{X}_{\text{diff}} =$	4.9
		$s_{\text{diff}} =$	4.7

(b)

FIGURE 8.10 (a) Results of musical training of identical twins, treated as two independent samples. (b) Results of musical training of identical twins, treated as a paired-difference experiment.

standard errors out on the tail of a t distribution with $n - 1 = 10 - 1 = 9$ degrees of freedom. From the table of t distributions, the observed significance of the test is $p < .01$. Were the level to reject .01 or greater, you would decide to reject the null hypothesis and conclude that method 2 is superior to method 1 for musical training.

. . .

CAUTION: THE SIGNIFICANCE OF "SIGNIFICANCE"

Any time the word "significant" or the phrase "statistically significant" is used, it means the researcher has conducted a test of a hypothesis about a population parameter and has rejected a null hypothesis. If a researcher says a test is "not significant," that means he or she failed to reject the null hypothesis. The *level of significance*, which a researcher usually makes explicit, is simply the probability of the person's being wrong in deciding to reject the null hypothesis.

Just to make certain you understand this point, consider a final example. Suppose someone says to you that the difference between mean schizophrenia scores of those with authoritarian fathers and those with nonauthoritarian fathers is "significant at the .05 level." Then this person adds that the difference between mean schizophrenia scores for those with authoritarian mothers and those with non-authoritarian mothers is "significant at the .001 level." There is a temptation to think that mothers' authoritarianism is the stronger determinant of schizophrenia. You cannot, however, say this from the information given. Both statements simply mean that in the populations from which the samples were drawn, parental authoritarianism is *probably not unrelated* to schizophrenia score. The null hypothesis of equal population means can be rejected. There is a smaller chance of the decision to reject the null hypothesis being wrong in the case of mothers' authoritarianism than in the case of fathers' authoritarianism. That is what the different levels of significance tell you. But neither of these statements says anything about the strength of the relationship or even about the direction of the relationship between variables. From the information given, you cannot tell whether either parent's authoritarianism is strongly or weakly associated with the likelihood of developing schizophrenia. Nor can you tell whether the likelihood of developing schizophrenia goes up or down with increased levels of parental authoritarianism. The word "significant" means only one thing: The null hypothesis has been rejected. The level of significance tells you only the probability that you have incorrectly decided to reject the null hypothesis.

One writer was especially critical of overreliance on hypothesis testing and the observed significance of a test. David D. Salsburg, writing in *The American*

Statistician, aimed his barbs at the medical profession, but his comments apply with equal force to those in any field who go through the ritualized motions of statistical analysis without understanding what they are doing. Salsburg says,

> After 17 years of interacting with physicians, I have come to realize that many of them are adherents of a religion they call *Statistics*. It bears some resemblance to the mathematical theories and practices described in journals like this one [*The American Statistician*], using many of the same words, but it reflects activity in only a small portion of the statistical world— the use of hypothesis tests. To the physician who practices this religion, Statistics refers to the seeking out and interpretation of *p* values. Like any good religion, it involves vague mysteries capable of contradictory and irrational interpretation. It has a priesthood and a class of mendicant friars. And it provides Salvation: Proper invocation of the religious dogmas of Statistics will result in publication in prestigious journals. This form of Salvation yields fruit in this world (increases in salary, prestige, invitations to speak at meetings) and beyond this life (continual references in the citation indexes) . . . .
>
> The practitioner [of the religion of Statistics] engages in a ritual known as "hunting for *p* values." He manipulates the data derived from an experiment according to a set of apparently irrational rules . . . . Once the calculations are completed, the computer output (or the screen of the minicomputer, the crystal liquid diodes of the calculator, or the final line of the tally sheets) will present the practitioner with a *p* value.
>
> At this point, the practitioner must be prepared to suffer the wrath of the angry gods of Statistics. If the *p* value is bigger than .05, he will not be allowed to publish. It may even mean running another experiment. If he is clever, the practitioner may find ways to modify the original data (leaving out numbers that are obviously wrong is the most common practice) and invoke the gods again. The gods are a bit stupid. Even if you run various modifications of the data through the same computer program again and again, the gods never catch on and keep presenting you with new *p* values. Sometimes, however, no manipulation of the data will produce a *p* value of less than .05. The sensible practitioner will remember that we live in an unfair and irrational world and accept his defeat. Salvation comes to an elect few, but the religion is not unrelenting. Perhaps it will present the practitioner with a *p* value of less than .05 for the next experiment.[2]

But now that you understand the somewhat convoluted but precise logic of hypothesis testing, you will never get trapped by such gods as these, because you will never have to worship at their altar.

• • •

KEY CONCEPTS IN THIS CHAPTER

• • •

NOTES

1. R. A. Fisher, *Design of Experiments,* Olive and Boyd, Edinburgh, Scotland, 1935.

2. David S. Salsburg, "The Religion of Statistics as Practiced in Medical Journals," *The American Statistician* 39: 220, August 1985.

• • •

EXERCISES

Chapter 8

1. Here are regions of rejection for a test about a single population mean. Draw a picture of the sampling distribution for y if the sample is large. Shade the area under the distribution, and put a line under the region of rejection. Finally, determine the level to reject implied by the rejection region.

    a. $y > 1.645$
    b. $y < -1.645$ or $y > 1.645$
    c. $y < -2.32$
    d. $y < -2.32$ or $y > 2.32$
    e. $y > 2.58$
    f. $y < -2.58$ or $y > 2.58$

    2. Here are regions of rejection for a test about a single population mean. Draw a picture of the sampling distribution for y if the sample is of size n. Shade the area under the distribution, and put a line under the region of rejection. Finally, determine the level to reject implied by the rejection region.

    a. $y > 3.078$, $n = 2$
    b. $y < -2.353$ or $y > 2.353$, $n = 4$
    c. $y < -2.718$ or $y > 2.718$, $n = 12$
    d. $y > 1.746$, $n = 17$
    e. $y < -1.96$, $n = 42$
    f. $y < -2.807$ or $y > 2.807$, $n = 24$

    3. With the information given about random samples of size n drawn from populations with unknown μ and σ, construct the alternative hypothesis and decide if the null hypothesis can be rejected at a level to reject of .05.

    a. H_0: $\mu = 0$, $n = 60$, $\bar{X} = 2.34$, $s = 2.34$
    b. H_0: $\mu = 100$, $n = 1000$, $\bar{X} = 106.4$, $s^2 = 4.9$
    c. H_0: $\mu = -7.7$, $n = 45$, $\bar{X} = 0$, $s = 14.2$
    d. H_0: $\mu = 6.3$, $n = 13$, $\bar{X} = 8.5$, $s^2 = 2.8$
    e. H_0: $\mu = 45.8$, $n = 10$, $\bar{X} = 48.9$, $s = 1.0$
    f. H_0: $\mu = 0$, $n = 6$, $\bar{X} = 0$, $s = 0.001$
    g. H_0: $\mu = 2.3$, $n = 30$, $\bar{X} = 7.3$, $s^2 = 10$

    4. With the information given about random samples of size n drawn from populations with unknown μ and σ, construct the alternative hypothesis and decide if the null hypothesis can be rejected at a level to reject of .01.

    a. H_0: $\mu = 0$, $n = 60$, $\bar{X} = 2.34$, $s = 2.34$
    b. H_0: $\mu = 100$, $n = 1000$, $\bar{X} = 106.4$, $s^2 = 4.9$
    c. H_0: $\mu = -7.7$, $n = 45$, $\bar{X} = 0$, $s = 14.2$
    d. H_0: $\mu = 6.3$, $n = 13$, $\bar{X} = 8.5$, $s^2 = 2.8$
    e. H_0: $\mu = 45.8$, $n = 10$, $\bar{X} = 48.9$, $s = 1.0$
    f. H_0: $\mu = 0$, $n = 6$, $\bar{X} = 0$, $s = 0.001$
    g. H_0: $\mu = 2.3$, $n = 30$, $\bar{X} = 7.3$, $s^2 = 10$

    5. With the information given about two random samples of sizes n_1 and n_2 taken from two populations with unknown means and variances, construct the alternative hypothesis and decide if the null hypothesis can be rejected at the level to reject α shown.

   a. $H_0: \mu_1 = \mu_2$, $n_1 = 30$, $n_2 = 30$, $\bar{X}_1 = 15.4$, $\bar{X}_2 = 18.3$,
      $s_1 = 1.46$, $s_2 = 1.64$, $\alpha = .01$
   b. $H_0: \mu_1 < \mu_2$, $n_1 = 15$, $n_2 = 15$, $\bar{X}_1 = 1064$, $\bar{X}_2 = 1178$,
      $s_1 = 10.8$, $s_2 = 18.9$, $\alpha = .05$
   c. $H_0: \mu_1 > \mu_2$, $n_1 = 89$, $n_2 = 99$, $\bar{X}_1 = 11.9$, $\bar{X}_2 = 12.7$,
      $s_1 = 3.8$, $s_2 = 4.0$, $\alpha = .10$
   d. $H_0: \mu_1 = \mu_2$, $n_1 = 11$, $n_2 = 13$, $\bar{X}_1 = 1.106$, $\bar{X}_2 = 1.724$,
      $s_1 = .12$, $s_2 = .34$, $\alpha = .05$

   6. With the information given about a random sample of size n taken from a population with an unknown population proportion, p, construct the alternative hypothesis and decide if the null hypothesis can be rejected at the level to reject α shown.

   a. $H_0: p = .20$, $n = 450$, $\hat{p} = .28$, $\alpha = .05$
   b. $H_0: p = .50$, $n = 1500$, $\hat{p} = .39$, $\alpha = .01$
   c. $H_0: p = .98$, $n = 400$, $\hat{p} = .96$, $\alpha = .05$
   d. $H_0: p = .82$, $n = 1458$, $\hat{p} = .75$, $\alpha = .01$
   e. $H_0: p < .30$, $n = 350$, $\hat{p} = .38$, $\alpha = .01$

   7. For purposes of this problem, you should think of the countries in Appendix A as the population. Draw a random sample of size $n = 10$ from the population.

   a. What is the population mean μ of per capita income?
   b. What is the sample mean of per capita income for the sample?
   c. What is the population standard deviation of per capita income?
   d. Does your sample provide evidence that the sample came from a population with a mean different from the overall mean of per capita income? Test the null hypothesis, using the first sample with a level to reject of .10.
   e. Explain why the question in part (d) is not as silly as it sounds.
   f. If all the students in your class did this problem, about how many would you expect to reject the null hypothesis?

   8. Suppose our man in Dublin did a small experiment in brewing. He brewed some beer with a short fermentation time and other beer with a longer fermentation time. He let the beer set, properly stored, and measured its "shelf life." He had eight samples from each batch, and here, in days, is the shelf life:

Batch	1	2	3	4	5	6	7	8
Short ferment	22	19	26	24	28	26	20	19
Long ferment	21	20	16	13	19	29	12	19

If you knew that the average shelf life of a barrel of beer from Dublin was, in fact, 20.5 days and the standard deviation around that mean was 2.1 days, would you say there is evidence that the sample of 16 batches drawn for this experiment is unrepresentative of all beer brewed in terms of its central shelf-life value?

> **a.** Calculate the sample mean.
> **b.** Construct a null hypothesis and an alternative designed to answer the question.
> **c.** Do the necessary calculations, using appropriate statistics, and answer the question.

9. Is there a difference between the shelf life of short-fermentation beer and that of long-fermentation beer?

10. Would you do a one-tailed or a two-tailed test on the following hypotheses?

> **a.** Catholics have a lower suicide rate than Protestants.
> **b.** Costs to patients who see a specialist are higher than those to patients who see a general practitioner.
> **c.** Low-urbanization countries tend to have higher per capita incomes than high-urbanization countries.
> **d.** Female athletes have a greater heart-stroke volume than male athletes.
> **e.** Heart-stroke volume is associated with the risk of heart disease.
> **f.** Smoking is related to deaths from lung cancer.

For all the following problems, choose a level to reject at which you want to conduct each test. Justify your choice in terms of the kind of error—Type I or Type II—you would rather make.

11. There are 12 doctors who discharged patients in DRG 384. There seems to be considerable variation in the percentages of the total charges devoted to "material and technology." This variation may be due to specialization: More specialized physicians spend a higher percentage of their total charges on material and technology. Is there a significant difference in the percentages of the total charges in DRG 384 devoted to "material and technology" for the two groups of physicians formed on the basis of specialization score?

12. Is there a significant difference between the work and the leisure groups on the amount of "time spent on word game" in the first internal-motivation experiment? Interpret your results.

13. Create two sets of countries, one with low male life expectancy and one with high male life expectancy. Is there a significant difference between literacy rates for these two groups. Interpret your results.

14. In the first internal-motivation experiment, create two groups of subjects by dividing them on the basis of Protestant work ethic. Is there a statistically significant difference in Type A personality scores of the two groups? Interpret your results.

15. If the federal reimbursement scheme allows hospitals to charge for 2 days in hospital for discharges in DRG 373 and the data in Appendix A are representative of patients paid for by federal schemes, is there evidence in the data that this hospital will make a profit in DRG 373 patients? That is, is there evidence that the hospital from which these data came discharges patients in significantly less time than 2.0 days?

16. This question refers to Exercise 9 in Chapter 4. Are average total costs for procedures with complications significantly greater than those for procedures without complications?

17. This question refers to Exercise 10 in Chapter 4. Are physician 02's average charges significantly different from physician 01's charges?

18. This question refers to Exercise 6 in Chapter 3. Are these patients' temperatures, on average, significantly different from normal?

19. This question refers to Exercise 7 in Chapter 3. If these were randomly chosen stocks, is there evidence in the sample that the market changed on this day?

20. This question refers to Exercise 8 in Chapter 3. Are people with children at home significantly older than people without children at home?

21. This question refers to Exercise 9 in Chapter 3. Do gardens that use a lot of fertilizer produce significantly larger ears of corn than gardens that use little fertilizer? (Make the break between "little" and "a lot" of fertilizer however you wish, but justify your decision.)

22. This question refers to Exercise 10 in Chapter 3. If you know that in the whole school 15 percent of the students get A's, is there evidence in the sample for concluding that this sample is unrepresentative of the overall student population?

23. This question refers to Exercise 11 in Chapter 3. Do older people have significantly different IQs from younger people?

24. Draw a random sample of 20 countries from the list in Appendix A.

    a. Calculate the proportion of countries with a literacy rate greater than 50 percent.

    b. Is there a significant difference between the proportion of countries in the sample with a literacy rate of greater than 50 percent and the proportion of countries in the population of countries with literacy rates greater than 50 percent? Test this at the .05 level.

    c. If everyone in your class did this problem, approximately how many would reject the null hypothesis?

25. Draw a random sample of 30 countries from the list in Appendix A.

    a. Calculate the proportion of countries with a literacy rate greater than 50 percent.

b. Is there a significant difference between the proportion of countries in the sample with a literacy rate of greater than 50 percent and the proportion of countries in the population of countries with literacy literacy rates greater than 50 percent? Test this at the .50 level.

c. If everyone in your class did this problem, what proportion of the students would reject the null hypothesis?

d. Find out what proportion of students in the class had evidence on which to reject the null hypothesis.

e. Let the proportion you stated in part (**c**) be P, and let the sample proportion found in part (**d**) be P^*. If p is the true proportion of students who would reject the null hypothesis in the population of students from which your class came, is there evidence that allows you to reject the null hypothesis that $H_0: p = P$ based on the sample proportion P^*? Test at the .05 level.

26. If you knew that, across the country, hospital charges for surgery in obstetrical DRGs was 8.4 percent of the bill, is there evidence that the patients in the hospital from which these data came are charged a greater proportion of their bills for surgery than the national average proportion?

27. Doctors in the hospital from which these data came have an overall specialization score of 72 percent. Is there evidence that physicians who provide obstetrical care tend to specialize more than their colleagues?

CHAPTER

9

▼

· · ·

Point and Interval Estimation

Tests of statistical hypotheses allow you to say where a population parameter is not—probably. If you are able to reject the null hypothesis, you can say, "I reject the null hypothesis, and therefore the difference in methods of musical training is *not equal* to zero (probably)," or, based on the evidence, "The population mean score on the Type A personality test among Chinese-speaking students is *not greater than or equal to* 80.5 (probably)," or "I conclude that Beth is *not* playing with fair dice (probably)."

Once you know where a parameter is not, it is natural to ask where it is. It may be helpful for partying purposes to reject the hypothesis that the mean of the population of throws of two dice from which Beth "sampled" her 50 rolls is not equal to 7.0. But it may be interesting to know, then, where the mean of the population from which Beth was sampling is located. It is only fair to complement a negative statement with a positive statement about a parameter. Of course, you can never know the true value of a population parameter unless you have data on the entire population, but you can develop *estimates* of population parameters based on sample statistics. This chapter discusses *parameter estimation*.

David Salsburg, the critic of overreliance on hypothesis testing, wrote of medical studies:

> Great effort has been expended on the planning and execution of large-scale studies in the U.S. and elsewhere . . . , and the result has been the accumulation of banks of well-structured data from carefully controlled and followed experiments . . . . In none of these studies, however, will the authors cast off the awkward cloak of hypothesis testing and treat the data as an exercise in *estimation of parameters* and the identification of reasonable subsets of patients [emphasis added].

Salsburg notes that physicians and policymakers alike need to know how long it will take a patient to respond to treatment (if a response is [probably] to be forthcoming). They do not need to know that the mean response time is "not less than or equal to zero (probably)." They need to know how large a change in symptoms might reasonably be expected and what those changes might be. They do not need to know that the change in symptoms is "not equal to zero (probably)." They need to know what kinds of side effects might appear and in what kinds of patients these effects are likely to occur, not just that "Older people do not experience the same side effects as younger people (probably)." Salsburg urges people in medicine and, by extension, other users of statistical studies to make estimates of population parameters, and not just try to reject null hypotheses about them.[1]

There are two types of estimates of population parameters, point estimates and interval estimates.

· · ·

POINT ESTIMATES

You have already estimated population parameters. In some hypothesis tests, s_x is used to estimate σ. In that case, a single number was used to estimate a parameter. This is a common way to estimate a population parameter: Simply give a single point on the number line as your estimate. Such estimates are called *point estimates* of population parameters.

There are many different ways to pick a single point on the number line as the estimate of a parameter. Some ways are good, others are less good.

For example, suppose you wanted to estimate the mean score on a final examination taken by a chemistry class of 400 people. The population consists of the class of 400 students. One way to estimate the mean is to pick a number at random. Go to a random number table and select the numbers 5, 0, and 6. Is 506 a good estimate of the mean score of the 400 students in the class? Probably not, since it is just a random number picked without any knowledge of the nature of the test or of the people who took it. If you were told the minimum possible score on the test was zero and the maximum possible score was 100, you would probably change your randomly chosen estimate so that it fell somewhere between 0 and 100. If you knew, furthermore, that the minimum and maximum actual scores on the test by members of the class were 14 and 87, respectively, you would change your randomly chosen estimate again, this time so that it was between 14 and 87.

All these randomly chosen numbers are *estimates* of the mean score, and the rule "Pick a random number that lies within the constraints imposed by what you know of the test and/or the results" is an *estimator rule*. The estimator tells you how to make an estimate of the mean score. You make estimates by using an estimator.

You could probably get a better estimate of the true mean if you made some effort to find out how some of the people in the population scored. For example, you could ask five people as they were leaving the test site how they think they scored. Then you could develop an estimator rule such as "Find the arithmetic average of the five guesses, and add 5 points (since students tend to underestimate their own examination scores)." Say you were told the following five scores: 17, 28, 65, 95, 54. Your estimate of the mean score, following the estimator rule, is $(17 + 28 + 65 + 95 + 54)/5 + 5 = 56.8$. You would have used some knowledge of the test and of some of the people who took it to develop an estimator rule that, in combination with some data, gave an estimate of the mean score.

Alternatively, you could ask the professor of the class for a random sample of 10 actual scores. Your estimator rule for estimating the overall population mean score might then be "Find the mean of this sample of 10 actual scores." Suppose the professor says, "I chose 10 students using a random number table. Here are their scores: 56, 17, 48, 65, 82, 81, 39, 49, 59, 84." Your point estimate of the mean will be 58.0 because the estimator rule says to calculate the sample mean of the sample of 10 scores you are given.

Obviously, you could develop many different estimates of the population mean because you could invent many different estimators. The question arises, How does one choose from among estimators and which estimate is the best?

Bias and Efficiency

As with anything, choosing the "best" requires that you specify the criteria by which "best" is to be judged. In the matter of point estimates of population parameters, statisticians have two principal criteria that together determine what is best: *bias* and *efficiency*.

The first criterion concerns an estimator's *bias*. The less biased an estimator, the better the estimates of a population parameter that it gives. An *estimator is unbiased* if the mean of the sampling distribution of the estimator is equal to the population parameter. An *estimator is biased* if the mean of the sampling distribution of the estimator is not equal to the population parameter.

The sample mean $\bar{X}$ is an unbiased estimator of the population mean μ. Why? Because the mean of the sampling distribution of $\bar{X}$, or $\mu_{\bar{x}}$, is equal to the population mean μ. And s_x^2, where

$$s_x^2 = \frac{\sum_{i=1}^{n} (X_i - \bar{X})^2}{n - 1}$$

is an unbiased estimator of the population variance σ_x^2, where

$$\sigma_x^2 = \frac{\sum_{i=1}^{N} (X_i - \mu)^2}{N}$$

because the mean of the sampling distribution of s_x^2, with $n - 1$ in the denominator, is equal to σ_x^2. That is, $\mu_{s_x^2}^2 = \sigma_x^2$.

If n is substituted for $n - 1$ in the denominator of the formula for s_x^2 above, the result has a sampling distribution with a mean smaller than the actual population variance. Using n in the denominator yields a "negatively biased" estimate of σ_x^2.

The bias of an estimator is sometimes dependent on the nature of the population whose parameters you are trying to estimate. For example, if the population is symmetrically distributed, the sample median is an unbiased estimator of the population mean μ. If the population is symmetrically distributed and the distribution has only one mode, the mode is also an unbiased estimator of the population mean μ. If the population is skewed, the median and the mode both provide biased estimates of μ while $\bar{X}$ remains an unbiased estimator of μ.

There may be several unbiased estimators of a population parameter. A second criterion for judging estimators may allow you to choose the "best" of the unbiased estimators. The second criterion in the selection of a point estimator of a population parameter is the *efficiency* of the estimator. One estimator is more efficient than another if the variance of the sampling distribution of the first estimator is smaller than the variance of the sampling distribution of the second estimator.

If both $\bar{X}$ and the median are unbiased estimators of μ in symmetrically distributed populations, which should you choose as a point estimator of μ? You should choose the estimator with the smaller variance of its sampling distribution. That is, you should choose the estimator that, on average, comes closer to the population mean. You should select the more efficient estimator. You know the standard deviation of the sampling distribution of the sample mean $\bar{X}$. It is equal to the population standard deviation of X divided by the square root of the sample size n. That is,

$$\sigma_{\bar{X}} = \frac{\sigma}{\sqrt{n}}$$

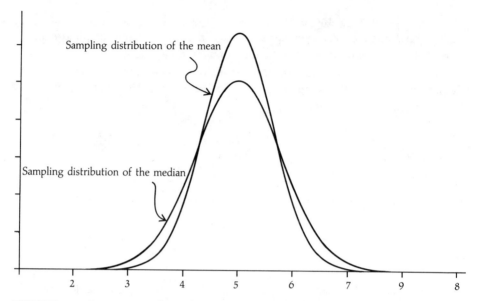

FIGURE 9.1 Comparison of sampling distributions of mean and of median of variable that is symmetrically distributed.

The variance of the sampling distribution is then

$$\sigma_{\overline{X}}^2 = \left(\frac{\sigma}{\sqrt{n}}\right)^2 = \frac{\sigma^2}{n}$$

If the population is symmetrically distributed, the sampling distribution of the median is normal and has a mean of μ (that is, the median is an unbiased estimate of μ), but it has a variance of $1.57\sigma^2/n$. The variance of the sampling distribution of the median is more than one and one-half times the variance of the sampling distribution of $\overline{X}$. The sampling distribution of $\overline{X}$ and the sampling distribution of the median, each for samples of size 10 for a symmetrically distributed variable with a population mean of 5 and population standard deviation of 2, are shown in Figure 9.1. You can see that, on average, a single $\overline{X}$ from the sampling distribution of the mean will be closer to μ than a single selection from the distribution of the median. Therefore $\overline{X}$ is a more efficient estimator of μ than is the median. In fact, $\overline{X}$ is the best estimator of the population mean μ.

$\cdot$ $\cdot$ $\cdot$

INTERVAL ESTIMATES

Point estimates of parameters are helpful, but they are not terribly useful for indicating where a population parameter *probably* is. There is no probability that the population parameter is equal to the point estimate. Either the estimate is equal to the parameter or it is not; furthermore, there is no way to tell. Inferential statistics has another approach to estimation that tells you where a population parameter may be and how much confidence you can have that the parameter is where the estimate says it is. *Interval estimates* provide a range of values in which the population parameter may lie and a statement of the confidence you may have that the parameter actually is in the interval.

Interval Estimates of the Population Mean

Where is μ? You can construct an interval estimate of μ around a point estimate of μ. Interval estimates are constructed around sample statistics. Sample statistics, remember, vary around their corresponding true population parameter. That variation is described by the sampling distribution of the sample statistic. In a specifiable proportion of times you construct an interval estimate of a parameter around a sample statistic, the interval will contain the parameter.

Consider the problem of estimating the population mean. The best point estimate of μ is $\bar{X}$. Figure 9.2 shows the sampling distribution of $\bar{X}$. It has a mean of μ and a standard deviation of $\sigma/\sqrt{n}$. It is a normal distribution, so about 68 percent of the area under the distribution is contained between 1 standard deviation above the mean and 1 standard deviation below the mean. Between 2 standard deviations on either side of the mean lies approximately 95 percent (more accurately, 95.44 percent) of the area under the distribution. That is, 68 percent of the time a sample mean $\bar{X}$ will lie within 1 standard deviation of the true population mean μ, and about 95 percent of the time a sample mean $\bar{X}$ will lie within 2 standard deviations of the true population mean μ. [Actually, 95 percent of the time $\bar{X}$ will lie within 1.96 standard deviations of μ. At z = 1.96, 0.025 (or 2.5 percent) of the area under

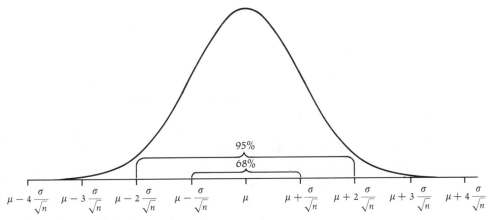

FIGURE 9.2 Sampling distribution of the mean with percentages of the area under the distribution shown.

the normal distribution lies under the tail beyond z. Therefore, 5 percent of the area under the distribution lies under the two tails, one below $z = -1.96$ and one above $z = 1.96$.]

The step from understanding the area under the normal distribution to constructing a confidence interval is only a little tricky. If $\bar{X}$ lies within 1.96 standard deviations of μ some 95 percent of the time, then 95 percent of the intervals that extend from 1.96 standard-error units below $\bar{X}$ to 1.96 standard-error units above $\bar{X}$ will contain the actual mean of the sampling distribution, which is the mean of variable X. To put it a little more mathematically, if you construct an interval around $\bar{X}$ that extends from $\bar{X} - 1.96\sigma_{\bar{X}}$ to $\bar{X} + 1.96\sigma_{\bar{X}}$, that interval will contain the actual mean of the distribution, μ, some 95 percent of the time. Put another way, μ will lie in the interval $\bar{X} - 1.96\sigma/\sqrt{n}$ to $\bar{X} + 1.96\sigma/\sqrt{n}$ some 95 percent of the times you construct intervals that are 3.92 standard errors wide around a sample mean $\bar{X}$. [The intervals are 3.92 standard errors wide since $\bar{X} + 1.96\sigma/\sqrt{n} - (\bar{X} - 1.96\sigma/\sqrt{n}) = 3.92\sigma/\sqrt{n}$.]

The interval from $\bar{X} - 1.96\sigma/\sqrt{n}$ to $\bar{X} + 1.96\sigma/\sqrt{n}$ is an *interval estimate* of the population parameter μ. Does this interval estimate of μ actually contain the parameter μ? Not necessarily, but you can be relatively confident that it does. The probability is .95 that μ actually lies in an interval constructed in this manner around a specific sample mean $\bar{X}$. That probability of .95 is called a *confidence coefficient*, and the interval constructed around a point estimate so that it has a probability of .95 of containing μ is called a *95 percent confidence interval*. You can have a 95 percent level of confidence that an interval constructed around a single sample mean $\bar{X}$ that is constructed as $\bar{X} + 1.96\sigma/\sqrt{n}$ contains μ.

An example will help. I randomly select 35 countries from the list of 142 in Appendix A. The sample mean per capita income (PCI) is $2140, so $2140 is a point estimate of the actual population mean of per capita income, μ_{PCI}, of the 142 countries. You can build an interval around this point estimate to create an interval estimate of the mean per capita income μ_{PCI}.

If I wanted to have a confidence level of 95 percent that the interval would contain μ_{PCI}, I would construct the interval to extend from $2140 - 1.96\sigma_{PCI}/\sqrt{n}$ to $2140 + 1.96\sigma_{PCI}/\sqrt{n}$. I known from previous work that $\sigma_{PCI} = 3270$. The sample size is $n = 35$, so the standard error of the mean is $3270/\sqrt{35} = 553$. Thus, a 95 percent confidence interval of μ_{PCI} is the interval $2140 - (1.96)(533)$ to $2140 + (1.96)(553)$, or $1056 to $3224. Does this interval contain μ_{PCI}? If I knew nothing about the population, I would know only that the probability that μ_{PCI} lies between $1056 and $3224 is .95. In this example, I know that $\mu_{PCI} = 2335, and the population mean does, in fact, lie in the interval.

I had a computer select 20 random samples of 35 countries each from the population of 142 countries in Appendix A. I constructed a 95 percent confidence interval around each of the 20 sample means. The results are shown below the sampling distribution of the mean in Figure 9.3. The mean of the sampling distribution is $\mu = 2335.4$, and the standard error is still $3270/\sqrt{35} = 553$. The 20 means

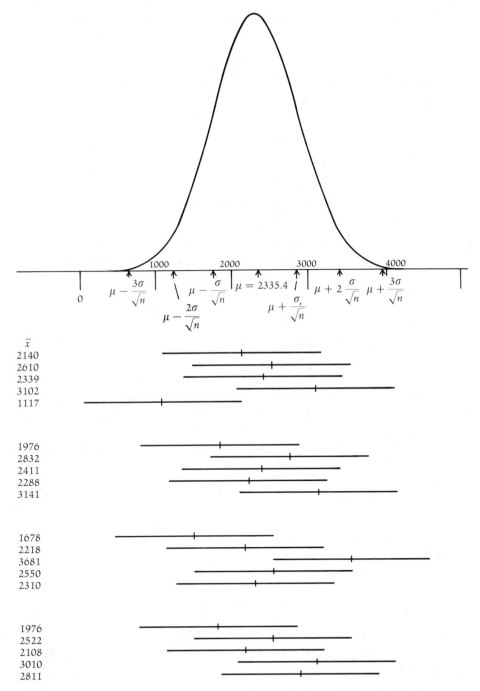

FIGURE 9.3 Twenty confidence intervals constructed around 20 means of random samples of size 35.

are shown on the left side of the figure. Each interval is the same width—2 ×
1.96 × 553 = 2168—but the intervals center at different spots, each on its own
sample mean $\bar{X}$. Eighteen of the intervals constructed in this way contain μ, the
population mean. That is, 90 percent of these 20 intervals capture the population
parameter that is being estimated. But this is just 20 samples and twenty 95 percent
confidence intervals. Over the very long run, 95 percent of the intervals constructed
in this way would contain the population parameter μ.

Figure 9.3 displays all the principles of interval estimation. To repeat: Intervals
are constructed around a sample statistic. The sample statistic varies around the
parameter. In a proportion of instances specified by the confidence coefficient, the
interval estimate will contain the population parameter.

In practice, you have only one sample (not 20), one sample mean $\bar{X}$ (not 20),
and thus one point estimate of μ. Therefore, you can only calculate one interval
estimate of μ. If your interval extends from $\bar{X} - 1.96\sigma/\sqrt{n}$ to $\bar{X} + 1.96\sigma/\sqrt{n}$, then
you can be 95 percent confident that this one interval contains the population
parameter μ.

You can change the level of confidence you wish to have that the interval
contains the parameter. Suppose you wanted to be only 90 percent confident that
the interval you constructed around a particular $\bar{X}$ contained μ. How wide would
the interval be? Go back to Figure 9.2. Of the area under the distribution, 68
percent is contained between 1 standard deviation below the mean and 1 standard
deviation above the mean; 95 percent lies within 1.96 standard deviations of either
side of the mean. So something more than 1 standard deviation but less than 1.96
standard deviations of either side of the mean μ contains 90 percent of the area. But
where exactly is that point? Look at the table of the standard normal distribution,
Appendix Table B.3. You want to find the point z^* where 5 percent of the area
lies under the tail beyond that point, so that 90 percent of the area under the normal
distribution will lie under the distribution between $\mu - z^*\sigma/\sqrt{n}$ and $\mu + z^*\sigma/\sqrt{n}$.
z^* is approximately equal to 1.645. A 90 percent confidence interval around $\bar{X}$ extends from $\bar{X} - 1.645\sigma/\sqrt{n}$ to $\bar{X} + 1.645\sigma/\sqrt{n}$. And 90 percent of the time this
interval will contain the population mean μ. The 90 percent confidence interval for
the mean per capita income based on samples of size 35 is from $\bar{X} - 1.645(3270)/\sqrt{35}$ to $\bar{X} + 1.645(3270)/\sqrt{35}$. In the case of the first sample, $\bar{X} = 2140$, so the
90 percent confidence interval extends from 1230 to 3050.

Notice that the 90 percent confidence interval is smaller than the 95 percent
confidence interval. This makes sense. If you want to be more confident that the
interval will contain the actual population parameter, you have to make the interval
wider. As you narrow an interval (and thereby get a better idea of where the
parameter might be located), the confidence you can have that the interval contains
the parameter must, necessarily, go down.

Salsburg has an intriguing proposal about estimating parameters. You want to
know if a drug or other treatment has some effect on a patient's condition. Suppose

patients tend to improve, $\theta > 0$. If patients tend to get worse as a result of the treatment, $\theta < 0$. If an interval estimate of θ contains zero, which indicates "no change," then you cannot conclude that the drug or treatment has a salutary effect on patients. Salsburg says, "Suppose we routinely compute three levels of confidence with coverage of 50 percent, 80 percent, and 99 percent . . . . [With a 50 percent confidence interval] we are more sure that the true value of the parameter is within that interval than outside it. The 80 percent interval contains information of which we are reasonably sure. The 99 percent interval contains information of which we are quite sure. Surely," he asserts, "a medical treatment can be considered worth using on the basis of a 50 percent interval . . . ." That is, if the 50 percent confidence interval does not contain $\theta = 0$, then you can be more certain than not that the drug or treatment has some beneficial effect. Salsburg continues: "[And we can argue for] wide use if [a treatment] does not involve serious adverse consequences on the basis of a 75 to 80 percent interval." A 75 to 80 percent interval is much wider than a 50 percent interval and so has a better chance of capturing $\theta = 0$ in it. If such a wide interval does not capture $\theta = 0$, then Salsburg thinks a treatment ought to get "wide use" if there are no serious side effects. Finally, he writes, "99 percent intervals [ought to be left] for issues in which the use of the treatment might entail very serious consequences."[2] If there are serious adverse effects of the drug or treatment, one ought to be quite sure that $\theta > 0$, he is saying. The way to do this is to construct a very wide interval—a 99 percent confidence interval. If that interval does not capture $\theta = 0$, you can be pretty sure it will have some positive effect on patients.

Constructing Intervals

As with hypothesis testing, a general scheme is followed in the construction of confidence intervals around point estimates of any parameter. This scheme has five steps.

1. Calculate the point estimate of the parameter. Call this sample statistic *E*. Now *E* should be the best point estimate—the most efficient of the unbiased estimators—of the parameter.

2. Choose the level of confidence with which you wish to assert that the interval contains the parameter. Call this level of confidence $1 - \alpha$. So for a .95 confidence coefficient, set α (the same alpha encountered as the level to reject) to .05 so that $1 - \alpha = 1 - .05 = .95$. The confidence interval is the "$100(1 - \alpha)$ percent confidence interval" since confidence intervals are expressed in percentages.

Remember, the greater the confidence with which you will claim the parameter is in the interval, the wider the interval and thus the less precise will be your statement about the location of the parameter. The more precise your statement (i.e., the narrower the confidence interval), the less confident you will be that the parameter is in the interval.

3. Determine the nature of the sampling distribution of the estimator. The sampling distribution may be a normal distribution, a t distribution, or some other distribution. You need to know the shape of the distribution, its mean, and its standard error. Call the standard error S.

4. Determine the distance on the sampling distribution—in standard errors— you have to move from the mean to capture the amount of area under the distribution equal to the confidence coefficient $1 - \alpha$ you selected in step 2. This distance—call it D—is the distance you have to move from the mean to capture $\alpha/2$ of the area under the distribution in one tail. On a normal distribution or on a t distribution, this distance D is equal to the boundary of the region of rejection in a two-tailed test with a level to reject of α. The table below lists the number of standard errors you need to move away from the mean of a standard normal distribution to capture the specified proportion of the area under the distribution:

Confidence $1 - \alpha$	α	Distance D
.50	.50	0.675
.80	.20	1.281
.90	.10	1.645
.95	.05	1.960
.99	.01	2.580

5. Form the confidence interval. If E is your point estimator, D is the distance from the mean that captures the appropriate area under the distribution, and S is the standard error of the estimator, then the interval ranges from $E - DS$ to $E + DS$. The $100(1 - \alpha)$ percent confidence interval estimate of the population parameter is the interval $E \pm DS$.

· · ·

ESTIMATING THE POPULATION MEAN

As with hypothesis testing, the construction of intervals varies from situation to situation even though the approach stays the same. In the example concerning per capita income, the interval was designed to estimate a population mean. The estimate was based on a large sample ($n = 35$) with a known population standard deviation σ. In that case the interval extends from $\bar{X} - z_{\alpha/2}\sigma/\sqrt{n}$ to $\bar{X} + z_{\alpha/2}\sigma/\sqrt{n}$, where $z_{\alpha/2}$ is the point on a standard normal distribution that captures $\alpha/2$ of the area under the distribution in one tail. And $z_{\alpha/2}$ is the lower bound of a rejection region for a two-tailed test with a level to reject of α, or equivalently the lower bound of rejection region for a one-tailed test with a level to reject of $\alpha/2$. The case of the per capita income estimate was a *large-sample* estimate of a population mean with a *known* σ. You may also encounter situations in which these two conditions—large sample and/or known σ—are not met.

Unknown Population Standard Deviation σ

If you do not know σ but the sample is large, then s_x is used to estimate σ, and the standard error of the mean is approximated by $s_x/\sqrt{n}$. Then the 100 $(1 - \alpha)$ percent confidence interval is

$$\bar{X} \pm z_{\alpha/2} \frac{s_x}{\sqrt{n}}$$

where, once again, $z_{\alpha/2}$ is the point in the tail of a normal distribution which bounds $\alpha/2$ of the area under the distribution.

As an example, let me return to a situation discussed in Chapter 8. I decided that the Chinese-speaking students in the second internal-motivation experiment did not come from a population whose mean work-ethic score was equal to the U.S. national norm of 80.5. If the mean of their population is not 80.5, what is it?

First, find a point estimate of the population mean. The sample mean is 84.25.

Second, choose the level of confidence $1 - \alpha$ which you want to have that the interval you construct will contain the actual population work-ethic mean score. Choose a level of confidence of .95, and construct a 95 percent confidence interval estimate of the mean.

Third, describe the sampling distribution. The sampling distribution of the mean is normal with an estimated standard error of $s/\sqrt{n}$, or $9.334/\sqrt{40} = 1.48$.

Fourth, since $\alpha = .05$, you need to know the point on a normal distribution that captures $\alpha/2 = .05$ of the area of the distribution in each tail. That point is $z_{\alpha/2} = 1.96$.

Fifth, construct the interval. The interval estimate of the population mean of the work-ethic score is $84.25 - 1.96(1.48) = 81.35$ to $84.25 + 1.96(1.48) = 87.15$. You can be 95 percent confident that the population mean score on "work ethic" is between 81.35 and 87.15. (Note that the U.S. national norm of 80.5 is not in this interval.)

Small Samples

You use the *t* distribution to construct interval estimates of a mean when the sample size is small. Recall the sample of five throws of two dice. I will construct a 90 percent confidence interval estimate of the mean of the population from which this sample came. In that case (the data are in Chapter 8), $n = 5$, $\bar{X} = 9.2$, $s = 2.17$, and the standard error of the mean is estimated as $s/\sqrt{n} = 2.17/\sqrt{5} = 0.97$. In this case, $\alpha = .10$, so you need to find the point on a *t* distribution with 4 degrees of freedom that contains $\alpha/2$, or .05, of the area under the distribution in each tail. To find that point, you look at the two-tailed t distribution with df $= 5 - 1 = 4$ and a level to reject of 0.10, which in Appendix Table B.5 is equivalent to a one-tailed test with a level to reject of .05. At that point, $t_{\alpha/2} = 2.13$. The confidence interval, in general, is

$$\bar{X} \pm t_{\alpha/2} \frac{s}{\sqrt{n}}$$

In this particular case, the 90 percent confidence interval is $\bar{X} \pm 2.13(0.97) =$ 9.2 $\pm$ 2.07. You can be 90 percent confident that the true mean of the population from which this sample came lies between 7.13 and 11.27. To be 95 percent confident that the interval contains the mean of the population from which this sample came, you have to enlarge the interval to $\bar{X} \pm 2.78(0.97)$, that is, the interval would extend from 6.50 to 11.90

· · ·

INTERVAL ESTIMATES OF A POPULATION PROPORTION

Do you ever read the fine print in those ubiquitous opinion polls? They always say something like, "Based on a sample of 1500 adults phoned at home between March 5 and 7. Percentages accurate within 3 percent." Or simply, "± 3 percent accuracy." Now you are in a position to understand what that means. It is—you guessed—an expression of an interval estimate of the true population proportion that is estimated by the proportion of people in the sample who gave a particular answer.

This is going to be easy now that you have been through the logic of interval estimation several times. But let's estimate the true proportion of the U.S. population that believes abortion should be okay for any reason.

Recall that in the General Social Survey (GSS) of 1406 people, 578 people said yes to the question, "Do you think abortion should be okay for any reason?" The sample proportion $\hat{p}$ is a good estimator of the true population proportion p. That is, the point estimate of p is $\hat{p} = 578/1406 = .411$.

Suppose you want to construct a 99 percent confidence interval to be very confident that the interval actually contains p, the true proportion of the U.S. population that approves of abortion. The sampling distribution of $\hat{p}$ is a binomial distribution; but as long as the sample is large ($n\hat{p} > 5$, $n\hat{q} > 5$, and $n > 20$), it is well approximated by a normal distribution. The standard error of $\hat{p}$ is estimated by $\sqrt{\hat{p}\hat{q}/n}$. In this case, the estimate of the standard error of the sample proportion is $\sqrt{(.411)(.589)/1406} = .013$. For a 99 percent confidence interval with an underlying normal distribution, the distance from the mean that captures $\alpha/2 = 0.01/2 = .005$ of the area under the distribution is $z_{\alpha/2} = 2.58$ standard errors from the mean. The 99 percent confidence interval for a population proportion extends from $\hat{p} - 2.58\sqrt{\hat{p}\hat{q}/n}$ to $\hat{p} + 2.58\sqrt{\hat{p}\hat{q}/n}$. The interval estimate of the proportion of people who said abortion should be okay for any reason is $.411 \pm (2.58)(0.013)$, or the interval from .377 to .445. Very likely, at least 37.7 percent of the people in the United States approved of abortion for any reason.

Opinion polls seem to come in two sorts. The quick-and-dirty type that newspapers and local TV stations conduct usually has about 400 respondents. Sophisticated network polls and national polling organizations usually have samples of about 1500. In the quick-and-dirty variety, if $\hat{p}$ were .5, the standard error of the sampling distribution would be $\sqrt{(.5)(.5)/400} = .025$. A 95 percent confidence interval would extend $(1.96)(.025) = .049$, or about 5 percent, in either direction from the sample proportion. That is why polls of this sort often carry a footnote like, "Accurate within ± 5 percent." They really mean that the 95 percent confidence interval is 10 percent wide and centers on the sample proportion. Under similar circumstances, the standard error of the sample proportion for a large national poll would be $\sqrt{(.5)(.5)/1500} = 0.13$. A 95 percent confidence interval estimate of the population proportion in their case would extend $(1.96)(0.013) = .025$, or 2.5 percent, in either direction from the sample proportion. That is why their caveat says, "Accurate within ± 3 percent." (*Note:* $\hat{p} = .5$ provides the conservative case. As $\hat{p}$ gets larger or smaller, the standard error of the sample proportion decreases, as does the "margin of error.")

· · ·

INTERVAL ESTIMATES OF THE DIFFERENCE BETWEEN MEANS

We can move more quickly now since the logic of interval construction remains the same throughout other varieties of interval estimation. This section shows how to construct interval estimates of differences between two means. Three situations are possible: The samples may be independent and large, the samples may be independent and small, or the samples may be dependent on one another.

If two independent samples are large, then the difference between means ($\bar{X}_1 - \bar{X}_2$) has a sampling distribution that is normal, centered at $\mu_1 - \mu_2$, with a standard error of

$$\sigma_{\bar{X}_1 - \bar{X}_2} = \sqrt{\frac{\sigma_1^2}{n_1} + \frac{\sigma_2^2}{n_2}}$$

If you do not know the population variances, then the standard error is estimated by

$$\sigma_{\bar{X}_1 - \bar{X}_2} \cong \sqrt{\frac{s_1^2}{n_1} + \frac{s_2^2}{n_2}}$$

A 95 percent confidence interval for the difference in per capita income for low and high-urbanization countries can be constructed around the difference in sample means, which was $4161.67 − $737.62 = $3424.05. The interval will extend 1.96 standard errors in either direction from this point estimate of the actual difference in means $\mu_1 - \mu_2$. An estimate of the standard error is

$$\sqrt{\frac{s_1^2}{n_1} + \frac{s_2^2}{n_2}} = \sqrt{\frac{(1103.5)^2}{53} + \frac{(3549.3)^2}{52}} = 515.0$$

The interval extends from 3424.05 − (1.96)(515.0) to 3424.05 + (1.96)(515.0), or from $2414.65 to $4433.45. You can be 95 percent confident that minimally the true difference in mean per capita incomes of the two populations of countries is $2414.

If two independent samples are small, the sampling distribution of the difference between two sample means is a t distribution with $n_1 + n_2 - 2$ degrees of freedom which has a standard error estimated by

$$\sqrt{\frac{(n_1 - 1)s_1^2 + (n_2 - 1)s_2^2}{n_1 + n_2 - 2}\left(\frac{1}{n_1} + \frac{1}{n_2}\right)}$$

In the case of the teacher who claimed that men score better than women in his classes, we failed to reject the null hypothesis that there is a difference between the mean test scores of the populations of men and women. Failing to reject the null hypothesis means that the true difference between population means *may* be equal to zero. But what else might the difference $\mu_m - \mu_f$ equal? To answer this question, you can construct a confidence interval around the difference in sample means, which was $\bar{X}_m - \bar{X}_f = 5.76$. The estimate of the standard error of the difference between sample means was 10.85. A 90 percent confidence interval using a t distribution with $n_1 + n_2 - 2 = 8$ degrees of freedom (df) would extend $t_{\alpha/2} = 1.86$ standard errors in either direction from the point estimate of the difference between population means. (The point $t_{\alpha/2} = 1.86$ is the boundary that captures $\alpha/2 = .05$ of the t distribution, with df = 8, in each tail.) So the 90 percent confidence interval estimate of the difference between population means is 5.76 $\pm$ (1.86)(10.85) which is the interval from −14.4 to 25.9. You can say with 90 percent confidence that the actual difference between population means lies somewhere between the point where women outscore men by about 14 points and the point where men outscore women by about 26 points. In this context, this does not say much for the teacher's assertion.

Finally, return to the musical training of twins. Recall that this is a paired-difference experiment. Instead of treating the data as two samples (since the samples were dependent on each other), we subtracted, within each pair, the score of one subject from the score of the other subject. That left 10 difference scores which were used to test a hypothesis that the mean difference score in the population from which this *single* sample of size $n = 10$ came was zero. I rejected the null hypothesis at the .01 level. That meant that the actual difference in scores was not zero (probably).

How much difference, though, does method 2 make over method 1? Let me construct a 95 percent confidence interval around the point estimate of the difference $\bar{X}_{diff} = 4.9$. This is a small sample, so the sampling distribution of the mean difference score is distributed as a t distribution with $n - 1 = 9$ degrees of freedom. The distribution's standard error is estimated by $s_{diff}/\sqrt{n} = 4.7/\sqrt{10} = 1.49$. The point $t_{\alpha/2}$ on a t distribution with df $= 9$ that captures $\alpha/2 = 2.5$ percent of the area in each tail is $t_{\alpha/2} = 2.26$ standard errors from the mean. Therefore, the 95 percent confidence interval estimate of the mean difference score μ_{diff} is $\bar{X}_{diff} \pm (2.26) s_{diff}/\sqrt{n} = 2.9 \pm (2.26)(1.49)$, which is the interval from 3.4 to 6.4. You can say with 95 percent confidence that the actual difference between method 2 and method 1, or μ_{diff}, lies in the interval from 3.4 to 6.4.

· · ·

RELATIONSHIP BETWEEN HYPOTHESIS TESTING AND CONFIDENCE INTERVALS

You have probably guessed that there is a relationship between hypothesis testing and the construction of confidence intervals, since you use the same tables and many of the same statistics for both. The relationship is straightforward.

Suppose you have the null hypothesis that

$$H_0: \mu = 0$$

and your level to reject the null hypothesis is set at some specified α value, say α^*. Now suppose you construct a confidence interval around the sample mean $\bar{X}$ at a confidence level of $100(1 - \alpha^*)$ percent. If the interval you construct contains zero, the hypothesized value of the parameter, then you cannot reject the null hypothesis that $\mu = 0$ because μ *may* equal zero, among other values. In general, if a $100(1 - \alpha)$ percent confidence interval does not contain the value of the parameter specified in the null hypothesis, you can reject the null hypothesis at the α level of significance. If the interval does contain the value of the parameter against which you are testing the null hypothesis, then you cannot reject the null hypothesis at the α level of significance.

· · ·

DETERMINING SAMPLE SIZE

Suppose a researcher does use data, as I did earlier, from the internal-motivation experiments to conduct an investigation of Type A personality scores among Chinese-speaking students. The researcher decides that, in the experiments,

Chinese-speaking students scored above the U.S. national average Type A score (probably). This kind of study is a *preliminary study* of the Type A score since the data were not collected specifically to study Type A personality. But after the results of this preliminary investigation, the researcher may very well decide to do a full-blown study of Type A personality among Chinese-speaking students to estimate just how high their Type A scores are. A typical first question when one thinks about doing a study is, how many cases are needed, and how large should the sample be? With the tools acquired in this chapter, you can answer that question now.

An interval estimate of the mean Type A personality score of Chinese-speaking students is constructed as

$$\bar{X} \pm z_{\alpha/2} \frac{s_x}{\sqrt{n}}$$

Once you have a value of s_x and n, the $100(1 - \alpha)$ percent confidence interval estimate of μ extends

$$z_{\alpha/2} \frac{s_x}{\sqrt{n}}$$

units to either side of the point estimate $\bar{X}$. Call this length B, so that

$$B = z_{\alpha/2} \frac{s_x}{\sqrt{n}}$$

This equation gives you an initial insight into the answer to the question, "How large should the sample be?" You can see that as n increases, the width of the interval decreases, but the relationship is not linear. B decreases in proportion to the square root of n. So the larger n is, the more cases you have to add to the sample to achieve the same reductions in B, something like a case of decreasing marginal returns in economics.

But the equation above can provide an exact answer to the question of sample size. Squaring both sides and rearranging terms reveals that

$$n = \frac{z_{\alpha/2}^2 s_x^2}{B^2}$$

If you can specify how exact you want an interval estimate of μ to be (B), if you can specify the level of confidence you wish to have in your estimate [$100(1 - \alpha)$ percent, which requires a specification of α which leads to $z_{\alpha/2}$], and if you have a guess of s_x or some other way to specify s_x, then the sample size required of the experiment is given by the equation.

For example, suppose you want to do the study to estimate the mean Type A personality score among Chinese-speaking students, you want the estimate accurate within 1 test-score point, and you want to be 90 percent confident that the interval estimate of the mean score μ will actually contain μ. How large should the sample be? The information says $B = 1$ and $100(1 - \alpha)$ percent = 90 percent (so $\alpha = .10$). Because $\alpha = .10$, $z_{\alpha/x} = 1.645$. You have an estimate of s_x from the preliminary study: $s_x = 9.334$. Substituting these values into the equation, you find

$$n = \frac{z_{\alpha/2}^2 s_x^2}{B^2} = \frac{(1.645)^2 (9.334)^2}{1^2} = 235.8$$

You would need Type A personality scores from 236 students to have 90 percent confidence that an interval estimate of μ that is 2 test units wide constructed around the sample mean score of $\bar{X}$ actually contains μ.

The logic of determining sample sizes extends to all other situations. One more example should show you how to make the extension.

Suppose you want to conduct an opinion poll that will give a very accurate estimate of a true population proportion p. You want to be 95 percent confident that the interval estimate that is a total of 1 percentage point wide contains p. How large should the sample be?

If an interval estimate is a total of 1 percentage point wide, then $B = .005$. A 95 percent confidence interval has $\alpha = .05$. You know that

$$B = z_{\alpha/2} \sigma_{\hat{p}}$$

and that σ_p is estimated by $\sqrt{\hat{p}\hat{q}/n}$, so

$$B = z_{\alpha/2} \sqrt{\frac{\hat{p}\hat{q}}{n}}$$

Consequently,

$$n = \frac{z_{\alpha/2}^2 \hat{p}\hat{q}}{B^2}$$

To use the extreme case, let $\hat{p} = .5$. Then $n = (19.6)^2(.5)(.5)/(.005)^2 = 9.604/.000025 = 38,416$. You would need 38,416 cases to get a level of accuracy of $\pm .5$ percent. Do you see why national opinion polls settle for an accuracy level of ± 3 percent?

• • •

KEY CONCEPTS IN THIS CHAPTER

$\cdots$

NOTES

1. David S. Salsburg, "The Religion of Statistics as Practiced in Medical Journals," *The American Statistician* 39: 220–222, August 1985.
    2. Ibid., p. 223.

$\cdots$

EXERCISES

Chapter 9

Since there is a direct relationship between hypothesis testing and parameter estimation, there is a direct relationship between problems at the end of Chapter 8 and the problems here.

1. With the information given about random samples of size n drawn from populations with unknown μ and σ, construct 95 percent confidence interval estimates of the mean μ.

    a. $n = 60$, $\bar{X} = 2.34$, $s = 2.34$
    b. $n = 1000$, $\bar{X} = 106.4$, $s^2 = 4.9$
    c. $n = 45$, $\bar{X} = 0$, $s = 14.2$
    d. $n = 13$, $\bar{X} = 8.5$, $s^2 = 2.8$
    e. $n = 10$, $\bar{X} = 48.9$, $s = 1.0$
    f. $n = 6$, $\bar{X} = 0$, $s = 0.001$
    g. $n = 30$, $\bar{X} = 7.3$, $s^2 = 10$

2. With the information given about random samples of size n drawn from populations with unknown μ and σ, construct 99 percent confidence interval estimates of the mean μ.

    a. $n = 60$, $\bar{X} = 2.34$, $s = 2.34$
    b. $n = 1000$, $\bar{X} = 106.4$, $s^2 = 4.9$
    c. $n = 45$, $\bar{X} = 0$, $s = 14.2$
    d. $n = 13$, $\bar{X} = 8.5$, $s^2 = 2.8$
    e. $n = 10$, $\bar{X} = 48.9$, $s = 1.0$
    f. $n = 6$, $\bar{X} = 0$, $s = 0.001$
    g. $n = 30$, $\bar{X} = 7.3$, $s^2 = 10$

3. With the information given about two random samples of sizes n_1 and n_2 taken from two populations with unknown means and variances, construct a confidence interval estimate of the difference between means μ_1 and μ_2. Construct a $100(1 - \alpha)$ percent confidence interval using the α shown.

    a. $n_1 = 30$, $n_2 = 30$, $\bar{X}_1 = 15.4$, $\bar{X}_2 = 18.3$, $s_1 = 1.46$, $s_2 = 1.64$,
        $\alpha = .01$
    b. $n_1 = 15$, $n_2 = 15$, $\bar{X}_1 = 1064$, $\bar{X}_2 = 1178$, $s_1 = 10.8$, $s_2 = 18.9$,
        $\alpha = .05$
    c. $n_1 = 89$, $n_2 = 99$, $\bar{X}_1 = 11.9$, $\bar{X}_2 = 12.7$, $s_1 = 3.8$, $s_2 = 4.0$, $\alpha = .10$
    d. $n_1 = 11$, $n_2 = 13$, $\bar{X}_1 = 1.106$, $\bar{X}_2 = 1.724$, $s_1 = 0.12$, $s_2 = 0.34$,
        $\alpha = .05$

4. With the information given about a random sample of size n taken from a population with an unknown population proportion p, construct the $100(1 - \alpha)$ percent confidence interval estimate of the population proportion p.

    a. $n = 450$, $\hat{p} = .28$, $\alpha = .05$
    b. $n = 1500$, $\hat{p} = .39$, $\alpha = .01$
    c. $n = 400$, $\hat{p} = .96$, $\alpha = .05$
    d. $n = 1458$, $\hat{p} = .75$, $\alpha = .01$
    e. $n = 350$, $\hat{p} = .38$, $\alpha = .01$

5. For purposes of this exercises, you should think of the countries in Appendix A as the population. Draw a random sample of size $n = 10$ from the population.

    a. What is the population mean of per capita income?
    b. What is the sample mean of per capita income for the sample?
    c. What is the population standard deviation of per capita income?
    d. Construct a 90 percent confidence interval estimate of the mean of per capita income around the sample mean.
    e. Does your confidence interval capture the true population mean per capita income?
    f. If all the students in your class did this problem, about how many confidence intervals would capture the true population mean per capita income?

6. For this exercise, use the data on the brewing experiment in Exercise 8, Chapter 8.

   a. Construct a 90 percent confidence interval estimate of the shelf life of the beer.
   b. Construct a 95 percent confidence interval estimate of the shelf life of the beer.
   c. Construct a 95 percent confidence interval of the difference between the mean shelf life of short-fermentation beer and the mean shelf life of long-fermentation beer. Interpret your results.

7. This exercise is related to Exercise 11, Chapter 8, concerning the 12 doctors who discharged patients in DRG 384. Construct an estimate of the difference between percentages of the patients' bills devoted to "material and technology" for the two groups of physicians formed on the basis of specialization score. For this estimate let $\alpha = .10$.

8. Construct a 95 percent confidence interval estimate of the difference between the work and the leisure groups on the amount of time spent on word game in the first internal-motivation experiment. Interpret your results.

9. Create two sets of countries, one with low male life expectancy, the other with high male life expectancy. Construct a 99 percent confidence interval estimate of the difference between literacy rates for these two groups. Interpret your results.

10. In internal-motivation experiment 1, create two groups of subjects by dividing them on the basis of Protestant work ethic. Construct a 95 percent confidence interval estimate of the difference in Type A personality scores of the two groups. Interpret your results.

11. Construct a confidence interval estimate of the number of days patients are kept in the hospital if they are eventually discharged under DRG 373. As a hospital administrator who has to live with federal reimbursement schemes, should you make α large or small?

12. This question refers to Exercise 9 in Chapter 4. Construct a 95 percent confidence interval estimate of the difference in total costs for procedures with complications and the total costs for procedures without complications. Interpret your results.

13. This question refers to Exercise 10 in Chapter 4. Develop a 95 percent confidence interval estimate of the difference between physician 02's average charges and physician 01's charges. Interpret your results.

14. This question refers to Exercise 6 in Chapter 3. Construct an 85 percent confidence interval estimate of the mean temperature of the population of patients from which this sample came. Interpret your results.

15. This question refers to Exercise 7 in Chapter 3. If these stocks were randomly chosen, what is your estimate of the percentage change in the market for this day? Use $\alpha = .05$. Interpret your results.

16. This question refers to Exercise 8 in Chapter 3. Construct a 90 percent confidence interval estimate of the difference in ages of people with children at home and people without children at home. Interpret your results.

17. This question refers to Exercise 9 in Chapter 3. Construct a 99 percent confidence interval estimate of the difference in length of ears of corn harvested from gardens that use a lot of fertilizer and from gardens that use little fertilizer. (Make the break between "little" and "a lot" of fertilizer however you wish, but justify your decision.) Interpret your results.

18. This question refers to Exercise 10 in Chapter 3. Using these data, construct an 80 percent confidence interval estimate of the proportion of people in the school who get A's.

19. This question refers to Exercise 11 in Chapter 3. Construct a 50 percent confidence interval estimate of the difference in IQs between older and younger people. Interpret your results. Construct a 30 percent confidence interval estimate of the same difference. Interpret your results.

20. Draw a random sample of 20 countries from the list in Appendix A. Construct a 90 percent confidence interval estimate of the proportion of countries in the whole list that have literacy rates greater than 50 percent.

    a. Does your estimate contain the actual proportion of countries with a literacy rate greater than 50 percent?

    b. If everyone in your class did this exercise, approximately how many of their intervals would contain the actual population proportion.

21. Construct a 95 percent confidence interval estimate of the percentage of total hospital costs devoted to surgery. If you knew that across the country hospital charges for surgery in obstetrical DRGs is 8.4 percent of the bill, interpret your results.

22. Construct a 90 percent confidence interval estimate of the specialization score of the physicians represented in Appendix A. If you knew that doctors in the hospital from which these data came had an overall specialization score of 72 percent, interpret your results.

CHAPTER

10

▼

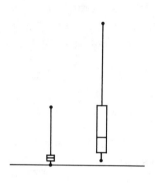

• • •

Introduction to Association and Statistical Independence

After so many pages, we have dealt primarily with statistics of one variable. The inferential tests about two population means allowed you to introduce a second variable into the analysis. For example, I used the variable "urbanization" in the analysis of another variable, "per capita income," in one instance in the last two chapters. Now it is time to take up two-variable analysis in a systematic way. This chapter moves from the discussion of *uni*variate statistics to a discussion of *bi*variate statistics. This chapter is an introduction to the concept of statistical association between variables. Specific techniques for measuring association are discussed in subsequent chapters.

Science asks, What makes things happen? Why do things change? Why are things different? Why is one case in one category of a variable and another case in another category? Are there similarities among the cases that are in one category and systematic differences between cases in different categories? Do these similarities and differences account for the observed distribution of cases across categories of a variable?

For early statisticians, questions of difference and change were pragmatic. For those working in agriculture, questions centered on the problem of producing better crop yields. Does more or less water improve production? Should one use more fertilizer or less? How is temperature related to yield? How is geographical orientation of the land related to yield?

For W. S. Gosset, our researcher at the Arthur Guinness and Son Brewery in Dublin, the question was, What influences the length of time beer remains palatable? Gosset conducted experiments to determine the relationships between length of fermentation, the amount of hops added, temperature at bottling—all independent variables to him—and the dependent variable, "shelf life" of the beer. He wanted to know if one variable or a combination of variables could be manipulated to produce longer-lasting brew.

G. Udny Yule, another student of Pearson, wondered what variables were associated with better health and living conditions. He was particularly interested in checking the spread of disease and ameliorating the lot of the poor by specific interventions.

Many of the early statisticians were eugenicists. They were interested in what makes people "well born" (well [*eu-*] born [*genesis-*]). Their eugenic interests made them ask what variables were related to intelligence and personal development. Eugenicists, of course, began with the hypothesis that personal traits are inherited. Their hypothesis was that people in the upper tail of the Law of Error tend to be born of parents from the upper tail, and those in the lower tail—those who were "dull"—tend to be born of parents who were themselves "dull."

Early statisticians developed their statistics in large part to test the eugenics hypothesis. They needed statistics that described relationships between two variables such as parents' intellectual abilities and offspring's intellectual abilities. They needed statistics that told them whether two variables varied together. They wanted to know if those cases in one category of one variable—e.g., "bright" on "offspring's ability"—tended to be in one category on another variable—"bright" on "parents' ability." They invented statistics that measured the degree to which two variables are associated with each other.

Statistics that measure the extent to which variables are associated, the extent to which they are correlated, the extent to which variables vary together—all of these terms mean the same thing—are called *measures of association.* This chapter discusses the concept of association and the related concept of statistical independence. It also shows how, in general, to measure the strength of association between two variables.

$\cdot \ \cdot \ \cdot$

ASSOCIATION AND STATISTICAL INDEPENDENCE

Before I discuss specific measures of association, the basic concept of "association" itself must be clear. This concept is the ground on which the remaining chapters of the text builds.

Always try to begin scientific investigations with a falsifiable statement of a relationship between two variables. Always begin with a hypothesis, if possible. Let me return to the example concerning the hypothesis about the relationship between per capita income and urbanization.

You know that the distribution of per capita income has one mode (in the $0–$1000 area), has a mean of $2335, and is skewed to the right (positively). Why are the 142 countries distributed in this manner? Is there another variable that might explain the overall shape of this distribution? That is, can you imagine another variable on which countries with high per capita income would tend, on average, to be either high or low and on which countries with low per capita income would tend, on average, to be either low or high? Is there a variable that is related to "per capita income," a variable that tends to vary with income?

My candidate for this variable is "urbanization." I think that countries with high urbanization rates tend to have high per capita incomes because of their tendency to have a vigorous industrial base; their tendency to have an available, mobile supply of labor; their tendency to have a banking system to mobilize capital investment; their ability to resist economic colonization; and so on. Countries with low urbanization tend not to have these things and would, I think, tend to have low per capita incomes. My hypothesis is that urbanization and per capita income are positively related to each other. Per capita income is, according to my hypothesis, dependent on urbanization. We write this as

$$\text{Urbanization} \overset{+}{\rightarrow} \text{Per capita income}$$

I may be wrong, but in order for this statement of relationship between two variables to be a hypothesis, it must be possible for the statement to be wrong.

To test this hypothesis, you just follow the logic that led to its formulation. Low urbanization rates tend, on average, to go with low per capita incomes, and high urbanization rates tend to go with high per capita incomes, the hypothesis says. So, as I did in Chapter 9, I will separate the 142 countries into those with low urbanization rates and those with high urbanization rates by breaking them at the median urbanization of 42.8 percent.

After dividing the countries into low- and high-urbanization countries, the question becomes, Is the average per capita income of low-urbanization countries lower than, higher than, or equal to the average per capita income of high-urbanization countries? You already have the tools to answer this question. You only need to calculate two sample means—the sample mean per capita income for the 52 low-urbanization countries and the sample mean per capita income of the 53 high-urbanization countries—and compare them.

The mean per capita income for the low-urbanization countries is $738, and the mean per capita income for the high-urbanization countries is $4097. The means are different. On average, then, high-urbanization countries tend to have much higher per capita incomes than low-urbanization. countries. *Conclusion*: The two variables "urbanization" and "per capita income" are related to each other. They vary together.

I have not done anything that is unfamiliar. I calculated two *conditional sample means* for "per capita income" and compared them.

Testing for a relationship between per capita income and urbanization was completely analogous to the dice game in which I "conditioned" the throws of the dice on the name of the thrower. I just separated countries into two conditional groups, groups conditioned on categories of the independent variable "urbanization," and compared the central tendencies of the two conditional distributions. I found them to be different. On average, high-urbanization countries have high per capita incomes, and low-urbanization countries have low per capita incomes. Urbanization and per capita income are positively related to each other. The hypothesis with which this investigation began is supported in the sample data.

Figures 10.1 and 10.2 are two ways to present the two conditional distributions of per capita income. In both figures, one distribution is of cases with urbanization

Per Capita Income (thousands)	Urbanization Less than 42.8				More than 42.8	
	10	20	30	40	5	10
0	4015606037425133042271035124413313 52432145				9887477867	
1	454210				65991181217	
2	2				3175067	
3	1				396031	
4	4				909	
5						
6	3 (Libya)				7036	
7					799	
8					46	
9		Leaves indicate the number			852	
10		in the hundreds' place of a			820	
11		country's per capita income				
12						
13						
14						
15						

FIGURE 10.1 Conditional distributions of per capita income for low- and high-urbanization countries.

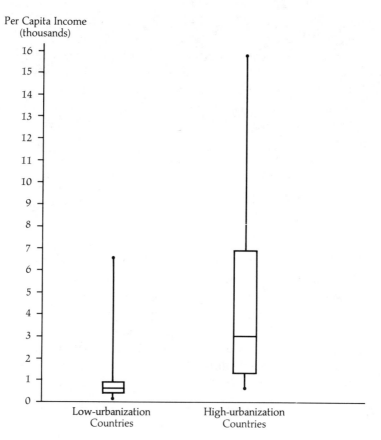

FIGURE 10.2 Box-and-whisker plot of per capita income for low- and high-urbanization countries.

lower than 42.8 percent, and one is a distribution of cases with urbanization greater than or equal to 42.8 percent. Figure 10.1 shows stem-and-leaf diagrams while Figure 10.2 shows box-and-whisker plots.

You can see in Figure 10.2 that the median per capita income of the low-urbanization countries is $397; the median income of the high-urbanization countries is $2711. The two plots "center" at different levels on the scale. Figure 10.2 shows, in a different way from Figure 10.1, that high-urbanization countries center higher on the per-capita-income scale and tend to be more dispersed than low-urbanization countries. Urbanization and per capita income are associated.

Even though the variables are associated, not all low-urbanization countries have low per capita incomes, and not all high-urbanization countries have high per capita incomes. That is okay. Association is concerned only with the tendency of cases to fall in a particular way, not principally with consistency.

In general, two variables are *associated* if conditional distributions of the dependent variable (conditioned on the categories of the independent variable) differ from one another. If cases are separated into groups based on the category that a case occupies on the independent variable, and if the conditional measures of central tendency of those groups differ from one another, then the variables are associated with, or related to, one another. Conditional distributions differing from one another is the definition of *association*. You have to accept this definition as a definition, but by now you should understand why the definition makes sense.

If conditional distributions formed by conditioning the dependent variable on the categories of the independent variable are the same, then the two variables are said to be *independent* of each other. Two variables that are independent of each other are not associated.

(*Caution*: Statistical "independence," or the fact that one variable is "independent" of another, is different from a variable's being an "independent variable" in a hypothesis. Make sure you understand the distinction.)

If conditional distributions differ, two variables are associated *in the sample*. Whether you can make the claim that two variables are associated in the population from which the sample came, based on information about association between the variables in the sample, is an inferential question. That problem is discussed later.

Consider one other example. This one uses discrete variables. Look at Table 10.1. It contains the data from the 1980 General Social Survey (GSS) on attitudes regarding abortion. These data can be used to test the hypothesis that sex is related to one's opinion on whether abortion should be okay for any reason. More women than men (325 versus 253) answered yes to the question, "Should it be okay for a woman to have an abortion for any reason?" But there are more women than men in the sample to begin with (790 versus 616). The *percentage* of women answering yes is the same as the percentage of men answering yes to the question. In fact, the conditional distribution of the dependent variable for men is the same as the conditional distribution for women: 41 percent say yes, 59 percent say no regardless of the category on the independent variable "sex" to which the respondent happens to belong. (Also 62 people said they didn't know or gave no answer. They were excluded from this analysis.) Once the overall distribution of

TABLE 10.1 Relationship Between Sex and Opinion on Abortion, GSS, 1980

| Sex | Abortion Okay? | | Total |
	Yes	No	
Female	41% (325)	59% (465)	790
Male	41% (253)	59% (363)	616
Total	41% (578)	59% (828)	$n = 1406$

the dependent variable "opinion" is conditioned on the categories of the independent variable "sex," the conditional distributions are the same and are identical to the overall distribution of "opinion." Having information on sex makes no difference in the distribution of responses to the question. This means that sex and opinion on abortions are *statistically independent* in the sample. The variables tend not to vary together in the sample. Whether the respondent is a man or a woman tends to make no difference in the likelihood he or she will answer no to the question. Sex and opinion are *not associated* with each other.

Remember: Two variables are associated if conditional distributions of the dependent variable (conditioned on the categories of the independent variable) differ. If conditional distributions are the same, the variables are statistically independent.

• • •

MEASURING STRENGTH OF ASSOCIATION

According to the definition, two variables are associated if conditional distributions differ *at all*. Technically, the variables "sex" and "opinion" in Table 10.1 *are* associated, if you figure the percentages out to the hundredth of a percent. The conditional distribution for males is actually that 58.93 percent say no, 41.07 percent say yes. The conditional distribution for females is that 58.86 percent say no, 41.14 percent say yes. There is a difference of 0.07 percent in the distributions. The difference is very small, but the conditional distributions are different, and technically you would have to say the variables are associated in this sample from the U.S. population. However, they are not strongly associated. Women tend to answer yes or no with a relative frequency virtually identical to that of men.

Statistics called *measures of association* or *measures of correlation* describe the strength of a relationship. They help distinguish between situations like that shown in Table 10.1, where there is very little relationship, and other situations, like the relationship between urbanization and per capita income, in which the variables are strongly related.

Let's begin with a very simple example, one of those instructors who believes that in his class there is a relationship between a student's sex and his or her test score. Men do better than women on his tests, he believes. Sex is the independent variable and score is the dependent variable in the instructor's mind. By saying sex is associated with test score, the instructor is saying that having information on a person's sex would allow him to predict that person's score more accurately than if he did not know a person's sex. If the instructor were told that a person was female, the instructor would guess this student had a lower test score than if he were told that the person was male. If two variables are related to each other, having information about the independent variable should help one better predict the dependent variable. To put it another way, having information about the independent variable should reduce one's error in predicting the dependent variable.

The instructor collected these data to test his hypothesis concerning sex and test score:

Sex	M	F	F	M	F	F	M	M	M	M
Score	88	52	97	82	65	74	91	48	79	78

There are 10 cases, 6 males and 4 females.

Consider, for the moment, just the dependent variable in this example, "score." The mean score is 75.4, and the median is 78.5. If you had to predict, or guess, a randomly selected person's score without having any other information, what would you guess? You should guess somewhere near the middle of the distribution. You might, for example, guess the median score of 78.5. You would tend to miss the lower scores by a lot since this is a slightly skewed distribution.

If your task in such a guessing game were to minimize error around your guess over the long run, what would you guess a person's score was if you did not have any other information? You might guess the mean score since the mean is the balance point of the distribution that equalizes the units of deviation on either side of itself. The mean would, on average, miss by the least amount over the long run if you took the size of your misses into consideration.

So if someone said, "I have randomly selected a case. Guess his or her score so as to minimize your error over many such guesses," I would guess the score was 74.5. I would be wrong every time, but over the long run I would minimize the amount by which I missed.

How much error is there in my guesses if I always guess the mean? In this kind of a guessing game, one measure of error around my guess of the mean is the variance. The variance is a standardized measure of the size of my miss (standardized by the number of cases, n, minus 1). If I always guessed that the score of a randomly selected case was 75.4, then, on average, my "error" could be measured as $[(88 - 75.4)^2 + (52 - 75.4)^2 + (97 - 75.4)^2 + (82 - 75.4)^2 + (65 - 75.4)^2 + (74 - 75.4)^2 + (91 - 75.4)^2 + (48 - 75.4)^2 + (79 - 75.4)^2 + (78 - 75.4)^2]/(10 - 1) = 260$. So 260 is the variance of the dependent variable "score," and it is a measure of the error of my prediction of "score" without having any other information on the cases.

If sex is associated with score, then having information on sex should reduce the error of my predictions. I should be able to come closer, on average, to a person's score if I know his or her sex than if I do not have such information.

The guessing game begins again with someone saying, "I have randomly selected a case. *It is male.* What do you guess his score is?" I would guess not the mean of all the scores (the *grand mean*), but I would guess the conditional mean score for males, which is $(88 + 82 + 91 + 48 + 79 + 78)/6 = 77.66$. If the case were female, I would guess the conditional mean for females, which is 72.00. Females tend to score lower than males. The conditional means differ, so the conditional distributions of score conditioned on sex are different, so the variables "sex" and "score" are associated. But how strongly associated? To what degree does having information on sex improve my predictions?

A measure of error for guesses that *uses information on the independent variable* is the sum of the squared deviations around conditional means divided by the number of cases minus 1 $(n - 1)$. So the error that remains after using information on sex is $[(88 - 77.66)^2 + (52 - 72.00)^2 + (97 - 72.00)^2 + (82 - 77.66)^2 + (65 - 72.00)^2 + (74 - 72.00)^2 + (91 - 77.66)^2 + (48 - 77.66)^2 + (79 - 77.66)^2 + (78 - 77.66)^2]/(10 - 1) = 251.5$. The error around the two conditional means is 251.5, which is less than 260, the error around the grand mean. By using information on sex, I have reduced the error of my prediction by 8.5 "error units."

By itself, a reduction in error of "8.5 units" does not mean much because the units in which error is expressed are dependent on the units in which the variable is measured. So to say that a reduction of 8.5 units of error has been achieved is not very informative. What is more informative is to know that having information on sex allowed a reduction of *8.5 out of the original 260 units of error.* That is a $8.5/260 = 0.033$, or 3.3 percent, reduction in error.

The *proportionate reduction in error* of predictions of the dependent variable that is achieved by having information on an independent variable is a *measure of the strength of association* between the two variables. The *proportionate reduction in error is the ratio of the absolute reduction in error to the total error with which one begins.* The greater the proportionate reduction in error, the more strongly are the independent and dependent variables associated.

The proportionate reduction in error (PRE) is

$$PRE = \frac{\text{Total error} - \text{Remaining error}}{\text{Total error}} \tag{10.1}$$

Most measures of association or correlation are measures of proportionate reduction in error. Differences among the many measures of association are due usually to differences in the definition of "error." Before you start learning the formulas for different measures of association, make certain you understand the logic of association completely. The same logic lies behind every measure of association you encounter in this text.

One more example should cement the concept of association in your mind. You know per capita income and urbanization are associated, but how strongly associated are they? Table 10.2 contains the information necessary to determine the strength of this positive association. The error with which you begin is the variance of per capita income for the 105 cases for which values of urbanization are available. That variance is 9,745,410.

TABLE 10.2 Calculating the Strength of Association Between Urbanization and Per Capita Income

Total error (variance)	9,754,410	
Average remaining error within groups (conditional variances)	Low urbanization $s_1^2 = 1,217,742$	High urbanization $s_2^2 = 12,338,681$
Number of cases	52	53
Total remaining error	$\dfrac{(52 - 1)1,241,620 + (53 - 1)12,575,967}{105 - 1} = 6,896,855$	
Proportionate reduction in error	$\dfrac{9,745,410 - 6,896,855}{9,745,410} = 0.29$	

The remaining error is the total squared deviations around the conditional means divided by the number of cases minus 1. The total squared deviations around each conditional mean can be found from the conditional variances s_L^2 and s_H^2, where s_L^2 is the total squared deviations around the conditional mean per capita income for low-urbanization countries, divided by 1 less than the number of countries in that group. So

$$s_L^2 = \frac{\text{total squared deviations around } \bar{X}_L}{52 - 1}$$

where $\bar{X}_L$ is the conditional mean per capita income for low-urbanization countries. From that equation, you can see that the total squared deviations around $\bar{X}_L$ are $(52 - 1)s_L^2 = 51(1,241,620) = 63,322,620$. By similar reasoning, the total squared deviations around the conditional mean per capita income for high-urbanization countries $\bar{X}_H$ are $(53 - 1)s_H^2 = 52(12,575,967) = 653,950,284$. The total squared deviations around the conditional means are $63,322,620 + 653,950,284 = 717,272,904$. Divide that by the total number of cases minus 1 to get the total remaining error: $717,272,904/(105 - 1) = 6,896,855$.

Then the proportionate reduction in error is 0.29, as shown in Table 10.2. Urbanization and per capita income are much more strongly associated than are sex and score in the teacher's class discussed earlier.

• • •

ASSOCIATION AND CAUSATION

The fact that two variables are associated does not imply they are causally related. "Name of thrower" was related to "sum of two dice" in the dice game, but the name of the thrower did not *cause* Beth's set of dice to come up with higher sums, on average, than Bill's. Urbanization is related to per capita income, but high urbanization is not necessarily a cause of high per capita income. In this modern world, there is a tendency to think always in terms of cause-and-effect relationships. In fact, the word "relationship" is often used as shorthand for "cause-and-effect relationship." You must distinguish carefully between the notion of a statistical relationship between two variables and the notion of a causal relationship. Association is just one aspect of causality.

Two variables are causally related if the relationship between them satisfies *all three* of these criteria:

1. The variables are associated.
2. There is a consistent temporal ordering of the variables.
3. The relationship between the variables is not spurious.

The first criterion is one you understand now. Two variables are associated if conditional distributions of the dependent variable differ.

The second criterion requires that the independent variable come before the dependent variable in time. It makes much more sense to say that an earthquake caused buildings to collapse than to claim that the buildings' falling down caused an earthquake. The variables "earthquake" and "building condition" are associated, and earthquakes generally come before buildings fall down. The relationship between these variables satisfies at least the first two criteria of causality.

Determining that a relationship is not spurious is very hard. One of John Stuart Mill's canons of scientific logic has it that if two events have only one factor in common, that factor must be the cause of the two events. If events have more than one factor in common, then the relationship between the event and one of the common factors might be, in fact, produced by some other common factor. If a third variable is producing an observed relationship between two variables, then the relationship between the two variables is said to be spurious.

The early days of the famous "Pepsi® challenge" provide an instructive example of a spurious relationship.[1] Pepsi asked Coke® drinkers in Dallas to choose between a glass of Coke marked simply with the letter Q and a glass of Pepsi marked with the letter M. A majority of the Coke drinkers said they preferred the glass with the Pepsi in it over the glass with the Coke in it. Pepsi used the results to try to lure Coke drinkers away from their cola drink.

Now obviously the dependent variable in the Pepsi Challenge is "preference," and it consists of the two mutually exclusive and totally inclusive categories "glass with Pepsi" and "glass with Coke." (The respondent had to state a preference for one and only one glass.) Pepsi believed—and asserted in subsequent advertising—that the independent variable was "beverage taste." They premised their advertising campaign on the notion that the only factor common to cases in which the glass with Coke was chosen was the "taste of Coke" and that the only factor common to the cases in which the glass with Pepsi was chosen was the "taste of Pepsi." Pepsi believed that

$$\text{Beverage taste} \rightarrow \text{Preference}$$

was a causal relationship.

But was taste the only factor common among those selecting the glass with Pepsi or among those selecting the glass with Coke? The answer is no. The glass with Pepsi in it not only always had the taste of Pepsi but always had an M on it. The Coke glass always had the taste of Coke, but it also had a Q on it every time. A person's preference for one glass over the other might have been caused by the preference for different letters, not by the preference for one taste over the other. There was a second factor common to all stated preferences, "letter." "Letter" was a variable that was perfectly correlated with "taste," and so the effects of "letter preference" on "preference" as expressed by the choice of one glass over the other could not be distinguished from the effects of "beverage taste." "Letter preference" might have been producing a *spurious* relationship between "beverage taste" and "(glass) preference," the relationship of which Pepsi was so proud.

To see if the relationship between taste and preference was, indeed, spurious, Coke did their own test. They also asked people to choose between glasses of cola beverage marked M and Q, but they put Coke in both glasses. People tended to prefer the glass marked M to the glass marked Q. This result suggests that "letter" might have been causing the differences in preference that Pepsi had attributed to taste. Coke controlled for the effects of the variable "taste" (by putting the same beverage in each glass), and Coke showed that it was reasonable to say that the relationship between beverage taste and (glass) preference in the original Pepsi Challenge was, indeed, spurious. Once taste was controlled, the only factor common to all the M glasses was the letter M, and the only factor in common among the Q glasses was the letter Q. The original relationship Pepsi touted was not necessarily a causal one.

(The more modern version of the Pepsi Challenge switched the letters L and S randomly between the two beverages. Half the time Pepsi is marked with an L, and half the time it is marked with an S. Random assignment of the letters controls for the effects of the variable "letter.")

In order for a relationship to be considered nonspurious, the researcher must be able to convince the reader of a study that *no third variable* is producing the observed relationship between the independent variable and the dependent variable. This is often very hard to do since *all reasonable* possibilities must be considered; but the attempt must be made if science is to progress.

As you study relationships between two variables, keep in mind that saying "There is a causal relationship between X and Y" is a very strong statement. It should be made only with great care and thoughtfulness. Discovering and reporting a statistical relationship between X and Y is a comparatively weak statement. A statistical relationship between X and Y is a prerequisite of saying there is a causal relationship between X and Y, but association is only one of the three criteria of causality. The (true) cliché to remember is, *Correlation is not causation.*

• • •

AN INFERENTIAL TEST ABOUT ASSOCIATION: CHI SQUARED

There are tests that allow you to make inferences about association between two variables. As usual, you use sample data to make inferences into the population from which the sample was drawn.

This section discusses a chi-squared (χ^2) test about association between two discrete variables. The chi-squared test about an association between two variables is a *nonparametric* test. All the inferential tests discussed in Chapters 8 and 9 were tests about population parameters; they were *parametric* tests. You could reject (or not) a null hypothesis about the size of a particular parameter, and then you could develop estimates of the size of the parameter. With a chi-squared test about association, you can only decide if there is sufficient evidence to reject a null hypothesis of no association between two variables. There is no parameter to estimate.

Look at Table 10.3. It shows the relationship between religious preference and attitude toward abortion. There is some association between these two variables because the conditional distributions differ from one another. For example, the modal response for Jews and people who expressed no religious preference or a preference not on the questionnaire is yes while the modal response for Protestants and Catholics is no. The inferential question is, Are the two variables "religious preference" and "attitude toward abortion" related to each other in the noninstitutional population of the United States, the population from which the GSS drew its sample? In other words, is there evidence in the sample to argue that

TABLE 10.3 Observed Table Showing the Relationship Between Religious Preference and Opinion on Abortion, GSS, 1980

Religious Preference	Abortion Okay?		Total
	Yes	No	
Protestant	39% (355)	61% (545)	900
Catholic	32% (109)	68% (237)	346
Jewish	77% (23)	23% (7)	30
None	73% (73)	27% (27)	100
Other	64% (18)	36% (10)	28
Total	41% (578)	59% (826)	$n = 1404$

if you had a table just like that in Table 10.3 but it contained information on every noninstitutionalized person in the United States 18 years old or older, then the conditional distributions of attitude toward abortion would be different across the categories of religious preference?

Suppose our belief is that religious preference and attitude toward abortion are related in the population. So I formulate the alternative hypothesis:

> H_A: There is some association between religious preference and attitude toward abortion (i.e., the conditional distributions differ) in the population.

The logical complement is the null hypothesis

> H_0: There is no association between religious preference and attitude toward abortion (i.e., the conditional distributions are the same) in the population.

The second step of a chi-squared test for association, after you have framed the null hypothesis and its alternative, involves a what-if statement. What if the null hypothesis is true? What would the sample look like if it exactly reflected a population in which the null hypothesis were true, i.e., in which there was no association between variables? What would a table structured like Table 10.3 look like if there were no association between variables? You must, in this step, construct a table that you would expect to get if the null hypothesis were true. Chi squared is a statistic based on a comparison of an *observed table*, the table containing data from the sample, and an expected table, a table *expected* under an assumption of statistical independence of the variables in the population.

Constructing an expected table is not difficult if you remember what it means for two variables to be statistically independent of each other. Two variables are statistically independent of each other if the conditional distributions of the dependent variable (conditioned on the categories of the independent variable) are all the same. To construct a table expected under an assumption of independence, you must construct a table in which the conditional distributions are all the same. If the conditional distributions all are to be the same, they must all be identical to the overall distribution of the dependent variable.

In Table 10.3, the overall frequency distribution of attitude toward abortion is 41 percent say yes, 59 percent say no. To be exact, the distribution is yes — $578/1404 = .4117$ and no — $826/1404 = .5883$. If the sample exactly reflected a population in which religious preference and attitude toward abortion were not associated, each conditional distribution of the dependent variable would have exactly .4117 of its cases in the "Yes" column and exactly .5883 of its cases in the "No" column.

For example, in this sample there are 900 Protestants. Under an assumption of independence of religious preference and attitude toward abortion, .4117 of these 900 would have said yes. That is, $.4117(900) = 370.53$ cases would be in the Protestant–Yes cell of the table. Similarly, .5883(900) = 529.47 cases would be in the Protestant–No cell. The fractions of cases are not a problem since this is a purely hypothetical table constructed under a what-if situation. The conditional distribution for Protestants in a table expected if the null hypothesis were true would be 370.53 yes and 529.47 no.

You must do the same calculations for the other four conditional distributions to complete the construction of the "expected table," the table expected if the sample were drawn from a population in which the variables are not related and if the sample exactly reflected the population. There are 346 Catholics. And .4117(346) = 142.45 Catholics should be in the "Yes" column and .5883(346) = 203.55 should be in the "No" column. The calculations for the other three conditional distributions are as follows:

Jewish: Yes − .4117(30) = 12.35   No − .5883(30) = 17.65

None: Yes − .4117(100) = 41.17   No − .5883(100) = 58.83

Other: Yes − .4117(28) = 11.53   No − .5883(28) = 16.47

The expected table, the table expected under an assumption of independence of religious preference and attitude toward abortion, is shown in Table 10.4a. All the conditional distributions are exactly the same, so the variables in this hypothetical table are not associated.

In general, to construct the expected table, you need to respect the general makeup of the sample (578 people who said yes, 826 who said no; 900 Protestants, 346 Catholics, etc.), but you redistribute the cases in each category of the independent variable as they would be distributed if the two variables in the table were statistically independent. You construct conditional distributions that are identical to the overall frequency distribution of the dependent variable. You do this by multiplying the proportion of cases that should be in each column of the table by the total number of cases in each row. The proportion of cases that should be in each column (under an assumption of statistical independence) is the proportion of the total number of cases that is in each column of the table.

The third step in a chi-squared test for association is to compare the sample table that was *observed* to the table that would be *expected* if the null hypothesis were true. Look at Tables 10.3 and 10.4a. They are different. It would be convenient to have a single number that indicates just how different they are. For reasons that will be made clear, statisticians use χ^2 (chi squared) to make this comparison. Chi squared is defined as

$$\chi^2 = \sum_{i=1}^{k} \frac{(o_i - e_i)^2}{e_i}$$

with k the number of cells in the observed and expected tables; o_i, where $1 \leq i \leq k$, is the number of cases in cell i of the observed table; and e_i, where $1 \leq i \leq k$, is

TABLE 10.4a Expected Table Showing the Relationship Between Religious Preference and Opinion on Abortion. If the Null Hypothesis Is True (marginals from Table 10.1)

| | Abortion Okay? | | |
Religious Preference	Yes	No	Total
Protestant	41.17% (370.53)	58.83% (529.47)	900
Catholic	41.17% (142.45)	58.83% (203.55)	346
Jewish	41.17% (12.35)	58.83% (17.65)	30
None	41.17% (41.17)	58.83% (58.83)	100
Other	41.17% (11.53)	58.83% (16.47)	28
Total	41.17% (578.00)	58.83% (826.00)	1404

the number of cases in the corresponding cell of the expected table. To calculate χ^2, you subtract the expected frequency e_i from the observed frequency o_i in a cell, square that quantity, and divide by the expected frequency e_i. You sum those values over all k cells in the two tables. The sum, by definition, is χ^2.

I will calculate χ^2 for this set of data. Table 10.4b shows the observed and expected frequencies next to each other for each cell. For the cell in the upper left corner, the Protestant–Yes cell, the term is $(355 - 370.53)^2/370.53 = 0.65$. For the Catholic–Yes cell, the term is $(109 - 142.45)^2/142.45 = 7.85$. Continuing down the "Yes" column and then down from the top of the "No" column, the necessary

TABLE 10.4b Expected and Observed Frequencies from Tables 10.3 and 10.4a

| | Abortion Okay? | | | |
| | Yes | | No | |
Religious Preference	o_i	e_i	o_i	e_i
Protestant	355	370.53	545	529.47
Catholic	109	142.45	237	203.55
Jewish	23	12.35	7	17.65
None	73	41.17	27	58.83
Other	18	11.53	10	16.47
Total	578	578.00	826	826.00

calculations are:

Jewish–Yes:
$$\frac{(23 - 12.35)^2}{12.35} = 9.18$$

None–Yes:
$$\frac{(73 - 41.17)^2}{41.17} = 24.61$$

Other–Yes:
$$\frac{(18 - 11.53)^2}{11.53} = 3.63$$

Protestant–No:
$$\frac{(545 - 529.47)^2}{529.47} = 0.46$$

Catholic–No:
$$\frac{(237 - 203.55)^2}{203.55} = 5.50$$

Jewish–No:
$$\frac{(7 - 17.65)^2}{17.65} = 6.43$$

None–No:
$$\frac{(27 - 58.83)^2}{58.83} = 17.22$$

Other–No:
$$\frac{(10 - 16.47)^2}{16.47} = 2.54$$

Chi squared is, by definition, equal to the sum of these terms. The sum is approximately equal to 78.1. That single number is a measure of the difference between the observed table and the table expected under an assumption of independence of the variables in the table.

The more different the observed table is from the expected table, the larger chi squared will be. If there were near-zero association between variables in the sample, the observed table would differ little from the expected table and chi squared would be small. If variables are strongly associated in the sample, the observed table will differ greatly from the table constructed by assuming the variables are not associated, and chi squared will be large. Chi squared is *not* a good measure of association, however. In fact, you can increase chi squared simply by multiplying all the cells in a table by a constant, an operation that has no effect on the degree of association. Or you can increase chi squared by adding cells to the table in such a way that does not affect the degree of association. Chi squared is not a measure of association. It is just a convenient number that gives an overall assessment of the difference between the table that you observe and the table that would be expected if the null hypothesis were true and if the sample exactly reflected a population in which the variables were not associated.

The fourth step in the chi-squared test of association is to determine the probability of getting a χ^2 at least as large as that calculated from the data if the sample was randomly drawn from a population in which there is no association between variables. As you already know, there is a table showing the probabilities of getting a chi squared of any size if, in fact, the sample for which χ^2 was calculated was drawn from a population in which the null hypothesis is true.

Recall that in Table B.6 in the Appendix the P across the top of the table refers to probability or "proportion of the area under the curve to the right of . . . ." The ellipses in this statement are completed by the number in the body of the table. You need to know the degrees of freedom (df) in order to decide which row of the table to use. For our example, df $= 4$. (Just accept that for the moment.) Since df $= 4$, you use the fourth row of the table:

P	.99	.975	.95	.90	.80	.70	.50	.30	.20	.10	.05	.025	.01	.001
χ^2	.30	.48	.71	1.06	1.65	2.20	3.36	4.88	5.99	7.78	9.49	11.143	13.28	18.46

Our $\chi^2 = 78.06$. What is the probability p of getting a chi squared at least that large if the null hypothesis is true? The probability is smaller than .99 because our chi squared is way, way past 0.30, the entry under $P = .99$, the first column in the table. So 99 times out of 100 a random sample drawn from a population in which the null hypothesis is true will have a χ^2 of at least 0.30 when df $= 4$. The probability of getting a chi squared of 78.1 is also smaller than 1 in 2 ($P = .50$) because our chi squared is larger than 3.36. One out of every two samples drawn from a population in which the null hypothesis is true will have a chi squared of at least 3.36. In fact, since our chi squared is larger than 18.46, the value of chi squared associated with a probability of .001, the probability of getting a chi squared of at least 78.1 is much smaller than .001, or 1 in 1000. Only 1 out of 1000 times will a sample drawn from a population in which the null hypothesis is true have a chi squared of 18.46 or larger. There is still a chance that our sample was drawn from a population in which the null hypothesis is true. But the chance is very small, less than 1 in 1000.

Finally, we go back to the two hypotheses framed in the first step:

> H_A: There is some association between religious preference and attitude toward abortion in the population.

and

> H_0: There is no association between religious preference and attitude toward abortion in the population.

I decide to reject the null hypothesis of no association. I may be doing so incorrectly. My sample still may have come from a population in which the null hypothesis is true. The chance is less than 1 in 1000 that it did, but there is still that small probability. I acknowledge the possibility, decide to reject the null hypothesis, and I am left with the alternative H_A: There is some association between religious preference and attitude toward abortion.

I could summarize everything done so far in a simple statement: Religious preference and attitude toward abortion are related to each other ($\chi^2 = 78.1$, df $= 4$, $p < .001$). To a person who knows the language of statistics, this statement is crystal-clear. It contains the results of the inferential test concerning the likelihood that these two variables are associated in the population from which the sample was drawn. The statement $p < .001$ means "The probability that decision to reject the null hypothesis will be incorrect is less than .001, less than 1 in 1000." (This statement does not contain—as it should—a measure of the strength of association between variables in the sample. That topic is addressed in Chapter 11.)

Degrees of Freedom

The only part of the statement above that is not crystal-clear at this stage is that df $= 4$. We must know how many degrees of freedom (df) you have in order to use Appendix Table B.6 to determine the probability associated with a given χ^2. The "freedom" in "degrees of freedom" refers to how free you are to put numbers into a blank table of the sort that describes the relationship between two variables, if you are constrained in this activity by only the values in the margins of the table. (The values in the margins are sometimes called just *the marginals*.) And df is a measure of how much freedom can be exercised until a table is completely determined.

Consider Figure 10.3 which shows, in panel 1, a blank version of Table 10.3 with only the marginals in place. You are completely free to put any number you like into any cell you like, with the single constraint that you cannot exceed the row or column marginal of the cell you choose to fill. I choose freely to put a number in the Jewish–No cell. The marginals indicate that the number must be less than 826 (the number of people who said no) *and* less than 30 (the number of Jewish respondents). Obviously, the number must be smaller than 30. I choose freely to put 15 in the Jewish–No cell. In doing so, I use 1 degree of freedom. So Table 10.3 has at least 1 degree of freedom.

Putting a 15 in the Jewish–No cell causes the Jewish–Yes cell to be determined. Since there are 30 Jewish people in the sample and I have chosen to say 15 of them responded no, 15 of them must have responded yes. After using 1 degree of freedom, the table looks like panel 2 in Figure 10.3. The table is not completely determined yet, so it must have more degrees of freedom.

I will choose to use a second degree of freedom by putting a number in the Protestant–Yes cell. It must be less than the smaller of 900 (the number of Protestants) and $578 - 15 = 563$ (the number of people who said minus the number already in that column). I choose to put 463 in that upper left cell. This move causes the upper right cell to become $900 - 463 = 437$. After using 2 degrees of freedom, the table looks like panel 3 in Figure 10.3.

I use a third degree of freedom by putting a number in the none–Yes cell. The number must be less than the smaller of 100 and $578 - 15 - 463 = 100$.

PANEL 1

Religious Preference	Abortion Okay? Yes	No	Total
Protestant			900
Catholic			346
Jewish			30
None			100
Other			28
Total	41% (578)	59% (826)	$n = 1404$

PANEL 2

Religious Preference	Abortion Okay? Yes	No	Total
Protestant			900
Catholic			346
Jewish	15	15	30
None			100
Other			28
Total	41% (578)	59% (826)	$n = 1404$

☐ = Number inserted on this step.

PANEL 3

Religious Preference	Abortion Okay? Yes	No	Total
Protestant	463	437	900
Catholic			346
Jewish	15	15	30
None			100
Other			28
Total	41% (578)	59% (826)	$n = 1404$

☐ = Number inserted on this step.

FIGURE 10.3 Determining the number of degrees of freedom for Table 10.3.

PANEL 4

	Abortion Okay?		
Religious Preference	Yes	No	Total
Protestant	463	437	900
Catholic			346
Jewish	15	15	30
None	75	25	100
Other			28
Total	41% (578)	59% (826)	$n = 1404$

□ = Number inserted on this step.

PANEL 5

	Abortion Okay?		
Religious Preference	Yes	No	Total
Protestant	463	437	900
Catholic	0	346	346
Jewish	15	15	30
None	75	25	100
Other	25	3	28
Total	41% (578)	59% (826)	$n = 1404$

□ = Number inserted on this step.

FIGURE 10.3 (Continued)

I will put a 75 in the none–Yes cell, and the table looks like panel 4 of Figure 10.3.

I will use a fourth degree of freedom by putting a number in the other–No cell. It appears that the number must be less than the smaller of 28 and 826 − 437 − 15 − 25 = 349. What happens if I choose to put a 0 in that cell? Putting 0 in the other–No cell causes the other–Yes cell to be filled with 28. But wait. If I put 28 in the other–Yes cell, there will be 463 + 15 + 75 + 28 = 581 people in the cells of the "Yes" column. But there can be only 578 in the "Yes" column according to the "Yes" column marginal. I must use my freedom wisely and recognize constraints from both marginals simultaneously. I can put a number in the other–No cell, but that number, call it x, must not only be less than the smaller of 28 and 349, but also satisfy the condition that 28 − x plus all the other people already designated as saying yes must not exceed the "Yes" column marginal of 578. So 463 + 15 + 75 + 28 − x must be less than or equal to 578. So x must be greater than or equal to 3 in addition to being less than 28. I will put a 3 in the other–No cell. That puts a 25 in the other–Yes cell.

Once 25 is in the other–Yes cell, we can calculate the number that must go in the Catholic–Yes cell. It must be 578 (the "Yes" column marginal) minus the number of people already in the "Yes" column, which is $463 + 15 + 75 + 25 = 578$. So a 0 must go into the Catholic–Yes cell.

But, then, if there is a 0 in the Catholic–Yes cell, all 346 Catholics must go into the "No" column. The table, then, is completely filled. The table is completely determined after using 4 degrees of freedom. I say, "my table has 4 degrees of freedom" or, simply, df = 4.

There is a simple way to calculate the number of degrees of freedom of a table. In general,

$$df = (R - 1)(C - 1) \tag{10.2}$$

where R is the number of rows in the table and C is the number of columns in the table. In Table 10.1 there are 5 rows and 2 columns, so $df = (5 - 1)(2 - 1) = (4)(1) = 4$. Sure, it would have been a lot easier just to say $df = (R - 1)(C - 1)$, but "degrees of freedom" is not an entirely frivolous choice of words. You can now understand the meaning of "degrees of freedom".

A Quicker Example

Working through another example quickly may help you understand the logic better. Table 10.5 allows me to test the hypothesis that men and women have

TABLE 10.5 Relationship Between Sex and Attitude toward Homosexual Relations, GSS, 1980

Sex	Attitude toward Homosexuality		Total
	Always Wrong	Other Response	
Observed Relationship			
Female	69.5% (575)	30.5% (252)	827
Male	70.4% (449)	29.6% (189)	638
Total	69.9% (1024)	30.1% (441)	1465
Expected Relationship If Null Hypothesis Is True			
Female	69.9% (578.05)	30.1% (248.95)	827
Male	69.9% (445.95)	30.1% (192.05)	638
Total	69.9% (1024.00)	30.1% (441.00)	1465

different attitudes toward homosexuality, i.e., that the variables "sex" and "attitude toward homosexual relations" are related. According to Table 10.5, they *are* related, but only weakly. There is only a 1 percent difference between male and female opinion, with men saying homosexual relations are "always wrong" slightly more often than women. On the basis of these data, am I justified in asserting that sex and attitude toward homosexual relations are related in the U.S. population?

First, I must construct the alternative hypothesis and its logical complement, the null hypothesis. The alternative hypothesis is that sex and attitude toward homosexual relations are related in the population. The null hypothesis is that sex and attitude are unrelated. So

H_A: There is some association between sex and attitude toward homosexual relations.

H_0: There is no association between sex and attitude toward homosexual relations.

The lower part of Table 10.5 shows the table that would be expected if the null hypothesis were true. That table also contains 638 men and 827 women, 1024 people who said homosexual relations are "always wrong," and 441 people who gave some other response. But the internal parts of the table show how these 1465 cases would be distributed among the four cells if there were no association between sex and attitude toward homosexual relations.

Now χ^2 is used to compare the observed to the expected table:

$$\chi^2 = \frac{(449 - 445.95)^2}{445.95} + \frac{(189 - 192.05)^2}{192.05} + \frac{(575 - 578.05)^2}{578.05}$$

$$+ \frac{(252 - 248.95)^2}{248.95} = .122$$

What is the probability of getting a chi squared at least that large strictly by chance if, in fact, the sample was drawn randomly from a population in which the null hypothesis is true? First, determine the number of degrees of freedom in the table: df $= (2 - 1)(2 - 1) = 1$. Then turn to the table of critical values in the Appendix (Table B.6). We look at the first row where df $= 1$. Between which columns of the table does our χ^2 fall? Our χ^2 of .122 lies between the column where $P = .80$ (and $\chi^2 = .064$) and $P = .70$ (and $\chi^2 = .15$). So the probability of getting a chi squared of at least .122 is greater than 0.70. More than 7 times out of 10, you would get a χ^2 of at least .122 if, in fact, the sample were drawn from a population in which sex and attitude were unrelated. That is a very high probability.

Remember, I *can still reject* the null hypothesis. That is a decision I have to make. If I choose to reject the null hypothesis, there is a greater than 7-in-10 chance that I am doing so *incorrectly*. I prefer not to make that decision and take that kind of risk, so I choose not to reject the null hypothesis. I decide not to claim that in the U.S. population there is a difference between men's and women's attitudes toward homosexual relations.

. . .

A TEST ABOUT TWO POPULATION PROPORTIONS

Chi squared can be used to decide if there is sufficient evidence to claim that two population proportions are different from each other. It does not permit you to estimate the size of the difference, but it does permit you to say that the difference is not zero. This is the kind of test that was used in the chronic stable angina study mentioned in Chapter 1.

Recall that in that study 596 eligible patients were randomly assigned to have medical or surgical treatment for their condition. At the end of 36 months, 88 percent of the surgically treated group was alive, and 87 percent of the medically treated group was alive. Does the sample supply evidence on which to base a claim that the proportion of people who survive with surgery is different from the proportion of people who survive with medical treatment?

Table 10.6 shows data based on the information in the report. Some 41 medical patients died, and 35 surgical patients died. If the medically treated sample and the surgically treated sample came from populations in which the proportions of survivors were the same, then if the samples perfectly represented the populations from which they came, the conditional distribution of the medically treated group and the conditional distribution of the surgically treated group on the dependent

TABLE 10.6 Results of the Chronic Stable Angina Study
36 Months after Assignment

Treatment Group	Status 36 Months after Assignment		
	Alive	Dead	Total
	Observed Results		
Medical	269	41	310
Surgical	251	35	286
Total	520	76	596
	Expected Frequencies		
Medical	270.48	39.52	310
Surgical	249.54	36.46	286
Total	520 (.8725)	76 (.1275)	596 (1.000)

variable "status at 36 months" would be the same. By definition, there would be no association between the variables "treatment group" and "status at 36 months." If χ^2 is used as a test about association between the variables shown in Table 10.6, it is thereby being used as a test about the difference between population proportions. If there is evidence to support the claim that treatment group and status are related, then there is evidence to support the claim that the proportions of survivors in the two groups are different.

Let's conduct the test with the level to reject set at $\alpha = .10$. The hypotheses are

H_A: "Treatment group" and "status" are associated.
H_0: "Treatment group" and "status" are not associated.

The bottom part of Table 10.6 shows the table of expected frequencies. From that you can calculate

$$\chi^2 = \frac{(269 - 270.48)^2}{270.48} + \frac{(41 - 39.52)^2}{39.52} + \frac{(251 - 249.54)^2}{249.54} + \frac{(35 - 36.46)^2}{36.46} = .13$$

The probability of getting a chi squared that large if the null hypothesis is true is $p > .70$. That is, the observed significance of the test is $p > .70$, much larger than the level to reject. I do not reject the null hypothesis. That means that I do not conclude that treatment group and status are related. And so I do not conclude that the proportions of survivors in the medically treated population and in the surgically treated population are different. My conclusion—the same as the researchers made—is that there is "no statistically significant difference between surgical and medical treatment of chronic stable angina."

• • •

KEY CONCEPTS IN THIS CHAPTER

. . .

NOTE

1. This example is described in greater detail in Schuyler W. Huck and Howard M. Sandler, *Rival Hypotheses: Alternative Explanations of Data Based Conclusions,* Harper and Row, New York, 1979, pp. 11, 158. This book is an excellent and entertaining introduction to problems of designing research to eliminate variables that might compete with the independent variable for the claim of being a "cause" of the distribution of cases on the dependent variable.

. . .

EXERCISES

Chapter 10

1. Here's another our-man-in-Dublin experiment in brewing. He varied the fermentation time for the beer so that there were three batches—one with a short fermentation time, one with a moderate fermentation time, and one with a long fermentation time. Then he let the beer set, properly stored, and had it tasted every day to determine how long it lasted. He had 5 barrels from each batch, and the number of days each barrel lasted before going bad is shown below:

Days before Beer Went Bad ("Shelf Life")					
	Barrel in Batch				
Batch	1	2	3	4	5
Short fermentation	23	18	27	25	29
Moderate fermentation	25	19	19	22	21
Long fermentation	17	12	18	28	11

    a. What was the hypothesis that motivated this study? What was the independent variable? What was the dependent variable? What, if any, was the expected relationship between the independent and dependent variables?

b. Find the total error of the dependent variable. The following steps will help you answer this question:

   (i) What is the average number of days a barrel of beer lasts?

   (ii) What is the variance of the number of days that a barrel of beer lasts? That is, what is the total error around the central value of the dependent variable?

c. Statistically, what is the nature of the relationship between fermentation time and shelf life?

   (i) Find the conditional mean of shelf life for each batch.

   (ii) Decide if there is any systematic relationship between the level of one variable and the average level of the other variable. Describe that relationship.

d. How much error is there in each of the three groups formed by conditioning "shelf life" on the categories of "batch" or "fermentation time"? Calculate each conditional variance.

e. Calculate the strength of the relationship between the independent and dependent variables in this exercise. That is, calculate the proportionate reduction in error (PRE) achieved by having information on the independent variable.

   (i) Calculate the remaining error from the conditional variances calculated in part (**d**).

   (ii) Calculate the PRE, using the formula.

f. How would you describe the relationship between the two variables? What is the direction of the relationship? What is the strength of the relationship?

g. If extending shelf life of the beer were Gosset's only concern, how would he recommend that the beer be brewed? What other factors might he take into consideration before making his recommendation?

h. Look closely at the raw data. Are there any data that would cause you to worry about the conclusion you reached in part (**g**)?

2. This problem is related to Exercise 11, Chapter 8. There are 12 doctors who discharged patients in DRG 384. There seems to be considerable variation in the percentages of the total charges in DRG 384 devoted to material and technology. I have the idea that this variation might be due to specialization: More specialized doctors spend a higher percentage of the total charges on material and technology. See if this idea is supported by the sample data. The following steps will help you answer this question:

a. Frame my idea as a hypothesis: "The [higher or lower] the specialization score, the [higher or lower] will be the percentage of the total cost devoted to material and technology." Which variable is the dependent variable? Which is the independent variable?

b. Divide the 12 physicians into two groups based on specialization scores. Do the division in whatever way seems useful or appropriate.

c. Describe the conditional distributions of percentage of the total cost devoted to material and technology for the two groups of physicians. Use measures of centrality and dispersion to make these descriptions.

d. Is there a strong relationship between these two variables? Calculate the PRE in guessing the dependent variable that is achieved by having information on the independent variable.

e. Is this relationship, if there is one, a causal relationship? What other variables should be considered before concluding that this relationship is a causal relationship?

3. This question uses data from internal-motivation experiment 1 and is related to Exercise 12, Chapter 8.

a. Is there a strong association between task label and time spent on word game?

b. Is there a strong association between task label and the number of anagrams solved?

c. Explain the difference between a relationship that is "strong" and one that is "significant." Consider, for example, whether a relationship can ever be "weak" *and* "significant."

4. How strongly is literacy rate associated with per capita income among the first 15 countries that have a value for literacy rate? See Exercise 13, Chapter 8.

5. There seems to be a relationship between a faculty member's rank in a university and the number of books in his or her office.

a. Do you think there is a causal relationship between the variables?

b. If there is potentially a causal relationship, which way does causality flow?

c. If the relationship might be spurious, what third variable(s) might be bringing the original observed bivariate relationship into existence?

6. There is a relationship between the eruption of a solar flare and changes in the shape of the earth's magnetic field. What would you need to know to determine if the eruption of a solar flare caused the changes in the earth's magnetic field?

7. I played racquetball with Paul. We played on a court that seemed to have an inordinate amount of dust and dirt in it. He lost two games. We changed courts in order to play on a cleaner surface, so that we would not slide as much as we had. Paul said, as we entered the second court, "I lost because of the dirt in the other court. Look out now!" Paul lost two more games. What would you say to Paul if you had to use the word "spurious"?

8. Consider the table showing the relationship between one's sex and one's judgment of who won the Bush-Ferraro debate in 1984:

Respondent's Sex	Who Won?		Total
	Bush	Ferraro	
Female	37% (109)	63% (182)	291
Male	67% (158)	33% (79)	237
Total	51% (267)	49% (261)	528

a. What is the dependent variable? What is the independent variable? What hypothesis do you think motivated this study?

b. Construct the null hypothesis for this pair of variables.

c. Construct the table that would be expected if the null hypothesis were true, i.e., if, in the population from which this sample of 528 people was drawn, there were no association between sex and judgment of the who won. That is, fill in the following table as if these two variables were not associated:

Respondent's Sex	Who Won?		Total
	Bush	Ferraro	
Female	( )	( )	291
Male	( )	( )	237
Total	51% (267)	49% (261)	528

d. Calculate χ^2 for the original table.

e. Calculate the degrees of freedom for the table.

f. Determine the probability of drawing a sample with a χ^2 as large as this one from a population in which the null hypothesis is true.

g. Is the relationship between sex and winner significantly different from zero?

h. Write a sentence describing the results of this study.

9. Here are two tables like the one in Exercise 8. One shows the relationship between sex and the respondent's judgment of who won among Republicans only. The other is for Democrats only.

	Republicans		
	Who Won?		
Respondent's Sex	Bush	Ferraro	Total
Female	42	38	80
Male	78	32	110
Total	120	70	190

	Democrats		
	Who Won?		
Respondent's Sex	Bush	Ferraro	Total
Female	70	141	211
Male	77	50	127
Total	147	191	338

    a. Is there a statistically significant relationship between sex and winner among Republicans?

    b. Is the same relationship statistically significant among Democrats?

    c. Interpret the results.

    10. Here is a table showing the relationship between the day of the week and breakfast for a family:

Hypothetical Relationship Showing a Perfect Relationship between Day of Week and Breakfast Entree for 1 Year at the Robinsons

Day of Week	Entree			
	Eggs	Cereal	Rolls	Waffles
Monday	—	100% (52)	—	—
Tuesday	—	—	100% (52)	—
Wednesday	—	100% (52)	—	—
Thursday	100% (52)	—	—	—
Friday	—	100% (52)	—	—
Saturday	—	—	—	100% (52)
Sunday	100% (53)	—	—	—
Total	29% (105)	43% (156)	14% (52)	14% (52)

a. Construct the table that you would expect if there were no relationship between day of the week and the breakfast entree.

b. Does it make sense to do the calculations to determine if there is a statistically significant relationship between these two variables? If so, do the calculations and discuss the meaning of the results. If not, say why.

11. This question refers to Exercise 17, Chapter 8. Describe the strength of the relationship between the variable "physician" that has only the two categories "physician 01" and "physician 02" and the variable "average total cost." Interpret the results by writing a sentence incorporating these results with the results obtained in Chapter 8.

12. This question refers to Exercise 16, Chapter 8. Describe the strength of the relationship between the variable "complications," which has the categories "procedures with complications" and "procedures without complications," and the variable "average total cost." Interpret the results.

13. This question refers to data in Exercise 9, Chapter 3, and to the analysis of that data conducted in Exercise 21, Chapter 8. Describe the strength of the relationship between the length of the ears of corn and whether a person uses a lot of fertilizer or only a little. Combine the results of all the analyses of this data set to develop a short interpretation of the results.

CHAPTER

11

▼

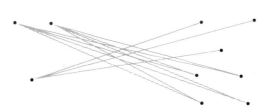

• • •

Measures of Association for
Discrete Variables

The previous chapter introduced the general concept of association and the logic behind measuring the strength of association between two variables. Strength of association is the proportionate reduction in error (PRE) of predicting the dependent variable achieved by having information on an independent variable. The examples in the section on measuring strength of association in Chapter 10 were peculiar because the dependent variable was always a continuous variable and the independent variables was always discrete. "Per capita income" is a ratio variable, and "urbanization" was formulated in that example so it was an ordinal variable with only two categories. Test "score" was at least an interval variable (we don't know if a 0 score was meaningful), and "sex," the independent variable, was a nominal variable. Not all bivariate problems of analysis fit this pattern.

There are measures of association for other situations—situations in which both variables are nominal, both variables are ordinal, or both variables are continuous, say. This chapter discusses measures of association for the first two situations. All measures of association discussed here measure proportionate reduction in error. What "error" means varies with the circumstances of the problem, but the underlying logic of all measures of association remains constant.

• • •

NOMINAL VARIABLES: LAMBDA

Table 11.1 presents again the data from the National Opinion Research Center's 1980 General Social Survey (GSS). It shows the relationship between one's religious preference and one's answer to a question about abortion. Both variables are nominal variables. There is no inherent order to the categories "Yes-No" or to the categories "Protestant-Catholic-Jewish-None-Other."

If you were to guess a randomly selected person's answer to the question about abortion, without having any other information, what would you guess? Look at the overall frequency distribution in the bottom margin of the table, the row marked "Total." Of the respondents 41 percent said yes, abortion is okay, and 59 percent said no. To minimize your error over the long run, you should guess the response of a randomly selected person is no. "No" is the modal response. The mode is a measure of central tendency for nominal variables just as the mean is a measure of central tendency for continuous variables. Guessing the mode when the dependent variable is nominal is like guessing the mean when the dependent variable is ratio or interval.

TABLE 11.1 Relationship Between a Person's Religious Preference and Opinion on Abortion, GSS, 1980

Religious Preference	Abortion Okay?		Total
	Yes	No	
Protestant	39% (355)	61% (545)	900
Catholic	32% (109)	68% (237)	346
Jewish	77% (23)	23% (7)	30
None	73% (73)	27% (27)	100
Other	64% (18)	36% (10)	28
Total	41% (578)	59% (826)	$n = 1404$

If you guess that a randomly selected case responded in the modal category, what is your error? If you always guess the mode, you will be wrong 578 times out of the 1404 cases. The number of cases in the nonmodal category (or categories) of the dependent variable is a measure of error in this situation. So 578 is the *total error* in predicting the dependent variable with which you begin this analysis.

Now, add information on the independent variable, "religious preference." To add information on the independent variable means to condition the distribution of the dependent variable on the categories of the independent variable. You obtain five conditional distributions of "opinion." These five conditional distributions are the five rows of Table 11.1. If the independent variable has the value "Protestant," then the distribution of opinion is 39 percent say yes and 61 percent say no. If the value of the independent variable is "Catholic," then the distribution of opinion is 32 percent say yes, 68 percent say no. If the value of the independent variable is "Jewish," the distribution of opinion is 77 percent say yes, 23 percent say no, and so on. Table 11.1 is a set of five conditional distribution of opinion, one for each of the five categories of religious preference.

Now you can return to the guessing game. Suppose a person randomly selects a case, but gives you information on the independent variable by saying, "This case has a religious preference of 'Protestant.'" What would you guess the case's opinion is? You should guess the *conditional mode* for Protestants, which is "no." What is your error if you always guess "no" when the case is "Protestant"? Error is measured by the number of cases in the nonmodal categories, so the error for Protestants is 355, the number of Protestants who responded yes. If a case is "Catholic" on religious preference, you should also guess that case said no. You would be wrong 109 times because 109 Catholics said yes. If a case is "Jewish" or "Other" or expresses no religious preference, then you should guess the conditional mode of each of these three categories, which is "yes." Your error for these three categories is equal to the number of Jewish, other, or no-preference cases who answered no. The error for these three categories is 7 + 27 + 10 = 44.

The error that remains after information on the independent variable is added is the number of people not in the modal categories of the five conditional distributions. The error remaining after conditioning is 355 + 109 + 7 + 27 + 10 = 508.

If you know the total error with which you began, which is 578, and the error that remains after conditioning on the categories of the independent variable, which is 508, the proportionate reduction in error is easy to calculate from Formula (10.1):

$$\text{PRE} = \frac{\text{total error} - \text{remaining error}}{\text{total error}}$$

$$= \frac{578 - 508}{578} = 0.12$$

You achieve a 12 percent reduction in error of guesses of attitude by knowing religious preference. Religious preference and attitude toward abortion are associated, but not very strongly.

The measure of association calculated as it was for religious preference and attitude toward abortion is called *lambda*, the Greek letter λ. Lambda is a measure of association for two nominal variables. It is a measure of PRE, but lambda is distinguished from other measures of association by the way "error" is measured. Error, for lambda, is the number of cases in nonmodal categories. The total error with which you begin is the number of cases in the nonmodal categories of the frequency distribution of the dependent variable. The remaining error is the total number of cases in the nonmodal categories of the conditional distributions formed by conditioning the dependent variable on the categories of the independent variable. The proportionate reduction in error, which is lambda, is calculated in the usual way:

$$PRE = \frac{\text{total error} - \text{remaining error}}{\text{total error}}$$

Table 11.2 allows you to examine the hypothesis that attitude toward abortion varies with region of residence. Lambda for this table is

$$\lambda = \frac{578 - (138 + 119 + 171 + 110)}{578} = .07$$

This indicates that religion and attitude toward abortion are more strongly associated than region and attitude. So what?

By itself, this statistical analysis means little. It is valuable to know that your ability to predict opinion increases if you know the region of the country from which a person comes, but what is really important is the nature of the association between the two variables. Which categories of "region" go with which categories of "attitude"? People in the east and west are more likely to approve abortion for any reason than people in the midwest and south. *This* is the important statement made by Table 11.2. There is no way you can discern the nature of this association just from lambda, a measure of strength of association. The lesson is this: *Do not become mesmerized by statistics and let your interpretations of data stop with the gross descriptions statistics provide. Look at the data; interpret them intelligently; use statistics only to the degree they assist you toward this end.*

Lambda is a measure of association, so it varies from 0 to 1. If lambda is 1, all the cases in each category of the independent variable are in one category of the dependent variable. If lambda is 1, conditioning the distribution of the dependent variable on the categories of the independent variable allows for errorless prediction of a case's value on the dependent variable once you know the case's value on

TABLE 11.2 Relationship Between Region of Residence
and Opinion on Abortion, GSS, 1980

| Region of Residence | Abortion Okay? | | Total |
	Yes	No	
East	50% (139)	50% (138)	277
Midwest	30% (119)	70% (273)	392
South	36% (171)	64% (307)	478
West	57% (149)	43% (110)	259
Total	41% (578)	59% (828)	$n = 1406$

the independent variable. Lambda equals 1 if two nominal variables are *perfectly associated* like the hypothetical variables in Table 11.3. The Robinson family is a very routinized and predictable family. Every week for a whole year, a member of the Robinson family could predict without error what was for breakfast if he or she knew the day of the week.

If lambda equals 0, the two nominal variables in a table may be unrelated to each other, but they do not necessarily have to be absolutely unrelated. That is, lambda can equal 0 when conditional distributions of the dependent variable differ, when the variables are, in fact, associated with each other according to the definition of association.

TABLE 11.3 Hypothetical Relationship Showing a Perfect Relationship Between Day of Week and Breakfast Entree for 1 Year at the Robinsons

| Day of Week | Entree | | | |
	Eggs	Cereal	Rolls	Waffles
Monday	—	100% (52)	—	—
Tuesday	—	—	100% (52)	—
Wednesday	—	100% (52)	—	—
Thursday	100% (52)	—	—	—
Friday	—	100% (52)	—	—
Saturday	—	—	—	100% (52)
Sunday	100% (53)	—	—	—
Total	29% (105)	43% (156)	14% (52)	14% (52)

TABLE 11.4 Relationship Between Sex and Opinion on Pornography, GSS, 1980

| | Does Pornography Lead to Rape? | | |
Sex	Yes	No	Total
Male	51% (303)	49% (288)	591
Female	66% (487)	34% (250)	737
Total	59% (790)	41% (538)	$n = 1328$

Consider more data from the GSS shown in Table 11.4. The variables "sex" and one's view of whether pornography leads to rape are associated because the conditional distribution of the dependent variable for women is different from that for men. Some 15 percent more women than men said yes, pornography tends to lead to rape. Lambda, however, is 0. The total error with which one begins is the number of cases in the nonmodal category of the dependent variable, or 538. The remaining error is the sum of cases in the nonmodal categories in the two conditional distribution, or $288 + 250 = 538$. And PRE $= (538 - 538)/538 = 0$, which is lambda for this table.

This little example provides another caution not to become too fond of the statistics: There *is* a relationship between sex and one's view of the effects of pornography, but the descriptive statistic used to measure the strength of that association superficially suggests there is "zero" association. Remember that statistics have their limitations. Lambda has the limitation that it sometimes equals zero when, in fact, two variables are associated with each other. Sometimes the limitations of one summary statistic are overcome by other statistics, but this reassurance should not keep you from attending closely to the data.

· · ·

TWO-BY-TWO TABLES: YULE'S Q

There is a measure of association that does not share lambda's problem of equaling zero when there is some association between two variables. Yule's Q can be used to measure association if the two variables of interest each have only two categories. G. Udny Yule invented Q to measure association in two-by-two 2×2 tables, tables that show the relationship between two variables when both variables have two categories.[1] Table 11.4 is a 2×2 table.

Now Q is a measure of PRE, but "error" is not the same for Q as it was for lambda. To define "error" for Q, first we must have a special definition of the term "pair to cases." A *pair of cases* taken from a 2×2 table is defined as two cases that differ from each other on both variables. (Look closely at Table 11.4 as you read the following discussion.) A case taken from the upper left cell of Table 11.4 is a male who said yes. This case can be "paired," according to this special definition of "pair," only with cases from the lower right cell of Table 11.4, cases that are female and said no. Cases from the upper right cell cannot be "paired" with cases from the upper left cell because both cases would be males. Cases from the upper left cell cannot be "paired" with cases from the lower left cell because both would have said yes. Such pairs would not differ on both variables. Cases from the upper right cell can be paired only with cases from the lower left cell.

Two kinds of pairs of cases can be constructed according to this special definition of "pair": (1) pairs in which one case comes from the upper left cell and one case comes from the lower right cell and (2) pairs in which one case comes from the lower left cell and one case comes from the upper right cell. The first kind of pair is called a *major-diagonal pair* because the pair lies on the *major diagonal* of a 2 × 2 table. The second kind of pair is called a *minor-diagonal pair* because it lies on the minor diagonal of a 2 × 2 table. As shown in Figure 11.1, major-diagonal pairs come from cells that form the northwest-southeast axis of the table, and minor-diagonal pairs come from cells that form the southwest-northeast axis of the table.

I shall call pairs that lie on the major diagonal *concordant pairs*. Pairs that lie on the minor diagonal are *discordant pairs*. These names make sense if you think of the categories of each variable as if they had an order to them. Think about the category in the left-hand column as the "low" category of the dependent variable and the category in the right-hand column as the "High" category. Similarly, think of the first row as the low category of the independent variable and the second row as the high category of the independent variable. Then major-diagonal cases consist of one case that is, for example, low on one variable and low on the other variable plus a case that is high on both variables. This kind of pair is, obviously, *concordant* since it contains cases that are consistently high or low. *Discordant* pairs are formed from one case that is low on the dependent variable and high on the independent variable and one case that is high on the dependent

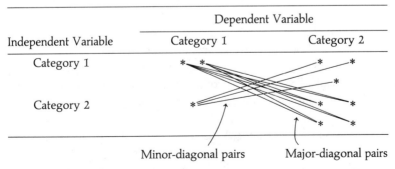

FIGURE 11.1 Major-diagonal and minor-diagonal pairs in a 2 × 2 table.

variable and low on the independent variable. A discordant pair is two cases that occupy inconsistent categories on the two variables. (Pairs that lie on the major diagonal will be called concordant pairs even if the order of the categories does not fit this definition, because most computer programs calculate Q as if this were the case.)

Once you understand the special definition of "pair," you can determine how many of each kind of pair there are. Look at Figure 11.1. There are two cases in the upper left cell. Both those cases can be paired, according to the definition of "pair," with each of the four cases in the lower right cell. Each line from the upper left corner to the lower right corner of the figure represents one concordant pair. There are $2 \times 4 = 8$ lines, so there are eight concordant pairs in this figure. The one case in the lower left can be paired with each of the three cases in the upper right cell, so there are $1 \times 3 = 3$ discordant pairs.

The number of concordant pairs is designated C, and the number of discordant pairs is designated D. For Figure 11.1, $C = 8$ and $D = 3$.

In general, C is equal to the number of cases in the upper left cell of a 2×2 table times the number of cases in the lower right cell and D is the product of the number of cases in the lower left cell and the cases in the upper right cell. For Table 11.4, the table showing the relationship between sex and opinion on pornography, $C = 303(250) = 75{,}750$ and $D = 487(288) = 140{,}256$.

Now I can return to the question of what constitutes error for Yule's Q. Error for Q is determined according to the results of a guessing game involving pairs of cases. If you had no information about the relationship between an independent variable and a dependent variable, then you would have no basis on which to guess whether a randomly selected pair of cases was a concordant pair or a discordant pair. Without any information from the insides of a 2×2 table, you should respond to a person who says, "I have randomly selected a *pair* of cases from the table. What kind of pair is it?" by guessing "concordant" one-half the time and "discordant" the other half of the time. You should guess randomly since you have no information on which to make any other choice. If you did this, over the long run you would be wrong about half the time. That is, you would be wrong 0.5 times the total number of pairs. The total error with which you would begin, then, is $0.5(C + D)$. For Figure 11.1, the total error with which one begins is $0.5(8 + 3) = 5.5$. For Table 11.4, the total error with which one begins is $0.5(75{,}750 + 140{,}256) = 108{,}003$.

Adding information on the independent variable means knowing the conditional distributions of the dependent variable for the two categories of the independent variable. From the two conditional distributions one can calculate the number of concordant and discordant pairs. If one or the other kind of pair predominates, then you should respond to the person saying, "I have randomly selected a pair from a 2×2 table. What kind of pair is it?" by guessing the kind of pair that predominates. If there are more concordant pairs—if $C > D$ as in Figure 11.1—you should guess concordant all the time. The remaining error would be equal to the number of discordant pairs D. If $D > C$, as in Table 11.4, you should always guess discordant, and our error would be C, the number of concordant pairs.

Once you have the total error and the remaining error, you can calculate the PRE. For Figure 11.1, where concordant pairs predominate, the remaining error is the number of minor-diagonal pairs; remaining error $= D = 3$. Therefore,

$$PRE = \frac{\text{total error} - \text{remaining error}}{\text{total error}}$$

$$= \frac{0.5(8 + 3) - 3}{0.5(8 + 3)} = \frac{5.5 - 3}{5.5} = .45$$

For Table 11.4, the remaining error is $C = 75{,}750$, so

$$PRE = \frac{0.5(75{,}750 + 140{,}256) - 75{,}750}{0.5(75{,}750 + 140{,}256)} = .30$$

Based on these calculations, one would say that the variables in Figure 11.1 were more strongly associated than the variables in Table 11.4. The proportionate reduction in error give an indication of the improvement in ability to guess how the data tend to lie in a 2×2 table after information on the independent variable is added.

There is a more general method for calculating Yule's Q. If $C > D$, then

$$Q = \frac{0.5(C + D) - D}{0.5(C + D)}$$

To simplify this expression, multiply it by $2/2$:

$$Q = \frac{0.5(C + D) - D}{0.5(C + D)} \left(\frac{2}{2}\right)$$

$$= \frac{C + D - 2D}{C + D}$$

$$= \frac{C - D}{C + D} \qquad\qquad (11.1)$$

If $D > C$, then by the same logic

$$Q = \frac{D - C}{C + D} \qquad\qquad (11.2)$$

But notice: Formula (11.2) is just the negative of Formula (11.1). That is,

$$\frac{D - C}{C + D} = (-1)\frac{C - D}{C + D}$$

Instead of remembering both Formulas (11.1) and (11.2) and having to remember that one applies when $C > D$ and the other applies when $D > C$, statisticians have adopted the convention that Q is defined as

$$Q = \frac{C - D}{C + D} \tag{11.3}$$

With this definition, Q is greater than 0 when the cases in a 2×2 table lie mostly on the major diagonal (that is, $C > D$), and Q is less than 0 when the cases lie mostly on the minor diagonal (that is, $D > C$). So Q for Figure 11.1 is positive, and Q for table 11.4 is negative. For Figure 11.1, $Q = +0.45$, and $Q = -0.30$ for Table 11.4.

Now Q is a measure of association that indicates both the strength *and* the direction of a relationship. It measures strength of association since it varies from 0 to 1. It measures direction since it is positive when concordant pairs predominate and negative when discordant pairs predominate. And Q is 0 when there is no association between the two variables in a table. That is, Q is 0 when the two conditional distributions in a 2×2 table are the same.

Let's calculate Q for Table 10.1 in which the conditional distributions of attitude toward abortion for men and women are almost identical. (Recall, there was a difference of 0.07 percent in the conditional distributions, so there was a slight association of the two variables according to the definition of "association.") There are $253 \times 465 = 117,645$ concordant pairs and $325 \times 363 = 117,975$ discordant pairs. So $Q = (117,645 - 117,975)/(117,645 + 117,975) = -0.0014$. This means sex and attitude are virtually unassociated even though the discordant pairs predominate slightly. Women tend, ever so slightly, to say no more than men. Q is very small and indicates the small degree of association.

Q equals 1 or -1 when two variables are perfectly associated. If knowing a case's value on the independent variable allows us to predict the case's value on the dependent variable without error, then Q will equal $+1$ or -1. That is, Q will equal $+1$ if all the cases fall into the upper left and lower right cells, and Q will equal -1 if all the cases fall into the lower left and upper right cells only.

Q also equals 1 or -1 in some other circumstances, and you need to be aware of this peculiarity of Yule's Q. If there is a 0 in any one of the four cells of a 2×2 table, then either C or D will equal 0 and Q will equal -1 or $+1$. Look at Table 11.5. It shows the relationship between getting a vaccination against a disease and dying of that disease within 1 year. If you know that a person got the vaccine, you can predict without error that the person would not die of the disease within

TABLE 11.5 Relationship Between Getting a Vaccination against a Disease and Dying of that Disease within 1 Year

Got Vaccine?	Died? Yes	No	Total
Yes	—	100% (520)	520
No	12% (116)	88% (850)	966
Total	8% (116)	92% (1370)	$n = 1486$

the year. If you knew the person did not get the vaccine, then you would also tend to predict that the person did not die of the disease, but there would be some error in this prediction. The variables are not perfectly associated. Yet—and this is the peculiarity of Q—Q is equal to -1 [that is, $Q = (0 \times 850 - 116 \times 520)/(0 \times 850 + 116 \times 520) = -1$].

Some people say this peculiarity of Q indicates that Q "overestimates" the association between two variables. After all, they argue, the two variables in Table 11.5 are strongly associated, but they are not perfectly associated, in the usual sense of "perfect predictability of the dependent variable for *all* categories of the independent variable." As far as G. Udny Yule, the statistic's inventor, was concerned, however, the variables in Table 11.5 *are* perfectly correlated. Yule was one of the early statisticians who wanted to know how to intervene in processes to make improvements in a situation *now*. He did not side with the eugenicists who were willing to help nature do its selecting so that living conditions would improve five generations down the road. Yule studied data just like those shown in Table 11.5, and if he ever found an independent variable, one of the categories of which seemed to lead *without exception* to a better life (not dying, improved living standard, not returning to the poor house), he was willing to say that variable was perfectly associated with the dependent variable. He constructed his measure of association around the value he placed on social activism. You should remember that Q has a peculiarity to it, but Q's peculiarity is based on the political orientation of its inventor.

· · ·

ORDINAL VARIABLES IN TABLES THAT ARE LARGER THAN TWO-BY-TWO: GOODMAN AND KRUSKAL'S GAMMA

Frankly, Yule did not invent Q by applying the logic of PRE to 2 × 2 tables. Yule needed a statistic for studying data on the effects of innoculation, social programs, and the like, and he invented Q (naming it after Quetelet) because it met his needs.

The logic of PRE came later. The logic can be discerned in a 1954 paper by Goodman and Kruskal,[2] who saw that Q followed the PRE logic. Goodman and Kruskal then extended that logic to tables that were larger than 2 × 2. Goodman and Kruskal invented the statistic called *gamma*, denoted by the Greek letter γ, to describe the relationship between two ordinal variables when at least one of the variables has more than two categories.

Gamma is appropriate only for ordinal variables. To see why this restriction on gamma is necessary, think about the reason Q can be calculated for any 2 × 2 table regardless of whether the table contains nominal or ordinal variables or one of each. It makes little sense, on the face of it, to say, "Sex and one's opinion of whether pornography leads to rape are negatively associated" or "Innoculation and whether one lives or dies are *negatively* associated" even though the Q's were less than zero. Why? Because the variables "sex," "attitude," "innoculation," and "lives or dies" have no order to their categories by which one can judge positive and negative direction. However, once you decide which category to put first, the order of the two categories is completely determined. If you put "male" first, "female" must come second if there are only two categories. Once you put "died" first, "lived" must come second. In a 2 × 2 table, both variables *acquire* an order to their categories, and that order allows one to speak about the direction of an association. If male is placed before female on sex and yes before no on opinion, then a negative relationship between sex and opinion means that females (the "higher" category on sex) tend to say yes (the "lower" category on opinion) and males tend to say no. The direction of a relationship in a 2 × 2 table can be reversed by interchanging the two categories of one variable. The sign of Q changes if you flip the categories of one variable, but the interpretation of Q remains the same because the nature of the relationship remains the same.

If there are more than two categories to a nominal variable, there is no defensible way to determine an ordering among the categories. If you must describe the relationship between two nominal variables and one of them has more than two categories, you must use lambda as your measure of association. If you want to describe the relationship between two ordinal variables and at least one of them has more than two categories, the statistic of choice is Goodman and Kruskal's gamma.

Consider Table 11.6. It shows the relationship between urbanization and per capita income (PCI) for the 105 countries in Appendix A that have values for both variables. The categories of both variables have been reduced to 4 by dividing each variable at its quartiles. For urbanization, $Q_1 = 21.3$, $Q_2 = 42.8$, and $Q_3 = 60.5$. (For purposes of this analysis, Ecuador, the country whose value of urbanization is the median, was put in the second category.) For per capita income, $Q_1 = 333.5$, $Q_2 = 787.5$, and $Q_3 = 2741.5$. To construct Table 11.6, each case was examined to determine which quartile group it fell into on each variable. Then the case was placed in the cell that describes the case's joint placement on the two variables. So Albania with an urbanization of 38 percent falls into the second quar-

TABLE 11.6 Urbanization and Per Capita Income with Both Variables Divided at the Quartiles

| | Per-Capita-Income Quartile | | | | |
Urbanization Quartile	1st	2d	3d	4th	Total[1]
1st	67% (18)	30% (8)	4% (1)	—	27
2d	15% (4)	50% (13)	23% (6)	11% (3)	26
3d	—	15% (4)	58% (15)	27% (7)	26
4th	—	4% (1)	23% (6)	73% (19)	26
Total	21% (22)	25% (26)	27% (28)	28% (29)	$n = 105$

[1] Some rows do not sum to 100 percent due to rounding.

tile of that variable. With a per capita income of $490, Albania falls into the second quartile on that variable. Albania is one of the 13 countries in the cell that is in the second row and second column of Table 11.6, the "2d-2d" cell. Barbados falls into the first quartile on urbanization and the third quartile on per capita income. It is the only case in the 1st-3d cell of the table.

You can see from the four conditonal distributions of Table 11.6 that urbanization and per capita income are related. As urbanization increases, there is a tendency for cases to fall into higher quartiles of per capita income. Gamma provides a measure of the strength of this relationship. Gamma, like Q has the formula

$$\gamma = \frac{C - D}{C + D} \tag{11.4}$$

You just have to generalize the manner in which "concordant pairs" and "discordant pairs" are calculated. The special definition of "pair," however, remains the same. (A pair consists of two cases whose values on the two variables are different.)

Begin calculations of gamma for Table 11.6 by considering the 18 cases in the 1st–1st cell, the cell in the upper left corner. You can pair these 18 cases with many cases that lie in the general northwest-southeast orientation of the major diagonal. How many? All the cases in the nine cells that lie below and to the right of the 1st–1st cell. That is, you can pair the 17 cases in the 1st–1st cell with all the cases in the 2d–2d cell, the 2d–3d cell, the 2d–4th cell, the 3d–2d cell, the 3d–3d cell, the 3d–4th cell, the 4th–2d cell, the 4th–3d cell, and the 4th–4th cell. These $13 + 6 + 3 + 4 + 15 + 7 + 1 + 6 + 19 = 74$ cases are all different from the 18 cases in the 1st–1st cell on both variables, and they lie in the general direction of the major diagonal with respect to one another. So you can form $18 \times 74 = 1332$ concordant pairs using the 18 cases from the 1st–1st cell.

But there are more concordant pairs in the table. Consider the eight cases in the 1st–2d cell. You can pair each of these cases with all the cases that lie below and to the right of them to form concordant pairs. You can form $8(6 + 3 + 15 + 7 + 6 + 19) = 448$ concordant pairs in this way. That is a total of $1332 + 448 = 1780$ concordant pairs so far.

You are not finished yet, however. With the one case in the 1st–3d cell you can form concordant pairs with the cases from the 2d–4th, 3d–4th, and 4th–4th cells, or with the $3 + 7 + 19 = 29$ cases that lie below and to the right of the 1st–3d cell. That is another 1×29 pairs for a total of 1809. There are no cells that lie below and to the right of the 1st–4th cell, so even if there were cases in that cell, no concordant pairs could be formed with them.

To form even more concordant pairs, follow the same procedure on the second row of Table 11.6. Calculate concordant pairs by multiplying the number of cases in each cell by the number of cases below and to the right of the cell. For the second row there are $4(4 + 15 + 7 + 1 + 6 + 19) + 13(15 + 7 + 6 + 19) + 6(7 + 19) = 975$. For the two rows, that makes a total of $1809 + 975 = 2784$ concordant pairs. There are no cells below and to the right of the three cases in the 2d–4th cell, so no concordant pairs can be forced by using that cell.

For the third row there are $0(1 + 6 + 19) + 4(6 + 19) + 15(19) = 385$ concordant pairs. The concordant pairs for the three rows, then, total 3169.

No cases lie below the cases in the fourth row, so there are no concordant pairs that can be formed with cases in that row. For the whole table, then, there are 3169 concordant pairs, or $C = 3169$.

In general, to find C for Formula (11.4) you work your way through an entire table, cell by cell, multiplying the number of cases in each cell by the number of cases in all cells *below and to the right* of the cell in question. The sum of all these multiplications is C.

Discordant pairs are formed by cases that lie in a southwest-northeast orientation to one another. To find D, work your way through a table, cell by cell, multiplying the number of cases in each cell by the number of cases that lie *above and to the right* of the cell in question, and sum all the products. in Table 11.6, there are no cells above the first row, so you begin this procedure with the cells in the second row. There are nine cases above and to the right of the four cases in the 2d–1st cell, so you begin with $4 \times 9 = 36$ discordant pairs. There is one case above and to the right of the 13 cases in the 2d–2d cell, so there are 13 more discordant pairs. There are no cases above and to the right of the five cases in the 2d–3d cell, so a total of $36 + 13 = 49$ discordant pairs are formed by using cases in the second row of Table 11.6. For the third and fourth rows there is a total of $0(8 + 1 + 13 + 6 + 3) + 4(1 + 6 + 3) + 15(3) + 0(8 + 1 + 13 + 6 + 3 + 4 + 15 + 7) + 1(1 + 6 + 3 + 15 + 7) + 6(3 + 7) = 177$. Then D for the whole table, is the sum of the discordant pairs formed with cases in the second row, 49, and discordant pairs forms with cases in the third and forth rows. 177, or $D = 177 + 49 = 226$.

With D and C it is a straightforward matter to calculate gamma for Table 11.6;

$$\gamma = \frac{3169 - 226}{3169 + 226} = \frac{2943}{3395} = .87$$

$\gamma = .87$ is a very large gamma, close to its maximum value of 1.0. This gamma is even larger than the measure of association calculated in Chapter 10 for these same two variables. Once again, this is not an example of lying with statistics; it is an example of the statistics themselves being different. You can compare two relationships to each other if you use the same statistic to measure the strength of both. It was perfectly legitimate to compare the strength of association of urbanization and per capita income calculated in Chapter 10 to the strength of the relationship of sex and test score measured in the same way. It is not legitimate to compare the strength of association of urbanization and per capita income calculated in Chapter 10 to the strength of the relationship calculated here. Here γ was used; Chapter 10 took a different approach.

As a concluding exercise regarding gamma, let's test a hypothesis using the hospital cost data in Appendix A. My hypothesis is this: The more specialized a physician is, the more likely he or she is to care for patients who suffer complications. Figure 11.2 contains the raw data I shall use to test this hypothesis.

The specialization number, recall, is the percentage of DRGs which a physician used to discharge patients who are not in the obstetrical group of DRGs. The *higher* the percentage, the *less* specialized the physician. These numbers range from 47 to 97 percent. There are nine physicians with specialization scores below 70 percent. For this example, I will call them the *specialists*. The other 13 physicians, 7 of whom had scores above 90 percent and another 5 of whom scored between 80 and 89 percent, I will call *generalists*. I put an S or a G next to the specialization score in Figure 11.2.

I determined the number of patients with complications treated by each physician by adding the number of patients each physician discharged in DRG 370, 372, or 383. This variable's range is from 0 to 16. I decided to divide this variable into four categories: no patients discharged in DRG 370, 372, or 383; 1 or 2 patients discharged; 3 to 10 patients discharged; and 11 or more patients discharged in a DRG with a complicating diagnosis. Five physicians are in the first category, nine are in the second, six are in the third, and two are in the fourth. I put the category number (1 = no patients; 2 = 1 or 2 patients; 3 = 3–10 patients; 4 = 11 or more patients) in parentheses next to the actual number of patients a physician discharged.

The hypothesis is

Specialization → Discharges with complicating diagnoses

Number of discharges is the dependent variable. Whether a physician is a specialist or generalist is the independent variable. The hypothesis is that the specialists

Physician	Specialization,[1] %		Number of Patients with Complications[2]	
01	50	(S)	2	(2)
02	47	(S)	4	(3)
03	61	(S)	16	(4)
04	63	(S)	2	(2)
05	95	(G)	0	(1)
06	94	(G)	1	(2)
07	55	(S)	8	(3)
08	92	(G)	0	(1)
09	93	(G)	2	(2)
10	75	(G)	2	(2)
11	62	(S)	6	(3)
12	67	(S)	1	(2)
13	90	(G)	4	(3)
14	90	(G)	1	(2)
15	86	(G)	3	(3)
16	97	(G)	0	(1)
17	63	(S)	14	(4)
18	84	(G)	3	(3)
19	85	(G)	1	(2)
20	89	(G)	2	(2)
21	63	(S)	0	(1)
22	88	(G)	0	(1)

[1] Specialization score from the data set. Here S is a specialist; anyone who scores below 70 percent is so designated. And G is a generalist; a specialization score of 70 percent and above merits this designation.
[2] Patients discharged in DRG 370, 372, or 383. The number in parentheses is the group to which each case was assigned: 1 = no patients treated; 2 = 1 or 2 patients treated; 3 = 3–10 patients treated; 4 = 11 or more patients treated.

FIGURE 11.2 Raw data to test a hypothesis concerning the relationship between specialization and number of complicated cases treated.

TABLE 11.7 Relationship Between Specialization and Number of Patients Discharged with Complicating Diagnosis (DRG 370, 372, or 383)

Specialization	Number of Discharges			
	0	1–2	3–10	11 or more
Specialists	11% (1)	33% (3)	33% (3)	22% (2)
Generalists	31% (4)	46% (6)	23% (3)	— (0)
Total	23% (5)	41% (9)	27% (6)	9% (2)

will tend to discharge more patients with complicating diagnoses than will the generalists.

Table 11.7 shows a cross tabulation of specialization with number of discharges in DRGs 370, 372, and 383. A case is a physician. The total number of cases is 22. The conditional distributions—the one for specialists and the one for generalists—differ, so specialization is associated with the number of complicated cases handled. What is the nature of that association? Look at the rows of Table 11.7. Specialists tend to fall into the higher categories on the dependent variable. One specialist treated no patients with complications, but 55 percent of the specialists treated three or more cases with complications. Only 23 percent of the generalists treated three or more cases in DRG 370, 372, or 383. The hypothesis appears to be supported by the sample data.

Which statistic would you use to describe the relationship between these two variables? The dependent variable is ordinal and has more than two categories, so gamma is a candidate. The independent variable is not ordinal, but it only has two categories. If you interpret the sign of gamma in light of the order imposed on those two categories, then you may use gamma as a descriptive statistic. That is, if the hypothesis is supported, then gamma for Table 11.7 should be negative since "lower-valued" cases on the independent variable ("specialists") would tend to go with higher-valued cases on the dependent variable. Gamma for Table 11.7 is, in fact, -0.58 ($C = 18$; $D = 68$). The hypothesis is supported, and you would say that the variables are moderately strongly associated ($\gamma = -0.58$).

$\cdot\ \cdot\ \cdot$

INFERENTIAL TESTS ABOUT G, THE POPULATION PARAMETER CORRESPONDING TO THE SAMPLE STATISTIC GAMMA

If you know γ for the association between two discrete variables in a sample, you can calculate an interval estimate for G, the population parameter corresponding to gamma. All you need to know is that the sampling distribution of γ is normal with a maximum standard error of

$$\sqrt{\frac{n(1 - \gamma)}{C + D}}$$

You can conduct a hypothesis test about G using the test statistic

$$\frac{\gamma - G}{\sqrt{\dfrac{n(1 - \gamma)}{C + D}}}$$

and you can construct confidence interval estimates of G.

TABLE 11.8 Relationship Between an NBA
Player's Race and Percentage of Population
of Player's Team's City That Is Black

Black Population of Player's Team City, %	Player's Race		Total
	Black	White	
< 10	56	32	88
10–20	80	30	110
> 20	48	7	55
Total	184	60	253

As an example, consider the data in Table 11.8. They come from a newspaper story about two Harvard professors who were trying to claim that in the National Basketball Association (NBA) there is a leaguewide pattern that teams in cities with especially large white populations tend to have a lot of white players and teams in cities with especially large black populations tend to have a large number of black players. The two variables in this table are "black population of player's team's city" and the "player's race." If the data support the hypothesis, how should the cases—players—be arrayed in the table? Of course, there should be a higher proportion of black players in the cities with larger proportions of blacks in the population. That is, the cases should tend to array themselves in a general south-west-northeast direction in the table. Calculating a value for the table should yield a negative gamma. Indeed, gamma for the table is −0.36, so the sample data support the hypothesis.

Remember, these data are only a sample. They were drawn from a population. In this case, the sample consists of one year of NBA players. The population is the players in the NBA without regard to year. Does this sample provide evidence to make the claim that in general there is a relationship between a player's race and the racial composition of the city in which the player plays? That is the inferential question: Is $G < 0$, where G is the "gamma" parameter for the entire population?

First, we can conduct a hypothesis test about G. Let's conduct this test with a level to reject of $\alpha = .05$. The alternative hypothesis is

$$H_A: G < 0$$

and the null hypothesis is

$$H_0: G \geq 0$$

Since $C = 2632$ and $D = 5536$, the maximum standard error of gamma, the sample statistic is

$$\sqrt{\frac{245[1 - (-0.36)]}{2632 + 5536}} = .20$$

Then the test statistic is

$$\frac{-.36 - 0}{.20} = -1.80$$

With a level to reject of .05 in a one-tailed test, the critical value of z is -1.645. The test statistic lies below that point on the distribution. So you can reject the null hypothesis and accept the alternative. In the population from which the data in Table 11.8 came, there is a relationship between the proportion of a team city's population that is black and an NBA player's race.

Now let's construct a 95 percent confidence interval estimate of G for the relationship between an NBA player's race and the percentage of the population in the player's team city that is black. The standard error is still .20. The 95 percent confidence interval extends 1.96 standard errors out from the sample of -0.36. You can be 95 percent confident that the population parameter G is in the interval $-0.36 \pm 1.96(0.20)$ or between -0.75 and 0.03. Notice that the interval contains $G = 0$. The variables may be unrelated in the population from which this sample came.

But wait! We rejected the null hypothesis in the first step, but now an interval estimate of the parameter G contains 0, which says the variables may be unrelated. That seems contradictory. That happens because a 95 percent confidence interval is constructed by using the normal deviate that corresponds to a *two*-tailed test of the hypothesis. The hypothesis test was conducted by using only a one-tailed test. That is why there is a seeming contradiction here.

There is one other caution in the interpretation of these results. Remember that the estimate of the standard error gives a *maximum* standard error. That makes a test of a null hypothesis about G a conservative test, but it makes an interval estimate of G the widest it might be.

• • •

SUMMARY

Lambda, Yule's Q, and Goodman and Kruskal's gamma are statistics used to describe the relationship between two discrete variables. They are bivariate descriptive statistics. Lambda is used to measure association between two nominal variables; Q is a measure of association in 2×2 tables; γ is a measure of association for ordinal variables that is used if one or both of the variables have more than two categories.

• • •

KEY CONCEPTS IN THIS CHAPTER

Gamma   298
    Defined [Formula (11.4)]   299
Inferential tests for tables larger than 2×2 303

· · ·

NOTES

1. G. Udny Yule, "On the Methods of Measuring Association between Two Attributes," *Journal of the Royal Statistical Society* 75:579–642, 1912.

2. Leo Goodman and William Kruskal, "Measures of Association for Cross Classifications," *Journal of the American Statistical Association* 49: 732–764, 1954.

· · ·

EXERCISES

Chapter 11

1. Let's go back to the table that resulted from a quick survey following the 1984 Vice Presidential debate between Geraldine Ferraro and George Bush:

Respondent's Sex	Who Won?		Total
	Bush	Ferraro	
Male	158	79	237
Female	109	182	291
Total	267	261	528

a. Who won the debate? Why do you say that?

b. Find the error around the overall modal response to the question, Who won?

c. What is the conditional modal response for females? What is the remaining error for that category of the independent variable?

d. What is the conditional mode for males? What is the remaining error for that category of the independent variable?

e. What is the remaining error for the whole table?

f. What is the PRE in guessing "who won" achieved by knowing a person's sex? That is, what is lambda for this table?

g. What does it mean for lambda to be this size?

h. Interpret your results by writing a sentence describing the strength of the relationship and incorporating the results of inferential tests.

2. Calculate Yule's Q for the 2 × 2 table in Exercise 1.

a. How many concordant pairs are there?

b. How many discordant pairs are there?

c. What is Q?

d. How do you interpret this result?

e. What does it mean that Q is different from lambda for this table, if there is a difference between them?

3. Here is a table showing the relationship between visiting one's physician during the first trimester of pregnancy and the birth weight of the child that results from the pregnancy.

Relationship Between Having First-Trimester Prenatal Visits and Giving Birth to a Low-Birth-Weight Infant, Hypothetical Data

Prenatal Visits in First Trimester	Birth Weight(g)		Total
	< 2500	≥ 2500	
Yes	20% (425)	80% (1735)	2160
No	42% (615)	58% (865)	1480
Total	29% (1040)	71% (2600)	3640

a. Describe the data shown in this table. What is the nature of the relationship between the two variables?

b. What is the most appropriate measure of association for this table? Calculate it. Use it to describe the relationship.

   c. Do you think there is a causal relationship between visiting one's physician early in pregnancy and the birth weight of the child? If yes, why? If not, what other variables might be bringing about this spurious relationship?

   4. Consider the first 75 countries in the first data set in Appendix A. This analysis concerns male life expectancy and literacy rate.

   a. Reconstruct each variable so that both have three categories and each category has roughly the same number of countries in it.
   b. Construct a 3 × 3 joint frequency distribution (table) showing the relationship between these two variables.
   c. Calculate the appropriate measure of association for the table. Describe the relationship, using this statistic.
   d. Conduct appropriate inferential tests and describe the results.
   e. Interpret your results. Decide if there is a causal relationship between these two variables or if there might be other variables at work in this relationship.

   5. Consider the following table that shows the relationship between religious preference and attitude toward abortion only for those who say their religious intensity is "very strong."

Relationship Between Religious Preference and Attitude toward Abortion for Those of Very Strong Religious Intensity, GSS, 1980

	Abortion Okay?		
Religious Preference	Yes	No	Total
Protestant	28% (101)	72% (262)	363
Catholic	21% (32)	79% (118)	150
Jewish	67% (10)	33% (5)	15
None[1]	—	—	—
Other	50% (3)	50% (3)	6
Total	27% (146)	73% (388)	534

[1] Excluded from this analysis.

   a. What hypothesis probably motivated the construction of this table?
   b. Calculate the appropriate measure of association for the table. Describe the relationship between the two variables, using this statistic.

c. Conduct the appropriate inferential tests to see if the sample provides evidence for claiming the variables are associated in the population from which the sample came.

d. Interpret the results. Decide if there is a causal relationship between the variables or if there might be other variables at work in this relationship.

6. Consider the following table that shows the relationship between religious preference and attitude toward abortion only for those who say their religious intensity is "not so strong."

Relationship Between Religious Preference and Attitude toward Abortion for Those Whose Religious Intensity Is "Not So Strong"

Religious Preference	Abortion Okay?		Total
	Yes	No	
Protestant	48% (216)	52% (230)	446
Catholic	40% (64)	60% (95)	159
Jewish	75% (6)	25% (2)	8
None[1]	—	—	—
Other	69% (11)	31% (5)	16
Total	47% (297)	53% (332)	629

[1] Excluded from this analysis.

a. What hypothesis probably motivated the construction of this table?

b. Calculate the appropriate measure of association for the table. Describe the relationship between the two variables, using this statistic.

c. Conduct the appropriate inferential tests to see if the sample provides evidence for claiming the variables are associated in the population from which the sample came.

d. Interpret the results. Decide if there is a causal relationship between the variables or if other variables might be at work in this relationship.

7. Consider the following table that shows only the relationship between religious intensity and attitude toward abortion.

Relationship Between Religious Intensity and Attitude
toward Abortion, GSS, 1980

	Abortion Okay?		
Religious Intensity	Yes	No	Total
Very strong	27% (146)	73% (388)	534
Not so strong	47% (297)	53% (332)	629
Total	38% (443)	62% (720)	1163

- **a.** What hypothesis probably motivated the construction of this table?
- **b.** Calculate the appropriate measure of association for the table. Describe the relationship between the two variables, using this statistic.
- **c.** Conduct the appropriate inferential tests to see if the sample provides evidence for claiming the variables are associated in the population from which the sample came.
- **d.** Interpret the results. Decide if there is a causal relationship between the variables or if other variables might be at work in this relationship.

   8. Consider the relationship between one's occupation and one's attitude toward homosexuality expressed in the following table.

Relationship Between Occupation and Attitude toward
Homosexual Relations, GSS, 1980

	Attitude toward Homosexual Relations		
Occupation	Always Wrong	Other Response	Total
White-collar	62% (435)	38% (267)	702
Blue-collar	78% (501)	22% (143)	644
Total	70% (936)	30% (410)	1346

- **a.** What hypothesis probably motivated the construction of this table?
- **b.** Calculate the appropriate measure of association for the table. Describe the relationship between the two variables, using this statistic.
- **c.** Conduct the appropriate inferential tests to see if the sample provides evidence for claiming the variables are associated in the population from which the sample came.

d. Interpret the results. Decide if there is a causal relationship between the variables or if there might be other variables at work in this relationship.

9. Consider the relationship between one's occupation and one's own personal earnings (i.e., not total family income) as expressed in the following table.

Relationship Between Occupation and Earnings, GSS, 1980

| Occupation | Respondent's Earnings in 1977 | | Total |
	Less than $15,000	$15,000 or more	
White-collar	59% (279)	41% (192)	471
Blue-collar	70% (287)	30% (124)	411
Total	64% (566)	36% (316)	882

a. What hypothesis probably motivated the construction of this table?
b. Calculate the appropriate measure of association for the table. Using this statistic, describe the relationship between the two variables.
c. Conduct the appropriate inferential tests to see if the sample provides evidence for claiming the variables are associated in the population from which the sample came.
d. Interpret the results. Decide if there is a causal relationship between the variables or if there might be other variables at work in this relationship.

10. Consider the same relationship as that shown in Exercise 9—the relationship between one's occupation and one's own earnings—but only among males.

Relationship Between Occupation and Earnings for Males

| Occupation | Respondent's Earnings in 1977 | | Total |
	Less than $15,000	$15,000 or more	
White-collar	33% (69)	67% (142)	211
Blue-collar	57% (159)	43% (119)	278
Total	47% (228)	53% (261)	489

a. What hypothesis probably motivated the construction of this table?
b. Calculate the appropriate measure of association for the table. Describe the relationship between the two variables, using this statistic.

    c. Conduct the appropriate inferential tests to see if the sample provides evidence for claiming the variables are associated in the population from which the sample came.

    d. Interpret the results. Is there a causal relationship between the variables, or might there be other variables at work in this relationship?

11. Consider the same relationship as shown in Exercise 10—the relationship between occupation and earnings—but only among females.

Relationship Between Occupation and Earnings for Females

Occupation	Respondent's Earnings in 1977		Total
	Less than $15,000	$15,000 or more	
White-collar	81% (210)	19% (50)	260
Blue-collar	96% (128)	4% (5)	133
Total	86% (338)	14% (55)	393

    a. What hypothesis probably motivated the construction of this table?

    b. Calculate the appropriate measure of association for the table. Using this statistic, describe the relationship between the two variables.

    c. Conduct the appropriate inferential tests to see if the sample provides evidence for claiming the variables are associated in the population from which the sample came.

    d. Interpret the results. Decide if there is a causal relationship between the variables or if there might be other variables at work in this relationship.

12. Consider the relationship between religious intensity and the question of whether a person wants laws prohibiting interracial marriage.

Relationship Between Religious Intensity and Desire for Laws Prohibiting Interracial Marriage, GSS, 1980

Religious Intensity	Desire Laws Prohibiting Intermarriage?		Total
	Yes	No	
Very strong	35% (188)	65% (348)	536
Not so strong	27% (175)	73% (467)	642
Total	31% (363)	69% (815)	1178

a. What hypothesis probably motivated the construction of this table?

b. Calculate the appropriate measure of association for the table. Describe the relationship between the two variables, using this statistic.

c. Conduct the appropriate inferential tests to see if the sample provides evidence for claiming the variables are associated in the population from which the sample came.

d. Interpret the results. Decide if there is a causal relationship between the variables or if there might be other variables at work in this relationship.

13. Consider the relationship between one's race and the question of whether one wants laws prohibiting interracial marriage.

Relationship Between Race and Desire for Laws
Prohibiting Interracial Marriage

Race	Desire Laws Prohibiting Intermarriage?		
	Yes	No	Total
Whites	32% (340)	68% (717)	1057
Nonwhites	19% (23)	81% (98)	121
Total	31% (363)	69% (815)	1178

a. What hypothesis probably motivated the construction of this table?

b. Calculate the appropriate measure of association for the table. Describe the relationship between the two variables, using this statistic.

c. Conduct the appropriate inferential tests to see if the sample provides evidence for claiming the variables are associated in the population from which the sample came.

d. Interpret the results. Decide if there is a causal relationship between the variables or if other variables might be at work in this relationship.

14. Consider the relationship between task label and the time spent on word games among those with a low Protestant work-ethic score in internal-motivation experiment 1.

Relationship Between Task Label and Time Spent for a
Low Level of Protestant Work Ethic, Internal-Motivation
Experiment 1

Task Label	Time Spent, s		
	Low (< 205.5 s)	High (≥ 205.5 s)	Total
Work	64% (9)	36% (5)	14
Leisure	46% (6)	54% (7)	13
Total	56% (15)	44% (12)	27

a. What hypothesis probably motivated the construction of this table?
b. Calculate the appropriate measure of association for the table. Describe the relationship between the two variables, using this statistic.
c. Conduct the appropriate inferential tests to see if the sample provides evidence for claiming the variables are associated in the population from which the sample came.
d. Interpret the results. Decide if there is a causal relationship between the variables or if there might be other variables at work in this relationship.

15. Consider the relationship between task label and the time spent on word games among those with a high Protestant work-ethic score in internal-motivation experiment 1.

Relationship Between Task Label and Time Spent for a
High Level of Protestant Work Ethic, Internal-Motivation
Experiment 1

Task Label	Time Spent, s		
	Low (< 205.5 s)	High (≥ 205.5 s)	Total
Work	29% (4)	71% (10)	14
Leisure	62% (8)	38% (5)	13
Total	44% (12)	56% (15)	27

a. What hypothesis probably motivated the construction of this table?
b. Calculate the appropriate measure of association for the table. Using this statistic, describe the relationship between the two variables.
c. Conduct the appropriate inferential tests to see if the sample provides evidence for claiming the variables are associated in the population from which the sample came.

   d. Interpret the results. Decide if there is a causal relationship between the variables or if there might be other variables at work in this relationship.

16. Here is a table showing the relationship between the number of magazine subscriptions a person has and the amount of junk mail the person receives per week.

Relationship Between Subscriptions and Junk Mail

Subscriptions	Junk Mail Pieces				
	0–2	3–6	7–10	11+	Total
0–1	58	75	15	7	155
2–3	42	88	107	85	322
4 or more	13	76	145	178	412
Total	113	239	267	270	889

   a. What hypothesis probably motivated the construction of this table?
   b. Calculate the appropriate measure of association for the table. Describe the relationship between the two variables, using this statistic.
   c. Conduct the appropriate inferential tests to see if the sample provides evidence for claiming the variables are associated in the population from which the sample came.
   d. Interpret the results. Decide if there is a causal relationship between the variables or if there might be other variables at work in this relationship.

17. Here is a table showing the relationship between a city's economic growth and an index showing business confidence among the city's business leaders.

Relationship Between Economic Growth and Business Confidence

Growth	Confidence			
	Low	Moderate	High	Total
Low	14	32	44	90
Moderate	12	27	41	80
High	7	41	24	72
Total	33	100	109	242

a. What hypothesis probably motivated the construction of this table?
b. Calculate the appropriate measure of association for the table. Describe the relationship between the two variables, using this statistic.
c. Conduct the appropriate inferential tests to see if the sample provides evidence for claiming the variables are associated in the population from which the sample came.
d. Interpret the results. Decide if there is a causal relationship between the variables or if there might be other variables at work in this relationship.

18. Here is a table showing the relationship between a university's endowment and the number of students it places in medical schools on average each year.

Relationship Between Endowment and Medical School Placements

Endowment Size	Medical School Placements			
	0–10	11–50	51–120	121+
$0	3	13	11	8
$0 < Endowment < $1 million	7	17	18	6
$1 million ≤ Endowment < $10 million	5	42	13	10
Endowment ≥ $10 million	1	32	27	0

a. What hypothesis probably motivated the construction of this table?
b. Calculate the appropriate measure of association for the table. Describe the relationship between the two variables, using this statistic.
c. Conduct the appropriate inferential tests to see if the sample provides evidence for claiming the variables are associated in the population from which the sample came.
d. Interpret the results. Decide if there is a causal relationship between the variables or if there might be other variables at work in this relationship.

C

▼

Statistical Doubletalk?[1]

• • •

Consider the percentage. If you want to "lie with statistics." if you want to "prove anything with statistics," you do not need all the sophistication of the recent chapters. You need only study closely this lowly transformation. It is the best weapon in the arsenal used against the statistically unarmed. As with any language, you can use statistics to deceive the uninitiated, those who do not and will not try to understand. And the primary path to deception begins with the percentage.

• • •

PERCENTAGE CHANGE AND PERCENTAGE POINTS

What is a "percentage"? Simple. A percentage is 100 times the ratio of a quantity to a base. To know what a percentage describes, you need to know the quantity and the base on which the quantity is being expressed.

You received a 6 percent raise this year. So you are being paid R more dollars this year than last year, when you were receiving B dollars, where 100 times the ratio of the raise R to the base salary B is equal to 6. That is, $100(R/B) = 6$ percent. Simple and familiar.

But be careful. Things can get a little tricky—especially when you are talking about "percentage changes."

A new president of a company sends a memorandum to the secretarial pool whose average pay was $14,000 when he arrived one year ago. The memorandum says, "I'm very pleased that the raises received by the secretarial staff are 50 percent more than the raises received last year." "Fifty percent?" a secretary thinks. "I only got a 3 percent raise to $14,420 this year. If any of my friends are making $21,000 and didn't tell me, they'll be wearing their word processors." But the memorandum said nothing about "50 percent raises." It just said that this year's raises are 50 percent more than last year's. The base of the boss's percentage was not salary but last year's *percentage increase* in salary. Last year, all the secretaries received 2 percent raises. This year, they all received 3 percent raises. Voilà! This year's percentage increase is $3 - 2 = 1$ percent (1 *percentage point*) greater than last year's percentage increase and

$$100\left(\frac{1\%}{2\%}\right) = 50\%$$

So this year's increase was 50 percent greater than last year's raise.

There is a big difference between "percentage change" and percentage points. The boss could have written, "Your raises are 1 percentage point greater than last year's raises. Enjoy." He chose to write about the percentage change in the percentage increase. He probably took a course in "happy memorandum writing." Part of the syllabus was called "Good News Looks Better with a Different Base in the Percentage."

· · ·

DIFFERENT BASES

Over a 4-month period, your broker takes you on a seesaw stock market ride. At the end of the first month, he phones and says, "Bad news. Your portfolio fell 20 percent this month." At the end of the second month, he phones and says, "Good news. Your portfolio rose 20 percent this month." Third month: "Bad news. Down 30 percent this month." Fourth month: "Good news. Up 30 percent this month." Down 20 percent, up 20 percent, down 30 percent, up 30 percent. You are even, right? Wrong.

Figure 1 charts the progress of your portfolio value that had a beginning value of $5000. A 20 percent decrease from the base of $5000 means a decrease in value

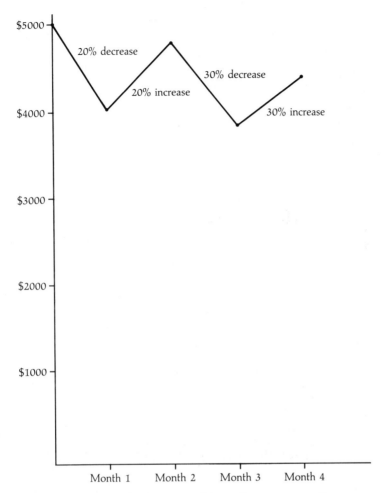

FIGURE 1 Changes in portfolio value over 4 months.

of (20 percent)($5000) = $1000. At the end of 1 month, the value of your port-folio is $4000. The value goes up 20 percent the next month, but this increase is from the new base of $4000. That means an increase of (20 percent)($4000) = $800. The value of the portfolio is now $4800. A 30 percent decrease from *this* base is a loss of $1440, down to $4800 − $1440 = $3360. A rise of 30 percent from this yet again new base means an increase in value of $1008 to $4368. So 20 percent down, 20 percent up, 30 percent down, and 30 percent up equals 12.64 percent down for a 4-month loss of $632.

This example shows how percentages can be used to compare apples and oranges. A percentage is a unitless number, so alone it offers no indication of that to which it refers. The decreases and increases mentioned in your broker's phone calls are all relative to different bases, so they are not comparable numbers.

Here is another common example of changing bases. The vice president in charge of finances in a new company reports to the president, "Last quarter's total sales increased 20 percent over the previous quarter while expenditures rose only 15 percent over the previous quarter. Looks good, J. B." What the vice president fails to tell J. B. is that at the start of the quarter expenditures were 80 percent higher than sales. Sales started at $10,000 per week, and expenditures were $18,000 per week. Sales increase 20 percent to $12,000. Expenditures rise "only 15 percent" from the base of $18,000, which means that expenditures increase by $2700 ($700 more than the increase in sales) to $20,700.

Think of all the ways you could use the humble percentage to talk about these changes:

1. The rise in expenditures was 35 percent greater than the rise in sales.

2. Total expenditures as a percentage of total sales dropped from 180 to 172.5 percent.

3. Total sales as a percentage of total expenditures rose from about 56 percent to 58 percent.

4. The increase in expenditures was 135 percent of the increase in sales.

5. The difference between the increase in expenditures and the increase in sales was only 5.8 percent of total sales.

You can compare and compare so that the bottom line moves farther and farther down the page, perhaps even out of sight. The company is still losing money.

· · ·

COMPOUNDING AND ANNUALIZING

"Inflation this month was reported to be 1 percent for an annual inflation rate of . . . "—12 percent, right? Wrong. It is an annual rate of 12.68 percent. This is a familiar problem in compounding percentage increases. Applying the increase to this month's base increases next month's base, to which the same percentage increase is applied, which makes the base increase proportionately more than the previous month . . . and so on for 12 months. So 1 percent applied 12 times equals 12.68 percent, not 12 percent.

Banks use this aspect of percentage changes to market their interest rates. "CDs: 9.2% = 9.69%," says the sign outside a bank. "Is this a true/false quiz?" I wonder. No, it's just compounded percentage increases at work "if you leave your money and interest payments on deposit for the full term of the certificate," as the fine print says.

With big changes in inflation from month to month, as occurred in Israel and some Third World nations, the overall changes can be astonishing. If inflation ran at 40 percent per month for 12 months, as has happened, the 1-year increase in consumer prices would be *5,569 percent*, not $12 \times 40 = 480$ percent.

You can get some odd-sounding results from compounding good news. "The Commerce Department reported today that consumer prices in January fell 0.3 percent for an annual inflation rate of −3.6 percent. Prices for the 12 months ending in January rose 4.3 percent, a spokesperson said." What? Well, such double-talk is easy to unravel if you keep track of the bases and the time period to which the percentage applies. The *negative inflation rate* is an annualized figure based on the single, 1-month decrease in prices. If that same decrease occurred in the next 11 months, the overall decrease for the year beginning in January would be −3.6 percent. For the year that had just passed, "the 12 months ending in January," prices actually increased by 4.3 percent (even with the January decrease taken into consideration).

· · ·

CHARTING CHANGES

Graphs and charts are marvelously convincing means for conveying statistical "truths" to those who do not understand the language. Consider the data on salaries of managers and workers in plant XYW shown in Figure 2a. The following charts show four ways to present those data. All the charts present the same data. They do not convey the same message.

Year	Workers' Salary, $	Managers' Salary, $
1977	400	1000
1978	440	1100
1979	484	1204
1980	532	1313
1981	586	1425
1982	644	1539
1983	709	1654
1984	779	1770
1985	857	1894
1986	943	1997
1987	1038	2108

(a)

FIGURE 2 (a) Monthly salaries of workers and managers in plant XYW. (b) Graph of salaries in (a). (c) Graph of salaries in (a); logarithmic scale. (d) Graph of salaries in (a); each set of salaries is indexed to a starting point of 100. (e) Graph of salaries in (a) shows percentage increases from one year to the next.

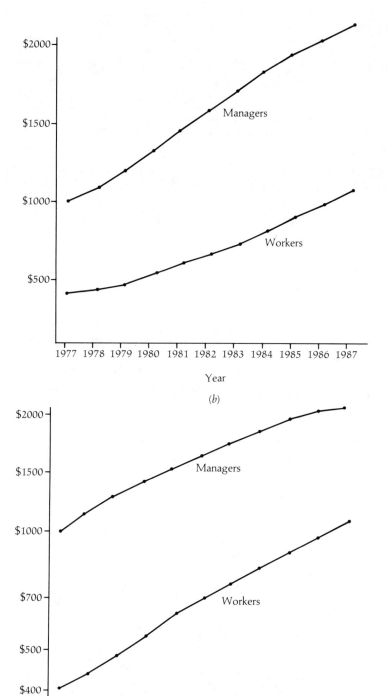

Year

(b)

Year

(c)

FIGURE 2 (Continued)

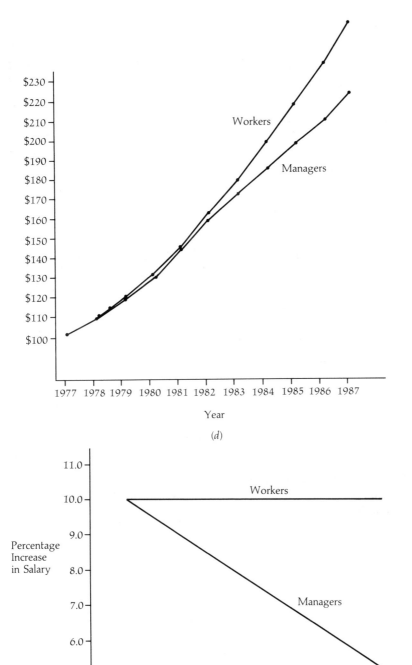

(d)

(e)

FIGURE 2 (Continued)

Figure 2b is just an ordinary chart of salaries over time. It shows that the abso-luate gap between the salary of workers and the salary of managers is increasing over time.

Figure 2c plots the same data on a logarithmic scale. Logarithms increase 1 unit for every multiplicative change in the underlying variable. A logarithmic graph is useful for charting changes in the rate of change. Figure 2c shows that the salaries of both workers and managers are increasing, but it suggests that over time the managers are doing less well than the workers. It shows this because the rate of change for the managers' salaries is lower, overall, than the rate of change for workers' salaries.

Figure 2d presents the same data but in an "indexed" form. Each data point is revalued relative to an index score of 100 for the workers' wages in 1977 and for the managers' wages in 1977. This chart, in effect, is a graph of percentage change from the initial salary levels. The managers' line rises less rapidly than the workers' line.

Figure 2e shows for each year the percentage change from the previous year. In Figure 2d, the base is always the 1977 salary. In Figure 2e, the base changes from year to year and is always the previous year's salary. This chart seems to suggest that managers are falling very far behind workers.

· · ·

CAUTION

The percentage is a slippery device. It can be used in attempts to deceive. Your surest protection against being deceived is close reading of statistical claims and a critical understanding of the data that lie behind summary statements.

· · ·

NOTE

1. Inspired by "Statistics Brief: Playing with Numbers," *The Economist*, May 31, 1986.

CHAPTER

12

▼

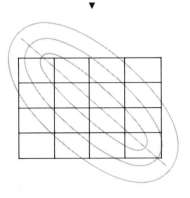

• • •

Measures of Association for Continuous Variables

In Chapter 11, I discussed techniques for the analysis of bivariate relationships for discrete variables. Sometimes variables contain more information than can be reflected through discrete categorizations. This chapter discusses techniques for analyzing the relationship between two continuous variables.

For example, urbanization and per capita income, whose relationship was analyzed in Chapter 11, are continuous variables. It is possible to display and analyze the relationship between them in much finer detail than was possible with the techniques of Chapter 11. Look at the panels of Figure 12.1. They show progressively finer resolution of the category sizes for both variables. The tables move from a 2 × 2 size to 4 × 4, 8 × 8, and finally to 16 × 16. The larger tables

Panel 1

INC1

COUNT	$8000 1.00I	$16,000 2.00I	ROW TOTAL
URBAN1 1.00 (50%)	66		66 / 62.9
2.00 (100%)	30	9	39 / 37.1
COLUMN TOTAL	96 / 91.4	9 / 8.6	105 / 100.0

NUMBER OF MISSING OBSERVATIONS = 38

Panel 2

INC1

COUNT	$4000 1.00I	$8000 2.00I	$12,000 3.00I	$16,000 4.00I	ROW TOTAL
URBAN1 1.00	30				30
2.00 (25%)	33	3			36
3.00 (50%)	17	3	3	1	24
4.00 (75%)	5	5	5		15
COLUMN TOTAL (100%)	85	11	8	1	105

NUMBER OF MISSING OBSERVATIONS = 38

Panel 3

INC1 COUNT

	$2000 1.00I	$4000 2.00I	$6000 3.00I	$8000 4.00I	$10,000 5.00I	$12,000 6.00I	$14,000 7.00I	$16,000 8.00I	ROW TOTAL
1.00 (0%)	11								11
2.00 (12.5%)	19								19
3.00 (25%)	12		1	1					14
4.00 (37.5%)	17	4		1					22
5.00 (50%)	7	6		1	2				16
6.00 (62.5%)	1	3		2	1	1			8
7.00 (75%)	2	3	2	3	2	1			13
8.00 (87.5%)						1		1	2
COLUMN TOTAL (100%)	69	16	3	8	5	3	0	1	105

NUMBER OF MISSING OBSERVATIONS = 39

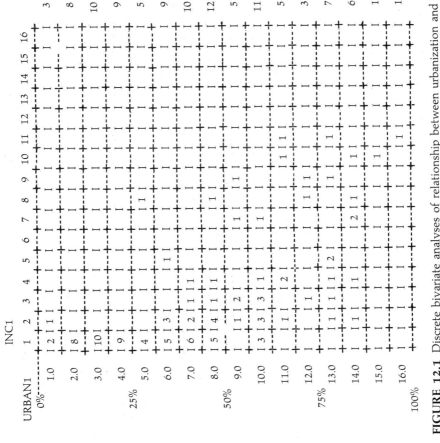

FIGURE 12.1 Discrete bivariate analyses of relationship between urbanization and per capita income with decreasing cell widths (transition to bivariate analysis of continuous variables).

are harder to read, but they give you a better idea of the overall pattern of the relationship between the two variables.

You can make the transition from the bivariate analysis of discrete variables to the bivariate analysis of continuous variables by imagining that the process represented in Figure 12.1 countries indefinitely so that the categories for each variable become infinitely small. Eventually, each case would occupy a single point in two-dimensional space. The result would be an even finer resolution than that shown in Figure 12.2, which is a computer plot of the two variables. The computer's typewriterlike output consists not of points in a space but "boxes" in which several cases might be grouped. In fact, you can see one "box" that has

PLOT OF INC WITH URBAN

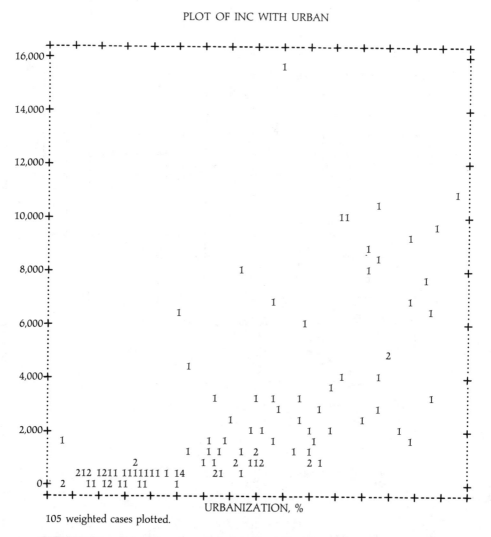

105 weighted cases plotted.

FIGURE 12.2 Computer-generated plot of urbanization and per capita income.

four cases in it. Figure 12.10 on page 345 shows a two-dimensional plot of the two continuous variables "per capita income" and "urbanization." On that graph, each case occupies a single point in the two-dimensional space.

Notice that the orientation of the variables in Figure 12.2 is different from the orientation in Figure 12.1. By convention, with continuous variables the dependent variable is displayed on the vertical axis (the ordinate), and the independent variable is displayed on the horizontal axis (the abscissa).

Special statistical techniques are used to analyze data like those in Figure 12.2 (or, more accurately, Figure 12.10). This chapter discusses linear regression, a technique that describes relationships between two continuous variables by using a straight line, and correlation, a technique for describing the strength of the relationship between two continuous variables.

$$\bullet \quad \bullet \quad \bullet$$

BACKGROUND

Sir Francis Galton was the first person to develop the general concept of association. His work on linear regression and correlation analysis, written in the last part of the nineteenth century, forms the basis for most techniques used today in the analysis of continuous variables. Galton's inventions were remarkable. As Helen Walker said of Galton in 1929,

> [T]here were others in that century who hovered on the verge of the discovery of correlation. Any one of them might have discovered it. None of them did. A French mathematician, an Italian astronomer, a German mathematician, and a French physicist each approached the problem from the point of view of mathematical analysis, but failed to see the practical significance of the formulas they derived. This may have been indeed because their attention was focused too closely upon the theory and not enough directed toward empirical data.[1]

Galton says the idea of association came to him in a flash as he wandered the grounds of Naworth Castle.[2] After that, for the next dozen years or so, Galton dedicated himself to fleshing out the concept.

Galton's work began with sweet peas. He divided sweet pea seeds into groups according to size, planted them, and measured the size of the seeds produced by the resulting plants. He recorded the results of his initial experiments in 5 × 5 tables in his notebooks of 1875. Small seeds tended to produce small seeds, but they also produced some large seeds. Moderate-size seeds produced a lot of moderate-size seeds while also producing some small seeds and some large. Larger seeds tended to produce large seeds, but there was some variation in the size of their offspring as well. Galton enlisted friends to grow peas for him so that he would have a lot of data with which to test his ideas. Later Galton applied his techniques to people and correlated a person's stature with the average height of that person's parents, among other things from his store of anthropomorphic data.

Galton initially treated the size of his sweet pea seeds and the heights of people as discrete variables, and he did his analysis by using tables like those in Chapter 11. Then, in a true stroke of genius that occurred, Galton tell us, "while waiting at a roadside station near Ramsgate for a train," Galton "smoothed" the data in his tables by placing on the intersections of the dividing lines in his tables the average frequency of the four cells around each intersection. Then he connected the points of roughly equal frequency in his tables with curves. The result appeared to be a set of concentric ellipses.

In Figure 12.3 I have tried to replicate Galton's procedure, using data from Table 11.6. The results—mine as well as Galton's—are crude, but genius often involves the capacity to see elegance and simplicity where others see crudeness and complexity. Galton realized that when data are presented in this way, cases seem to lie around the line that forms the major axis of the set of ellipses. Galton asked J. D. Hamilton Dickson of Cambridge to work out the equation of the line

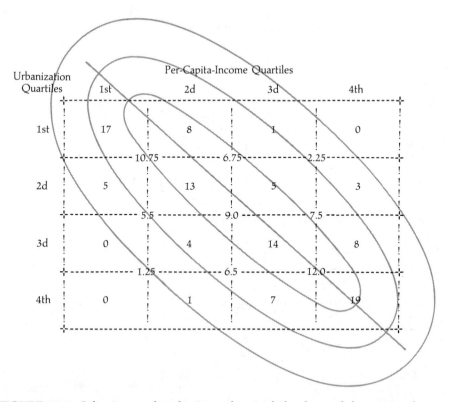

FIGURE 12.3 Galton's procedure for "smoothing" tabular data and discovering the regression line. This figure uses data on urbanization and per capita income from Table 11.6.

and the ellipses around it. Dickson's equations, which formalized Galton's ideas, are the basis of bivariate regression and correlation analysis, two of the most widely used statistical techniques today.

Galton's practical concern involved heredity. He wanted to know the extent to which personal characteristics were inherited. He was particularly intrigued by the fact that the distributions of most variables remained stable from generation to generation. That distributions of personal characteristics remain stable over generations is somewhat counterintuitive. Personal attributes were, everyone knew, distributed according to the Law of Error. Since there was some dispersion among the offspring of one generation, it seemed to Galton that the distribution of the attribute ought to expand gradually over the generations. People in the upper and lower tails of the distribution ought to produce some offspring who were more extreme cases than those present in the parent generation. They ought to produce cases who were farther out in the tails than any cases before them, and over time the tails of the distribution would creep outward. The distribution of heights, say, ought to get wider and wider.

What kept distributions stable over time, Galton finally reasoned, was "reversion," or the general tendency of the offspring to be nearer the mean of the distribution than were their parents. Reversion countered the effects of expansion at the extremes, and the result was intergenerational stability of the overall distribution.

"Reversion," a term from biology, later became "regression," and Galton wrote, for example, of *"Regression* toward mediocrity in hereditary stature."[3] The relationship between two variables arrayed like those in Figure 12.3 is described by a *regression line*, the line that forms the axis of the set of concentric ellipses that surround data on two variables.

There was a related concept that eventually captured Galton's attention—correlation. Correlation, as you already know, is the extent to which two variables vary together. The measurement of correlation between two continuous variables and the description of the relationship between two continuous variables using a regression line are the subjects of this chapter.

· · ·

DESCRIBING DATA WITH A LINE

Figure 12.4 contains a simple data set of eight cases on three continuous variables.[4] It also shows a *scattergram* of two of the variables, X and Y.

You probably know how to construct a scattergram that shows the plot of one variable against another on the two-dimensional set of coordinates formed by the X and Y axes. In the example in Figure 12.4, for every case i, $1 \leq i \leq 8$, place a mark in the two-dimensional space that is X_i units away from the origin on the X axis and Y_i units up or down on the Y axis. The first case in this simple data set, for example, has coordinates $X_i = -4$ and $Y_1 = -5$. This first case is farthest

Case i	X	Y	Z
1	-4	-5	30
2	-2	-7	30
3	-2	-1	10
4	0	-3	10
5	0	3	-10
6	2	1	-10
7	2	7	-30
8	4	5	-30

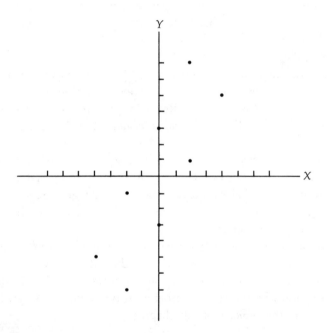

FIGURE 12.4 Three variables and a scattergram of X and Y.

to the left in the lower left quadrant in Figure 12.4. The second case has coordinates $X_2 = -2$ and $Y_2 = -7$. It is the "lowest" case on the graph.

The data in Figure 12.4 seem to lie in a nice, straight line. That is, a straight line would seem to be a good device with which to describe the general way the data are arrayed in the two-dimensional space. No single straight line will hit all eight points in the space, but several different lines would seem to provide good summary descriptions of how the data tend to lie.

A straight line, you will recall from algebra courses, always has the equation

$$Y = a + bX$$

where Y is conventionally the variable plotted on the vertical axis (the ordinate) and X is the variable plotted on the horizontal axis (the abscissa). a is the Y *intercept*, the point where the line cuts through the Y axis. The Y intercept a is the value of Y when X equals zero. b is the *slope* of the line, the rise over the run, the number of Y units the line goes up or down for every unit increase in X. Every line is defined by two numbers a and b, the y intercept and the slope.

If you could find a line that describes the data in Figure 12.4 well, you would have described the eight cases, which take two numbers each to say where they are on the scattergram, using only two numbers a and b. Remember that descriptive statistics ought to accomplish a data reduction. Describing eight cases consisting of two numbers each with only two numbers is a sizable data reduction.

To review the concept of a line and to see how a line can be used to describe data, pick a line—any line—that seems to describe the data in Figure 12.4. Just put a ruler on the page in a way that seems to capture the general form that the set of data assumes on the scattergram. Then draw a line that seems to describe the data well. Finally, estimate as carefully as you can the y intercept a and the slope b of the line you drew.

In Figure 12.5, there are three lines on the scattergram. Each describes the data in a slightly different way. The first line is $Y = 0 + 2X = 2X$. It has a y intercept of 0 and a slope of 2. It is parallel to the two "lines" formed by the cases in Figure 12.4. This line, $Y = 2X$, comes close to several points but hits none of them. The

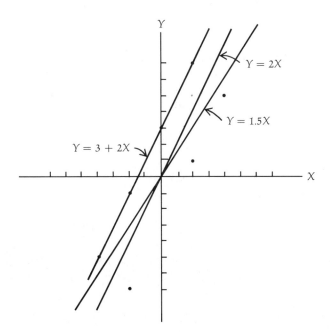

FIGURE 12.5 Data on X and Y from Figure 12.4 with three lines used to describe the data.

second line is $Y = 1.5X$. It also has an intercept of 0, but its slope is slightly less steep than the first line's slope. The third line, $Y = 3 + 2X$, hits four points exactly. It is not a particularly good descriptor of all eight cases, but it is a perfect descriptor of half the cases since it tells you exactly where four cases are.

You should put your own line on the graph, too, and do the following calculations with your line as I try to decide which line of the three on Figure 12.5 provides the best description of the data.

You can think of each line as a device for predicting Y if you know the value of a case on the variable X. So if someone says, "A case has been chosen. It has an X value of -2. What is its Y value"? then you should use your line to predict the Y value.

Using my first line, $Y = 2X$, I would predict the Y value of a case where $X = -2$ is $\hat{Y} = 0 + 2(-2) = -4$. (A $\hat{}$ over the Y indicates a value of Y *predicted* using information on the independent variable. So $\hat{Y}$, or "y hat," is a predicted Y.) By using the second line, $\hat{Y} = 1.5(-2) = -3$ when $X = -2$. By using the third line, $\hat{Y} = 3 + 2(-2) = -1$ when $X = -2$. The predictions are shown in the second rows of the third columns of the panels of Figure 12.6. The predictions are designated Y_i, $1 \leq i \leq 8$. Most of the predictions in Figure 12.6 miss the exact Y values of the cases. That is, there is some error in the predictions.

You can measure "error" in a way that is similar to the way you measured error in Chapter 10. The *total error* with which I begin this analysis is simply the variance of Y. Remember that the mean of Y, designated $\bar{Y}$, would be your best guess of Y if you had no information on X or on the relationship between X and Y. The total error then is $\sum_{i=1}^{8} (Y_i - \bar{Y})^2/(8 - 1) = 24$. The remaining error is the "variance" around your predictions since the predictions can be thought of as "conditional means" for the various levels of the independent variable X. The *variance* around the predictions—in keeping with the approach used in Chapter 10—is the sum of the squared errors (SSE) around the predictions divided by the number of cases minus 1.

To calculate the sum of the squared errors (SSE) around the predictions, first we need the absolute deviation of each actual value of Y_i from each prediction $\hat{Y}_i$. The deviation around each prediction is $Y_i - \hat{Y}_i$. The absolute deviations are shown in the fourth column of each panel in Figure 12.6. For the first case, the deviation of the prediction using the line $Y = 2X$ is $Y_i - \hat{Y}_i = Y_i - 2X_i = -5 - 2(-4) = -5 + 8 = 3$. At $X = -4$, the line $Y = 2X$ misses the actual value of Y by 3 units. The deviation of the prediction of a case with $X = -4$, using the second line $Y = 1.5X$, is $Y_i - 1.5X_i = -5 - 1.5(-4) = -5 + 6 = 1$. It misses by only 1 unit. The third line, $Y = 3 + 2X$, hits the point exactly since $Y = 3 + 2(-4) = -5$ at $X = -4$, and $-5 - (-5) = 0$. (Make sure you understand the calculation of deviations, and make sure you see what a deviation means on the scattergram in Figure 12.5.)

Once you have the absolute deviations, finding the SSE of the predictions around the three lines is easy. We simply square each deviation and add them.

Prediction on the Basis of $Y = 2X$

X_i	Y_i	$\hat{Y}_i$	$Y_i - \hat{Y}_i$	$(Y_i - \hat{Y}_i)^2$
−4	−5	−8	+3	9
−2	−7	−4	−3	9
−2	−1	−4	+3	9
0	−3	0	−3	9
0	3	0	+3	9
2	1	4	−3	9
2	7	4	+3	9
4	5	8	−3	9
Sum = 0	0			72
Mean = 0	0	Variance around predictions = 10.29		

Prediction on the Basis of $Y = 1.5X$

X_i	Y_i	$\hat{Y}_i$	$Y_i - \hat{Y}_i$	$(Y_i - \hat{Y}_i)^2$
−4	−5	−6	+1	1
−2	−7	−3	−4	16
−2	−1	−3	+2	4
0	−3	0	−3	9
0	3	0	+3	9
2	1	3	−2	4
2	7	3	+4	16
4	5	6	−1	1
Sum = 0	0			60
Mean = 0	0	Variance around predictions = 8.57		

Prediction on the Basis of $Y = 3 + 2X$

X_i	Y_i	$\hat{Y}_i$	$Y_i - \hat{Y}_i$	$(Y_i - \hat{Y}_i)^2$
−4	−5	−5	0	0
−2	−7	−1	−6	36
−2	−1	−1	0	0
0	−3	3	−6	36
0	3	3	0	0
2	1	7	−6	36
2	7	7	0	0
4	5	11	−6	36
Sum = 0	0			144
Mean = 0	0	Variance around predictions = 20.57		

FIGURE 12.6 Prediction of Y from X using data in Figure 12.4 on the basis of three different lines (errors are shown for each prediction).

These calculations are shown in Figure 12.6. To make these calculations consistent with the approach in Chapter 10, I have divided the SSE by $n - 1 = 8 - 1 = 7$ to determine the "variance" around the predicted Y's. You should carry out the same calculations for your line.

Each line has a different "variance" around the predictions. That is, each line has a different amount of remaining error associated with it. The remaining error for the first line, $Y = 2X$, is 10.29 units; the remaining error for the second line, $Y = 1.5X$, is 8.57 units; the remaining error for the third line, $Y = 3 + 2X$, is 20.57 units. On the basis of this analysis, we would have to say that $Y = 1.5X$ is the best descriptor of the data since it has the smallest error remaining after you use information on the independent variable and the relationship between variables to predict the dependent variable. On average, it comes closer to the points in the scattergram than the other two lines. The line $Y = 1.5X$ describes the data best and provides the best device of the three lines for predicting Y for any given X.

How does your line compare to each of the three lines used in this example?

You can easily calculate the proportionate reduction in error (PRE) achieved by each line. The errors calculated in Figure 12.6 are the *remaining errors* after predictions have been made using each line. The *total error* was the sample variance of Y, which was 24. The PRE, in each case, is the total error minus the remaining error divided by the total error [Formula (10.1)]. The PRE values are as follows:

Line	Total Error	Remaining Error	PRE
$Y = 2X$	24	10.29	0.57
$Y = 1.5X$	24	8.57	0.64
$Y = 3 + 2X$	24	20.57	0.14

The second line, $Y = 1.5X$, achieves the highest PRE of the three lines used in this example.

How does the PRE for your line compare to the PREs for these three lines?

• • •

STRAIGHT-LINE MODEL

Describing data with a line provides a *model* of the relationship between two variables. A model is not an exact representation. There are differences between a model and the "real thing." But, as noted above, it is very useful to have a description of a large amount of data (two numbers for each point in the XY plane) that consists of only two numbers. It is like having a model airplane with only 32 plastic pieces while the real thing would have thousands of pieces.

The lines used in the previous section are *deterministic models*. They predict, in a completely determined way, the value of Y for a given value of X. The value of Y is determined by the value of X without any room for variation in the predicted value of Y. But, as you know by now, there is a lot of variation in the world. For any given X, there could be a lot of different values of Y; that is, there could be considerable variation in the value of the predicted Y. For such a situation, a *probabilistic model*, one that allows for uncertainty in the predicted value of Y, would be more appropriate. A probabilistic model is a little more complicated than a deterministic model, but it provides a better representation of the "real" relationship. It is something like having a model airplane with 150 parts instead of 32.

Consider now the best deterministic model of the data in Figure 12.4. Of the three deterministic models of that data set, $Y = 1.5X$ is the best. To make this into a probabilistic model, which admits uncertainty (probability is the science of uncertainty) about the predicted value of Y for a specified level of X, you have to add a *random-error* component. So a probabilistic model of the relationship between X and Y would be

$$Y = 1.5X + \text{random error}$$

In general, a probabilistic model of Y has the form

$$Y = \text{deterministic model} + \text{random error}$$

If you assume that the mean value of the random-error term is zero, which is one of the assumptions of this sort of modeling, then the mean value of the predicted Y's, or $E(Y)$, is equal to the deterministic model:

$$E(Y) = \text{deterministic model}$$

In simple linear regression, the deterministic model always has the form of a straight line, so a straight-line probabilistic model of Y in terms of X has the form

$$Y = A + BX + \varepsilon$$

where Y is the dependent variable, X is the independent variable, A is the y intercept of the straight line relating X and Y, B is the slope of that line, and ε (the Greek letter "epsilon") is a random-error component.

The general form of the straight-line model can be used to represent the relationship between Y and X in a population. The mean value of the predicted Y for a given value of X is

$$E(Y) = \mu_{Y.X} = A + BX$$

where $\mu_{Y.X}$ is the conditional mean of Y for a specified X. In practice, as usual, you use sample data to estimate population parameters A and B. These estimates, from the sample data, are a and b. After you have estimates of A and B, you can make certain assumptions about the distribution of the random-error component ε, assess the utility of the model, and use the model to estimate and predict values of Y for given X's.

· · ·

ESTIMATING *A* AND *B*: THE REGRESSION LINE

For every set of data consisting of two continuous variables, there is one line around which the average squared deviation is minimized. That line is called the *regression line*. You fit the regression line through the data according to the criterion of *ordinary least squares*. The regression line is the line for which the "squares" around it are the least. (Those of you who have had calculus know that one function of the calculus is to determine the minimum and maximum values of mathematical functions. The first supplement to this chapter shows how to derive the equation of the regression line by using calculus. There is no practical reason to know how to derive the regression line; but do not think that the origins of the equations for the slope and y intercept of the regression line, which you are about to learn, are a magical mystery. Think of the supplement as the statistical analog of a linguistic etymology for the term "regression line.")

The regression line, like any other line, is defined by its slope b and its y intercept a. The regression line for a sample is defined as

$$\hat{Y} = a + bX$$

And the task of regression analysis is to calculate a and b, where a and b are estimates of parameters A and B, $\hat{Y}$ is an estimate of the conditional mean of Y for a given X, or, put another way, $\hat{Y}$ is an estimate of $\mu_{Y.X}$ in the model

$$\mu_{Y.X} = A + BX$$

To find b, the sample statistic for the slope, use Formula (12.1a) or (12.1b):

$$b = \frac{\sum_{i=1}^{n}(X_i - \bar{X})(Y_i - \bar{Y})}{\sum_{i=1}^{n}(X_i - \bar{X})^2} \tag{12.1a}$$

$$b = \frac{n\sum_{i=1}^{n}X_iY_i - \sum_{i=1}^{n}X_i\sum_{i=1}^{n}Y_i}{n\sum_{i=1}^{n}X_i^2 - \left(\sum_{i=1}^{n}X_i\right)^2} \tag{12.1b}$$

These two formulas yield the same results in every case. [Supplement 12.2 proves that b calculated by using Formula (12.1a) will always equal b calculated by using Formula (12.1b).] The second formula is the *computational formula* for b since it requires only one pass through the data.

Once your know b, a is easy to find because the least-squares regression line always passes through the point $(\bar{X}, \bar{Y})$, the point on the scattergram defined by the means of the two variables. That is, it is always true that $\bar{Y} = a + b\bar{X}$. So if you know b, $\bar{X}$, and $\bar{Y}$, you can find the y intercept a from

$$a = \bar{Y} - b\bar{X} \tag{12.2}$$

An example will help. Let's calculate the slope and the y intercept of the regression line for the data in Figure 12.4. All the relevant calculations using both formulas are shown in Figure 12.7.

The three leftmost columns at the top of the figure display the data once again and show calculations of the means of the two variables. The next two columns show the calculations of the deviations from $\bar{X}$ and the squared deviations around $\bar{X}$. At the bottom of the fifth column is the sum of the squared deviations around $\bar{X}$, and it is equal to 48. This is the quantity needed for the denominator of Formula (12.1a). The sixth column of Figure 12.7 calculates the deviations around the mean of Y. The final column shows the *cross products*, the product of each deviation from the mean of X and the corresponding deviation from the mean of Y. The sum of the cross products is used as the numerator of Formula (12.1a). The sum of the cross products, which is 72, is shown at the bottom of the last column.

The numerator of Formula (12.1a) is 72. The denominator is 48. Therefore, $b = 72/48 = 1.5$. Since $b = 1.5$, $\bar{X} = 0$, and $\bar{Y} = 0$, you can use Formula (12.2) to find that $a = 0 - 1.5(0) = 0$. So the equation of the regression line for the data in Figure 12.4 is

$$\hat{Y} = 0 + 1.5X$$

The second line used in the example above was, in fact, the line that minimizes the squared deviations around itself. The remaining error of 7.5 units that the line $Y = 1.5X$ achieved was the smallest error that could remain after any line was used to describe the data. No other line would have fit the data better than $Y = 1.5X$.

The bottom part of Figure 12.7 shows how to calculate b by using the computational formula (12.1b). Clearly this is much easier to use if we are doing calculations by hand. The results are the same.

The sample statistic b is called the *regression coefficient*. It is *not* a measure of association since b does not measure proportionate reduction in error. The slope b can assume any value; b is a number that tells the average increase or decrease in Y for every 1-unit increase in X in the sample. Coefficient b is positive if Y increases with a unit increase in X and negative if Y decreases with a unit increase

Using Formula (12.1a)

i	X_i	Y_i	$X_i - \bar{X}$	$(X_i - \bar{X})^2$	$Y_i - \bar{Y}$	$(X_i - \bar{X})(Y_i - \bar{Y})$
1	-4	-5	-4	16	-5	20
2	-2	-7	-2	4	-7	14
3	-2	-1	-2	4	-1	2
4	0	-3	0	0	-3	0
5	0	3	0	0	3	0
6	2	1	2	4	1	2
7	2	7	2	4	7	14
8	4	5	4	16	5	20

$$\sum_{i=1}^{n} X_i = 0 \qquad \sum_{i=1}^{n} Y_i = 0 \qquad \qquad \sum_{i=1}^{n} (X_i - \bar{X})^2 = 48 \qquad \qquad \sum_{i=1}^{n} (X_i - \bar{X})(Y_i - \bar{Y}) = 72$$

$$\bar{X} = 0 \qquad \bar{Y} = 0$$

Calculations:

$$b = \frac{\sum_{i=1}^{n} (X_i - \bar{X})(Y_i - \bar{Y})}{\sum_{i=1}^{n} (X_i - \bar{X})^2} = \frac{72}{48} = 1.5$$

$$a = \bar{Y} - b\bar{X} = 0 - 1.5(0) = 0$$

Using Formula (12.1b)

i	X_i	Y_i	X_iY_i	X_i^2
1	−4	−5	20	16
2	−2	−7	14	4
3	−2	−1	2	4
4	0	−3	0	0
5	0	3	0	0
6	2	1	2	4
7	2	7	14	4
8	4	5	20	16
	$\sum_{i=1}^{n} X_i = 0$	$\sum_{i=1}^{n} Y_i = 0$	$\sum_{i=1}^{n} X_iY_i = 72$	$\sum_{i=1}^{n} X_i^2 = 48$

Calculations:

$$b = \frac{n \sum_{i=1}^{n} X_iY_i - \sum_{i=1}^{n} X_i \sum_{i=1}^{n} Y_i}{n \sum_{i=1}^{n} X_i^2 - \left(\sum_{i=1}^{n} X_i\right)^2} = \frac{8(72) - 0(0)}{8(48) - 0^2} = 1.5$$

$$a = \bar{Y} - b\bar{X} = 0 - 1.5(0) = 0$$

FIGURE 12.7 Calculating the regression line of Y on X for data in Figure 12.4.

in X. The size of b depends to a large extent on the units in which the two variables are measured. You must examine the data to understand the meaning of b.

Consider Figure 12.8 which shows the relationship between the variables X and Z from the inset table in Figure 12.4. The regression line for that figure, which is $\hat{Z} = -8.33X$, has a negative slope since higher values of X tend to go with lower values of Z. Also the line is steeply negative. The absolute value of b for these data is much larger than b for the data in Figure 12.4 simply because Z is of a different order of magnitude than Y.

Conventionally, in a bivariate analysis using continuous variables, the dependent variable is displayed on the vertical axis. Variables Y and Z were the dependent variables in the two examples discussed so far. To put it in statistically proper terms, $\hat{Y} = 1.5X$ is the result of the "regression of Y on X." And $\hat{Z} = -8.33X$ is the result of the regression of Z on X. You always speak of the regression line as showing the regression of the dependent variable *on* the independent variable.

This terminology—"regression of Y on X"—brings us to another characteristic of b that is important. Since the regression coefficient b_{YX}—the notation used for the regression of Y on X—is expressed in terms of units of variable Y over units of variable X, you might expect $b_{YX} = \dfrac{1}{b_{XY}}$. However, the regression coefficient obtained by regressing Y on X will not necessarily be the reciprocal of

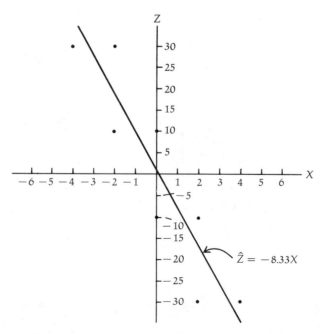

FIGURE 12.8 Scattergram of X and Z from Figure 12.4, with regression line inserted.

the regression coefficient obtained by regressing X on Y. This surprised Francis Galton. If he regressed offspring's stature on parent's stature, the regression coefficient was usually about $\frac{2}{3}$. If he turned the variables around and regressed parental stature on offspring's stature, he found that the regression coefficient was about $\frac{1}{3}$. The regression coefficient is an *asymmetric* descriptor of a relationship between two variables.

The regression coefficient is an asymmetric descriptor of a bivariate relationship because of the way "error" around the regression line is measured. Ordinary least-squares regression analysis measures error from the regression line by "dropping" a line perpendicular to the X axis from a case to the regression line. (Sometimes the perpendicular has to be "dropped" upward from the case to the regression line, since some data points lie below the regression line.) Errors for the regression of Y on X from the data in Figure 12.4, which are constructed in this way, are shown in Figure 12.9. If you regress X on Y, then deviations or "errors" are constructed by dropping a line sideways toward the Y axis, so that it is perpendicular to the Y axis. The two kinds of deviations are not necessarily equal. That is why the regression coefficient of Y on X is not necessarily equal to the reciprocal of the regression coefficient of X on Y. In fact, using the data from Figure 12.4 but regressing X on Y yields a regression line $\hat{X} = 0.43Y$. The y intercept of zero is the same as when Y was regressed on X, but the coefficient $b_{XY} = .43$ is different from what Galton expected, namely, $1/b_{YX} = 1/1.5 = .67$.

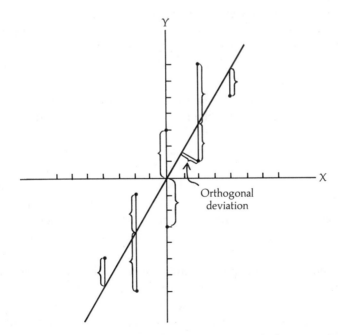

FIGURE 12.9 Scattergram of X and Y from Figure 12.4 with deviations from the regression line shown.

There is another way to construct the deviations from the regression line that yields yet another kind of regression coefficient. Instead of dropping a line perpendicular to one of the axes, you could drop a line perpendicular to the regression line itself. This kind of deviation is shown for the point $(2, -1)$ in Figure 12.9. A regression line that minimizes the squares of this kind of error around the line is called an *orthogonal* regression line because it satisfies the *orthogonal least-squares* criterion. ("Orthogonal" means "having to do with right angles.") An orthogonal regression coefficient, unlike an ordinary regression coefficient, is a symmetric descriptor of a relationship. That is,

$$b_{YX}^* = \frac{1}{b_{XY}^*}$$

if b^* is an orthogonal regression coefficient. You need to know that ordinary least-squares regression coefficients are *asymmetric* descriptors of a relationship, but that there is a form of regression analysis that provides symmetric coefficients. All regressions in this book are done under the *ordinary* least-squares criterion.

$$\bullet \quad \bullet \quad \bullet$$

A PRACTICAL EXAMPLE

As an example of how regression is used on a real data, let's return to a familiar problem, the relationship between urbanization and per capita income (PCI). Figure 12.10 is a scattergram of all 105 countries that have values for both urbanization and per capita income. For the first time in this text, both these variables are being treated as continuous variables. For the first time, we are not losing information from the outset by collapsing categories of one or both variables. The analysis begins with all the information contained in these two variables.

The first thing to notice about Figure 12.10 is that the data tend to lie generally in a line. If you are going to describe data with a line, you must make sure that a line is an appropriate descriptor. Some pairs of variables are related in a *curvilinear* fashion, as are the number of doctors per 100,000 inhabitants of a country and the male life expectancy of the country. The graph in Figure 12.11 supports the hypothesis that male life expectancy is associated with the number of doctors per 100,000, but the variables are not linearly related to each another. A straight line is *not* a good way to describe the relationship between doctor density and life expectancy.

A line is not a bad descriptor of the relationship between urbanization and per capita income, however. There is a tendency for cases above the regression line to be farther from the line than cases below the regression line, and there is one obvious outlier that is very high in per capita income and in the midrange of urbanization. But the array of data is not obviously curvilinear. Consequently, you can reasonably use a line to describe this relationship.

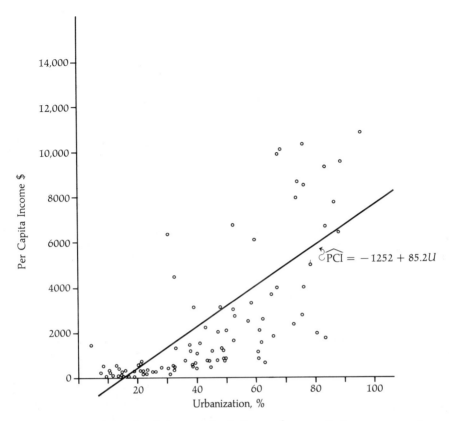

FIGURE 12.10 Relationship between urbanization and per capita income; regression line is shown.

Before doing a regression, always look at a scattergram of the two variables to make sure the relationship is roughly linear. A computer or a calculator will calculate a regression line for any two variables. However, as the regression line in Figure 12.11 demonstrates, in some cases it is foolish to do so because a line is sometimes not a good device for describing data.

Once you know that a line is an appropriate way to describe a relationship, calculate the regression line and interpret the results. The regression line for Figure 12.10 is

$$\widehat{\text{PCI}} = -1252 + 85.2U$$

where U is urbanization. The intercept is -1252, and the slope is 85.2.

The slope of the regression line indicates that for every 1 percent increase in urbanization, per capita income increases by \$85.20, on the average. The regression line gives you a description of the relationship between two variables once you have determined that line is a good means for describing the relationship in the first place.

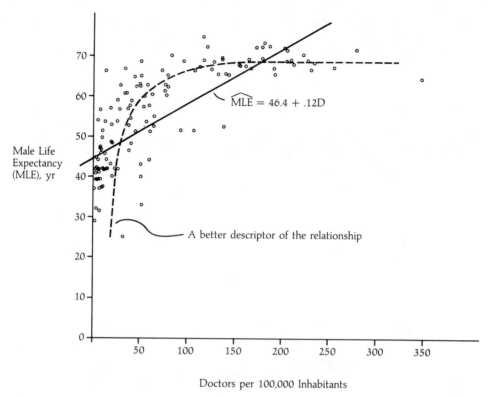

FIGURE 12.11 Relationship between doctors per 100,000 inhabitants and male life expectancy. Regression line is shown. Relationship is curvilinear.

The regression line can be used to predict the dependent variable if you have information on an independent variable. If you knew that a country had an urbanization rate of 30 percent, what would you predict its per capita income to be? You can use the regression line on Figure 12.10 to make your prediction. Go up the abscissa (the X axis) to 30 percent urbanization, then go straight up to the regression line and determine the level of per capita income that the line predicts. The line is at a level between $1000 and $1500 when urbanization equals 30 percent. Being more precise than that just by eyeballing the line is difficult. But you know the exact equation of the line, so you should be able to find the exact level of the regression line when urbanization equals 30 percent. Just put 30 percent into the equation of the line to find

$$\widehat{PCI} = -1252 + 85.2(30) = \$1304$$

If a country had an urbanization of 30 percent, you would predict its per capita income to be $1304. Its "expected value of per capita income," or equivalently the estimate of the conditional mean value of income given that urbanization is equal to 30 percent, is $1304.

What if a country had an urbanization of 2 percent? What would you predict its per capita income to be? Just put 2 percent into the regression equation to find

$$\widehat{PCI} = -1252 + 85.2(2) = -\$1082$$

To say a country has per capita income of $-\$1082$ makes little sense. But remember: Regression is not about countries. A regression line is a description of a *relationship between variables*. The prediction of a negative per capita income for a hypothetical country with an urbanization of 2 percent is based on the overall relationship between urbanization and per capita income as it is described by a line that minimizes the squared deviations around itself. The prediction is not based on anything in reality. It is based on a fiction, but the fiction is a useful one because it allows you to describe a relationship by using two numbers, a y intercept and a slope, instead of using the 210 numbers (an urbanization and a per capita income value for each of 105 countries) with which this analysis started.

• • •

ASSUMPTIONS OF LINEAR REGRESSION MODELS

The general model for the regression of Y on X is

$$Y = A + BX + \varepsilon$$

and the estimate of the deterministic part of the model gives a prediction of Y for any X by

$$\hat{Y} = a + bX$$

where a and b are least-squares estimates of A and B, respectively. If four assumptions about the error component of the model are reasonable in a particular application of regression analysis, then you can say something about how well the regression line $\hat{Y} = a + bX$ based on the sample data describes the true relationship between X and Y in the population from which the sample came.

The assumptions are these:

1. The mean of the probability distribution of the error component ε is zero. This assumption is necessary if the expected value of Y, or $E(Y)$, is to be equal to the deterministic component, i.e., if $E(Y)$ is to equal $a + bX$.

2. The variance of the probability distribution of the error component ε is the same for all values of X and is equal to σ_{ε}^2.

3. The error component ε is normally distributed.

4. The errors associated with the observations are independent of one another.

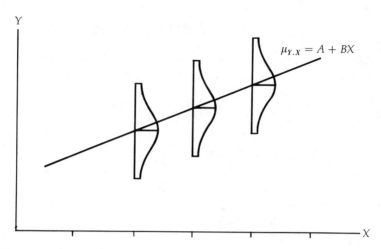

FIGURE 12.12 The population regression line conceived as a series of conditional means with the assumptions of homoscedasticity illustrated.

Before discussing these assumptions, it is important to say that regression is "robust against" these assumptions. That means that even if the assumptions are violated in a particular application, the technique still yields good results.

The first three assumptions of regression analysis are represented pictorially in Figure 12.12. The regression line is an estimate of a series of conditional means of the dependent variable Y. In the population

$$\mu_{Y.X} = A + BX$$

where $\mu_{Y.X}$ is the conditional mean of Y for any given X. There is dispersion around the conditional mean of Y, estimated by the regression line, at any level on the independent variable X. The assumptions of regression analysis stipulate that the variance around any point $\mu_{Y.X}$ for any value of X be the same as for any other value of X and that the error be normally distributed. The variances around the conditional means that make up the line are said to be *homoscedastic* (from the Greek meaning "same spread"). This way of thinking about the regression line and the assumption of homoscedasticity are illustrated in Figure 12.12.

You rarely know the variance of the error component σ_ε^2, so, as usual, you use the sample data to estimate its value. The estimate of σ_ε^2 is the sum of the squared errors of the values of Y around the predicted values of Y divided by the number of degrees of freedom associated with the error. That is,

$$\sigma_\varepsilon^2 \cong s_\varepsilon^2 = \frac{\text{sum of squared errors}}{\text{degrees of freedom for error}} = \frac{\text{SSE}}{\text{df}}$$

You know the sum of the squared errors around the predicted Y's is

$$\text{SSE} = \sum_{i=1}^{n} (Y_i - \hat{Y}_i)^2$$

The degrees of freedom for error is $n - 2$. You begin with n degrees of freedom, one for each case in the sample and you lose 1 degree of freedom for each parameter estimate. In the case of simple linear regression, you estimate two parameters—A and B are estimated by a and b—so you lose 2 degrees of freedom. To put it in the terms of the previous chapters, if you know a and b, then you are free to choose the first $n - 2$ numbers in a sample of size n before all n cases in the sample are determined by the $n - 2$ numbers and the two "constraints" a and b. Therefore, df $= n - 2$ and

$$\sigma_\varepsilon^2 \cong s_\varepsilon^2 = \frac{\sum_{i=1}^{n} (Y_i - \hat{Y}_i)^2}{n - 2}$$

The square root of this estimate of the error variance is

$$s_\varepsilon = +\sqrt{s_\varepsilon^2} = +\sqrt{\frac{\sum_{i=1}^{n} (Y_i - \hat{Y}_i)^2}{n - 2}}$$

and it is called the *standard error of the estimate* or the *standard deviation of the residuals*. In regression, the standard error of the estimate is *not* a standard deviation of a sampling distribution as all other "standard errors" are. Unfortunately this is a confusing use of terminology, but no language is confusion-free. The standard error of the estimate in regression is the sample standard deviation of the residuals around the series of conditional means that the regression line estimates. The standard error of the estimate is sometimes denoted $s_{Y.X}$, so

$$s_{Y.X} = \sqrt{\frac{\sum_{i=1}^{n} (Y_i - \hat{Y}_i)^2}{n - 2}}$$

where $\hat{Y} = a + bX$ for any given X. $s_{Y.X}$ is a measure of dispersion around the sample regression line. You can calculate $s_{Y.X}$ by

$$s_{Y.X} = \sqrt{\frac{\sum_{i=1}^{n} Y_i^2 - a \sum_{i=1}^{n} Y_i - b \sum_{i=1}^{n} X_i Y_i}{n - 2}}$$

Thinking of the standard error of the estimate as the "standard deviation of the residuals" helps you understand the concept. If the residuals—the left overs from the regression, the deviations around the line like those shown in Figure 12.9—are normally distributed, as one of the assumptions requires, then about 68 percent of the deviations should lie within 1 standard deviation of the regression line. A little more than 95 percent of the deviations should lie within 2 standard deviations of the regression line. For the example using the simple data,

$$s_{Y.X} = \sqrt{\dfrac{\displaystyle\sum_{i=1}^{n} Y_i^2 - a \sum_{i=1}^{n} Y_i - b \sum_{i=1}^{n} X_i Y_i}{n-2}}$$

$$= \sqrt{\dfrac{168 - 0(0) - 1.5(72)}{8-2}} = 3.16$$

In this case, six of the eight residuals (or deviations from the regression line) lie within 1 standard deviation (3.16 units) of the regression line, and all eight lie within 2 standard deviations ($3 \times 3.16 = 7.32$ units) of the line.

$$\bullet \quad \bullet \quad \bullet$$

A TEST ABOUT COEFFICIENTS *A* AND *B*

By using the standard error of the estimate, it is possible to conduct hypothesis tests about the size of the slope of the line that describes the true relationship between X and Y. In many cases, a researcher wants to know if he or she can conclude that the population parameter for the slope B in a regression relating variables X and Y is different from some specified value. Recall that the regression equation between two variables in the population is

$$\mu_{Y.X} = A + BX$$

The alternative hypothesis is

$$H_A: B \neq B^*$$

where B^* is the specified value. The null hypothesis, of course, is that

$$H_0: B = B^*$$

To see if there is evidence for claiming that two continuous variables are associated, we examine the null hypothesis that

$$H_0: B = 0$$

Why 0? Think about what it means for variables to be related or associated: The conditional distributions of the dependent variable are the same for every value of the independent variable. In particular, the conditional *means* of the dependent variable—all the values of $\mu_{Y.X}$—must be the same. In order for that to be true, the B in the equation $\mu_{Y.X} = A + BX$ must be equal to zero, so that the conditional means are all equal to a constant ($\mu_{Y.X} = A$). Two continuous variables are independent of each other if $B = 0$.

If all four assumptions of a regression model are reasonable in a particular application, then the sampling distribution of the sample regression coefficient b_{yx} is normal with a standard deviation of

$$\sigma_{b_{yx}} = \frac{\sigma_\varepsilon}{\sqrt{\sum_{i=1}^{n} (X_i - \bar{X})^2}}$$

In practice, σ_ε is usually not known, so we estimate $\sigma_{b_{yx}}$ with

$$s_{b_{yx}} = \frac{\sqrt{\sum_{i=1}^{n} (Y_i - \hat{Y})^2 / (n - 2)}}{\sqrt{\sum_{i=1}^{n} (X_i - \bar{X})^2}}$$

$$= \frac{\sqrt{\left(\sum_{i=1}^{n} Y_i^2 - a \sum_{i=1}^{n} Y_i - b \sum_{i=1}^{n} X_i Y_i\right) \Big/ (n - 2)}}{\sqrt{\sum_{i=1}^{n} X_i^2 - \left(\sum_{i=1}^{n} X_i\right)^2 \Big/ n}}$$

The test of the null hypothesis is conducted by using a t distribution with $n - 2$ degrees of freedom. The test statistic is

$$t = \frac{b_{yx} - B^*}{s_{b_{yx}}}$$

Let's use the simple data set in Figure 12.4 to test the null hypothesis that

$$H_0: B \leq 0$$

and set the level to reject for this one-tailed test at .05. I calculated the standard error of the estimate above and found that $s_{Y.X} = 3.16$. The standard deviation of the sampling distribution of b_{yx} is estimated by

$$s_{b_{yx}} = \frac{s_{Y \cdot X}}{\sqrt{\sum\limits_{i=1}^{n} (X_i - \bar{X})^2}} = \frac{3.16}{\sqrt{48}} = .46$$

The sample regression coefficient of $b_{yx} = 1.5$ lies $1.5 - 0 = 1.5$ raw units from the mean of the sampling distribution (if the null hypothesis is true), and

$$t = \frac{b_{yx} - B^*}{s_{b_{yx}}} = \frac{1.5 - 0}{0.46} = 3.26$$

standard error units above the mean of the sampling distribution. The test statistic is $t = 3.26$. With $df = n - 2 = 8 - 2 = 6$ and a level to reject of .05 in a one-tailed test, the test statistic has to be greater than 1.943 to reject the null hypothesis. It is. I decide to reject the null hypothesis and accept the alternative that

$$H_A: B > 0$$

The slope of the line relating these variables in the population from which this sample of eight cases came is (probably) greater than zero.

You can construct a confidence interval around the regression coefficient b in a way completely analogous to the construction of all other confidence intervals. You know that the standard error of the regression coefficient is

$$s_{b_{yx}} = \frac{\sqrt{\left.\sum\limits_{i=1}^{n} (Y_i - \hat{Y})^2 \middle/ (n - 2)\right.}}{\sqrt{\sum\limits_{i=1}^{n} (X_i - \bar{X})^2}}$$

and that the sampling distribution is distributed as a t distribution with $n - 2$ degrees of freedom. Therefore, to construct an interval estimate of B, you construct an interval around b such that the bounds are $b_{yx} \pm ts_{b_{yx}}$, where t is chosen from the table of t distributions for $df = n - 2$ at the appropriate level of confidence. For example, for the regression line relating X and Y in the simple data set, the 95 percent confidence interval for b is constructed by using a t value for a two-tailed test with $df = 6$. Now $b_{yx} = 1.5$, $t = 2.447$, and $s_{b_{yx}} = .46$, so the 95 percent confidence interval is $1.5 \pm (2.447)(.46)$, which is the interval from 0.37 to 2.63.

Recall that you can use a regression model to predict levels of the dependent variable for given levels of the independent variable. The true conditional mean of

Y for a given X, denoted $\mu_{Y.X'}$ is estimated by

$$\hat{Y} = a + bx$$

where $\hat{Y}$ is a point estimate of $\mu_{Y.X}$. Around this point estimate you can construct an interval estimate of $\mu_{Y.X}$ if you know the standard error of the conditional mean. The standard error of the conditional mean $\sigma_{\hat{Y}}$ for a given X is estimated by $s_{\hat{Y}}$ which is

$$s_{\hat{Y}} = s_{Y.X} \sqrt{\frac{1}{n} + \frac{(X - \bar{X})^2}{\sum\limits_{i=1}^{n} (X_i - \bar{X})^2}}$$

The sampling distribution of the conditional mean estimate Y has a mean of $\mu_{Y.X'}$ and a standard error of $s_{\hat{Y}}$ and is distributed according to a t distribution with $n - 2$ degrees of freedom.

Let's return to the same simple data set and construct confidence intervals around the predictions of Y at several levels of X. For $X = 0$, the predicted Y is $Y = 1.5(0) = 0$. The standard error of this conditional mean is

$$s_{\hat{Y}} = s_{Y.X} \sqrt{\frac{1}{n} + \frac{(X - \bar{X})^2}{\sum\limits_{i=1}^{n} (X_i - \bar{X})^2}} = 3.16 \sqrt{\frac{1}{8} + \frac{(0.0)^2}{48}} = 1.12$$

A 95 percent confidence interval at $X = 0$ with df $= 6$ extends $t = 2.447$ standard error units from the estimate $Y = 0$, so the interval extends from $0 - (2.447)$ $(1.12) = -2.74$ to $0 + (2.447)(1.12) = 2.74$.

What about the interval estimate of $\mu_{Y.X}$ at $X = 2$? The estimate of $\mu_{Y.X}$ is $\hat{Y} = 1.5 \ (2) = 3$, and the standard error of $\hat{Y}$ is estimated by

$$s_{\hat{Y}} = 3.16 \sqrt{\frac{1}{8} + \frac{(2 - 0)^2}{48}} = 1.44$$

So the interval extends from $3.0 - (2.447)(1.44) = -0.52$ to $3 + (2.447)(1.44) = 6.52$.

Notice that the interval at $X = 2$ is $6.52 - (-0.52) = 7.04$ units wide while the interval at $X = 0$ is $2.74 - (-2.74) = 5.48$ units wide. As you move out from the mean of the independent variable, the interval estimate of the level of the dependent variable gets wider. The farther from the mean you make a prediction, the less accurate your prediction will be. Here are the 95 percent confidence interval estimates for all levels of X shown in the original, simple data set. These

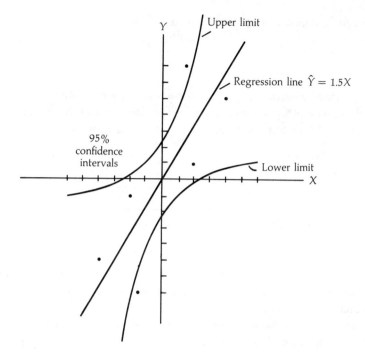

FIGURE 12.13 A 95 percent confidence interval around the regression line for the data in Figure 12.4.

estimates are plotted in Figure 12.13. The interval estimates of the predicted level of a dependent variable look like an expanding band.

X	$\hat{Y}$	$s_{\hat{Y}}$	95% Confidence Interval
−4	−6	2.14	−11.24 to −0.76
−2	−3	1.44	−6.52 to 0.52
0	0	1.12	−2.74 to 2.74
2	3	1.44	−0.52 to 6.52
4	6	2.14	0.76 to 11.24

Reprise: Urbanization and Per Capita Income

Let's return, once again and finally, to the relationship between urbanization and per capita income. The scatterplot is shown in Figure 12.10, and the regression line is

$$\widehat{PCI} = -1252 + 85.2U$$

EQUATION NUMBER 1   DEPENDENT VARIABLE .. INC   INCOME PER CAPITA

BEGINNING BLOCK NUMBER   1.   METHOD: ENTER
VARIABLE(S) ENTERED ON STEP NUMBER

1 ..   URBAN   URBANIZATION PERCENTAGE

---------------- VARIABLES IN THE EQUATION ----------------

VARIABLE	B	SE B	95% CONFDNCE INTRVL B		BETA
URBAN	85.25328	9.61993	66.17445	104.33212	.65774
(CONSTANT)	− 1252.52148	475.55538	− 2195.67243	− 309.37054	

--------- IN ---------

VARIABLE	T	SIG T
URBAN	8.862	.0000
(CONSTANT)	− 2.634	.0097

FIGURE 12.14 Computer printout of regression analysis of urbanization and per capita income.

Figure 12.14 shows a computer printout of the regression analysis. The slope B associated with the independent variable "URBAN" is "85.25328" and the CONSTANT is − 1252.52148. Of concern here are the inferential statistics included in the printout.

Across the row form URBAN you see the number 9.61993 under "SE B." That is the standard error of the regression coefficient. From that number the computer calculates a 95 percent confidence interval estimate of B, the true slope of the line relating these variables. With df $= 105 − 2 = 103$, you use the bottom line of the table of t distributions and find that the confidence interval extends 1.96 standard errors out from the point estimate of B, which is 85.2. So the interval extends from $85.2 − (1.96)(9.62) = 66.4$ to $85.2 + (1.96)(9.62) = 104.2$ or as the computer, with its own rounding errors, has it, from "66.17445" to "104.33212."

Across from the constant under the column headed "SE B" is the number 475.55538. This is not the standard error of the regression coefficient. That was in the first row. This is the standard error of the predicted level of the dependent variable at the point where the independent variable equals zero. The 95 percent confidence interval given directly after that is an interval estimate of the true y intercept. You can say with 95 percent confidence that the true y intercept A lies in the interval bounded by − 2195.7 and − 309.4.

Finally, at the bottom of Figure 12.14 is the information you need to conduct a test of the null hypothesis about the slope

$$H_0: B = 0$$

The sample regression coefficient lies $85.2 − 0 = 85.2$ absolute units away from the hypothesized value of the parameter. The standard error of the regression coefficient is, from above, 9.62, so the sample regression coefficient lies $85.2/9.62 = 8.87$ standard-error units above the mean of its sampling distribution. The test statistic is $t = 8.87$ with df $= 105 - 2 = 103$. Under "SIG T" (the "significance of t," or the observed significance of the test) you see ".0000." That means that the observed significance of this test is $p < .0001$. You may reject the null hypothesis and conclude that in the population from which this sample came, the slope of the line relating urbanization and per capita income is probably not equal to zero.

Aren't computers great?

· · ·

CORRELATION

Usually some error remains in the predictions of the dependent variable that you make by using the regression line. One hopes that having information on an independent variable and having a regression line with which to make predictions reduce the error of predictions, but whether a reduction is achieved or not is a question that a measure of the strength of association between two continuous variables can answer. The measure of association for two continuous variables is r^2 ("r squared"), the square of *Pearson's product-moment correlation coefficient r*. Sometimes r is called simply the *correlation coefficient*. But remember that it is the correlation coefficient one usually uses with two continuous variables.

Now r^2 is called the *coefficient of determination*. Like many measures of association, r^2 is a measure of proportionate reduction in error (PRE). You already know that the total error with which one begins a problem in which the dependent variable is continuous is the sample variance of the dependent variable s_y^2. And s_y^2 is the total squared deviations around the grand mean of the dependent variable divided by the number of cases in the sample minus 1. The remaining error, after information on the independent variable is added, is the total squared deviations around the regression line divided by the number of cases minus 1.

Recall that in Chapter 10 the remaining error was the conditional variances measured within categories of the independent variable. In each instance in that chapter, you conditioned the distribution of the dependent variable on the two categories of the independent variable, and calculated the remaining error around those two conditional means. To develop an analogy when the independent variable is continuous and has an infinite number of categories, you can think of the regression line as an infinite series of conditional means, the $\hat{Y}$'s. The sum of the squared deviations around this series of conditional means divided by the number of cases minus 1 is the remaining error.

If $\hat{Y}_i$ is the value of Y predicted by the regression line for a case with an X-value of X_i, then the deviation of the actual value of the case from the value predicted by the regression line is $Y_i - \hat{Y}_i$. Then the total squared deviations around the regression line divided by $n - 1$ is

$$\frac{\sum_{i=1}^{n} (Y_i - \hat{Y}_i)^2}{n - 1}$$

This is the error that remains in the predictions of the dependent variable after information on the independent variable is added.

With the total error—the sample variance of Y—and the remaining error (shown above) you can calculate PRE by using Formula (10.1). The PRE is equal to r^2:

$$\text{PRE} = r^2 = \frac{\left(\sum_{i=1}^{n} (Y_i - \bar{Y})^2 \middle/ (n - 1)\right) - \left(\sum_{i=1}^{n} (Y_i - \hat{Y})^2 \middle/ (n - 1)\right)}{\sum_{i=1}^{n} (Y_i - \bar{Y})^2 \middle/ (n - 1)}$$

$$= \frac{\sum_{i=1}^{n} (Y_i - \bar{Y})^2 - \sum_{i=1}^{n} (Y_i - \hat{Y})^2}{\sum_{i=1}^{n} (Y_i - \bar{Y})^2} \qquad (12.2)$$

Figure 12.15 shows how to use this formula to calculate r^2 for X and Y in Figure 12.4. $\sum_{i=1}^{n} (Y_i - \bar{Y})^2$ is called the *sum of squares around the grand mean* while

X_i	Y_i	$(Y_i - \bar{Y})^2$	$\hat{Y}_i = 1.5X_i$	$(Y_i - \hat{Y}_i)^2$
-4	-5	25	-6	1
-2	-7	49	-3	16
-2	-1	1	-3	4
0	-3	9	0	9
0	3	9	0	9
2	1	1	3	4
2	7	49	3	16
4	5	25	6	1
		Sum = 168		Sum = 60

$$r^2 = \frac{168 - 60}{168} = .64$$

FIGURE 12.15 Calculation of r^2 for X and Y in Figure 12.4 using the PRE approach of Formula (12.2).

$\sum_{i=1}^{n} (Y_i - \hat{Y}_i)^2$ is called the *sum of squares around the predicted Y's*. The sum of squares around the predictions of the dependent variable based on the regression line is 60. The PRE is $r^2 = (168 - 60)/168 = .64$.

The numerator of Formula (12.2) is the variation in Y that is accounted for by the regression line. So r^2 is a measure of the proportion of the total *variance in Y that is accounted for by the regression line*. And r^2 says that the independent variable, X in this case, accounts for .64, or 64 percent, of the original variation in Y.

The X and Y data from Figure 12.4 are displayed again in Figure 12.16 in a manner that lets you see what "accounted for" refers to. It also shows what remains "unaccounted for" and should give you a sense of what the common statistical phrase "decomposition of variance" means. For the point (2, 7), the deviation from the grand mean of Y is $Y_i - \bar{Y} = 7 - 0 = 7$. This deviation is decomposed in Figure 12.16 into two parts:

1. That accounted for by the regression line at $X = 2$. This part is $\hat{Y}_i - \bar{Y}$, the difference between the prediction of Y at $X = 2$ and the grand mean; $\hat{Y}_i - \bar{Y} = a + bX_i - \bar{Y} = 1.5(2) - 0 = 3$.

2. That which remains unaccounted for. The deviation of the case from the prediction $Y_i - \hat{Y}_i$, which in this instance is $7 - 3 = 4$.

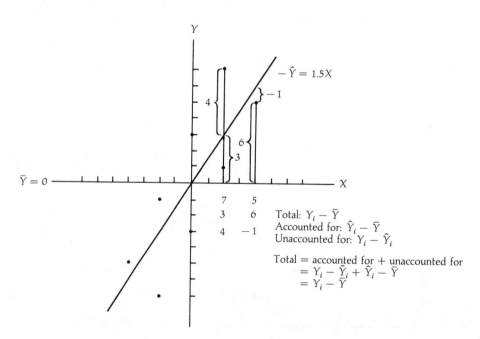

FIGURE 12.16 Illustration of decomposition of variance, variance accounted for, and variance unaccounted for.

The part of the deviation accounted for by the regression line and the part that remains unaccounted for add to the whole deviation: $4 + 3 = 7$. The deviation is composed of two parts: that which is accounted for by the regression line and that which remains unaccounted for. If a deviation is composed of two parts, it can be "decomposed" into two parts. Consequently, the variance—which is based on the sum of these deviations squared—can be "decomposed" into two parts, the part accounted for by the regression and the part that remains unaccounted for.

If the data points tend to lie close to the regression line, distances between the cases and the grand mean will be large relative to distances between cases and the line. If that is true, a large proportion of the variance will be accounted for by the regression line. If cases tend to lie far away from the regression line, a large portion of the variance remains unaccounted for. The data in Figure 12.8 have an $r^2 = 0.83$. They lie, as you can see, closer to the regression line than the data in Figure 12.4, and so the proportion of the variance accounted for by the line is higher than in the earlier example.

The *correlation coefficient r* is the square root of r^2:

$$r = \pm \sqrt{r^2}$$

A positive number always has two square roots, a positive one and a negative one. The correlation coefficient r takes its sign from the slope of the regression line. If the slope of the regression line is positive, then r is the positive square root of r^2. If the slope of the regression line is negative, r is the negative square root of r^2.

There is a direct way to calculate r. The formula for Pearson's product-moment correlation coefficient is

$$r = \frac{\sum_{i=1}^{n} (X_i - \bar{X})(Y_i - \bar{Y})}{\sqrt{\sum_{i=1}^{n} (X_i - \bar{X})^2 \sum_{i=1}^{n} (Y_i - \bar{Y})^2}} \qquad (12.3a)$$

The computation formula for r, which allows you to calculate r with one pass through a data set, is

$$r = \frac{n \sum_{i=1}^{n} X_i Y_i - \sum_{i=1}^{n} X_i \sum_{i=1}^{n} Y_i}{\sqrt{\left[n \sum_{i=1}^{n} X_i^2 - \left(\sum_{i=1}^{n} X_i \right)^2 \right]\left[n \sum_{i=1}^{n} Y_i^2 - \left(\sum_{i=1}^{n} Y_i \right)^2 \right]}} \qquad (12.3b)$$

There is no reason whatsoever to remember either formula. You can always look them up. It is important to understand the concept of correlation and to know that the correlation coefficient can be calculated.

There are a few characteristics of the correlation coefficient that should not be surprising to you since it is a measure of association. First, r varies from -1

to $+1$, and r^2 obviously varies from 0 to $+1$. Second, r is equal to 1 or -1 if two variables are perfectly associated, i.e., if all the points in a scattergram lie exactly on a straight line. Third, $r = 0$ if the data on a scattergram are arrayed in a perfectly random fashion. That is, if $r = 0$, there is no tendency for high values of the independent variable to be associated with either high or low values of the dependent variable. Fourth, r^2 is sometimes just called the *variance accounted for*, since it measures how well you can predict the dependent variable on the basis of the independent variable.

There is one characteristic of r that is not so obvious: r is a symmetric measure of association. That is, the correlation coefficient of variables X and Y, taken in that order, is the same as the correlation coefficient for variables Y and X. The regression coefficient b is an asymmetric descriptor of a relationship; r is a symmetric measure of association.

High values of r^2 are few and far between. Look again at the relationship between urbanization and per capita income in Figure 12.10. You know r is positive since the slope of the regression line is positive. Do you think r^2 is smaller or larger than the values of r^2 for the data in Figures 12.4 and 12.8? The points in Figure 12.10 are spread widely around the regression line, so you should expect the r^2 to be fairly small. In fact, $r = .66$ and $r^2 = .43$. Even these are fairly high correlation coefficients.

The size of a correlation coefficient is not terribly important. The important issue in research is whether a hypothesis is supported by data. Hypotheses are falsifiable statements of a relationship between variables. A correlation coefficient tells you whether there is a data-based relationship between variables. If there is a nonzero correlation between two variables, there is at least some support for a hypothesis about a relationship. Inferential statistics answer the question, How big is big enough?

By now, to do a test of a hypothesis, all you should need to know is the shape, the mean, and standard deviation of the sampling distribution of the sample statistic. For example, suppose you want to test the null hypothesis that the true product-moment correlation between two variables in the population ρ (the Greek letter "rho," pronounced "row") is equal to zero. All we need to know is that if the null hypothesis is true, then the sampling distribution is a t distribution with $n - 2$ degrees of freedom, it has a mean of $\rho = 0$, and the standard error is

$$s_{r_{xy}} = \sqrt{\frac{1 - r_{xy}^2}{n - 2}}$$

Consider the relationship between Protestant work ethic and the score on the leisure-ethic scale in the internal-motivation experiments. The correlation between the two scales in the first experiment is $r = -.316$. It is negative, as theory would predict (the higher one's work ethic, the lower one's leisure ethic should be), but is it significantly less than zero? Is it enough below zero that it is reasonable to

conclude that work ethic and leisure ethic are negatively correlated in the population from which the sample was drawn?

First, set up the appropriate hypotheses for conducting a one-tailed test ("*wl*"
stands for "*work ethic*" and "*leisure ethic*"):

$$H_0: \rho_{wl} \geq 0$$

$$H_A: \rho_{wl} < 0$$

Next, calculate the standard error of the correlation coefficient:

$$s_{r_{wl}} = \sqrt{\frac{1 - (-0.316)^2}{60 - 2}} = 0.12$$

The sample correlation coefficient is $-0.316/0.12 = 2.6$ standard units away from
the mean of $\rho = 0$ on a t distribution with df $= 60 - 2 = 58$. The observed significance of the test is $p < .01$.

You should reject the null hypothesis and conclude that indeed work ethic
and leisure ethic are probably negatively correlated in the population from which
this sample was drawn.

The test just described is useful only if you are testing a hypothesis that the
correlation coefficient in the population is equal to zero. In some cases you want
to test the hypothesis that the population parameter ρ_{xy} is equal to some specified value ρ_a that is not zero. R. A. Fisher worked out a procedure for doing just
that. If the null and alternative hypotheses are

$$H_0: \rho_{xy} = \rho_a \qquad \text{or} \qquad \rho_{xy} - \rho_a = 0$$

and

$$H_A: \rho_{xy} \neq \rho_a \qquad \text{or} \qquad \rho_{xy} - \rho_a \neq 0$$

then, Fisher showed, there is no convenient way to express the distribution of the
difference $r_{xy} - r_a$. However, he found, if the correlation coefficient r_{xy} and the
specified value r_a are transformed by using a Z transformation, then the difference
$Z_{xy} - Z_a$ (where Z_{xy} is the transformation of r_{xy} and Z_a is the transformation of
r_a) is distributed normally with mean zero and standard error $1/\sqrt{n - 3}$. The Z
transformation is

$$Z = \ln \sqrt{\frac{1 + r}{1 - r}}$$

So

$$Z_{xy} = \ln \sqrt{\frac{1 + r_{xy}}{1 - r_{xy}}} \qquad \text{and} \qquad Z_a = \ln \sqrt{\frac{1 + r_n}{1 - r_n}}$$

The use of this procedure is demonstrated in "A Concluding Example."

Interval Estimates of the Correlation Coefficient, ρ

The correlation between work ethic and leisure ethic in the internal-motivation experiments is $r_{wl} = -0.316$. What is the interval that you can be 95 percent confident contains ρ_{wl}, the true correlation coefficient between scales in the population from which the sample was drawn?

Since you do not know anything about the population parameter, you need to use the Z transformation of r, construct an interval around $Z_{r_{wl}}$, and then transform the bounds of the interval from Z's back to correlation coefficients r.

There is a table of Z transformations, Appendix Table B.7. From that table, you find the Z transformation of $r = -0.316$ is $Z = -.327$. The sampling distribution of Z is normal and has a standard error of $\sqrt{1/(n-3)} = \sqrt{1/(60-3)} =$ .132 in this case. The 95 percent confidence interval around $Z = -.327$ is $-.327 \pm$ 1.96(.132) or $Z = -.586$ to $Z = .068$. Using Table B.7, you can find the r that corresponds to each of these Z's. For $Z = -.586$, r is approximately $-.53$. For $Z = .068$, $r = .07$ approximately. So a 95 percent confidence interval for the population correlation coefficient between "work ethic" and "leisure ethic" extends from $-.53$ to .07. You can be 95 percent confident that ρ_{wl} lies in this interval.

· · ·

A CONCLUDING EXAMPLE

Using the hospital cost data in Appendix A, I can test a hypothesis that, for a long time, I have believed is true. I think that specialists in medicine "do more medicine" than generalists. I think they order more tests, are quicker to intervene, and so on. In terms of the data I have, my hypothesis can be framed as, "Specialists are more costly than generalists" (not costly in terms of physician's fees, but costly in terms of hospital charges to patients under their care). Specifically, to express the hypothesis in terms of the variables in the data set, I claim that the lower a physician's "specialization percentage" (i.e., the more specialized the practice), the higher the hospital charges that physician's patients. The hypothesis is

$$\text{Specialization score} \longrightarrow \text{Average total cost}$$

where the minus sign indicates a negative relationship between variables.

To test this hypothesis, I calculated the average total cost to patients for each of the 22 physicians in the data set. The data I need to test this hypothesis are presented in Figure 12.17.

What is the relationship between specialization score and average total cost? The data are shown in a scattergram in Figure 12.18. In fact, lower specialization scores tend to go with higher average costs. The data seem to support the hypothesis. In fact, the variables appear to be linearly related to each other, so a line will provide a good description of the relationship between specialization and cost

Physician	Specialization, %	Average Total Cost, $	Cost for DRG 373, $
01	50	1125	1074
02	47	1306	990
03	61	1516	973
04	63	1186	1095
05	95	807	860
06	94	990	1054
07	55	1662	1636
08	92	857	956
09	93	1016	1000
10	75	682	1075
11	62	1313	1035
12	67	1764	1126
13	90	1118	901
14	90	1104	1078
15	86	1079	1272
16	97	992	992
17	63	1841	1709
18	84	623	767
19	85	1164	1143
20	89	1347	964
21	63	983	1098
22	88	718	914

FIGURE 12.17 Raw data to test the hypotheses concerning specialization and cost.

in the sample. I calculated the equation of the regression line and found

$$\hat{C} = 2010.5 - 11.3S$$

where S is the specialization score and C is the average total cost. For every 1 percent increase in specialization score, the average cost to the patient decreases by more than $11. The correlation coefficient is $-.55$, so the data are moderately well grouped around the regression line. $r^2 = .30$, so the specialization score accounts for about 30 percent of the variation in the dependent variable "total cost." My hypothesis is supported by the sample data.

The zero-order correlation between specialization score and average cost to patients is $r = -.55$. Is it significantly less than zero? Notice that I want to conduct a one-tailed test. Using ρ_{sc} (where s = specialization score and c = cost), I

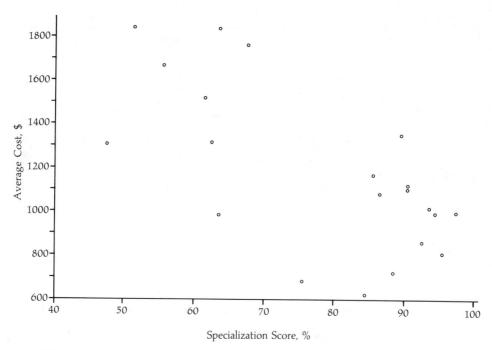

FIGURE 12.18 Relationship between specialization score and average cost to patients of 22 physicians.

construct the alternative hypothesis

$$H_A: \rho_{sc} < 0$$

and the null hypothesis

$$H_0: \rho_{sc} \geq 0$$

If the null hypothesis is true, then r_{sc} is $-.55 - 0 = -.55$ raw unit away from the mean of the sampling distribution. The standard error is

$$s_{r_{sc}} = \sqrt{\frac{1 - (-.55)^2}{22 - 2}} = .19$$

So the correlation coefficient is $-.55/.19 = -2.9$ standard units away from the mean. By using a one-tailed test against a t distribution with df $= n - 2 = 20$ the probability of being incorrect in a decision to reject the null hypothesis is less than .005. I reject the null hypothesis, accept the alternative, and conclude that the correlation between specialization score and cost in the population from which this sample was drawn is probably less than zero.

My hypothesis—a statement about a relationship between variables—is supported, but does that mean that my rationale (the reasoning that led to the formulation of the hypothesis) is supported? Does this statistical result show that, in truth, specialists "do more medicine"? No. It simply means that the patients of specialists, on average, are charged more than patients of less specialized physicians. There are reasons other than "specialists do more medicine" that might account for this relationship. In fact, we already have learned that specialists tend to treat more complicated cases than generalists. More complicated cases are probably more costly than routine cases. (This is a relationship you could examine, using this data set.) So specialists may have higher charges to their patients simply because they are treating more complicated cases than generalists. The relationship between specialization and cost may be spurious and dependent on the complexity of the case.

There is a way to get around this problem and to test the hypothesis in a different way. Why not see if patients of specialists are charged more than patients of generalists *for the same procedures*? You can do this by examining the relationship between specialization and cost for a single, common procedure like vaginal delivery without medical complications, DRG 373. Figure 12.17 also lists each physician's average charge for patients in DRG 373.

What is the relationship between specialization and cost to patients in DRG 373? Figure 12.19 shows the data in a scattergram. There still appears to be a

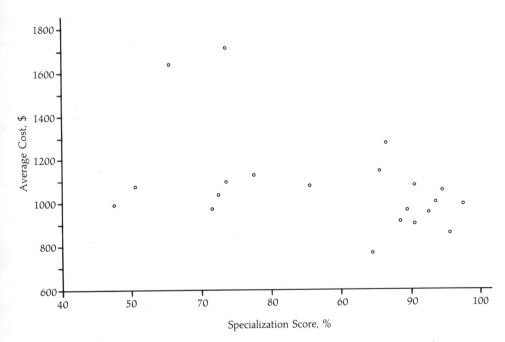

FIGURE 12.19 Relationship between specialization score and average costs of patients in DRG 373 for 22 physicians.

negative relationship between the variables. The regression line for that figure is

$$\widehat{C373} = 1512.1 - 5.7S$$

where $C373$ is cost for DRG 373. There is a negative relationship, but the slope of the regression line is much smaller for the cost of a routine childbirth than for overall costs. The correlation between variables is $-.42$, so specialization accounts for only 18 percent of the variation in costs for a routine childbirth. My hypothesis is still supported by the sample data. Indeed, I can still reject the null hypothesis of a zero correlation coefficient with an observed significance of the test of $p < .025$, but the support is a little weaker than before.

Note that there are two physicians, both relatively specialized, who have very high charges for patients in DRG 373. Their existence on the scattergram is exerting considerable influence on the slope of the regression line since they are way up in the upper left corner of the chart. I wondered what would happen if I eliminated these two outliers from this analysis. Once I did that, the regression line became

$$\widehat{C373^*} = 1157.4 - 1.8S$$

where $C373^*$ is average cost to patients in DRG 373 for the 20 physicians remaining after physicians 07 and 17 are eliminated. The relationship between specialization and cost for the remaining physicians is very small: There is a decrease of less than \$2 for every unit change in specialization score.

Let's perform some inferential tests on the regressions. First, let's construct confidence intervals around several conditional means, given by the regression of costs to patients on physicians' specialization scores. The regression for the sample of 22 physicians is

$$\hat{C} = 2010.5 - 11.3S$$

The standard error of the estimate is $s_{C.S} = 289.6$. And $\sum_{i=1}^{n}(X_i - \bar{X})^2 = 5575.9$, $n = 22$, and $\bar{X} = 76.77$. So for any S

$$s_{\hat{C}} = 289.6 \sqrt{\frac{1}{22} + \frac{(S - 76.77)^2}{5575.9}}$$

You can use this to calculate $s_{\hat{C}}$ for several values of specialization score S:

S	$s_{\hat{C}}$
$\bar{S} = 76.77$	61.7
50	120.8
60	89.7
80	63.0
90	80.3

Then you can calculate the 95 percent interval for $\mu_{C.S}$ for each of these S's as $\hat{C} \pm ts_{\hat{C}}$, where $\hat{C} = 2010.5 - 11.3S$ and t is determined for 95 percent confidence on a t distribution with df $= n - 2 = 22 - 2 = 20$

S	Lower Bound $\hat{C} - 2.086s_C$	Upper Bound $\hat{C} + 2.086s_C$
$\bar{S} = 76.77$	1014.3	1271.7
50	1193.5	1697.5
60	1145.4	1519.6
80	975.1	1237.9
90	826.0	1161.0

These values are plotted, along with the regression line $\hat{C} = 2010.5 - 11.3S$, on a scatterplot of the data in Figure 12.20. You can be 95 percent confident that the true regression line lies within the band sketched on Figure 12.20.

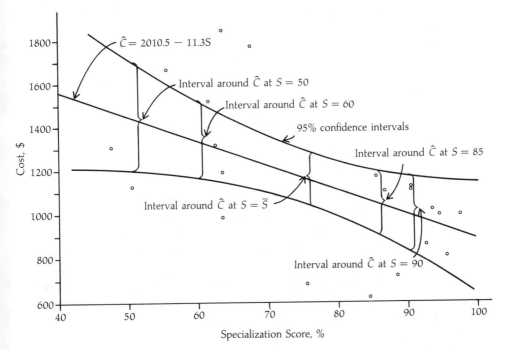

FIGURE 12.20 Regression of cost on specialization score; sample regression line shown with five confidence intervals around five conditional means.

Let's now test a hypothesis concerning the regressions of costs on specialization score. The regression of cost on specialization score shows that

$$\hat{C} = 2010.5 - 11.3S$$

And for the regression of costs to patients in DRG 373 on specialization score with the two high-priced physicians (07 and 17) eliminated, the regression is

$$\widehat{C373^*} = 1157.4 - 1.8S$$

Are the slopes in these two regressions significantly different from zero?

For the first regression the alternative hypothesis is that the regression coefficient is greater than zero:

$$H_A: B_{cs} > 0$$

And the null hypothesis is

$$H_0: B_{cs} \leq 0$$

The standard error of the regression coefficient is

$$s_b = \frac{\sqrt{\left(\sum_{i=1}^{n} Y_i^2 - a \sum_{i=1}^{n} Y_i - b \sum_{i=1}^{n} X_i Y_i\right)/(n-2)}}{\sqrt{\sum_{i=1}^{n} (X_i - \bar{X})^2}}$$

$$= \frac{\sqrt{31,182,773 - 50,650,526 + 21,145,532/(22-2)}}{\sqrt{5575.9}}$$

$$= \frac{289.6}{74.7} = 3.88$$

Therefore, the regression coefficient for the sample is $-11.3/3.88 = -2.91$ standard units below the mean of zero on a t distribution with 20 degrees of freedom. I reject the null hypothesis with an observed significance of the test of $p < .02$. The regression coefficient relating cost and specialization score in the population is probably greater than zero.

What about the relationship between costs to patients in DRG 373 and specialization score with physicians 07 and 17 eliminated? The null hypothesis and the alternative are the same as above:

$$H_A: B_{cs} > 0 \qquad H_0: B_{cs} \leq 0$$

The standard error is

$$s_b = \frac{\sqrt{20,979,475 - 23,572,766 + 2,864,239/(20 - 2)}}{\sqrt{4848.9}} = \frac{122.7}{69.6} = 1.76$$

The regression coefficient is only $-1.8/1.76 = -1.02$ standard units away from the mean of $B_{cs} = 0$ on a t distribution with $20 - 2 = 18$ degrees of freedom. I do not reject the null hypothesis, so I cannot conclude that specialization score and costs to patients in DRG 373 are related in the population from which this sample was drawn.

My conclusion from all this is that I am not convinced that specialists necessarily "do more medicine." It seems that, with a couple of exceptions, virtually all physicians cause their patients to incur just about the same hospital charges for a common procedure. I would, however, like to know more about physicians 07 and 17 whose charges are so very different from those of their colleagues before I gave up my original belief entirely.

Suppose, finally (and principally to illustrate the use of the Z transformation), for some reason you wanted to test the hypothesis that the sample in which the coorelation between specialization score and cost to patients discharged in DRG 373 came from a population in which the variables were correlated with $\rho = -.20$. That is, your alternative hypothesis is

$$H_A: \rho_{sc} < -.20$$

and the null hypothesis is

$$H_0: \rho_{sc} \geq -.20$$

Since the test is not against a hypothesized value of $\rho = 0$, you must do the Z transformations

$$Z_{r_{sc}} = Z_{-.42} = \ln \sqrt{\frac{1 + (-.42)}{1 - (-.42)}} = -.448$$

$$Z_{r_a} = Z_{-.20} = \ln \sqrt{\frac{1 + (-.20)}{1 - (-.20)}} = -.203$$

(You don't have to do these calculations. The Z transformations of positive-valued correlation coefficients are in the Appendix.) Second, calculate the difference $Z_{r_{sc}} - Z_{r_a} = -.448 - (-.203) = -.245$. Third, find the standard error $s = \sqrt{1/(n - 3)} = \sqrt{1/(22 - 3)} = .229$. The difference of $-.245$ raw (Z) unit is

$-.245/.229 = -1.07$ standard units away from the mean of zero. Using the normal distribution, we see there is a high likelihood that you would be incorrect to reject the null hypothesis. We decide not to reject it. We conclude that the sample correlation of $-.42$ is not significantly less than $-.20$.

$$\bullet \quad \bullet \quad \bullet$$

KEY CONCEPTS IN THIS CHAPTER

$$\bullet \quad \bullet \quad \bullet$$

NOTES

1. Helen Mary Walker, *Studies in the History of Statistical Method*, Williams and Williams Co., Baltimore, Md., 1929, pp. 92–93.

2. Ibid., p. 103.

3. Francis Galton, "Regression towards Mediocrity in Hereditary Stature," *Journal of the Anthropological Institute* 15: 246–263, 1885.

4. This data set is adapted from the article by Gary M. Mullet, "A Graphical Illustration of Simple (Total) and Partial Regression," *American Statistician* 26: 25–27, 1972.

· · ·

SUPPLEMENT 12.1

Using the Calculus to Obtain the Regression Line

The task is to find the line that minimizes the squared deviations of cases around itself. Any line has the form $Y = a + bX$, so the task is to find a and b, the y intercept and the slope, such that the squared error around the line is minimized. The resulting line is called the *regression line*.

Expressed mathematically, the task is to minimize

$$\frac{\sum_{i=1}^{n} (Y_i - \hat{Y}_1)^2}{n - 1}$$

It is sufficient to minimize just the numerator since the denominator is a constant. Since $\hat{Y}_1 = a + bX_i$, the sum to be minimized can be rewritten as

$$f(a, b) = \sum_{i=1}^{n} [Y_i - (a + bX_i)]^2$$

which is a function of the two unknowns a and b. The task is to find a and b such that f is at a minimum. Calculus is used to find minima and maxima of functions.

The first thing to do is to expand the sum by squaring the term indicated:

$$f(a, b) = \sum_{i=1}^{n} (a^2 + abX_i - aY_i + abX_i + b^2X_i^2 - bX_iY_i - aY_i - bX_iY_i + Y_i^2)$$

Collecting terms and dropping the subscript i to simplify matters, we have

$$f(a, b) = \sum (a^2 + 2abX - 2aY + b^2X^2 - 2bXY + Y^2)$$

To minimize f, we must take the partial derivatives of f with respect to both a and b and set the partials equal to zero. At that point (or points), f assumes either a maximum or a minimum:

$$\frac{\partial f}{\partial a} = \sum (2a + 2bX - 2Y)$$

$$= 2an + 2b\sum X - 2\sum Y = 0 \tag{1}$$

$$\frac{\partial f}{\partial b} = \sum (2aX + 2bX^2 - 2XY)$$

$$= 2a\sum X + 2b\sum X^2 - 2\sum XY$$

$$= 2an\bar{X} + 2b\sum X^2 - 2\sum XY \tag{2}$$

We have two equations in two unknowns a and b. The system is soluble. Multiply Equation (1) by $\bar{X}$ or $\sum X/n$ and subtract (2) from (1):

$$2an\bar{X} + 2b\frac{(\sum X)^2}{n} - 2\frac{\sum X\sum Y}{n} = 0$$

$$-\;\frac{2an\bar{X} + 2b\sum X^2 - 2\sum XY = 0}{2b\frac{(\sum X)^2}{n} - 2b\sum X^2 - 2\frac{\sum X\sum Y}{n} + 2\sum XY = 0}$$

Collecting terms and eliminating the 2s give

$$b\left(\frac{(\sum X)^2}{n} - \sum X^2\right) = \frac{\sum X\sum Y}{n} - \sum XY$$

So

$$b = \frac{\sum X_i \sum Y_i - n\sum X_i Y_i}{(\sum X_i)^2 - n\sum X_i^2}$$

If we took the second partial derivatives of f with respect to a and b, we would find they are positive, which indicates that this solution is indeed a minimum of f. This is the computational formula for the regression coefficient b. We can show that this is equal to Formula (12.1b), the computational formula in the text, by multiplying this by $(-1)/(-1)$.

· · ·

SUPPLEMENT 12.2

The Computational and Basic Formulas for b are Equal

The computational formula for the regression coefficient was derived in Supplement 12.1. The task in this supplement is to show that the computational formula equals the basic formula for the regression coefficient, which is

$$b = \frac{\displaystyle\sum_{i=1}^{n} (X_i - \bar{X})(Y_i - \bar{Y})}{\displaystyle\sum_{i=1}^{n} (X_i - \bar{X})^2}$$

If we carry out the multiplication in the numerator and complete the square in the denominator, we get

$$b = \frac{\sum\limits_{i=1}^{n}(X_iY_i - \bar{X}Y_i - X_i\bar{Y} + \bar{X}\bar{Y})}{\sum\limits_{i=1}^{n}(X_i^2 - 2X_i\bar{X} + \bar{X}^2)}$$

$$= \frac{\sum\limits_{i=1}^{n}X_iY_i - \bar{X}\sum\limits_{i=1}^{n}Y_i - \bar{Y}\sum\limits_{i=1}^{n}X_i + n\bar{X}\bar{Y}}{\sum\limits_{i=1}^{n}X_i^2 - 2\bar{X}\sum\limits_{i=1}^{n}X_i + \left(\sum\limits_{i=1}^{n}X_i\right)^2 \Big/ n}$$

$$= \frac{\sum\limits_{i=1}^{n}X_iY_i - \dfrac{\sum\limits_{i=1}^{n}X_i\sum\limits_{i=1}^{n}Y_i}{n} - \dfrac{\sum\limits_{i=1}^{n}X_i\sum\limits_{i=1}^{n}Y_i}{n} + \dfrac{\sum\limits_{i=1}^{n}X_i\sum\limits_{i=1}^{n}Y_i}{n}}{\sum\limits_{i=1}^{n}X_i^2 - 2\dfrac{\left(\sum\limits_{i=1}^{n}X_i\right)^2}{n} + \dfrac{\left(\sum\limits_{i=1}^{n}X_i\right)^2}{n}}$$

$$= \frac{n\sum\limits_{i=1}^{n}X_iY_i - \sum\limits_{i=1}^{n}X_i\sum\limits_{i=1}^{n}Y_i}{n\sum\limits_{i=1}^{n}X_i^2 - \left(\sum\limits_{i=1}^{n}X_i\right)^2}$$

which is the computational formula for b. The techniques used here can also be used to show that the two formulas for the correlation coefficient, Formulas (12.3a) and (12.3b), are equal.

$$\bullet \quad \bullet \quad \bullet$$

SUPPLEMENT 12.3

Relationship Between the Regression Coefficient and the Correlation Coefficient

Formula (12.1a), the formula for the regression coefficient b, and Formula (12.3a) for the correlation coefficient look similar. It is very easy to discover the mathematical relationship between b and r.

Consider first Formula (12.1a), the coefficient of regression of Y on X. If we divide both the numerator and the denominator by $n - 1$, we get

$$b_{yx} = \frac{\sum\limits_{i=1}^{n}(X_i - \bar{X})(Y_i - \bar{Y})/(n - 1)}{\sum\limits_{i=1}^{n}(X_i - \bar{X})^2/(n - 1)}$$

The denominator is familiar enough. It is the variance of the independent variable X. The numerator is the average cross products of deviation of X from its mean and of Y from its mean. The numerator is the *covariance* of X and Y, denoted cov_{xy}. Using this notation, we can rewrite the formula for b as

$$b_{yx} = \frac{cov_{xy}}{s_x^2}$$

(It is clear from this representation why b is an asymmetric descriptor of a relationship. The regression coefficient of Y on X is equal to the regression coefficient of X on Y *only if* the variances of the two variables are equal. That is, if $s_y^2 = s_x^2$, then

$$b_{yx} = \frac{cov_{xy}}{s_x^2} = \frac{cov_{xy}}{s_y^2} = b_{xy}$$

But that is a diversion from the question of the relationship between b and r.)

Consider next Formula (12.3a). We divide its numerator and denominator by n − 1;

$$r = \frac{\sum_{i=1}^{n} (X_i - \bar{X})(Y_i - \bar{Y})/(n - 1)}{\sqrt{\sum_{i=1}^{n} (X_i - \bar{X})^2/(n - 1)} \sqrt{\sum_{i=1}^{n} (Y_i - \bar{Y})^2/(n - 1)}}$$

This says that the correlation coefficient is equal to the covariance of X and Y divided by the product of the standard deviations of X and Y, or

$$r = \frac{cov_{xy}}{s_x s_y}$$

To get from r to b, we have to multiply r by the standard deviation of Y over the standard deviation of X:

$$r\frac{s_y}{s_x} = \frac{cov_{xy}}{s_x s_y} \cdot \frac{s_y}{s_x} = \frac{cov_{xy}}{s_x^2} = b_{yx}$$

So there is a direct relationship between b and r:

$$b = r\frac{s_y}{s_x} \quad \text{or} \quad r = b\frac{s_x}{s_y}$$

These equations can be very useful if, for example, you have a calculator that will calculate a bivariate regression coefficient, standard deviations, and variances, but will not calculate the correlation coefficient.

· · ·

EXERCISES

Chapter 12

1. Here is a hypothetical data set with 10 data points:

X	− 2.0	− 1.5	− 1.0	1.0	1.5	2.0	3.0	4.0	5.0	5.0
Y	1	4	−2	1	−5	3	−3	1	−2	−5

  a. Draw a scattergram of these points.
  b. Is a straight line a good descriptor of these data?
  c. Does the regression line describing the data have a positive or a negative slope? (Don't calculate the coefficients of the regression line yet; just look at the data and answer.)
  d. Do you think the correlation coefficient is large or small?
  e. Draw a line that describes the data well. Just eyeball it.
  f. Determine the equation of the line you drew. What is its y intercept a? What is its slope b? Express the line as an equation of the form $Y = a + bX$.
  g. Determine the total error in variable Y. That is, calculate the variance of Y.
  h. Use a procedure like that illustrated in Figure 12.6 to determine the remaining error around the line you have drawn to describe the data. The following steps will help you answer this question.
    (i) Using your line, determine the values of Y that would be predicted for each value of X. That is, calculate the 10 values of $\hat{Y}_i$, $1 \leq i \leq 10$.
    (ii) Calculate the 10 squared deviations of the actual Y values from the predicted values. That is, calculate the 10 values $(Y_i - \hat{Y}_i)^2$, $1 \leq i \leq 10$.
    (iii) Calculate the total squared deviation of the actual Y values around the predicted Y values divided by $n - 1$. That is the remaining error.
  i. Calculate the PRE achieved by your line.
  j. Is your line a good descriptor of the data?

2. Calculate the regression line for the data in Exercise 1. The following steps will help you answer this question.

  a. Following a procedure like that in Figure 12.7, calculate the mean of X, or $\bar{X}$, and the mean of Y, or $\bar{Y}$. Then calculate the squared deviation of each X value around $\bar{X}$, the deviation of each Y value around $\bar{Y}$, and the cross product of each X and Y deviation. That is, calculate $X_i - \bar{X}$, $Y_i - \bar{Y}$, and $(X_i - \bar{X})(Y_i - \bar{Y})$ for $1 \le i \le 10$.

b. Use Formula (12.1*a*) to find the slope of the regression line.

c. Use Formula (12.2) to find the *y* intercept of the regression line.

d. Express the regression line as an equation of the form $Y = a + bX$.

e. Calculate the proportionate reduction in error r^2, using the formulas in Supplement 12.2. Since you know the slope of the regression line, you can calculate the correlation coefficient r by $r = bs_x/s_y$, where s_x and s_y are the sample standard deviations of X and Y, respectively. The proportionate reduction in error is r^2, the square of the correlation coefficient r.

f. Compare your line from Exercise 1 to the regression line.

g. If you were asked to predict the value of Y at $X = 2.5$, what would you predict it to be, based on the regression line?

3. What is the relationship between Protestant work ethic and Type A personality scores? The following steps will help you answer this question:

a. What do you think the relationship is? Treat Type A personality score as the dependent variable and form a hypothesis.

b. Select a random sample of 10 subjects from internal-motivation experiment 1.

c. Construct a scattergram of Protestant work ethic and Type A personality score for those 10 subjects.

d. Calculate the regression line for those 10 subjects.

e. Is your hypothesis supported?

f. Select five more subjects randomly. Use the regression line calculated in part (**d**) to predict their Type A personality scores.

g. Assess the accuracy of your predictions. The following steps will help you answer this question.

   (i) What would you predict the value of the Type A peersonality score to be for a randomly selected case if you had no other information about the case?

   (ii) What is the total error involved in the prediction of the five randomly selected cases if you use the prediction from part (**f**) to predict each of the five scores? (Calculate the variance of the five scores around the mean you use for the prediction. That is a measure of the total error.)

   (iii) What is the remaining error of your predictions from part (**f**)? (Calculate the total squared deviations of the actual Type A personality score, around the regression line, and divide that number by the number of cases minus 1.)

   (iv) By how much did the regression line and information on Protestant-work-ethic scores improve your prediction of Type

A personality over the predictions made in part (**f**)? (Calculate the PRE achieved by using the regression line.)

4. Use regression analysis to assess the relationship between a physician's specialization score and either the percentage of the total cost for DRG 379 (threatened abortion) devoted to diagnosis or the percentage of the total cost of DRG 379 devoted to material and technology. (Note that only seven physicians discharged patients in DRG 379.)

  a. Which relationship is more interesting to you?
  b. Formulate a hypothesis about the relationship.
  c. Conduct the analyses necessary to test the hypothesis.
  d. Is your hypothesis supported? Write a paragraph describing this study that you have just completed.

5. Ten counties had the following unemployment rates and rates of families (per 1000 population) reported to the state's child protective services (CPS) program:

County	1	2	3	4	5	6	7	8	9	10
Unemployment, %	7.0	6.1	2.4	10.7	14.1	7.2	6.1	5.4	8.9	11.2
CPS rate	1.2	1.6	7.1	12.2	10.1	2.4	3.1	1.4	1.6	8.4

  a. Is there a relationship between the variables? (Describe the relationship and decide if there is evidence for claiming that there is a relationship between these variables in the population from which this sample came.)
  b. Interpret the results. (What other variables might be of interest in your effort to understand the relationship that might exist between these variables?)

6. Here are data on stock market changes:

	Change in Dow Jones Industrial Average				
Day of Week	Week 1	Week 2	Week 3	Week 4	Week 5
Monday	−10.2	−4.2	−7.4	−21.1	−5.4
Tuesday	−6.1	−8.2	22.7	15.1	10.2
Wednesday	7.5	4.1	21.6	10.6	11.8
Thursday	−4.2	−3.1	−10.2	−5.4	12.9
Friday	5.1	15.6	15.3	28.3	21.2

a. Is there a relationship between changes in the Dow Jones Industrial Average (DJIA) and the day of the week? (Just number the days of the week 1 to 5 and treat "day of week" as if it were a continuous variable.) Do both descriptive and inferential statistical analyses.

b. Are all the assumptions of regression analysis reasonable in this instance?

7. A clinical trial of a drug found the following "time to relief" of symptoms for the eight patients given the amount of drug, in milligrams (mg), shown.

Patient	1	2	3	4	5	6	7	8
Drug dose, mg	0.5	1.2	4.0	5.2	2.5	3.8	5.0	1.7
Response, min	75	45	25	20	32	26	20	28

a. Is there a relationship between dose and time to relief?

b. Develop a 95 percent confidence interval estimate of the slope of the line relating these two variables.

c. What would you expect to be the response time to 4.0 mg of the drug? Construct a 95 percent confidence interval estimate of the response time.

d. What would you expect to be the response time to 7.5 mg of the drug? Construct a 95 percent confidence interval estimate of the response time.

e. In which estimate, (c) or (d), would you have more confidence? Without reference to the relative sizes of the confidence intervals, explain why you answered as you did.

8. Is there a relationship between an automobile's average speed on a 2000-mile (mi) trip and its oil consumption? The following data are from 10 cars that made just such a trip.

Auto	1	2	3	4	5	6	7	8	9	10
Average speed, mi/h	46.2	50.1	55.7	48.7	62.1	60.0	49.8	56.1	53.2	59.8
Oil, qt	0.8	0.9	1.1	1.2	1.0	0.7	1.5	1.2	1.3	0.8

a. Answer the question.

b. Develop a 95 percent confidence interval estimate of oil consumption at 55 mi/h.

c. Describe and interpret all the results.

9. What is the relationship between years of schooling and starting salary? Use the following data to answer the question. Salary is in thousands of dollars.

Case	Years of Schooling	Starting Salary, $1000s	Case	Years of Schooling	Starting Salary, $1000s
1	12	10.4	11	12	14.2
2	13	10.5	12	10	9.5
3	12	12.6	13	18	13.0
4	11	18.0	14	16	17.5
5	12	10.9	15	16	14.2
6	12	14.5	16	14	18.5
7	16	19.6	17	14	13.6
8	15	19.9	18	12	10.7
9	16	21.5	19	19	21.5
10	16	10.6	20	12	18.6

10. How strongly is starting salary related to salary 10 years after the beginning of work? Calculate r^2 and r for the following data. Calculate a 95 percent confidence interval for r, and answer the question. Interpret the results. Salary is in thousands of dollars.

Case	Starting Salary, $1000s	Salary at 10 yr, $1000s	Case	Starting Salary, $1000s	Salary at 10 yr, $1000s
1	10.7	35.7	9	6.7	18.7
2	8.5	17.8	10	8.9	27.5
3	8.7	24.2	11	12.7	15.2
4	7.4	29.6	12	8.4	8.9
5	9.5	21.2	13	3.6	14.7
6	5.6	18.9	14	6.5	20.7
7	11.8	18.6	15	11.8	36.8
8	4.6	24.5	16	9.9	17.9

11. What is the relationship between the performance of a mutual fund in one year and its performance in the following year? Use these data on percentage changes from the beginning of the year to the end of the year for 10 mutual funds.

Fund	Year 1	Year 2	Fund	Year 1	Year 2
1	35.4	−6.2	6	16.7	−12.7
2	15.6	−8.9	7	32.7	−2.6
3	17.5	−10.6	8	14.8	−7.8
4	40.2	−4.2	9	81.7	−0.1
5	110.7	3.8	10	12.8	1.2

12. Here are data from 10 beer-brewing experiments. Which variable, temperature during fermentation or length of fermentation, is the better predictor of shelf life?

Batch	Average Temperature, °F	Length of Fermentation	Shelf Life, wk
1	104	39	22
2	108	36	19
3	107	32	26
4	102	40	24
5	110	39	28
6	114	48	26
7	99	45	20
8	101	47	19
9	107	41	21
10	104	52	20

13. Here are actual data from 10 stations along Vermont roads. One variable is "damage units from trucks." It is an index based on the number of trucks passing the station, the weight of each truck, and the number of axles on the truck. Roughly speaking, the higher the "damage units," the more truck traffic there was past the station. The other variable is the average annual maintenance cost per mile of road in the immediate vicinity of the station. (The annual average was calculated over a 5-year period.) Describe the relationship between the variables. What might cause the data to present the picture they do?

Station Code	Damage Units from Trucks	Average Annual Maintenance Cost per Mile, $
D2	25	317
W2	35	3
P4	3	688
C10	9	1266
C28	4	686
X74	19	35
C7	5	440
D23	0	1280
W89	39	49
F94	35	36

14. Refer to Exercise 9, Chapter 3. What is the nature of the relationship between fertilizer use and ear length of corn? What would you predict to be the ear length of corn if you used 7.0 units of fertilizer on a 100-ft^2 garden?

15. A wine merchant has regular "tastings" during which she gives out free samples of five wines. Here are the data on the number of bottles used for free distribution during the tastings and sales during the time of the tasting. Describe the relationship between the variables, using appropriate statistics, and write a narrative explaining the results and why they might have occurred (e.g., what other variables might be at work here).

Tasting	Bottles Used	Sales, $
1	15	525
2	46	1658
3	12	350
4	18	700
5	27	1001
6	32	1040
7	26	828
8	8	300
9	35	1200
10	27	945
11	51	1850
12	13	425

16. A person considers opening a boating business. He hypothesizes that there is a relationship between days of sunshine in the year and boat sales. He collects the following data.

Year	Days of Sun	Boat Sales, Units
1979	108	5067
1980	153	4320
1981	175	3833
1982	110	3627
1983	156	3758
1984	132	4529
1985	109	5138
1986	187	5859

a. Should he pray for sunshine?

b. Based on these data, what other factors might the man consider as he thinks about entering the boat business?

D

▼

Political History of Correlation

. . .

In Chapter 11, we mentioned that some people say that Yule's Q "overestimates" the correlation of two variables. Karl Pearson, Yule's mentor, was the first person to say that. In an argument that lasted years and irreparably damaged their friendship, Yule and Pearson battled over the proper way to measure correlation or association between two *discrete* variables. Yule used and lobbied for Q. Pearson developed a different method, called the *tetrachoric correlation coefficient*, to measure association between discrete variables.

Pearson's approach to correlation between discrete variables was based on the principles that lay behind his product-moment correlation coefficient for continuous variables. Pearson argued that underlying any discrete variable, with its finite number of categories, there is a continuous variable with an infinite number of categories, and it is the relationship between the underlying continuous variables that is of primary interest to a researcher.

Pearson's argument is unassailable for urbanization measured as "high" and "low," for example, since there is a continuous variable from which the discrete variable was constructed. But, Yule countered, for variables like "died" or "didn't die," it does not make sense even to think there might be an underlying continuous variable. You are either dead or not dead. There is no imaginable, underlying continuity to some variables, Yule said.

Why did these two friends, student and teacher, get so worked up over what seems to be an esoteric problem in mathematics? As Donald Mackenzie has shown,[1] there was much more at stake than just having a widely used statistic to carry one's name. Yule was a social activist. He wanted to find variables and relationships that he could use to bring about change now. Yule's Q suited his needs and his political orientation. On the other side, Pearson's product-moment correlation coefficient (and the tetrachoric coefficient) suited Pearson's needs and his political orientation, which were different from Yule's. *Differences in political orientation led to the development of different statistics.*

Pearson was a eugenicist. He wanted to use his statistics to uncover the way nature selected certain traits in people, so that he could help nature select the "right" traits. He was somewhat discouraged by Galton's notion of regression which seemed to suggest that, over the long run, populations would become more homogeneous and the people in them would tend to become more mediocre. Galton's work seemed to say that subsequent generations tended to revert or regress to the mean. Thus, evolution tended to undo the selection of people of talent and character that nature had accomplished in the past.

Pearson fastened his fortunes on the counterpart of regression, correlation, because the idea of correlation suggested that at least a portion of the attributes of one generation carried over to the next generation. Tall people tend, on average, to produce taller offspring than short people. Pearson felt certain the argument extended to socially valued traits like intelligence and moral development. Pearson believed that if one read the correlation coefficients properly, one would understand that in order to produce a better nation, certain people should not be allowed to reproduce while others should be encouraged to do so. Pearson felt that science could help nature select the right people for building a strong nation. Evolution, said Pearson, "is not merely a passive intellectual view of nature; it applies to man in his communities as it applies to all forms of life. It teaches us the art of living, of building up stable and dominant nations."[2] Pearson spent a large portion of his life studying correlation because it formalized the theory of evolution and seemed to base the theory in hard fact. Donald Mackenzie comments,

> Such a theory [the theory of evolution] had to be presented as based on hard, solid, preferably quantitative fact, in order to obtain maximum

plausibility and to combat people like Lord Salisbury [who mounted a religious argument against evolution and claimed that the theory could never be demonstrated]; hence the necessity to develop it in a statistical form, free from speculative, theoretical elements.[3].

Pearson's work was, in large part, an effort to take the "theoretical" and the speculative out of the theory that had motivated Galton's work in the first place. Pearson wanted to turn the theory of evolution into the law of evolution and then make sure everyone conformed to the law.. Yule's work was a dire threat to Pearson's because Yule wanted to develop a *theoretical* understanding of change that could bring about changes that were probably "contrary to nature." The different approaches to measuring correlation were only the tip of a very deep political difference between these two men. The statistics we use today came out of a turbulent time and were motivated by different sets of political interests.

. . .

NOTES

1. Donald A. Mackenzie, *Statistics in Britain, 1865–1930: The Social Construction of Scientific Knowledge*, Edinburgh University Press, Scotland, 1981, pp. 153–182.

2. Ibid., p. 90.

3. Ibid.

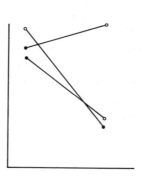

• • •

Analysis of Variance: The Case of Multiple Means

Statistics was a social phenomenon as well as a new discipline. As a social phenomenon, it had its share of social sidelight stories like the one about the feud between Pearson and Yule described in Interlude D. Another statistical feud involved Pearson and one of the other statistical giants, R. A. Fisher. Fisher was keenly interested in the analysis of data from carefully constructed experiments, particularly agricultural experiments. The feud began with Pearson's disputing one of Fisher's earliest findings, but the feud was exacerbated when Fisher refused a job offer at Pearson's statistical laboratory at University College, London, in order to work at the agriculture Experimental Station at Rothamsted. While at Rothamsted Fisher developed a series of techniques for analyzing experimental data and published them in his famous *Statistical Methods for Research Workers*. His fights with Pearson were so fierce and so petty that Pearson would not allow Fisher to use a table of chi-squared values in his book. This chapter introduces you to some of the techniques Fisher developed and to a new distribution, the F distribution, a distribution that takes it name from Fisher himself.

The techniques described here are called *analysis-of-variance* techniques. They are used to test for differences among multiple means.

You know how to conduct a test of statistical significance of the difference between two independent sample means. That test is called the *t test of the difference between means* or sometimes just the *t test*. In many instances, you face the problem of having to compare several means at once. For example, in internal-motivation experiment 2, the researchers, Professors Tang and Baumeister, decided to divide the subjects into *three* groups based on their work ethic scores. Fourteen subjects were in the low-work-ethic group. Their scores were below the median work-ethic scores of subjects in experiment 1. The remaining 26 subjects in experiment 2 were divided into two groups: 13 were assigned to a medium-work-ethic group, and 13 were assigned to a high-work-ethic group. Table 13.1 shows the mean time spent on the word game during the observation period by members of these three groups. (The table also shows the standard deviation of time spent for each group.) The medium-work-ethic group clearly spent more time, on average, on the word game than either members of the low or high-work-ethic groups. But, by now, you are statistically sophisticated enough not to stop with a mere description of the data. You are probably already wondering if there is a *significant* difference among the means of the three groups.

You might be tempted to use a tool like the *t* test to examine differences between the three pairs of means in Table 13.1. You could, you might think, conduct a *t* test of the difference between the mean of the low group and the mean of the medium group, a test of the difference between the low and high groups, and a test of the difference between the medium and high groups. If you did this, however, you would be biasing the results of each test in your favor.

TABLE 13.1 Means and Standard Deviations of Time Spent on Word Game for Three Groups Determined by Work-Ethic Score

Work Ethic	n	Mean Time Spent, s	Standard Deviation
Low	14	324.1	361.6
Medium	13	608.1	325.8
High	13	380.2	349.9
Total	40	434.6	359.6

Data are from internal-motivation experiment 2.

To understand why doing *multiple t tests* biases the results of each test in your favor is a little complicated, but it is worth thinking about for just a moment. The probability of being incorrect in your decision to reject a null hypothesis in a *t* test is based on the assumption that you are conducting a single, solitary test of the difference of two sample means. The procedure you might be tempted to employ with Table 13.1 involves three *t* tests that are *inter*dependent. For example, the first two tests both involve the low-work-ethic group. The first test—between the low group's mean and the medium group's mean—has a much greater chance of showing a "significant" difference than the second test—the test of the low- and high-work-ethic group means—even though the means do not change and the structure of the test does not change. If one tests showed a "significant" difference and the other did not, how would you interpret such a result? A result from one test of three interdependent tests cannot be interpreted in a straightforward way. If you conduct more than one *t* test, the probability of incorrectly rejecting at least one null hypothesis of the several you test is greater than the probability of incorrectly rejecting a null hypothesis in a single test. Consequently, if you conduct several interdependent *t* tests, the actual observed significance of each test will be slightly higher than the table of *t* distributions indicates. So if you do multiple *t* tests, the probability of incorrectly rejecting a null is higher than your formulation of the test would indicate.

· · ·

ANALYSIS OF VARIANCE: BASICS

There is a solution to this problem of conducting multiple comparisons among means. The solution is a statistical technique called *analysis of variance*. Analysis of variance, sometimes abbreviated as ANOVA (*analysis of variance*), allows you to examine the null hypothesis that more than two independent sample means were drawn from populations with equal means.

You begin with data like those in Table 13.1 where several sample means are different from one another. This leads you to formulate an alternative hypothesis that

$$H_A: \mu_f \neq \mu_g \qquad \text{for some } f \text{ and } g$$

That is, there is at least one pair of populations whose means μ_f and μ_g are not equal. For data like those in Table 13.1, the alternative hypothesis is

$$H_A: \mu_{low} \neq \mu_{medium} \quad \text{and/or} \quad \mu_{medium} \neq \mu_{high} \quad \text{and/or} \quad \mu_{low} \neq \mu_{high}$$

The null hypothesis for Table 13.1 is that all the population means are equal, i.e., that

$$H_0: \mu_{\text{low}} = \mu_{\text{medium}} = \mu_{\text{high}}$$

In general, ANOVA provides a test of the null hypothesis that

$$H_0: \mu_1 = \mu_2 = \cdots = \mu_J$$

where J is the number of groups involved. (In this chapter (capital) J is an integer that is equal to the number of groups involved, and (small) j is used as an index on summations. In the summations, j will vary from 1 to j.)

Analysis of variance provides a method for the comparison of multiple means. ANOVA is often used in psychology and other disciplines that rely heavily on experimental methods since it is a technique that assumes the independent variable(s) is (are) discrete, as in the case of experimental treatments, and the dependent variable is continuous.

Analysis of variance rests on several assumptions. First, it assumes cases have been randomly and independently assigned to each of the groups. Second, the distribution of cases around each population mean is assumed to be normal. Third, the variance around each population mean is assumed to be equal across all the populations. Finally, the residuals around each population mean are assumed to be uncorrelated with residuals around all other population means. These assumptions are the same as in regression analysis. Analysis of variance is robust against the violation of the second assumption, the assumption of normality. The assumption of homoscedasticity, however, cannot be violated.

The homoscedasticity assumption is crucial because ANOVA is dependent on the comparison of two estimates of the common variance of the dependent variable σ^2. One estimate of σ^2 is based on variation among sample means. This variation is called the *between-group variation*. In the example in Table 13.1, it would be an estimate of the common variance based on differences among the means of the times spent on the word game by groups formed on the basis of their work-ethic scores. A second estimate of the common variance is formed on the basis of variation within groups, variation around the sample means. In the example in Table 13.1, this estimate would use the information contained in the conditional standard deviations shown in the rightmost column. If the comparison of these variance estimates shows that the between-group variation is large relative to the within-group variation, you have evidence to support the hypothesis that the population means, of which the sample means are estimates, are different from one another. If there is little difference between these two estimates of the variance, there is no evidence on which to base a claim of difference in the population means. In this way, an analysis of *variance* provides a test of differences among *means*, odd as that may sound.

TABLE 13.2a Hypothetical Outcomes of an
Experiment to Test Three Methods of CPR
Instruction, Example 1

	Method of Instruction		
Case	A	B	C
1	21	44	64
2	21	44	64
3	21	44	64
4	21	44	64
5	21	44	64
6	21	44	64
7	21	44	64
8	21	44	64
9	21	44	64
10	21	44	64
Mean:	21	44	64
Standard deviation:	0	0	0

Consider this example: Suppose you conduct an experiment in which 10 people are instructed in cardiopulmonary resuscitation (CPR) using method *A*, 10 are instructed using method *B*, and 10 are taught by method *C*. The results of the instruction are measured on a 100-point scale. Suppose the results of the assessment are as shown in Table 13.2a. These data present a strong basis for making the claim that there are (probably) some differences among the population mean outcome scores. Why? Because there are big differences between the group sample means and no differences among cases in each group. The variation between groups is (infinitely) large compared to the variation within groups.

In contrast, suppose the results of the experiment were as shown in Table 13.2b. These data provide less strong support for the claim that there are differences among the population mean outcome scores. Why? Because the outcome scores from one group "overlap" the scores from the other groups (as shown in the stem-and-leaf diagram in Figure 13.1). There are differences between the group mean outcome scores—the same difference as in Table 13.2a—but there are considerable differences among the individual outcome scores. The variation within groups is much larger than in Table 13.2a.

Analysis of variance compares variation attributable to differences between group means to variation attributable to differences that remain in the groups. If the differences between groups are large relative to the differences within groups,

TABLE 13.2*b* Hypothetical Outcomes of an
Experiment to Test Three Methods of CPR
Instruction, Example 2

| | Method of Instruction | | |
Case	A	B	C
1	5	17	81
2	40	82	99
3	78	4	100
4	7	18	37
5	13	62	47
6	51	45	81
7	4	71	99
8	2	57	12
9	10	81	44
10	0	3	40
Mean:	21	44	64
Standard deviation:	26.3	31.1	31.7

as in Table 13.2a, ANOVA gives you a basis for claiming that there are differences among population means. If the differences between groups are small relative to differences within groups, as in Table 13.2b, ANOVA suggests caution in deciding to reject the null hypothesis of no differences among population means.

	Example 1	Example 2
0–10		*AAAAAABB*
11–20		*AB B C*
21–30	*AAAAAAAAAA*	
31–40		*AC C*
41–50	*B B B B B B B B B B*	*BC C*
51–60		*AB*
61–70	*CCCCCCCCCC*	*B*
71–80		*AB*
81–90		*BBCC*
91–100		*CCC*

FIGURE 13.1 Stem-and-leaf diagrams of outcome scores shown in Table 13.2*a* and *b*.

• • •

ONE-WAY ANALYSIS OF VARIANCE

The problems described above, and illustrated in Tables 13.1 and 13.2, are all *one-way analysis-of-variance* problems. They are called *one-way* because there is one independent variable, work ethic in one example and teaching method in the other. The independent variable in both examples is conditioned on three categories of a "treatment" variable, and the question is whether there is a any significant difference among the means of the populations from which the three groups in Table 13.1 or Table 13.2a or Table 13.2b were drawn.

ANOVA begins with the null hypothesis that

$$H_0: \mu_1 = \mu_2 = \cdots = \mu_J$$

i.e., that the J conditional means of the dependent variable are all equal. The alternative hypothesis is *not* that all the means are different from one another. The null hypothesis is that one mean is different from *at least* one other mean:

$$H_A: \mu_f \neq \mu_g \qquad \text{for some } f \text{ and } g$$

If the null hypothesis is true, then it is also true that

$$H_0: \mu_1 - \mu = \mu_2 - \mu = \cdots = \mu_J - \mu$$

where μ is the grand mean of the dependent variable. But then, if this hypothesis is true, then all the conditional means equal one another *and* all the conditional means equal the grand mean as well. So all the differences in this series of equivalences are equal to zero. If all the differences in the series equal zero, then the sum of the squared differences must also equal zero. That is, another way to state the null hypothesis is

$$H_0: \sum_{j=1}^{J} (\mu_j - \mu)^2 = 0$$

You do not know the population parameters involved in this summation, but you can estimate this sum by using the sample mean of the variable $\bar{X}$ and the conditional means obtained after conditioning the dependent variable on the categories of the independent variable. These conditional means are denoted $\bar{X}_j$, $1 \leq j \leq J$. If the null hypothesis, stated in the form shown above, is true, then the summation given above for the between-group sum of squared deviations (SS_B) should be close to zero. That is, SS_B should be close to zero where

$$SS_B = \sum_{j=1}^{J} n_j(\bar{X}_j - \bar{X})^2 \qquad (13.1)$$

SS_B is called the *between-group sum of squares* because it gives an indication of the variation in the data attributable to differences among the means of the groups.

One way to test the null hypothesis about differences among means might be to ask whether SS_B is significantly different from zero. But this is not a useful approach because SS_B increases as (1) the number of groups J increases, (2) the number of cases within groups n_j increases, and (3) as the unit of measure of the dependent variable increases. There is no statistically sound way to assess the difference of SS_B from zero. But SS_B is a crucial element in the ANOVA comparison of two estimates of the common population variance.

Data from the internal-motivation experiment 2 provide an example to show how ANOVA tests its null hypothesis. Table 13.3 shows a layout of the data from internal-motivation experiment 2 for this one-way ANOVA problem, the same data as summarized in Table 13.1. Here i is the index of cases within groups, j is the group number index; i varies from 1 to n_j, the number of cases within group

TABLE 13.3 Data Layout for One-Way Analysis of Variance of Time Spent by Work Ethic in Experiment 2

	Work-Ethic Group ($J = 3$)		
Case i	Low ($j = 1$)	Medium ($j = 2$)	High ($j = 3$)
1	$X_{1\,1} = 30$	$X_{1\,2} = 815$	$X_{1\,3} = 900$
2	$X_{2\,1} = 397$	$X_{2\,2} = 820$	$X_{2\,3} = 182$
3	$X_{3\,1} = 767$	$X_{3\,2} = 885$	$X_{3\,3} = 665$
4	$X_{4\,1} = 756$	$X_{4\,2} = 392$	$X_{4\,3} = 275$
5	$X_{5\,1} = 583$	$X_{5\,2} = 225$	$X_{5\,3} = 570$
6	$X_{6\,1} = 0$	$X_{6\,2} = 700$	$X_{6\,3} = 130$
7	$X_{7\,1} = 25$	$X_{7\,2} = 897$	$X_{7\,3} = 871$
8	$X_{8\,1} = 292$	$X_{8\,2} = 0$	$X_{8\,3} = 0$
9	$X_{9\,1} = 0$	$X_{9\,2} = 502$	$X_{9\,3} = 900$
10	$X_{10\,1} = 3$	$X_{10\,2} = 109$	$X_{10\,3} = 176$
11	$X_{11\,1} = 900$	$X_{11\,2} = 900$	$X_{11\,3} = 35$
12	$X_{12\,1} = 0$	$X_{12\,2} = 760$	$X_{12\,3} = 208$
13	$X_{13\,1} = 785$	$X_{13\,2} = 900$	$X_{13\,3} = 30$
14	$X_{14\,1} = 0$		
n_j:	14	13	13
Sum:	4538	7905	4942
Mean $\bar{X}_j$:	324.1	608.1	380.2
Standard deviation:	361.6	325.8	349.9

j. In the example, $n_1 = 14$ while $n_2 = n_3 = 13$. And j varies from 1 to J, the number of groups. In this instance, $J = 3$, since the cases are divided into low-, medium-, and high-work-ethic groups. X_{ij} refers to case i in group j. For example, $X_{10\ 2}$ refers to the value of the 10th case—the case in the 10th row of Table 13.3—in the second group, the medium-work-ethic group. So $X_{10\ 2} = 109$.

Let us examine the hypothesis that there are differences among the mean times spent by the three groups formed on the basis of work-ethic score. Let us test the null hypothesis with a level to reject of $\alpha = .05$.

The between-group sum of squared deviations is calculated from Formula (13.1)

$$SS_B = \sum_{j=1}^{J} n_j(\bar{X}_j - \bar{X})^2$$

where SS_B is the total squared deviations due to the differences of the conditional sample means $\bar{X}_j$, $1 \leq j \leq J$, from the grand sample mean $\bar{X}$. For the data in Table 13.3

$$SS_B = 14(324.1 - 434.6)^2 + 13(608.1 - 434.6)^2 + 13(380.2 - 434.6)^2$$
$$= 170,944 + 391,329 + 38,471 = 600,744$$

Since SS_B is a measure of variation, it is converted to a variance by dividing SS_B by the number of degrees of freedom associated with the between-group sum of squared deviations. The degrees of freedom associated with SS_B is

$$df_B = J - 1$$

where df_B is called the *degrees of freedom between* and J is the number of groups, or conditional means, involved in the analysis. In our example, $J = 3$, so $df_B = 3 - 1 = 2$. (There are $J - 1$ degrees of freedom associated with the between-group variation because the calculation begins with J conditional means $\bar{X}_1, \bar{X}_2, \ldots, \bar{X}_J$ and one constraint, the grand mean $\bar{X}$. You are free to choose $J - 1$ conditional means before you are constrained by the grand mean to a mathematically determined Jth conditional mean. Hence, there are $J - 1$ degrees of freedom associated with SS_B.)

In analysis of variance, the first estimate of the common variance—the between-group variation SS_B divided by the number of degrees freedom between df_B—is called the *mean squares between*. The mean squares between is denoted MS_B and

$$MS_B = \frac{SS_B}{df_B} \tag{13.2}$$

In our example, MS_B is equal to

$$MS_B = \frac{SS_B}{df_B} = \frac{600,745}{3-1} = 300,372$$

ANOVA is based on a comparison of the mean squares between to a similar estimate of the variance based on differences within groups after the dependent variable has been conditioned on the categories of the independent variable.

The *within-group sum of squared deviations* is denoted SS_W. There are two ways to calculate SS_W, the direct method and the indirect method. The direct method uses Formula (13.3):

$$SS_W = \sum_{j=1}^{J} \sum_{i=1}^{n_j} (X_{ij} - \bar{X}_j)^2 \tag{13.3}$$

where X_{ij} is the ith case in the jth group, $\bar{X}_j$ is the conditional mean of the jth group, and n_j is the number of cases in the jth group. This double summation says: (1) take the difference of every case in group j, X_{ij}, from the conditional mean of its group $\bar{X}_j$; (2) square that difference; (3) sum all n_j squared deviations for group j; and (4) sum all those sums for the J groups. So SS_W is the total squared deviations around conditional means after the dependent variable has been conditioned on the categories of the independent variable.

You could carry out those calculations to find SS_W directly if you wish. I don't recommend it, since there is a much simpler approach, the indirect method of calculating SS_W. The total sum of squared deviations SS_T around the grand mean is

$$SS_T = \sum_{j=1}^{J} \sum_{i=1}^{n_j} (X_{ij} - \bar{X})^2 = (n-1)s_x^2$$

But the total sum of squared deviations SS_T is composed of the sum of squared deviations between groups plus the sum of squared deviations within groups. That is,

$$SS_T = SS_B + SS_W$$

If you know the between-group variation SS_B and the total variation SS_T, then you can find the within-group variation by simple subtraction:

$$SS_W = SS_T - SS_B$$

For this example, Table 13.1 contains the standard deviation s_x for the variable "time spent": $s_x = 359.6$. The variance is

$$s_x^2 = (s_x)^2 = (359.6)^2 = 129,312$$

Since $n = 40$, the total squared deviations around the mean are

$$SS_T = (n - 1)s_x^2 = 39(129,312) = 5,043,168$$

The total squared deviations around the grand mean are 5,043,168. By subtracting the between-group sum of squares from this total sum of squares, you can find the within-group sum of squares;

$$SS_W = SS_T - SS_B = 5,043,168 - 600,745 = 4,442,423$$

This within-group sum of squares, a measure of variation, is converted to a variance estimate by dividing by the number of *degrees of freedom within*:

$$df_W = n - J$$

The degrees of freedom associated with the within-group variation is equal to the number of cases in the sample n minus the number of groups involved in the analysis. Why? Because you needed to calculate J conditional means in order to calculate SS_W. You lose 1 degree of freedom for each conditional mean you calculate. Put another way, each conditional mean places one constraint on our freedom to choose the n numbers that constitute the overall sample. If, as in our example, there are 3 conditional means and the sample size is 40, you can only choose $40 - 3 = 37$ numbers before the other three numbers are determined by the constraints. The within-group sum of squares divided by the associated degrees of freedom

$$MS_W = \frac{SS_W}{df_W} \tag{13.4}$$

is called the *mean squares within.* In the example

$$MS_W = \frac{4,442,423}{37} = 120,065$$

Now you are ready to compare the between-group variance estimate to the within-group variance estimate. The comparison is made by dividing MS_B by MS_W since they are both expressed in the same units of analysis. If the independent variable has a strong main effect on the dependent variable, the between-group variation will be significantly larger than the within-group variation and the ratio of MS_B to MS_W will be significantly greater than 1.00. In our example

$$\frac{MS_B}{MS_W} = \frac{300,372}{120,065} = 2.502$$

This ratio is greater than 1.0, which indicates that the between-group variance estimate is larger than the within-group variance estimate, so you know work ethic has some effect on time spent on the word game during the observation period. But is the ratio *significantly* greater than 1.0? To answer that question, you need to know how the ratio is disturbed. That is, you need to know the sampling distribution of the ratio of mean squares between to mean squares within if, in fact, the null hypothesis that all group means are equal is true.

The ratio MS_B/MS_W is distributed according to an F distribution with $J - 1$ and $n - J$ degrees of freedom, the degrees of freedom associated with the numerator of the ratio and the degrees of freedom associated with the denominator of the ratio, respectively. (The order in which the two sets of degrees of freedom are listed for reference to the F distribution is important; $J - 1$ is the first set of degrees of freedom, and $N - J$ is the second.) To determine whether MS_B is significantly greater than MS_W, and thereby to determine whether or not you can reject the null hypothesis, you need to use the F distribution in Appendix Table B.8 to find the probability of getting an $F_{J-1, n-j} = F_{2,37} = 2.501$ if, in fact, the null hypothesis is true.

Look at Appendix Table B.8. The critical value of F is in the second column (since the first degrees of freedom $= 2$) and lies between the batches of F statistics marked 30 and 40 in the leftmost column. Our $F_{2,37} = 2.501$ is greater than the larger of those two values, $F_{2,30} = 1.45$, for $\alpha = .25$. Consequently, the observed significance of the test is at least $p < .25$. But then the probability of being incorrect in the decision to reject is 1/4. Look at the row for $x = .10$. Our F is still larger than the $F_{2,30} = 2.49$, so the observed significance of the test is at least $p < .10$. Drop down one more row. Our $F_{2,37} = 2.501$ is not larger than either $F_{2,30} = 3.32$ or $F_{2,40} = 3.23$, so you *cannot* reject the null hypothesis at the $p < .05$ level of significance. If the level to reject were a conventional .05, you should not reject the null hypothesis that

$$H_0: \mu_{low} = \mu_{medium} = \mu_{high}$$

The sample does not provide sufficient evidence to claim that there are differences among the group population means.

Narrative Summary

Analysis of variance obviously involves a lot of computation. It will be helpful at this point to have an overview of the process of decision making that uses the example above but without including calculations.

You begin with a research question: Is one's score on a work-ethic scale related to the time one would spend on the word game during a postexperimental period during which one is required to do nothing? The dependent variable is the continuous variable "time spent" measured in seconds. The independent variable is "work ethic," and it consists of three categories, low, medium, and high. The sample consists of 40 Chinese-speaking people. Roughly one-third of the sample falls into each of the three categories of the independent variable.

The conditional means of "time spent" are shown in Table 13.1. There is a difference among the sample means. In particular, people with a medium work ethic seem to spend considerably more time on the word game than either the low- or high-work-ethic subjects. However, the inferential question is this: Is there enough difference among the three means to make it reasonable to assert that the three groups of subjects came from populations at least one of which has a population mean on "time spent" that is different from one of the others? That is, is it reasonable to reject the null hypothesis that

$$H_0: \mu_{\text{low}} = \mu_{\text{medium}} = \mu_{\text{high}}$$

and accept the alternative that

$$H_A: \mu_f \neq \mu_g \qquad \text{for some } f \text{ and } g$$

where f and g are low, medium or high?

This inferential question calls for a one-way analysis of variance. The results of the ANOVA are presented in Table 13.4. The statistic of principal interest is the F value. The results shown in Table 13.4 are summarized by saying simply, "We cannot reject the null hypothesis. We cannot conclude that the groups were drawn from populations that have unequal mean times spent on the word game $(F_{2,37} = 2.501, .05 < p < .10)$." Once again, the relevant statistics, so painstakingly calculated, are relegated to parentheses, but a person who understands the language of statistics will get the message. By making such a statement, you have been concise, accurate, and clear, and Tables 13.1 and 13.4 present all the material you need to back up your conclusion.

One small caution: If you run the data through an analysis-of-variance computer program, your results may be ever so slightly different from those shown

TABLE 13.4 One-Way ANOVA to Assess the Effect of Work Ethic on Time Spent on Word Game in Postexperimental Observation Period

Source of Variation	Sum of Squares	df	Mean Squares	F
Work ethic	600,745	2	300,372	2.502
Residual	4,442,423	37	120,065	
Total	5,043,168	39	129,312	

Original data are in Tables 13.1 and 13.3.

in Table 13.4. I did the calculations described in the narrative, using the numbers shown in the tables. Computer programs deal with many more decimal places of accuracy. The roundoff error in my hand calculations may make the summary statistics in Table 13.4 different from your computer-generated numbers.

. . .

EXAMINING EFFECTS IN ONE-WAY ANOVA

Let's return to the hypothetical data on three methods of CPR instruction shown in Table 13.2b. Recall that the mean outcome scores were the same as shown in Table 13.2a, but there was more variation within "treatment" groups. Statistically, we should ask whether there is so much variation that it is impossible to distinguish between the means of the populations from which these three samples were drawn. To express it formally, we should ask whether there is support in the data for accepting the alternative hypothesis that

$$H_A: \mu_A \neq \mu_B \quad \text{and/or} \quad \mu_A \neq \mu_C \quad \text{and/or} \quad \mu_B \neq \mu_C$$

or whether the sample data leave us in the position of failing to reject the null hypothesis that

$$H_0: \mu_A = \mu_B = \mu_C$$

A further question should be asked. If the data allow us to accept the alternative hypothesis that there is some difference between at least two means, we ought to ask where that (those) difference (differences) is (are). Which of the three pairs of means demonstrate a statistically significant difference?

The one-way ANOVA table for these data is shown in Table 13.5. The mean squares between ($MS_B = 4630$) is more than 5 times the mean squares within ($MS_W = 888.2$). And $F_{2,27} = 5.21$. The computer I used said the exact observed significance of the test was $p = .012$. With a level to reject of $\alpha = .05$, we can

TABLE 13.5 One-Way Analysis of Variance to Assess the Effects of Instructional Method on CPR Skills and Knowledge

Source of Variation	Sum of Squares	df	Mean Squares	F
Instructional method	9,260	2	4,630	5.21
Residual	23,982	27	888.2	
Total	33,242	29	1,146.3	

Data are from Table 13.2b.

reject the null hypothesis and claim that at least two of the three sample means shown in Table 13.2b came from populations with different mean scores on the CPR assessment.

Just as one moved from the relatively weak statements of hypothesis testing to the relatively strong statements of point and interval estimation, now that we know there is (probably) at least one difference between two population means, we should ask where that difference is. Is instructional method B significantly better than method A, is C distinguishable from B, or can we perhaps only honestly separate method C from method A? There are many ways to assess differences. Here I discuss two.

Using Interval Estimates of μ_j

One method for assessing differences involves the use of interval estimates of each μ_j, $1 \le j \le J$. You construct an interval estimate of each population mean around each sample mean. Those intervals give you an idea of where each population mean (probably) is. If the interval estimates of a pair of means overlap, then you must agree that the two are statistically indistinguishable from each other. If the intervals overlap, the means may be equal. If, however, the interval estimates of two means do not overlap, you have a basis for claiming that those means are statistically different.

Let's return to the CPR example. The mean scores from each instructional group are, from Table 13.2b, method A, 21; method B, 44; and method C, 64. Let us construct 95 percent confidence intervals around each sample mean.

A confidence interval estimate of a mean, recall, is constructed by

$$\mu \cong \bar{X} \pm t_{\alpha/2} \frac{s}{\sqrt{n}}$$

where $(s/\sqrt{n})^2$ is an estimate of the unknown population variance. In analysis of variance, a better estimate of the population variance is given by the unexplained variance following conditioning on the categories of the independent variable. That is, the mean squares within MS_W is a better estimate of the population variance than is a single sample variance s_j^2. The divisor is n, the number of cases in a treatment condition. So an interval estimate of a population mean for a treatment in a one-way analysis of variance can be constructed by

$$\mu_j = \bar{X}_j \pm t_{\alpha/2} \sqrt{\frac{MS_W}{n}} \tag{13.5}$$

and the degrees of freedom associated with t are $J(n-1)$.

For the example in Tables 13.2b and 13.5, the mean squares within is 888.2 (from Table 13.5). Since $n = 10$, df $= 3(10 - 1) = 27$, and $t_{\alpha/2}$ where $\alpha = .05$ is

2.052. The intervals for each instructional group are as follows:

Instructional Method	Estimate of	Interval	Minimum	Maximum
A	μ_A	$21 \pm 2.052\sqrt{\dfrac{888.2}{10}}$	1.7	40.3
B	μ_B	$44 \pm 2.052\sqrt{\dfrac{888.2}{10}}$	24.7	63.3
C	μ_C	$64 \pm 2.052\sqrt{\dfrac{888.2}{10}}$	44.7	83.3

The interval estimates of μ_A and μ_B overlap. So do the interval estimates of μ_B and μ_C. The only pair that this test shows is different is instructional methods A and C. Method C is significantly better than method A, but that is the only difference for which we can find support in the data.

Tukey's Honestly Significant Difference

Tukey has a different way to assess significant differences among means after ANOVA says it is reasonable to reject the null hypothesis. He constructs the *honestly significant difference* (HSD) for a particular experimental design. Then he compares the absolute difference between each pair of means to the HSD. Those differences that exceed the HSD are significantly different, honestly.

The formula is

$$\text{HSD} = q_\alpha \sqrt{\frac{\text{MS}_W}{n}} \tag{13.6}$$

The MS_W and n are familiar—they are the mean-squares-within (or the error or the residual variance) from a one-way ANOVA and the number of cases in each treatment group. But q_α is not familiar. It is a number that varies depending on three factors: the degrees of freedom associated with the error component df_W, the number of means estimated J, and the level to reject α. Values for q_α are in Appendix Table B.9. You look up the appropriate value of q_α, plug everything else into the formula, and compare the differences between means to the calculated HSD. If there are J means in an experiment, there will be $J(J-1)/2$ pairs of means to compare to the HSD.

For the example involving CPR scores, $J = 3$, $df_W = 27$, $\text{MS}_W = 888.2$, and $n = 10$. For an $\alpha = .05$, from the table q_α is between 3.53 (for $df_W = 24$) and 3.49

(for $df_W = 30$). Let's use the harshest test and set $q_\alpha = 3.53$. So

$$HSD = 3.53 \sqrt{\frac{888.2}{10}} = 33.3$$

Means in the example have to have an absolute difference of 33.3 points between them to be declared honestly significantly different. The following chart shows the absolute differences between mean CPR scores:

Method

		A	B	C
	A	—	23	43*
Method	B	—	—	20
	C	—	—	—

Once again, only the difference between treatments *A* and *C*—the difference marked with an asterisk—is significantly different.

$\cdot\ \cdot\ \cdot$

TWO-WAY ANALYSIS OF VARIANCE: AN INTRODUCTION

The relationship between one independent variable and one dependent variable is often interesting, particularly in experiments. Careful experimental design can allow the researcher to control the effects of all theoretically relevant variables except one. So one-way analysis of variance is a useful and powerful tool. However, multivariate statistical techniques open new dimensions in data analysis. Higher-order analysis of variance allows you to assess the effects of more than one independent variable on the dependent variable. This section introduces you to the most basic form of higher-order analysis of variance—*two-way analysis of variance for balanced designs*. The technique is used when you have a continuous dependent variable and two independent variables that are both discrete.

Recall once again the original hypothesis of Professors Tang and Baumeister concerning internal motivation. It involves two independent variables. They wrote:

> We reasoned that a task label may shape the interpretation of the task, but the *evaluation* of the task depends on both that interpretation *and* the personal values of the individual. Defining a task as work might well *increase* its attractiveness to a person who endorses the value of work. . . . We predicted that among subjects who endorse the work ethic, labeling the task as work would increase their tendency to choose to perform that activity

later on. Among subjects who do not endorse the value of work, however, "turning play into work" by means of labeling the task may, we predicted, reduced their subsequent inclination to perform the task.[1]

They are saying that personal values—specifically, whether a person endorses the work ethic—affect the *relationship* between the definition of a task and the subsequent inclination to continue doing the task. The relationship between a task's label and continuing to work on the task is dependent on one's work-ethic orientation. Tang and Baumeister want to examine more than just the separate, zero-order relationship of each independent variable on the dependent variable. They want to examine the *joint* effects of the two independent variables on the dependent variable in this experiment. Two-way analysis of variance is perfectly suited to help them do that since work ethic can be made a discrete variable, task label is a discrete variable with subjects assigned randomly to one of two conditions (label = work or leisure), and the dependent variable, time spent on the word game in the postexperimental observation period, is a continuous variable measured in seconds.

Table 13.6 shows how the data must be arrayed for a two-way analysis of variance. *Note:* Two cases were eliminated, randomly, from the work group so that 26 subjects are assigned to the work group and 26 are assigned to the leisure group. That leaves 13 cases in each of the four conditions shown in Table 13.6. If the number of cases in each condition in the data layout is the same for a two-way ANOVA, it is a *balanced design*. The mathematics of unbalanced designs—in which treatment conditions have unequal numbers of subjects in them—is difficult and the interpretation of the results is a little trickier. For all these reasons, I will describe two-way analysis of variance only for balanced designs. I "balanced" the design for the data in Table 13.6 by randomly selecting two cases in the "work label" condition for elimination—cases 7 and 13.

Look carefully at Table 13.6. The addition of a second independent variable requires the addition of one more subscript on X, the symbol for the dependent variable "time spent." Now X_{ijk} refers to the ith case, where $i = 1, 2, \ldots, 13$, in the jth group on the first independent variable "work ethic," where j is 1 (low work ethic) or 2 (high work ethic), *and* in the kth group on the second independent variable "task label," where k is 1 (work) or 2 (leisure). This design is called a 2×2 *two-way analysis of variance*. The "2×2" refers to the fact that there are two categories for the first independent variable and two categories for the second independent variable.

In general, a two-way ANOVA can be used to analyze data in a $J \times K$ design where the first independent variable has J categories and the second independent variable has K categories. n_{jk} refers to the number of cases in a jointly defined category, the category containing cases that are in category j on the first independent variable and in category k on the second independent variable. In a balanced design, all the n_{jk}'s are equal. For all j and k, $n_{jk} = 13$.

TABLE 13.6 Data Layout for Two-Way ANOVA of Time Spent by Work Ethic and Task Label in Experiment 1; Balanced Design with Cases 7 and 13 Eliminated

	Task Label ($K = 2$)			Task Label ($K = 2$)	
Case i	Work ($k = 1$)	Leisure ($k = 2$)	Case i	Work ($k = 1$)	Leisure ($k = 2$)
	Work ethic = low ($j = 1$)			Work ethic = high ($j = 2$)	
1	$X_{111} = 80$	$X_{112} = 331$	1	$X_{121} = 40$	$X_{122} = 0$
2	$X_{211} = 254$	$X_{212} = 40$	2	$X_{221} = 327$	$X_{222} = 295$
3	$X_{311} = 0$	$X_{312} = 388$	3	$X_{321} = 630$	$X_{322} = 85$
4	$X_{411} = 350$	$X_{412} = 30$	4	$X_{421} = 210$	$X_{422} = 520$
5	$X_{511} = 170$	$X_{512} = 0$	5	$X_{521} = 135$	$X_{522} = 50$
6	$X_{611} = 220$	$X_{612} = 35$	6	$X_{621} = 205$	$X_{622} = 120$
7	$X_{711} = 150$	$X_{712} = 165$	7	$X_{721} = 330$	$X_{722} = 245$
8	$X_{811} = 360$	$X_{812} = 290$	8	$X_{821} = 95$	$X_{822} = 510$
9	$X_{911} = 85$	$X_{912} = 130$	9	$X_{921} = 370$	$X_{922} = 352$
10	$X_{1011} = 30$	$X_{1012} = 505$	10	$X_{1021} = 555$	$X_{1022} = 205$
11	$X_{1111} = 3$	$X_{1112} = 520$	11	$X_{1121} = 440$	$X_{1122} = 140$
12	$X_{1211} = 0$	$X_{1212} = 300$	12	$X_{1221} = 250$	$X_{1222} = 40$
13	$X_{1311} = 355$	$X_{1312} = 330$	13	$X_{1321} = 545$	$X_{1322} = 143$
n_{1k}:	13	13	n_{2k}:	13	13
Sum:	2037	3064	Sum:	4132	2705
Mean $\bar{X}_{1k}$:	156.7	235.7	Mean $\bar{X}_{2k}$:	317.8	208.1
Standard deviation:	136.6	181.3	Standard deviation:	185.4	169.9

Also $\bar{X}_{jk}$ is the conditional mean of the dependent variable for cases in category j on the first independent variable and category k on the second. As usual, $\bar{X}$ is the grand mean of all cases.

With the triple-subscript notation, it is easy to define the grand mean and four joint conditional means. For the grand mean,

$$\bar{X} = \frac{\sum\limits_{k=1}^{K} \sum\limits_{j=1}^{J} \sum\limits_{i=1}^{n_{ik}} X_{ijk}}{n_{jk}JK}$$

The conditional means are even simpler:

$$\bar{X}_{jk} = \frac{\sum\limits_{i=1}^{n_{jk}} X_{ijk}}{n_{jk}}$$

Table 13.7 shows four conditional means for the variable "time spent" in a 2×2 table. It also shows the grand mean $\bar{X}$ in the lower right-hand corner.

In addition to the grand mean and four conditional means "inside" the table, there are four conditional means designated by a notation system that is different from what you have seen so far. The means in the margins of the table each have a dot in one subscript position. Thus, $\bar{X}_{1.}$ is the conditional mean of all cases in the low-work-ethic group, group 1 on the first independent variable. The first subscript, j, is set to 1 to refer to the first category of the first independent variable. A dot is placed in the position of the second subscript to indicate that a category of the second independent variable is not being specified. A dot means, "This statistic is calculated without regard to the categories of the indicated variable." So to calculate $\bar{X}_{1.}$, you need to add all the "time spent" values for all the low-work-ethic cases in both the work and leisure groups on the second independent variable,

TABLE 13.7 All Conditional Means of Time Spent by Work Ethic and Task Label for Experiment 1; Balanced Design with Cases 7 and 13 Eliminated

Work Ethic	Task Label		
	Work ($k = 1$)	Leisure ($k = 2$)	Total ($k = .$)
Low ($j = 1$)	156.7 $\bar{X}_{11}$	235.7 $\bar{X}_{12}$	196.2 $\bar{X}_{1.}$
High ($j = 2$)	317.8 $\bar{X}_{21}$	208.1 $\bar{X}_{22}$	262.9 $\bar{X}_{2.}$
Total ($j = .$)	237.3 $\bar{X}_{.1}$	221.9 $\bar{X}_{.2}$	229.6 $\bar{X}$

"task label," and divide the sum by the number of cases in the low-work-ethic group. That is,

$$\bar{X}_{1.} = \frac{\sum\limits_{k=1}^{2} \sum\limits_{i=1}^{n_{ij}} X_{i1k}}{2n_{jk}}$$

In general, a conditional mean in the margins of the rows is equal to

$$\bar{X}_{j.} = \frac{\sum\limits_{k=1}^{K} \sum\limits_{i=1}^{n_{jk}} X_{ijk}}{Kn_{jk}}$$

A conditional mean in the margins of the columns is equal to

$$\bar{X}_{.k} = \frac{\sum\limits_{j=1}^{J} \sum\limits_{i=1}^{n_{jk}} X_{ijk}}{Jn_{jk}}$$

You might want to check a few of the entries in Table 13.7, using the data in Table 13.6, just to make certain that you understand this new notation system.

Main Effects and Interaction Effects

In a two-way analysis of variance, the total variation of the dependent variable around the grand mean is decomposed (or analyzed) into several components. One part is called, as it was in a one-way ANOVA, the *within-group variation*. There is still variation around the conditional means in the four groups shown in Table 13.6. This is the variation left over after time spent is conditioned on the joint categories of the two independent variables. Since this variation is "left over," it is sometimes called the *residual* or *error variation*.

In a two-way analysis of variance, the other component of the variation is *not* called between-group variation. Instead, the variation that is not the residual variation is itself divided into two parts, the *main effects* of each of the two independent variables and the *interaction effect* of the two independent variables taken together.

The concept of "main effects" is already familiar from your work with one-way analysis of variance. Assessing the main effects of each independent variable begins with the hypothesis of the equality of conditional means for the groups formed by conditioning the dependent variable on the categories of the independent variable of interest. Expressed in terms of the notation introduced above, the problem of assessing main effects begins with the two, separate null hypotheses:

$$H_0: \mu_{1.} = \mu_{2.} = \cdots = \mu_{J.}$$

and

$$H_0: \mu_{.1} = \mu_{.2} = \cdots = \mu_{.K}$$

The first null hypothesis says the means in the margins of the rows of a table like Table 13.7 for the whole population are equal. The second says that the means in the margins of the columns are equal. If you do an analysis of variance and conclude there are grounds for rejecting one or both of these null hypotheses, you have decided to accept one or both alternative hypotheses and assert that

$$H_A: \mu_{f.} \neq \mu_{g.} \quad \text{for some } f \text{ and } g$$

and/or

$$H_A: \mu_{.f} \neq \mu_{.g} \quad \text{for some } f \text{ and } g$$

Assessing main effects in a two-way ANOVA is a straightforward extension of the logic used in a one-way ANOVA.

Interaction effects are slightly more difficult to understand, so an example might help. Tang and Baumeister's hypothesis concerning the data in Tables 13.6 and 13.7 is that "Among subjects who endorse the work ethic, labeling the task as work would increase their tendency to perform that task later on." They are talking about a relationship between one variable (task label) and another (time spent) within one category of the third variable (work ethic). Figure 13.2 shows how the mean times spent by the work group and the leisure group among those who endorse the work ethic might be related to one another if Tang and Baumeister's

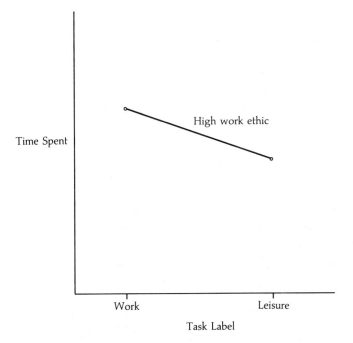

FIGURE 13.2 Hypothetical relationship of mean time spent on word game/task in observation period for people who endorse the work ethic.

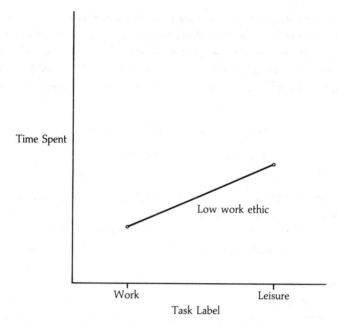

FIGURE 13.3 Hypothetical relationship of mean time spent on word game/task during observation period for people who do not endorse the work ethic.

hypothesis is correct. Time spent solving anagrams by high-work-ethic people should be lower among those people who think they are doing a leisuretime activity than among those who think they are doing work.

What about low-work-ethic people? We might expect low-work-ethic people to spend less time on a task if it is called work than if it is called leisure. That relationship between task label and time spent for low-work-ethic people is shown in Figure 13.3.

Figure 13.4 combines Figures 13.2 and 13.3. The (hypothesized) *relationship* between task label and time spent is different for high- and low-work-ethic subjects. The direction of the relationship (if we may speak of "direction" given that task label is a nominal variable with only two categories) in one group is the opposite of the direction for the other group. (At least, that is the hypothesis.) *Whenever the relationship between one independent variable and the dependent variable differs depending on the category of the second independent variable, there is an interaction effect of the two independent variables on the dependent variable.* This is the definition of *interaction.* If Tang and Baumeister's hypothesis is correct, then there should be an interaction effect of task label and work ethic on time spent.

It is easy to tell if there is an interaction effect if you graph conditional means on a graph like Figure 13.4. Put the dependent variable on the vertical axis and the categories of one independent variable on the horizontal axis, and plot a sepa-

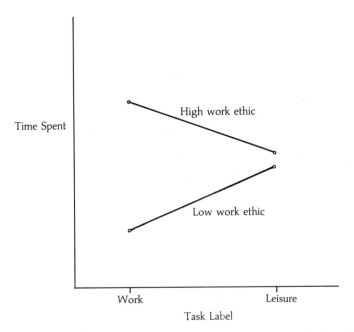

FIGURE 13.4 Relationship between mean time spent on word game/task in the observation period if the hypothesis is true.

rate set of conditional means for each category of the second independent variable. (Try it for the data in Table 13.7. You see that the actual sample data support the hypothesis of an interaction effect because the lines form a pattern somewhat similar to that in Figure 13.4.) If the lines on the graph are all parallel to one another, there is no interaction effect. If not all the lines are parallel, then the relationship between the independent variable graphed on the horizontal axis and the dependent variable differs across the categories of the second independent variable. By definition, then, there is an interaction effect if the lines on a graph like that in Figure 13.4 are not parallel.

Mathematically and conceptually, what does it mean for there to be an interaction effect? Perhaps it is easier to begin with a different question: What does it mean for there to be *no* interaction effect? Look at Figure 13.5a. It shows the relationship between variable *A* and variable *C* for two categories of the third variable, variable *B*. (This is a plot of the hypothetical data in Figure 13.5b.) The lines which connect conditional means within categories of variable *B* are parallel. According to the definition offered above, there is no interaction effect. The figure does show there is a main effect of both variables *A* and *B* on variable *C*. You can tell there are main effects because the conditional means of *C*, following conditioning on the categories of each variable, are unequal. That is,

$$\bar{X}_{.1} \neq \bar{X}_{.2} \quad \text{or} \quad \bar{X}_{.1} - \bar{X} \neq \bar{X}_{.2} - \bar{X}$$

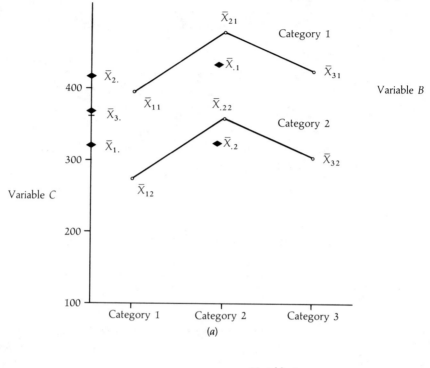

FIGURE 13.5 (*a*) Conditional means of variable *C* after conditioning on the categories of variables *A* and *B*; hypothetical data. (*b*) Conditional means of variable *C*, conditioned on the two categories of variable *B* and the three categories of variable *A*. Hypothetical data are graphed in (*a*).

and

$$\bar{X}_{1.} \neq \bar{X}_{2.} \neq \bar{X}_{3.} \quad \text{or} \quad \bar{X}_{1.} - \bar{X} \neq \bar{X}_{2.} - \bar{X} \neq \bar{X}_{3.} - \bar{X}$$

But what does "no interaction" mean? If there is no interaction effect, then there is a very special relationship among all the conditional means shown in Figure 13.5. Any joint conditional mean $\bar{X}_{jk}$ is equal to the grand mean $\bar{X}$ plus the main effect of the first independent variable for category *j*, which is $\bar{X}_{j.} - \bar{X}$, plus the main effect of the second variable for category k, which is $\bar{X}_{.k} - \bar{X}$. That is, if there is no interaction effect, then for any j and k

$$\bar{X}_{jk} \quad \bar{X} + (\bar{X}_{j.} - \bar{X}) + (\bar{X}_{.k} - \bar{X})$$

So

$$\bar{X}_{jk} = \bar{X}_{j.} + \bar{X}_{.k} - \bar{X} \qquad \text{for all } j \text{ and } k$$

if there is no interaction effect.

You should check this equation for the hypothetical data given in Figure 13.5b. For example, $\bar{X}_{32}$ should equal

$$\bar{X}_{32} = \bar{X}_{3.} + \bar{X}_{.2} - \bar{X}$$

and, indeed,

$$\bar{X}_{32} = 360 + 310 - 370 = 300$$

which is the value of the conditional mean $\bar{X}_{32}$. Try the equation on the other five conditional means.

If the relationship above holds when there is no interaction in the sample data, it gives us a basis for formulating a null hypothesis concerning interaction effects in the population. We should say that there are no interaction effects in the population from which the sample was drawn if

$$H_0 \colon \mu_{jk} = \mu_{j.} + \mu_{.k} - \mu$$

for all $j = 1, 2, \ldots, J$ and $k = 1, 2, \ldots, K$.

Restatement of the Three Null Hypotheses

In a two-way analysis of variance, then, there are three null hypotheses: one concerns the main effect of the first independent variable (sometimes called the first *factor*), one concerns the main effect of the second independent variable or second factor, and one concerns the interaction effect of the two factors together. These hypotheses can be stated as follows:

For factor 1: $\quad H_0 \colon \mu_{1.} = \mu_{2.} = \cdots = \mu_{J.}$

For factor 2: $\quad H_0 \colon \mu_{.1} = \mu_{.2} = \cdots = \mu_{.K}$

For interaction: $\quad H_0 \colon \mu_{jk} = \mu_{j.} + \mu_{.k} - \mu \qquad$ for all j and k

Just as in one-way analysis of variance, the first two null hypotheses can be rewritten so that they point toward a way of testing them statistically by using components of the variance of the dependent variable.

For factor 1: $H_0: \mu_{j.} - \mu = 0$ for $j = 1, \ldots, J$

or $H_0: \sum\limits_{j=1}^{J} (\mu_{j.} - \mu)^2 = 0$

For factor 2: $H_0: \mu_{.k} - \mu = 0$ for $k = 1, \ldots, K$

or $H_0: \sum\limits_{k=1}^{K} (\mu_{.k} - \mu)^2 = 0$

In a similar way, we can rewrite the null hypothesis concerning interaction effects. If it is true that

$$H_0: \mu_{jk} = \mu_{j.} + \mu_{.k} - \mu \qquad \text{for all } j \text{ and } k$$

then it is also true that

$$H_0: \mu_{jk} - (\mu_{j.} + \mu_{.k} - \mu) = 0 \qquad \text{for all } j \text{ and } k$$

or $H_0: (\mu_{jk} - \mu_{j.} - \mu_{.k} + \mu)^2 = 0 \qquad \text{for all } j \text{ and } k$

or $H_0: \sum\limits_{j=1}^{J} \sum\limits_{k=1}^{K} (\mu_{jk} - \mu_{j.} - \mu_{.k} + \mu)^2 = 0$

Sums of Squares and Degrees of Freedom

You can develop estimates of the sums of squares based on the final forms of the three null hypotheses stated above and do the calculations for the experimental data in Table 13.6. For factor 1, the sum of squared deviations would be

$$SS_1 = n_{jk}K \sum\limits_{j=1}^{J} (\bar{X}_{j.} - \bar{X})^2$$

The summation is of the J squared deviations of the conditional means around the grand mean. The multiplier $n_{jk}K$ is used to find the total deviations. There are n_{jk} (the number of cases per cell) times K (the number of groups formed by the categories of the second independent variable) cases whose average deviation from the grand mean is $\bar{X}_{j.} - \bar{X}$. For the data in Table 13.7, where the first factor is work ethic,

$$
\begin{aligned}
SS_1 &= 13(2) \sum\limits_{j=1}^{2} (\bar{X}_{j.} - \bar{X})^2 \\
&= 26[(\bar{X}_{1.} - \bar{X})^2 - (\bar{X}_{2.} - \bar{X})^2] \\
&= 26[(196.2 - 229.6)^2 + (262.9 - 229.6)^2] \\
&= 26(1115.6 + 1108.9) = 57{,}837
\end{aligned}
$$

The sum of squares for factor 2 is analogous to that for factor 1:

$$SS_2 = n_{jk}J \sum_{k=1}^{K} (\bar{X}_{.k} - \bar{X})^2$$

For the data in Table 13.7, factor 2 is task label, and

$$
\begin{aligned}
SS_2 &= 13(2) \sum_{k=1}^{2} (\bar{X}_{.k} - \bar{X})^2 \\
&= 26[(237.3 - 229.6)^2 + (221.9 - 229.6)^2] \\
&= 3083
\end{aligned}
$$

The sum of squares for interaction effects is simple to estimate. The sum of squares for interaction is denoted $SS_{1,2}$ and, in general, is equal to

$$SS_{1,2} = n_{jk} \sum_{j=1}^{J} \sum_{k=1}^{K} (\bar{X}_{jk} - \bar{X}_{j.} - \bar{X}_{.k} + \bar{X})^2$$

The multiplier n_{jk} is there because there are n_{jk} cases whose average deviation from the grand mean plus the main effects of the two independent variable is $\bar{X}_{jk} - \bar{X}_{j.} - \bar{X}_{.k} + \bar{X}$. For the example in Table 13.7,

$$
\begin{aligned}
SS_{1,2} = 13 \sum_{j=1}^{2} \sum_{k=1}^{2} (\bar{X}_{jk} &- \bar{X}_{j.} - \bar{X}_{.k} + \bar{X})^2 \\
= 13[(156.7 - 196.2 &- 237.3 + 229.6)^2 & \text{when } j = 1, k = 1 \\
+ (317.8 - 262.9 &- 237.3 + 229.6)^2 & \text{when } j = 2, k = 1 \\
+ (235.7 - 196.2 &- 221.9 + 229.6)^2 & \text{when } j = 1, k = 2 \\
+ (208.1 - 262.9 &- 221.9 + 229.6)^2] & \text{when } j = 2, k = 2 \\
= 115{,}725 &
\end{aligned}
$$

Finally, it is a simple matter to calculate the within-group sum of squares SS_W because SS_W is simply the total squared deviations of all cases in all jointly defined categories around the conditional mean of each category. In general,

$$SS_W = \sum_{j=1}^{J} \sum_{k=1}^{K} \sum_{i=1}^{n_{jk}} (X_{ijk} - \bar{X}_{jk})^2$$

If you have the conditional standard deviations of each group $s_{x_{jk}}$, as you do in Table 13.7, then you can find the total squared deviations by multiplying the squared standard deviation by the denominator used in the calculation of the variance $(n - 1)$ to find the total within-group variation for each group. Then the total within-group variation is

$$SS_W = \sum_{j=1}^{J} \sum_{k=1}^{K} (n-1)s_{x_{jk}}^2$$

For the data in Table 13.5,

$$SS_W = 12(136.6)^2 + 12(185.4)^2 + 12(181.3)^2 + 12(169.9)^2$$
$$= 1{,}377{,}221$$

All the sums of squared deviations are converted to variance estimates by dividing by the various degrees of freedom (df) associated with them. For the two sums of squares for main effects, there is one constraint, the grand mean. There are J conditional means used in the calculation of the sum of squared deviations for factor 1, so there are $J-1$ degrees of freedom associated with SS_1. That is, $df_1 = J-1$. There are K conditional means used in the calculation of SS_2, and there is the one constraint of the grand mean, so $df_2 = K-1$.

In the calculation of $SS_{1,2}$, the sum of squares for interaction, there are JK conditional means of interest, so you begin with JK degrees of freedom. The conditional means in the margins of a layout like that in Table 13.7 are the constraints placed on the calculation of $SS_{1,2}$. If you know all the "dot" means in a two-way analysis of variance, then you are free to choose $(J-1)(K-1)$ of the JK conditional means "inside" the table before the rest are determined by the combination of the $(J-1)(K-1)$ choices you make and the constraints. Therefore, $(J-1)(K-1)$ degrees of freedom are associated with the sum of squares for interaction $SS_{1,2}$. That is, $df_{1,2} = (J-1)(K-1)$.

The within-group variation begins with $n_{jk}JK$ degrees of freedom, the number of cases in the sample. You lose JK degrees of freedom since all JK conditional means inside the table (the means in each of the JK cells of the table) must be used in the calculation of SS_W. So the degrees of freedom associated with the sum of squared deviations within groups are

$$df_W \sim n_{jk}JK - JK = (n_{jk}-1)JK$$

All the formulas for degrees of freedom are summarized as

$$df_1 = J-1 \qquad df_{1,2} = (J-1)(K-1)$$
$$df_2 = K-1 \qquad df_W = (n_{jk}-1)JK$$

For the data in Table 13.6,

$$df_1 = 2-1 = 1 \qquad df_{1,2} = (2-1)(2-1) = 1$$
$$df_2 = 2-1 = 1 \qquad df_W = (13-1)(2)(2) = 48$$

The *mean squares* for main effects, interaction effects, and within-group variation are calculated in a way analogous to the calculation of mean squares within and mean squares between in a one-way ANOVA. The mean squares is equal to the sum of squared deviations divided by the degrees of freedom associated with the sum of squares. In our example,

$$MS_1 = \frac{SS_1}{df_1} = \frac{57{,}837}{1} = 57{,}837$$

$$MS_2 = \frac{SS_2}{df_2} = \frac{3083}{1} = 3083$$

$$MS_{1,2} = \frac{SS_{1,2}}{df_{1,2}} = \frac{115{,}725}{1} = 115{,}725$$

$$MS_W = \frac{SS_W}{df_W} = \frac{1{,}337{,}221}{48} = 28{,}692$$

F Test for Significance

A two-way ANOVA answers the questions of whether there is evidence to claim that there are main effects of either independent variable or interactions effects of the two independent variables on the dependent variable in the population from which the sample was drawn. To answer these questions, you need to compare the two mean squares for main effects and the mean squares for interaction to the mean squares within. The comparisons are made by division, just as in a one-way ANOVA. You use the resulting F statistic, with its two sets of degrees of freedom, to decide if the sum of squares either for main effects or for interaction is significantly larger than the sum of squares within. In a two-way ANOVA, there are three F statistics to calculate, one for each null hypothesis to be tested.

For factor 1:
$$F_{J-1,\ n(n_{jk}-1)JK} = \frac{MS_1}{MS_W}$$

For factor 2:
$$F_{K-1,\ (n_{jk}-1)JK} = \frac{MS_2}{MS_W}$$

For interaction:
$$F_{(J-1)(K-1),\ (n_{jk}-1)JK} = \frac{MS_{1,2}}{MS_W}$$

In practice, one assesses interaction effects first. If the null hypothesis for interaction can be rejected, it is difficult to assess main effects. For illustrative, introductory purposes, I shall carry out the test of each hypothesis in the following paragraphs.

For each hypothesis F statistics are compared to the critical values of F in Appendix Table B.8 to determine the observed significance of the test for any given effect. If the F for factor 1 is larger than the critical value in the F table for the preset level to reject, you may reject the null hypothesis that

$$H_0: \mu_1 = \mu_2. = \cdots = \mu_J.$$

If the F for factor 2 is larger than the critical value in the distributions of F for the preset level to reject, then you may reject the null hypothesis that

$$H_0: \mu_{.1} = \mu_{.2} = \cdots = \mu_{.K}$$

If the F for interaction is larger than the critical value in the F table for the preset level to reject, you may reject the null hypothesis that

$$H_0: \mu_{jk} = \mu_{j.} + \mu_{.k} - \mu \qquad \text{for some } j \text{ and } k$$

Let's do the tests for the data in Table 13.5, all with a level to reject of .05. For factor 1, the work-ethic score, the F statistic is

$$F_{J-1,\,(n_{jk}-1)JK} = F_{1,48} = \frac{MS_1}{MS_W} = \frac{57,837}{28,892} = 2.02$$

Refer to Table B.8 of critical values for F. Notice that with an $F_{1,48} = 2.02$, you can reject the null hypothesis concerning the equality of conditional means (after conditioning time spent on the categories of work ethic) at the .25 level of significance, but you cannot reject it at the .10 level of significance. So the observed significance of the test is $.10 < p < .25$. I decide not to reject the null hypothesis, and do not conclude that the sample was drawn from a population in which the mean values of time spent solving anagrams during the observation period were unequal for various levels of work ethic.

The F for task label, the second factor, is

$$F_{1,48} = \frac{MS_2}{MS_W} = \frac{3083}{28,692} = .11$$

When an F statistic is less than 1.00, the mean squares for that factor is less than the mean squares within, so we know there is no effect from that factor. You say, "F is trivial, and there is not a significant effect." In this case, there is no statistically significant effect of task label on time spent.

The F for interaction is

$$F_{(K-1)(J-1),\,(n_{jk}-1)JK} = F_{1,48} = \frac{MS_{1,2}}{MS_W} = \frac{115,725}{28,692} = 4.03$$

TABLE 13.8 Results of Two-Way ANOVA for Time Spent by Work Ethic and Task Label for Experiment 1; Balanced Design with Cases 7 and 13 Eliminated

Source of Variation	Sum of Squares	df	Mean Squares	F	p
Main effects					
1. Work ethic	57,837	1	57,837	2.02	< .25
2. Task label	3,083	1	3,083	0.11	< .75
Interaction effect					
1, 2: Task label and work ethic	115,725	1	115,725	4.03	< .05*
Within group (residual)	1,377,221	48	28,692		
Total	1,553,867	51	30,468		

* See the note in text concerning the determination of this level of significance.

This F falls between the critical values of $F_{1,40} = 4.08$ and $F_{1,60} = 4.00$ shown in Table B.8 for rejection of the null hypothesis with an observed significance of the test of $p < .05$. The computer program I used to check my hand calculations indicated that the level of confidence with which I can reject the null hypothesis concerning interaction effects is, indeed, ever so slightly less than .05. I reject the null hypothesis and conclude there is probably an interaction effect of task label and work ethic on time spent.

Table 13.8 summarizes the results of this two-way analysis of variance. It contains all the sums of squared deviations (for main effects, for the two-variable interaction effect, for the residual variation, and for the whole data set), the degrees of freedom associated with each component of the variation, the mean squares, the three F statistics, and the observed significance of the test. The only null hypothesis that can be rejected concerns the interaction effect. ANOVA simply tells you that you can reject, in this case, the null hypothesis that

$$H_0: \mu_{jk} = \mu_{j.} + \mu_{.k} - \mu \quad \text{for some } j \text{ and } k$$

We must look back at the data to describe the nature of any effect. In the words of the researcher, the conclusion from all this analysis is, "For subjects who agreed with the work ethic (half our sample) the label 'work' resulted in subsequent intrinsic motivation that was . . . greater than that following the label 'leisure.'" If you "turn play into work" for those who like work, you will get more work from them.

Another Example

To reinforce your understanding of two-way analysis of variance, let's work through the analysis of the data from the internal-motivation experiment 2 without doing the tedious calculations. You should be able to see, from this example, how elegant and concise the presentation of an analysis of variance can be.

The purpose of the second experiment was to test two competing hypotheses that each might explain the results of the first experiment. "The preference for the task labeled 'work' that was found among subjects who endorsed the work ethic may have been due to intrinsic motivation *or* to the desire to impress the experimenter." So the researcher made all the subjects in the second experiment think they were doing "work," divided them into three work-ethic groups based on their work-ethic scores, and then randomly assigned them to an experimental condition in which they thought they might be under surveillance by the researcher (a "public" condition) or in which they had no indication that they would be watched during the postexperiment observation period (a "private" condition). In the words of the researchers,

> If the differential preference for the "work" activity was mediated by
> self-presentational concerns (that is, the desire to impress the experimenter
> in certain ways), then it would be obtained only in the public condition.
> If it was due to intrinsic motivation, then it would obtain in the private
> condition as well.[2]

The first possibility is a hypothesis concerning the existence of an interaction effect. If there is a different association between work ethic and time spent in the public condition than there is in the private condition, there is an interaction effect of work ethic and surveillance on time spent. If the relationship between one independent variable and the dependent variable is the same for both categories of the surveillance variable, as the second part of the paragraph above suggests might be the case, then there is no interaction effect. If there is an interaction effect, then the desire to impress the researcher is at work. If there is no interaction effect, then intrinsic motivation is the prime mover.

Table 13.9 presents the results of the experiment, and Figure 13.6 shows the results in graphical form. This is a 3×2 design since there are three categories of the first independent variable and two categories of the second independent variable. This is an unbalanced design because there are from five to eight subjects in each of the six experimental conditions. Even though it is difficult to describe and justify the calculations for a two-way ANOVA with an unbalanced design, you can interpret the results of such an analysis in somewhat the same way you interpret the results from a balanced design.

The ANOVA results for experiment 2 are shown in Table 13.10. There is probably a main effect of experimental condition ("surveillance" = "public" or "private") on time spent. Look at Table 13.9. In the bottom row (marked "Total") there is

TABLE 13.9 Conditional Means of Time Spent by Work Ethic and Surveillance for Experiment 2; Unbalanced Design

Work Ethic	Surveillance		Total $(k = .)$ $\overline{X}_{j.}$ $(n_{j.})$
	Public $(k = 1)$ $\overline{X}_{j1}$ (n_{j1})	Private $(k = 2)$ $\overline{X}_{j2}$ (n_{j2})	
Low $(j = 1)$	510.0 (6)	184.8 (8)	324.1 (14)
Medium $(j = 2)$	562.0 (8)	681.8 (5)	608.1 (13)
High $(j = 3)$	656.8 (6)	143.0 (7)	380.2 (13)
Total $(j = .)$	574.9 (20)	294.4 (20)	434.6 (40)

a big difference between the conditional mean for those subjects who thought they were observed and the conditional mean for those who had no reason to believe they were observed. Based on the F statistic, you can reject the null hypothesis concerning a main effect for factor 2, surveillance. It seems as though people will continue to do the work task more if they think they are observed. This should not be surprising to students or teachers.

The main effect of work ethic is not statistically significant. You cannot conclude that there is a significant difference among the means in the column of Table 13.9 marked "Total," even though the medium-work-ethic subjects spent more time on the word game than the others.

The most interesting result of this experiment concerns the interaction effect. The interaction effect is statistically significant at the .05 level. You can get the

TABLE 13.10 Results of Two-Way ANOVA for Time Spent by Work Ethic and Surveillance for Experiment 2; Unbalanced Design

Source of Variation	Sum of Squares	df	Mean Squares	F	p
Main effects					
1. Work ethic	408,914	2	204,457	2.18	<.25
2. Surveillance	594,863	1	594,863	6.36	<.05
Interaction effect					
1, 2: Surveillance and work ethic	665,000	2	332,500	3.55	<.05
Within group (residual)	3,181,965	34	93,587		
Total	4,850,742	39	129,292		

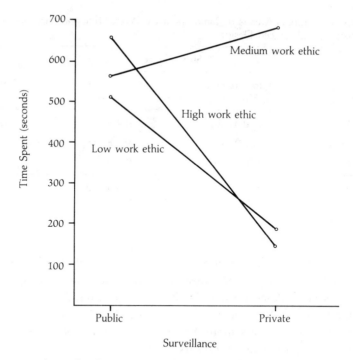

FIGURE 13.6 Relationship between surveillance condition and time spent on word game/task during observation session for three work-ethic groups; experiment 2.

best idea of the nature of the interaction by looking at Figure 13.6. The means of all the work-ethic groups are high for the public condition. The means of the low- and high-work-ethic groups are low in the private condition. But the mean for the medium-work-ethic group is high even in the private condition. The researchers stated their conclusion this way:

> It appears that subjects who surpassed Experiment 1's criterion for "high" endorsement of the work ethic fall into two distinct groups. One group appears to be motivated chiefly by the desire to *appear* to be work-oriented persons. These show extremely high advocacy of the value of work, and when others are watching, they show behavioral preference for activities that have been explicitly labeled as "work." However, when these subjects believe themselves to be unobserved, their preference for "work" vanishes. Thus, this group cannot be said to be guided by genuinely intrinsic motivation to perform work activities.
>
> The second group, on the other hand, does appear to prefer "work" labeled activities due to a genuine intrinsic attraction to work. These subjects show high but not extremely high endorsement of the value of work. Their behavioral preference for an activity labeled "work" obtains even when they

believe no one else is interested in (or even aware of) their allotment of time.[3]

This kind of study has obvious implications in education and for the structure of work situations.

. . .

KEY CONCEPTS IN THIS CHAPTER

. . .

NOTES

1. Thomas Li-Ping Tang and Roy F. Banmeister, "Effects of Personal Values, Perceived Surveillance, and Task Labels on Task Preference: The Ideology of Turning Work into Play," *Journal of Applied Psychology* 68: 99–105, Copyright c 1984 by the American Psychological Association. Reprinted by permission.

2. Ibid., p. 102.
3. Ibid., p. 105.

$$\bullet \quad \bullet \quad \bullet$$

EXERCISES

Chapter 13

1. Refer to Exercise 1, Chapter 10. Do a one-way analysis of variance to determine if there are any significant differences among mean shelf lives based on fermentation times.

  a. Formulate the appropriate alternative hypothesis and a corresponding null hypothesis.
  b. Calculate the three sample means $\bar{X}_1$ (1 = short fermentation), $\bar{X}_2$ (2 = moderate fermentation), and $\bar{X}_3$ (3 = long fermentation).
  c. Calculate the grand mean $\bar{X}$.
  d. Calculate SS_B.
  e. Calculate SS_W.
  f. Calculate the degrees of freedom associated with each of the sums of squares df_B and df_W.
  g. Calculate MS_B and MS_W.
  h. Calculate the appropriate F statistic.
  i. Choose a level to reject.
  j. Determine if the null hypothesis can be rejected or if it must be accepted.
  k. Display your results in an ANOVA table like Table 13.4.
  l. Conduct a test of difference between pairs of means, if appropriate.
  m. Interpret your results in terms of the hypothesis that motivated the experiment.

2. Return to the raw data in Figure 12.17. It shows the average total cost for patients treated by each physician. Physicians with a higher physician number were granted privileges to practice at the hospital in question later than the physicians with lower numbers. On average, the higher-numbered physicians (16 to 22) are probably younger, closer to their medical school training, more likely to be women, perhaps more up to date medically, and so on. Divide the physicians into "younger" (numbers 16 to 22), "medium" (numbers 8 to 15), and "older" (numbers 1 to 7) groups.

  a. Formulate a hypothesis about the relationship between this new variable, called "age," and total cost to the patient.
  b. Conduct a one-way analysis of variance to test your hypothesis. Fill in the following table, conduct a test of difference between pairs of means (if appropriate), and discuss the results.

Source of Variation	Sum of Squares	df	Mean Squares	F	p
Age					
Residual					

3. A researcher decided to examine suicide rates of counties. Her dependent variable was suicide rate, and her independent variables were "urban-rural," a variable with two categories into which each county was placed based on its population density, and "income," a variable with three categories into which a county was placed based on its per capita income. The sample consisted of 180 counties. In each of the six conditions shown in the table below 30 counties were randomly selected from all counties in each condition.

Mean Suicide Rates per 100,000 Population for Counties Divided according to Population Density and Per Capita Income

	Population Density		
Income	Rural (n)	Urban (n)	Total (n)
Low	31.0 (30)	37.2 (30)	34.1 (60)
Medium	17.9 (30)	19.3 (30)	18.6 (60)
High	27.1 (30)	23.5 (30)	25.3 (60)
Total	25.3 (90)	26.7 (90)	26.0 (180)

a. Plot the six conditional means and say if there is an interaction effect.

b. Fill in the remainder of the following ANOVA table:

Source of Variation	Sum of Squares	df	Mean Squares	F	P
Main effects					
1. Income					
2. Rural-urban					
Interaction effects					
1, 2: Income and rural-urban					
Within group (Residual)	786.5				
Total					

c. Interpret the results. How do these results relate to Durkheim's theory of suicide?

4. Here are data related to clients' psychosocial functionality (rated on a 200-point scale). Thirty patients were randomly assigned to one of three treatment schemes: 10 received psychoactive drugs only, 10 received only psychotherapeutic counseling, and 10 received a combination of drugs and counseling. Is there evidence that there are differences in the effectiveness of the modes of treatment?

		Treatment Modality	
Case	Drugs	Drugs and Counseling	Counseling
1	45	75	142
2	58	79	131
3	67	82	121
4	92	89	95
5	41	46	45
6	38	35	110
7	74	32	152
8	81	85	160
9	42	92	111
10	68	98	112

5. Here is the weight loss by each of six people randomly enrolled in four weight loss programs. Is there evidence that there are differences among the programs in terms of effectiveness?

	Weight Loss in Program			
Case	A	B	C	D
1	3	−5*	2	17
2	4	10	1	16
3	−1	15	0	4
4	7	17	0	17
5	5	13	−1	22
6	6	4	4	21

* Negative numbers indicate a weight gain.

6. A factory manager conducted an experiment to determine the impact of various social organizations of workers on the quality of the products they produced. He assigned workers randomly to (1) a strict factory-line scheme, (2) a Japanese-style quality-circle approach, or (3) a liberal, employee-determined organization scheme. The following table shows the errors attributed to each of the seven individual employees during the first week of the program. Is there any evidence in these data that there are differences among the organizational schemes?

Employee	Factory Line	Quality Circle	Employee-Determined
1	3	0	3
2	4	2	2
3	8	1	4
4	1	2	6
5	0	7	5
6	7	1	4
7	9	0	9

7. The same manager mentioned in Exercise 6 continued the experiment for 8 weeks. These data show the proportion of products that were defective produced under each scheme for each of the 8 weeks. Is there evidence in these data of a difference in the organizational schemes' impacts on quality? Is there anything in the data or in your analysis that would make you want to ask other questions or conduct further experiments?

Week	Factory Line	Quality Circle	Employee-Determined
1	.15	.05	.19
2	.20	.06	.25
3	.16	.05	.16
4	.19	.19	.11
5	.10	.04	.04
6	.05	.02	.02
7	.19	.07	.01
8	.15	.05	.02

8. A book company conducted an experiment to see if different kinds of covers had an effect on romance book sales. The company marketed one book with four different covers and randomly assigned each cover to six bookstores that distributed its books. Here are data on the first 6 months of sales. Is there evidence that the cover art has an impact on sales?

	Cover Art			
Store	Explicit	Romanticized	Abstract	Photograph
1	65	45	20	.72
2	87	43	21	71
3	95	52	25	73
4	20	95	36	111
5	36	150	15	97
6	72	57	41	135

9. A company buys five types of rechargeable batteries. It purchases four batteries of each type. It keeps track of the number of times each battery can be recharged. Is there evidence in the data that there are differences among the types of batteries purchased?

	No. Recharges for Battery:				
Purchase	*A*	*B*	*C*	*D*	*E*
1	115	90	145	99	87
2	215	106	148	141	146
3	150	115	149	115	152
4	172	120	152	122	201

10. This question refers to data in Exercise 10, Chapter 3. Assign a number to each grade (A = 4.0, B = 3.0, C = 2.0, D = 1.0). Is there evidence in the data to support the claim that there is a difference in grades based on the time students spent studying?

11. Here are the grade-point averages (GPAs) of 32 students. They are divided into four groups on the basis of two variables: (1) whether the student is an athlete and (2) sex.

a. Calculate and plot the conditional mean GPAs for the four groups.

b. Do a two-way analysis of variance to determine if there is any effect of either or both independent variables on grade-point average.

Case	Females		Males	
	Athletes	Nonathletes	Athletes	Nonathletes
1	3.21	4.00	2.63	2.93
2	2.15	3.95	2.17	3.42
3	2.78	3.21	2.98	3.00
4	3.45	2.86	3.45	3.86
5	3.98	2.90	3.52	2.45
6	3.10	2.45	3.86	2.97
7	2.90	1.98	2.97	3.62
8	2.00	3.65	3.00	4.00

Appendix A: Data Sets

SOCIAL INDICATORS

Country	Doctors per 100,000	Urbanization, %	Per Capita Income, $	Male Life Expectancy, Years	Literacy Rate, %
Afghanistan	51	—	168	39.9	12
Albania	—	38.0	490	64.9	75
Algeria	19	52.0	1,600	52.9	36
Angola	6	—	500	37.0	12
Argentina	192	72.0	2,331	65.2	93
Australia	154	86.0	7,720	67.6	98
Austria	233	52.0	6,739	68.1	99
Bahamas	—	58.0	3,310	64.5	—
Bahrain	62	78.0	4,967	—	40
Bangladesh	8	9.0	85	45.8	29
Barbados	76	4.0	1,450	62.7	97
Belgium	211	95.0	10,800	67.8	99
Benin	3	14.0	162	44.8	20
Bhutan	23	—	70	42.0	—
Bolivia	38	—	477	46.5	55
Botswana	14	12.3	544	44.3	27
Brazil	59	61.2	1,523	57.6	70
Bulgaria	226	60.5	2,100	68.7	95
Burma	19	—	113	48.6	70
Cameroon	6	20.3	628	41.9	20
Canada	178	75.5	10,296	69.3	98
Central African Republic	52	—	257	33.0	16

(*continued*)

Country	Doctors per 100,000	Urbanization, %	Per Capita Income, $	Male Life Expectancy, Years	Literacy Rate, %
Chad	2	18.4	73	29.0	15
Chile	62	79.8	1,950	60.5	90
China–PRC	33	—	232	60.7	70
China–Taiwan	33	—	1,300	66.8	85
Colombia	51	59.5	986	65.0	80
Congo	14	—	500	41.9	40
Costa Rica	72	40.6	1,512	66.3	90
Cuba	94	60.3	840	68.5	94
Cyprus	82	42.2	2,200	70.0	86
Czechoslovakia	254	66.7	3,985	67.0	99
Denmark	204	66.9	9,869	71.1	99
Djibouti	—	—	1,000	—	—
Dominica	18	—	460	57.0	—
Dominican Republic	53	49.1	841	57.2	68
Ecuador	64	42.8	741	54.9	74
Egypt	92	44.1	448	51.6	44
El Salvador	27	38.8	639	56.6	63
Ethiopia	1	12.9	91	37.0	7
Fiji	50	37.2	1,440	68.5	75
Finland	160	59.0	6,090	67.4	99
France	164	73.0	7,908	69.2	99
Gabon	32	32.0	4,487	25.0	45
Germany–East	190	75.5	4,000	66.8	99
Germany–West	204	—	9,278	68.6	99
Ghana	10	31.4	380	41.9	30
Greece	221	64.8	3,665	70.1	84
Guatemala	40	35.6	749	48.3	47
Guinea	6	—	140	39.4	15
Guinea-Bissau	—	—	330	37.0	—
Guyana	25	29.6	437	59.0	85
Haiti	7	24.3	260	47.1	22
Honduras	137	31.4	528	52.4	57
Hungary	230	51.8	3,000	66.5	98

(continued)

Country	Doctors per 100,000	Urbanization, %	Per Capita Income, $	Male Life Expectancy, Years	Literacy Rate, %
Iceland	180	87.4	6,392	73.0	99
India	26	21.2	150	41.9	36
Indonesia	7	18.2	304	47.5	62
Iran	39	46.8	1,986	57.6	50
Iraq	44	—	1,561	51.2	30
Ireland	116	52.2	2,711	68.8	99
Israel	277	87.2	3,332	71.3	88
Italy	208	—	3,076	68.9	94
Ivory Coast	4	32.4	1,293	41.9	22
Jamaica	28	37.1	1,143	62.6	86
Japan	119	75.9	8,460	72.1	99
Jordan	37	—	552	52.6	54
Kenya	8	9.9	337	46.9	40
Korea–North	40	—	570	58.8	85
Korea–South	49	48.4	1,187	63.0	91
Kuwait	124	—	11,431	66.4	60
Laos	6	14.7	85	39.1	28
Lebanon	75	60.1	1,142	61.4	70
Lesotho	8	—	240	46.7	50
Liberia	12	27.6	453	45.8	18
Libya	106	29.8	6,335	51.4	40
Luxembourg	112	67.9	10,040	67.0	98
Madagascar	10	14.1	275	37.5	45
Malawi	2	10.1	220	40.9	25
Malaysia	12	20.6	714	66.2	60
Maldives	—	11.3	150	—	36
Mali	5	16.6	96	39.4	10
Malta	127	—	2,036	68.3	85
Mauritania	7	22.8	376	39.4	10
Mauritius	44	43.6	738	60.7	80
Mexico	57	65.2	1,800	62.8	80
Mongolia	209	46.4	750	59.1	95
Morocco	9	37.9	555	51.4	24
Mozambique	6	—	170	41.9	10
Nepal	3	4.0	114	42.2	19

Country	Doctors per 100,000	Urbanization, %	Per Capita Income, $	Male Life Expectancy, Years	Literacy Rate, %
Netherlands	172	88.4	9,500	72.0	99
New Zealand	135	83.0	6,650	69.0	98
Nicaragua	60	48.6	825	51.2	58
Niger	2	—	250	39.4	5
Nigeria	7	—	523	37.2	25
Norway	186	44.2	7,949	72.1	99
Pakistan	25	25.5	280	53.7	23
Panama	78	56.6	1,116	62.3	82
Papua New Guinea	7	12.9	480	47.5	32
Paraguay	77	39.6	1,038	60.3	82
Peru	64	62.5	655	52.6	72
Philippines	36	31.8	457	56.9	85
Poland	166	57.0	2,500	66.9	98
Portugal	142	—	2,000	65.3	72
Rumania	135	47.5	3,100	69.3	98
Rwanda	13	3.5	178	41.8	25
Sampa	35	21.3	320	60.8	—
Saudi Arabia	60	—	11,500	44.2	15
Senegal	2	31.7	342	39.4	10
Sierra Leone	6	—	199	41.8	15
Singapore	78	—	2,279	65.1	76
Somalia	3	—	105	39.4	5
South Africa	6	47.9	1,296	56.6	50
Spain	176	—	5,500	69.7	93
Sri Lanka	43	22.4	168	64.8	81
Sudan	50	20.4	320	43.0	20
Surinam	49	—	1,240	62.5	—
Swaziland	11	7.9	530	41.8	36
Sweden	178	82.7	9,274	72.1	99
Switzerland	201	54.6	15,455	71.8	99
Syria	39	48.8	702	54.5	45
Tanzania	20	7.3	253	40.0	37
Thailand	12	13.2	444	53.6	82
Togo	6	15.2	319	31.6	18
Tonga	5	—	430	—	—

(continued)

Country	Doctors per 100,000	Urbanization, %	Per Capita Income, $	Male Life Expectancy, Years	Literacy Rate, %
Trinidad	54	49.4	2,090	60.1	92
Tunisia	4	—	934	54.0	40
Turkey	56	44.6	1,140	53.7	60
Uganda	20	7.1	240	48.3	25
United Arab Emirates	130	—	16,000	—	21
United Kingdom	153	77.7	4,955	67.8	99
United States	176	73.5	8,612	68.7	99
Upper Volta	3	—	75	32.1	7
Uruguay	139	83.0	1,710	65.5	94
USSR	346	62.0	2,600	64.0	99
Venezuela	107	75.1	2,772	66.4	82
Vietnam	18	—	150	43.2	75
Yemen	8	—	475	37.3	12
Yugoslavia	131	38.6	3,109	65.4	85
Zaire	2	30.3	127	41.9	30
Zambia	5	39.3	414	44.3	49
Zimbabwe	9	19.6	579	49.8	30

INTERNAL-MOTIVATION EXPERIMENTS

Experiment 1

Task Label*	Protestant Work Ethic	Leisure Ethic	Type A Personality	Anagrams Solved	Time Spent on Word Game
1	66	59	51	13	80
1	98	39	45	37	—†
1	82	43	48	17	40
1	101	49	47	20	—†
1	74	46	52	10	—†
1	71	52	56	15	254
1	95	50	57	14	327

* 1 = work, 2 = leisure.
† Case excluded from all further analyses. The authors write, "For the first six subjects [those marked with a dagger in this list], the instructions ... permitted the subject to do 'anything you want.' Several subjects did their homework assignments. This obviously ruined the measure of intrinsic motivation, because homework is a 'work' activity and could be motivated by either extrinsic or intrinsic motivations. The instructions were therefore modified to specify that the subject should either work the task or do nothing (relax)."

(continued)

Experiment 1 (*continued*)

Task Label*	Protestant Work Ethic	Leisure Ethic	Type A Personality	Anagrams Solved	Time Spent on Word Game
1	68	54	35	21	0
1	92	40	47	10	630
1	90	41	39	25	385
1	69	38	43	10	350
1	77	47	35	26	170
1	92	52	40	13	210
1	82	60	52	20	135
1	78	58	45	20	220
1	73	43	26	26	85
1	89	53	43	11	205
1	75	51	30	19	150
1	87	41	43	11	330
1	88	48	34	13	95
1	73	45	40	17	360
1	82	48	49	27	370
1	86	55	43	15	555
1	95	53	53	30	440
1	96	46	56	13	250
1	84	60	39	22	545
1	73	53	53	27	85
1	65	57	31	11	30
1	62	60	35	24	3
1	59	55	28	11	0
1	65	50	43	11	335
2	77	55	49	31	—†
2	94	35	49	10	—†
2	61	54	49	15	—†
2	71	52	24	29	331
2	93	59	41	16	0
2	75	44	44	8	40
2	69	53	29	14	388
2	57	61	51	24	30
2	78	49	38	7	0
2	59	54	19	4	35
2	78	50	36	19	165

(*continued*)

Task Label*	Protestant Work Ethic	Leisure Ethic	Type A Personality	Anagrams Solved	Time Spent on Word Game
2	88	40	34	16	295
2	83	40	38	5	85
2	90	42	38	12	520
2	66	39	48	10	290
2	65	58	27	34	130
2	98	45	49	18	50
2	83	40	37	3	120
2	99	47	38	16	245
2	65	46	37	27	505
2	73	49	39	17	520
2	82	57	47	20	510
2	87	45	50	6	352
2	79	44	40	21	300
2	103	55	52	16	205
2	92	37	38	13	140
2	91	37	42	8	40
2	60	39	35	19	330
2	97	46	52	24	143

Experiment 2

Observation Type*	Protestant Work Ethic	Leisure Ethic	Type A Personality	Time Spent on Word Game
1	102	31	51	900
1	100	47	47	665
1	96	50	50	570
1	94	51	41	871
1	90	42	52	900
1	89	37	43	35
1	88	37	37	815
1	88	41	41	820
1	87	48	38	392

* 1 = public, 2 = private. See Exercise 3 at the end of Chapter 2.

(continued)

Experiment 2 (continued)

Observation Type*	Protestant Work Ethic	Leisure Ethic	Type A Personality	Time Spent on Word Game
1	84	48	43	700
1	83	48	28	0
1	82	38	31	109
1	81	50	46	760
1	80	38	44	900
1	79	55	38	767
1	77	44	46	583
1	76	44	46	25
1	74	48	45	0
1	70	34	48	900
1	69	39	51	785
2	101	45	59	182
2	99	30	49	275
2	97	32	39	130
2	94	47	50	0
2	94	46	46	176
2	89	51	55	208
2	89	42	52	30
2	88	39	46	885
2	87	40	37	225
2	85	35	38	897
2	81	38	42	502
2	80	41	47	900
2	79	43	38	30
2	79	46	43	397
2	78	47	42	756
2	76	55	28	0
2	72	50	57	292
2	72	47	18	3
2	71	52	33	0
2	70	58	45	0

HOSPITAL COSTS

Doctor	DRG	Complications[1]	Discharges	ALOS,[2] days	Specialization[3]	Total Cost,[4] $	Surgery, % of Total Cost	Diagnosis, % of Total Cost	Material and Technology, % of Total Cost
01	370	1	1	5.0	50	2527	2	3	20
01	371	0	4	4.0	50	1962	3	8	17
01	372	1	1	2.0	50	740	2	2	6
01	373	0	28	1.9	50	1074	1	7	17
01	374	0	2	2.0	50	1434	30	2	11
01	378	0	1	6.0	50	3197	22	9	16
01	380	0	1	1.0	50	1053	0	20	8
01	382	0	2	1.0	50	158	0	4	3
01	384	0	6	1.0	50	521	0	9	6
02	370	1	2	4.0	47	1673	4	3	21
02	371	0	7	4.4	47	2513	7	9	14
02	372	1	1	1.0	47	986	2	4	14
02	373	0	24	2.0	47	990	2	5	11
02	374	0	1	3.0	47	1663	25	2	9
02	381	0	1	1.0	47	1491	15	10	16
02	382	0	1	1.0	47	240	0	39	18
02	383	1	1	1.0	47	536	0	24	15
03	370	1	4	4.8	61	4146	1	18	14

03	371	0	12	4.6	61	2736	6	11	18
03	372	1	5	2.0	61	1834	19	8	14
03	373	0	40	1.8	61	973	2	14	12
03	374	0	2	2.5	61	1499	29	3	14
03	378	0	1	6.0	61	5954	13	5	8
03	379	0	7	1.0	61	652	0	11	5
03	382	0	9	1.0	61	222	0	41	11
03	383	1	7	2.0	61	2766	0	13	9
03	384	0	4	1.0	61	1380	18	16	9
04	371	0	9	4.6	63	2109	3	4	27
04	372	1	2	2.0	63	1436	4	11	8
04	373	0	30	2.2	63	1095	1	16	10
04	374	0	1	3.0	63	1750	23	2	15
04	381	0	2	3.5	63	1198	10	6	8
04	382	0	3	1.0	63	88	0	7	10
04	384	0	4	1.0	63	344	0	3	18
05	371	0	1	4.0	95	2182	3	4	17
05	373	0	2	1.0	95	860	2	8	11
05	382	0	2	1.0	95	66	0	0	6
06	372	1	1	2.0	94	1177	1	6	26
06	373	0	11	2.0	94	1054	2	21	8

(continued)

HOSPITAL COSTS (continued)

Doctor	DRG	Complications[1]	Discharges	ALOS,[2] days	Specialization[3]	Total Cost,[4] $	Surgery, % of Total Cost	Diagnosis, % of Total Cost	Material and Technology, % of Total Cost
06	382	0	2	1.0	94	541	0	40	16
07	370	1	3	4.3	55	2531	2	3	15
07	371	0	11	4.5	55	2523	2	11	12
07	372	1	3	2.0	55	884	7	3	12
07	373	0	56	1.9	55	1636	1	15	6
07	378	0	5	3.0	55	3571	13	6	8
07	379	0	1	1.0	55	507	0	14	14
07	380	0	1	1.0	55	873	2	4	11
07	382	0	8	1.0	55	126	0	26	2
07	383	1	2	1.0	55	688	0	26	16
07	384	0	3	1.0	55	1104	26	26	14
08	373	0	8	2.1	92	956	2	8	11
08	382	0	1	1.0	92	67	0	0	10
09	373	0	2	2.0	93	1000	1	2	10
09	383	1	2	1.0	93	1031	0	14	26
10	372	1	2	2.0	75	1204	1	4	19
10	373	0	5	1.4	75	1075	1	15	9
10	382	0	2	1.0	75	63	0	0	0
10	384	0	3	1.0	75	92	0	0	0
11	371	0	18	3.9	62	2664	2	7	16

11	372	1	2	2.5	62	1143	1	16	11
11	373	0	66	1.9	62	1035	2	13	10
11	380	0	5	1.0	62	1075	0	8	7
11	381	0	3	1.0	62	1663	1	12	9
11	382	0	3	1.0	62	164	0	27	14
11	383	1	4	1.5	62	1671	27	4	16
11	384	0	5	1.0	62	619	0	30	13
12	371	0	2	5.0	67	2385	3	7	15
12	372	1	1	2.0	67	1224	1	3	10
12	373	0	9	1.9	67	1126	1	14	13
12	379	0	2	3.0	67	3535	18	9	13
12	382	0	2	1.0	67	327	0	7	42
12	384	0	4	3.5	67	2857	1	7	2
13	372	1	3	1.7	90	2065	1	12	18
13	373	0	5	2.2	90	901	2	5	14
13	383	1	1	1.0	90	282	0	10	0
13	384	0	1	1.0	90	199	0	48	0
14	371	0	2	5.0	90	2161	3	3	19
14	372	1	1	2.0	90	1099	1	5	16
14	373	0	5	1.6	90	1078	2	6	12
14	382	0	2	1.0	90	117	0	6	3

(continued)

HOSPITAL COSTS (*continued*)

Doctor	DRG	Complications[1]	Discharges	ALOS,[2] days	Specialization[3]	Total Cost,[4] $	Surgery, % of Total Cost	Diagnosis, % of Total Cost	Material and Technology, % of Total Cost
15	370	1	1	5.0	86	1699	4	4	24
15	372	1	1	1.0	86	1316	1	7	13
15	373	0	24	1.5	86	1272	1	17	8
15	374	0	1	4.0	86	1476	24	1	9
15	379	0	2	1.0	86	1122	0	14	0
15	382	0	8	1.0	86	337	0	44	19
15	383	1	1	1.0	86	1058	0	19	6
16	373	0	3	1.7	97	992	2	7	11
17	370	1	4	4.3	63	2213	3	5	22
17	371	0	23	3.9	63	3188	14	9	16
17	372	1	3	2.0	63	1433	1	3	15
17	373	0	65	1.9	63	1709	1	38	8
17	374	0	4	2.8	63	2086	23	4	9
17	376	0	1	4.0	63	491	0	9	12
17	378	0	1	4.0	63	3978	20	6	9
17	379	0	7	1.0	63	1627	0	13	1
17	380	0	3	1.0	63	1069	1	6	7
17	381	0	1	1.0	63	757	2	7	8
17	382	0	8	1.0	63	147	0	13	21

17	383	1	7	1.6	63	1089	0	25	17
17	384	0	7	1.0	63	1737	28	17	9
18	370	1	1	4.0	84	1874	3	5	20
18	372	1	1	1.0	84	1466	1	5	15
18	373	0	3	2.0	84	767	2	6	12
18	379	0	1	1.0	84	218	0	30	0
18	383	1	1	1.0	84	111	0	23	0
18	384	0	4	1.0	84	222	0	0	4
19	371	0	2	5.0	85	2378	3	4	16
19	372	1	1	1.0	85	1143	1	10	12
19	373	0	15	2.3	85	1143	1	8	10
19	382	0	1	1.0	85	145	0	10	0
19	384	0	1	1.0	85	98	0	0	0
20	370	1	1	5.0	89	7001	6	9	27
20	372	1	1	2.0	89	937	2	4	13
20	373	0	11	1.5	89	964	2	9	10
20	382	0	1	1.0	89	311	0	37	30
21	371	0	3	4.7	63	2596	2	4	15
21	373	0	12	2.6	63	1098	1	14	9
21	376	0	1	1.0	63	880	0	10	26
21	378	0	1	3.0	63	3424	18	6	8

(continued)

HOSPITAL COSTS (continued)

Doctor	DRG	Complications[1]	Discharges	ALOS,[2] days	Specialization[3]	Total Cost,[4] $	Surgery, % of Total Cost	Diagnosis, % of Total Cost	Material and Technology, % of Total Cost
21	379	0	3	1.0	63	103	0	0	0
21	382	0	7	1.0	63	136	0	0	2
22	373	0	13	2.1	88	914	2	8	13
22	382	0	3	1.0	88	70	0	0	0
22	384	0	1	1.0	88	115	0	49	10

[1] If the diagnosis contains the phrase "with complications" or "with complicating diagnosis," this variable is coded "1". Otherwise, it is coded "0".
[2] Average Length of Stay. The average number of days spent in the hospital by this doctor's patients discharged in this DRG.
[3] Specialization. This is the percentage of DRGs in which the physician discharged at least one patient that are not in the obstetrical group (DRG 370-384). The higher this percentage, the lower a physician's degree of specialization in obstetrical care.
[4] Total average cost per patient for this physician in this DRG.

List of DRG titles

DRG   Title
370   Cesarean section with complicating diagnosis.
371   Cesarean section without complicating diagnosis.
372   Vaginal delivery with complicating diagnosis.
373   Vaginal delivery without complicating diagnosis.
374   Vaginal delivery with sterilization and/or D&C.
376   Postpartum diagnosis without operative procedure.
377   Postpartum diagnosis with operative procedure.
378   Ectopic pregnancy.
379   Threatened abortion.
380   Abortion without D&C.
381   Abortion with D&C.
382   False labor.
383   Other antepartum diagnosis with medical complications.
384   Other antepartum diagnosis without medical complications.

Appendix B: Statistical Tables

TABLE B.1 Binomial Coefficients

n	$\binom{n}{0}$	$\binom{n}{1}$	$\binom{n}{2}$	$\binom{n}{3}$	$\binom{n}{4}$	$\binom{n}{5}$	$\binom{n}{6}$	$\binom{n}{7}$	$\binom{n}{8}$	$\binom{n}{9}$	$\binom{n}{10}$
0	1										
1	1	1									
2	1	2	1								
3	1	3	3	1							
4	1	4	6	4	1						
5	1	5	10	10	5	1					
6	1	6	15	20	15	6	1				
7	1	7	21	35	35	21	7	1			
8	1	8	28	56	70	56	28	8	1		
9	1	9	36	84	126	126	84	36	9	1	
10	1	10	45	120	210	252	210	120	45	10	1
11	1	11	55	165	330	462	462	330	165	55	11
12	1	12	66	220	495	792	924	792	495	220	66
13	1	13	78	286	715	1,287	1,716	1,716	1,287	715	286
14	1	14	91	364	1,001	2,002	3,003	3,432	3,003	2,002	1,001
15	1	15	105	455	1,365	3,003	5,005	6,435	6,435	5,005	3,003
16	1	16	120	560	1,820	4,368	8,008	11,440	12,870	11,440	8,008
17	1	17	136	680	2,380	6,188	12,376	19,448	24,310	24,310	19,448
18	1	18	153	816	3,060	8,568	18,564	31,824	43,758	48,620	43,758
19	1	19	171	969	3,876	11,628	27,132	50,388	75,582	92,378	92,378
20	1	20	190	1,140	4,845	15,504	38,760	77,520	125,970	167,960	184,756

If necessary, use the identity

$$\binom{n}{k} = \binom{n}{n-k}$$

From John E. Freund, *Statistics, A First Course*, Prentice-Hall, Englewood Cliffs, N.J., 1970, p. 313. Reprinted by permission.

TABLE B.2 Binomial Probabilities $\left[\binom{n}{x} \cdot p^x q^{n-x} \right]$

n	x	.01	.05	.10	.20	.30	.40	.50	.60	.70	.80	.90	.95	.99	x
2	0	980	902	810	640	490	360	250	160	090	040	010	002	0+	0
	1	020	095	180	320	420	480	500	480	420	320	180	095	020	1
	2	0+	002	010	040	090	160	250	360	490	640	810	902	980	2
3	0	970	857	729	512	343	216	125	064	027	008	001	0+	0+	0
	1	029	135	243	384	441	432	375	288	189	096	027	007	0+	1
	2	0+	007	027	096	189	288	375	432	441	384	243	135	029	2
	3	0+	0+	001	008	027	064	125	216	343	512	729	857	970	3
4	0	961	815	656	410	240	130	062	026	008	002	0+	0+	0+	0
	1	039	171	292	410	412	346	250	154	076	026	004	0+	0+	1
	2	001	014	049	154	265	346	375	346	265	154	049	014	001	2
	3	0+	0+	004	026	076	154	250	346	412	410	292	171	039	3
	4	0+	0+	0+	002	008	026	062	130	240	410	656	815	961	4
5	0	951	774	590	328	168	078	031	010	002	0+	0+	0+	0+	0
	1	048	204	328	410	360	259	156	077	028	006	0+	0+	0+	1
	2	001	021	073	205	309	346	312	230	132	051	008	001	0+	2
	3	0+	001	008	051	132	230	312	346	309	205	073	021	001	3
	4	0+	0+	0+	006	028	077	156	259	360	410	328	204	048	4
	5	0+	0+	0+	0+	002	010	031	078	168	328	590	774	951	5
6	0	941	735	531	262	118	047	016	004	001	0+	0+	0+	0+	0
	1	057	232	354	393	303	187	094	037	010	002	0+	0+	0+	1
	2	001	031	098	246	324	311	234	138	060	015	001	0+	0+	2
	3	0+	002	015	082	185	276	312	276	185	082	015	002	0+	3
	4	0+	0+	001	015	060	138	234	311	324	246	098	031	001	4
	5	0+	0+	0+	002	010	037	094	187	303	393	354	232	057	5
	6	0+	0+	0+	0+	001	004	016	047	118	262	531	735	941	6
7	0	932	698	478	210	082	028	008	002	0+	0+	0+	0+	0+	0
	1	066	257	372	367	247	131	055	017	004	0+	0+	0+	0+	1
	2	002	041	124	275	318	261	164	077	025	004	0+	0+	0+	2
	3	0+	004	023	115	227	290	273	194	097	029	003	0+	0+	3
	4	0+	0+	003	029	097	194	273	290	227	115	023	004	0+	4
	5	0+	0+	0+	004	025	077	164	261	318	275	124	041	002	5
	6	0+	0+	0+	0+	004	017	055	131	247	367	372	257	066	6
	7	0+	0+	0+	0+	0+	002	008	028	082	210	478	698	932	7
8	0	923	663	430	168	058	017	004	001	0+	0+	0+	0+	0+	0
	1	075	279	383	336	198	090	031	008	001	0+	0+	0+	0+	1
	2	003	051	149	294	296	209	109	041	010	001	0+	0+	0+	2
	3	0+	005	033	147	254	279	219	124	047	009	0+	0+	0+	3
	4	0+	0+	005	046	136	232	273	232	136	046	005	0+	0+	4
	5	0+	0+	0+	009	047	124	219	279	254	147	033	005	0+	5
	6	0+	0+	0+	001	010	041	109	209	296	294	149	051	003	6
	7	0+	0+	0+	0+	001	008	031	090	198	336	383	279	075	7
	8	0+	0+	0+	0+	0+	001	004	017	058	168	430	663	923	8

(continued)

TABLE B.2 (*continued*)

n	x	.01	.05	.10	.20	.30	.40	p .50	.60	.70	.80	.90	.95	.99	x
9	0	914	630	387	134	040	010	002	0+	0+	0+	0+	0+	0+	0
	1	083	299	387	302	156	060	018	004	0+	0+	0+	0+	0+	1
	2	003	063	172	302	267	161	070	021	004	0+	0+	0+	0+	2
	3	0+	008	045	176	267	251	164	074	021	003	0+	0+	0+	3
	4	0+	001	007	066	172	251	246	167	074	017	001	0+	0+	4
	5	0+	0+	001	017	074	167	246	251	172	066	007	001	0+	5
	6	0+	0+	0+	003	021	074	164	251	267	176	045	008	0+	6
	7	0+	0+	0+	0+	004	021	070	161	267	302	172	063	003	7
	8	0+	0+	0+	0+	0+	004	018	060	156	302	387	299	083	8
	9	0+	0+	0+	0+	0+	0+	002	010	040	134	387	630	914	9
10	0	904	599	349	107	028	006	001	0+	0+	0+	0+	0+	0+	0
	1	091	315	387	268	121	040	010	002	0+	0+	0+	0+	0+	1
	2	004	075	194	302	233	121	044	011	001	0+	0+	0+	0+	2
	3	0+	010	057	201	267	215	117	042	009	001	0+	0+	0+	3
	4	0+	001	011	088	200	251	205	111	037	006	0+	0+	0+	4
	5	0+	0+	001	026	103	201	246	201	103	026	001	0+	0+	5
	6	0+	0+	0+	006	037	111	205	251	200	088	011	001	0+	6
	7	0+	0+	0+	001	009	042	117	215	267	201	057	010	0+	7
	8	0+	0+	0+	0+	001	011	044	121	233	302	194	075	004	8
	9	0+	0+	0+	0+	0+	002	010	040	121	268	387	315	091	9
	10	0+	0+	0+	0+	0+	0+	001	006	028	107	349	599	904	10
11	0	895	569	314	086	020	004	0+	0+	0+	0+	0+	0+	0+	0
	1	099	329	384	236	093	027	005	001	0+	0+	0+	0+	0+	1
	2	005	087	213	295	200	089	027	005	001	0+	0+	0+	0+	2
	3	0+	014	071	221	257	177	081	023	004	0+	0+	0+	0+	3
	4	0+	001	016	111	220	236	161	070	017	002	0+	0+	0+	4
	5	0+	0+	002	039	132	221	226	147	057	010	0+	0+	0+	5
	6	0+	0+	0+	010	057	147	226	221	132	039	002	0+	0+	6
	7	0+	0+	0+	002	017	070	161	236	220	111	016	001	0+	7
	8	0+	0+	0+	0+	004	023	081	177	257	221	071	014	0+	8
	9	0+	0+	0+	0+	001	005	027	089	200	295	213	087	005	9
	10	0+	0+	0+	0+	0+	001	005	027	093	236	384	329	099	10
	11	0+	0+	0+	0+	0+	0+	0+	004	020	086	314	569	895	11
12	0	886	540	282	069	014	002	0+	0+	0+	0+	0+	0+	0+	0
	1	107	341	377	206	071	017	003	0+	0+	0+	0+	0+	0+	1
	2	006	099	230	283	168	064	016	002	0+	0+	0+	0+	0+	2
	3	0+	017	085	236	240	142	054	012	001	0+	0+	0+	0+	3
	4	0+	002	021	133	231	213	121	042	008	001	0+	0+	0+	4
	5	0+	0+	004	053	158	227	193	101	029	003	0+	0+	0+	5
	6	0+	0+	0+	016	079	177	226	177	079	016	0+	0+	0+	6
	7	0+	0+	0+	003	029	101	193	227	158	053	004	0+	0+	7
	8	0+	0+	0+	001	008	042	121	213	231	133	021	002	0+	8
	9	0+	0+	0+	0+	001	012	054	142	240	236	085	017	0+	9

TABLE B.3 Standard Normal Curve Areas

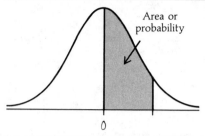

Area or probability

Entries in this table give the area under the curve between the mean and z standard deviations above the mean. For example, for $z = 2.25$, the area under the curve between the mean and z is .4878.

z	.00	.01	.02	.03	.04	.05	.06	.07	.08	.09
.0	.0000	.0040	.0080	.0120	.0160	.0199	.0239	.0279	.0319	.0359
.1	.0398	.0438	.0478	.0517	.0557	.0596	.0636	.0675	.0714	.0753
.2	.0793	.0832	.0871	.0910	.0948	.0987	.1026	.1064	.1103	.1141
.3	.1179	.1217	.1255	.1293	.1331	.1368	.1406	.1443	.1480	.1517
.4	.1554	.1591	.1628	.1664	.1700	.1736	.1772	.1808	.1844	.1879
.5	.1915	.1950	.1985	.2019	.2054	.2088	.2123	.2157	.2190	.2224
.6	.2257	.2291	.2324	.2357	.2389	.2422	.2454	.2486	.2518	.2549
.7	.2580	.2612	.2642	.2673	.2704	.2734	.2764	.2794	.2823	.2852
.8	.2881	.2910	.2939	.2967	.2995	.3023	.3051	.3078	.3106	.3133
.9	.3159	.3186	.3212	.3238	.3264	.3289	.3315	.3340	.3365	.3389
1.0	.3413	.3438	.3461	.3485	.3508	.3531	.3554	.3577	.3599	.3621
1.1	.3643	.3665	.3686	.3708	.3729	.3749	.3770	.3790	.3810	.3830
1.2	.3849	.3869	.3888	.3907	.3925	.3944	.3962	.3980	.3997	.4015
1.3	.4032	.4049	.4066	.4082	.4099	.4115	.4131	.4147	.4162	.4177
1.4	.4192	.4207	.4222	.4236	.4251	.4265	.4279	.4292	.4306	.4319
1.5	.4332	.4345	.4357	.4370	.4382	.4394	.4406	.4418	.4429	.4441
1.6	.4452	.4463	.4474	.4484	.4495	.4505	.4515	.4525	.4535	.4545
1.7	.4554	.4564	.4573	.4582	.4591	.4599	.4608	.4616	.4625	.4633
1.8	.4641	.4649	.4656	.4664	.4671	.4678	.4686	.4693	.4699	.4706
1.9	.4713	.4719	.4726	.4732	.4738	.4744	.4750	.4756	.4761	.4767
2.0	.4772	.4778	.4783	.4788	.4793	.4798	.4803	.4808	.4812	.4817
2.1	.4821	.4826	.4830	.4834	.4838	.4842	.4846	.4850	.4854	.4857
2.2	.4861	.4864	.4868	.4871	.4875	.4878	.4881	.4884	.4887	.4890
2.3	.4893	.4896	.4898	.4901	.4904	.4906	.4909	.4911	.4913	.4916
2.4	.4918	.4920	.4922	.4925	.4927	.4929	.4931	.4932	.4934	.4936
2.5	.4938	.4940	.4941	.4943	.4945	.4946	.4948	.4949	.4951	.4952
2.6	.4953	.4955	.4956	.4957	.4959	.4960	.4961	.4962	.4963	.4964
2.7	.4965	.4966	.4967	.4968	.4969	.4970	.4971	.4972	.4973	.4974
2.8	.4974	.4975	.4976	.4977	.4977	.4978	.4979	.4979	.4980	.4981
2.9	.4981	.4982	.4982	.4983	.4984	.4984	.4985	.4985	.4986	.4986
3.0	.4986	.4987	.4987	.4988	.4988	.4989	.4989	.4989	.4990	.4990
3.1	.4990	.4991	.4991	.4991	.4992	.4992	.4992	.4992	.4993	.4993
3.2	.4993	.4993	.4994	.4994	.4994	.4994	.4994	.4995	.4995	.4995
3.3	.4995	.4995	.4995	.4996	.4996	.4996	.4996	.4996	.4996	.4997
3.4	.4997	.4997	.4997	.4997	.4997	.4997	.4997	.4997	.4997	.4998
3.6	.4998	.4998	.4999	.4999	.4999	.4999	.4999	.4999	.4999	.4999
3.9	.5000									

Source: The National Bureau of Standards, *Tables of Normal Probability Functions*, Applied Mathematics Series, no. 23 (Washington Government Printing Office, 1953). The original contains probabilities for values of z from 0 to 8.285, mostly in increments of .0001, and for areas from $\mu - z$ to $\mu + z$.

TABLE B.4 Table of Random Numbers

I.	1–4	5–8	9–12	13–16	17–20	21–24	25–28	29–32
1	74 44	80 91	21 41	40 25	98 81	57 12	30 13	24 93
2	72 59	62 28	26 74	90 62	91 20	70 31	19 10	23 06
3	33 76	63 60	48 79	23 76	28 61	87 65	79 30	38 27
4	78 02	65 54	17 61	60 15	00 81	18 07	66 38	88 33
5	32 46	64 91	77 63	26 35	94 81	54 90	10 70	10 66
6	19 68	47 39	30 75	39 71	13 14	55 59	25 38	79 00
7	06 34	06 19	72 70	53 47	57 70	04 07	54 81	04 98
8	62 23	31 49	29 34	39 38	99 54	66 13	94 08	17 03
9	97 69	04 44	89 07	31 84	66 59	86 21	61 78	60 26
10	71 00	49 40	32 08	38 57	58 59	69 72	31 52	94 75
11	32 40	60 49	51 52	47 01	29 40	59 31	14 60	26 91
12	63 42	42 91	61 34	02 22	44 76	88 32	06 36	71 39
13	09 20	12 10	05 86	08 66	45 84	84 80	69 45	65 08
14	62 50	89 39	48 02	24 64	45 60	20 27	83 65	33 82
15	73 95	05 00	52 98	08 57	74 19	05 58	27 46	23 26
16	62 43	84 11	42 38	74 13	04 57	80 26	28 04	20 52
17	07 00	14 93	55 80	14 27	69 56	24 43	30 82	55 08
18	83 26	52 43	70 61	67 23	07 36	49 78	40 25	09 66
19	14 67	02 60	21 02	64 47	54 86	62 88	81 12	28 29
20	33 60	94 02	89 25	44 73	03 85	01 95	17 85	70 51
21	02 73	10 59	69 74	76 11	57 27	04 63	94 15	74 96
22	75 46	82 03	13 43	64 34	96 68	23 86	38 49	83 98
23	79 06	02 26	58 82	81 17	91 27	44 27	71 89	17 90
24	85 16	88 13	08 97	13 08	73 28	25 34	79 27	16 34
25	37 30	30 55	08 17	55 15	93 34	10 60	00 95	60 26

II.								
1	24 25	56 63	72 28	28 39	91 61	34 21	52 63	73 21
2	50 63	56 77	89 77	80 28	03 14	79 27	86 26	35 33
3	03 65	03 42	90 08	30 90	14 39	85 94	74 39	97 71
4	63 60	97 32	86 61	10 39	07 30	89 99	09 11	21 55
5	54 69	75 00	63 95	78 98	01 93	93 77	57 30	50 82
6	88 05	23 40	46 42	52 55	27 85	28 12	00 51	23 76
7	97 38	25 33	16 78	32 87	47 58	19 34	31 76	44 97
8	03 12	82 62	94 17	66 36	56 10	23 73	50 93	15 55
9	19 66	44 73	79 92	31 66	72 70	27 72	90 95	46 77
10	46 32	77 62	36 51	73 93	57 25	09 15	50 30	50 95
11	40 78	23 70	51 26	87 86	69 22	21 85	62 27	39 01
12	20 66	67 60	26 95	80 64	02 42	97 88	48 34	27 23
13	97 77	58 66	34 10	91 71	94 82	79 59	14 11	53 84
14	91 93	21 80	20 91	19 52	71 42	20 08	35 28	35 91
15	14 88	89 71	48 84	32 22	13 63	78 02	72 97	61 13
16	90 97	01 01	01 59	01 39	96 96	74 40	66 88	44 01
17	85 29	86 31	19 55	37 86	04 56	98 35	78 82	29 06
18	22 06	90 91	84 64	81 65	63 51	54 35	94 73	79 48
19	53 69	65 88	46 28	13 02	00 17	27 22	69 94	45 92
20	66 42	58 45	92 71	40 83	59 73	64 04	42 92	38 84
21	91 09	52 38	46 27	17 09	95 13	43 45	80 94	98 07
22	88 72	65 18	16 79	80 82	75 47	29 46	95 09	91 01
23	86 63	79 92	70 95	28 32	95 25	95 25	81 18	30 16
24	46 70	03 50	46 40	34 78	59 35	93 12	24 69	37 37
25	25 50	24 15	01 82	38 36	21 15	71 91	31 52	52 51

(continued)

TABLE B.4 Table of Random Numbers (*continued*)

III.	1–4	5–8	9–12	13–16	17–20	21–24	25–28	29–32
1	81 18	43 25	80 75	71 96	48 88	91 61	85 37	12 99
2	30 49	80 30	38 91	62 72	55 48	26 82	31 66	09 47
3	47 11	18 80	57 00	16 38	30 49	09 74	15 77	52 68
4	00 31	08 24	87 17	23 04	98 29	30 98	14 95	03 98
5	24 25	33 96	83 92	12 02	80 63	80 41	49 40	62 49
6	93 06	35 71	31 25	38 38	01 14	75 19	72 11	92 52
7	45 33	21 67	02 64	92 85	74 74	82 52	68 19	23 78
8	44 45	81 92	53 10	78 28	17 76	84 74	60 37	34 08
9	95 75	30 09	08 93	87 71	68 63	71 84	96 91	86 02
10	13 99	84 18	43 72	24 15	33 59	11 97	95 69	24 43
11	46 15	99 32	14 87	23 20	44 45	84 19	35 65	20 97
12	74 00	80 33	52 32	96 66	57 94	25 86	63 40	57 70
13	59 47	85 05	51 89	52 12	75 48	61 99	99 11	48 07
14	84 22	38 10	92 68	34 81	15 10	03 01	30 59	79 03
15	58 57	59 12	18 06	15 63	10 13	58 18	49 60	64 86
16	13 95	54 28	92 78	95 64	71 57	33 08	46 27	18 31
17	77 32	46 87	82 56	39 99	81 79	87 57	12 82	24 62
18	52 58	01 90	82 77	99 53	71 20	22 50	41 28	99 16
19	73 26	35 54	15 57	67 00	28 84	47 57	10 46	36 12
20	86 83	39 22	37 11	93 21	01 40	14 71	20 98	40 01
21	12 70	37 38	82 24	18 01	45 58	72 29	70 45	18 50
22	41 31	79 58	62 06	58 38	72 38	13 63	51 70	38 27
23	24 40	09 84	72 10	84 64	50 20	85 02	37 12	46 34
24	99 76	09 25	14 33	44 93	20 35	18 69	50 99	24 73
25	29 74	34 46	74 62	58 08	68 78	60 16	83 98	86 80

IV.	1–4	5–8	9–12	13–16	17–20	21–24	25–28	29–32
1	81 66	77 08	85 13	41 90	28 77	60 13	59 55	15 05
2	32 42	50 81	08 01	90 10	43 28	89 50	05 42	05 95
3	11 50	29 08	16 39	76 94	70 66	53 71	23 03	41 38
4	93 65	51 22	55 70	86 61	59 58	64 86	29 00	65 26
5	33 43	08 85	65 24	55 58	73 81	50 89	58 50	57 14
6	59 87	34 45	41 02	32 95	98 53	54 21	95 66	01 13
7	15 52	12 97	14 84	23 98	01 13	04 26	20 79	37 97
8	75 02	13 24	27 60	50 77	97 95	06 07	52 64	86 71
9	14 52	99 22	31 39	70 43	58 93	43 52	61 47	51 75
10	59 22	81 73	42 89	96 56	46 75	39 39	37 10	70 70
11	12 07	71 71	64 45	62 43	10 27	48 73	88 72	28 81
12	51 12	39 78	31 47	77 80	94 00	57 79	54 64	08 44
13	25 52	91 93	90 49	05 47	33 28	40 98	13 85	92 30
14	30 63	79 24	45 48	15 83	74 00	62 15	54 44	71 02
15	84 21	76 60	10 79	48 36	76 51	74 52	04 72	96 63
16	02 22	20 00	82 36	33 25	60 45	80 70	93 29	33 61
17	77 24	43 56	80 48	10 29	45 33	44 14	19 76	26 11
18	62 79	14 00	69 80	81 05	33 52	93 34	10 31	55 89
19	76 87	06 38	98 93	50 50	06 33	95 12	52 93	92 72
20	18 90	97 14	95 07	88 30	69 06	75 51	75 45	32 65
21	17 27	41 02	29 40	58 56	16 66	35 38	58 29	04 01
22	94 73	05 06	86 43	55 58	55 70	43 35	53 80	43 49
23	68 94	03 23	79 95	89 33	64 51	68 19	87 45	29 13
24	96 34	44 78	24 04	72 98	17 07	13 28	49 56	68 69
25	53 55	99 99	13 59	25 54	41 52	27 17	05 74	28 03

(*continued*)

TABLE B.4 Table of Random Numbers (*continued*)

V.	1–4	5–8	9–12	13–16	17–20	21–24	25–28	29–32
1	61 81	17 59	68 00	35 10	30 90	59 71	09 95	01 14
2	78 95	64 65	24 82	14 05	27 63	33 96	10 41	88 70
3	84 28	44 68	07 47	21 46	56 81	32 87	28 40	40 50
4	92 33	63 98	99 22	09 21	97 18	10 03	79 46	17 13
5	15 79	75 50	29 36	12 37	63 39	02 47	57 02	97 17
6	80 16	09 75	22 28	35 25	53 57	72 64	09 98	63 50
7	68 20	33 03	43 73	80 96	21 13	97 61	90 37	35 77
8	55 26	85 04	30 60	68 10	73 53	89 35	58 45	83 23
9	60 00	37 51	42 89	52 32	46 00	57 02	71 97	44 16
10	59 69	31 20	16 37	66 34	99 76	07 23	40 85	64 91
11	84 42	33 66	58 54	17 16	45 73	67 20	09 27	90 96
12	57 46	65 19	78 34	57 12	77 45	54 65	17 17	30 90
13	78 17	51 47	69 22	41 48	01 99	66 46	00 28	21 74
14	27 66	33 21	49 11	24 15	33 70	06 95	04 67	98 56
15	82 54	98 27	81 86	77 35	87 56	32 72	60 90	26 75
16	33 06	79 71	73 57	96 74	85 94	36 97	87 79	82 00
17	77 94	61 11	69 61	78 78	36 51	45 21	82 94	39 22
18	87 15	49 66	56 55	34 99	05 26	45 35	59 83	55 47
19	24 98	52 45	79 85	15 67	32 21	29 94	98 90	02 27
20	05 66	15 23	83 66	24 98	06 75	60 69	64 26	58 24
21	84 90	70 29	01 36	90 78	56 40	61 00	58 40	75 37
22	49 50	30 71	87 38	70 10	80 71	12 54	60 76	62 13
23	27 53	95 47	04 78	61 85	56 15	71 76	25 31	96 39
24	56 17	07 83	96 29	88 39	67 86	98 23	95 03	82 62
25	41 67	05 42	29 18	54 76	71 82	04 81	82 63	00 23
VI.								
1	59 63	29 38	35 59	02 05	68 55	03 47	95 17	41 48
2	11 94	21 16	54 90	92 80	80 91	71 76	54 03	81 00
3	97 62	76 15	96 67	40 92	96 85	18 84	70 89	87 05
4	07 02	78 73	21 58	12 95	04 96	66 91	42 11	11 86
5	13 40	90 19	67 10	34 15	62 59	21 10	30 33	62 02
6	45 48	25 79	20 34	96 33	32 28	66 64	75 37	10 31
7	41 01	61 47	38 60	24 86	08 42	37 27	16 65	20 86
8	49 89	46 70	52 25	93 67	00 76	10 78	72 86	63 18
9	83 90	36 74	50 40	54 90	71 78	80 65	48 29	01 80
10	94 53	17 86	40 96	47 83	02 53	42 68	21 55	96 13
11	73 09	63 85	30 66	78 74	91 82	64 54	81 95	50 35
12	42 47	76 36	12 49	28 49	39 61	49 16	69 42	98 75
13	36 77	54 32	75 18	69 35	54 26	99 87	86 21	94 49
14	65 15	36 03	51 29	64 85	08 56	58 27	32 20	94 21
15	25 25	78 24	08 31	20 26	82 28	54 65	30 00	70 33
16	61 33	06 70	01 51	70 43	38 01	21 94	08 89	77 54
17	59 55	83 53	92 99	57 59	52 24	07 21	82 57	97 42
18	54 63	59 93	45 39	87 90	49 18	71 36	19 88	79 46
19	42 26	36 54	15 06	45 23	61 47	59 31	30 37	08 64
20	84 41	06 96	39 93	14 09	66 32	58 24	55 92	10 76
21	77 00	01 88	33 81	04 10	26 96	38 07	08 44	34 62
22	92 12	15 04	18 73	45 98	64 20	60 93	35 60	29 32
23	59 19	35 73	78 60	18 44	27 97	71 69	44 70	30 76
24	83 17	41 05	62 05	10 84	51 42	68 31	85 75	87 63
25	74 41	13 36	38 79	52 23	86 67	34 06	15 75	62 86

(continued)

TABLE B.4 Table of Random Numbers (*continued*)

VII.	1-4	5-8	9-12	13-16	17-20	21-24	25-28	29-32
1	38 72	32 95	74 46	76 67	68 09	89 22	60 57	82 64
2	11 82	49 29	40 38	95 27	81 69	93 47	66 37	58 35
3	95 03	45 03	70 47	62 85	98 97	30 77	42 07	56 81
4	27 08	80 32	56 82	94 55	08 77	65 06	96 89	25 01
5	85 28	95 84	92 94	24 58	44 70	29 77	51 65	30 77
6	24 20	59 89	51 58	35 01	11 42	28 86	74 92	98 59
7	43 99	91 57	41 65	31 50	92 26	73 23	69 01	73 61
8	60 40	15 37	73 20	69 70	55 57	15 29	04 80	55 84
9	46 21	83 42	72 91	77 61	43 03	99 51	61 55	95 52
10	65 16	18 75	61 81	63 65	90 58	08 61	91 93	12 82
11	94 09	28 63	60 84	61 72	33 05	21 22	62 33	08 64
12	73 29	16 49	23 94	04 08	56 16	50 82	71 54	41 85
13	40 89	53 52	52 24	71 12	67 11	81 57	14 17	41 61
14	17 26	53 28	16 02	11 05	00 16	90 00	92 59	31 17
15	97 21	81 57	15 12	72 51	77 72	39 16	37 90	14 82
16	95 97	68 82	11 37	52 15	14 17	56 10	38 80	19 31
17	13 74	46 34	72 76	97 12	89 94	79 35	53 65	57 47
18	96 84	74 54	51 90	61 57	86 10	63 29	91 78	63 30
19	07 23	87 56	36 47	49 13	08 05	60 03	41 28	97 32
20	07 30	14 39	08 34	67 36	77 48	42 73	38 26	76 46
21	79 92	18 02	31 87	99 28	29 12	86 94	42 93	92 15
22	67 55	96 52	20 18	23 86	06 70	04 88	18 43	14 06
23	79 27	82 62	05 89	98 67	55 36	11 38	00 68	15 01
24	09 79	13 97	33 12	37 47	52 10	37 21	15 39	17 63
25	54 08	82 23	41 24	83 94	36 43	69 56	55 29	06 16
VIII.								
1	55 75	40 42	28 16	15 56	85 90	22 52	87 75	06 06
2	53 93	89 69	57 62	00 50	26 55	37 24	65 06	64 78
3	84 57	05 82	38 34	07 71	97 01	91 60	45 25	33 38
4	03 05	40 70	93 45	19 14	58 44	31 03	79 85	07 37
5	65 05	52 06	67 02	47 09	67 69	07 49	67 57	91 35
6	50 47	01 71	99 25	67 79	31 22	22 06	54 11	75 95
7	60 33	68 59	90 87	16 12	28 04	74 19	58 23	70 65
8	72 59	23 82	08 63	50 57	22 08	93 19	04 14	97 89
9	90 76	09 09	51 31	94 39	66 42	80 81	52 57	75 01
10	55 08	70 65	08 89	97 03	10 80	17 66	02 34	05 62
11	75 34	83 06	54 74	25 75	21 66	70 25	56 88	94 85
12	35 12	26 18	99 18	94 62	15 26	67 31	20 64	11 94
13	31 34	34 41	42 27	82 69	18 17	43 38	34 60	27 82
14	11 06	90 62	46 36	29 49	61 61	59 17	06 05	30 10
15	45 39	91 03	75 07	44 92	10 88	83 66	36 68	60 00
16	25 39	41 17	27 38	47 37	53 47	24 61	14 26	63 71
17	09 89	05 38	91 35	66 23	35 07	24 25	70 97	04 84
18	05 08	88 91	65 32	98 80	67 94	01 96	67 42	37 23
19	25 77	61 05	66 95	67 51	95 05	31 65	11 81	80 88
20	80 27	99 51	62 04	97 57	64 38	74 62	66 96	88 31
21	77 63	69 24	66 53	10 06	53 68	30 75	58 69	66 09
22	60 36	08 06	17 43	89 37	19 21	29 61	41 54	17 80
23	72 25	43 32	87 36	99 15	39 77	47 45	28 97	90 13
24	82 42	03 82	40 22	17 69	64 42	39 68	44 19	83 56
25	41 38	49 33	89 76	67 76	87 32	94 70	01 81	90 14

TABLE B.5 Student's *t* Distribution

	Level of Significance for One-Tailed Test					
	.10	.05	.025	.01	.005	.0005
	Level of Significance for Two-Tailed Test					
df	.20	.10	.05	.02	.01	.001
1	3.078	6.314	12.706	31.821	63.657	636.619
2	1.886	2.920	4.303	6.965	9.925	31.598
3	1.638	2.353	3.182	4.541	5.841	12.941
4	1.533	2.132	2.776	3.747	4.604	8.610
5	1.476	2.015	2.571	3.365	4.032	6.859
6	1.440	1.943	2.447	3.143	3.707	5.959
7	1.415	1.895	2.365	2.998	3.499	5.405
8	1.397	1.860	2.306	2.896	3.355	5.041
9	1.383	1.833	2.262	2.821	3.250	4.781
10	1.372	1.812	2.228	2.764	3.169	4.587
11	1.363	1.796	2.201	2.718	3.106	4.437
12	1.356	1.782	2.179	2.681	3.055	4.318
13	1.350	1.771	2.160	2.650	3.012	4.221
14	1.345	1.761	2.145	2.624	2.977	4.140
15	1.341	1.753	2.131	2.602	2.947	4.073
16	1.337	1.746	2.120	2.583	2.921	4.015
17	1.333	1.740	2.110	2.567	2.898	3.965
18	1.330	1.734	2.101	2.552	2.878	3.922
19	1.328	1.729	2.093	2.539	2.861	3.883
20	1.325	1.725	2.086	2.528	2.845	3.850
21	1.323	1.721	2.080	2.518	2.831	3.819
22	1.321	1.717	2.074	2.508	2.819	3.792
23	1.319	1.714	2.069	2.500	2.807	3.767
24	1.318	1.711	2.064	2.492	2.797	3.745
25	1.316	1.708	2.060	2.485	2.787	3.725
26	1.315	1.706	2.056	2.479	2.779	3.707
27	1.314	1.703	2.052	2.473	2.771	3.690
28	1.313	1.701	2.048	2.467	2.763	3.674
29	1.311	1.699	2.045	2.462	2.756	3.659
30	1.310	1.697	2.042	2.457	2.750	3.646
40	1.303	1.684	2.021	2.423	2.704	3.551
60	1.296	1.671	2.000	2.390	2.660	3.460
120	1.289	1.658	1.980	2.358	2.617	3.373
∞	1.282	1.645	1.960	2.326	2.576	3.291

* Adapted from Table III of R. A. Fisher and F. Yates, *Statistical Tables for Biological, Agricultural and Medical Research*, 1948 ed. (Edinburgh and London: Oliver & Boyd Limited) by permission of the authors and publishers.

TABLE B.6 Critical Values of χ^2

The first column contains the number of degrees of freedom. The values in the body of the table are the values of χ^2 required for the listed probability levels. For example, a χ^2 of 4.22 with 1 df exceeds the tabled value of 3.84 for 1 df at the .05 level and would be judged significant at that level.

df	P = .99	.98	.95	.90	.80	.70	.50	.30	.20	.10	.05	.02	.01	.001
1	.00016	.00063	.0039	.016	.064	.15	.46	1.07	1.64	2.71	3.84	5.41	6.64	10.83
2	.02	.04	.10	.21	.45	.71	1.39	2.41	3.22	4.60	5.99	7.82	9.21	13.82
3	.12	.18	.35	.58	1.00	1.42	2.37	3.66	4.64	6.25	7.82	9.84	11.34	16.27
4	.30	.43	.71	1.06	1.65	2.20	3.36	4.88	5.99	7.78	9.49	11.67	13.28	18.46
5	.55	.75	1.14	1.61	2.34	3.00	4.35	6.06	7.29	9.24	11.07	13.39	15.09	20.52
6	.87	1.13	1.64	2.20	3.07	3.83	5.35	7.23	8.56	10.64	12.59	15.03	16.81	22.46
7	1.24	1.56	2.17	2.83	3.82	4.67	6.35	8.38	9.80	12.02	14.07	16.62	18.48	24.32
8	1.65	2.03	2.73	3.49	4.59	5.53	7.34	9.52	11.03	13.36	15.51	18.17	20.09	26.12
9	2.09	2.53	3.32	4.17	5.38	6.39	8.34	10.66	12.24	14.68	16.92	19.68	21.67	27.88
10	2.56	3.06	3.94	4.86	6.18	7.27	9.34	11.78	13.44	15.99	18.31	21.16	23.21	29.59
11	3.05	3.61	4.58	5.58	6.99	8.15	10.34	12.90	14.63	17.28	19.68	22.62	24.72	31.26
12	3.57	4.18	5.23	6.30	7.81	9.03	11.34	14.01	15.81	18.55	21.03	24.05	26.22	32.91
13	4.11	4.76	5.89	7.04	8.63	9.93	12.34	15.12	16.98	19.81	22.36	25.47	27.69	34.53
14	4.66	5.37	6.57	7.79	9.47	10.82	13.34	16.22	18.15	21.06	23.68	26.87	29.14	36.12
15	5.23	5.98	7.26	8.55	10.31	11.72	14.34	17.32	19.31	22.31	25.00	28.26	30.58	37.70
16	5.81	6.61	7.96	9.31	11.15	12.62	15.34	18.42	20.46	23.54	26.30	29.63	32.00	39.25
17	6.41	7.26	8.67	10.08	12.00	13.53	16.34	19.51	21.62	24.77	27.59	31.00	33.41	40.79
18	7.02	7.91	9.39	10.86	12.86	14.44	17.34	20.60	22.76	25.99	28.87	32.35	34.80	42.31
19	7.63	8.57	10.12	11.65	13.72	15.35	18.34	21.69	23.90	27.20	30.14	33.69	36.19	43.82
20	8.26	9.24	10.85	12.44	14.58	16.27	19.34	22.78	25.04	28.41	31.41	35.02	37.57	45.32
21	8.90	9.92	11.59	13.24	15.44	17.18	20.34	23.86	26.17	29.62	32.67	36.34	38.93	46.80
22	9.54	10.60	12.34	14.04	16.31	18.10	21.34	24.94	27.30	30.81	33.92	37.66	40.29	48.27
23	10.20	11.29	13.09	14.85	17.19	19.02	22.34	26.02	28.43	32.01	35.17	38.97	41.64	49.73
24	10.86	11.99	13.85	15.66	18.06	19.94	23.34	27.10	29.55	33.20	36.42	40.27	42.98	51.18
25	11.52	12.70	14.61	16.47	18.94	20.87	24.34	28.17	30.68	34.38	37.65	41.57	44.31	52.62
26	12.20	13.41	15.38	17.29	19.82	21.79	25.34	29.25	31.80	35.56	38.88	42.86	45.64	54.05
27	12.88	14.12	16.15	18.11	20.70	22.72	26.34	30.32	32.91	36.74	40.11	44.14	46.96	55.48
28	13.56	14.85	16.93	18.94	21.59	23.65	27.34	31.39	34.03	37.92	41.34	45.42	48.28	56.89
29	14.26	15.57	17.71	19.77	22.48	24.58	28.34	32.46	35.14	39.09	42.56	46.69	49.59	58.30
30	14.95	16.31	18.49	20.60	23.36	25.51	29.34	33.53	36.25	40.26	43.77	47.96	50.89	59.70

Reproduced with permission from McNemar, Q.: *Psychological Statistics.* 3d Ed., New York: John Wiley and Sons, Inc. 1962.

TABLE B.7 Transformation of r to Z

r	.000	.001	.002	.003	.004	.005	.006	.007	.008	.009
.000	.0000	.0010	.0020	.0030	.0040	.0050	.0060	.0070	.0080	.0090
.010	.0100	.0110	.0120	.0130	.0140	.0150	.0160	.0170	.0180	.0190
.020	.0200	.0210	.0220	.0230	.0240	.0250	.0260	.0270	.0280	.0290
.030	.0300	.0310	.0320	.0330	.0340	.0350	.0360	.0370	.0380	.0390
.040	.0400	.0410	.0420	.0430	.0440	.0450	.0460	.0470	.0480	.0490
.050	.0501	.0511	.0521	.0531	.0541	.0551	.0561	.0571	.0581	.0591
.060	.0601	.0611	.0621	.0631	.0641	.0651	.0661	.0671	.0681	.0691
.070	.0701	.0711	.0721	.0731	.0741	.0751	.0761	.0771	.0782	.0792
.080	.0802	.0812	.0822	.0832	.0842	.0852	.0862	.0872	.0882	.0892
.090	.0902	.0912	.0922	.0933	.0943	.0953	.0963	.0973	.0983	.0993
.100	.1003	.1013	.1024	.1034	.1044	.1054	.1064	.1074	.1084	.1094
.110	.1105	.1115	.1125	.1135	.1145	.1155	.1165	.1175	.1185	.1195
.120	.1206	.1216	.1226	.1236	.1246	.1257	.1267	.1277	.1287	.1297
.130	.1308	.1318	.1328	.1338	.1348	.1358	.1368	.1379	.1389	.1399
.140	.1409	.1419	.1430	.1440	.1450	.1460	.1470	.1481	.1491	.1501
.150	.1511	.1522	.1532	.1542	.1552	.1563	.1573	.1583	.1593	.1604
.160	.1614	.1624	.1634	.1644	.1655	.1665	.1676	.1686	.1696	.1706
.170	.1717	.1727	.1737	.1748	.1758	.1768	.1779	.1789	.1799	.1810
.180	.1820	.1830	.1841	.1851	.1861	.1872	.1882	.1892	.1903	.1913
.190	.1923	.1934	.1944	.1954	.1965	.1975	.1986	.1996	.2007	.2017
.200	.2027	.2038	.2048	.2059	.2069	.2079	.2090	.2100	.2111	.2121
.210	.2132	.2142	.2153	.2163	.2174	.2184	.2194	.2205	.2215	.2226
.220	.2237	.2247	.2258	.2268	.2279	.2289	.2300	.2310	.2321	.2331
.230	.2342	.2353	.2363	.2374	.2384	.2395	.2405	.2416	.2427	.2437
.240	.2448	.2458	.2469	.2480	.2490	.2501	.2511	.2522	.2533	.2543
.250	.2554	.2565	.2575	.2586	.2597	.2608	.2618	.2629	.2640	.2650
.260	.2661	.2672	.2682	.2693	.2704	.2715	.2726	.2736	.2747	.2758
.270	.2769	.2779	.2790	.2801	.2812	.2823	.2833	.2844	.2855	.2866
.280	.2877	.2888	.2898	.2909	.2920	.2931	.2942	.2953	.2964	.2975
.290	.2986	.2997	.3008	.3019	.3029	.3040	.3051	.3062	.3073	.3084

From Albert E. Waugh, *Statistical Tables and Problems* (New York: McGraw-Hill, 1952, table A11, pp. 40–41), by permission of the publisher.

(continued)

TABLE B.7 *(continued)*

r	.000	.001	.002	.003	.004	.005	.006	.007	.008	.009
.300	.3095	.3106	.3117	.3128	.3139	.3150	.3136	.3172	.3183	.3195
.310	.3206	.3217	.3228	.3239	.3250	.3261	.3272	.3283	.3294	.3305
.320	.3317	.3328	.3339	.3350	.3361	.3372	.3384	.3395	.3406	.3417
.330	.3428	.3439	.3451	.3462	.3473	.3484	.3496	.3507	.3518	.3530
.340	.3541	.3552	.3564	.3575	.3586	.3597	.3609	.3620	.3632	.3643
.350	.3654	.3666	.3677	.3689	.3700	.3712	.3723	.3734	.3746	.3757
.360	.3769	.3780	.3792	.3803	.3815	.3826	.3838	.3850	.3861	.3873
.370	.3884	.3896	.3907	.3919	.3931	.3942	.3954	.3966	.3977	.3989
.380	.4001	.4012	.4024	.4036	.4047	.4059	.4071	.4083	.4094	.4106
.390	.4118	.4130	.4142	.4153	.4165	.4177	.4189	.4201	.4213	.4225
.400	.4236	.4248	.4260	.4272	.4284	.4296	.4308	.4320	.4332	.4344
.410	.4356	.4368	.4380	.4392	.4404	.4416	.4429	.4441	.4453	.4465
.420	.4477	.4489	.4501	.4513	.4526	.4538	.4550	.4562	.4574	.4587
.430	.4599	.4611	.4623	.4636	.4648	.4660	.4673	.4685	.4697	.4710
.440	.4722	.4735	.4747	.4760	.4772	.4784	.4797	.4809	.4822	.4835
.450	.4847	.4860	.4872	.4885	.4897	.4910	.4923	.4935	.4948	.4961
.460	.4973	.4986	.4999	.5011	.5024	.5037	.5049	.5062	.5075	.5088
.470	.5101	.5114	.5126	.5139	.5152	.5165	.5178	.5191	.5204	.5217
.480	.5230	.5243	.5256	.5279	.5282	.5295	.5308	.5321	.5334	.5347
.490	.5361	.5374	.5387	.5400	.5413	.5427	.5440	.5453	.5466	.5480
.500	.5493	.5506	.5520	.5533	.5547	.5560	.5573	.5587	.5600	.5614
.510	.5627	.5641	.5654	.5668	.5681	.5695	.5709	.5722	.5736	.5750
.520	.5763	.5777	.5791	.5805	.5818	.5832	.5846	.5860	.5874	.5888
.530	.5901	.5915	.5929	.5943	.5957	.5971	.5985	.5999	.6013	.6027
.540	.6042	.6056	.6070	.6084	.6098	.6112	.6127	.6141	.6155	.6170
.550	.6184	.6198	.6213	.6227	.6241	.6256	.6270	.6285	.6299	.6314
.560	.6328	.6343	.6358	.6372	.6387	.6401	.6416	.6431	.6446	.6460
.570	.6475	.6490	.6505	.6520	.6535	.6550	.6565	.6579	.6594	.6610
.580	.6625	.6640	.6655	.6670	.6685	.6700	.6715	.6731	.6746	.6761
.590	.6777	.6792	.6807	.6823	.6838	.6854	.6869	.6885	.6900	.6916
.600	.6931	.6947	.6963	.6978	.6994	.7010	.7026	.7042	.7057	.7073
.610	.7089	.7105	.7121	.7137	.7153	.7169	.7185	.7201	.7218	.7234
.620	.7250	.7266	.7283	.7299	.7315	.7332	.7348	.7364	.7381	.7398
.630	.7414	.7431	.7447	.7464	.7481	.7497	.7514	.7531	.7548	.7565
.640	.7582	.7599	.7616	.7633	.7650	.7667	.7684	.7701	.7718	.7736

(continued)

TABLE B.7 (*continued*)

r	.000	.001	.002	.003	.004	.005	.006	.007	.008	.009
.650	.7753	.7770	.7788	.7805	.7823	.7840	.7858	.7875	.7893	.7910
.660	.7928	.7946	.7964	.7981	.7999	.8017	.8035	.8053	.8071	.8089
.670	.8107	.8126	.8144	.8162	.8180	.8199	.8217	.8236	.8254	.8273
.680	.8291	.8310	.8328	.8347	.8366	.8385	.8404	.8423	.8442	.8461
.690	.8480	.8499	.8518	.8537	.8556	.8576	.8595	.8614	.8634	.8653
.700	.8673	.8693	.8712	.8732	.8752	.8772	.8792	.8812	.8832	.8852
.710	.8872	.8892	.8912	.8933	.8953	.8973	.8994	.9014	.9035	.9056
.720	.9076	.9097	.9118	.9139	.9160	.9181	.9202	.9223	.9245	.9266
.730	.9287	.9309	.9330	.9352	.9373	.9395	.9417	.9439	.9461	.9483
.740	.9505	.9527	.9549	.9571	.9594	.9616	.9639	.9661	.9684	.9707
.750	.9730	.9752	.9775	.9799	.9822	.9845	.9868	.9892	.9915	.9939
.760	.9962	.9986	1.0010	1.0034	1.0058	1.0082	1.0106	1.0130	1.0154	1.0179
.770	1.0203	1.0228	1.0253	1.0277	1.0302	1.0327	1.0352	1.0378	1.0403	1.0428
.780	1.0454	1.0479	1.0505	1.0531	1.0557	1.0583	1.0609	1.0635	1.0661	1.0688
.790	1.0714	1.0741	1.0768	1.0795	1.0822	1.0849	1.0876	1.0903	1.0931	1.0958
.800	1.0986	1.1014	1.1041	1.1070	1.1098	1.1127	1.1155	1.1184	1.1212	1.1241
.810	1.1270	1.1299	1.1329	1.1358	1.1388	1.1417	1.1447	1.1477	1.1507	1.1538
.820	1.1568	1.1599	1.1630	1.1660	1.1692	1.1723	1.1754	1.1786	1.1817	1.1849
.830	1.1870	1.1913	1.1946	1.1979	1.2011	1.2044	1.2077	1.2111	1.2144	1.2178
.840	1.2212	1.2246	1.2280	1.2315	1.2349	1.2384	1.2419	1.2454	1.2490	1.2526
.850	1.2561	1.2598	1.2634	1.2670	1.2708	1.2744	1.2782	1.2819	1.2857	1.2895
.860	1.2934	1.2972	1.3011	1.3050	1.3089	1.3129	1.3168	1.3209	1.3249	1.3290
.870	1.3331	1.3372	1.3414	1.3456	1.3498	1.3540	1.3583	1.3626	1.3670	1.3714
.880	1.3758	1.3802	1.3847	1.3892	1.3938	1.3984	1.4030	1.4077	1.4124	1.4171
.890	1.4219	1.4268	1.4316	1.4366	1.4415	1.4465	1.4516	1.4566	1.4618	1.4670
.900	1.4722	1.4775	1.4828	1.4883	1.4937	1.4992	1.5047	1.5103	1.5160	1.5217
.910	1.5275	1.5334	1.5393	1.5453	1.5513	1.5574	1.5636	1.5698	1.5762	1.5825
.920	1.5890	1.5956	1.6022	1.6089	1.6157	1.6226	1.6296	1.6366	1.6438	1.6510
.930	1.6584	1.6659	1.6734	1.6811	1.6888	1.6967	1.7047	1.7129	1.7211	1.7295
.940	1.7380	1.7467	1.7555	1.7645	1.7736	1.7828	1.7923	1.8019	1.8117	1.8216
.950	1.8318	1.8421	1.8527	1.8635	1.8745	1.8857	1.8972	1.9090	1.9210	1.9333
.960	1.9459	1.9588	1.9721	1.9857	1.9996	2.0140	2.0287	2.0439	2.0595	2.0756
.970	2.0923	2.1095	2.1273	2.1457	2.1649	2.1847	2.2054	2.2269	2.2494	2.2729
.980	2.2976	2.3223	2.3507	2.3796	2.4101	2.4426	2.4774	2.5147	2.5550	2.5988
.990	2.6467	2.6996	2.7587	2.8257	2.9031	2.9945	3.1063	3.2504	3.4534	3.8002

TABLE B.8 Critical Values of F^a

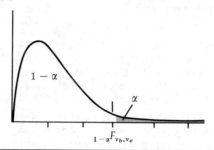

v_e for Denominator	α	v_b (Degrees of Freedom for Numerator)											
		1	2	3	4	5	6	7	8	9	10	12	15
1	.25	5.83	7.50	8.20	8.58	8.82	8.98	9.10	9.19	9.26	9.32	9.41	9.49
	.10	39.9	49.5	53.6	55.8	57.2	58.2	58.9	59.4	59.9	60.2	60.7	61.2
	.05	161	200	216	225	230	234	237	239	241	242	244	246
	.025	648	800	864	900	922	937	948	957	963	969	977	985
	.01	4052	5000	5403	5625	5764	5859	5928	5982	6022	6056	6106	6157
	.001	b	b	b	b	b	b	b	b	b	b	b	b
2	.25	2.57	3.00	3.15	3.23	3.28	3.31	3.34	3.35	3.37	3.38	3.39	3.41
	.10	8.53	9.00	9.16	9.24	9.29	9.33	9.35	9.37	9.38	9.39	9.41	9.42
	.05	18.5	19.0	19.2	19.2	19.3	19.3	19.4	19.4	19.4	19.4	19.4	19.4
	.025	38.5	39.0	39.2	39.3	39.3	39.3	39.4	39.4	39.4	39.4	39.4	39.4
	.01	98.5	99.0	99.2	99.3	99.3	99.3	99.4	99.4	99.4	99.4	99.4	99.4
	.001	998.5	999.0	999.2	999.2	999.3	999.3	999.4	999.4	999.4	999.4	999.4	999.4
3	.25	2.02	2.28	2.36	2.39	2.41	2.42	2.43	2.44	2.44	2.44	2.45	2.46
	.10	5.54	5.46	5.39	5.34	5.31	5.28	5.27	5.25	5.24	5.23	5.22	5.20
	.05	10.1	9.55	9.28	9.12	9.01	8.94	8.89	8.85	8.81	8.79	8.74	8.70
	.025	17.4	16.0	15.4	15.1	14.9	14.7	14.6	14.5	14.5	14.4	14.3	14.3
	.01	34.1	30.8	29.5	28.7	28.2	27.9	27.7	27.5	27.4	27.2	27.1	26.9
	.001	167	149	141	137	135	133	132	131	130	129	128	127
4	.25	1.81	2.00	2.05	2.06	2.07	2.08	2.08	2.08	2.08	2.08	2.08	2.08
	.10	4.54	4.32	4.19	4.11	4.05	4.01	3.98	3.95	3.94	3.92	3.90	3.87
	.05	7.71	6.94	6.59	6.39	6.26	6.16	6.09	6.04	6.00	5.96	5.91	5.86
	.025	12.2	10.7	9.98	9.60	9.36	9.20	9.07	8.98	8.90	8.84	8.75	8.66
	.01	21.2	18.0	16.7	16.0	15.5	15.2	15.0	14.8	14.7	14.6	14.4	14.2
	.001	74.1	61.3	56.2	53.4	51.7	50.5	49.7	49.0	48.5	48.1	47.4	46.8
5	.25	1.69	1.85	1.88	1.89	1.89	1.89	1.89	1.89	1.89	1.89	1.89	1.89
	.10	4.06	3.78	3.62	3.52	3.45	3.40	3.37	3.34	3.32	3.30	3.27	3.24
	.05	6.61	5.79	5.41	5.19	5.05	4.95	4.88	4.82	4.77	4.74	4.68	4.62
	.025	10.0	8.43	7.76	7.39	7.15	6.98	6.85	6.76	6.68	6.62	6.52	6.43
	.01	16.3	13.3	12.1	11.4	11.0	10.7	10.5	10.3	10.2	10.1	9.89	9.72
	.001	47.2	37.1	33.2	31.1	29.8	28.8	28.2	27.6	27.2	26.9	26.4	26.9
6	.25	1.62	1.76	1.78	1.79	1.79	1.78	1.78	1.78	1.77	1.77	1.77	1.76
	.10	3.78	3.46	3.29	3.18	3.11	3.05	3.01	2.98	2.96	2.94	2.90	2.87
	.05	5.99	5.14	4.76	4.53	4.39	4.28	4.21	4.15	4.10	4.06	4.00	3.94
	.025	8.81	7.26	6.60	6.23	5.99	5.82	5.70	5.60	5.52	5.46	5.37	5.27
	.01	13.8	10.9	9.78	9.15	8.75	8.47	8.26	8.10	7.98	7.87	7.72	7.56
	.001	35.5	27.0	23.7	21.9	20.8	20.0	19.5	19.0	18.7	18.4	18.0	17.6
	α	1	2	3	4	5	6	7	8	9	10	12	15

[a] Critical values with v_b of 50, 100, 200, 500, and 1000, or with v_e for denominator of 200, 500, and 1000 determined via computer thanks to Frank B. Baker, James R. Morrow, and Gregory Camilli. Other values are reprinted from table 18 in E. S. Pearson and H. O. Hartley (eds.), *Biometrika Tables for Statisticians*, 3d ed. (1966), by permission of the *Biometrika* Trustees.

[b] To obtain critical values for $\alpha = .001$ with 1 degree of freedom in the denominator, multiply critical values at $\alpha = .01$ by 100.

Note: As an example, the critical value of F with $J = 3$ and $n = 2$ $(n = 6)$ with $\alpha = .05$ is $_{1-\alpha}F_{v_b},\ v_e = {_{1-\alpha}}F_{(J-1)},\ (n.-J) = {_{.95}}F_{2,3} = 9.55$.

					v_b (Degrees of Freedom for Numerator)									
20	24	30	40	50	60	100	120	200	500	1000	∞	α	v_e
9.58	9.63	9.67	9.71	9.74	9.76	9.78	9.80	9.82	9.84	9.85	9.85	.25	1
61.7	62.0	62.3	62.5	62.7	62.8	63.0	63.1	63.2	63.3	63.3	63.3	.10	
248	249	250	251	252	252	253	253	254	254	254	254	.05	
993	997	1001	1006	1010	1010	1010	1014	1020	1020	1019	1018	.025	
6209	6235	6261	6287	6300	6313	6330	6339	6350	6360	6363	6366	.01	
b	b	b	b	b	b	b	b	b	b	b	b	.001	
3.43	3.43	3.44	3.45	3.45	3.46	3.47	3.47	3.48	3.48	1.39	3.48	.25	2
9.44	9.45	9.46	9.47	9.47	9.47	9.48	9.48	9.49	9.49	2.31	9.49	.10	
19.4	19.5	19.5	19.5	19.5	19.5	19.5	19.5	19.5	19.5	3.00	19.5	.05	
39.5	39.5	39.5	39.5	39.5	39.5	39.5	39.5	39.5	39.5	3.70	39.5	.025	
99.5	99.5	99.5	99.5	99.5	99.5	99.5	99.5	99.5	99.5	4.63	99.5	.01	
999	999	999	999	999	999	999	999	999	999	6.95	999	.001	
2.46	2.46	2.47	2.47	2.47	2.47	2.47	2.47	2.47	2.47	1.37	2.47	.25	3
5.18	5.18	5.17	5.16	5.15	5.15	5.14	5.14	5.14	5.14	2.09	5.13	.10	
8.66	8.64	8.62	8.59	8.58	8.57	8.55	8.55	8.54	8.53	2.61	8.53	.05	
14.2	14.1	14.1	14.0	14.0	14.0	14.0	14.0	13.9	13.9	3.13	13.9	.025	
26.7	26.6	26.5	26.4	26.4	26.3	26.2	26.2	26.2	26.1	3.80	26.1	.01	
126	126	125	125	125	125	124	124	124	124	5.46	123	.001	
2.08	2.08	2.08	2.08	2.08	2.08	2.08	2.08	2.08	2.08	1.35	2.08	.25	4
3.84	3.83	3.82	3.80	3.80	3.79	3.78	3.78	3.77	3.76	1.95	3.76	.10	
5.80	5.77	5.75	5.72	5.70	5.69	5.66	5.66	5.65	5.64	2.38	5.63	.05	
8.56	8.51	8.46	8.41	8.38	8.36	8.32	8.31	8.29	8.27	2.80	8.26	.025	
14.0	13.9	13.8	13.8	13.7	13.7	13.6	13.6	13.5	13.5	3.34	13.5	.01	
46.1	45.8	45.4	45.1	44.9	44.8	44.5	44.4	44.3	44.1	4.65	44.1	.001	
1.88	1.88	1.88	1.88	1.88	1.87	1.87	1.87	1.87	1.87	1.33	1.87	.25	5
3.21	3.19	3.17	3.16	3.15	3.14	3.13	3.12	3.12	3.11	1.85	3.10	.10	
4.56	4.53	4.50	4.46	4.44	4.43	4.41	4.40	4.39	4.37	2.22	4.36	.05	
6.33	6.28	6.23	6.18	6.14	6.12	6.08	6.07	6.05	6.03	2.58	6.02	.025	
9.55	9.47	9.38	9.29	9.24	9.20	9.13	9.11	9.08	9.04	3.04	9.02	.01	
25.4	25.1	24.9	24.6	24.4	24.3	24.1	24.1	23.9	23.8	4.14	23.8	.001	
1.76	1.75	1.75	1.75	1.75	1.74	1.74	1.74	1.74	1.74	1.74	1.74	.25	6
2.84	2.82	2.80	2.78	2.77	2.76	2.75	2.74	2.73	2.73	2.72	2.72	.10	
3.87	3.84	3.81	3.77	3.75	3.74	3.71	3.70	3.69	3.68	3.67	3.67	.05	
5.17	5.12	5.07	5.01	4.98	4.96	4.92	4.90	4.88	4.86	4.86	4.85	.025	
7.40	7.31	7.23	7.14	7.09	7.06	6.99	6.97	6.93	6.90	6.89	6.88	.01	
17.1	16.9	16.7	16.4	16.3	16.2	16.0	16.0	15.9	15.8	15.8	15.8	.001	
20	24	30	40	50	60	100	120	200	500	1000	∞	α	v_e

(continued)

TABLE B.8 (*continued*)

v_e for Denominator	α	1	2	3	4	5	6	7	8	9	10	12	15
						v_b (Degrees of Freedom for Numerator)							
7	.25	1.57	1.70	1.72	1.72	1.71	1.71	1.70	1.70	1.69	1.69	1.68	1.68
	.10	3.59	3.26	3.07	2.96	2.88	2.83	2.78	2.75	2.72	2.70	2.67	2.63
	.05	5.59	4.74	4.35	4.12	3.97	3.87	3.79	3.73	3.68	3.64	3.57	3.51
	.025	8.07	6.54	5.89	5.52	5.29	5.12	4.99	4.90	4.82	4.76	4.67	4.57
	.01	12.3	9.55	8.45	7.85	7.46	7.19	6.99	6.84	6.72	6.62	6.47	6.31
	.001	29.3	27.1	18.8	17.2	16.2	15.5	15.0	14.6	14.3	14.1	13.7	13.3
8	.25	1.54	1.66	1.67	1.66	1.66	1.65	1.64	1.64	1.63	1.63	1.62	1.62
	.10	3.46	3.11	2.92	2.81	2.73	2.67	2.62	2.59	2.56	2.54	2.50	2.46
	.05	5.32	4.46	4.07	3.84	3.69	3.58	3.50	3.44	3.39	3.35	3.28	3.22
	.025	7.57	6.06	5.42	5.05	4.82	4.65	4.53	4.43	4.36	4.30	4.20	4.10
	.01	11.3	8.65	7.59	7.01	6.63	6.37	6.18	6.03	5.91	5.81	5.67	5.52
	.001	25.4	18.5	15.8	14.4	13.5	12.9	12.4	12.0	11.8	11.5	11.2	10.8
9	.25	1.51	1.62	1.63	1.63	1.62	1.61	1.60	1.60	1.59	1.59	1.58	1.57
	.10	3.36	3.01	2.81	2.69	2.61	2.55	2.51	2.47	2.44	2.42	2.38	2.34
	.05	5.12	4.26	3.86	3.63	3.48	3.37	3.29	3.23	3.18	3.14	3.07	3.01
	.025	7.21	5.71	5.08	4.72	4.48	4.32	4.20	4.10	4.03	3.96	3.87	3.77
	.01	10.6	8.02	6.99	6.42	6.06	5.80	5.61	5.47	5.35	5.26	5.11	4.96
	.001	22.9	16.4	13.9	12.6	11.7	11.1	10.7	10.4	10.1	9.89	9.57	9.24
10	.25	1.49	1.60	1.60	1.59	1.59	1.58	1.57	1.56	1.56	1.55	1.54	1.53
	.10	3.29	2.92	2.73	2.61	2.52	2.46	2.41	2.38	2.35	2.32	2.28	2.24
	.05	4.96	4.10	3.71	3.48	3.33	3.22	3.14	3.07	3.02	2.98	2.91	2.85
	.025	6.94	5.46	4.83	4.47	4.24	4.07	3.95	3.85	3.78	3.72	3.62	3.52
	.01	10.0	7.56	6.55	5.99	5.64	5.39	5.20	5.06	4.94	4.85	4.71	4.56
	.001	21.0	14.9	12.6	11.3	10.5	9.92	9.52	9.20	8.96	8.75	8.45	8.13
11	.25	1.47	1.58	1.58	1.57	1.56	1.55	1.54	1.53	1.53	1.52	1.51	1.50
	.10	3.23	2.86	2.66	2.54	2.45	2.39	2.34	2.30	2.27	2.25	2.21	2.17
	.05	4.84	3.98	3.59	3.36	3.20	3.09	3.01	2.95	2.90	2.85	2.79	2.72
	.025	6.72	5.26	4.63	4.28	4.04	3.88	3.76	3.66	3.59	3.53	3.53	3.33
	.01	9.65	7.21	6.22	5.67	5.32	5.07	4.89	4.74	4.63	4.54	4.40	4.25
	.001	19.7	13.8	11.6	10.4	9.58	9.05	8.66	8.35	8.12	7.92	7.63	7.32
12	.25	1.46	1.56	1.56	1.55	1.54	1.53	1.52	1.51	1.51	1.50	1.49	1.48
	.10	3.18	2.81	2.61	2.48	2.39	2.33	2.28	2.24	2.21	2.19	2.15	2.10
	.05	4.75	3.89	3.49	3.26	3.11	3.00	2.91	2.85	2.80	2.75	2.69	2.62
	.025	6.55	5.10	4.49	4.12	3.89	3.73	3.61	3.51	3.44	3.37	3.28	3.18
	.01	9.33	6.93	5.95	5.41	5.06	4.82	4.64	4.50	4.39	4.30	4.16	4.01
	.001	18.6	13.0	10.8	9.63	8.89	8.38	8.00	7.71	7.48	7.29	7.00	6.71
13	.25	1.45	1.55	1.55	1.53	1.52	1.51	1.50	1.49	1.49	1.48	1.47	1.46
	.10	3.14	2.76	2.56	2.43	2.35	2.28	2.23	2.20	2.16	2.14	2.10	2.05
	.05	4.67	3.81	3.41	3.18	3.03	2.92	2.83	2.77	2.71	2.67	2.60	2.53
	.025	6.41	4.97	4.35	4.00	3.77	3.60	3.48	3.39	3.31	3.25	3.15	3.05
	.01	9.07	6.70	5.74	5.21	4.86	4.62	4.44	4.30	4.19	4.10	3.96	3.82
	.001	17.8	12.3	10.2	9.07	8.35	7.86	7.49	7.21	6.98	6.80	6.52	6.23
14	.25	1.44	1.53	1.53	1.52	1.51	1.50	1.49	1.48	1.47	1.46	1.45	1.44
	.10	3.10	2.73	2.52	2.39	2.31	2.24	2.19	2.15	2.12	2.10	2.05	2.01
	.05	4.60	3.74	3.34	3.11	2.96	2.85	2.76	2.70	2.65	2.60	2.53	2.46
	.025	6.30	4.86	4.24	3.89	3.66	3.50	3.38	3.29	3.21	3.15	3.05	2.95
	.01	8.86	6.51	5.56	5.04	4.69	4.46	4.28	4.14	4.03	3.94	3.80	3.66
	.001	17.1	11.8	9.73	8.62	7.92	7.43	7.08	6.80	6.58	6.40	6.13	5.85
15	.25	1.43	1.52	1.52	1.51	1.49	1.48	1.47	1.46	1.46	1.45	1.44	1.43
	.10	3.07	2.70	2.49	2.36	2.27	2.21	2.16	2.12	2.09	2.06	2.02	1.97
	.05	4.54	3.68	3.29	3.06	2.90	2.79	2.71	2.64	2.59	2.54	2.48	2.40
	.025	6.20	4.77	4.15	3.80	3.58	3.41	3.29	3.20	3.12	3.06	2.96	2.86
	.01	8.68	6.36	5.42	4.89	4.56	4.32	4.14	4.00	3.89	3.80	3.67	3.52
	.001	16.6	11.3	9.34	8.25	7.57	7.09	6.74	6.47	6.26	6.08	5.81	5.54
	α	1	2	3	4	5	6	7	8	9	10	12	15

					v_b (Degrees of Freedom for Numerator)									
20	24	30	40	50	60	100	120	200	500	1000	∞	α	v_e
1.67	1.67	1.66	1.66	1.66	1.65	1.65	1.65	1.65	1.65	1.65	1.65	.25	7
2.59	2.58	2.56	2.54	2.52	2.51	2.50	2.49	2.48	2.48	2.47	2.47	.10	
3.44	3.41	3.38	3.34	3.32	3.30	3.27	3.27	3.25	3.24	3.23	3.23	.05	
4.47	4.42	4.36	4.31	4.28	4.25	4.21	4.20	4.18	4.16	4.15	4.14	.025	
6.16	6.07	5.99	5.91	5.86	5.82	5.75	5.74	5.70	5.67	5.66	5.65	.01	
12.9	12.7	12.5	12.3	12.2	12.1	11.9	11.9	11.8	11.7	11.7	11.7	.001	
1.61	1.60	1.60	1.59	1.59	1.59	1.58	1.58	1.58	1.58	1.58	1.58	.25	8
2.42	2.40	2.38	2.36	2.35	2.34	2.32	2.32	2.31	2.30	2.29	2.29	.10	
3.15	3.12	3.08	3.04	3.02	3.01	2.97	2.97	2.95	2.94	2.93	2.93	.05	
4.00	3.95	3.89	3.84	3.81	3.78	3.74	3.73	3.70	3.68	3.68	3.67	.025	
5.36	5.28	5.20	5.12	5.07	5.03	4.96	4.95	4.91	4.88	4.87	4.86	.01	
10.5	10.3	10.1	9.92	9.80	9.73	9.57	9.53	9.46	9.39	9.35	9.33	.001	
1.56	1.56	1.55	1.55	1.54	1.54	1.53	1.53	1.53	1.53	1.53	1.53	.25	9
2.30	2.28	2.25	2.23	2.22	2.21	2.19	2.18	2.17	2.17	2.16	2.16	.10	
2.94	2.90	2.86	2.83	2.80	2.79	2.76	2.75	2.73	2.72	2.71	2.71	.05	
3.67	3.61	3.56	3.51	3.47	3.45	3.40	3.39	3.37	3.35	3.34	3.33	.025	
4.81	4.73	4.65	4.57	4.52	4.48	4.42	4.40	4.36	4.33	4.32	4.31	.01	
8.90	8.72	8.55	8.37	8.26	8.19	8.04	8.00	7.93	7.86	7.83	7.81	.001	
1.52	1.52	1.51	1.51	1.50	1.50	1.49	1.49	1.49	1.48	1.48	1.48	.25	10
2.20	2.18	2.16	2.13	2.12	2.11	2.09	2.08	2.07	2.06	2.06	2.06	.10	
2.77	2.74	2.70	2.66	2.64	2.62	2.59	2.58	2.56	2.55	2.54	2.54	.05	
3.42	3.37	3.31	3.26	3.22	3.20	3.15	3.14	3.12	3.09	3.09	3.08	.025	
4.41	4.33	4.25	4.17	4.12	4.08	4.01	4.00	3.96	3.93	3.92	3.91	.01	
7.80	7.64	7.47	7.30	7.19	7.12	6.98	6.94	6.87	6.81	6.78	6.76	.001	
1.49	1.49	1.48	1.47	1.47	1.47	1.46	1.46	1.46	1.45	1.45	1.45	.25	11
2.12	2.10	2.08	2.05	2.04	2.03	2.00	2.00	1.99	1.98	1.98	1.97	.10	
2.65	2.61	2.57	2.53	2.51	2.49	2.46	2.45	2.43	2.42	2.41	2.40	.05	
3.23	3.17	3.12	3.06	3.03	3.00	2.96	2.94	2.92	2.90	2.89	2.88	.025	
4.10	4.02	3.94	3.86	3.81	3.78	3.71	3.69	3.66	3.62	3.61	3.60	.01	
7.01	6.85	6.68	6.52	6.41	6.35	6.21	6.17	6.10	6.04	6.01	6.00	.001	
1.47	1.46	1.45	1.45	1.44	1.44	1.43	1.43	1.43	1.42	1.42	1.42	.25	12
2.06	2.04	2.01	1.99	1.97	1.96	1.94	1.93	1.92	1.91	1.91	1.90	.10	
2.54	2.51	2.47	2.43	2.40	2.38	2.35	2.34	2.32	2.31	2.30	2.30	.05	
3.07	3.02	2.96	2.91	2.87	2.85	2.80	2.79	2.76	2.74	2.73	2.72	.025	
3.86	3.78	3.70	3.62	3.57	3.54	3.47	3.45	3.41	3.38	3.37	3.36	.01	
6.40	6.25	6.09	5.93	5.83	5.76	5.63	5.59	5.52	5.46	5.44	5.42	.001	
1.45	1.44	1.43	1.42	1.42	1.42	1.41	1.41	1.40	1.40	1.40	1.40	.25	13
2.01	1.98	1.96	1.93	1.92	1.90	1.88	1.88	1.86	1.85	1.85	1.85	.10	
2.46	2.42	2.38	2.34	2.31	2.30	2.26	2.25	2.23	2.22	2.21	2.21	.01	
2.95	2.89	2.84	2.78	2.74	2.72	2.67	2.66	2.63	2.61	2.60	2.60	.025	
3.66	3.59	3.51	3.43	3.38	3.34	3.27	3.25	3.22	3.19	3.18	3.17	.01	
5.93	5.78	5.63	5.47	5.36	5.30	5.17	5.14	5.07	5.00	4.98	4.97	.001	
1.43	1.42	1.41	1.41	1.40	1.40	1.39	1.39	1.39	1.38	1.38	1.38	.25	14
1.96	1.94	1.91	1.89	1.87	1.86	1.83	1.83	1.82	1.80	1.80	1.80	.10	
2.39	2.35	2.31	2.27	2.24	2.22	2.19	2.18	2.16	2.14	2.14	2.13	.05	
2.84	2.79	2.73	2.67	2.64	2.61	2.56	2.55	2.53	2.51	2.49	2.49	.025	
3.51	3.43	3.35	3.27	3.22	3.18	3.11	3.09	3.06	3.03	3.01	3.00	.01	
5.56	5.41	5.25	5.10	5.00	4.94	4.80	4.77	4.70	4.69	4.62	4.60	.001	
1.41	1.41	1.40	1.39	1.39	1.38	1.38	1.37	1.37	1.36	1.36	1.36	.25	15
1.92	1.90	1.87	1.85	1.83	1.82	1.79	1.79	1.77	1.76	1.76	1.76	.10	
2.33	2.29	2.25	2.20	2.18	2.16	2.12	2.11	2.10	2.08	2.07	2.07	.05	
2.76	2.70	2.64	2.59	2.55	2.52	2.47	2.46	2.44	2.41	2.40	2.40	.025	
3.37	3.29	3.21	3.13	3.08	3.05	2.98	2.96	2.92	2.89	2.88	2.87	.01	
5.25	5.10	4.95	4.80	4.70	4.64	4.51	4.47	4.41	4.35	4.32	4.31	.001	
20	24	30	40	50	60	100	120	200	500	1000	∞	α	v_e

(continued)

TABLE B.8 (*continued*)

v_e for Denominator	α	\multicolumn{12}{c}{v_b (Degrees of Freedom for Numerator)}

v_e	α	1	2	3	4	5	6	7	8	9	10	12	15
16	.25	1.42	1.51	1.51	1.50	1.48	1.47	1.46	1.45	1.44	1.44	1.43	1.41
	.10	3.05	2.67	2.46	2.33	2.24	2.18	2.13	2.09	2.06	2.03	1.99	1.94
	.05	4.49	3.63	3.24	3.01	2.85	2.74	2.66	2.59	2.54	2.49	2.42	2.35
	.025	6.12	4.69	4.08	3.73	3.50	3.34	3.22	3.12	3.05	2.99	2.89	2.79
	.01	8.53	6.23	5.29	4.77	4.44	4.20	4.03	3.89	3.78	3.69	3.55	3.41
	.001	16.1	11.0	9.00	7.94	7.27	6.81	6.46	6.19	5.98	5.81	5.55	5.27
17	.25	1.42	1.51	1.50	1.49	1.47	1.46	1.45	1.44	1.43	1.43	1.41	1.40
	.10	3.03	2.64	2.44	2.31	2.22	2.15	2.10	2.06	2.03	2.00	1.96	1.91
	.05	4.45	3.59	3.20	2.96	2.81	2.70	2.61	2.55	2.49	2.45	2.38	2.31
	.025	6.04	4.62	4.01	3.66	3.44	3.28	3.16	3.06	2.98	2.92	2.82	2.72
	.01	8.40	6.11	5.18	4.67	4.34	4.10	3.93	3.79	3.68	3.59	3.46	3.31
	.001	15.7	10.7	8.73	7.68	7.02	6.56	6.22	5.96	5.75	5.58	5.32	5.05
18	.25	1.41	1.50	1.49	1.48	1.46	1.45	1.44	1.43	1.42	1.42	1.40	1.39
	.10	3.01	2.62	2.42	2.29	2.20	2.13	2.08	2.04	2.00	1.98	1.93	1.89
	.05	4.41	3.55	3.16	2.93	2.77	2.66	2.58	2.51	2.46	2.41	2.34	2.27
	.025	5.98	4.56	3.95	3.61	3.38	3.22	3.10	3.01	2.93	2.87	2.77	2.67
	.01	8.29	6.01	5.09	4.58	4.25	4.01	3.84	3.71	3.60	3.51	3.37	3.23
	.001	15.4	10.4	8.49	7.46	6.81	6.35	6.02	5.76	5.56	5.39	5.13	4.87
18	.25	1.41	1.49	1.49	1.47	1.46	1.44	1.43	1.42	1.41	1.41	1.40	1.38
	.10	2.99	2.61	2.40	2.27	2.18	2.11	2.06	2.02	1.98	1.96	1.91	1.86
	.05	4.38	3.52	3.13	2.90	2.74	2.63	2.54	2.48	2.42	2.38	2.31	2.23
	.025	5.92	4.51	3.90	3.56	3.33	3.17	3.05	2.96	2.88	2.82	2.72	2.62
	.01	8.18	5.93	5.01	4.50	4.17	3.94	3.77	3.63	3.52	3.43	3.30	3.15
	.001	15.1	10.2	8.28	7.26	6.62	6.18	5.85	5.59	5.39	5.22	4.97	4.70
20	.25	1.40	1.49	1.48	1.46	1.45	1.44	1.43	1.42	1.41	1.40	1.39	1.37
	.10	2.97	2.59	2.38	2.25	2.16	2.09	2.04	2.00	1.96	1.94	1.89	1.84
	.05	4.35	3.49	3.10	2.87	2.71	2.60	2.51	2.45	2.39	2.35	2.28	2.20
	.025	5.87	4.46	3.86	3.51	3.29	3.13	3.01	2.91	2.84	2.77	2.68	2.57
	.01	8.10	5.85	4.94	4.43	4.10	3.87	3.70	3.56	3.46	3.37	3.23	3.09
	.001	14.8	9.95	8.10	7.10	6.46	6.02	5.69	5.44	5.24	5.08	4.82	4.56
22	.25	1.40	1.48	1.47	1.45	1.44	1.42	1.41	1.40	1.39	1.39	1.37	1.36
	.10	2.95	2.56	2.35	2.22	2.13	2.06	2.01	1.97	1.93	1.90	1.86	1.81
	.05	4.30	3.44	3.05	2.82	2.66	2.55	2.46	2.40	2.34	2.30	2.23	2.15
	.025	5.79	4.38	3.78	3.44	3.22	3.05	2.93	2.84	2.76	2.70	2.60	2.50
	.01	7.95	5.72	4.82	4.31	3.99	3.76	3.59	3.45	3.35	3.26	3.12	2.98
	.001	14.4	9.61	7.80	6.81	6.19	5.76	5.44	5.19	4.99	4.83	4.58	4.33
24	.25	1.39	1.47	1.46	1.44	1.43	1.41	1.40	1.39	1.38	1.38	1.36	1.35
	.10	2.93	2.54	2.33	2.19	2.10	2.04	1.98	1.94	1.91	1.88	1.83	1.78
	.05	4.26	3.40	3.01	2.78	2.62	2.51	2.42	2.36	2.30	2.25	2.18	2.11
	.025	5.72	4.32	3.72	3.38	3.15	2.99	2.87	2.78	2.70	2.64	2.54	2.44
	.01	7.82	5.61	4.72	4.22	3.90	3.67	3.50	3.36	3.26	3.17	3.03	2.89
	.001	14.0	9.34	7.55	6.59	5.98	5.55	5.23	4.99	4.80	4.64	4.39	4.14
26	.25	1.38	1.46	1.45	1.44	1.42	1.41	1.39	1.38	1.37	1.37	1.35	1.34
	.10	2.91	2.52	2.31	2.17	2.08	2.01	1.96	1.92	1.88	1.86	1.81	1.76
	.05	4.23	3.37	2.98	2.74	2.59	2.47	2.39	2.32	2.27	2.22	2.15	2.07
	.025	5.66	4.27	3.67	3.33	3.10	2.94	2.82	2.73	2.65	2.59	2.49	2.39
	.01	7.72	5.53	4.64	4.14	3.82	3.59	3.42	3.29	3.18	3.09	2.96	2.81
	.001	13.7	9.12	7.36	6.41	5.80	5.38	5.07	4.83	4.64	4.48	4.24	3.99
28	.25	1.38	1.46	1.45	1.43	1.41	1.40	1.39	1.38	1.37	1.36	1.34	1.33
	.10	2.89	2.50	2.29	2.16	2.06	2.00	1.94	1.90	1.87	1.84	1.79	1.74
	.05	4.20	3.34	2.95	2.71	2.56	2.45	2.36	2.29	2.24	2.19	2.12	2.04
	.025	5.61	4.22	3.63	3.29	3.06	2.90	2.78	2.69	2.61	2.55	2.45	2.34
	.01	7.64	5.45	4.57	4.07	3.75	3.53	3.36	3.23	3.12	3.03	2.90	2.75
	.001	13.5	8.93	7.19	6.25	5.66	5.24	4.93	4.69	4.50	4.35	4.11	3.86
	α	1	2	3	4	5	6	7	8	9	10	12	15

						v_b (Degrees of Freedom for Numerator)							
20	24	30	40	50	60	100	120	200	500	1000	∞	α	v_e
1.40	1.39	1.38	1.37	1.37	1.36	1.36	1.35	1.35	1.34	1.35	1.34	.25	16
1.89	1.87	1.84	1.81	1.79	1.78	1.76	1.75	1.74	1.73	1.72	1.72	.10	
2.28	2.24	2.19	2.15	2.12	2.11	2.07	2.06	2.04	2.02	2.02	2.01	.05	
2.68	2.63	2.57	2.51	2.47	2.45	2.40	2.38	2.36	2.33	2.32	2.32	.025	
3.26	3.18	3.10	3.02	2.97	2.93	2.86	2.84	2.81	2.78	2.76	2.75	.01	
4.99	4.85	4.70	4.54	4.45	4.39	4.25	4.23	4.16	4.10	4.08	4.06	.001	
1.39	1.38	1.37	1.36	1.35	1.35	1.34	1.34	1.34	1.33	1.33	1.33	.25	17
1.86	1.84	1.81	1.78	1.76	1.75	1.73	1.72	1.71	1.69	1.69	1.69	.10	
2.23	2.19	2.15	2.10	2.08	2.06	2.02	2.01	1.99	1.97	1.97	1.96	.05	
2.62	2.56	2.50	2.44	2.40	2.38	2.33	2.32	2.29	2.26	2.26	2.25	.025	
3.16	3.08	3.00	2.92	2.87	2.83	2.76	2.75	2.71	2.68	2.66	2.65	.01	
4.78	4.63	4.48	4.33	4.24	4.18	4.04	4.02	3.95	3.89	3.87	3.85	.001	
1.38	1.37	1.36	1.35	1.34	1.34	1.33	1.33	1.32	1.32	1.32	1.32	.25	18
1.84	1.81	1.78	1.75	1.74	1.72	1.70	1.69	1.68	1.67	1.66	1.66	.10	
2.19	2.15	2.11	2.06	2.04	2.02	1.98	1.97	1.95	1.93	1.92	1.92	.05	
2.56	2.50	2.44	2.38	2.35	2.32	2.27	2.26	2.32	2.20	2.20	2.19	.025	
3.08	3.00	2.92	2.84	2.78	2.75	2.68	2.66	2.62	2.59	2.58	2.57	.01	
4.59	4.45	4.30	4.15	4.05	4.00	3.86	3.84	3.77	3.71	3.69	3.67	.001	
1.37	1.36	1.35	1.34	1.33	1.33	1.32	1.32	1.31	1.31	1.31	1.30	.25	19
1.81	1.79	1.76	1.73	1.71	1.70	1.67	1.67	1.65	1.64	1.63	1.63	.10	
2.16	2.11	2.07	2.03	2.00	1.98	1.94	1.93	1.91	1.89	1.88	1.88	.05	
2.51	2.45	2.39	2.33	2.30	2.27	2.22	2.20	2.18	2.15	2.14	2.13	.025	
3.00	2.92	2.84	2.76	2.71	2.67	2.60	2.58	2.55	2.51	2.50	2.49	.01	
4.43	4.29	4.14	3.99	3.90	3.84	3.71	3.68	3.61	3.55	3.53	3.51	.001	
1.36	1.35	1.34	1.33	1.33	1.32	1.31	1.31	1.30	1.30	1.30	1.29	.25	20
1.79	1.77	1.74	1.71	1.69	1.68	1.65	1.64	1.63	1.62	1.61	1.61	.10	
2.12	2.08	2.04	1.99	1.97	1.95	1.91	1.90	1.88	1.86	1.85	1.84	.05	
2.46	2.41	2.35	2.29	2.25	2.22	2.17	2.16	2.13	2.10	2.09	2.09	.025	
2.94	2.86	2.78	2.69	2.64	2.61	2.54	2.52	2.48	2.44	2.43	2.42	.01	
4.29	4.15	4.00	3.86	3.77	3.70	3.58	3.54	3.48	3.42	3.39	3.38	.001	
1.34	1.33	1.32	1.31	1.31	1.30	1.30	1.30	1.29	1.29	1.28	1.28	.25	22
1.76	1.73	1.70	1.67	1.65	1.64	1.61	1.60	1.59	1.58	1.57	1.57	.10	
2.07	2.03	1.98	1.94	1.91	1.89	1.85	1.84	1.82	1.80	1.79	1.78	.05	
2.39	2.33	2.27	2.21	2.17	2.14	2.09	2.08	2.05	2.02	2.01	2.00	.025	
2.83	2.75	2.67	2.58	2.53	2.50	2.42	2.40	2.36	2.33	2.32	2.31	.01	
4.06	3.92	3.78	3.63	3.53	3.48	3.35	3.32	3.25	3.19	3.17	3.15	.001	
1.33	1.32	1.31	1.30	1.29	1.29	1.28	1.28	1.27	1.27	1.26	1.26	.25	24
1.73	1.70	1.67	1.64	1.62	1.61	1.58	1.57	1.56	1.54	1.54	1.53	.10	
2.03	1.98	1.94	1.89	1.86	1.84	1.80	1.79	1.77	1.75	1.74	1.73	.05	
2.33	2.27	2.21	2.15	2.11	2.08	2.02	2.01	1.98	1.95	1.94	1.94	.025	
2.74	2.66	2.58	2.49	2.44	2.40	2.33	2.31	2.27	2.24	2.22	2.21	.01	
3.87	3.74	3.59	3.45	3.35	3.29	3.16	3.14	3.07	3.01	2.99	2.97	.001	
1.32	1.31	1.30	1.29	1.28	1.28	1.26	1.26	1.26	1.25	1.25	1.25	.25	26
1.71	1.68	1.65	1.61	1.59	1.58	1.55	1.54	1.53	1.51	1.51	1.50	.10	
1.99	1.95	1.90	1.85	1.82	1.80	1.76	1.75	1.73	1.71	1.70	1.69	.05	
2.28	2.22	2.16	2.09	2.05	2.03	1.97	1.95	1.92	1.90	1.89	1.88	.025	
2.66	2.58	2.50	2.42	2.36	2.33	2.25	2.23	2.19	2.16	2.14	2.13	.01	
3.72	3.59	3.44	3.30	3.21	3.15	3.02	2.99	2.92	2.86	2.84	2.82	.001	
1.31	1.30	1.29	1.28	1.27	1.27	1.26	1.25	1.25	1.24	1.24	1.24	.25	28
1.69	1.66	1.63	1.59	1.57	1.56	1.53	1.52	1.50	1.49	1.48	1.48	.10	
1.96	1.91	1.87	1.82	1.79	1.77	1.73	1.71	1.69	1.67	1.66	1.65	.05	
2.23	2.17	2.11	2.05	2.01	1.98	1.92	1.91	1.88	1.85	1.84	1.83	.025	
2.60	2.52	2.44	2.35	2.30	2.26	2.19	2.17	2.13	2.09	2.08	2.06	.01	
3.60	3.46	3.32	3.18	3.08	3.02	2.89	2.86	2.80	2.73	2.71	2.69	.001	
20	24	30	40	50	60	100	120	200	500	1000	∞	α	v_e

(continued)

TABLE B.8 (continued)

v_e for Denominator	α	\multicolumn{13}{c}{v_b (Degrees of Freedom for Numerator)}
		1	2	3	4	5	6	7	8	9	10	12	15
30	.25	1.38	1.45	1.44	1.42	1.41	1.39	1.38	1.37	1.36	1.35	1.34	1.32
	.10	2.88	2.49	2.28	2.14	2.05	1.98	1.93	1.88	1.85	1.82	1.77	1.72
	.05	4.17	3.32	2.92	2.69	2.53	2.42	2.33	2.27	2.21	2.16	2.09	2.01
	.025	5.57	4.18	3.59	3.25	3.03	2.87	2.75	2.65	2.57	2.51	2.41	2.31
	.01	7.56	5.39	4.51	4.02	3.70	3.47	3.30	3.17	3.07	2.98	2.84	2.70
	.001	13.3	8.77	7.05	6.12	5.53	5.12	4.82	4.58	4.39	4.24	4.00	3.75
40	.25	1.36	1.44	1.42	1.40	1.39	1.37	1.36	1.35	1.34	1.33	1.31	1.30
	.10	2.84	2.44	2.23	2.09	2.00	1.93	1.87	1.83	1.79	1.76	1.71	1.66
	.05	4.08	3.23	2.84	2.61	2.45	2.34	2.25	2.18	2.12	2.08	2.00	1.92
	.025	5.42	4.05	3.46	3.13	2.90	2.74	2.62	2.53	2.45	2.34	2.29	2.18
	.01	7.31	5.18	4.31	3.83	3.51	3.29	3.12	2.99	2.89	2.80	2.66	2.52
	.001	12.6	8.25	6.60	5.70	5.13	4.73	4.44	4.21	4.02	3.87	3.64	3.40
60	.25	1.35	1.42	1.41	1.38	1.37	1.35	1.33	1.32	1.31	1.30	1.29	1.27
	.10	2.79	2.39	2.18	2.04	1.95	1.87	1.82	1.77	1.74	1.71	1.66	1.60
	.05	4.00	3.15	2.76	2.53	2.37	2.25	2.17	2.10	2.04	1.99	1.92	1.84
	.025	5.29	3.93	3.34	3.01	2.79	2.63	2.51	2.41	2.33	2.27	2.17	2.06
	.01	7.08	4.98	4.13	3.65	3.34	3.12	2.95	2.82	2.72	2.63	2.50	2.35
	.001	12.0	7.76	6.17	5.31	4.76	4.37	4.09	3.87	3.69	3.54	3.31	3.08
120	.25	1.34	1.40	1.39	1.37	1.35	1.33	1.31	1.30	1.29	1.28	1.26	1.24
	.10	2.75	2.35	2.13	1.99	1.90	1.82	1.77	1.72	1.68	1.65	1.60	1.55
	.05	3.92	3.07	2.68	2.45	2.29	2.17	2.09	2.02	1.96	1.91	1.83	1.75
	.025	5.15	3.80	3.23	2.89	2.67	2.52	2.39	2.30	2.22	2.16	2.05	1.95
	.01	6.85	4.79	3.95	3.48	3.17	2.96	2.79	2.66	2.56	2.47	2.34	2.19
	.001	11.4	7.32	5.79	4.95	4.42	4.04	3.77	3.55	3.38	3.24	3.02	2.78
200	.25	1.33	1.39	1.38	1.36	1.34	1.32	1.31	1.29	1.28	1.27	1.25	1.22
	.10	2.73	2.33	2.11	1.97	1.88	1.80	1.75	1.70	1.66	1.63	1.57	1.52
	.05	3.89	3.04	2.65	2.42	2.26	2.14	2.06	1.98	1.93	1.88	1.80	1.72
	.025	5.10	3.76	3.18	2.85	2.63	2.47	2.35	2.26	2.18	2.11	2.01	1.90
	.01	6.76	4.71	3.88	3.41	3.11	2.89	2.73	2.60	2.50	2.41	2.27	2.13
	.001	11.2	7.15	5.63	4.81	4.29	3.92	3.65	3.43	3.26	3.12	2.90	2.67
500	.25	1.33	1.39	1.37	1.35	1.33	1.31	1.30	1.28	1.27	1.26	1.24	1.22
	.10	2.72	2.31	2.10	1.96	1.86	1.79	1.73	1.68	1.64	1.61	1.56	1.50
	.05	3.86	3.01	2.62	2.39	2.23	2.12	2.03	1.96	1.90	1.85	1.77	1.64
	.025	5.06	3.72	3.14	2.81	2.59	2.43	2.31	2.22	2.14	2.07	1.97	1.86
	.01	6.69	4.65	3.82	3.36	3.05	2.84	2.68	2.55	2.49	2.36	2.22	2.07
	.001	11.0	7.00	5.50	4.69	4.17	3.81	3.54	3.33	3.16	3.02	2.80	2.51
1000	.25	1.33	1.39	1.37	1.35	1.33	1.31	1.29	1.28	1.27	1.26	1.24	1.22
	.10	2.71	2.31	2.09	1.95	1.85	1.78	1.72	1.68	1.64	1.61	1.55	1.49
	.05	3.85	3.00	2.61	2.38	2.22	2.10	2.02	1.95	1.89	1.84	1.76	1.64
	.025	5.04	3.70	3.13	2.80	2.58	2.42	2.30	2.20	2.13	2.06	1.96	1.85
	.01	6.66	4.62	3.80	3.34	3.04	2.82	2.66	2.53	2.43	2.34	2.20	2.06
	.001	10.9	6.95	5.46	4.65	4.14	3.78	3.51	3.30	3.13	2.99	2.77	2.54
∞	.25	1.32	1.39	1.37	1.35	1.33	1.31	1.29	1.28	1.27	1.25	1.24	1.22
	.10	2.71	2.30	2.08	1.94	1.85	1.77	1.72	1.67	1.63	1.60	1.55	1.49
	.05	3.84	3.00	2.60	2.37	2.21	2.10	2.01	1.94	1.88	1.83	1.75	1.67
	.025	5.02	3.69	3.12	2.79	2.57	2.41	2.29	2.19	2.11	2.05	1.94	1.83
	.01	6.63	4.61	3.78	3.32	3.02	2.80	2.64	2.51	2.41	2.32	2.18	2.04
	.001	10.8	6.91	5.42	4.62	4.10	3.74	3.47	3.27	3.10	2.96	2.74	2.51
	α	1	2	3	4	5	6	7	8	9	10	12	15

v_b (Degrees of Freedom for Numerator)													
20	24	30	40	50	60	100	120	200	500	1000	∞	α	v_e
1.30	1.29	1.28	1.27	1.26	1.26	1.25	1.24	1.24	1.23	1.23	1.23	.25	30
1.67	1.64	1.61	1.57	1.55	1.54	1.51	1.50	1.48	1.47	1.46	1.46	.10	
1.93	1.89	1.84	1.79	1.76	1.74	1.70	1.68	1.66	1.64	1.63	1.62	.05	
2.20	2.14	2.07	2.01	1.97	1.94	1.88	1.87	1.84	1.81	1.80	1.79	.025	
2.55	2.47	2.39	2.30	2.25	2.21	2.13	2.11	2.07	2.03	2.02	2.01	.01	
3.49	3.36	3.22	3.07	2.98	2.92	2.79	2.76	2.69	2.63	2.61	2.59	.001	
1.28	1.26	1.25	1.24	1.23	1.22	1.21	1.21	1.20	1.19	1.19	1.19	.25	40
1.61	1.57	1.54	1.51	1.48	1.47	1.43	1.42	1.41	1.39	1.38	1.38	.10	
1.84	1.79	1.74	1.69	1.66	1.64	1.59	1.58	1.55	1.53	1.52	1.51	.05	
2.07	2.01	1.94	1.88	1.83	1.80	1.74	1.72	1.69	1.66	1.65	1.64	.025	
2.37	2.29	2.20	2.11	2.06	2.02	1.94	1.92	1.87	1.83	1.82	1.80	.01	
3.15	3.01	2.87	2.73	2.64	2.57	2.44	2.41	2.34	2.28	2.25	2.23	.001	
1.25	1.24	1.22	1.21	1.20	1.19	1.17	1.17	1.16	1.15	1.15	1.15	.25	60
1.54	1.51	1.48	1.44	1.41	1.40	1.36	1.35	1.33	1.31	1.30	1.29	.10	
1.75	1.70	1.65	1.59	1.56	1.53	1.48	1.47	1.44	1.41	1.40	1.39	.05	
1.94	1.88	1.82	1.74	1.70	1.67	1.60	1.58	1.54	1.51	1.49	1.48	.025	
2.20	2.12	2.03	1.94	1.88	1.84	1.75	1.73	1.68	1.63	1.62	1.60	.01	
2.83	2.69	2.55	2.41	2.31	2.25	2.12	2.08	2.01	1.94	1.91	1.89	.001	
1.22	1.21	1.19	1.18	1.17	1.16	1.14	1.13	1.12	1.11	1.10	1.10	.25	120
1.48	1.45	1.41	1.37	1.34	1.32	1.27	1.26	1.24	1.21	1.20	1.19	.10	
1.66	1.61	1.55	1.50	1.46	1.43	1.37	1.35	1.32	1.28	1.27	1.25	.05	
1.82	1.76	1.69	1.61	1.56	1.53	1.45	1.43	1.39	1.34	1.33	1.31	.025	
2.03	1.95	1.86	1.76	1.70	1.66	1.56	1.53	1.48	1.42	1.40	1.38	.01	
2.53	2.40	2.26	2.11	2.02	1.95	1.80	1.76	1.68	1.60	1.57	1.54	.001	
1.21	1.20	1.18	1.16	1.14	1.12	1.11	1.10	1.09	1.08	1.08	1.06	.25	200
1.46	1.42	1.38	1.34	1.31	1.29	1.24	1.22	1.20	1.17	1.16	1.14	.10	
1.62	1.57	1.52	1.46	1.41	1.39	1.32	1.29	1.26	1.22	1.21	1.19	.05	
1.78	1.71	1.64	1.56	1.51	1.47	1.39	1.37	1.32	1.27	1.25	1.23	.025	
1.97	1.89	1.79	1.69	1.63	1.58	1.48	1.45	1.39	1.33	1.30	1.28	.01	
2.42	2.29	2.15	2.00	1.90	1.83	1.68	1.64	1.55	1.46	1.43	1.39	.001	
1.20	1.18	1.17	1.15	1.14	1.13	1.10	1.10	1.08	1.06	1.05	1.05	.25	500
1.44	1.40	1.36	1.31	1.28	1.26	1.21	1.19	1.16	1.12	1.11	1.09	.10	
1.59	1.54	1.48	1.42	1.38	1.35	1.28	1.26	1.21	1.16	1.14	1.11	.05	
1.74	1.67	1.60	1.52	1.46	1.42	1.34	1.31	1.25	1.19	1.17	1.14	.025	
1.92	1.83	1.74	1.63	1.57	1.52	1.41	1.38	1.31	1.23	1.20	1.17	.01	
2.33	2.19	2.05	1.90	1.80	1.73	1.57	1.53	1.43	1.32	1.28	1.23	.001	
1.19	1.18	1.16	1.15	1.13	1.25	1.10	1.09	1.07	1.05	1.04	1.03	.25	1000
1.43	1.39	1.35	1.30	1.27	1.33	1.20	1.18	1.15	1.10	1.06	1.06	.10	
1.58	1.53	1.47	1.41	1.36	1.41	1.26	1.24	1.19	1.13	1.11	1.08	.05	
1.72	1.65	1.58	1.50	1.44	1.50	1.32	1.29	1.23	1.16	1.13	1.10	.025	
1.89	1.81	1.71	1.61	1.54	1.69	1.38	1.35	1.28	1.19	1.16	1.11	.01	
2.30	2.16	2.02	1.87	1.77	1.72	1.53	1.49	1.38	1.27	1.22	1.15	.001	
1.19	1.18	1.16	1.14	1.13	1.12	1.09	1.08	1.07	1.04	1.03	1.00	.25	∞
1.42	1.38	1.34	1.30	1.26	1.24	1.18	1.17	1.13	1.08	1.06	1.00	.10	
1.57	1.52	1.46	1.39	1.35	1.32	1.24	1.22	1.17	1.11	1.08	1.00	.05	
1.71	1.64	1.57	1.48	1.43	1.39	1.30	1.27	1.21	1.13	1.09	1.00	.025	
1.88	1.79	1.70	1.59	1.52	1.47	1.36	1.32	1.25	1.15	1.11	1.00	.01	
2.27	2.13	1.99	1.84	1.73	1.66	1.50	1.45	1.34	1.21	1.15	1.00	.001	
20	24	30	40	50	60	100	120	200	500	1000	∞	α	v_e

TABLE B.9 Tabular Values of q_α for the Tukey Test

The row and column headings identify the appropriate values of q_α according to the degrees of freedom within (df_w) and the number of means k, respectively. These values are formally known as the percentage points of the Studentized range. The table shows the values of q_α corresponding to the .05 level of significance (regular type) and the .01 level of significance (**boldface** type). These values of q_α are entered in the equation for the HSD statistic of Tukey to determine the minimum difference between pairs of means that would be significant. The difference between a pair of means is significant if it is equal to or greater than the HSD value determined by the equation.

		J = number of means																	
df_w	α	2	3	4	5	6	7	8	9	10	11	12	13	14	15	16	17	18	19	20
	.05	18.0	27.0	32.8	37.1	40.4	43.1	45.4	47.4	49.1	50.6	52.0	53.2	54.3	55.4	56.3	57.2	58.0	58.8	59.6
	.01	**90.0**	**135**	**164**	**186**	**202**	**216**	**227**	**237**	**246**	**253**	**260**	**266**	**272**	**277**	**282**	**286**	**290**	**294**	**298**
2	.05	6.09	8.3	9.8	10.9	11.7	12.4	13.0	13.5	14.0	14.4	14.7	15.1	15.4	15.7	15.9	16.1	16.4	16.6	16.8
	.01	**14.0**	**19.0**	**22.3**	**24.7**	**26.6**	**28.2**	**29.5**	**30.7**	**31.7**	**32.6**	**33.4**	**34.1**	**34.8**	**35.4**	**36.0**	**36.5**	**37.0**	**37.5**	**37.9**
3	.05	4.50	5.91	6.82	7.50	8.04	8.48	8.85	9.18	9.46	9.72	9.95	10.15	10.35	10.52	10.69	10.84	10.98	11.11	11.24
	.01	**8.26**	**10.6**	**12.2**	**13.3**	**14.2**	**15.0**	**15.6**	**16.2**	**16.7**	**17.1**	**17.5**	**17.9**	**18.2**	**18.5**	**18.8**	**19.1**	**19.3**	**19.5**	**19.8**
4	.05	3.93	5.04	5.76	6.29	6.71	7.05	7.35	7.60	7.83	8.03	8.21	8.37	8.52	8.66	8.79	8.91	9.03	9.13	9.23
	.01	**6.51**	**8.12**	**9.17**	**9.96**	**10.6**	**11.1**	**11.5**	**11.9**	**12.3**	**12.6**	**12.8**	**13.1**	**13.3**	**13.5**	**13.7**	**13.9**	**14.1**	**14.2**	**14.4**
5	.05	3.64	4.60	5.22	5.67	6.03	6.33	6.58	6.80	6.99	7.17	7.32	7.47	7.60	7.72	7.83	7.93	8.03	8.12	8.21
	.01	**5.70**	**6.97**	**7.80**	**8.42**	**8.91**	**9.32**	**9.67**	**9.97**	**10.24**	**10.48**	**10.70**	**10.89**	**11.08**	**11.24**	**11.40**	**11.55**	**11.68**	**11.81**	**11.93**
6	.05	3.46	4.34	4.90	5.31	5.63	5.89	6.12	6.32	6.49	6.65	6.79	6.92	7.03	7.14	7.24	7.34	7.43	7.51	7.59
	.01	**5.24**	**6.33**	**7.03**	**7.56**	**7.97**	**8.32**	**8.61**	**8.87**	**9.10**	**9.30**	**9.49**	**9.65**	**9.81**	**9.95**	**10.08**	**10.21**	**10.32**	**10.43**	**10.54**
7	.05	3.34	4.16	4.68	5.06	5.36	5.61	5.82	6.00	6.16	6.30	6.43	6.55	6.66	6.76	6.85	6.94	7.02	7.09	7.17
	.01	**4.95**	**5.92**	**6.54**	**7.01**	**7.37**	**7.68**	**7.94**	**8.17**	**8.37**	**8.55**	**8.71**	**8.86**	**9.00**	**9.12**	**9.24**	**9.35**	**9.46**	**9.55**	**9.65**
8	.05	3.26	4.04	4.53	4.89	5.17	5.40	5.60	5.77	5.92	6.05	6.18	6.29	6.39	6.48	6.57	6.65	6.73	6.80	6.87
	.01	**4.74**	**5.63**	**6.20**	**6.63**	**6.96**	**7.24**	**7.47**	**7.68**	**7.87**	**8.03**	**8.18**	**8.31**	**8.44**	**8.55**	**8.66**	**8.76**	**8.85**	**8.94**	**9.03**
9	.05	3.20	3.95	4.42	4.76	5.02	5.24	5.43	5.60	5.74	5.87	5.98	6.09	6.19	6.28	6.36	6.44	6.51	6.58	6.64
	.01	**4.60**	**5.43**	**5.96**	**6.35**	**6.66**	**6.91**	**7.13**	**7.32**	**7.49**	**7.65**	**7.78**	**7.91**	**8.03**	**8.13**	**8.23**	**8.32**	**8.41**	**8.49**	**8.57**
10	.05	3.15	3.88	4.33	4.65	4.91	5.12	5.30	5.46	5.60	5.72	5.83	5.93	6.03	6.11	6.20	6.27	6.34	6.40	6.47
	.01	**4.48**	**5.27**	**5.77**	**6.14**	**6.43**	**6.67**	**6.87**	**7.05**	**7.21**	**7.36**	**7.48**	**7.60**	**7.71**	**7.81**	**7.91**	**7.99**	**8.07**	**8.15**	**8.22**
11	.05	3.11	3.82	4.26	4.57	4.82	5.03	5.20	5.35	5.49	5.61	5.71	5.81	5.90	5.99	6.06	6.14	6.20	6.26	6.33
	.01	**4.39**	**5.14**	**5.62**	**5.97**	**6.25**	**6.48**	**6.67**	**6.84**	**6.99**	**7.13**	**7.25**	**7.36**	**7.46**	**7.56**	**7.65**	**7.73**	**7.81**	**7.88**	**7.95**

12	.05	6.21	6.15	6.09	6.03	5.95	5.88	5.80	5.71	5.62	5.51	5.40	5.27	5.12	4.95	4.75	4.51	4.20	3.77	3.08
	.01	7.73	7.66	7.59	7.52	7.44	7.36	7.26	7.17	7.06	6.94	6.81	6.67	6.51	6.32	6.10	5.84	5.50	5.04	4.32
13	.05	6.11	6.05	6.00	5.93	5.86	5.79	5.71	5.63	5.53	5.43	5.32	5.19	5.05	4.88	4.69	4.45	4.15	3.73	3.06
	.01	7.55	7.48	7.42	7.34	7.27	7.19	7.10	7.01	6.90	6.79	6.67	6.53	6.37	6.19	5.98	5.73	5.40	4.96	4.26
14	.05	6.03	5.97	5.92	5.85	5.79	5.72	5.64	5.55	5.46	5.36	5.25	5.13	4.99	4.83	4.64	4.41	4.11	3.70	3.03
	.01	7.39	7.33	7.27	7.20	7.12	7.05	6.96	6.87	6.77	6.66	6.54	6.41	6.26	6.08	5.88	5.63	5.32	4.89	4.21
15	.05	5.96	5.90	5.85	5.79	5.72	5.65	5.58	5.49	5.40	5.31	5.20	5.08	4.94	4.78	4.60	4.37	4.08	3.67	3.01
	.01	7.26	7.20	7.14	7.07	7.00	6.93	6.84	6.76	6.66	6.55	6.44	6.31	6.16	5.99	5.80	5.56	5.25	4.83	4.17
16	.05	5.90	5.84	5.79	5.72	5.66	5.59	5.52	5.44	5.35	5.26	5.15	5.03	4.90	4.74	4.56	4.33	4.05	3.65	3.00
	.01	7.15	7.09	7.03	6.97	6.90	6.82	6.74	6.66	6.56	6.46	6.35	6.22	6.08	5.92	5.72	5.49	5.19	4.78	4.13
17	.05	5.84	5.79	5.74	5.68	5.61	5.55	5.47	5.39	5.31	5.21	5.11	4.99	4.86	4.71	4.52	4.30	4.02	3.63	2.98
	.01	7.05	7.00	6.94	6.87	6.80	6.73	6.66	6.57	6.48	6.38	6.27	6.15	6.01	5.85	5.66	5.43	5.14	4.74	4.10
18	.05	5.79	5.74	5.69	5.63	5.57	5.50	5.43	5.35	5.27	5.17	5.07	4.96	4.82	4.67	4.49	4.28	4.00	3.61	2.97
	.01	6.96	6.91	6.85	6.79	6.72	6.65	6.58	6.50	6.41	6.31	6.20	6.08	5.94	5.79	5.60	5.38	5.09	4.70	4.07
19	.05	5.75	5.70	5.65	5.59	5.53	5.46	5.39	5.32	5.23	5.14	5.04	4.92	4.79	4.65	4.47	4.25	3.98	3.59	2.96
	.01	6.89	6.84	6.78	6.72	6.65	6.58	6.51	6.43	6.34	6.25	6.14	6.02	5.89	5.73	5.55	5.33	5.05	4.67	4.05
20	.05	5.71	5.66	5.61	5.55	5.49	5.43	5.36	5.28	5.20	5.11	5.01	4.90	4.77	4.62	4.45	4.23	3.96	3.58	2.95
	.01	6.82	6.76	6.71	6.65	6.59	6.52	6.45	6.37	6.29	6.19	6.09	5.97	5.84	5.69	5.51	5.29	5.02	4.64	4.02
24	.05	5.59	5.54	5.50	5.44	5.38	5.32	5.25	5.18	5.10	5.01	4.92	4.81	4.68	4.54	4.37	4.17	3.90	3.53	2.92
	.01	6.61	6.56	6.51	6.45	6.39	6.33	6.26	6.19	6.11	6.02	5.92	5.81	5.69	5.54	5.37	5.17	4.91	4.54	3.96
30	.05	5.48	5.43	5.38	5.33	5.27	5.21	5.15	5.08	5.00	4.92	4.83	4.72	4.60	4.46	4.30	4.10	3.84	3.49	2.89
	.01	6.41	6.36	6.31	6.26	6.20	6.14	6.08	6.01	5.93	5.85	5.76	5.65	5.54	5.40	5.24	5.05	4.80	4.45	3.89
40	.05	5.36	5.31	5.27	5.22	5.16	5.11	5.05	4.98	4.91	4.82	4.74	4.63	4.52	4.39	4.23	4.04	3.79	3.44	2.86
	.01	6.21	6.17	6.12	6.07	6.02	5.96	5.90	5.84	5.77	5.69	5.60	5.50	5.39	5.27	5.11	4.93	4.70	4.37	3.82
60	.05	5.24	5.20	5.16	5.11	5.06	5.00	4.94	4.88	4.81	4.73	4.65	4.55	4.44	4.31	4.16	3.98	3.74	3.40	2.83
	.01	6.02	5.98	5.93	5.89	5.84	5.79	5.73	5.67	5.60	5.53	5.45	5.36	5.25	5.13	4.99	4.82	4.60	4.28	3.76
120	.05	5.13	5.09	5.05	5.00	4.95	4.90	4.84	4.78	4.72	4.64	4.56	4.48	4.36	4.24	4.10	3.92	3.69	3.36	2.80
	.01	5.83	5.79	5.75	5.71	5.66	5.61	5.56	5.51	5.44	5.38	5.30	5.21	5.12	5.01	4.87	4.71	4.50	4.20	3.70
∞	.05	5.01	4.97	4.93	4.89	4.85	4.80	4.74	4.68	4.62	4.55	4.47	4.39	4.29	4.17	4.03	3.86	3.63	3.31	2.77
	.01	5.65	5.61	5.57	5.54	5.49	5.45	5.40	5.35	5.29	5.23	5.16	5.08	4.99	4.88	4.76	4.60	4.40	4.12	3.64

Answers to Selected Exercises

Chapter 2

Note: Where "(*for example*)" is added, there are other acceptable answers to the question.

1. **a.** Jewish-other (*for example*).

   b. Protestant-Catholic-Jewish-other-no reported religion (*for example*).

   d. Nominal. No.

2. **a.** A class.

   b. Catholic most popular, Protestant most popular, Jewish most popular, other most popular (*for example*).

   c. Assign a class to one of the four categories based on which religion was named by the most people in the class. In case of a tie, assign a class to a category based on alphabetical order of the two religions that were tied (*for example*).

3. **a.** "Self presentational concerns important," "Internal motivation paramount" (*for example*).

   b. Those in the private mode will spend less time on the anagram game than those in the public mode (*for example*).

   c. Nominal.

   d. High Protestant work ethic: There will be no relationship between observation type and time spent (*for example*). Low Protestant work ethic: same answer as in (**b**) (*for example*).

   f. Name: level of deception of subjects. Category 1: low (experiment 1); Category 2: high (experiment 2) (*for example*).

4. a. Ratio.

    b. Not a variable. It is a constant.

    c. Ratio. Over time the rate will vary.

    d. Ratio.

    e. Nominal.

    f. Nominal.

    g. Nominal (probably, but can you think of a variable that would be ordinal?)

    h. Nominal certainly; arguably ordinal (what's the argument?)

    i. Depends on what characteristics of the cards one pays attention to.

5. a. No.

    b. No, at least not by a human being in the story.

    c. Well. . . . That's a hard question. The answer depends on how you think of the status of a story. If griffins were real, then the answer would be no. If not, . . . well, it's a hard question.

7. a. Case: a river or a section of a river. Hypothesis: Trout population increases linearly to 58 degrees Fahrenheit, then decreases with increasing temperature. Consider: time of day the temperature is measured, the difficulty of counting trout (*for example*).

    c. Case: a person. Hypothesis: The older a person, the higher would be the person's test score (*for example*).

    d. Case: a person. Hypothesis: People of moderate power will have the most keys. People with great power (e.g., the president) and people with little power (e.g. janitors) will have few keys (*for example*).

    e. Case: section of roadway. Hypothesis: The more cars, the higher the maintenance costs. Consider: number of trucks, part of the country (*for example*).

    g. Case: a college. Hypothesis: The lower the number of catalogs mailed, the higher the enrollment. Reason: High prestige colleges attract a lot of people on the basis of reputation (*for example*). Remember: Hypotheses only have to be falsifiable, not true or even well reasoned.

    h. Case: an area. Hypothesis: The greater the number of admissions, the higher the death rate. Consider: How to define an area. Must an area contain a hospital? Wouldn't it be better to measure an area's admission *rate* to standardize for population differences?

    l. Case: a state. Hypothesis: The higher the state's prison population, the shorter the average length of prison sentences. Reason: judges take account of problems of prison space availability in sentencing decisions.

    m. Ha.

Chapter 3

1. a. Private: 59, 49, 39, 50, 46, 55, 52, 46, 37, 38, 42, 47, 38, 43, 42, 28, 57, 18, 33, 45.

b. 18, 59.

c. Class interval = 5 (*for example*).

d.

Class	15–19	20–24	25–29	30–34	35–39	40–44	45–49	50–54	55–59
f_i	1	0	1	1	4	3	5	2	3

e.

Class	f_i
15–19	X
20–24	
25–29	X
30–34	X
35–39	X X X X
40–44	X X X
45–49	X X X X X
50–54	X X
55–59	X X X

f. For the public condition:

Class	15–19	20–24	25–29	30–34	35–39	40–44	45–49	50–54	55–59
f_i	0	0	1	1	3	5	6	4	0

Class	f_i
15–19	
20–24	
25–29	X
30–34	X
35–39	X X X
40–44	X X X X X
45–49	X X X X X X
50–54	X X X X
55–59	

g. No reason to expect a difference if, in fact, subjects were randomly assigned to the two conditions. They appear different. The public condition histogram is less spread out. They could be different due to "the luck of the draw" or due to some systematic assignment problem.

2. a. I chose classes of width 10.0 beginning at 0.0. The frequency distribution is

i	0–10.0	10.1–20.0	20.1–30.0	30.1–40.0	40.1–50.0
f_i	8	14	12	16	16

i	50.1–60.0	60.1–70.0	70.1–80.0	80.1–90.0	90.1–100.
f_i	10	11	10	7	1

b. Here is a histogram:

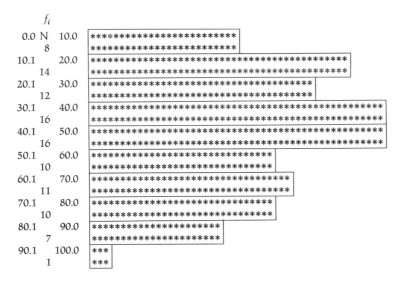

3. a. Here is a histogram with class intervals of 100 for time spent:

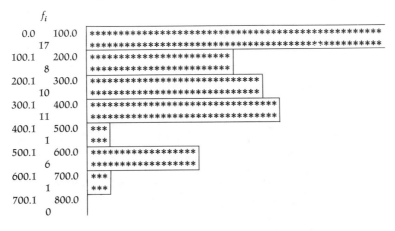

b. Here is the histogram for those who thought they were doing "work:"

```
      f_i       Time
0.0   100.0   **************************************************
      9        **************************************************
100.1 200.0   *****************
      3        *****************
200.1 300.0   ****************************
      5        ****************************
300.1 400.0   ****************************************
      7        ****************************************
400.1 500.0   ******
      1        ******
500.1 600.0   ***********
      2        ***********
600.1 700.0   ******
      1        ******
700.1 800.0   |
      0
```

c. Here is the histogram for those who thought they were doing "play:"

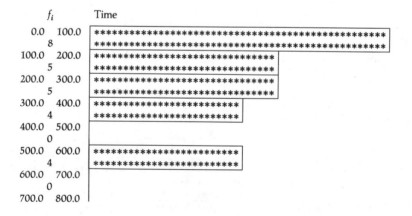

```
      f_i       Time
0.0   100.0   ***************************************************
      8        ***************************************************
100.0 200.0   *******************************
      5        *******************************
200.0 300.0   *******************************
      5        *******************************
300.0 400.0   ************************
      4        ************************
400.0 500.0
      0
500.0 600.0   ************************
      4        ************************
600.0 700.0
      0
700.0 800.0   |
```

d. I divided those who thought they were doing "work" into two groups based on their Protestant work ethic score. Those 14 people who scored 82 or higher were high work ethic people. Those 14 people who scored lower than 82 were low work ethic people. Here are the two histograms for their time spent on the word game:

High work ethic

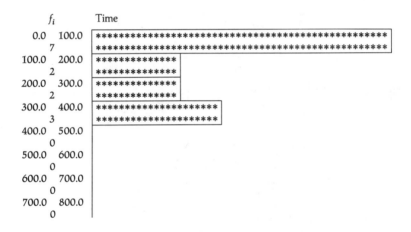

f_i		Time
0.0	100.0	*************************
2		*************************
100.0	200.0	*************
1		*************
200.0	300.0	***************************************
3		***************************************
300.0	400.0	**
4		**
400.0	500.0	*************
1		*************
500.0	600.0	*************************
2		*************************
600.0	700.0	*************
1		*************
700.0	800.0	
0		

Low work ethic

f_i		Time
0.0	100.0	**
7		**
100.0	200.0	**************
2		**************
200.0	300.0	**************
2		**************
300.0	400.0	**********************
3		**********************
400.0	500.0	
0		
500.0	600.0	
0		
600.0	700.0	
0		
700.0	800.0	
0		

Conclusion: Among those who thought they were doing work, those with high work ethics spent more time on a task labeled work than did those who have a low work ethic. The hypothesis is supported in the sample.

5. a. Frequency distribution of pets owned:

i	0	1	2	3	4	5	6	7
f_i	20	15	8	3	2	1	0	1

b. Histogram

```
Class

  0  │ X X X X X X X X X X X X X X X X X X X X X
  1  │ X X X X X X X X X X X X X X X
  2  │ X X X X X X X X
  3  │ X X X
  4  │ X X
  5  │ X
  6  │
  7  │ X
```

c. It makes little sense to form classes for these data.

6. a. Histogram with one degree class intervals

```
    Class       f_i
 97.0− 97.9      1  │ X
 98.0− 98.9     20  │ X X X X X X X X X X X X X X X X X X X X
 99.0− 99.9      4  │ X X X X
100.0−100.9      3  │ X X X
101.0−101.9      2  │ X X
102.0−102.9      3  │ X X X
103.0−103.9      1  │ X
104.0 +          2  │ X X
```

b. Histogram with half-degree class intervals

```
    Class        f_i
 97.0− 97.4       0  │
 97.5− 97.9       1  │ X
 98.0− 98.4       7  │ X X X X X X X
 98.5− 98.9      13  │ X X X X X X X X X X X X X
 99.0− 99.4       3  │ X X X
 99.5− 99.9       1  │ X
100.0−100.4       3  │ X X X
100.5−100.9       0  │
101.0−101.4       1  │ X
101.5−101.9       1  │ X
102.0−102.4       1  │ X
102.5−102.9       2  │ X X
103.0−103.4       0  │
103.5−103.9       1  │ X
104.0−104.4       1  │ X
104.5 +           1  │ X
```

c. It is difficult to assert that "helpful information" is gained by decreasing the class size without any context. Perhaps the first would be helpful in the context of a study interested in the percentage of "abnormal temperatures" seen in the emergency room. The second would be helpful in the context of a study interested in the distribution of "high temperatures" seen in the emergency room.

d. The distribution is unimodal and skewed positively.

e. (i) Variable = sex. Hypothesis = Women have higher temperatures than men.

(ii) Variable = white blood count. Hypothesis = People with a high white blood count tend to have higher temperatures than those with low white blood count.

(iii) Variable = number of children. Hypothesis = The more children one has, the higher one's temperature.
Remember: Hypotheses do not have to be correct. They just have to be falsifiable.
Question: Is "People who are sick will have a higher temperature than those who are not" a hypothesis?

8. a. Families with children present will tend to have an older head of household.

b.

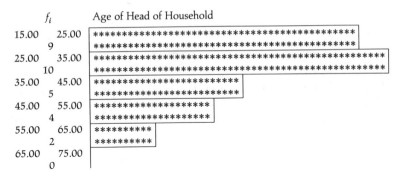

c. With children.

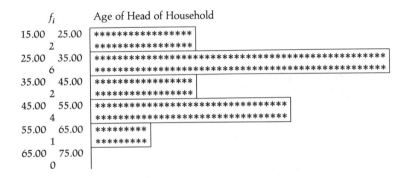

Without children.

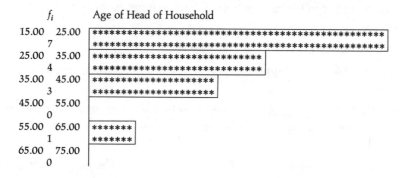

f_i		Age of Head of Household
15.00	25.00	
7		
25.00	35.00	
4		
35.00	45.00	
3		
45.00	55.00	
0		
55.00	65.00	
1		
65.00	75.00	
0		

d. Age   Y = Children present   N = Children not present

15–25	N N N N N N Y Y N
26–35	Y Y Y Y N Y Y N N N
36–45	Y N N Y N
46–55	Y Y Y Y
56–65	Y N
66–75	

e.

Class	Yes	No
f_i	15	12

f.

No	222353334652244
Yes	212441211423316

g. For purposes of *my* hypothesis, the conditional distributions in (**c**) or the stem-and-leaf diagram in (**d**) is the appropriate presentation. I prefer the conditional distributions in this case because they show, pretty clearly, that the age of the head of household is, on average, lower when children are not present.

9. a. Hypothesis: The more fertilizer, the higher the corn.

b. Here are histograms (with frequency distributions on the side) of each variable.

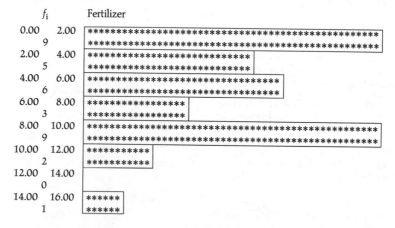

f_i		Fertilizer
0.00	2.00	
9		
2.00	4.00	
5		
4.00	6.00	
6		
6.00	8.00	
3		
8.00	10.00	
9		
10.00	12.00	
2		
12.00	14.00	
0		
14.00	16.00	
1		

f_i		Corn Length

5.000	5.500	*****
	1	*****
5.500	6.000	*********
	2	********
6.000	6.500	************************************
	8	************************************
6.500	7.000	**
	11	**
7.000	7.500	*******************************
	7	*******************************
7.500	8.000	******************
	4	******************
8.000	8.500	*********
	2	*********

c. I divided the independent variable, fertilizer, into two categories. Seventeen cases are in the low fertilizer category and have values of 5.4 or less. Eighteen cases are in the high fertilizer category with values above 5.4.

d. For high fertilizer gardens

Class	5.0–5.5	5.6–6.0	6.1–6.5	6.6–7.0	7.1–7.5	7.6–8.0	8.0–8.5
f_i	1	2	3	6	4	2	0

For low fertilizer gardens

Class	5.0–5.5	5.6–6.0	6.1–6.5	6.6–7.0	7.1–7.5	7.6–8.0	8.0–8.5
f_i	0	0	5	5	3	2	2

e. Stem-and-leaf of corn length with leaves indicating high (H) or low (L) fertilizer use:

Class	
5.0–5.5	H
5.6–6.0	H H
6.1–6.5	H L L L H L L H
6.6–7.0	H H L L L H L H L H L L H
7.1–7.5	H L H H L L H
7.6–8.0	H L H L
8.1–8.5	L L

f. I conclude from the data that the hypothesis is not supported. From the conditional distributions in particular larger ears tend to come from low fertilizer gardens. That is a little harder to see from the stem-and-leaf plot.

11. a. Hypothesis: There should be no difference in IQ based on age.

b. Here are conditional distributions of IQ scores for young people and for older people.

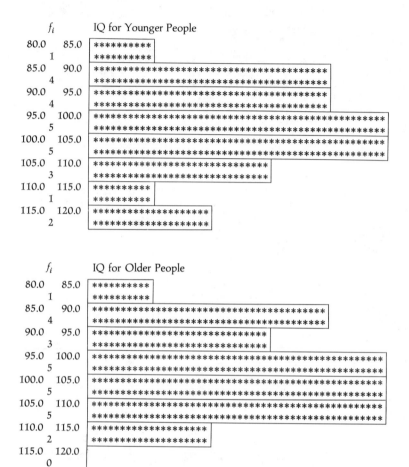

The hypothesis seems to be supported in the sample. Note: Don't be misled by the two cases in the last class in the histogram for younger pepple. The point is that the general shape and the general distribution of cases appears the same in both distributions.

Chapter 4

1. a. I selected the last ten countries on the list, from U.S.A. through Zimbabwe.

b. The mean per capita income is $1802.30.

c. I selected ten countries randomly. (See Chapter 7.) They are Tanzania, Spain, Sudan, New Zealand, Mexico, Laos, Greece, Barbados, China (Taiwan), and Jordan.

d. $2157.50.

e. The two sample means are different from the overall per capita income. Why? Because selecting a sample from a population introduces error into the estimation of population characteristics. If you want errorless estimation of population characteristics, you must have knowledge about the entire population.

2. a. 84.05

b. 84.45

c. There was no reason to expect the means to differ. It seems to me that the important thing is *not* that these two means differ; rather, the important thing is that they differ by so little.

d. I find comparing means easier. The histogram comparison may be better since it gives a "bigger picture."

3. a. The mode in that histogram is at 30–50.

b. 43.23

c.

Whisker Plot for Urban

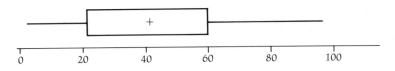

4. a. For the subjects assigned to the "work" condition, the mean Protestant work ethic score is 80.23. For those assigned to the "play" condition, the mean is 79.76.

b. The means must differ simply because of the "luck of the draw." There is no reason to expect the means to differ because of anything having to do with the experiment since the subjects were randomly assigned to the two experimental conditions.

c. If the means were very different, we would say that the groups resulting from the random assignment of subjects to the experimental conditions are not comparable groups. Therefore, you could not attribute differences in the dependent variable strictly to the experimental manipulation of the independent variable. The experiment would be compromised from the outset. If the means are the same, or nearly so as they are in this case, the experiment can proceed. A critic would not have available to him or her the argument of non-comparability between experimental groups.

6. a. The mean time spent on the word game for those who thought they were doing "work" is 237.1 seconds. The mean time spent for those who thought they were doing "play" is 221.9 seconds. Among those who thought they were doing "work," those with a Protestant work ethic score of 82 or higher, spent an average of 322.6 seconds on the word game while those with a Protestant work ethic score lower than 82 spent an average of 151.6 seconds on the word game.

b. The hypothesis is supported in the sample. Those with a high work ethic spend more time on a task labeled "work" than do those with a low work ethic.

8. a. Average length of stay in DRG 373 using the physician as a unit of analysis is 1.89 days.

b. Average length of stay in DRG 373 using the patient as a unit of analysis is 1.92 days.

c. The slight difference is attributable to physicians who tend, on average, to keep patients in the hospital longer having more patients than other physicians. If all the physicians had the same number of patients, there would be no difference in these two means.

10. $1305.60. Perhaps he or she keeps his or her patients in the hospital longer. This could be checked by calculating the average ALOS for each physician. Perhaps he or she deals with more complicated cases. This could be checked in the data.

12. Hypothesis: Procedures with complications will tend to have a higher proportion of the total cost captured in "material" and technology. The average percentage of total expenditures devoted to material and technology for physician-DRG pairs in which there is a complication is 14.9%. The average percentage of total expenditures devoted to material and technology for physician-DRG pairs in which there is no complication is 10.8%. The hypothesis is supported by the data in this sample.

13. Because the specialization score is a characteristic of a physician. The physician is a constant across all physician-DRG pairs identified by the physician's number, so the specialization score is constant across the physician-DRG pairs identified by each physician's number.

14. a. The minimum is 47; the maximum is 97. The range is $(97 - 47) + 1 = 51$.

b. $Q_1 = 63.0$; $Q_2 = 84.5$; $Q_3 = 90.0$.

c. 13.5.

d. 265.4.

e. The distribution is bi-modal with one mode in the 60–70 area and another in the 80–90 area. The distribution is skewed negatively.

f. Box-and-whisker plot for specialization score with outliers shown with asterisks:

42	52	62	72	82	92

16. Refer to the histograms in response to Exercise 3, Chapter 3.

   a. The distributions center at slightly different places. For the "work" condition, the mean time spent on the word game is 237.1 seconds and the median time spent is 215 seconds. For the "leisure" condition, the mean time spent is 221.9 seconds and the median time spent is 185 seconds.

   b. The distributions are shaped a little differently. The "work" distribution is bi-modal. Both are positively skewed.

   c. The ranges are slightly different. For the "work" condition, "time spent" ranges from 0 to 630 seconds. For the "leisure" condition, the range is 0–520 seconds for a range of 521 seconds.

   d. The standard deviations of the two distributions are slightly different. The standard deviation of "time spent" for those in the "work" condition is 177.5 seconds while the standard deviation for those in the "leisure" condition is 172.7 seconds.

   Conclusion: The distributions differ slightly.

18. a. Protestant work ethic, first ten scores: Mean = 83.7, standard deviation = 13.16, variance = 173.

   b. Type A personality, first ten scores: Mean = 47.7, standard deviation = 6.91, variance = 47.8.

   c. Coefficients of variation: work ethic = 0.16; Type A personality = 0.14.

   d. The scores on work ethic are slightly more variable than the scores on the Type A personality scale, but the variation is remarkably similar.

20. a. 57.5%.

   b. 12%–99%. Range = 88%.

   c. 1174.

   d. 34.3.

   f.

Income	Mean	Range	Variance	Standard Deviation
Low	32.9	12–75	558	23.6
High	79.0	36–99	733	27.1

g.

Whisker Plot for Lit for Low Income, $n = 7$

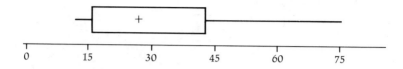

Whisker Plot for Lit for High Income, $n = 8$

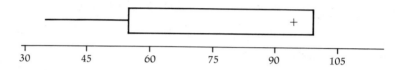

h. The statistics for the subgroups are each different from the overall group. The low income countries have lower literacy than the overall average literacy rate. The high income countries have, on average, higher literacy than the overall average literacy rate.

i. The high income group has a much higher average literacy rate than the low income group of countries. The high income countries have slightly more variation in literacy rates than does the low income group.

21. a. mode = 0.

b. mean = 1.2.

c. Since the mean is greater than the mode, the distribution is skewed positively. Yes, this agrees with the histogram.

d. Box-and-whisker plot

Whisker Plot for Pets

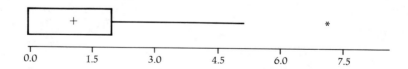

23. a. Mean = -0.48; Median = -0.9, Mode (using histogram with 2% class intervals) = 0.1–2.0% class; variance = 11.0; standard deviation = 3.32.

b. The best estimate of the percentage change in the whole market is the mean change in the sample: -0.48%.

c. It would shatter my confidence in my estimate. Estimating population characteristics depends on the assumption that the sample is representative of the population with which one is concerned. This statement says that the sample is not at all representative of the whole market.

25. a.

Whisker Plot for Corn for High Fertilizer Gardens, $n = 18$

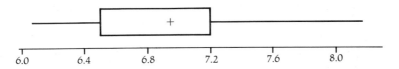

b.

Whisker Plot for Corn for Low Fertilizer Gardens, $n = 17$

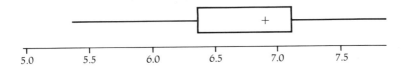

c. Note that the scales in (**a**) and (**b**) differ. To compare the two box-and-whisker plots, they should be on the same scales:

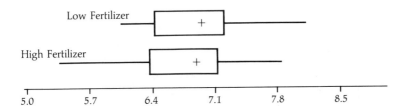

Using more fertilizer does not seem to increase corn ear length.

26. a.

Study Time	Conditional Mode	Conditional Median
High	A	B
Medium	C	B
Low	C	C

b. It is possible to determine conditional means if you are willing to assume that grades are an interval variable with, for example, A = 4.0, B = 3.0, C = 2.0, and D = 1.0. Using that scheme and making the required assumption, then the conditional mean grades are 3.07 for high study time students, 2.67 for medium study time students, and 2.53 for low study time students.

c. Yes, a higher level of study time is associated with higher grades, on average.

d. This is a tricky question. These data are cross-sectional data about the relationship between the amount of time an individual studies and the individual's grade. These data do *not* speak directly to the question of whether an individual who has low grades could *change* his or her grades by studying more. However, recall that decisions regarding time-based phenomena like "change" are made using non-time-based (cross-sectional) data by inferring a time dimension into the data. If you want to make that inference and if this sample is representative of the population that includes the individual in question, then you might want to urge the individual to study more.

Chapter 5

1. a. Sample space: {red, blue}. P(red) = .75. P(blue) = .25. P(yellow) = 0.

d. Sample space: {black-black, black-red, red-red}. (Do you understand why "red-black" is not in the sample space?) P(black-black) = 1/6. P(black-red) = 2/3.

2. a. Sample space: {0, 1, 2, 3, 4}

b. Sample space: {T-T-T-T, T-T-T-H, T-T-H-T, T-T-H-H, T-H-T-T, T-H-T-H, T-H-H-T, T-H-H-H, H-T-T-T, H-T-T-H, H-T-H-T, H-T-H-H, H-H-T-T, H-H-T-H, H-H-H-T, H-H-H-H}

3. a. (i) Sample space: {2, 4, 6, 8, 10}

(ii) P(6) = 1/3.

(iii) P(10) = 1/9.

(iv) Outcomes in the event "an even number": 2, 4, 6, 8, 10. P(even number) = 1.0.

(v) Outcomes in the event "a number greater than four": 6, 8, 10. P(a number greater than four) = 2/3.

b. (i) Sample space: (note—R3 means, e.g., "red die, three showing") {R1-W1, R1-W3, R1-W5, R3-W1, R3-W3, R3-W5, R5-W1, R5-W3, R5-W5}

(ii) P(R1-W3) = 1/3.

(iii) P(red die lower than three and white die 3 or higher) = 2/9.

(iv) P(an even number) = 0. (This event is not in the sample space of this experiment.)

(v) P(R5-W5) = 1/9.

4. a. Sample space: {coin = head and die = 1, coin = head and die = 3, coin = head and die = 5, coin = tail and die = 1, coin = tail and die = 3, coin = tail and die = 5}

5. a. Sample space: {0, 1, 2}

d.

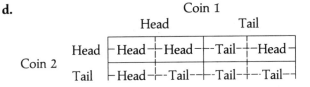

e. P(one head) = 1/4.

6. a. $P(7) = .15$.

b. Outcome 7 should occur three times as frequently as outcome 6.

c. $P(6 \text{ or } 7) = .05 + .15 = .20$.

d. Outcome 7 should occur with equal frequency as the event (outcome 4 or outcome 5 or outcome 6).

e. If there are other mutually exclusive outcomes in the sample space, the probability of each one occurring is zero since one of these outcomes must, with certainty, occur.

7. b. $P(H \text{ or } K) = .8$

c. $P(\bar{H}) = 0.3$.

f. $P(H \text{ and } K) = 0$ if the experiment is structured so that only one outcome is selected on each trial. In general, this probability cannot be assessed with the information given since we know nothing about the independence of the events.

8. The events "being a mother" and "works" are not mutually exclusive. One cannot assess P("being a mother" and "works") without knowing either the conditional probability of working given that one is a mother [P(works|mother)] or the conditional probability of being a mother given that one works [P(mother|works)].

9. a. (i) The events are mutually exclusive.

(ii) The events are mutually exclusive.

(iii) The events are mutually exclusive.

(iv) The events are not mutually exclusive.

(v) The events are not mutually exclusive.

   b. (i) The events are not mutually exclusive.

   (ii) The events are mutually exclusive.

   c. (i) The events are not mutually exclusive.

   (iv) The events are mutually exclusive.

10. a. $P(H \text{ and } K) = P(H) \cdot P(K) = 0.21$.

   c. $P(H|K) = P(H) = 0.3$.

11. a. no.

   b. $P(H \text{ and } K) = P(K) \times P(H|K) = 0.04$.

   c. $P(H \text{ or } K) = P(H) + P(K) - P(H \text{ and } K) = .3 + .4 - .04 = .66$.

   e. no.

12. a. 0.6.

   b. 0.4.

   c. 0.7.

   d. 0.5.

   e. 0.2.

   f. 0.

   h. R and S are not mutually exclusive events. S and T are mutually exclusive events.

   i. R and S are independent. S and T are not independent.

14. a. $P(\text{male}) = 0.35$.

   b. $P(\text{female and teenager}) = P(\text{teen}) \times P(\text{female}|\text{teen}) = 0.85 \times 0.7 = 0.595$.

   c. $P(\text{male and not teen}) = 0.095$.

15. a. With replacement, the probability of getting three red balls is 0.125.

   b. Without replacement, the probability is $(0.5)(0.4)(0.25) = 0.05$.

18. a. 0.03125.

   b. 0.3125.

   c. 0.5.

19. a. 0.00098.

   b. 0.264.

   c. 0.896.

21. a. 0.16.

   b. 0.80.

   c. 0.77.

22. a. 0.55.

   b. 0.55.

   c. 0.40.

   d. 0.20.

   e. 0.73.

   f. 0.27.

24. a. 0.243.

   b. 0.271.

   c. The store can expect about 27 of the 100 customers to have a packet with at least one defective widget. It will give two packets to each person, so it will distribute about 54 packets free for every 100 sold.

26. Without spelling checker: 500 words. With (defective) spelling checker: 10 words.

29. Probability of getting exactly one double-6 = 0.0788. Probability of getting at least one double-6 = 0.101. The probability of getting a double-6 on one throw, which is 1/36 = .0278, is independent of the outcomes of previous throws.

Chapter 6

1. a. (i) You can simply map the "number of red balls drawn" onto a number in the sample space, $\{0, 1, 2, 3, 4\}$.

   (ii) Map onto the numbers in the sample space, $\{0, 1, 2, 3\}$.

   b. (ii) A binary number is an excellent way to express heads and tails in the order obtained. Map T-T-T-T onto 0000, T-T-T-H onto 0001, T-T-H-T onto 0010, and so on up to H-H-H-H onto 1111.

   c. (ii) A random variable technically does not map from a single event into a set of numbers. It is a map from an entire sample space. However, in this case the sample space consists of all elements in the event "an even number." So you can use the same map as you created in (i). Alternatively, you could use the map $y = x/2$ where x is the random variable created in (i).

2. **a.** continuous.

   b. discrete.

   c. continuous.

   e. If this means "the number you own *right now*" this is, technically, not a variable. It is a constant.

3. **a.** Not a probability distribution. Can't have a negative probability.

   b. Is a probability distribution.

   c. Not a probability distribution. The probabilities of the outcomes sum to more than 1.0.

4. **a.** 1/4

   b. $E(x) = 2.25$.

   c. $E(x^2) = \sum_x x^2 \cdot P(x^2)$

   $= (0)(.125) + (1)(.25) + (4)(.125) + (9)(0) + (16)(0) + (25)(0) = .75$.

   d. $\sigma_x^2 = 1.80$. $\sigma_x = 1.34$.

5. **c.** (i) 0.016.

   (iii) 0.134.

   (iv) 0.288.

   (v) 0.712.

   d.

Number	3	4	5	6	7	8	9	10
Prob.	.0046	.014	.028	.046	.069	.097	.116	.125

Number	11	12	13	14	15	16	17	18
Prob.	.125	.116	.097	.069	.046	.028	.014	.0046

f. (i) $P(4) = .028$.

(iii) 0.083.

(iv) 0.259.

(v) 0.741.

6. a. It is a probability distribution because the area under the distribution is equal to 1.0 and there are no probabilities outside the range 0–1.0.

b. mean = 8.5, variance = 5.58.

c. (viii) 0.

7. a.

Number drawn	0	1	2
Probability	0.5625	0.3750	0.0625

b. mean number of black balls drawn = 0.5. variance = .234.

.e. The two distributions are different because of the initial probability associated with each color ball.

8. a.

Number of twin births	0	1	2	3
Probability	.9127	.0847	.0026	.000027

b. mean number of twin births = 0.09.

c. 3.09

10. a.

Clear Marbles	0	1	2	3	4	5
Probability	.0313	.156	.313	.313	.156	.0313

b. 2.5.

c. 0.5.

12. a.

Defective Widgets	0	1	2	3
Probability	.729	.243	.027	.001

b. mean number of defective widgets per packet = 0.3.

13. a. 0.10.

b. 0.95.

c. 0.814.

14. a. 0.0668.

   b. 0.9953.

   c. 0.1336.

   g. 1.0.

   h. 0.5.

15. a. 0.0918.

   b. 0.0027.

   e. 0.726.

16. a. $x = 0$.

   b. $x = .676$.

   d. $y = 1.96$.

   e. $y = 1.645$.

18. a. 79.7%.

   b. 14%.

19. a. The company should write a warranty for approximately 18.9 months.

   b. About 1.4 out of every thousand will run 2 years before their first failure.

21. Hint: This is not a question about probability.

22. a. 0.021.

   b. 0.48.

   c. 0.0066.

   d. Tricky question. Given the information in this problem, the answer is, zero.

25. a. I chose $p = 0.5$. $P(x \geq 7) = 0.387$.

   b. If $p = 0.5$, the mean of the distribution with $n = 12$ is $np = 6$ and the variance is $npq = 3.0$, so the standard deviation is 1.73. The approximate probability is 0.39.

26. a. $(32)(0.49) = 15.7$.

   b. 2.83.

   c. The question asks the probability of getting an outcome of more than 19.5 on a normal distribution with mean 15.7 and standard deviation of 2.83. The probability is 0.09.

   d. 0.0002.

27. a. The company will fill an average of $(0.2)(400) = 80$ jobs. The standard deviation is the square root of $(400)(0.2)(0.8)$ or 8. The probability of filling 100 slots is 0.0075.

b. 0.9793.

c. This is a difficult problem. The answer is approximately 579 applications.

28. a. 0.05.

b. Depends on what happens after a cup is broken. If it is replaced at the end of the year, then the probability that Jane's cup will not be broken in either of the two years is 0.9025. The probability that her cup will be broken in one of the two years is 0.095. The probability that her cup will be broken in both of the two years is 0.0025.

c. and d. The normal approximation of the binomial does not apply since $np = 2.5$, less than 5. So these questions cannot be answered using the approximation.

30. Approximately 75.5% of batches of 100 fillipsies produced by the machine will contain four or more defective fillipsies. The machine will have to be adjusted after three of every four batches of 100 fillipsies. This is not a very good machine.

Chapter 7

1. a. 0-0, 0-4, 0-6, 0-10, 0-12, 4-4, 4-6, 4-10, 4-12, 6-6, 6-10, 6-12, 10-10, 10-12, 12-12.

b. *eliminate* 0-4, 4-4, 6-6, 10-10, 12-12.

c.
```
 0 | X
 1 |
 2 | X
 3 | X
 4 | X
 5 | X X
 6 | X X
 7 | X
 8 | X X
 9 | X
10 | X
11 | X
12 | X
```

d. same

e. They are the same because the mean of each sample of size $n = 2$ is equal to the median of the sample.

f.

```
 0 |
 1 | X X X X X
 2 |
 3 | X X
 4 |
 5 | X X
 6 |
 7 | X X X
 8 |
 9 | X
10 |
11 | X
12 |
13 | X
```

g. Expected value of the mean is 6.4, which is equal to the mean. Expected value of the median is 6.4, which is greater than the median of 6. This bias is expected. The expected value of the range is 5, which is much less than the actual range of 13.

3. 51-59-54-16, 68-45-96-33, 83-77-05-15, 40-43-34-44, 89-20-69-31, 67-80-20-31, 03-69-30-66, 55-80-10-72, 74-76-82-04, 31-23-93-42, 16-29-97-86, 21-92-36-62, 86-93-86-11, 35-60-28-56, 95-41-66-88, 99-43-15-86, 01-35-52-90, 13-23-73-34, 57-35-83-94, 56-67-66-60, 77-82-60-68, 75-28-73-92, 07-95-43-78, 24-84-59-25, 96-13-94-14 were my choices.

a. 45, 60.5, 45, 40.25, 52.25, 49.5, 42, 54.25, 59, 47.25, 57, 52.75, 69, 44.75, 72.5, 60.75, 44.5, 35.75, 67.25, 62.25, 71.75, 67, 55.75, 48, 54.25.

b.

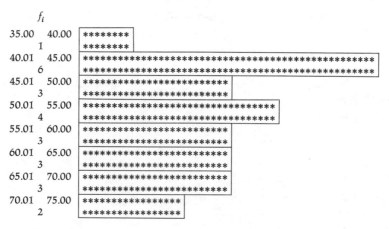

	f_i	
35.00	40.00	*******
	1	*******
40.01	45.00	**
	6	**
45.01	50.00	*************************
	3	*************************
50.01	55.00	*********************************
	4	*********************************
55.01	60.00	**************************
	3	**************************
60.01	65.00	*************************
	3	*************************
65.01	70.00	*************************
	3	*************************
70.01	75.00	*****************
	2	*****************

c. 54.33.

d. 49.5.

e. The mean of the 25 sample means is larger than the theoretical mean. The difference is due to error, sampling error.

4. a., b., and c.

(a) Sample	(b) Mean	(c) Probability	(a) Sample	(b) Mean	(c) Probability
0-0-0	0	.036	2-0-0	.66	.018
0-0-1	.33	.036	2-0-1	1	.018
0-0-2	.66	.018	2-0-2	1.33	.009
0-0-3	1	.018	2-0-3	1.66	.009
0-1-0	.33	.036	2-1-0	1	.018
0-1-1	.66	.036	2-1-1	1.33	.018
0-1-2	1	.018	2-1-2	1.66	.009
0-1-3	1.33	.018	2-1-3	2	.009
0-2-0	.66	.018	2-2-0	1.33	.009
0-2-1	1	.018	2-2-1	1.66	.009
0-2-2	1.33	.009	2-2-2	2	.005
0-2-3	1.66	.009	2-2-3	2.33	.005
0-3-0	1	.018	2-3-0	1.66	.009
0-3-1	1.33	.018	2-3-1	2	.009
0-3-2	1.66	.009	2-3-2	2.33	.005
0-3-3	2	.009	2-3-3	2.66	.005
1-0-0	.33	.036	3-0-0	1	.018
1-0-1	.66	.036	3-0-1	1.33	.018
1-0-2	1	.018	3-0-2	1.66	.009
1-0-3	1.33	.018	3-0-3	2	.009
1-1-0	.66	.036	3-1-0	1.33	.018
1-1-1	1	.036	3-1-1	1.66	.018
1-1-2	1.33	.018	3-1-2	2	.009
1-1-3	1.66	.018	3-1-3	2.33	.009
1-2-0	1	.018	3-2-0	1.66	.009
1-2-1	1.33	.018	3-2-1	2	.009
1-2-2	1.66	.009	3-2-2	2.33	.005
1-2-3	2	.009	3-2-3	2.66	.005
1-3-0	1.33	.018	3-3-0	2	.009
1-3-1	1.66	.018	3-3-1	2.33	.009
1-3-2	2	.009	3-3-2	2.66	.005
1-3-3	2.33	.009	3-3-3	3	.005

d.

M	0	.33	.66	1.0	1.33	1.66	2.0	2.33	2.66	3.0
P(M)	.036	.108	.162	.198	.189	.135	.086	.041	.013	.005

e. $E(\bar{X}) = 1.13$ on the basis of the figures above. $E(X) = 1.16$. The difference is due to rounding errors in the calculation of the probability distribution.

7. The sampling distribution of the mean would be normal, have a mean of 1.0, and a standard error of 0.76.

9. The sampling distribution of the mean will be approximately normal with a mean of 180 and a standard error of 0.19.

11. **a.** standard deviation of the population.

    b. population mean.

12. **a.** mean = 0, standard deviation of the sampling distribution = 7.07.

    c. mean = 0, standard deviation of the sampling distribution = 1.58.

    e. mean = 0, standard deviation of the sampling distribution = 0.71.

    g. mean = 0, standard deviation of the sampling distribution = 0.30.

13. **a.** Sampling distribution of the mean is normally distributed with a mean of 40 and a standard error of 3.16.

    d. Sampling distribution of the mean is approximately normally distributed with a mean of 14 and a standard error of 0.28.

14. Note: The resulting sampling distribution of the mean is a standard normal distribution.

    a. 0.50.

    c. almost zero.

15. **a.** The mean of the sample is 9.56. From the previous chapter you know that the mean of the distribution is 8.5 and the variance is 5.58. The sampling distribution is approximately normal with a mean of 8.5 and a standard error of $\sqrt{5.58}/\sqrt{32} = 0.4176$. The sample mean is $9.56 - 8.5 = 1.06$ raw units above the mean and $1.06/0.4176 = 2.54$ standard units above the mean of the sampling distribution. The probability of getting that far out on the tail of the normal distribution is about 0.0055. I would claim that this sample did *not* come from that population. The chance of my being wrong in my claim is 0.0055.

    b. This sample *definitely* did not come from that population. The dice described by that population cannot produce a 3.

17. The problem asks the probability of drawing a sample of 100 bars with an average weight of 3.95 oz. when the machine is operating according to the information given. The sampling distribution of mean weights for samples of 100 is approximately normal with a mean of 4.0 oz. and a standard error of 0.01 oz. The probability is very small (nearly zero) that the machine will produce a sample that is 5 standard error units away from the mean if it is operating according to its usual standards.

19. **a.** 0.16.

    b. 0.023.

c. This is the same question as in (a). The wording is different, but it is the same question.

d. The standard error of the sampling distribution of mean lengths for samples of size 10 is $1/\sqrt{10} = 0.316$. The probability of a sample of ten ears averaging more than 8" in length is 0.0008.

e. Probably zero. The standard error of the sampling distribution for mean lengths with samples of 25 is 0.2. A sample would have to be *five* standard deviations above the mean in order to get visited. The probability of that is small, nearly zero.

f. Divide the garden into 3 foot squares. Use a random number table to select the square. Number the stalks in the chosen square. Randomly select the stalk from which the ear is to be taken. Number the ears on the stalk and randomly select the ear to be chosen. Pick that ear. Measure it.

20. a. $(1.645)(12) + 50 = 69.74$.

b. 53.6.

c. They are equally difficult to get. Five percent of all individuals and five percent of all classes should get certificates.

Chapter 8

1. a.

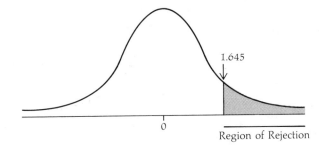

Implied level to reject $\alpha = 0.05$, one-tailed test.

b.

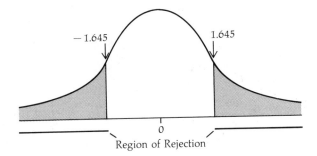

Implied level to reject $\alpha = 0.10$, two-tailed test.

f.

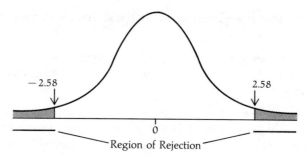

Implied level to reject $\alpha = 0.01$, two-tailed test.

2. a.

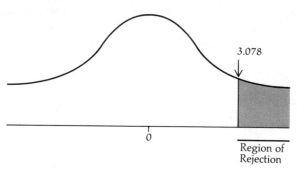

Implied level to reject $\alpha = 0.10$, one-tailed test.

b.

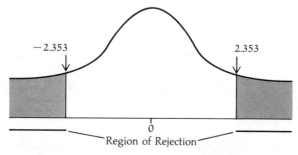

Implied level to reject $\alpha = 0.10$, two-tailed test.

c.

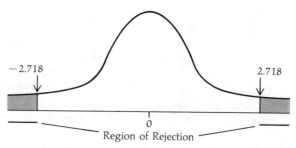

Implied level to reject $\alpha = 0.02$, two-tailed test.

e.

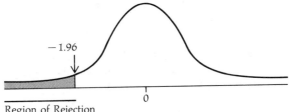

-1.96

0

Region of Rejection

Implied level to reject $\alpha = 0.028$, two-tailed test.

f.

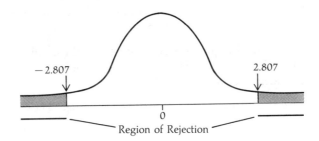

-2.807

2.807

0

Region of Rejection

Implied level to reject $\alpha = 0.01$, two-tailed test.

3. a. $H_A: \mu \neq 0$, reject.

   b. $H_A: \mu \neq 100$, reject.

   d. $H_A: \mu \neq 6.3$, reject.

   f. $H_A: \mu \neq 0$, fail to reject (and you don't have to conduct the test on this one since the sample mean is equal to the mean in the null hypothesis).

4. c. $H_A: \mu \neq -7.7$, reject.

   e. $H_A: \mu \neq 45.8$, reject.

   g. $H_A: \mu \neq 2.3$, reject.

5. a. $H_A: \mu_1 \neq \mu_2$. Take the samples of size 30 to be "large." Then the standard error of the difference between means is estimated as 0.40. The difference between sample means is 2.9, which is a difference of 7.25 standard errors. You may reject the null hypothesis.

   d. $H_A: \mu_1 \neq \mu_2$. The samples are small. The standard error of the difference between means is estimated as 0.108. The test statistic is $t_{22} = 5.72$. You may reject the null hypothesis.

6. a. $H_A: p \neq .20$. The standard error is 0.019. The test statistic is equal to 4.24. You may reject the null hypothesis.

   c. $H_A: p \neq .98$. The standard error is 0.007. The test statistic is equal to 2.86. You may reject the null hypothesis.

7. My sample consists of Bahamas ($3310), Chile ($1950), Congo ($500), Fiji ($1440), Greece ($3665), Japan ($8460), Maldives ($150), Panama ($1116), Singapore ($2279), and Trinidad ($2090).

  a. $2335.

  b. $2496.

  c. $3293.

  d. No. The standard error is $1041. The test statistic is $t_9 = .15$. You cannot reject the null hypothesis that the mean of the population from which this sample came is different from the mean of the set of countries.

  e. This is not a silly question because you might obtain evidence that says you should reject the null hypothesis even though you know you drew this sample from the specified population.

  f. Using a level to reject of .10, you would expect about 10% to reject the null hypothesis.

8. a. 20.8 days.

  b. $H_0: \mu = 20.5$
      $H_A: \mu \neq 20.5$

  c. The standard error is 0.525. The test statistic is $t_{15} = 0.57$. You should not reject the null hypothesis. There is no evidence for concluding that the sample came from a population with a mean different from the Dublin mean. There is no evidence from this test that the 16 batches are unrepresentative.

9. Depends on the level to reject and the nature of the test. The question asks just about "difference" so you can reasonably conduct a two-tailed test. The absolute difference in mean shelf lives is 4.375 days. The standard error of the difference between means is 2.25. The test statistic is $t_{14} = 1.94$. Were the level to reject set at $\alpha = 0.10$, you could reject the null hypothesis of no difference between the means and conclude that the samples probably came from populations with different means. Were the level to reject set at 0.05, you would fail to reject the null hypothesis of no difference and you could not claim, on the basis of this evidence, that the samples came from populations with different means.

10. a. one tailed.

  c. one tailed.

  e. two tailed.

11. I select a level to reject of $\alpha = 0.05$. There is a difference in the percentage of the total cost that is due to materials and technology. The six high specialization physicians (low scores on the specialization index) averaged 11.5% of the total cost due to materials and technology. Low specialization physicians averaged 2.67%. The standard error of the difference between means is 2.39. The test statistic is $t_{10} = 3.70$. Using a one tailed test, I reject the null hypothesis of no difference. The observed significance of the test is $p < 0.005$.

13. My hypothesis is that countries with a high male life expectancy will have a high literacy rate. I choose a level to reject of 0.10. I divided the sample into countries with male life expectancy (MLE) below the median MLE of 59.6 and countries above the median MLE. The average literacy rate for countries with low MLE is 33.0%. The average literacy rate for high MLE countries is 88.5%. This difference is so great that you should not even have to resort to a statistical test. However, I did so anyway. The standard error is 2.83. The test statistical is $z = 19.6$. You can reject the null hypothesis of no difference.

15. The average length of stay is 1.886 days. The sample standard deviation is 0.343. With a sample of size $n = 22$, the standard error of the mean is 0.073. The test statistic is $t_{21} = 1.56$. The problem calls for a one-tailed test. If you chose a level to reject of $\alpha = .05$ you cannot reject the null hypothesis of a difference between the ALOS in this DRG and the payment period of 2 days. If, however, you relaxed the level to reject to $\alpha = 0.10$, you would reject the null hypothesis and conclude that the ALOS in this DRG is significantly less than the 2 day payment period.

18. The question calls for a test of the null hypothesis that

$$H_0: \mu \neq 98.6.$$

The test is a two-tailed test. I chose a level to reject of 0.10. The average temperature is 99.69 with a standard deviation of 1.84. The standard error is 0.31. The test statistic is $(99.69 - 98.6)/0.31 = 3.52$. I reject the null hypothesis. The observed significance of the test is $p < .005$.

21. The question calls for a test of the hypothesis:

$$H_0: \mu_{low} < \mu_{high}$$

for corn length means. I divided the sample into two groups, one with gardens that used less than the median amount of fertilizer (Md = 5.4), one with more than the median amount of fertilizer. There were 17 and 18 gardens in the groups, respectively. There was a difference in the sample means. The low-fertilizer gardens' average corn length was 6.99 inches; the high-fertilizer gardens' corn length was 6.74 inches. Since the low-fertilizer gardens' corn length was *greater* than the corn length from high-fertilizer gardens it makes little sense to go further. There is no support in the data for rejecting the null hypothesis. If you did conduct the test, you would find that the standard error is 0.21, the test statistic is $t_{33} = -1.23$, and the observed significance of the test is $p = .73$.

22. This question calls for a test of the hypothesis that

$$H_0: p \neq 0.15.$$

There are 14 A's in the sample of 45 students, so the sample proportion is 0.31. The standard error is 0.07. The test statistic is $(0.31 - 0.15)/0.07 = 2.28$. The observed significance of the (two-tailed) test is $p < 0.03$. If you chose a level to reject larger than this observed significance of the test, you could reject the null hypothesis and conclude that this sample came from a population that had a proportion of A students different from that of the school overall.

23. No. The observed significance of the test is $p > 0.95$.

26. No. The average percentage of the total bill devoted to surgery for the 125 DRG-physician pairs is 4.35%, below the national average. The average percent of a patient's bill devoted to surgery for the 773 patients discharged by these 22 physicians is 3.03%. There is no evidence in these data to claim that the patients in this hospital are charged a greater proportion of their bills for surgery than the national average.

Chapter 9

1. a. 1.75 to 2.93.

   c. −41.5 to 4.15.

   e. 48.2 to 49.6.

   g. 6.1. to 8.5.

2. b. 106.2 to 106.6.

   d. 7.1 to 9.9.

   f. −0.00165 to 0.00165.

3. b. −126.8 to −101.2.

   c. −1.74 to 0.14

4. a. 0.24 to 0.32.

   c. 0.94 to 0.98.

   e. 0.31 to 0.45.

5. I used the same sample as I drew for Exercise 7, Chapter 8.

   a. $2335.

   b. $2496.

c. $3293.

d. $783 to $4209.

e. yes.

f. about 90%.

6. a. 19.9 to 21.7 days.

b. 19.7 to 21.9 days.

c. −.5 to 9.2 days. The 95% confidence interval contains zero. Therefore, you cannot be sure (with 95% confidence) that the difference between sample means is significantly different from zero. You cannot state with 95% confidence that the samples came from populations with different means.

7. A 90% confidence interval extends from 4.5 to 13.2.

9. The 99% confidence interval estimate of the difference between population means extends from 48.2 to 62.8. Since this interval does not contain zero, you can be 99% confident that there is a difference in the literacy rates of the populations from which these two samples (formed on the basis of male life expectancy) come.

11. I would want to have fairly high confidence that my estimate contains the actual population parameter. So I would set alpha at 0.01 and construct a fairly wide, 99% confidence interval. The interval is $1.886 \pm (2.831)(0.073)$, which extends from 1.68 days to 2.09 days.

14. Treating this as a large sample (since $n > 30$), the interval estimate is $99.69 \pm (1.44)(0.31)$, which is the interval from 99.2 degrees to 101.1. You can say with 85% confidence that this sample comes from a population whose mean is greater than normal.

17. See Exercise 21, Chapter 8. To do this in light of the hypothesis is a little silly. However, silliness notwithstanding, we can construct the interval as follows: The difference between sample means is −0.25 inches. The standard error is 0.21, so the 99% confidence interval estimate is $-0.25 \pm (2.58)(0.21)$, which is the interval from −0.79 inches to .29 inches. You cannot claim, on the basis of these data, that there is a difference in the mean lengths of corn ears in the populations from which these two samples came since the interval estimate contains zero.

18. If these were the only data you had with which to estimate the proportion of the students who got A's, you could be 80% confident that between 22% and 40% of the students got A's.

19. A 50% interval extends from −4.4 to 4.5. The interval contains zero, so there is no basis in these data for claiming a difference in IQ based on age. A 30% interval extends from −3.4 to 3.6. Same interpretation.

21. Using the DRG-physician pair as the unit of analysis, the mean percentage of the bill devoted to surgery is 4.35%. (See Exercise 26, Chapter 8.) The standard deviation is 7.645, so the standard error of the mean is 0.68. A 95% confidence interval estimate of the percentage of the total bill devoted to surgery extends from $4.35 - (1.96)(0.68) = 3.0\%$ to $4.35 + (1.96)(0.68) = 5.7\%$. Based on these data, you can be 95% confident that the percentage of the bill devoted to surgery in the population from which this sample came is less than the national average of 8.4%.

22. Since the standard error of the mean specialization score is 3.47 for this sample of size $n = 22$, the 90% confidence interval estimate of the specialization score extends $(1.721)(3.47)$ percentage points on either side of the point estimate of the mean which is 76.77%. So a 90% confidence interval extends from 70.8% to 82.7%. There is no basis in these data for claiming that the mean specialization score for the population from which this sample came is any different from the mean specialization score (72%) of all the physicians in this hospital since the interval contains the overall mean.

Chapter 10

1. a. Hypothesis: Fermentation time and shelf life are associated.

    b. (i) 20.9 days.

       (ii) 29.2.

    c. (i) Mean shelf life for short fermentation $= 24.4$ days; mean shelf life for moderate fermentation $= 21.2$ days; mean shelf life for long fermentation $= 17.2$ days.

       (ii) There is a systematic relationship between the variables. The longer the fermentation, the shorter the shelf life, on average.

    d. short $= 17.8$; moderate $= 6.2$; long $= 45.7$.

    e. (i) 19.9.

       (ii) PRE $= 0.32$.

    f. The relationship is of moderate to low strength and is negative (the longer the fermentation, the shorter the shelf life).

    g. Brew the beer shorter. There are probably a lot of other variables to take into consideration in extending shelf life, but the principal concern would be the effect of short fermentation times on taste (or marketability).

    h. Yes, there is an outlier in the long fermentation group. One batch lasted 28 days, the second longest shelf life in the whole group of 15. I would investigate that batch in particular. Also, there is quite a lot of variation in the shelf life of the short fermentation group. That might concern me a little.

2. a. The higher the specialization score, the lower will be the percentage of the total cost devoted to material and technology. (NB: This hypothetical relationship is, in part, an artifact of the way "specialization score" is coded. The higher the "specialization score," the lower one's specialization.)

b. I divided the group of 12 at the median so that each group has six physicians in it.

c. For specialists (those with low "specialization scores"), the mean percentage of the total bill devoted to material and technology is 11.5%; the variance around that mean is 18.7. For generalists (those with high "specialization scores"), the mean percentage of the total bill devoted to material and technology is 2.7%; the variance around that mean is 15.5.

d. The total error with which the analysis began is 36.8. The remaining error after taking specialization score into consideration is 15.5. The proportionate reduction in error is $(36.8 - 15.5)/36.8 = 0.58$. This indicates the relationship between specialization score and the percentage of the bill devoted to material and technology is moderately strong. It is also in line with the hypothesis.

e. It would be hard to say that the relationship is a causal one. Specialists might treat more complicated cases than generalists. That alone would drive up the percentage of the bill devoted to material and technology. They also might do more surgery. That, too, could contribute to material and technology usage.

3. a. There is not a strong relationship. The two means are: "work" group = 237.1 seconds; "leisure" group = 221.9 seconds. The proportionate reduction in error is 0.0017, less than one percent.

b. The PRE is 0.019. The relationship is very weak.

4. You should expect, on the basis of the previous analysis, that these two variables would be moderately strongly related. Indeed, they are. The following table summarizes the analysis:

Literacy Rate	Overall	Low Income	High Income
N	15	7	8
Mean	57.5%	32.9%	79.0%
Variance	1173.7	558.5	733.1

From this information, you can calculate the remaining error as 605.9. From that, you find the PRE = 0.48, a relationship of moderate strength.

6. First, you would want to know that the magnetic field changed whenever there was a solar flare (or at least that there was a change every time a flare larger than some threshold magnitude occurred). Second, you would want to know that the changes in the magnetic field occurred after the eruption of the flare. Third, you would want to know that no other variables were associated with the correlated occurrence of the appearance of a flare and the changes in the magnetic field.

7. His assumed relationship between the existence of dirt on the court and the outcome of the games was a spurious relationship (and a rather poor excuse).

8. a. Dependent variable is "who won." The independent variable is "respondent's sex." Hypothesis: There is an association between the respondent's sex and his or her judgment of who won the vice-presidential debate in 1984.

b. H_0: There is no relationship between a respondent's sex and his or her judgment of who won the debate.

c.

Respondent's Sex	Who Won?		Total
	Bush	Ferraro	
Male	(119.8)	(117.2)	237
Female	(147.2)	(143.8)	291
Total	51% (267)	49% (261)	528

d. $\chi^2 = 44.69$.

e. df = 1.

f. The probability is very small, much less than 0.001.

g. Yes.

h. The respondent's sex is related to his or her perception of who won the Bush-Ferraro debate. Males tended to think Bush won while females tended to think that Ferraro won.

9. a. There is a statistically significant relationship between "sex" and "winner" among Republicans. Chi-squared = 6.746, $p < 0.01$.

b. There is a statistically significant relationship between "sex" and "winner" among Democrats. Chi-squared = 24.32, $p < 0.001$.

c. This interpretation is not based on the tests of significance in (**a**) and (**b**). It is based on an examination of the tables. Among Republicans, Bush was dubbed the winner by majorities of both males and females. However, among females the majority was narrow. Among Democrats, males thought Bush (the Republican) was the winner. Female Democrats thought Ferraro won but the majority they gave her was somewhat smaller than the majority male Republicans gave Bush.

12. Using the DRG-physician pair as the unit of analysis:

Cost	Overall	No Complications	Complications
N	125	92	33
Mean	$1335	$1238	$1606
Variance	1,285,956	1,170,724	1,552,516

From this information, you can find that the remaining error is 1,259,810. The proportionate reduction in error is 0.02. You would conclude that, while the relationship is in the direction one might expect (with higher average cost for those diagnoses involving complications), the relationship is not a strong one. Indeed, it is very weak.

13. There is no relationship between the use of fertilizer and the length of corn ears produced.

Chapter 11

1. a. In the sample, Bush won by a slight amount. A statement about who won in the population from which this sample came would be based on a test of the null hypothesis, $H_0: p_{Bush} > .50$. The sample proportion is .505. The standard error is 0.02. Using a level to reject of, say, $= 0.10$, the test statistic is $z = 0.25$, and you should not reject the null hypothesis. On the basis of these data, there is no reason to claim that either side won the debate (if "won" means "received a majority").

b. 261.

c. Modal response for females is "Ferraro." Remaining error $= 109$.

d. Conditional mode for males is "Bush." Remaining error $= 79$.

e. Remaining error for the table $= 188$.

f. Proportionate reduction in error $= (261 - 188)/261 = 0.28$.

g. It means there is a moderately weak relationship between the sex of the respondent and the respondent's perception of who won the debate.

h. Although there was no clear-cut winner of the debate, there was a statistically significant relationship between the sex of the person surveyed and his or her perception of who won the debate ($\lambda = 0.28$, $\chi^2 = 44.69$, $p < 0.001$).

2. a. 28,756.

b. 8,502.

c. $(28,756 - 8,502)/(28,756 + 8,502) = 0.54$.

d. There is a moderate relationship between the sex of the respondent and the person's perception of who won the debate. The direction of the relationship indicates that women tend to think that Ferraro won and men think that Bush won.

e. The difference between lambda and Q is of little consequence. They are different statistics.

3. a. The data show that women who have prenatal visits in the first trimester have low-birth-weight babies about one-fifth of the time. The chance of a woman having a low-birth-weight baby is doubled if she does not have prenatal visits in the first trimester of her pregnancy. Having prenatal visits is associated with the birth weight of the baby resulting from the pregnancy.

b. Yule's Q. $Q = (367,625 - 1,067,025)/(367,625 + 1,067,025) = -0.49$. Prenatal visits in the first trimester of a pregnancy are negatively associated with infant birth weight ($Q = -.49$).

c. This is probably not a direct causal relationship. Women who tend not to have prenatal visits in the first trimester tend to be economically disadvantaged, less well nourished, and in less good health than those who do. The variable "prenatal visits in the first trimester" is probably a good indicator for women and children "at risk" of having some complications, but it is probably not causing low birth weight itself.

5. **a.** Hypothesis: Among those who profess strong religious beliefs, there are differences in support for abortion based on one's religion.

b. lambda $= 0.03$.

c. $\chi^2 = 16.0$, df $= 3$ (since you can eliminate the "None" row), $p < .002$. There is a relationship between the variables in the population from which this sample came.

d. Strong Christians tend to think that abortion is not okay while Jews and people who profess other beliefs think that it is okay.

7. **a.** Hypothesis: Those who have strong religious beliefs (regardless of the nature of those beliefs) think abortion is wrong.

b. $Q = -.41$.

c. $\chi^2 = 48.39$, df $= 1$, $p < 0.001$. You can reject the null hypothesis of no association in the population from which this sample came.

d. People with strong religious beliefs tend to disapprove of abortion more than people of not so strong beliefs (even though a majority of both groups disapprove). The relationship is moderate and significantly different from zero.

9. **a.** Hypothesis: One's occupation and one's earnings are associated.

b. $Q = -.23$. White collar workers tend to be more likely to be in the higher income category.

c. $\chi^2 = 10.71$, df $= 1$, $p < 0.002$. You can reject the null hypothesis of no association between occupation and earnings in the population from which this sample came.

d. There is a moderately weak, statistically significant (significantly different from zero) relationship between one's occupational category and one's earnings.

10. **b.** $Q = -.47$.

c. $\chi^2 = 28.92$, df $= 1$, $p < 0.001$. You can reject the null hypothesis of no association between occupation and earnings among males in the population from which this sample came.

d. The relationship between occupation and earnings is stronger for males than it is in the overall population.

11. b. $Q = -.72$.

c. $\chi^2 = 17.50$, df $= 1$, $p < 0.001$. You can reject the null hypothesis of no association between occupation and earnings among females in the population from which this sample came.

d. The relationship between occupation and earnings is stronger for females than it is either in the overall population or among males. The overall analysis from Exercises 9, 10, and 11 shows that lumping the two sexes together in the analysis of the relationship between occupation and earnings tends to *suppress* the relationship (the underlying relationship) between these two variables. You should examine these three tables closely to see how the relationship between the two variables of interest can be suppressed by adding in a third variable. Look especially at the table for females. It shows that they tend to be in lower income category *regardless* of their occupational classification. Adding all of those low paid, white collar workers tends to affect the overall relationship between occupational classification and earnings.

13. a. There is a difference between the races on wanting laws to prohibit interracial marriage.

b. $Q = 0.34$.

c. $\chi^2 = 8.18$, df $= 1$, $p < 0.005$. In the population from which this sample was drawn, you can reject the null hypothesis of no relationship between race and one's desire for laws prohibiting interracial marriage. While nearly 70% of people do not want such laws, whites, more than non-whites, express a desire for laws prohibiting interracial marriage.

15. a. Hypothesis: Among those with a high Protestant work ethic score, those who are engaged in an activity labeled "work" will be likely to do the job more than those who think they are doing a leisure-time activity.

b. $Q = -.6$.

c. $\chi^2 = 2.97$, df $= 1$, $p < .10$. If you set the level to reject at a conventional $\alpha = 0.05$, you could not reject the null hypothesis of no association between task label and time spent on the word game (among those with high Protestant work ethic scores) in the population from which this sample came.

d. Even though the relationship is fairly strong, you cannot conclude that the hypothesis is supported in the population from which this sample was drawn.

17. a. Hypothesis: The higher the growth rate, the more business confidence the city's business leaders will have.

b. $\gamma = -.10$.

c. $\chi^2 = 10.42$, df $= 2$, $p < 0.05$. You can reject the null hypothesis of no association between economic growth and confidence of the business community in the population from which this sample was drawn.

d. If you just assumed that the result of (c) confirmed the hypothesis, you would be badly mistaken. Gamma shows that the relationship is negative, but only slightly so. The result of the inferential test shows *only* that there is a non-zero relationship between the variables in the population from which this sample came. It tells you nothing about the nature of that relationship. Examining the data in the table shows that, contrary to the hypothesis, confidence does not rise with increasing economic growth. In fact, these leaders tend to be confident in times of low growth and in times of moderate growth. The only difference worth noting in the table is the last row: In times of high growth, the level of confidence is lower than at other times. Moral: Always pay close attention to the data, not to the statistics.

Chapter 12

1. a., e., and f.

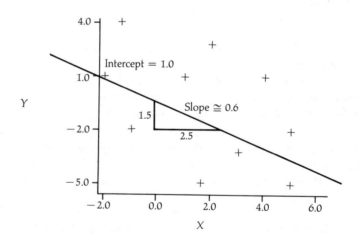

b. Yes, it appears as though it would be.

c. Negative.

d. Small to moderate.

f. See diagram. The slope of that line is approximately -0.6 and the intercept is approximately 1.0.

g. $s_y^2 = 10.11$.

h. $\hat{Y} = 1 - .6\ X$.

X	Y	$\hat{Y}$	$(Y_i - \hat{Y}_i)^2$
-2.0	1	2.2	1.44
-1.5	4	1.9	4.41
-1.0	-2	1.6	12.96
1.0	1	0.4	.36
1.5	-5	0.1	26.01
2.0	3	-0.2	10.24
3.0	-3	-0.8	0.64
4.0	1	-1.4	5.76
5.0	-2	-2.0	0
5.0	-5	-2.0	9.0

78.38

Remaining error $= 78.38/9 = 8.71$

i. PRE $= (10.11 - 8.71)/10.11 = .14$

j. Not a very good descriptor, but I don't know from these exercises whether it is very different from the *best* descriptor. That is, I don't know if any line is a good descriptor.

2. a. $\bar{X} = 1.7$, $\bar{Y} = -0.7$

$(X_i - \bar{X})$	$(Y_i - \bar{Y})$	$(X_i - \bar{X})^2$	$(X_i - \bar{X})(Y_i - \bar{Y})$
-3.7	1.7	13.69	-6.29
-3.2	4.7	10.24	-17.39
-2.7	-1.3	7.29	3.51
$-.7$	1.7	.49	-1.19
$-.2$	-4.3	.04	.86
.3	3.7	.09	1.11
1.3	-2.3	1.69	-2.99
2.3	1.7	5.29	3.91
3.3	-1.3	10.89	-4.29
3.3	-4.3	10.89	-14.19

$\sum = 60.51$ -36.95

b. $b = -36.95/60.51 = -.61$

c. $a = -.7 - (-.61)(1.7) = -.34$

d. $\hat{Y} = -.34 - .61\ X$

e. $r = (-.61)(2.595/3.164) = -.50.$ $r^2 = .25$

g. -2.225

Note: The calculations above were all done by hand, as shown. There is round-off error introduced in this way. A computer will derive different answers for this problem.

3. a. Hypothesis: The higher one's work ethic score, the higher will be one's Type A personality score.

b.

Subject	1	2	3	4	5	6	7	8	9	10
Work Ethic	82	69	82	89	75	86	69	78	66	103
Type A	48	43	52	43	30	43	29	36	48	52

c.

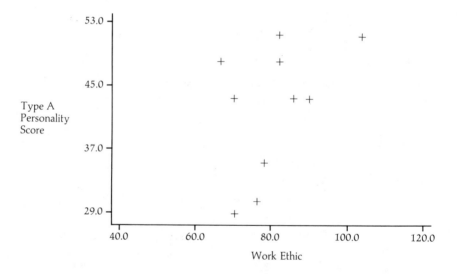

d. $\widehat{\text{Type A}} = 14.07 + .354 \text{ Work Ethic}$

e. In the sample, the data lie in the predicted relationship to one another. The standard error of the regression coefficient is .232. The test statistic t (to test the null hypothesis that the slope in the population from which this sample came is zero) is 1.53 with 8 degrees of freedom. The observed significance of the test, using a one-tailed test of the hypothesis, is $p = .08$. Using a conventional level to reject of $\alpha = 0.05$, one would not reject the null hypothesis. This sample does not provide evidence for claiming that these two variables are related to one another in the population from which this sample was drawn. (If the level to reject were set at $\alpha = 0.10$, one would reject the null hypothesis.)

f.

Subject	1	2	3	4	5
Work Ethic	88	77	83	87	92
Type A	34	49	38	50	38

g. (i) Pred. Type A   45.2   41.3   43.5   44.9   46.6

(ii) $(A_i - \bar{A})^2$ 60.8   51.8   14.4   67.2   14.4   Sum = 208.6
                        Total Error = 52.15

(iii) $(A_i - \hat{A}_i)^2$ 125.4   59.3   30.3   26.0   74.0   Sum = 315
                        Remaining Error = 78.7

(iv) This is an odd case. For *my* particular random sample of five other subjects, the prediction using the regression line (calculated from the first ten randomly selected cases) is worse than the prediction using just the mean. This shows you one of the problems of projecting from the sample into cases outside the sample. How did your sample do?

5. a.

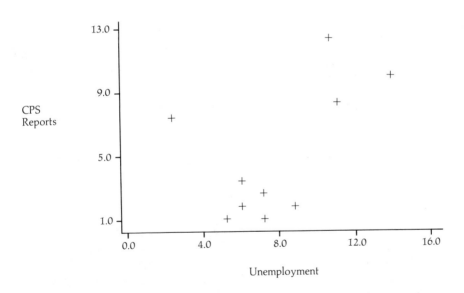

In the sample, the regression line is $\widehat{CPS} = -.64 + .7$ Unemp. The relationship is positive, as the hypothesis suggested. Using a one-tailed test of the null hypothesis that the regression coefficient relating these two variables in the population from which this sample came, is zero. One can conclude that the unemployment rate is probably related to the rate of reports to CPS ($t = 1.97$, df $= 8$, $p = .042$).

b. I would be interested in variables such as the staffing levels provided by CPS in each of the counties, average education in the counties, rate of mental illness, and so forth. I would also want to investigate what seems to be an outlier in the data. Case 3 has the lowest unemployment and a moderately high level of CPS reporting. I would not eliminate this from the data for that would be playing at the religion of Statistics that Salsburg describes, but it may provide some ideas for further hypotheses if it were investigated closely.

7. a.

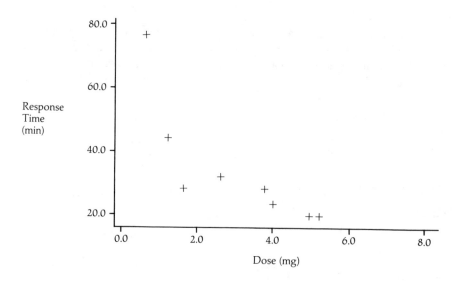

The equation of the regression line is

$$\widehat{\text{Response Time}} = 59.5 - 8.57 \text{ Dose}$$

The null hypothesis that the slope is zero in the population from which this sample came can be rejected ($t = -3.54$, df $= 6$, $p = 0.006$ for a one-tailed test). The only problem I have in conducting this regression analysis is suggested by the scatterplot. There may be a curvilinear relation between these two variables, not a linear one. I would be more comfortable using a linear relationship to describe these data if I had more points in the dose range 0–2 mg.

b. The standard error of the regression coefficient is 2.42. A 95% confidence interval extends 2.447 standard errors on either side of the sample regression coefficient when df $= 6$. So the interval is from $-8.57 - (2.447)(2.42)$ to $-8.57 + (2.447)(2.42)$ or from -14.5 to -2.6.

c. At 4.0 mg, the predicted response time is $59.5 - (8.57)(4) = 25.2$ min.

d. At 7.5 mg, the predicted response time is $59.5 - (8.57)(7.5) = -4.8$ min. (That is, relief begins in anticipation of taking that much of the drug!)

e. I would place more confidence in estimate (**c**). The reason is that the hypothetical dose in (**c**) is in the range of doses in the sample. The dose in (**d**) is outside the range of doses in the sample. Thus, that prediction is actually a projection beyond the sample. I would be especially suspicious of projection (**d**) since there may be a curvilinear relationship between the two variables.

9. The higher one's level of education, the higher one's starting salary:

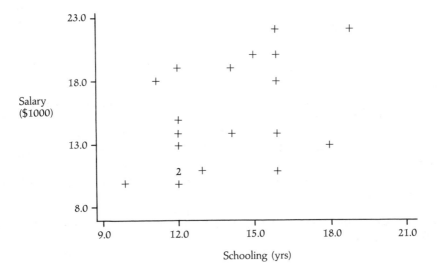

A line appears to be a good descriptor of these data. The regression equation is

$$\widehat{\text{Salary}} = 4.2 + .78 \text{ School}$$

For every extra year of school, one's starting salary goes up by approximately $780. The standard error of the regression coefficient is 0.34 and, using a one-tailed test of the null hypothesis, one can reject the null hypothesis of no relationship between these variables in the population from which this sample came ($t = 2.29$, $df = 18$, $p < 0.02$).

10. The correlation between one's starting salary and one's salary ten years later is weak ($r = .242$, $r^2 = .059$). You can see from the scatter plot, below, that there is not a strong relationship between the variables:

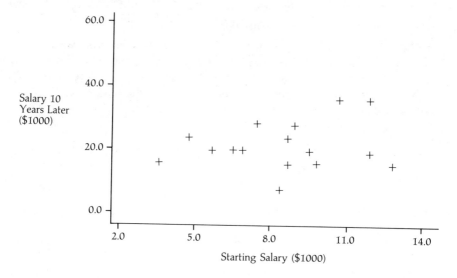

The 95% confidence interval is constructed using a Z-transformation. The Z-transformation of $r = .242$ is $Z = .2469$. The standard error is $\sqrt{1/(16 - 3)} = .2773$. The interval extends from $Z = .2469 - (1.96)(.2773) = -.2996$ to $Z = .2469 + (1.96)(.2773) = .7904$. The interval, expressed in terms of the correlation coefficient, r, is $-.288 < r < .658$. This interval captures $r = 0$, so one cannot confidently claim that the correlation coefficient in the population from which this sample came is not equal to zero.

11. The scatterplot, below, suggests that there may be a curvilinear relationship between performance in one year and performance in the next year.

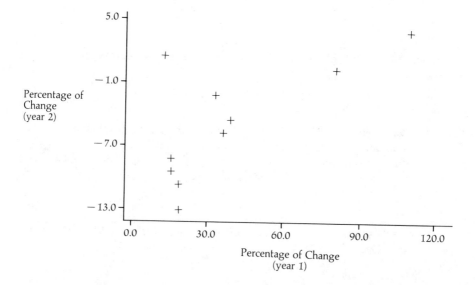

However, if you want to use a line to describe the relationship, the regression line is

$$\widehat{Yr2} = -9.14 + .115 \; Yr1$$

The relationship is signficant at the $p < 0.02$ level ($t = 2.79$, df $= 8$, one-tailed test).

13. Here is the scatterplot:

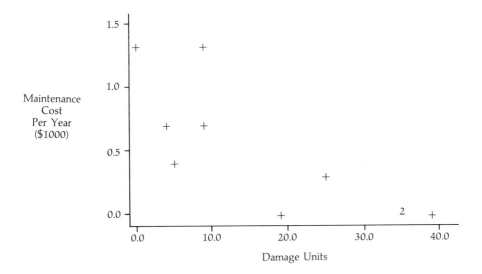

The relationship is negative! The more damage, the *lower* the cost. The relationship appears to be curvilinear, but there is a natural floor at maintenance cost = $0.

In fact, this pattern is due to the fact that the data contains two types of roads. Interstate highways are very durable once they are built and carry a lot of truck traffic (which increases the damage index). The data points that are low and to the right are interstate highways. The other highways are state and federal highways. They are not so durable and require high yearly maintenance. (If you had data over a much longer term, the relationship would, no doubt, change since the interstates are going to be *very* expensive to repair once they begin to fail.)

16. The following scatterplot suggests that there is no relationship between the days of sun and boat sales:

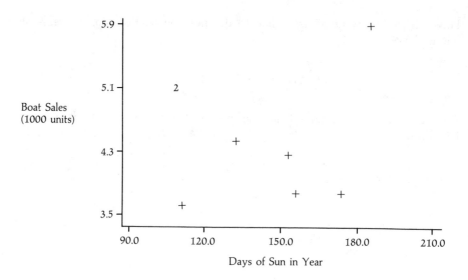

The correlation coefficient is $r = .08$, showing that the relationship is nearly zero in the sample. The man should consider the following graph showing the relationship between year and sales.

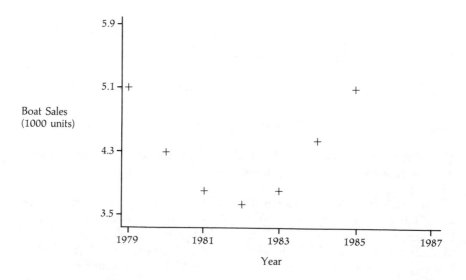

Boat sales seem to be on the upswing over the past 5 years. The graph may contain a cautionary note, however, if boat sales are cyclical. The man would not know, from these data, where in the business cycle sales are.

Chapter 13

1. a. $H_0: \mu_s = \mu_m = \mu_l$

$H_A: \mu_s \neq \mu_m$ or $\mu_s \neq \mu_l$ or $\mu_m \neq \mu_l$

b. $\bar{X}_s = 24.4$; $\bar{X}_m = 21.2$; $\bar{X}_l = 17.2$

c. $\bar{X} = 20.93$

d. $SS_B = 5 \times (24.4 - 20.93)^2 + 5 \times (21.2 - 20.93)^2 + 5 \times (17.2 - 20.93)^2$
$= 130.13$.

e. $SS_W = 71.2 + 24.8 + 182.8 = 278.8$

f. $df_W = 2$; $df_B = 12$

g. $MS_B = 130.13/2 = 65.07$; $MS_W = 278.8/12 = 23.23$

h. $F_{2,12} = 65.07/23.23 = 2.80$

i. $\alpha = .10$

j. Fail to reject the null hypothesis. (You would also fail to reject if you set $\alpha = .05$.)

k.

Source of Variation	Sum of Squares	df	Mean Squares	F
Fermentation Time	130.13	2	65.07	2.80
Residual	278.80	12	23.23	
Total	408.93	14	29.21	

l. Not appropriate since you cannot reject the null hypothesis.

m. There are no significant differences among shelf life lengths based on fermentation time.

2. a. Hypothesis: The older the physician, the higher the cost. (Rationale: the younger ones have been raised in the era of cost consciousness in medical care.)

b. The mean costs are $1227 for older physicians, $1117 for physicians in the middle age group, and $1095 for younger physicians. The hypothesis is supported in the sample. The null hypothesis is that the mean costs for the populations from which these three samples came are equal. The following ANOVA table presents information to test this hypothesis:

Source of Variation	Sum of Squares	df	Mean Squares	F	p
Age	71,200	2	35,600	0.30	.75
Residual	2,262,000	19	119,100		
Total	2,333,200	21	111,105		

The null hypothesis of no difference between means should not be rejected. There is no evidence for claiming that there is a difference in cost based on the age (or, more accurately, time in practice in this hospital) of the physician.

3. a.

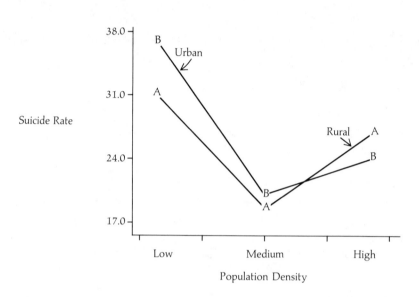

There is some interaction since the lines are not parallel.

b.

Source of Variation	Sum of Squares	df	Mean Squares	F	p
Main Effects					
1. Income	7222.7	2	3611.4	799	<.001
2. Rural-Urban	88.2	1	88.2	19.5	<.001
Interaction Effects					
1,2. Income and Rural-Urban	720.6	2	360.3	79.7	<.001
Within Group (Residual)	786.5	174	4.52		
Total	8818	179	49.3		

5. The null hypothesis is that there is no difference among the mean weight losses of the four populations from which these three samples came. The mean weight losses for the samples are

Sample	A	B	C	D
Weight Loss	4.0	9.0	1.0	16.17

ANOVA Table:

Source of Variation	Sum of Squares	df	Mean Squares	F	p
Program	791.1	3	263.7	8.78	.0006
Residual	600.8	20	30.0		
Total	1391.9	23	60.5		

Tukey's Honestly Significant Difference Test for a level to reject of $\alpha = .05$:

$$\text{HSD} = q_\alpha \sqrt{\frac{\text{MS}_W}{n}} = (3.96)(\sqrt{30.0/6}) = (3.96)(2.24) = 8.85$$

Differences (with honestly significant differences marked with *)

	A	B	C	D
A	—	5	3	12.17*
B	—	—	8	7.17
C	—	—	—	15.17*

There is a distinguishable difference between methods A and D and between methods C and D.

7. The null hypothesis is that there is a difference in average rate of defective parts produced by the three types of work groups. The sample means are different with the factory line group's average defect rate being .159, the quality circle group rate being .066, and the employee determined rate being .105. The following ANOVA table lets one test the null hypothesis:

Source of Variation	Sum of Squares	df	Mean Squares	F	p
Group	.0275	2	.0138	3.01	.07
Residual	.0961	21	.0046		
Total	.1236	23			

Based on this evidence, one should reject the null hypothesis only if α is larger than .07. But the manager really ought to look at the trend in defect rates over the three weeks:

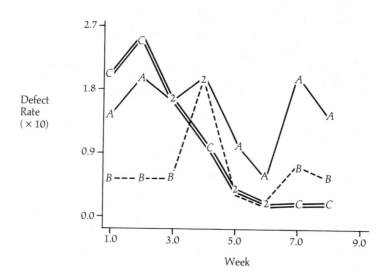

The factory line group bounces all over and remains at a moderately high level. The quality circle group starts at a fairly low defect level, has one bad week, and returns to and remains at its beginning low level. The employee determined group begins at the highest level, moves higher, and then trends rapidly down to the lowest defect level of the three groups (and seems to stabilize there). This shows why it is important to look at the data. There is much in these data to think about.

10. No. The mean grade points of the three groups are:

Study Time	High	Medium	Low
GPA	3.07	2.67	2.53

The following ANOVA table shows that there is no evidence on which to reject the null hypothesis of no difference among the mean GPAs in the populations from which these samples came:

Source of Variation	Sum of Squares	df	Mean Squares	F	p
Study Time	2.31	2	1.16	1.16	.32
Residual	42.00	42	1.00		
Total	44.31	44	1.01		

11. **a.** Male Athletes = 3.05; Male Nonathletes = 3.28; Female Athletes = 2.95; Female Nonathletes = 3.13.

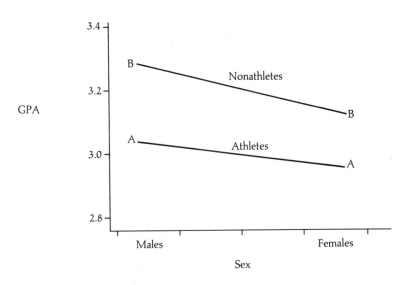

The following ANOVA table shows there is no basis for claiming any statistically significant differences among the population means from which these four groups came:

Source of Variation	Sum of Squares	df	Mean Squares	F	p
Sex	.160	1	.160	.42	.521
Athlete/Nonathlete	.300	1	.300	.80	.380
Interaction (Sex, Ath.)	.002	1	.002	.005	.945
Residual	10.565	28	.377		
Total	11.027	31	.356		

Index